The Child as Social Person

Questions about how children grow up in their social worlds are of enormous significance for parents, teachers, and society at large, as well as for children themselves. Clearly children are shaped by the social world that surrounds them but they also shape the social worlds that they, and those significant to them, encounter. But exactly how does this happen, and what can we do to ensure that it produces happy outcomes?

This book provides a critical review of the psychological literature on the development of personality, social cognition, social skills, social relations and social outcomes from birth to early adulthood. It was Bronfenbrenner's model of the development of the person and up-to-date evidence to analyse normal and abnormal social development, prosocial and antisocial behaviour, within and across cultures. As well as outlining the theory, the book addresses applied issues such as delinquency, school failure, and social exclusion.

Using a coherent theoretical structure, *The Child as Social Person* examines material from across the biological and social sciences to present an integrated account of what we do and do not know about the development of the child as a social actor.

The Child as Social Person provides an integrated overview of the exciting field of developmental social psychology, and as such will be essential reading for advanced undergraduate students in psychology, education and social work, as well as postgraduates and researchers in these disciplines.

Sara Meadows works in the Graduate School of Education of the University of Bristol. As a psychologist she uses the concepts and the methods of developmental psychology as a way of understanding what children are experiencing at home and in their other social settings and the ways in which they grow up as effective social actors. Much of her current research is with the Avon Longitudinal Study of Parents and Children (ALSPAC), also known as the 'Children of the Nineties' study.

The Child as Social Person

Sara Meadows

Routledge
Taylor & Francis Group

LONDON AND NEW YORK

First published 2010
by Routledge
27 Church Road, Hove, East Sussex BN3 2FA

Simultaneously published in the USA and Canada
by Routledge
270 Madison Avenue, New York, NY 10016

Routledge is an imprint of the Taylor & Francis Group, an Informa business

Copyright © 2010 Psychology Press

Typeset in Times by Garfield Morgan, Swansea, West Glamorgan
Printed and bound in Great Britain by TJ International Ltd, Padstow,
Cornwall
Cover design by Anú Design

British Library Cataloguing in Publication Data
A catalogue record for this book is available from the British Library

Library of Congress Cataloging-in-Publication Data
Meadows, Sara.
   The child as social person / Sara Meadows.
       p. cm.
    ISBN 978-0-415-45199-4 (hardback) – ISBN 978-0-415-45200-7 (pbk.)
1. Socialization. 2. Social skills in children. 3. Social interaction in children.
I. Title.
   HQ783.M377 2010
   303.3'2083–dc22

                                                            2009027233

ISBN: 978-0-415-45199-4 (hbk)
ISBN: 978-0-415-45200-7 (pbk)

Dedicated with love and wonder to my daughter Anne, who has been from infancy an excellent thinker and a lovely social person, and who has enabled me to bask to the full in parental pride and reflected glory. Born in a tempest, she might well have been called 'Miranda'.

Contents

A note for the reader

I have tried to represent the literature fairly and clearly, but I am very anxious that readers should go on from this book to the more detailed information that lies behind what I have said here. I have therefore tried to give a good range of references to begin this further reading. I have included review papers, key texts, and a selection of papers and books which should, together, equip the reader with a sense of the field and knowledge of key words, and of authors, to search for. A few non-psychology books are included, mainly because they provide insights and enjoyment complementary to that gained from the standard works.

Chapter 1

Beginning to look at the development of the child as social person

1.1 Introduction

The study of 'the child as social person' is one of the major areas of child psychology – a complement to the study of 'the child as thinker' which I wrote about in an earlier book (Meadows 2006) – and it is also at the core of discussions of what causes and what can prevent mental health problems and antisocial behaviour. The aim of this book is to provide an informed and accessible overview of the area that will encourage the reader to think usefully about what children do as social persons and how their different social careers build up, allowing the reader access to research literature and current burning issues. There have been various interesting shifts and widenings in what children's social development is thought to be, and this book is intended to review the field and, as far as possible, suggest what answers to the issues involved might be like. In this chapter I present the core psychological model that I am going to use in an attempt to synthesise different bodies of evidence, and raise some issues from other standpoints.

There is relevant research in a wide range of disciplines. These have tended to be isolated from each other, and I am convinced that workers in each field need to be better informed about each other's progress. Recent work has generated new data and new explanatory models that I want to juxtapose, and it has shown that some of the assumptions we have left unquestioned need to be re-examined. I hope to give students who are new to the field of social development a sense of what is going on, to allow researchers who are more dug into it to access the relevant research flowering outside their own areas, and to fork over and refresh the general compost heap: which may all, finally, help us to grow children's social lives better than we do at present.

Here, in the first chapter, I will present, briefly, some of the issues that will surface for closer examination elsewhere. The first is fundamental for how we describe people's social lives; it is the question of what a 'social person' is. This may seem to be capable of a clear answer, but there are different components. We act socially, interacting with other people – for example we talk to our children. We have social agency, social purposes, goals and intentions – for example we encourage our children to work hard in school so that they will get into good universities. And we tell a narrative of ourselves and of our social partners, a combination of autobiography and biography of others – for example that our talking to our child early in her life has contributed to, but not entirely caused, her academic success. These components interact, but do not have identical developmental paths, as we will see. Nor do our frames of reference include them all easily. In fact there are a number of problems in the background, stretching right back to psychology's unresolved tension between its two definitions as 'the science of mental life' and 'the science of behaviour'. At one level when we look at the 'social' or the 'person' we are concerned with what people can be observed to do when they act socially or think of themselves or other people or social systems and so forth; at another it is the system behind these different abilities. Researchers tend to focus on one level rather than another, the within-person or the interpersonal or the group or the culture, with less commitment to understanding how different levels interact. Sometimes this is because different researchers are using different, albeit allied, disciplines; the user of neurophysiological research is probably not dealing with quite the same question about personality or emotional functioning as the users of research in social psychology or anthropology. I am going to argue that there would be more progress in the study of children's social development if practitioners who differed in their focus on the subject nevertheless took into account the illumination that other focuses provided. The study of emotional resilience in childhood and adulthood is a shining example of the advances that arise when different disciplines, in this case developmental psychology, cognitive neurophysiology, and comparative psychology, are brought together intelligently.

Another uncertainty stretching back to the early days of psychology is about what the limits of social psychology are in the sense of what is not 'social'. Virtually every human action involves both oneself and other people and will therefore be both social and personal. One nineteenth century division of psychology's subject matter, still perceptible in the literature, was into 'affective' (or emotional), 'conative' (or motivational) and 'cognitive' (or intellectual). The problem with this division is that it underplays the links between cognition, emotion and motivation, and these links have been largely neglected in research, which is regrettable. Nor does the traditional division easily accommodate the social dimension of behaviour, and here another problematic issue about psychology is relevant: is it a matter of each individual constructing his or her own individual social and personal system, or are such systems constructed within and by social interaction? Again, much of the literature tends to focus on either individual or social without giving the other adequate consideration, and many of the descriptive studies do not help with the problem because they seek to describe a generalised child and do not examine the variation between individuals with different powers of construction or different experience of social interaction. Further, there is ambivalence among us all, psychologists included, about whether to deal with humanity as part of the animal kingdom, subject to the same general biological laws, or as a unique species, whose similarities to for example primates or laboratory rats are trivial and uninteresting. And these debates happen also in the other social sciences, often with an even stronger dismissal of the relevance of biology.

A whole set of even more unresolved issues arise about the parallel question of what 'development' is. These interact with the problems of the nature and limits of 'the social' that I have just mentioned; if these are difficulties when we look at completed social development in adults, they are much more delicate when we look at social development in childhood, because in childhood we have to explain both development and stability. Even when we have a stable state of social behaviour or personal identity, it may be the result of dynamic processes that maintain that stability within a permanent process of change. Development is not just about how X becomes Y or gives rise to Y, but about how X maintains itself as X. As I will discuss, there are theoretical accounts of both development and stability which need to be brought to bear on descriptions of the ways in which children behave.

The introduction is not the place to discuss these difficult issues. They will be implicit (occasionally explicit) in my description of 'the child as social person', and are more fully addressed in the later parts of the book, in which I look at accounts of 'social development' and what pushes, pulls and mauls it. I hope readers will read the descriptive sections to get a reasonably firm sense of what has to be explained, but be able to enjoy a bit of uncertainty about what sorts of explanation might work. Very little indeed is at the level of scientific certainty that we would like, but there is enough clarity to allow some suggestion of what further knowledge is needed, and quite often of what practice should be.

There are, I think, three good reasons for studying the development and acquisition of social cognition, skills, attitudes and practices, and of personhood, in childhood. First, they are there, interesting in themselves. Second, understanding them is going to make a major contribution to understanding human social life: as J. M. Baldwin (1895) said 'the study of children is often the only means of testing the truth of our mental analyses'. Third, understanding development should illuminate our activities as people interacting with children and influencing their social functioning in both formal and informal settings. I think we can already draw ideas from the field about how to facilitate their social development, and about what could impede it, even though we are some way from a rigorous under-standing (and even further from implementing it).

There is a vast and varied range of phenomena and theory about 'children as social persons', diverse as to intellectual roots, methods and applications. This raises problems of organisation for a book like this. It is impossible to produce a linear account with a series of one-off discussions topic by topic. Dealing with children as social persons topic by topic – friendships separate from sibling relationships, attachment separate from achievement, bullying separate from prosocial behaviour – risks overlooking the associations between different areas of behaviour and may miss opportunities to clarify common processes. A chronological organisation, all about each age in succession, is equally unsatisfactory. Talking about 'the infant', 'the toddler', middle childhood', 'adolescence' would misrepresent the variation that there is in individuals' development (there is much evidence of developmentally significant differences between individuals of the same age); and would also obscure the important and fascinating issues that arise over what continuity and what change there is over time. Studies of social behaviour and social development develop from a wide range of theoretical roots, and dealing with these discipline by discipline would make it harder to see where disciplines overlap or reinforce or contradict each other, which in my view is one of the most important things we need to clarify in order to progress. They reflect a wide range of practical issues, and again it is often the case that we cannot solve a social problem by addressing only one aspect of it. Because of all of this, many topics need to be addressed from more than one angle, and relate to other topics. No single way of cutting the cake appeals: none easily incorporates ideas from outside mainstream Anglo-American psychology, and none easily ties development and social action to coherent theory. I have come to the conclusion that the only intellectually honest course is to insist on the need for continual cross-referencing between topics, approaches and ages.

I have therefore organised my material in terms of the child in different contexts or social systems, with copious cross-references to where similar topics are addressed in different settings. The index is also constructed in such a way as to facilitate finding relevant work on a topic even if it is embedded in another section. In general, I hope readers will read with an eye to making comparisons and constructing links across fields, and in particular will test the assertions made within fields against those from other disciplines. (Part of my writing process has been to seek advice from specialists in different areas about whether my non-specialist account of their field made adequate sense in the context of this book: I have been grateful for their corrections and reassurance.)

The book is long, full of cross-references and linked to an enormous bibliography. A reviewer of my last book, *The Child as Thinker*, said it was more like an enormous Victorian novel than something from which 'the important stuff' could be filleted out in the half hour between lectures. *The Child as Social Person* is even more like this, inescapably because the different aspects of 'social personhood' are intricately inter-related; it would be a serious mistake to think that there are 'important bits' that make sense all by themselves and irrespective of much else. However, just as there is in even the longest Victorian novels, there is a plan to the book. The core of the structure derives from the theory proposed by Urie Bronfenbrenner. This is presented in the first chapter, which also briefly presents the disciplinary approaches to children's social action that modulate a Bronfenbrenner approach – ways of understanding social development as influenced by evolution, genes, social systems and culture. With Bronfenbrenner's model and the range of relevant disciplines always in mind, I have tried to provide niches for detailed discussion of important topics such that a reader will find related theories or topics following on from each other. The cross-referencing should make it easier to find where the same character turned up or will re-appear.

Because we all experience life as social persons, we all have experience and opinions to draw on when we think about the subject matter of this book. We are also dealing with issues that have big personal repercussions for ourselves, and enormous social implications. I have therefore been anxious above all to tie my assertions to systematic evidence. The text is lavishly referenced, and my intention is that interested readers will be able to use these references to test how substantial what I say really is. 'Lavish' has not meant unselective, but neither does it necessarily mean that I have cited only what is most important – being especially vivid, or especially current, or addressing a neglected area, or being among the most cited papers or authors in the field, all entered into decisions about what to keep in. The bibliography contains important books but primarily useful review papers, theoretical critiques, and empirical papers from a wide range of journals – thank you to my university for buying us access to so many. Readers will, I hope, develop an awareness of big themes, key authors, and unanswered questions that will take them forward into their own developing understanding of 'the child as social person'. I hope they will also develop the enthusiasm to search out their own material.

As I will describe shortly, Bronfenbrenner proposed a model of concentric or overlapping social settings, with the child at the centre amid successively wider and more varied patterns of interaction and influence. This is the basis for the organisation of this book. Things about being a social person that we commonly think of as being located largely within the child are discussed first. Successive chapters begin with the child and what he or she brings to social settings; move on to social interaction in which the parents are the other main players; then to relationships of the child and others within the wider family, the peer group, the school; then to the influence of social settings which affect the child although the child does not act in them. Typically within chapters and sections earlier periods of development are discussed before later ones. Resilience has a chapter of its own at the end of the book, which allows for explicit recapitulation of the themes derived from Bronfenbrenner and the base disciplines, and brings together considerations of all sorts of factors discussed earlier.

Throughout, I have been interested in both accounts of current social behaviour and experience and in how these carry forward in the life history of the individual. Developmental principles begin to appear here, and get some discussion in terms of how well they could account for children's social behaviour. But whatever general principles there are in development and in social functioning, they result in an important and fascinating range of individual differences – differences which result from individuals being innately different from each other, from individuals meeting different circumstances within the same social system, from individuals living in different social systems – and, no doubt, from developmental principles being probabilistic rather than extremely deterministic. I have tried to deal with both generality and variation in a principled way.

1.2 Bronfenbrenner's model of Person–environment interaction in development

The book that is the main intellectual ancestor of this book is Bronfenbrenner (1979), which sets out the parameters of an understanding of children's development as social persons that would be full enough to guide our efforts to make that development a positive process reaching positive ends. Describing Bronfenbrenner's ideas is my next task, and his distinctions structure my book. After doing that, I turn briefly to three other areas of theory that have also been influential, evolutionary psychology, developmental behaviour genetics, and the sociology of childhood, whose ideas will crop up at intervals throughout the book.

The core of Bronfenbrenner's model is the position that individuals and environments have to be seen as mutually–shaping systems, each changing over time, each reacting to changes in the other. Although it is possible to look at components of systems separately, and I will use research that does, there are enormous benefits for our understanding if we can maintain this view. Bronfenbrenner was sometimes quite caustic about research that conceived of children in ways far removed from the everyday realities of their experience in social settings – 'much of contemporary research can be characterized as the study of development-out-of-context' (Bronfenbrenner 1979: 21). The more we understand the multiple contexts of any piece of behaviour, the better we understand that behaviour.

Bronfenbrenner developed his model of the ecology of human development from psychological and anthropological studies of children, and from his own experience of children growing up in Soviet Russia and in the USA in one of its most anti-communist periods (e.g. Bronfenbrenner 1971), but it obviously relates to the evolution of the human species, which has also been a matter of adaptation between individual and environment. I develop this point later in this chapter (pp. 20–22).

In his book-length account of his model (Bronfenbrenner 1979) he begins by offering a series of definitions. Firstly,

> The ecology of human development involves the scientific study of the progressive, mutual accommodation between and active, growing human being and the changing properties of the immediate settings in which the developing persons lives, as this process is affected by relationships between these settings, and by the larger contexts in which the settings are embedded. [. . .] the growing person is viewed not merely as a tabula rasa on which the environment makes its impact, but as a growing, dynamic entity that progressively moves into and restructures the milieu in which it resides. Since the environment also exerts its influence, requiring a process of mutual accommodation, the interaction between person and environment is viewed as two-directional, that is characterized by *reciprocity*. [. . .] the environment defined as relevant to developmental processes is not limited to a single, immediate setting but is extended to incorporate interconnections between such settings, as well as to external influences emanating from the larger surroundings.
>
> (Bronfenbrenner 1979: 21–22)

Children growing up in different settings have access to different, and similar, interpersonal, economic, social and cultural resources, and experience the broader socio-cultural world in different, and similar, ways. What their contexts offer or do not offer them, or make more or less easily available to them, or just allow them to pick up themselves, will contribute to and even mould the development of all their psychological and social characteristics. What their contexts define as desirable will shape their goals and values, and thus their achievements, and thus their self-esteem: their own behaviour will evoke reactions and shape their context, especially their social context (Baumeister *et al.* 2003; Ge 1996; Salmivalli *et al.* 1999; Serbin and Karp 2004; Shaw 2003; Spencer and Blades 2006; Thornberry *et al.* 2003). 'No child is an island, entire of itself; every child is a part of a continent, attached to the main', if I may adapt John Donne to my own purposes. Children are persons, in relationships, engaging in activities; and so are the people they relate to, react to and engage with.

Children are not, as we will see, born as little blank slates on which their experience can write anything at all: by birth, maybe even at conception, they have some little peculiarities that could affect their entire later lives. We will look at inborn characteristics later (pp. 30–36, 50–51) while recognising the child's potential for change. I am going to use a model of child development that emphasises the role of children's everyday experience in both normal and abnormal developmental change. Developmentally, the child's experience of the world begins with the interaction between the babe in arms (or *in utero*) and the quite specialised and restricted world that is provided for it by its parents. As children grow older, they encounter more and more varied social worlds: perhaps just what is available with more mobility, more skills and more autonomy at home, perhaps entry into daycare; eventually entry into schooling, peer groups, employment and adult life. Each of these environments makes different demands on the individual, and children have to learn to negotiate their way through each. The environment affects the child, but the child is active and affects the environment too; and there may be effects of one environment on another.

Just after the definition I have just quoted, Bronfenbrenner wrote 'The *ecological environment* is conceived topologically as a nested arrangement of concentric structures, each contained within the next' (Bronfenbrenner 1979: 22). One of the metaphors that commentators have used follows on from this statement (and from Bronfenbrenner's own studies of education in Soviet Russia). It compares children's environments to a set of nested Russian dolls. The tiniest doll, typically the child–mother dyad, is located within a slightly larger doll, perhaps the nuclear family group: this is contained in a larger one, perhaps the whole extended family, and this in larger ones up to and including the whole society or even all of mankind. Although certainly it is better to recognise the existence of multiple contexts, the Russian dolls metaphor unhelpfully suggests that they are separate and do not influence each other, thus contradicting the point that Bronfenbrenner had just made. More recent research has confirmed, as we will see, Bronfenbrenner's point that it is often precisely the relations between the child's social systems that are most interesting for development (pp. 12, 62, 82, 143, 208–12, 221–23). It is rare for any social context to be completely immune from influence from any other.

Bronfenbrenner's model insists that for a full understanding of human development we need to examine several levels of social systems.

> Human development is the process through which the growing person acquires a more differentiated and valid conception of the ecological environment, and becomes motivated and able to engage in activities that reveal the properties of, sustain, or restructure that environment at levels of similar or greater complexity in form and content.
>
> (Bronfenbrenner 1979: 27)

1.2.1 Person, process, environment, activity, and time

Bronfenbrenner's definition of human development notes essential points to be considered in looking at the child as social person – differentiation of the person and of his or her ecology; motivation, engagement and activity;

complexity of form and content. Dealing with it thoroughly is the task of this book; but as a preliminary I note the importance of person, process, environment, activity and time.

1   **Persons** – individuals with unique arrangements of personal resources, particular levels of development, and personal histories, expectations, and characteristics. Each individual will have obvious personal characteristics – 'demand resources' – that shape the ways that other people behave towards them; for example their gender, or age, or apparent emotional state. As we will see, some of these operate in very predictable ways, for example the infant's softness, roundness and lack of co-ordination tend to suppress aggressive behaviour in adults (pp. 50–51). Individuals also have social and emotional resources that vary more in the population, and may have to be gradually inferred from their actions rather than responded to immediately – differences in intelligence and emotional stability, or differences in social capital such as access to good schooling or good parenting or possession of an extensive network of supportive friends and allies (pp. 91, 146, 155). And they will differ in 'force characteristics', qualities such as persistence, initiative, and temperament that contribute to the internal motivation of their development (pp. 77–78, 87–90). I will be presenting evidence on how complex the origins of these characteristics are, and they are certainly constituted by factors outside the individual, but for convenience I shall follow Bronfenbrenner (e.g. Bronfenbrenner and Evans 2000) and begin by locating them in the person.

Developmentally we know that there will be a general increase in personal psychological complexity (for example more history, self-consciousness, reflection, expectations, skills). There will also be both changes and continuities in persons' interactions with others, due to the development of their psychological processes, to developments in the roles they play, to developments in the settings they engage with, and due to the impact of historical events. The characteristics of the person influence social action at multiple levels, and when more than one person is involved, relationships between persons, individuals' views of each other, may become important. As the child develops, the personal characteristics of the other people that he or she interacts with also change; firstly in that the range of persons widens and the number increases, but also because even the persons who have been there from the beginning change because of their own development and because of their interactions with the child. The experienced mother of a teenager, for example, should have developed from when she was the naïve mother of a new baby – in her parenting skills, in her expectations, in the social influences and institutions she has to deal with, in her self-concept, in her view of her child, to name but a few.

2   **Processes** – how do persons acquire more knowledge, more social skills, different expectations of social interaction? What leads a toddler to recover from a tantrum? What persuades teenagers that it is crucially important to have the latest electronic gadget, or that it is OK to smoke, to drink, to carry a knife? Why have these particular individuals turned into career criminals and these other individuals into dedicated altruists? Attention could be focused especially on small moment-by-moment experiences or one-off dramatic ones; on different sorts of 'cause' (Meadows 2006). Developmentally what is, I think, particularly powerful for most people's development is the small quiet un-noticed '*proximal*' process – regular reciprocal person/other/environment interactions occurring over and over again for years and years. (Much of this book documents such processes.) Bronfenbrenner sees these as powerful engines of increases in the development of competence and dysfunction, for example in aggressive behaviour (pp. 120, 136, 168–69, 230) or sense of oneself as competent or helpless (pp. 46, 74, 77–78, 88, 90, 169, 192, 203, 214, 215, 217, 221) or difficulties in maintaining control and integration of behaviour across situations and domains of development (pp. 62–63, 76–77, 93–94, 119–121). This emphasis on regular and repeated proximal processes reminds us to look for issues about exposure (duration, frequency, predictability, timing, intensity) of these little everyday experiences, as well as bigger or unusual or more dramatic events.

We should note also that the combined effect of person and process may be non-additive. What looks like the same processes may have different impacts on different individuals because of their different personal characteristics. Individuals with a particular gene may be more vulnerable to the effects of abuse from their parents, for example (pp. 37, 55–56, 61–62, 129–30, 141–44, 147, 266, 267), or babies who have had experience of brief, pleasant separations from their mothers may be more able to withstand the experience of a further separation (Goldberg 2000; Rutter 1981, pp. 54, 59, 125, 126, 277–78), or heritability may be higher in environments where most people experience 'good enough' proximal processes such as encouragement of socialisation for activities that could support positive development than in environments where such support is rarer (Turkheimer *et al.* 2003, pp. 18, 30–34).

3   **Environments** – the third key point Bronfenbrenner reminds us of is the importance of environments, or contexts, for development. Developmental contexts may differ in size and complexity, and in their relationship to other developmental contexts. They differ too in the resources, objects and symbols, that are used. The context of the babe in arms, for example, centres on experience with the parents and a relatively small number of toys etc., and the personal characteristics focally involved are those of the baby, the parents, and of the probably

small number of others who have close and repeated contact with the baby; but even this small cocooned context is affected by other contexts – there may be an interface with the health services, with the parents' employment, with the culture's enthusiasm for having more babies to refresh an ageing population or its concern about over population or births to 'unsuitable' parents. Later developmental contexts, in ever-widening social worlds, are ever more permeated by other contexts, current ones, and ones experienced in the past, and ones anticipated in the future.

Bronfenbrenner's model, therefore, includes not just the immediate context of the child's experience but those other contexts that impinge upon it, sometimes far away from the child's experience. (It will be marginal to this book, but a case can be made that even non-human geographical factors can affect not just economies but psychological functioning (Clark and Uzzell 2006; Spencer and Blades 2006; Van de Vliert 2007).)

1.2.2 Contexts – microsystems, mesosystems, macrosystems, exosystems

The core level of context for development is the level of Microsystems. A microsystem is 'a pattern of activities, roles and interpersonal relations experienced by the developing person in a given setting with given particular physical and material characteristics.' (Bronfenbrenner 1979: 22). Typically microsystems are actual day-to-day settings where people engage in face-to-face interaction e.g. at home with mum, in the classroom, in the workplace). The word 'experience' is key; both in that if an individual does not have direct experience of a particular context then it is not a microsystem for that individual, although it could have an influence on the individual's actual microsystems, as I describe shortly; and in the sense that we need to attend to the individual's subjective or phenomenological experience of the microsystem as well as its objective characteristics. For example, as I discuss below, siblings commonly report that their parents treat them differently, although to the parents and to outside observers it appears that all the siblings receive much the same parenting (pp. 167–69). In some respects, siblings' development can be examined in terms of shared experiences of parenting, but for other outcomes the subjective experience of being favoured or not may be a better predictor.

Within microsystems what matters is the activities, roles and interpersonal relations that the participants engage in, learn and incorporate into their personal stories: these are the elements or building blocks of settings. We need to recognise patterns of enduring reciprocal interaction and relationships (c.f. Hinde 1979); interactions have a history of past experiences and involve expectations for the future. We also need to remember something Bronfenbrenner made explicit; that if one member of a micro-system is learning and developing, the other member probably is too.

Different microsystems tend to exist in a system of relations between microsystems – these are *mesosystems* e.g. child–home–school, or patient–family–medics. A particular individual, for example me, operates in the microsystems of her family (those family members surviving from her childhood in her family of origin and those acquired in adulthood), her employment (as colleague, scholar and teacher), her various voluntary activities, her friendship groups, her neighbourly relations, etc., etc. The different microsystems are connected via individuals' experience of each, via communications between settings, via the formal and informal knowledge of each setting about each other, and via the place of each in the entire social network. Quite commonly in my microsystems with partner and with best friend, for example, we talk about each other's work lives – this is a safe place to work off frustration with colleagues, and the activity both provides ideas about dealing with difficulties at work and sympathetic warmth about how much more effective, reasonable, and generally nice we are than our antagonists. This mesosystem of how the work microsystem is understood by individuals engaged with in other microsystems facilitates our functioning in all the microsystems involved. Bronfenbrenner proposes that stronger and more diverse links between microsystems are better for development than lack of connectedness. Linkage is probably good for non-developmental functioning too, though that is not our immediate concern here. Chaotic connections between microsystems, or some micro-systems being so demanding they exclude the possibility of successful participation in others, may be a serious problem.

Separate from microsystems, but nevertheless sometimes exerting a powerful influence on what happens within the microsystem and on what effects it has, are *exosystems* – situations with a bearing on individuals in which they don't play a direct role. An example is the parent's workplace, which is a microsystem for the parent but also affects the child, perhaps through the parent's energy level or level of satisfaction with life, or through the amount of time the parents can spend being parents rather than being workers, or through the cash their employment provides for purchases for the child. Similarly school staff meetings rarely involve the pupils, but they are an important exosystem for what happens in the classroom, and hence may have a significant impact on the child.

At a somewhat higher-order there are *macrosystems* – e.g. cultural ideologies, practices, proscriptions, and expectations about behaviour and development – which are consistencies in the shared values, belief systems, lifestyles, social options and so forth that lower-order settings afford to the child. These exist at cultural or subcultural level and have a significant impact on individuals and microsystems. Possible examples might include a consistent emphasis on educational achievement and accreditation, for example the current emphasis on assessment in British schools, a government policy which has arguably diverted teacher and child effort towards achieving a high rate of success in public examinations and tests; or gender discrimination, for example the exclusion of women from higher education in nineteenth century Britain (justified at the time by arguments that too much education would make young women infertile); or the rules of a dominant religious group about who may own property, be educated, drive their own car, aspire to a position of religious leadership, etc. Macrosystem effects are by no means confined to public activity, they may even define what are unacceptable personal characteristics – for example cultures have differed in beliefs about whether it was the right thing to do to kill newborns who were visibly deformed or part of a multiple birth (de Mause 1976). And they may define what is morally acceptable behaviour, for example whether children should be unquestioningly obedient to their parents.

Bronfenbrenner was always strongly interested in making people's lives 'better'. He said that for optimum development the child needs to experience 'good' and 'consistent' and 'co-ordinated systems' at all these levels. We will examine whether this is the case. We have to be careful to think critically about what we consider to be 'good' development – it is all too easy to assume that what we have experienced ourselves is the ideal, or that someone else's different development is not so good. Similarly for 'consistency' and 'co-ordination'; some chaos may be tolerable, some individuals may be more resilient in the face of chaos than others are. It is important to remember, too, that what is needed to adapt in one environment will not necessarily be adaptive in another.

1.2.3 Time

The final point I want to mention here is that we need to be alert to time. We need to consider the time period that we are studying in the individual's life (the same experience may have different effects at different ages), during an event (an intervention may have short-term effects different from longer-term effects), and beyond the individual. The impact of one-off events may be different, and produced differently, from the impact of 'chronic events', that have happened thousands of times over a long period. Individuals exist within a particular historical (and geographical) context, and such a context may differ from others. There are large-scale historical changes in expectations and practice (e.g. about urbanisation, about literacy, about the employment of women, about the acceptability and the circumstances of divorce, about technological access) that sweep across societies, and via macrosystems, exosystems and microsystems affect most individuals (although some may be more affected than others); and there is also a more local history of significant events (e.g. exposure to war or economic depression, rehousing in a different neighbourhood) which may have strong effects on those individuals who experience the events. An historical perspective can sometimes help to clarify processes (pp. 252–53, 275, 277; Elder 1974) and also make the direction and amount of change or of continuity more comprehensible.

This point about time applies particularly strongly when we are looking for effects of intermittent problems. The research on the effects of poverty, for example (Micklewright 2002; Newman and Massengill 2006; Ackerman *et al.* 2007; pp. 92–93, 148, 150–52), is complicated by the fact that if you assess a family's income level repeatedly over a period of time you are likely to find that it fluctuates. Some families may be considered to be living in poverty at one time but might be above the poverty level at another, for example because the head of the family is now in employment. And then at the third assessment, perhaps the employment has ended or another child has been born, and the family's income-to-needs ratio has fallen below the poverty line again. It is very typical for low-income families to have incomes that are unstable as well as low, so that their income varies and they do not have much opportunity to save resources that are surplus at one moment to cushion them during a future period of lack of cash. Clinical depression is another problem that can be intermittent. We have enough evidence to believe, for example, that exposure to their mother's depression can have an adverse effect on children, with more periods of maternal depression problems leading to worse results, but really precise evidence about the quantity and timing of problems and of their effects can be very hard to get.

1.2.4 Multiple factors at multiple levels

There are real questions about how to manage this intrinsic complexity in the data. Some theorists select a variable or level and treat all others as subsidiary to it, or as background noise (for example some evolutionary psychologists and some experimental social psychologists). This is a strategy that may illuminate a particular level or process but at the expense of failing to recognise what is important about others, and also precluding the possibility of interaction between variables. For example, although a substantial amount of research on the developmental effects of exposure to lead has indicated that it is significantly harmful to the nervous system and hence to cognitive and behavioural development (Meadows 2006; Hubbs-Tait *et al.* 2005), this research has also shown that the association between lead exposure and problematic outcome is affected by other variables, including what other neuro-toxicants the child is exposed to and also non-chemical factors. If you compare families from different social backgrounds, infants and children from families with low levels of socio-economic resources show more ill effects from the same level of lead exposure. This suggests that lead poisoning may be one contributor to the social class differences that are all too well known and hard to rectify, but also that if you want to look at, say, the effects of lead exposure on delinquency, you need to pay attention to the social factors relevant to delinquency as well as to the exposure to lead, lest the developmental effect of lead exposure be attributed to an social aspect of the family microsystem status or vice versa. Variables are likely to confound each other, and correlational evidence will not provide a firm picture of causality because of the presence of so many uncontrolled confounding variables. It has to be complemented by other sorts of studies. In the case of lead exposure, research on the physiological effects of lead on the nervous system and animal studies made complementary contributions, although it is not always straightforward to translate from one measure of nerve damage in animals to changes in their behaviour, and then to find the correct analogies in humans.

Careful attention to systems and collections of factors is especially important when the size of the effect of each factor is quite small. Unless we understand how it fits into other factors and their effects, we are at risk of concluding that it is not really terribly important. For example, even though it took quite a while for the evidence to influence policy, it is now believed that *high* levels of lead pollution are entirely undesirable for children and need to be eliminated (Meadows 2006; Hubbs-Tait *et al.* 2005). Exposure to *moderate* levels of lead seems to have a measurably damaging effect only in families with low educational achievements in the parents, with little or no effect evident when the child's parents are well-educated and value school highly. This may mean that there is a threshold effect with lead levels below the threshold being neutral for brain development, but it is more likely that education-focused families manage to teach their children to cope with subtle brain damage in ways that maintain their educational achievement, even though moderate levels are less than good for their brain development.

Allowing the study of several different variable levels simultaneously complicates matter enormously, and serious technical difficulties emerge. For example, if we are working in the field of possible neighbourhood effects on children's development, we can compare individuals living in neighbourhoods with high rates of poverty with those living in neighbourhoods where the incidence of poverty is moderate or low (e.g. Harding 2003). But we have to consider two things. Firstly, individuals live in areas with particular rates of poverty for reasons that might themselves affect outcomes – that these are areas where unemployed and low-income people can find affordable (but substandard) housing, that these are areas which professional highly educated parents choose to avoid, that these individuals in this neighbourhood have not been able to move out to a more prosperous neighbourhood – so that what looks like a 'neighbourhood effect' could be to some degree a result of social selection into both living in such a neighbourhood and the outcomes we are interested in. Secondly, if we try to get round the problem of selection by controlling for possible confounding variables, we may lose some of the indirect pathways between the causes and the effects. Controlling for quality of housing, for example, could obscure possible neighbourhood effects where overcrowding, or lack of access to safe outside space, or effects on health of damp and pollution, were part of the causal pathway. We need to be very cautious with our evidence and to think through our explanations of development equally carefully. In particular, we do need to identify associations between possible causes and their effects, but we also need to sort out what the causal pathways actually are.

This requires careful thought about what a 'cause' is. Something can be associated with another thing without causing it; for example lambs in the fields of Britain do not cause the Easter Eggs that appear at much the same time. A statistical association between A and B is very interesting, but we need further investigation if we are going to understand it. Quite often in the field of psychology and behaviour, an apparent 'cause' does not have a causal effect itself, it is associated with the outcome because it is itself associated with the real causes; social class or 'socio-economic status' (SES), for example, is strongly associated with differences in mortality, well-being, and educational achievement, but the association is more likely to be due to the range of risk factors that SES stands for than to the class identity itself. Questions about how could a factor actually work can be helpful in clarifying this. Ideally we have a clear theory and we understand how the whole thing actually works.

Ethologists distinguish between different sorts of causes in their studies of animal behaviour (e.g. Hinde 1982, 1987). The first is the proximal cause, the stimulus that immediately triggered the behaviour – for example I looked up because the doorbell rang because someone pushed it. Even this simple example makes it clear that there is a cluster of necessary conditions for the bell-pushing to have its effect – the bell and the bellpush have to be connected up correctly, for example. And there are other causal questions immediately rushing in – why did the person press the doorbell, for example? Why is there a doorbell? Why is there a door? Why am I being interrupted?

Ethologists are strongly interested in how behaviours develop, both in the life of the individual and in the evolution of the species. As social persons we have histories, which have developed from our earliest years and modify our behaviour. When we were younger we behaved differently from the way we behave now. Our individual ontogenetic histories will not change the bell-pushing /bell-ringing association itself, but they may make us more or less eager to press the doorbell, or to respond to it when we hear it. This second level of cause is central to developmental psychology.

There are two further levels of cause in the ethologists' concerns, however. One is the evolutionary history of the behaviour. Understanding this is likely to involve comparisons between related species, or discussion of how the behaviour might contribute to evolutionary adaptation. The other level of causation is to do with what the behaviour is for, what is its function. The function of the doorbell is to ring to attract attention. The function of pressing the doorbell is to make a socially acceptable noise to signal your arrival at the door. The function of having a doorbell is to know when someone wishes to tell you that they have arrived on the doorstep. The function of having a doorbell *and* a closed door is to allow you to choose whether or not to respond to people outside the door while maintaining a degree of social politeness. And so on. Purpose and intention may come in here.

Just as there are different sorts of causes, we cannot assume that there is only one pathway from cause to effect; or even from a set of causes to a set of effects. Most of social development involves multiple factors and multiple exposures to these factors, not one simple powerful characteristic or event that is the only cause. Two individuals may both start at A and end up at Z, but they could take largely different paths from one to the other because of their own different starting characteristics or their own experiences step-by-step on the way – there are multiple causal pathways. Two individuals may start out alike but end up differently – multifinality. Or they may start out unlike and end up in the same place – equifinality. Our research can identify key events in an individual's biography, or risk factors which make healthy development less likely for most of the individuals who encounter them, but it is very hard to link these different sorts of evidence. What is a risk factor for many may not be for me. What has been a catastrophe for me might not be for my more resilient neighbour or for the population as a whole. We are fairly safe in predicting that individuals with many risk factors are more likely to have life go badly than those who have few risk factors, but we still need to try to specify which were operative and in what ways.

All this implies interdisciplinary work, with for example psychologists, neuroscientists, and socio-cultural theorists paying serious attention to each other; and recognition of both the potential for and the complexity of interventions. So far as the development of the child as a social person is concerned, I believe what follows, and my concern is to specify it and act on it:

> to develop – intellectually, emotionally, socially and morally – a child requires, for all of these, the same thing: participation in progressively more complex activities, on a regular basis over an extended period in the child's life, with one or more persons with whom the child develops a strong, mutual emotional attachment, and who are committed to the child's well-being, preferably for life.
>
> (Bronfenbrenner 1994: 113)

I turn now to some of the theoretical perspectives that are relevant to the development of the child as a social person in order to introduce them before they crop up in later chapters.

1.3 Evolutionary psychology and socialisation

Clearly, contemporary human beings are the most recent stage of a very long history of earlier human beings, each generation of which has laid down legacies for its successors. At this point, I want to mention some of the ways in which evolutionary psychology conceptualises these legacies, focusing on those which are most relevant to the development of the child as a social person.

Darwin's account of evolution and the developments in evolutionary theory since 1859 have been among the most revolutionary and the most substantial theories ever. Not surprisingly, psychologists have tried to use evolution as a source of ideas and explanations for human behaviour. There is a large amount of theorising about how the evolution of the human species over time might account for some of the ways in which we behave (Beaulieu and Bugental 2007; Bjorklund and Pellegrini 2000, 2002). Some of this is subtle and interesting, some of it has, deservedly, been severely criticised; the social and political issues raised by evolutionary psychology today are potentially as earth-shaking as the implications of Darwin's original work were for nineteenth century religious thought.

Darwin's core idea was natural selection. This combined three self-evident truths. Firstly, individuals vary in how successfully they survive and reproduce – some have many descendants, some only a few. Secondly, individuals vary in physical and psychological characteristics – some are prettier, cleverer, stronger, more enthusiastic about football than others. Thirdly, some of the characteristics of the parents can be inherited by their children predictably and whether or not child or parent chooses – the family nose, the freckles, the big feet – and some may be passed on in a much less determined way, for example by teaching or modelling or imitation – fluency in English, an enthusiasm for opera or gardening, a preference for Bristol City over Bristol Rovers, a taste for fine wines. Those individuals who have lots of descendants will tend to have lots of copies of their own inheritable characteristics in future generations. Those individuals who have fewer descendants will tend to hand down fewer inheritable characteristics to the future population.

The theory of natural selection points out that there will, on the whole, be reasons why some individuals survive and reproduce more successfully than others. Some of the time, these reasons involve individuals possessing characteristics that improve their chances of meeting the challenges of the environment – they have better resistance to infection, they win more fights, they are better at getting hold of limited resources, they get preferential treatment from others – and if these characteristics are heritable they will pass on these advantages to their descendants. Individual characteristics that enhance the chances of leaving descendants will become more common in the succeeding generations, whereas characteristics which reduced the ancestors' chances of having descendants will not be passed on so frequently (as there are fewer descendants to carry these characteristics) and may, sooner or later, become vanishingly rare in the population. What we are like now is a mixture of acquired and inherited characteristics, and we come pre-packed with inherited characteristics that were useful to our ancestors.

1.3.1 Explaining inherited characteristics

Thus the level of explanation at the focus of evolutionary psychology is beyond the level of what happened to an individual a moment ago, or when they were a baby, or at any narrow time period. It does not outlaw explanations at such 'proximate' levels, but prefers to go for what Beaulieu and Bugental (2007) call the 'ultimate' level, reproductive success over the course of the evolutionary history of the human species. (There could of course be other levels of 'ultimate cause'; reproductive success over the course of the evolutionary history of living things including non-humans, for example; or causes dependent on the will of a Creator God; or evolutionary causes within the sphere of recent history; but I am not aware of evolutionary psychology that pays very much attention to these.)

'Reproductive success' is typically the theorists' main criterion of the evolutionary success of individuals, or, at different levels, of the evolutionary success of genes or species. Individuals cannot survive forever, and species change over time, but genes, being little bits of deoxyribonucleic acid (DNA), can potentially remain unchanged for millennia. We can trace human ancestry back through analysis of bits of DNA to establish that someone living in the Somerset village of Cheddar at the end of the twentieth century has the same particular bit of DNA as an individual whose bones were found in a cave near Cheddar but who was living there nine thousand years ago; or that contemporary Europeans have some of the genes found in the fossils of Neanderthals (hence they and we may not be two completely separate species, as was previously thought); or even that the species family tree going back to the first emergence of life on earth is of this shape rather than this other shape (Dawkins 2005). Geneticists' answer to the joke of 'which came first, the chicken or the egg?' could be that the chicken is merely the way in which the genes in the egg make another lot of genes. As psychologists or educators we are of course interested in the life of the 'merely' bit, rather than the life of the genes; but nevertheless we need to pay some attention to the evolutionary scale over which the genes replicate themselves.

Genes survive only if individuals who carry them reproduce successfully. This can only happen if the genes help, or at least allow, the individuals who have them to solve the day-to-day problems of living with enough success that they can mate and reproduce, thus producing offspring who carry the parent's genes; and if those genes then allow or help those offspring themselves to survive, mate and reproduce. In all generations, individuals have to solve the problems associated with survival and reproduction. Evolutionary psychology stresses that some of the variation in what solutions to problems are possible comes about because of the different genes that individuals have, although what is a good solution to a survival problem depends on the problem and the environment, as well as on the resources of the individual. If having a particular gene helps individuals solve a problem that threatens their survival or reproduction, then individuals who carry that gene may be more likely to survive and reproduce than individuals who lack it. By reproducing, these individuals will pass on this gene that was helpful to them to the next generation, who may in their turn find their ability to solve this problem is improved because they have the useful gene. Those individuals who carry a less useful gene may have fewer offspring, and consequently in future generations there will be fewer individuals that carry the variant that has been less useful.

We assume that the gene/person combination acts so as to perpetuate/ reproduce itself rather than just giving up and dying off. Individuals thus can be expected to make all sorts of effort to survive, and to reproduce. Reproductive effort will include finding a mate and perhaps retaining a mate, and ensuring the survival of one's genes in one's offspring (and in other related persons, p. 161).

1.3.2 Adaptation

Over enough generations, the result will be that those genetic variations which are really distinctly unhelpful for survival should tend to die out, and those which are maximally helpful for survival should tend to become more common. This is what is often called 'adaptation'; 'the evolutionary selection of genetic variation/s that demonstrate better ways of solving a problem associated with survival and/or reproduction' (Beaulieu and Bugental 2007: 72). However, it is very important to understand the nature of the process.

Firstly, it takes time. A genetic variation that is completely disastrous for those who carry it, so that not even one such individual survives to reproduce, could die out quite quickly, but mostly losing a gene from the gene pool of the population takes several generations. Conversely, if a particular challenge has only been around for a small number of generations, there may not have been time for particular genes to emerge as being either more successful or less successful in meeting it – we have no idea what genes might contribute to a more successful use of Facebook, for example, though of course we could speculate.

Secondly, the process of genetic selection is not goal-directed. Neither individual genes nor the whole genome nor the whole species can know in any sense which particular genes are going to be helpful or unhelpful, what would be the best sorts of genes to have; and if they did, they could not themselves do anything about it. (Gene therapy may change this, but so far the prospects are limited.)

Thirdly, not all characteristics that survive for generation after generation are adaptations in the sense of improving the individual's chances of survival and reproduction. They may survive because they are by-products of some other advantageous adaptive process, or because the genes that control them just happen to be next to an advantageous gene in the DNA string of genes. Or they may survive merely because they have been in the genome for a long time and they are not sufficiently harmful to be selected against – part of a default programme, for example, which is only partially activated in part of the population. That human males still have nipples, although they do not (usually) produce milk, is one example (Dawkins 2005; Gould 1977).

Fourthly, and very importantly, whether a particular gene helps or hinders survival and reproduction depends on both the environment in which the problem is faced, and other genes. For example, peppered moths vary genetically in how dark their wing colour is (Mallett 2004). In the days when heavy industrial pollution deposited a lot of soot on the trees where the moths perched, wings spread, it was advantageous to have dark coloured wings because you were then less visible against the dark trees and less likely to have your reproductive career shortened by being picked off and eaten by a bird: a high proportion of peppered moths were, effectively, black. Following the Clean Air Act in the UK (and equivalent legislation elsewhere) and the consequent reduction in soot on trees, peppered moths found themselves perching on a cleaner background, a lighter grey, and a paler wing colour was much better camouflage against predatory birds. The incidence of pale coloured wings in moths rose rapidly. Genes that made your wings darker were adaptive during the Industrial Revolution, and maladaptive following the Clean Air Act. Sickle cell anaemia offers an example of the co-action of genes. If individuals have only one copy of the gene concerned in sickle cell anaemia, they have some sickle-shaped blood cells but this does not seriously disadvantage them, while the gene also confers additional resistance to malaria and thus is adaptive in areas where there is a high risk of being bitten by a malaria-carrying mosquito. If an individual has two identical copies of this gene, however, there is a high risk of sickle cell anaemia, which is a painful and debilitating condition. The gene also carries little adaptive value if there are no malarial mosquitos in the environment. What is adaptive in one set of circumstances may not be in another. What is adaptive at one time may not be at another. And whether gene A is adaptive is dependent to some degree on whether or not the individual also has genes B, C, and D.

1.3.3 Neoteny, heterochrony and the timing of developmental events

A couple of biological points have to be made briefly here. Human beings as adults retain a uniquely high degree of juvenile characteristics. Basically, we grow up relatively slowly compared with other species and retain many of the characteristics that we had when we were immature. This is called 'neoteny' – holding on to the young – or, alternatively, 'juvenilisation'. Many of the examples commonly cited involve comparisons between development in humans and in chimpanzees: for example humans continue brain growth much later, retain relatively large heads and flat faces, and remain playful and flexible in learning much longer. These changes in the duration and rate of developmental change have been argued to be of the greatest importance in evolution, partly because they were associated with increased opportunities to learn and partly because of their association with retaining characteristics that induced protective behaviour from other members of the species (e.g. Gould 1977; Charlton 2006). These are points that I will return to later (pp. 27, 50–51, 108, 214–17).

Another couple of issues I must mention involve the timing of developmental events. In general, development can only work if the timing of developmental events is relatively favourable. But timing of the start and the end of changes, and the rate of change, can vary. In evolutionary biology, this is called 'heterochrony'. Differences in the timing of the onset and offset of development, and in the rate of development, may have important developmental effects, or they may on the whole even out and not result in differences between individuals. For example, brain growth and head growth starts at about the same time in the chimpanzee fetus as in the human fetus, but only the human continues rapid brain growth for an extended period postnatally. The result is that, on the whole, humans have grown larger brains than chimpanzees by continuing growth for longer. Arguably, the lower rates of dementia in humans who have regularly used their brains for complex cognition (and so maintained the development of new connections between neurones, even maybe the development of some new neurones) is a further example of the openness of development to the timing, in this case the continuation, of experience.

There may be issues if a particular developmental event occurs (or does not occur) at a particular time. For some developments, there may be what have been called 'critical periods' during which the individual is very much more sensitive to influences than before or after – in fact if the influence or experience that usually leads to a particular developmental change does not occur during this 'critical' time the individual may never be able to develop normally. There are numerous examples in the development of birdsong, in the development of human vision, and (probably) in the development of human discrimination and production of speech sounds. It is possible that there are issues about the timing of social contacts in young humans too. These I will return to when I discuss daycare and feral children. On a social rather than an evolutionary level, there are often expectations about the 'right' ages to do things – and anxieties about individuals who do not fit these timetables.

1.3.4 Developmental psychology and evolution

Bronfenbrenner's model draws on individual development (ontogeny) far more than it is related to the development of the human species (phylogeny). There is, however, some developmental psychology that bases itself in theories of how the human species has developed, drawing on ideas from evolutionary theory and research. I will try to integrate some of this into my discussion of children's development as seen from a Bronfenbrenner perspective, but it seemed to me to make sense to write about evolutionary psychology and developmental behaviour genetics in their own terms first. What follows is an attempt to show the sorts of issues and understandings that have emerged from these traditions of study.

So far as physical characteristics are concerned, evolution is broadly accepted by most scientists. Evolutionary psychology and sociobiology take it further by arguing that psychological characteristics evolve through natural selection much as physical ones do. Their argument has the following steps. During a species' evolutionary history, psychological mechanisms evolved to meet adaptive challenges. At any time, the population's present psychological mechanisms may be a result of the species' history of evolutionary adaptation. By examining current psychological processes, evolutionary psychology can show what the species' environment of evolutionary adaptiveness was; and by considering the species' environment of evolutionary adaptiveness, evolutionary psychology can identify what evolved psychological processes and biases we have. This shows, it is argued, what was 'natural' in the past and, finally, what is 'natural' now.

In practice, many examples of evolutionary psychology involve matching up some present day psychological characteristic with discussion of what life was like for early humans. Thus there is discussion of infants' fear of the dark, or children's fear of snakes, in terms of how such fears would have been advantageous to hunter–gatherer babies who needed to keep close to their parents in order not to be bitten or stolen by predators skulking beyond the light of the camp fire. The 'environment of evolutionary adaptiveness' that is focused on is usually the hunter–gatherer period; the period since is largely discounted as not long enough for significant genetic evolution, the (very much longer) earlier period is considered mainly in terms of comparisons with closely related species such as the great apes. The characteristics that are focused on are sometimes chosen because they are not easily explained in terms of contemporary problems – why our fear of snakes is stronger than our fear of motor cars, for example. But sometimes they are rather more contaminated with socio-political issues – sex differences in reproductive strategy and the 'natural' greater promiscuity of males, for example (pp. 187–91). This sort of argument becomes embroiled in assumptions about what is 'natural', and consequently also in the issue of whether what is 'natural' is 'better' than what is not. Such issues are rarely resolved, although attempts to clarify them, or at least to recognise the problem, can be very useful (e.g. Freese *et al.* 2003; Holland 2003).

1.3.5 Reproductive success, adaptation, and developmental challenge

However, the important point is that evolutionary processes may have led to the existence of *alternative* solutions to problems such as surviving and reproducing in a testing environment. The best solution will depend on the particular challenges of the environment and the particular resources of the individual, so that even if evolutionary selection has led to a preference for a particular type of solution, it will be advantageous to the individual to have other possibilities open. These other possibilities will carry some costs, and if they never need to be used they may not be worthwhile: but if they are needed, they could be invaluable. Probably what has evolved is a range of programmes for building and running bodies and minds, some programmes being heavily pre-determined and some very much more flexible in response to experience. We know, for example, that even heavily-programmed developments such as brain development are not completely hard wired. Brain development is partly 'experience expectant' and partly 'experience dependent' (Meadows 2006: 324–347). Some aspects of it vary very little between individuals and do not change during development; others are predictable but subject to fine tuning; yet others are open to extensive modification even into old age. We can be pretty sure that this makes us more able to learn from experience and adapt creatively than we could with an entirely pre-wired brain; and presumably the costs have been worthwhile.

Life history theory (e.g. Figueredo *et al.* 2006, 2007) seeks to provide a theory of individual differences that are underpinned by an evolved developmental strategy. This strategy is concerned with how to balance the need to survive and to maintain oneself and the need to reproduce and ensure the survival of one's genes in other people's bodies. Figueredo and his colleagues point out that the stability and predictability of the environment shape species' typical reproductive strategies, with species that live in relatively stable, relatively predictable, and relatively overpopulated environments being more likely to invest a lot of parenting effort in a small number of offspring, compared with species whose environments are challenging, unpredictable and underpopulated. They argue, further, that this could well apply to individuals too, and to a range of human psychosocial characteristics as well as to choices about number of offspring and how to parent them. I will present some examples of what they see as the implications of this elsewhere in this book (parenting, reproductive maturity, risk taking).

1.4 Genetic influences, the environment, and social development

I am going to go beyond biology shortly, but I will be keeping a biologically-based evolutionary model as one foundation of this book. To recapitulate, the general picture is as follows. Human children incorporate (metaphorically) evolved behavioural dispositions just as they incorporate (literally) evolved body structures. Development is a result of genes within environments. Genes exert their effects in fixed programmes that are coded in the DNA of the genotype, and in open programmes which are subject to environmental influence and prepared to acquire information from experience. Open programmes may progress using what is experienced only to fine tune development (experience expectant), or may be open to more radical influence (experience dependent) The structure and function of the developing brain are determined by how experiences shape the genetically programmed maturation of the nervous system. The social world, and especially the caregiver, will be crucial sources of experiences; these trim or enable genetic potentials by subtle differences in neuronal growth and neurotransmitter production. During critical periods in the early years psychoneuroendocrinological fine-tuning affects the workings of the brain – which may be particularly associated with the current interpersonal experiences of the infant and then with future interpersonal expectations, experience, and emotion. What we need to do is to examine how all this happens, co-ordinating our levels of description as far as we can.

> The expression of any one gene is embedded within a biological system influenced by a multitude of other genetic and environmental influences; concepts of gene regulation (expression) and epigenesis are now essential for understanding development.
>
> (Gottesman and Hanson 2005: 265)

Genes are sequences of DNA that, effectively, carry the instructions for constructing or maintaining some particular aspect of an organism (both structures such as skin colour and functions such as ability to digest milk). There may be slightly different versions of a particular gene: these are alleles of that gene. Not all the genes for a particular instruction are exactly the same, and they may result in slightly different outcomes, for example different skin colours or different proportions of digestive enzymes. As we have inherited one copy of each gene from each parent, we will sometimes have two alleles that are effectively identical and sometimes two that are different. If they are different, our outcome may be midway between them, or one allele may be expressed (be 'dominant') whereas the other ('recessive') gene is not. Often, one allele would have a damaging effect on development, but we do not in fact develop adversely because the other, normal, allele provides the instructions for normal development.

Our DNA provides genes that are handed down from generation to generation (sometimes with mistakes due to inaccurate copying, and sometimes subject to mutation). But DNA does not directly affect developmental outcome, rather it specifies the ribonucleic acid (RNA) that is involved in producing polypeptides which are transformed into proteins which then undergo protein folding, and then there is a long causal chain to the effect (including developmental sequences, timing, co-action of other genes, environmental influence etc.), and it is tissue specific and phase specific – hence we need a complex model to describe what is going on. It is always iffy to talk of genes 'for' something – at best a simplification, at worst a source of very serious misunderstandings.

Clearly, genes are important in development. Some genetic anomalies 'mess up' normal development in ways we are just beginning to understand. More subtle differences in genes, in partnership with other genes and with the non-genetic environment, undoubtedly make complex contributions to development as a social person too. Understanding these is going to require good data on people's genes, on their environments, and on their developmental histories, and subtle models and methodologies; it will take a lot of effort (and expense); and it will be of enormous political delicacy (Collins *et al.* 2000; Karmiloff-Smith and Thomas 2003; Scerif and Karmiloff-Smith 2005).

Parents may be seen to have a significant impact on their children's psychosocial development; but what parts of this similarity or this impact are due to their activity, what to the child's actions, what to shared genes and what to shared environment? I address this set of questions later (pp. 85–87, 146, 266–67, 270–71), but here I will just re-state two points that emerge from Bronfennbrenner's account of what a developmental model must look at: first different levels of analyses co-occur and mutually influence each other; second, we need to know about the proximal processes that accumulate to turn development into one pathway or another and to maintain it there or change it. Questions about 'how much' a single factor contributes mean less to this model (and to me) than questions about 'how' factors work and affect each other.

Genes and environment interact and have their effect in complex ways (e.g. Bishop *et al.* 2003; Cardon *et al.* 1992; Caspi *et al.* 2000; Plomin 1994; Rutter 1988a; Scarr 1992; Saudino and Plomin 2007). The complexity of causes of both the similarities and the differences between individuals, for example parents and children, is enormous; and there is extreme difficulty in finding decisive evidence to sort the causes out. It will be necessary to consider whether what seems to be an effect of experiencing a particular type of interaction or other social factor is not in fact largely genetically determined, and whether what seems to be largely genetically determined is not in fact an effect of experiencing a particular type of interaction or other social factor. There clearly is a great deal of genetic programming in development, but we cannot neglect the effect of the environment; for example, the physical environment has significant effects on the brain, and adoption into an advantaged social environment raises IQ (pp. 272–73). It is also necessary to consider which participant in a social interaction is having the crucial effect on the others; children influence their families and are not passive recipients of family influences.

There is no point in denying that genes can influence behaviour, that some of our characteristics as a social person are affected by the genes that we have. To quote Michael Rutter:

> genetic effects apply to all behaviours that have any kind of basis in the structure and functioning of the brain, and that applies to virtually all behaviours. Genetic effects are far from confined to disorders and diseases: on the contrary, they are all pervasive with respect to behaviour.
>
> (Rutter 2007a: 9)

Some genetic influences on behaviour are common to us all – for example our helpless state at birth and our tendency to mature slowly, compared with other species (pp. 27, 41, 51). Other genetic influences relate to differences between us as individuals – for example how liable we are to schizophrenia or hyperactivity, or our chance of depression or balding or a high soprano singing voice. But this is far from the whole story. Although we may be able to identify genes and developmental outcomes that are associated with each other, in that only people with those genes have that outcome, and only people with that outcome have those genes, this is only a small part of all that we need if we are to understand the association. Developmental approaches are fundamental; how have we got from the genes to the outcome? What do genes do that lead to particular outcomes? What else is involved?

1.4.1 Developmental approaches to understanding genetic influences

It is axiomatic that the individual's experience does not change his or her DNA. But the individual's experience does affect whether the individual's DNA is advantageous to their well-being or not. And it seems increasingly likely that experience does affect the expression of the individual's DNA in their body – and, presumably, their behaviour.

The importance of developmental approaches is increasingly well understood in work on the development of diseases and disorders. A biomedical example is the association between early nutrition and later diseases, for example nutrition *in utero* and heart disease in adulthood (Rickard and Lummaa 2007). Under nutrition before birth shows up as restricted growth and small size at birth; most such babies, given normal nutrition, then grow quickly and reach normal sizes. But as adults, these formerly small-for-dates individuals may be at increased risk of increased insulin resistance, heart disease and obesity (Barker 1997; Bateson *et al.* 2004; Power and Jefferis 2002). During development, environmental experiences such as fetal nutrition may have 'programmed' gene activity during later stages, resulting in different sets of genes being activated or silenced in the cells of the body according to a sort of 'expectation' that similar environmental experiences will happen late in life. Another example is the effect of the mother's smoking on the development of the fetus she is carrying (Adams, Harvey and Prince 2005; Alati *et al.* 2008; Fowler *et al.* 2008; Wiles *et al.* 2006). It is well established that there is a statistical association between maternal smoking during pregnancy and the incidence of malformation of the testes and penis, infertility and low levels of testosterone in males, and of infertility in females. I will not begin to pretend to understand the complexity of the processes involved, but in the paper just cited, Fowler *et al.* (2008) demonstrated that chemicals from the cigarette smoke were reaching the fetus and that there was lower expression of the 'desert hedgehog' gene, which is known to be involved in testis development, during the development of the fetuses of women who smoked. This might partly explain this pattern of association.

It has been known for a long time that mothers' smoking in pregnancy tends to produce restricted growth and lower birth weight in the babies (e.g. Butler, Goldstein and Ross 1972). More recent research (e.g. Adams, Harvey and Prince 2005; Al Mamun *et al.* 2006; Mendez *et al.* 2008) suggests that these babies may grow up to be at increased risk of obesity in childhood. In other studies, the researchers have looked at growth in the children of fathers who had started to smoke before the age of 11 (Learey *et al.* 2006a, 2006b; Pembrey *et al.* 2006). The children of these men were likely to have a higher Body Mass Index in middle childhood. It may therefore be the case that fathers' smoking affects their children and adds to the effect of mothers' smoking; although what the physiological mechanisms could be is not so clear (von Kries *et al.* 2008).

It appears that this sort of effect can both be very time specific and extend over more than one generation. In a recent stream of research (Pembrey *et al.* 2006; Kaati *et al.* 2007), individuals in a remote Swedish village who had experienced undernutrition during a particular period of development (between the ages of 9 and 12 for boys, and during this same age range but also during the fetal stage and infancy for girls) but had survived and reproduced, had grandchildren who lived longer than the grandchildren of individuals who were well fed during these periods. The timing of the sensitive periods suggests that the undernutrition was affecting the development of the individuals' eggs or sperm; thus we could infer that something was happening to the DNA that affected its expression and led to changes in the longevity of the next generation, or of the next few generations. Another recent paper (Painter *et al.* 2008) investigated the health of the children of the children who were exposed to maternal undernutrition *in utero*. In the first generation, women suffered undernutrition (as little as 400 calories a day) during pregnancy because of a famine in the Nazi-occupied Netherlands in 1944–5. The babies born from these pregnancies were smaller than normal at birth, although normal in height and weight at age 58, when they were followed up for this study. The children of the women in the group (grandchildren of the undernourished pregnancies of 1944–5) were shorter and fatter at birth and were more likely to be rated by their parents as 'unhealthy', and in fact more of them had died than in the comparison group where the grandmothers had not been starved in the famine. An increased risk of diabetes may be part of what is happening to worsen the health of these succeeding generations.

It would appear that in times of low food supply the expression of some genes can be reversibly modified in a way that changes the development or behaviour of the offspring so as to compensate for there being less food. Broadly, what seems to be happening is that the first generation experiences stress (undernutrition) at a particular stage of development, and as a consequence the next generations or generations will develop in a way that would compensate for this stress if they were to encounter it too. The development of the expression of the genes in the grandparents involved a short-term response to the lack of nutritional resources they encountered, which adjusted the ways the genes being copied into their sperm or eggs were programmed to develop; and this allowed subsequent generations to respond to the threats faced by their recent ancestors. This was advantageous if they did indeed meet the same risks, but might be less helpful if they did not, as in the case of individuals who grow slowly during gestation because of these sorts of genetic programming, but after birth are well fed by the standards of their ancestors – and because of having 'more food than expected' grow too fat and so are at risk of heart disease and diabetes.

1.4.2 Heritability and the interdependence of genes and environment

The more we look at people's functioning and at children's development, the more clearly we see that there is close mind–brain–body interdependence. There is therefore no point in theoretical claims prioritising genes over environment, or environment over genes (though in interventions we might focus on one or the other). This point applies very strongly to estimates of 'heritability'. Heritability is the proportion of population variation in a characteristic that is associated with characteristics inherited from the parent rather than with characteristics of the individual's experience of the environment post birth. Various researchers have tried to develop models which separate these two (e.g. Plomin and Rutter 1998; Rutter 2006, 2007a) and some have incautiously generalised to statements about the size or importance of genetic influences. But this can be seriously misleading. Firstly, heritability estimates are always specific to the particular population at the particular time with the particular measuring instruments, and are not generalisable to other populations, times, or measurements – the estimates will change if environments or genes (or measurements) change. Heritability estimates, also, are about individual differences *within* populations, and are not at all informative about differences *between* populations, or about particular individuals within populations. Secondly, in most models gene–environment interaction and gene–environment correlation (pp. 31, 33, 34, 38–39, 267) are included in heritability estimates, although they are clearly environmental as well as genetic. This inflates the apparent importance of heritability at the expense of the importance of the environment. Thirdly, although heritability estimates can suggest that a particular characteristic is affected by genetic influences – or by environmental ones – the estimate does nothing to show *how* genes work (or how environments work either). There is no point in fussing over whether heritable and non-heritable influences are 50/50 or 60/40 or whatever, even if the proportions are 99/1, as the best rule of thumb is that *always* both genes and environment are involved, and the proportion of influence of one or the other expressed as 'heritability' is irrelevant to understanding the causal mechanisms (and thus to deciding policy).

So heritability estimates have to be treated more cautiously than some researchers have managed. Nevertheless, two intriguing points come out of this approach. These analyses suggest that there is a significant genetic contribution to the development of most normal and pathological psychological traits, with heritabilities around 20 to 60 per cent, and these traits with some heritability include people's likelihood of experiencing certain stressful life events and the sort of childrearing they do. Secondly, the analyses suggest the possibility that heritability is lower in at-risk populations with tough environments than it is in populations whose environments are more benevolent (Malouff *et al.* 2008; Rutter 2006). These are points that I will return to elsewhere (pp. 31, 33, 34, 38–39, 267).

Thus so far as the development of a child as a psychological and social person is concerned, there are no 'genes for' differences in individual outcomes in the sense that having this allele, or particular version of a gene, completely predetermines the outcome. However, people's characteristics may make an outcome more likely or less likely. The characteristics that make the outcome more or less likely are not randomly distributed in the population, and most of them may be indirectly genetically influenced. Behaviours and opportunities that make experiencing key events more likely can be genetically influenced too, in so far as whether you experience them or not may be influenced by your genetic characteristics (my genetic gender makes it virtually impossible for me to be a Guardsman or to set foot on Mount Athos, for example). We need to examine the mechanisms by which characteristics, experiences and outcomes are associated, recognising that some of these mechanisms may be genetic. This need not be a matter of blaming the victim for his genes, or of excusing him either. Nor should we believe that we cannot change genetic influences (p. 35).

1.4.3 Co-action of genes and environments in development

We expect there to be co-action of genes and environments in everyday functioning, and in development. Given that environments are complex, challenging, changing, and somewhat unpredictable, an ability to adapt is essential. This is a key organising principle in ordinary everyday functioning and in every sort of development. Over the development of species, genomes which facilitate adaptation are selected for through evolution, and individuals' genes will play a role in their adaptation during their lives. Certain 'rogue' genes have fixed deleterious effects apparent in every individual with that gene – but most will operate via feedback loops with the environment, and it is the result of the interaction which determines how good or bad the outcomes are. It is important to remember also that each interaction between the organism and the environment need not lead to the same 'adaptation', or to equally successful adaptations; we may have what are in some way maladaptive responses e.g. to stress (pp. 53, 56, 61–63, 124, 278–79), or a particular adaptation may be positive in some ways but maladaptive in others, or good in the short term but not so good in the long term. I discuss some examples of this more fully in the chapter on resilience (pp. 274–87).

Like every sort of action, adaptation requires energy or resources, and part of the calculation of how to adapt will involve consideration of what resources are available. Hanson and Gottesman (2007) develop this point with reference to the second law of thermodynamics: all organised systems require energy to remain organised, and without it they become chaotic.

They argue that the same is true, perhaps even more true, of systems that are developing a more complex organisation than they had earlier; by analogy, unless enough energy is available and invested, the developing child will become more chaotic than well ordered. I have reservations about thinking of children's development in terms of thermodynamics, but I will return to the metaphor of resources for development later.

If we consider development as involving adaptation between organism and environment and as absolutely crucial to the interplay between genes and environment, we are talking about 'epigenesis'. This is a term that has some ancient roots (in Aristotle, for example) but was developed by the embryologist C. H. Waddington in the 1950s, and has been applied to post-embryonic stages of development too (it influenced Piaget's work (Piaget 1971)). In embryology, development begins with undifferentiated cells that take on differentiated forms and functions which they transmit through cell division to their daughter cells. All the cells in the body carry the same genetic information, but not all of this genetic information is at work in every cell or at every stage. In the development of two genetically identical cells in the fetus, one may develop into a liver cell, the other into a lung cell. Different parts of the genetic instructions are expressed in liver cells and lung cells; liver cells do not need to cope with the tasks of breathing, coughing etc., lung cells are not responsible for metabolising alcohol. The timing and the location of the developing cell can be what determines what the cell's daughter cells will become specialised as. Recent work on stem cells illustrates this; stem cells have the potential to develop into any specialised sort of cell, so that if you transplant them to part A of the body at the right time they can develop into cells appropriate for that part of the body, and not into cells appropriate for part B. Both the history of the cell itself, and the cells that it is neighbour to, affect the development; and examples of factors such as background radiation levels and levels of oestrogen in the water show how the environment can have a serious developmental effect too.

Much of our DNA is now thought to be regulating the expression of other DNA, rather than itself coding for the production of particular proteins, enzymes and so forth. Genes work very much with other genes and with other influences rather than being able to produce effects irrespective of everything else that is going on. Genetic influences on development include the regulation of gene expression. The expression of genes is tissue specific and developmental-phase specific, and affected by epigenetic processes – processes which do not change DNA, and hence are not 'genetic', but do bring about changes in expression of genes, changes which affect the development of the individual and which might in some cases be heritable. One of the processes involved is methylation; this applies to specific areas of the DNA and changes it temporarily so that specific genetic information is not read and used – e.g. genetic information about being a liver cell is only in use in the liver, not in other organs where it is not relevant. Known factors affecting methylation include diet, toxins, viral infections, ageing, and, importantly, chance. Effects known to be mediated by methylation include various rare specific syndromes, disorders such as diabetes, heart disease, cancer; and recent evidence is beginning to show, brain development, and consequently fine differences in behaviour. Nutrition and rearing experiences may perhaps be other sources of methylation effects (Cameron *et al.* 2005; Champagne *et al.* 2004; Weaver *et al.* 2004).

So normally in individual development, the early stages have rich potential which is not yet firmly specified, and there is progress towards differentiation, integration and elaboration in development, with earlier stages influencing later ones because they have changed the starting point for further development. We start off with the *genotype* that we have inherited from our parents, but what we live with throughout our lives is a *phenotype* which is derived from the original genotype and the genotype's existence in the specific environmental contexts it has experienced. What environments we experience may be in part a result of factors well outside our individual control – history, luck – but it can also be a result of personal choices, made for us by others in reaction to how they see us, and by ourselves.

As I have described, a small fraction of our DNA codes for structures, most of it codes for regulatory processes which also respond to environmental stimulation. The reaction range and the phenotype are determined within this by the influence of other genes and of environments. Which environments we get as we develop may be very much a result of chance ('stochastic'), or the result of past phenotypes, our own or other people's. But also there are clearly many different ways in which genes and environment can work together in the development of a child as a social person. Among these, the one most emphasised by some theorists (e.g. Harris 1995, 1998) is the 'passive' correlation. Genetically related individuals may have the same innate and genetic predisposition for particular sorts of environment or experience – the bookish parent fills the family's living space with books and its weekends with trips to the library, which suits the child with a similar 'bookish' genotype; the thrill-seeking brother involves his siblings in vigorous rough and tumble or mountaineering or driving fast cars. Harris argues that although the related people share the same environment it is not the environment that makes them alike, it is their genetic alikeness that makes them experience the same environment. She exaggerates her case, and sees gene–environment correlation as a component of heritability not as a component of environmental effects, but undoubtedly there could be passive gene–environment correlation.

There may also be 'evocative' or 'reactive' associations between genes and environment. The child has characteristics that *evoke* particular sorts of experience, or that other people *react* to in particular ways. For example, a child who is a bit fussy for genetic reasons may evoke irritability from its caretaker, a child who is female may be reacted to with more comments about appearance and gentleness than a male child receives. The child's own preferences for sporty or literary or social occupations may influence the social networks that they become part of and the social reputation that accrues to them – what has been called 'ecological niche-picking'. And the 'ecological niches' of course respond to the individual's characteristics as more or less valuable or detrimental to the inhabitants of the niche.

Which of these occurs will differ from individual to individual and from time to time – those with less power (small children, those in poverty, for example) have less opportunity to choose their own environments than the more powerful do (Newman and Massengill 2006; Ackerman *et al.* 2007).

In these ways, and in others, it is possible that the social environment mediates between the genes and the heritable characteristics that they lead to and the development of the phenotype of behaviour (or even physical characteristics). For example, if irritable or hostile parenting – originally evoked by children's characteristics – amplifies a characteristic that is initially trivial up to the problem level, then it becomes integrated or recruited into the mechanisms of how genetic influences find expression in children's subsequent problem behaviour – that is, it becomes a mediating factor in development. I think there is a considerable amount of evidence that the social environment, in addition to its main effects, is a crucial final pathway by which genetic influence is expressed in normal and pathological development. The implications of this suggest that planned interventions to alter the response of the social environment to heritable characteristics of children and adults might improve individual adjustment by affecting how genetic influences are expressed. The genes themselves are not changed, but the effects they bring about are.

As well as gene–environment *correlation* there is gene–environment *interaction*; people who have different genes will differ in the degree that they are affected by different environments. Environmental experiences sometimes moderate genetic effects to bring about normal, psychopathological, and resilient developmental outcomes. Genetic effects sometimes moderate environmental effects, to bring about normal, psychopathological, and resilient developmental outcomes. For example, genetic effects on functioning may be observed only under certain environmental contexts or in conjunction with different histories of experience; conversely, experience may only relate to what outcomes are like among individuals with specific genetic characteristics (e.g. Caspi *et al.* 2002, 2003, 2007; Nobile *et al.* 2007; Cicchetti *et al.* 2007; Thapar *et al.* 2007a, 2007b). Recognising that gene–environment interaction exists, and working to understand how it operates in particular instances, is important both for understanding development and for avoiding simplistic blaming of undesirable development on either genes or environments: 'an understanding of the complexities involved . . . may also help in avoiding misleading types of biological reductionism and stigma, whilst at the same time emphasizing the importance of genes in all risk and protection pathways' (Rutter *et al.* 2006: 252).

It can also help us if we want to develop interventions that prevent or remediate psychosocial disorders, or which promote resilience in the face of adverse genes or environments, not because some individuals are genetically predestined to disaster or success but because a particular intervention may work better for some individuals and a different intervention for others (e.g. Cicchetti and Blender 2006; Cicchetti and Curtis 2006; Luthar and Cicchetti 2000; Luthar, Cicchetti and Becker 2000; Luthar, Sawyer and Brown 2006).

There are, increasingly, clear, specific and well understood examples of this interaction (the journal *Development and Psychopathology*'s special issue of October 2007 presents several). For some gene–environment interactions the evidence is largely statistical, without there being as yet a detailed picture of how the interaction comes about at a biological level, and the examination of such patterns is not uncontroversial (Thapar *et al.* 2007a, 2007b; Rutter 2006). But in some cases the biological pathways are known. One of the earliest interactions to be understood is phenylketonuria (PKU), which is associated with an identified abnormal gene on chromosome 12 (Woo 1991). The defective gene leads to the absence from the individual's body of a particular enzyme, phenylalanine hydroxylase, which is needed to convert the phenylalanine from protein in the diet into tyrosine. In the absence of the enzyme, phenylalanine cannot be metabolised and used in the body, and cannot be got rid of. High concentrations of phenylalanine result in an excess of chemicals that are normally only present in minute quantities, but in the person with PKU they are present at toxic levels. They interfere with the development and growth of the central nervous system; the brain develops normally to birth, but once the baby starts a diet which contains phenylalanine in protein, the developing nerve cells are vulnerable, and the connections between nerve cells begin to be damaged and broken down. Reduced brain development, irreversible mental retardation and severe emotional and behavioural disturbance result. Thus the genetic anomaly leads to marked anomalies in development.

However, it only does so in the normal environment, specifically if the PKU baby receives a normal diet containing phenylalanine in protein. If a special dietary environment is provided during the period of brain development, so that the infant is fed on a diet which does not contain phenylalanine, no such excess of deleterious chemicals is built up, and the central nervous system can develop pretty much normally. The genetic defect is still there, but it has no effect in the special environment where there is little or no phenylalanine. PKU individuals still cannot produce phenylalanine hydroxylase, but if they do not need it to deal with phenylalanine because their diet contains none, they avoid the most serious consequences of their abnormality. Diets that contain even small amounts of phenylalanine may produce brain damage and some cognitive impairment even in late childhood (Smith, I., *et al.* 1990, 1991). But the impairment is dependent on the presence of two quite separate things, the genetic condition and the dietary environment; people who only have one of them are not impaired at all.

There must be many other examples of such interactions: different degrees of benefit from breastfeeding is one recent one (Caspi *et al.* 2007). This is what evolution works on, after all – you need to make an adaptation to the particular environment that you meet, and some are better at fitting in with one particular encountered environment than others are. Some genetic propensities are more helpful than others in adapting to particular environments (although they may be less helpful, or even very unhelpful, in adapting to others – for example some sickle cells protect against malaria but are no use in environments where there is no risk of malaria but increase the risk of serious anaemia). It is not easy to identify these gene–environment interactions, but evidence of some are emerging from research studies. I will introduce some examples briefly here; the outcomes are discussed more fully later (pp. 38–40, 55–56).

1.4.3.1 Gene–environment interaction and the development of depression

Research on the development of depression provides a very relevant example. Kendler *et al.* (1995) identified an association between genetic liability (as indexed by having a monozygotic twin who had depression) and the effect of a life event such as bereavement on the onset of depression (see also Kendler *et al.* 2005). Caspi *et al.* (2002) reported findings from a longitudinal study in Dunedin, New Zealand, which suggested there was interaction between a genetic variant linked to how much serotonin transporter protein is produced, a protein that is involved in the reuptake of serotonin from the synapse. Individuals with a short allelic form of this variant showed an increased risk of depression compared with those who carried the long allele, but only when they had been exposed to adverse life events. Thus, here there was no evidence of a main genetic effect for this variant; similar findings have since come from other studies, and the prevailing view appears to be that it is an *interaction* between the variants of the serotonin transport genes and experience of life events that is associated with major depression (e.g. Cicchetti *et al.* 2007; Gillespie *et al.* 2005; Kaufman *et al.* 2006; Kendler *et al.* 2005; Thapar *et al.* 2007a, 2007b; Willis-Owen *et al.* 2005; Goodyer 2008), although this is not without controversy (Munafo *et al.* 2009; Araya *et al.* 2009; Gillespie *et al.* 2005).

The gene implicated by Caspi *et al.* (2002) appears to be linked to stress response and sensitivity to anxiety, so there may be here some biological evidence of effects on the stress regulation system both postnatally and prenatally (Baler *et al.* 2008; Reiss *et al.* 2001; Reiss and Leve 2007: p. 54).

(There is also emerging evidence of the effects of maternal smoking on the development of the baby's brain systems: this is certainly relevant, even if its reliability is not yet certain.) However, more recent research has produced somewhat inconsistent findings: two large studies have failed to replicate Caspi *et al.*'s results (Gillespie *et al.* 2005) and the outcome is not yet clear (Thapar *et al.* 2007a, 2007b; Munafo *et al.* 2009). Araya *et al.* (2009) find stronger evidence for the effects of stress and exposure to mothers' depression than for the gene.

The link between genes and outcome regarding depression seems to be lower for adolescents who have experienced a high level of family conflict, whereas for individuals with low levels of family conflict genetic risk appeared to be the main source of risk (Rice *et al.* 2006). However, a study by Feinberg *et al.* (2007) did not find that family warmth and hostility interacted with genetic variation in risk of depression, if individuals have a higher genetic risk of depression. Clearly more research is needed.

I think it is currently reasonable to suppose that there may be evidence here of an interaction between a particular gene variant and environmental factors that together increase risk of depression. This could help us to explain why some individuals are not much affected by environmental events that produce strong negative effects in most of those who experience them. It is unlikely to suggest that the negative environment is not crucial, or that interventions to improve the environment are not worthwhile.

1.4.3.2 Gene–environment interaction and the development of attention-deficit hyperactivity disorder (ADHD)

There has also been a significant number of studies that examine the possibility of gene–environment interaction in the development of ADHD disorders (Taylor and Kim-Cohen 2007). A particular area of interest here is the variable number tandem repeat polymorphism in the promoter region of the *MAOA* gene, in interaction with serious family adversity. This was initially picked up in the Dunedin study (Caspi *et al.* 2002; Jaffee *et al.* 2005) and a meta-analysis by Taylor and Kim-Cohen (2007) suggests that a significant proportion of follow-up and replication studies have provided robust findings of an interaction between this genetic variation and susceptibility to parental abuse, with males being at serious risk of ADHD and other conduct disorders if they have both the genetic variation and a lifetime history of parental maltreatment (pp. 10, 55–56, 61–62, 129–30, 141–44, 147, 270–71). It will be very interesting to see whether further studies can clarify whether the effect depends on the age of the boy when the abuse is experienced, or on how long it continued, or whether other experiential factors moderate it, and thus give us a more exact understanding of the developmental mechanisms that contribute to development which is psychopathological or resilient.

For developmental disorders such as depression or ADHD, understanding gene effects is an interesting part of understanding the causes of these difficulties. Some individuals may be genetically at high risk, others genetically at low risk. But the effect of any single gene on risk is likely to be very small, and if we want to reduce the incidence of these disorders or help those who have developed them, we would do best to focus on preventing the environmental factors that are obviously relevant and well understood – maltreatment, neglect, abuse, lack of emotional support, as I shall describe. (pp. 85–86, 129–30, 141–42)

1.4.3.3 Parenting behaviour, children's behaviour, and gene–environment interaction

I discuss parenting at much more length in a section of its own. But clearly children's characteristics, including characteristics derived from genes, affect the behaviour of their parents. For example, highly irritable infants tend to receive less sensitive care and are at greater risk for developing insecure relationships (Crockenberg 1981; van den Boom 1994). Even sensitive parents may find that infant negativity makes attachment processes work less well. Attachment is enhanced when the child stimulates the mother and responds positively to her bids for interaction, and thus elicits more sensitive, warm caring and attention than children who are more irritable and less easy to soothe (Cox et al. 1992; Kochanska 2001; Shamir-Essakow et al. 2004). (This should not be taken as implying that it is always better for infants to be low in irritability. A classic study (deVries 1984) found that when an East African society was threatened by drought and famine it was the more irritable, more demanding babies who were most likely to survive, because they made demands on their caregivers and continued to receive what food there was whereas the less demanding babies died off quietly.) Equally clearly, the parents' characteristics affect their parenting behaviour – drug abuse, maternal depression and lack of social support, for example, all make it much harder to parent sensitively (pp. 56, 147–48, 278–79; Brody et al. 2002; Crockenberg and Leerkes 2003a; Espinosa et al. 2001; Meadows 2006; Valentino et al. 2008). There seems to be both more parent figure instability and more drug use and delinquency in children of substance abusers (Keller et al. 2008).

Change in dysfunctional parenting predicts changes in the children's attachment (Forbes et al. 2007). We do not, as yet, know much about whether particular specific genetic variations minimise or exacerbate the impact of parenting behaviour on particular children. A couple of studies have suggested that adoptive parents are more likely to parent negatively if their adopted child was born to a mother with a record of antisocial behaviour, but this is mediated by the child's own disruptive behaviour (O'Connor et al. 1998) and may only be the case in high-risk families

(Riggins-Caspers *et al.* 2003), where presumably there is less room for tolerating, and gently modifying, difficult behaviour. But we need more direct evidence about specific genes and their contributions to behaviour development. And we need to recognise that even if the infant is adopted very early indeed (and not all are), there may be effects from the intra-uterine environment which are innate but not genetic.

1.4.3.4 Variation in the severity of outcomes

When looking at the psychology of social development, a further com-plexity is that many risk factors and outcomes, including diagnosed diseases and disorders, are dimensional, not just a matter of having or not having a problem. It may not make sense to say that a person who has a particular level or range of difficulty definitely has a problem, and another whose level or range is slightly lower definitely does not. It also may not make sense to say that everyone who has more than the criterion level or range of difficulty is the same. Criterion levels may be arbitrary or variable, or something you move in and out of from time to time: e.g. people who suffer from depression are not depressed to the same degree all the time, people who go in for antisocial behaviour intermittently behave well, poverty is hard to eradicate partly because changes and interventions tend to leave people just above the poverty line and vulnerable to becoming poor again. Risk factors may be dimensional too, and there may be a dose–response pattern with bigger doses leading to worse outcomes – (e.g. psychosocial risk, smoking and ADHD: Baler *et al.* 2008; Linnet *et al.* 2003; Thapar *et al.* 2003). This may be true for genetic risks as well as environmental ones. Often there will be multiple causal pathways to the same endpoint – different starting points, risk factors and mechanisms but similar outcomes (Huston and Bentley 2010). Delinquency and school failure provide familiar examples (pp. 233–34, 264–67, 278–79; Newman and Massengill 2006). Environmental influences and risk factors may affect more than one outcome (Maughan and McCarthy 1997). For example, rarely being read to when you are a preschool child is associated with slower development of reading skills in school, and also with less closeness to the parent and more behaviour problems (Meadows 2006; CMPO (Centre for Market and Public Organisation) 2008); in abused children there may be higher rates of internalising symptoms, especially if there is a genetic vulnerability (Caspi *et al.* 2002, 2003; Feinberg *et al.* 2007; Moffitt, Caspi and Rutter 2005); children who suffered pervasive neglect showed a higher rate of inter-nalising problems and some difficulties with a memory task, especially if the children described their mothers in relatively negative terms (Valentino *et al.* 2008). Aspects of the wider social context influence the outcome of any particular risk, e.g. the availability and quality of any substitute that there is for a missing or 'inadequate' parent, e.g. the interface between school and home; the capacity of the home or the school to work positively with challenging behaviour.

Developmental psychology is not the only discipline to examine the 'wider social context'. I write as a psychologist, but it seems appropriate to focus briefly on some of these other disciplines before reverting to a psychology that has these other disciplines in the margins for most of what I have to say.

1.5 Sociology's perspectives on the child as social person

Where evolutionary psychology and developmental behaviour genetics focus on universals in child development, the sociology of childhood emphasises that 'childhood' is a social construction (Brannen and O'Brien 1995; Corsaro 2005; James, Jenks and Prout 1998; Jenks 2005; King 2007; Mayall 2002; Shanahan 2000; Shanahan 2007). Bronfenbrenner's model is perfectly compatible with this point. Childhood is defined, facilitated, restricted and evaluated by specific social, political, and cultural institutions. It is never independent of historical time, geographical space and ideological pressure. How children are seen, what they are expected to do, in what ways development is seen as 'normal or 'good' or 'a problem' – all these things are built up by the accumulated socio-cultural context and cannot be taken for granted. Even within a particular historical and socio-cultural context, different people see 'childhood' differently, as part of what they believe about human nature and social life. The meaning of 'childhood' cannot be extracted from the particular place, time, culture, and family structure within which it is embedded (Corsaro 2005; King 2007; McLanahan and Percheski 2008; Shanahan 2000, 2007).

Given this emphasis on childhood as a heavily interpreted concept, you will not be surprised by the variety of characteristics thought to be crucial to 'childhood'. However, among the variety a number of dilemmas crop up repeatedly, and are worth raising for their relevance to psychological research.

The first is a classic in European thought, circling round through millennia (Heywood 2001; James, Jenks and Prout 1998). Are children born full of 'original sin', so that society needs to work on them to control and eliminate innate impulses and faults, or born 'naturally' innocent and good, but then subjected to social training which reduces their freedom, warps their instinctive goodness, and generally tends to deprave and corrupt them? For the last three or four hundred years, most opinion has gone for the latter, following Rousseau's description of children's purity, innocence and goodness (Scott 2006), seeing childhood as separate from and different from adulthood, and reacting with more surprise, horror, and despair to serious bad behaviour committed by or on children than to the same behaviour committed by or on adults – teenagers who use guns to assert their status in gangs, for example, or children who kill other children, or child soldiers recruited into insurrectionary wars (James and Jenks 1996). Children are also seen as rightfully excluded from various sectors of social activity because of their innocence and purity – we have strong views about children's exposure to the sexual aspects of our culture, about their eligibility to be participants in political processes, about their employment. They are supposed to commit their time to the 'business of childhood' – notably play, education and family membership – although simultaneously these are supposed to prepare them for life after childhood. Once you look closely at public prescriptions about the rights of children and the responsibilities of parents and the wider society, deep concerns and ambivalence are evident that make even the best agreed and most altruistic formulations somewhat problematic (Christensen and James 2008).

A second dilemma, linked to the first, is the role of 'nature' and 'nurture' in development. Is 'nature' itself good, or something that needs to be civilised? It is a useful concept at all? Childhood is seen sometimes as explicitly a 'state of nature' and sometimes as a state through which it is natural to pass as part of the biological life cycle (Corsaro 2005; Hrdy 1999). For most psychologists, it seems self-evident and almost unproblematic to acknowledge that children are biologically immature and that they have to live in this state for a considerable period of time – that you have to get through being a caterpillar and do all the necessary caterpillar things before you can be a butterfly. Psychologists' anxieties here are largely about what is going on, what pushes this development along, moulds it, facilitates it, impedes it; in other words in detailed description of events, in detailed examination of mechanisms, in careful consideration of interventions. Reference to sociological and socio-cultural views, which are largely about the ways that development is nurtured, can be enormously helpful in checking and correcting speculations which take nature a bit too much for granted.

Another dilemma about childhood, one which can be seen in both humans and other animals, is around the vulnerability and the independence of children. Issues arise here both about helping children develop autonomy (how, when, in what areas), their need for protection (against what, when, where, for how long), and their status as autonomous persons responsible for their own actions rather than as the possession of their parents. There are issues also about the costs of children and the relative responsibilities of parents and others, and the tension between fairness and favouritism, or affection and objectivity. And the dilemma is very prominent in defining rights and responsibilities (King 2007; Mayall 2002). Here, particularly, the matter is complicated by the age of the child – younger children are seen as more vulnerable and as more dependent – and, in some cases, by the gender of the child, as in very many societies females are seen as more vulnerable and dependent than males even into adulthood. Adults' vested interests may have a powerful effect on definitions and policy here (James and James 2004; King 2007; Mayall 2002; Shanahan 2007), and we have to remember that the adults who have the power may be interested in something other than the nurture of the child. When we see a politician kissing a baby, we should probably not think that what is going on is simply a disinterested expression of delight in the baby.

It is as well to recognise that individuals and cultures may have a strong investment in childhood, and that this can be both emotional and practical. 'The child is a buffer against the profound loneliness of modernity' (Shanahan 2007: 415); of all our relationships, that of parent and child may be deepest and longest lasting and most important. We also believe that 'Childhood happiness secures adulthood happiness. Childhood is in no small part a set of adult aspirations, longings, and nostalgia, an untainted potential in the past and in the future of adults' (Shanahan 2007: 415). We invest in childhood not just for its own sake but because we believe it is of lifelong importance to us all. We see childhood as part of the transformation of imperfect societies for the better. We are nostalgic about it, and hopeful.

There is a powerful component in the sociology of childhood that centres on listening to children's own accounts of their lives (e.g. Mayall 2002; Pollard 1985, 2000; Pollard and Filer 1996, 1999, 2007; Christensen and James 2008) and on children's competence, autonomy, and right to self-determination. In some of this writing, there is both an emphasis on children's agency and an undertone of criticism of developmental psychology as being too focused on childhood as a preliminary for adulthood, as a stage of relative inadequacy which has to be grown out of on the way to greater competence (Mayall 2002 is particularly sharp-edged about this). Although I think the sociologists' picture of developmental psychology is unreasonable, applying only to a limited range of studies and models, I do share these theorists' interest in children's rights and the usefulness of studying children's views.

But there are major complications, which I must note here. Firstly, twentieth century sociology has developed a much stronger consciousness, and a more politicised consciousness, of identity politics than most psychology has done (King 2007). Identity in terms of gender, race, sexuality or religion is seen as politically important in determining people's experiences and status, and as something that needs to be fully considered in sociological and legal accounts of their characteristics and their rights. Children are, potentially, another such identity group; although they are unlike most of the other groupings in two ways. Few children are dedicated professional social scientists or social activists; the theorising and the political action are (mainly) done for them by adults. Conversely, these adults have themselves been children, but are children no longer. They may remember their own past experience of childhood, and they can observe the current childhoods of others – but they have moved out of the identity group. If they advocate for children, they are doing it for a group they no longer belong to.

Secondly, we have to remember that the systems that affect children and the ways that childhood is conceptualised are predominantly the work of adults: children do influence systems and ideas (often by behaving in ways that upset the expectations of adults, for example by resisting educational efforts or engaging in antisocial behaviour) but they are more often involved as indirect influence on social change than as the leaders of change. 'The child as social agent' rightly stresses children's rationality and competence, but there are limits to how far it can be extended into the sort of agency which directly changes social structures (and this may be a source of frustration to some children).

Thirdly, and partly as a consequence, children are often eager to leave the status of 'child', looking forward to the time when they have the status of 'grown-up'. Although childhood is in some ways a protected and privileged social status, and young people may retreat into it to protect themselves against demands for more responsible behaviour than they want to show, they are often conscious of how being a child restricts their autonomy, places controls and obligations on them, and excludes them from activities that they expect to be enjoyable. This in itself is an interesting ambivalence, and it can be looked at from biological as well as sociological angles, preferably while recognising that all this is inextricable from our idealisations about society and about childhood.

Ultimately, we have to recognise that 'childhood' is not just a matter of a complex and contradictory bundle of adults' views and actions. Children inhabit the social space and contribute to both social stability and social change. They creatively appropriate information and language and skills from the adult world, they produce and participate in their own culture, and they influence adult culture and behaviour by means of resistance, challenge, negotiation and creative participation in social life, cultural production, and social change. The remainder of this book is about the ways in which they do this, and how this has developmental outcomes for those concerned.

1.6 Socio-cultural perspectives

The last disciplinary tradition whose relevance I want to indicate is socio-cultural studies. There are wide levels of 'environment' relevant to children as social persons, operating on them without them having a responsibility for it or much of a voice in it – at the 'macrosystem' level of culture or political ideology. We operate within what I called earlier 'cultural ideologies, practices, proscriptions, and expectations about behaviour and development –

which are consistencies in the form and content of lower-order settings that exist at cultural or subcultural level and have a significant impact on microsystems' (pp. 12–13). Several examples of macrosystems that have been relatively well researched, partly because they seem to be close to the child's everyday experience, will be discussed later – gender rules (pp. 191, 194, 238), cultural expectations about children's and parents' behaviour (pp. 152–57). I also look more briefly at political macrosystems. But trying to see how cultures or macrosystems are involved in children's development as social persons involves me moving out from mainstream psychology towards other disciplines, notably socio-cultural studies, history and anthropology, and because the rules of how to do anthropology or history are not so clear to me, and my reading is less wide, my discussion is more tentative. I begin with some definitional work.

Much of the work that has been done on cultures as sites for child development and socialisation has been done by anthropologists; Montgomery (2009) provides a useful introduction to 'anthropological perspectives on children's lives'. These perspectives are not totally different from mainstream psychologists' perspectives, but they are derived mainly from ethnographic methods of careful observation and interviews with informants, and are often (but not always) sited in smallish cultures distinct from the Westernised ones that most of the readers of this book are familiar with. I have found this sort of evidence fascinating in many different ways – in richly detailed studies of one society after another, the naïve reader can enjoy both the titillating shock of difference and the reassuring comfort of similarity. A reader who is going beyond cultural tourism can begin to derive both underlying thematic similarities between cultures and a sense of the diversity of social structures and expectations that surround socialisation; to look at causal processes, not just what is happening on the surface; and to understand the conceptual difficulties that underlie some of our assumptions (e.g. Toren 1993; LeVine and New 2008). I want to review briefly here just a few of these issues; but as I have had to be selective in what I present, readers should move on to their own further reading and interpretation. Montgomery's introduction to the field, just mentioned, and journals such as *Childhood* and *Children and Society* will be useful sources.

Defining what 'culture' means and describing cultures are not in the least easy tasks. Broadly, culture refers to patterns of human activity and the symbolic systems that give these activities social significance and importance; as the combination of languages, beliefs, institutions, science, music, literature and art, manners, religions, rituals, worldviews, and artefacts that make up what we think, what we do and are, and what our ancestors thought and did and were, and what our descendants will think and will do and will be. Some are unique to a particular culture, others may be, more or less, universal. Schwartz and colleagues (Schwartz 1992, 1996; Schwartz and Bardie 2001; Schwartz and Boehnke 2004; Schwartz and Rubel 2005),

Table 1.1 Schwartz *et al.*'s typology of cultural value systems. Adapted from Schwartz 1992; Schwartz and Bardi 2001.

Value	Definition
Tradition	Degree to which there is respect, commitment and acceptance for the customs and Ideas provided by the traditional culture or religion, and to which the individual should be subordinate to traditional consensus
Benevolence	Emphasis on preserving and enhancing the welfare of known others with whom one is in frequent social contact by being loyal, helpful, honest, responsible
Universalism	Emphasis on understanding, appreciating, tolerating and protecting the welfare of all other people, known and unknown, and of nature
Self-direction	Emphasis on importance of independent thought and action – choosing, creating, exploring, being curious, choosing one's own goals
Stimulation	Valuing variety, having aspirations for change, challenge and excitement in life
Hedonism	Pursuit of personal and sensuous satisfaction for oneself, enjoying life
Achievement	Acquiring personal success through demonstrating competence according to social standards, and being seen to be successful and influential
Power	Aspiration for social status and prestige through gaining control and dominance over other people and resources, and preserving one's own image and reputation
Security	Need for protection of safety, harmony, and stability of the social structure, of relationships and of the self
Conformity	Limiting actions and urges that might upset or harm others and violate social expectations and norms, valuing politeness, obedience, self-discipline

for example, presented a typology of cultural value systems that they claim have emerged as approximately equivalent over many cultures (Table 1.1).

Individual actions that express each value will be likely to have practical, psychological, and social consequences, and these consequences may conflict with or be compatible with the actions that are motivated by other values. Schwartz and colleagues argue that these values relate to each other in a complex 'circumplex' model (Schwartz and Boehnke 2004) but they can also be seen as having two underlying dimensions: the first is self-enhancement (emphasis on power and achievement, and somewhat on hedonism) versus self-transcendence (emphasis on universalism and benevolence), and the second is openness (self-direction, stimulation, and possibly hedonism) rather than conservatism (security, tradition, conformity). (The first of these dimensions resembles the 'individualism/collectivism' model that has guided a considerable amount of research, as I discuss later (pp. 47, 81, 139, 156, 236–37).

The suggestion is (Schwartz and Bardi 2001) that value acquisition begins in the family, which like any close social network requires positive co-operative social values to run smoothly. Parents and others model benevolence, and reward it, from very early in children's lives (pp. 120–21, 130–33 parenting, moral development). Universalism, which emphasises being nice to the out-group as well as the in-group, becomes more important as the child's social networks widen, and it is often a great concern of primary school children and their adult mentors (p. 212). Valuing security, conformity and power may be in tension with valuing hedonism and self-direction from childhood on. (I remember my partner saying to me, when I was in despair over getting our small daughter to do what I wanted, 'But you wouldn't have wanted a little pudding, would you?'; at that moment I would have expressed a strong preference for her showing blind, unquestioning and immediate obedience, though in the long term he was quite right.) Valuing achievement could be seen as having two facets, one drawing on intrinsic motivation and doing things for one's own sake, the other drawing on achieving things in order to compare well with other people, and hence is relevant to Carol Dweck's work (1999) (pp. 77–78); probably self-direction is too.

Over a range of cross-cultural studies of people's expression of their personal values, the adult and student samples give most emphasis to values of benevolence, self-direction, and universalism; valuing power, tradition, and stimulation is least important; and security, conformity, achievement, and hedonism values are in between (Schwartz and Bardi 2001). That student samples endorse this hierarchy of values might be contrasted with the stereotype of students as hedonistic, iconoclastic and free-spirited that would be more familiar to some of us (p. 268); possibly we need to remember the potential discrepancy between expressed values and actual behaviour for any sample.

Although Schwartz and colleagues emphasise the cultural universality of their value set, and suggest that the value hierarchy and its origins are very similar over cultures and over genders, they acknowledge that there are some interesting differences (Schwartz and Bardi 2001; Schwartz and Rubel 2005; Knafo and Khoury-Kassabri 2008). The sub-Saharan African samples that they have studied tended to differ from other groups in placing a particularly high value on conformity and a relatively low value on self-determination. They propose that this emphasis arises developmentally, from the experience of family members as social persons in the traditional sub-Saharn African family. They describe large diverse multi-generational families with many members living closely together interdependently and with little privacy. A sample of teachers from Singapore also value conformity and benevolence very highly, and place power, hedonism and stimulation as the least cited values. Students from the USA value benevolence, achievement and power, but give a very low rating to universalism; Schwartz and colleagues relate this to the go-getting attitudes and absence of support for social welfare policies that are more characteristic in the USA than in European states, and to 'the centrality of the frontier experience'. Whatever the merits of such speculation, it does make the point that cultures have histories and may be among the ways in which history affects the life chances of individuals. Indeed, cultures differ in how explicitly historical sources, and history itself, are used as sources of values and in moral teaching (e.g. Wang 2008).

Hofstede (2001, 2005) discusses an alternative set of dimensions. The first, power–distance, is concerned with how power is distributed among the various levels of society. Western societies tend to have a fairly low power–distance index (PDI) whereas many non-Western societies, for example China, have a high PDI. Both parenting styles and practices, and political activity, are likely to be related to this dimension. Simply the degree to which a society is unequal is associated with the rate of problems for its members. The second dimension, individualism–collectivism (IC), involves whether people focus first on their individual needs and rights or whether individuals are felt to be secondary to collective needs. Individualism is said to dominate people's views and behaviour in Western societies, collectivism in the non-West. The third dimension is Masculinity–Femininity, whether the organisation of society reflects the stereotypical male attributes of aggression or the female attributes of consideration. More masculinist cultures (for example many Latin American or Islamic cultures) emphasise achievement and competition over more nurturant behaviour. The fourth dimension involves ideas about whether things can be changed or whether things are unchangeable or even fated to be the way they are, and is called *uncertainty avoidance*. This relates, I think, to ideas about one's own control of events, as well as to religious ideologies. Hofstede's fifth dimension is the balance of long-term and short-term perspectives. Both for individuals and for societies there may be many occasions when the short-term and the long-term good are discrepant from each other, and individuals will have to prioritise one or the other. Parenting is full of such experiences, and so is the experience of being a pupil. But the suggestion here is that cultures may differ in how they see the long-term/short-term balance, and in how they manage to convey this to individuals. A final dimension of cultural difference is the pattern of there being fixed rules which apply rigidly to interactions and equally to everyone involved, or there being more fluidity so that the immediate circumstances and the personal characteristics of participants can play a determining role in what is permitted. Politeness and hierarchy are obvious examples of this.

Toren (1993) points out the complexity and creativity of the interface between what we call 'cultural', what we call 'individual', and what we call 'biological'.

> Children have to live their lives in terms of their understandings, just as adults do; their ideas are grounded in their experience and thus equally valid. The challenge for the anthropologist [and the psychologist] is to analyse the processes that make it possible for children to lead effective

lives [. . .] An examination of this puzzle suggests that an analysis of, say, a politico-economic process is illuminated by a concurrent analysis of how children constitute cognitively the key concepts that inform that same politico-economic process. To understand this is to understand how people come to be 'enchanted', as Bourdieu would say, by meanings they themselves have made; how they come to take for granted their own concepts and practices. It is to understand, too, how this very process, as manifest in the concepts and practices of adults, structures the conditions in and through which children will come to maturity as particular, historically located persons, who will actively constitute a world which is at once the same as, *and different from*, the world their elders knew.

(Toren 1993: 463)

What adds to this complexity is that any given individual may be a member of more than one culture, with cultural identity fluctuating from moment to moment depending on, for example, the immediate social context. This applies in very visible ways in people emigrating from one country to another, and I make much the same point about self-concept later. And also cultures are not static, they are continually enacted by the people who live in them in ways that change from moment to moment. In particular, they change historically. The new generation growing into a culture will appropriate something of the old ways of doing things, and will develop them to fit the opportunities they have and the challenges they face. New ideologies and new expectations and new technologies may change this, sometimes gradually over several generations, sometimes abruptly. Sometimes we see these as positive changes, sometimes as frightening and destructive. Again, I return to this later (pp. 82–84, 220, 223–31, 252–55).

Discussions of culture and development drawn from cross-cultural studies may be found in later sections of this book (pp. 139–40, 152–57, 236–37).

1.7 Summary

Bronfenbrenner's model locates individual development within a set of social contexts. His model emphasises the sorts of interaction between different factors that emerge from studies of the effects of genes and the workings of evolution. The body of this book is organised in terms of his analysis of environments, with discussion at various points of evidence from genes, from evolution, and from other biological studies of how the individual's biological nature is drawn by nurture into the development of the child as a social person.

Coming at the question of development from a different direction, work in sociology, in anthropology, and in history raises all sorts of questions about how psychologists understand the environments of development.

Again, Bronfenbrenner's model requires discussion of many of these issues, and evidence from these disciplines will be fed into much of the rest of this book.

Chapter 2

Beginning with the child

In the Russian dolls metaphor of Bronfenbrenner's systems of developmental contexts, the smallest but central doll is the child himself or herself. This chapter is about this smallest doll; about the characteristics, states and processes which we attribute to the child itself (although it will become clear that these 'intrinsic' attributes are more often than not socially constituted and modified). It includes discussion of things about the child that are generally analysed in terms of biology – evolved characteristics, brain development, physiological self-regulation; but links these to characteristics where social and cultural pressures are increasingly evident as important determinants – personality and self-concept, conflict with siblings and others, taking on social roles. I begin with what might be evolutionary 'givens'; discuss self-regulation at some length; and proceed to ways of looking at the development of personality and of certain social emotions. The smallest doll will turn out to be a highly complex creature with a host of different factors affecting its development, some intrinsic to itself, most interacting with the outer dolls.

2.1 The evolved child: signals, neoteny and the uses of immaturity

I address some of the specifics about evolutionary givens elsewhere. The point I want to make briefly here is that children (reproductively immature humans) face a long period of surviving and developing and learning before they get to be able to pass on their genes. It is essential for them to survive in a world where they are, compared with some other species, rather helpless. It is in their interests to be good at learning and at evoking conditions in which they can learn. It is important for them not to be pushed aside (or worse) by other more mature humans. Because of all of this, they have evolved characteristics that signal that they are young (and so not yet competitors), that signal that they need help from related individuals (who should invest in them in order to enhance the survival of the genes that they share), and that enhance their ability to learn what they need to learn (often well before they actually need to use the skills and knowledge).

Human infants and young children have the big shiny eyes, high foreheads, soft skin, plump cheeks, round and chubby feet and hands, smell of milk, tendency to cuddle up, and uncoordinated movements that generally evoke automatic feelings of tenderness and nurturance in adults, and not to evoke feelings of hostility and fear. Similar signals operate in other species too; compare the adult chicken, bear, dog, horse, etc. and the immature one. (These characteristics are picked up and then exaggerated in various human art forms, too. Disney heroines have exaggerated large eyes and high foreheads, for example, and the villains are much more pointed than the good guys; teddy bears have evolved from quite a realistic humped and growly-looking prototype around 1900 to a much more baby-like soft round-faced big-eyed pastel-furred super-cub, pretty much unlike any actual bear.) The effect of signals like these is to mark the young individual as non-threatening, as not a competitor, as deserving more tolerance and more nurturance than an adult.

Typically, more mature humans react to these evolved characteristics by providing the developmental experiences that they think will give the immature individual a good chance of healthy development (parental 'frames', for example pp. 115–17, 130–33, 214, 242). They expect young individuals to need all sorts of care, help and support from adults: they do not expect them to be competent at everything that an adult is expected to be competent at. They may see childhood as a special period of life, to be enjoyed more than worked at, protected more than exploited.

We may be less positive towards individual children who do not show the expected childish characteristics, the precociously sexual child, for example, or the child who prefers private reading to engaging in social games. We may also exclude immature individuals from certain experiences or from equal status and respect on the grounds of their immaturity (schools are often problematic about this, and also parents and adolescents frequently have arguments about autonomy). Some individuals who are actually mature may exaggerate their own 'childlike' characteristics to elicit protection and favours from others (there is a vast make-up industry devoted to helping women display baby-smooth skin, big shiny eyes, rosy lips, for example). The assumptions about childhood, irresponsibility and protection that may have followed on from millennia of evolution but are culturally adopted may have costs as well as benefits for the individuals concerned.

2.2 Biological bases of systems for personality, emotion regulation and socialisation

So we tend to assume that children have characteristics in common that are different from characteristics of older individuals. Theories dating back to medieval Europe, or even earlier, attribute different personality types to physiological differences (e.g. the four temperaments Burrow 1986, pp. 64–65). Through to the present day, there are both common sense and formal psychological theories about body build and personality, or brain functioning and personality. For example, Shakespeare has Julius Caesar say 'let me have men about me that are fat' fearing that the 'lean and hungry' Cassius is dangerous. Researchers such as Sheldon linked body build and personality characteristics through a theory of subtle differences in the early development of the embryo. Another example is the model of introversion and extraversion based on brain functioning (in adults) proposed by Hans Eysenck (Eysenck 1967).

Both formal and informal ideas about personality and physiology have difficulties around the diagnosis of personality and the diagnosis of physiological differences, neither of which is straightforward There are major difficulties around cause–effect relationships – Cassius may be dangerous because he is treated with suspicion, as well as suspected because he is thin, 'thinks too much' and appears to be plotting. There are difficulties around causal pathways: how does a subtle difference in body build or brain functioning or physiology result in a difference in personality? Could a difference in 'personality' affect body build or brain functioning or physiology, as well as the other way round? And finally, there is the difficulty that most of the evidence (such as it is) is correlational, and the existence of even a more substantial correlation than is usually found in this area does not prove a causal relationship, whatever the models claim.

For all these reasons, there was a long period when biologically-based theories of personality development lacked general acceptance by research psychologists, even if the common sense versions linking obvious physical characteristics to underlying personality remained in use – cartoonists' drawings of politicians, for example, rest on these sorts of assumptions. But our understanding of the fine-tuning of physiological mechanisms, particularly in the nervous system, has expanded so much that current theory and research can use different and far more detailed physiological models, and a better range of evidence, to begin to provide an infinitely better understanding of causal pathways from physiology to personality. Some of the picture that is emerging is developmental and has massive implications for how we think about children and childrearing. The core of the issue is, I think, how people learn early in life to cope with stress.

2.2.1 Physiological systems for stress management

One central area of current research is on early experiences that guide the functioning and development of the central nervous system (CNS) and the endocrine and immune systems, resulting in a tendency to a differentiation of development, feelings, and behaviour because of these early experiences.

Experiences early in life may nudge the development of basic physiological systems in more or less favourable directions, with consequences for the individual which may be lifelong, and may even affect future generations through increasing individuals' tendency to provide the same sort of experience for their offspring.

One key area of interest is the development of physiological systems for stress management. 'Stress' is natural and not necessarily bad in itself, but we do need to avoid sustained or chronic stress which tends to be debilitating or even dangerous. Our bodies have ways of reacting to and reducing stress levels. 'Allostasis' is the process of activating neural, neuroendocrine and neuroendocrine–immune systems to adapt physiologically in face of potentially stressful challenges. Challenges increase arousal, but arousal needs to be followed by a period of recovery; too much arousal or a high level of arousal for too long tends to be damaging – chronic allostatic load can lead to disease and to changes in pattern of physiological regulation.

One important regulatory system that is being shown to be fine-tuned by early experience is the hypothalamic–pituitary–adrenocortical axis (HPA). This is critical in how we react to threat. The basal level of the activity of the HPA axis supports acute fight/flight reactions to events, but HPA activity also serves to modulate the impact of the events. In the short term this may be adaptive, but chronic HPA activity may overload the system and lead to worse functioning. If it becomes hyperresponsive then this influences the development of hypertension, cardiovascular disease, immune suppression, and insulin resistance hence susceptibility to diabetes. It may also be associated with anxiety disorders, depression, memory problems, developmental delay, and growth retardation. If it becomes hyporesponsive this is associated with autoimmune diseases such as rheumatoid arthritis and asthma. It appears that early life stress may lead to short-term hyperresponsivity and long-term lack of resiliency – showing up in behaviour as a short-term tendency to anxiety and longer-term psychic numbing. (pp. 274–87)

One set of physiological changes that are intimately related to the body's response to stress involve cortisol. Cortisol is a hormone produced by the adrenal gland that tends to increase blood pressure and blood sugar and reduces immune responses. After infancy, cortisol levels vary during the day with highest levels on waking; levels then fall gradually over the day, rise again in late afternoon, and gradually fall through the evening to be lowest a few hours after sleep begins at night. An individual person's rhythms of cortisol secretion tend to be consistent, but there is significant variation between individuals. Changes in cortisol levels have been seen in connection with illness, trauma, fear, pain, depression and stress.

Studies of other species allow a detailed look at what is going on in CNS development to produce calmer, more resilient individuals. What seems to be crucially important is the development of neurotransmitters. These provide diffuse modulatory systems over many parts of the brain, and they are important not just for cognition but also for a host of regulatory functions including stress management and meeting challenges. Important neurotransmitters include norepinephrine, dopamine, and serotonin. Norepinephrine is involved in (among other functions) attention, arousal, sleep–wake, learning, memory, anxiety, pain, mood, and brain metabolism. Serotonin is involved in sleep–wake cycles and sleep stages, mood, aggression, and depression. Dopamine is crucial for among other things voluntary movement (it is heavily implicated in Parkinsons, where individuals' movements are progressively disrupted and uncontrollable), appetite, temperature regulation, sexual behaviour, learning, and memory.

For example, early experience may affect the 'fight or flight' systems of the sympathetic nervous system, which are modulated primarily by norepinephrine and epinephrine. There may be risk factors for the functioning of the sympathetic nervous system and consequently heart disease and metabolic disorders. If there is maternal high anxiety in the second trimester of pregnancy or inter-parental conflict the child is more likely to have problems with vagal tone, heart rate variability, and sleep organisation. If the child experiences a lot of skin to skin contact ('kangaroo care') and more symmetrical mother–infant communication then they are likely to show better development in these areas, with more mature sleep cycles in babies, and with more quiet sleep/alert wakefulness) (e.g. Feldman et al. 2002; Weaver et al. 2004).

It is also known that separation of the infant from its mother suppresses its immune system and affects immune system development (although separation from mother may also involve a loss of breastfeeding which could be expected to affect the immune system). Possibly the context of the separation also needs to be considered – e.g. what alternative social attachments are present, what are the effects of prior mother–child relations. I will look at this in the section on attachment (pp. 121–27).

Other developmental processes seem to be modulated by early experience. Early rearing is known to impact on growth hormone production. Examples of effects in humans include deprivation dwarfism and failure to thrive (e.g. Kashani et al. 1992; Gardner et al. 1999; Hasselmann and Reichenheim 2006; Rutter 1998b). Another effect may be on the timing of puberty. Experiences of poor family relations or of father absence are associated with earlier puberty in girls (e.g. Belsky et al. 2007a; Bogaert 2005; Ellis and Garber 2000).

2.2.2 Mechanisms for developmental differences in self-regulation

Developmentally, we need to note the importance for infants of managing stress reduction and emotion regulation. A number of physiological and behavioural systems are available, some operated by the child itself (such as averting the gaze and peeping only briefly if something is too close or intrusive or frightening). Some of these systems appear to be fine-tuned after birth by parenting behaviour. Animal studies of early rearing conditions show effects of maternal deprivation, social isolation, and licking or grooming on the development of these regulatory systems. Handling of the young laboratory animals by humans is also associated with short-term changes in the efficiency of synaptic connections, and enables long-term potentiation of connections. Such experiences affect the expression of proteins which help with the establishment of brain connectivity and neurone development. Importantly, the mother rat's reaction to infants who have been taken away from her briefly and handled mediates the human handling effects: she reacts to the separation by providing more maternal licking and grooming.

Recent research on humans (see for example Kaffman and Meaney 2007) provides exciting evidence about the developmental impact of certain patterns of parental behaviour. There is emerging evidence that early rearing conditions affect gene expression. Being deprived of maternal care does not change the chemical/genetic content of your DNA, but it may affect how the DNA is expressed in the body (Kaffman and Meaney 2007). The structure of DNA in cells is folded in a complex way, and particular parts of the DNA sequence may be more or less accessible to do the work of building and maintaining the body and its functioning, as this building and maintenance work involves the transcription of the original DNA laid down at conception. Post-conception experience may modify exactly how this transcription proceeds. In rats (who are born immature compared with primates), more maternal licking and grooming in the first postnatal week of life reduces the methylation of the genes that determine how many hippocampus glucocortisoid receptors an animal will have. Methylated genes are not expressed. The well-licked rat pup may have fewer genes methylated and so more glucocortisoid receptors. Animals who develop more receptors are more able to control stress levels efficiently, whereas animals with few receptors have sluggish, inefficient, responses to stress, and more prolonged stress, and are at more risk of overload of the stress-response system. The developmental effects of maternal care seem to be irreversible in the normal lives of rats.

It looks as though there may be interaction between what genes you have and your rearing conditions. Kaffman and Meaney (2007) describe studies that found that the expression of genes was affected by early life differences in being parented. In work by Caspi and Moffitt and their colleagues (Caspi *et al.* 2002, 2003; Moffitt 2005; Moffitt *et al.* 2005, 2006; Moffitt and Caspi 2007) the researchers found interactions between genes and experience. Individuals who both had an unusual genetic variant linked to how much serotonin transporter protein is produced and were abused as children were highly likely to suffer adverse outcomes as adolescents or young adults. Individuals with the gene but with no experience of abuse were fine. I return to the effects of parental abuse of children elsewhere (pp. 85–86, 129–30, 141–42).

Another example of interesting research is the fine-grained analysis of the effects of breastfeeding. Breastfeeding has an extensive range of benefits for the infant. Obviously, it provides nourishment including key fatty acids, vitamins, and so forth that are so clearly implicated in favourable cognitive development (e.g. Caspi et al. 2007; Kramer et al. 2008) that baby food manufacturers are now adding them to formula milk. Breast milk also strengthens the immune system, giving better resistance to all sorts of infections at a time when the baby's own immune system is immature (M'Rabet et al. 2008). And breastfeeding involves closer physical contact, and perhaps more mutual gazing with the mother, than other ways of feeding.

Studies of rodents suggest that small amounts of stress (such as 15 minutes handling) seemed to lead to more resilience: long periods led to more vulnerability to stress – bigger startle reactions, more freezing and anxiety when exposed to the smell of a cat, higher levels of stress hormones, negative mood, mild cognitive impairments, and more consumption of alcohol. Brief separations were followed by more maternal licking and grooming, but longer separations disrupted maternal behaviour and reduce licking and grooming. There was some remediation if the young animal was exposed to interesting environmental and social stimulation (Kaffman and Meaney 2007). In primates too, conditions that impair or exclude maternal care are associated with attachment problems and changes in the neurobiology of stress hormone production.

Babies develop a buffering system against the disruptive effects of stress e.g. securely attached babies have more left frontal lobe activity compared with right, an asymmetry which is associated with positive emotions, whereas insecurely attached babies have more right frontal lobe activity, associated with negative emotions and inhibition (Dawson et al. 2001). Electroencephalogram (EEG) studies of humans (Dawson and Ashman 1999; Dawson et al. 1999) show that infants with depressed mothers are less likely to show left-hemisphere activation. Insensitive mothering seems to be mediating between depression and EEG. It appears that there may be differences between the brain responses to stress in infants with withdrawn, normal, and intrusive mothers (Halligan et al. 2004; Lupien et al. 2000; pp. 59, 146–47, 279).

2.2.3 Parenting behaviour and the development of stress regulation

Clearly, the experience of parenting that the baby and young child receive may contribute significantly and in many different ways to the child's development of stress-regulation systems. What may be emerging as developmentally important is responsive parenting, including breastfeeding. Breastfeeding is interesting because there are analogous findings in other species. It provides lots of skin-to-skin contact, and the human infant's experience of skin-to-skin contact is associated short term with reduction in stress, and long term with more rapid maturation of vagal tone (implicated in digestion, heart rate, facial expression) and more settled sleep cycles, maybe with better growth and behavioural development (Repetti, Taylor, and Saxbe 2007). Rats, mice, and monkeys who are low on such contact for a critical period soon after birth tend to be more fearful and to show greater physiological stress for the rest of their lives. Additionally, rodents and monkeys who have had little licking and grooming tend to parent their own litters in the same way, leading to similar patterns of stress in the next generation. Evidence from studies of rodents shows that even if overall contact is the same, fine differences in the quality of contact with the mother lead to a reduction in stress responses in the young animals and better learning of longer-term stress management strategies. One example, discussed by Kaffman and Meaney (2007), involves the maternal behaviour of rodents. Different strains of laboratory rats and mice show different amounts of licking, grooming and arched-back nursing (LG/ABN) during the first week after birth, and given the genetic differences between strains this might be a genetically programmed behaviour difference. Female offspring raised by mothers who do lots of LG/ABN treat their own offspring to lots of LG/ABN; those raised with little LG/ABN provide little of it for their own pups. However, the researchers were interested in the possibility that rates of LG/ABN were affected by experience. They also cross-fostered infant females with mothers of the other strain, so that animals born of high LG/ABN mothers were fostered by low LG/ABN mothers, and vice versa. When these fostered animals grew up and had litters of their own, they treated their litters to the same amount of LG/ABN that they had experienced themselves, acting like their foster mothers whatever their genetic background was. It looks, therefore, as if postnatal maternal care programmed later maternal behaviour and vulnerability to stress. The experiences of young females in generation one led them to behave in particular ways when they became mothers to the pups of generation two; this parenting shaped the development of generation two and thus their parenting of generation three; and so on, over succeeding generations.

Kaffman and Meaney (2007) suggest that this could be adaptive if environmental challenges encountered early in development are likely to persist through life, in which case neurodevelopmental programming might improve survival. A stressful environment, for example, where there are dangers such as an unreliable supply of food, would be expected to reduce the amount of LG/ABN that the mother can provide to her infants, as she will be busy coping with the challenges of the environment. The infants, receiving lower levels of LG/ABN, would tend to be fearful and responsive to stress. It might be advantageous for those infants to expect the environment to be full of challenges and so to be fearful as they grow up, and not waste their energy on superfluous LG/ABN towards their own offspring when the burning issue is survival itself. It might also be advantageous in a risky environment for human infants to be easily distressed, as distressed infants will do more to attract the care and attention of their parents. In a classic study of temperament in Kenyan infants during a time of food shortage (deVries 1984), it was the infants previously identified as having a difficult demanding temperament who survived the food shortage best, because they made more demands on their caregivers and consequently were less likely to be left short of food than the quieter more compliant babies.

Maestripieri (2005) describes research on maternal abuse by rhesus macaque monkeys. Some macaque mothers tend to abuse their young infants, typically by dragging, throwing, sitting on or biting them; the behaviour sometimes results in superficial injury and sometimes serious injury or death. These abusive mothers are not just being clumsy with their babies (as first-time mothers sometimes are), and they usually get on well enough with other adult macaques; abusive mothering seems to be a specific and socially limited set of maladaptive behaviours. This behaviour seems to run in families (daughters resemble mothers, sisters resemble sisters) and to occur across an individual mother's different pregnancies. Maestripieri reports a prospective study of macaque infant abuse, with females being observed during their own infancies and then as first-time mothers. In a cross-fostering study, some of the infants of mothers who had been abused in their own infancies were fostered by mothers who had not been abused, and some of the offspring of mothers who had not been abused were fostered by mothers who had been abused in infancy. Thus there were four groups: in group one neither birth mother nor foster mother had been abused; in group two birth mother had been abused in infancy but foster mother had not; in group three foster mother had been abused in infancy but birth mother had not; in group four both birth mother and foster mother had been abused. The groups of animals were similar in age and social status.

The results were striking. Not one of the infants reared by non-abused mothers suffered maternal abuse (groups one and two). Half of the infants reared by mothers who had themselves been abused as infants were abused by these mothers – four of the eight in group three and five of the eight in group four. It seemed to be the mothers' own experience of abuse that predicted whether they would abuse an infant, and it was the females who had suffered most abuse in their own infancies who were most likely to abuse their babies. The females may have learned their abusive mothering techniques from observing their own abusive mothers mistreating their siblings, but it is also highly possible that their own suffering from maternal abuse resulted in long-term changes in neural circuits or neuroendocrine processes that affected their own parenting behaviour.

Thus the emerging evidence from animal studies suggests increasingly strongly that maternal licking, grooming etc. modulate HPA activity. A lack of this care is worse for rats and primates throughout their lifetimes, and possibly there are similar effects in humans – especially for those who are at risk e.g. infants who have a fearful or irritable temperament. If the infant lacks reliable and affectionate parenting, there may be a chronic activation of basic stress-response mechanisms, leading to a 'cascade of risk', and cumulative effects. This 'risky families' model centres on change in allostatic load and a lifelong ability to cope with challenge and stress.

2.2.4 Developmental changes in reaction to stress

In humans, neonates react to pain or stress such as medical examinations with fussing and crying; and the secretion of cortisol and adrenocortico-trophic hormone (ACTH). Neonates do not have the adult daytime-related pattern of high cortisol levels in the morning getting lower throughout day but this is beginning to be established by three months. By one year, there tend to be diminished neurobiological reactions to stress, although infants produce the behavioural reaction of crying and fussing – perhaps less distress and more protest is involved? Evident distress does not necessarily mean high levels of stress hormones – for example securely attached babies may cry to elicit care but have low cortisol levels.

Attachment (pp. 121–27) will be crucial to this – secure attachments seem to be the best foundation for dealing with stress positively, insecure but consistent attachments are less helpful, insecure disorganised and unpredictable attachments are the most stressful in themselves and the least satisfactory foundation for development. Witnessing or exposure to parental conflict is also deleterious (pp. 62, 142–43) as is maternal depression leading to disrupted parenting (Halligan et al. 2004; Goodyer 2008; Lupien et al. 2000).

Sensitive and responsive parenting seems to influence regulatory processes in infants' immature regulatory systems, and to facilitate the long-term development of stress-response systems. The processes involved may affect neurodevelopment and the expression of genes. A lack of sensitive parenting and the experience of maternal separation stress the infant and simultaneously remove the person who normally de-stresses stress. Early experience of parenting may have long-term effects on social and emotional development, and also on cognitive development via affecting the child's ability to marshal cognitive resources to task, to sustain attention despite stress, and to lay down and access memory effectively. We might also expect risk-taking behaviour to be associated with early experience of stress and stress reduction.

Stress levels in young children are affected by peers as well as parents (Gunnar and Donzella 2002). Peer effects are evident in preschool daycare: normally secretion of cortisol shows a morning peak followed by a drop off, but for young children in daycare whose peer social skills are still developing, there can be increases in cortisol levels throughout the daytime spent with peers unless there is good supportive care from adults. In social settings later in childhood, peer-rejected children have higher levels of cortisol and behaviourally poor control of their aggression and negative emotions. Peer-neglected children start to show higher levels of cortisol in early adolescence, maybe because they have accumulated more aversive social experiences, or maybe because of the different social demands of the period.

Buffering seems to become less effective in smoothing out stress in adolescence. Some studies show a peak in basal glucocortisoids and reactivity around puberty, some more gradual increase; the evidence inconsistent as yet (Gunnar and Vazquez 2006). This may be associated with adolescence change in mood, behaviour, and disorder (Rutter and Smith 1995; pp. 195, 268, 281–82).

> One of the functions of the caregiving system is to moderate and enable control of physiological and behavioral responses to stressors. In humans, social modulation of physiological stress responses may lay the foundation for the development of emotion regulation competencies.
>
> (Gunnar and Vazquez 2006: 197)

2.2.5 Emotional self-regulation

I hope I have produced a convincing argument that there are very important physiological processes involved in emotion regulation, and that early experience in general, and experience of parenting in particular, may have profound effects on the fine-tuning of these systems. Self-regulation of emotions, cognitions, motivations and psychological processes in general is currently seen as one of the most important areas of the development of competence. All societies expect their members to regulate themselves so as to fit reasonably well with social expectations as to feelings, thoughtfulness, goals and social functioning, and socialisation therefore invests a great deal of effort in these areas (pp. 281–82; Bradley and Corwyn 2005). Measures of how children regulate their psychological processes to learn, or to cope with strong emotions or stress, predict their mental health and their achievement (Masten and Coatsworth 1998; Lengua and Sandler 1996; Lengua 2002; Compas et al. 2001; Meadows 2006). Undoubtedly there are many definitional questions about how general, how pervasive and how constant self-regulation is, or whether it might not often be specific to a limited range of settings. An individual might be able to be highly self-regulated in one setting or at one time or with one partner, but be very precariously self-regulating in another. Similarly it is likely that a wide range of complex mechanisms are involved in such behaviour, and in its development, and a large number of apparently different pathways might lead to indistinuishable outcomes. However, several researchers in this area are converging on a focus on 'effortful attentional control' (Dishion and Connell 2006; Rothbart and Bates 2006; Posner and Rothbart 2000; Frith and Frith 2001) as particularly important. Individual differences in the achievement of effortful attentional control seem to be associated with genetic predispositions in temperament plus experiences from infancy onwards (Rothbart and Bates 2006; Kagan and Fox 2006; Eisenberg *et al.* 2000, 2001; Eisenberg, Cumberland and Spinrad 1998; Eisenberg 2004), especially in interaction within the family. Effortful attentional control needs to be considered along with the achievement of joint attention (pp. 88, 112–13, 120–21, 130–33). The combination of mutually responsive orientation between mother and small child and lower levels of parental power assertion, for example, is associated with better self-regulation by the child, and by more positive development of interpersonal and moral behaviour (Bradley and Corwyn 2005; Kochanska 1997a, 1997b; Kochanska and Murray 2000; Kochanska, Murray and Coy 1997; Kochanska *et al.* 1996; Zhou *et al.* 2008).

2.2.5.1 Emotional self-regulation and psychosocial disorder

Lewis *et al.* (2006) review evidence that gives us reason to believe that difficulties with self-regulation of emotion may underlie a whole range of psychosocial disorders. If a child fails to develop ways to moderate feelings of anger and anxiety, such as shifting attention away from provoking events or inhibiting emotional impulses, he or she may be prone to start or to continue with aggressive or anxious behaviour, which may in turn damage their relations with parents, peers and teachers (pp. 93–95, 124–25, 176–77). Children who have better emotional self-regulation may be able to inhibit an immediate aggressive or anxious response, giving themselves time to find more constructive and positive ways of coping with the problem. Differences in emotion regulation and capacity for 'effortful control' can become deeply entrenched and difficult to change, in part because they are expressions of basic biological mechanisms, and in part because they may be grounded in relationships and interactions which pervade the child's development. Lewis *et al.* (2006) argue that both aggressive and anxious children tend to have experienced family interactions where both parent and child are 'stuck' in emotional exchanges that may bear little relation to the actual situation, whereas children who are not clinically impaired have more experience of parent–child interactions that shift flexibly according to the relevant context. This experience could have consequences for control at the cortical level, and neuroscience studies of brain functioning may be beginning to show what these are (although as Granger and Kivlighan (2003) argue, much more research is needed).

2.2.5.2 Emotion regulation and exposure to family conflict

It is worth noting briefly here that there is a literature on the effects on children's emotional regulation of their exposure to negative events such as conflict and violence between parents, or problems at school (e.g. Compas *et al.* 2001; Davies *et al.* 2002; Katz *et al.* 2007; Kitzmann *et al.* 2003; Sternberg *et al.* 2006; Zhou *et al.* 2008; pp. 59, 143). For example, children who have been exposed to higher levels of domestic violence have more problems with emotional regulation, which is in turn associated with more negative interactions with peers, more social problems such as being teased or excluded, and higher levels of both internalising and externalising behavior problems. They are also at risk of impaired emotional awareness, which may make it difficult for them to build and sustain intimate relationships either with friends or with romantic partners, and to work out positive resolutions to conflicts when these occur. Beijing children who had received particularly authoritarian parenting were more likely to show externalising behaviour problems if they also experienced negative school events and had low coping skills and low efficacy in emotional control (Zhou *et al.* 2008).

2.2.5.3 Maltreatment, abuse and neglect, and stress response systems

Adults who are suffering from post-traumatic stress disorder (PTSD) or depression, and have suffered abuse as children, seem to have hyperresponsive threat/stress response systems at cortico–limbic levels – possibly showing the cumulative effects of abuse/neglect (Gunnar and Quevedo 2007). Individuals who have suffered abuse but been resilient show evidence of reduced activity of stress neurobiology. The data do not show, however, if this low responsivity was there during childhood and protected them from the effects of the abuse, or whether it might be a risk factor for future disorder.

A common theme in stress research is that, consistent with other mammals, during development social relations play critical roles in regulating physiological stress reactions and protecting the developing brain from potentially deleterious effects of the hormones and neurochemicals associated with stress reactions. Disturbances in supportive care and care environments that are themselves threatening appear to rob children of an effective stress buffer and expose them to the consequences of biological stress responses that can have deleterious effects for later development. Caregivers and close relatives in a child's life are both potentially the strongest source of stress and the most powerful defense against harmful stressors. Complex patterns of social stimulation may be part of the experiential input that (in interaction with genetic predispositions) shapes children's emotional and biological reactivity. Children's stress responses are also sensitive to social experiences beyond the context of the family. Negotiating peer interactions in school settings is a potent challenge to the stress system, particularly at the stage in development where social skills are just emerging. Above and beyond these normative challenges, children who are less socially competent and/or rejected might be at risk for more frequent and prolonged activation of the stress response. One of the areas that need integration into models of developmental health and psychopathology is how stress activation that is associated with social status may affect children's later development and health.

(Gunnar and Quevedo 2007: 163)

There is more discussion of the effects of child abuse later (pp. 85–86, 129–30, 141–42).

2.2.6 Summary

I think this area of research is emerging as coherent in its picture of the effects of early experience of parenting on the long-term development of the young animal. I must nevertheless emphasise that more work needs to be done and there are possible problems of interpretation and detail. There are always problems with cross species comparisons. Comparing humans and animals gets us beyond correlational studies into experimental ones that can clarify causal patterns, but we cannot make uncritical extrapolations from one species to another. For example, there are questions about the timing of possible 'critical periods' for development, with changes in different sorts of early experience seeming to have more powerful effects if they come at one short period of time compared with earlier or later: but with differences in the precise timing between species. Similarly, some animals in research studies experience a laboratory cage environment that may not be comparable with a normal human one (or with the normal environment of that sort of animal); and we might (cf. Bronfenbrenner) expect the wider environment to be involved. There is as yet little work on infants' stress and other partners – little even on fathers, less still on other sorts of social settings. There are issues about brief stresses and chronic ones, and about different types of stress and adversity. How far are our stress management systems general and how far specific to particular sorts of stress? Are there lifetime changes? Are there systematic individual differences, such as gender effects or temperament-based effects? Are there shared genetic factors as well as or instead of parenting effects? Are there differences between individuals growing up in different socio-economic or socio-cultural environments? What is the generalisability of normative models to children in conditions of higher or lower risk? What evidence is there of ecological factors that are supportive or compromising of emotion regulation?

So at present we have an increasing body of very interesting findings, and the beginnings of a precise understanding of how certain sorts of early experience may have lifelong effects on emotion regulation and stress-management systems. I think that there may be rapid progress in this area, and we will soon have a secure grasp on how certain physiological systems come to operate in ways that amount to different personality types. I move on now to the contemporary model of temperament types. The ancient model (Burrow 1986) may not be validated by the self-regulation research, but the idea of subtle differences in 'humours' which the medieval model used may not turn out to be altogether ridiculous. Not the traditional humours of blood, black and yellow bile, and phlegm that the medieval scholars thought about, perhaps, but even Caesar's suspicion of Cassius's thinness may turn out to have justification, if Cassius's early experiences led to deficiencies in growth hormone, serotonin take-up and stress regulation!

2.3 Temperament

Clearly there is a lot going on developmentally inside the individual child's emotional system. I have discussed emotional self-regulation and stress management as developmentally important components of personality, but there are of course other ways of describing developmental differences in personality. The first body of work I want to mention focuses on 'temperament'. As a working definition, temperament is seen as biologically rooted individual differences in behaviour tendencies that are present early in life and are relatively stable across various kinds of situations and over the course of time (Eby, Maher and Butts 2010; Wachs and Bates 2001). Although temperament underlies predictable patterns of behaviour and of development, it does not determine them inexorably; it is a matter of pre-disposing characteristics which change over time and depend on the context that the child is working in. For example, it will often be easier to tease out someone's temperamental style in a situation that is not too familiar to them, because they will not be able to rely entirely on a very well-learned pattern of behaviour (cf. the assessment of attachment, p. 122).

Temperament has several dimensions, including negative emotionality, positive emotionality, how easy it is to soothe the individual when he or she is distressed, activity level, adaptability, the degree to which the individual approaches new situations or people enthusiastically rather than cautiously holding back, sociability, persistence, and behavioural rhythmicity, the ways in which a predictable timetable of feelings such as sleepiness, hunger and so forth develops in infancy (Bates and Pettit 2007; Rothbart and Bates

2006; Wachs and Bates 2001). Several of these clearly reflect differences in emotional reactivity and self-regulation (Rothbart and Bates 2006; pp. 54–59), and there is little doubt that they are influenced by both genetic and experiential factors. As our understanding of stress-reaction systems and neurotransmitters increases, we may become able to specify what temperament is in the sort of terms I used in the last section. This will help us link temperament, experience and outcome in more precise ways.

The temperament dimensions of negative emotionality, low adaptability, and extremely high levels of inhibition and of reactivity act as developmental risk factors, making behaviour problems a more likely development and reducing prospects of academic or social competence, particularly for individuals growing up in conditions of risk such as dysfunctional families or families facing high levels of stress and disadvantage. This was found in a study of Chinese children in Beijing as well as in European and American studies (Zhou *et al.* 2008). Whether temperament can also promote resilience in children is a question I address later (pp. 285–86).

2.4 The self-concept

One major set of our descriptions of individuals centres on the idea of 'self-concept'. I am locating my main discussion of 'self-concept' here because for many theorists it is a property of the individual, and our own experience of our 'self' is often that it sits inside our heads like the classic homunculus, providing a commentary on our actions and a narrative of our hopes, fears and dreams. But I shall be going on to show how social microsystems do a lot to build up individuals' self-concepts, and how individuals' self-concepts affect how they manage their social interactions.

The mainstream psychological model of the 'self' derives from the classic ideas of William James (1890, 1892/1985), developed by, amongst others, G. H. Mead (1934). This model incorporates the 'I', the subjective experiential features of being, hence the alternative name of the 'existential' self, and the 'Me' or 'categorical' self, the more objective material, social or psychological characteristics that make-up individual differences. The 'Me' is made up of labels – female, tall, green, intellectual, dislikes red cabbage, and so forth. The 'I' involves feelings and understandings such as awareness of oneself as an agent who has a unique life history and experience and who continues over time, distinct from others and capable of awareness of one's own awareness, that is, of self-reflection. It is the 'I' that we experience when we are not thinking about ourselves, and the 'me' that we call on when we are asked to tell someone who we are – so for example 'I' am enjoying the brightness of a spring day outside my window, and know 'I' experienced similar bright spring days last year; 'I' am also experiencing physical discomfort in my neck and shoulders as a result of sitting too long at my computer, which is a more serious discomfort than in previous years;

'I' know that 'I' am the only person who has this discomfort and that 'I' must use my ability to act to seek help with it, by going to a physiotherapist and by badgering my departmental administrator into providing a better chair. But if the focus is on the 'Me', category labels and personality characteristics would predominate, so it would be a matter of 'a gardener' rather than 'enjoying the sunlight on these new green leaves', 'usually able to persuade people' rather than 'a social agent', 'principled' rather than 'stiff-necked'. A moment's introspection will suggest both that 'I' and 'Me' intersect, and that the explicit content of each varies moment-to-moment. We are also getting dangerously near to issues about what 'consciousness' is; nonetheless, the classic distinction between 'I' and 'Me' will guide at least the beginning of my discussion of 'the self'.

2.4.1 The existential self

Theorists, particularly those influenced by psychoanalysis, used to propose that infants have little or nothing in the way of a sense of self, either 'me' or 'I', and that what 'self' they had was undifferentiated and disorganised. In particular, it was proposed that infants could not conceive of themselves as separate from their mothers (Mahler, Pine and Bergman 1975; Chodorow 1978). But more recent research on infants' early perception, cognition, attention etc. suggests otherwise (Laible and Thompson 2007; Trevarthen and Aitken 2003). From very early on, the infant has goals of mastery, autonomy, and connectedness (pp. 88, 120–22) that are hard to reconcile with the presumed capabilities and preferences of an undifferentiated infant–mother–world blob. It seems more likely that the I-self comes from basic biological and perceptual processes that are operative from quite early in the first year. For example, infants' capacity for imitation (Fenstermacher and Saudino 2006; McEwen *et al.* 2007), their developing perception of behavioural similarities, their attention to the visible bits of their bodies, and their special enthusiasm for events that are contingent on their own action (Trevarthen and Aitken 2003), their increasing interest in and pleasure in mastery (pp. 112–15; Messer *et al.* 1986), their involvement in joint activity with their parents in games and routines (pp. 120–21, 130–33), their use of their attachment figure (p. 124) as a reference point about what they are doing, all suggest a sense of existence in relation to the world and of agency within it that has roots very early in the first year. Probably these lead to increasing subjective self-awareness on several fronts: recognition of oneself in a mirror, and an increasing ability to use this recognition to operate in the world: awareness of oneself as agent, developing into mastery motivation and a sense of self-efficacy, but also to awareness of oneself as subject to judgement by others: ability to self-regulate, thus avoiding emotional distress (pp. 60–63, 128–29); and awareness of oneself as a social person, engaging in interaction with other social persons and developing scripts of how such interactions should proceed. Infants' and children's experience of affect and the modulation of their affect by parents and caregivers, their experience of social interaction games and routines with self-regulating others involving reciprocal exchange and caregiver scaffolding (Gauvain 2005; Jennings *et al.* 2008; Meadows 2006; Turner and Berkowitz 2005), the regularity of experience of affect–behaviour link, the early biographical narratives that parents offer to their children (Oppenheim *et al.* 2007; Slaughter *et al.* 2007; Wenner *et al.* 2008), the development of auto-biographical memory capacities (Bauer 2007; Fivush and Nelson 2004; Nelson 2003; Nelson and Fivush 2004), the stories children begin to tell (Nicolopoulou and Richner 2007) would all feed into a richer and more extensive sense of 'I'.

2.4.2 The categorical self-concept

I have just described the psychology of the 'I' self, which develops from early in infancy and results in us having a sense of being an entity which continues smoothly through time and space, which is a causal force in our world, which is related to but separate from other similar persons, and about whose experience and inner workings, both mental and physical, we have a different sort of knowledge than we have of other persons. But as we develop, increasingly we have a 'me' self-concept, the accumulation and organisation of labels that are appropriate for us (and a derivative of the biographical activites we are engaged in). We come to be able to experience ourselves as an object that can be thought about as well as subjectively lived, to develop a degree of reflexivity. Most theorists see this as being sub-stantially a matter of labels offered to us or imposed on us by others; hence the phrase the 'looking-glass self'. Such ideas were developed by symbolic interactionists (e.g. Mead 1934; Baldwin 1895). This 'self' is seen as a social construction, as a reflected self-internalisation of others' values, especially those presented to us verbally. We are constantly provided with such labels – 'who's a pretty baby then', 'clever girl', 'bad boy', 'people like us just don't do such things'. The model assumes that humans have a natural propensity to take on such labels, just as we seem to have a propensity to attend to and to imitate others. Certainly, as I will shortly describe, we have little difficulty in reporting such labels, and of, sometimes, living up (or down) to them. Our reflexivity is to some degree controlled by people other than ourselves, a point seen as particularly problematic by post-modernists (Callero 2003). Looking at people's ways of resisting this control is one of the fascinating areas of developmental psychology, particularly in ado-lescence (pp. 138, 141, 267–70).

So it is the predominant view (Eby, Maher and Butts 2010; Harter 2006; Leary 2007; Thompson 1998) that self-concept emerges as a result of a long-lasting interaction between emotional tendencies and interpersonal relationships, initially relationships with parents and increasingly relationships with other significant figures (maybe nowadays with virtual people (Dodge *et al.* 2008); a case is being made that interaction with avatars in virtual reality programs may powerfully affect individuals' self-concept (though bookish children may for centuries have developed their self-concepts in a sort of interaction with characters in literature, identifying with Antigone or Robin Hood or Alice in Wonderland or Harry Potter). Self-concept development involves assuming categorical labels and it also involves the internalisation, regulation and expression of emotions and motivations (pp. 85–95, 127–30; Leary 2007). Self-concept is seen as a powerful self-regulator, socially and personally. It continually crosses between the individual and the wider social environments.

2.4.3 Functions of self-concept

What point is there to having such a self-concept? Other animals seem to get by well enough without even the existential self-concept. I suspect the answer lies in the 'Me' concept's cognitive and social roots. Having a worked-out narrative of oneself could have organisational functions, giving rise to expectations which guide one's behaviour, to self-referent scripts, to clearer goals, perhaps to better regulation of affect. Self-concept theorists such as Conn (1997) suggest the person needs to:

1   maintain a favourable, or preferably enhanced, sense of Me-self;
2   maximise pleasure and minimise pain, as far as possible;
3   develop a coherent and related sense of the world and one's place in it;
4   maintain relatedness with others in balance with sense of self and transcendence;
5   avoid social exclusion.

Each of these needs may be involved in all sorts of psychological processes. For example, Baumeister (1998), in a chapter in *The Self*, discusses (I give an alphabetical list): self-control, self-deception, self-efficacy, self-enhancement, self-handicapping, self-image, self-knowledge, self-monitoring, self-presentation, self-regulation, and self-verification.

If something is so multifunctional it may be extremely pervasive. If something pervasive is favourable, one may be well set up for dealing with whatever one encounters. If I can say I am a good person, well regarded by others, able to keep out of trouble and able to get my fair share of what I need, this general belief will sustain a happiness and sense of competence that could be very positive for all of my social life and day-to-day experience. Having a general idea of one's self quite probably arises inevitably from our tendency to generalise about accumulated experiences (Meadows 2006) but would also mean we have a buffer against occasional negative experiences.

Having a negative general idea would, on the other hand, have negative consequences. So would having too much of a discrepancy between the real and the ideal. Some examples will follow at the end of this section.

I must note, however, the model of the 'self' that I have been using so far has been heavily criticised by post-modernists, who present the argument that it is a mistake, brought on by the European Enlightenment, to believe that we have a 'core, rational, unitary self, endowed with an essential nature and an independent consciousness' (Callero 2003: 117). Political power over the body, as exercised by institutions such as schools and workplaces (and families), coercively determines the self, bringing into existence a self that functions as a means of control with internalised modes of discourse that restrict, distort and dominate the possibility of the individual. The Enlightenment values of reason, rationality and scientific knowledge are not seen as positive, and particularly not as ways of emancipating individuals from earlier tyrannies of religion or state hierarchies, but as oppressive in their own way. What we call 'the self' is historically constructed, embedded in systems of knowing and of discourse, and the product of power relations across the social worlds that we inhabit. We cannot discover a 'true self', though we can deconstruct and reconstruct ourselves if we analyse our experience, how we understand it, and how we got to where we feel we are, and generally view ourselves as a knowledgeable, problem-solving actor.

The ways in which individual self and social setting are related is another area of debate and controversy, and we have to recognise that there may be influential cultural differences here (Bukobza 2007). Partitioning one's self into an individual private self and a public persona, dividing private experience and public experience, being individualist rather than part of a collective, indeed whether you see the self as individual at all may differ between cultures (Munro 2005; pp. 72–74, 80–84, 97–98, 236–39) and between ages, classes, genders, and, ultimately, moments. The different stories that we tell are likely to reflect these variations. The increased possibility of living a fictional life afforded by developments such as online role-playing games and 'second worlds' is not yet researched to the degree where we can examine the effects of engaging with such experience for one's 'real-world' self, but this could be an interesting area to examine (Dodge *et al.* 2008).

2.4.4 The development of self-concept in childhood

Harter (2006) summarises changes in the content and organisation of the 'Me' concept as children get older. The expressed self-concepts of toddlers and very young children tend to use concrete physical, active, and social terms rather than higher-order general abstract descriptions. Their self-descriptions often involve preferences and possessions; are often unrealistically optimistic; tend not to involve social comparisons and evaluations; and don't recognise their own internal contradictions of qualities, emotions and experience. Their spontaneous talk often involves putting themselves in the same category as a person who is important to them; apparently I said, age two or three, 'Mummy and Joe [my oldest brother] have curly hair; Daddy and I have nice soft [straight] hair', something which my adult me-self recognises as typical over a long time, both about the hair, and about my identification and contrasts with my parents.

Being mislabelled can be a source of distress if done by someone else – try mislabelling a preschooler about their species or gender, if you want to wind them up – or as a game (pp. 197–99). The time when self labels begin to be expressed by the child when asked to describe itself (Brown *et al.* 2008) is also the time at which infantile amnesia disperses and auto-biographical memory begins to emerge (Bauer 2007; Eby, Maher and Butts 2010; Fivush and Nelson 2004; Gauvain and Perez 2007; Meadows 2006; Wenner *et al.* 2008). Narratives of one's own life are often constructed in partnership with a parent, and in the same style, as are family myths (Fivush, Haden and Reese 2006; Reese, Hayne and Macdonald 2008; Wenner *et al.* 2008).

Bauer (2007) argues that children's autobiographical narratives develop particularly well if the parents support them with elaboration in the early stages, which may happen more in the context of a secure attachment relationship (pp. 72–74, 124–25). Cicchetti (2004) suggests that children who suffer abuse from their parents at this stage of developing a narrative of oneself may as a consequence develop a 'false' or 'impoverished' self; there may be problems also in achieving normal intersubjectivity for chil-dren whose parent is depressed and not communicative in the normal way or children who suffer hearing impairment, prematurity, or disorders such as autism, ADHD or Specific Language Impairment (Trevarthen and Aitken 2003).

The data provided by psychologists concerned with the development of descriptions of the 'me self' in childhood (for reviews see Harter 2006; Meadows 2006, and see Davis-Kean and Sandler 2001; Marsh, Ellis and Craven 2002 for discussion of methodological issues) broadly agree. As children pass through childhood, what they say about themselves becomes more integrated, involves more comparisons with other people, and includes more abstract higher-order descriptions. Even by age five personality self-descriptions are similar to the mothers' descriptions of their child in terms of timidity, agreeableness and negative affect (Brown *et al.* 2008). Young children sometimes make comparisons that help them have 'a triumphant sense of always being ahead' (Dunn and Kendrick 1982: 108–109). For example a child, Laura C., compares herself with her baby brother:

C to Mother (after M comments to Baby about cutting teeth): I was cutting teeth. I was walking before he was. I walked before him.
                                          (Dunn and Kendrick 1982: 108–109)

Young school children still tend to be positive in their self-descriptions, often unrealistically positive; possibly they have a sense of how rapidly they are learning new things and having new experiences, which gives them a sense of exciting possibilities being open for them. Being ahead of other classmates can be important; great prestige and self-satisfaction sometimes attaches to being the oldest in the class, for example. I knew a child who was happy at being one of the oldest and tallest in his primary school class, but became quite dismayed when classmates started to shed their baby teeth earlier and claimed this as a sign that they were more grown up. His wily parents engaged him in discussion of how long-lasting his own teeth were, and how his classmates were merely wearing out faster, and this restored his sense of superiority, but self-concept and prestige had been vulnerable for a while.

As children move further into school and spend more of their time with other children and with adults outside the family, their descriptions of themselves include more comparisons with others and incorporate more of others' views of themselves. As schooling progresses, since schools are full of experiences of being assessed and evaluated children show more sense of differentiating between the self they are and their ideal self. James (1890, 1892) discussed the relationship of the 'actual' self and the 'ideal self' as the basis for a person's 'self-esteem'. One's self-esteem will be comfortably high if one feels one is very like the self one would like to be, and low if one's actual self is felt to be discrepant with one's ideal self (discrepancies are likely to be in the direction of being worse than the ideal, rather than being better). The rather nice phrase encapsulating James' view is that 'self-esteem is the ratio of pretension to success'; you can be happy because you have reached a high-quality ideal self, or because you have set your standard less high and reached that (James 1892; Harter 2006; Rodriguez, Wigfield and Eccles 2003). Philosophers from Epicurus onwards have argued exactly the same thing – contentment lies with not wanting too much more than you have (e.g. De Botton 2000). Research on discrepancy between what one is and what one would like to be or ought to be, between the actual and the ideal, suggests that substantial discrepancy leads to dejection, or agitation if it is a matter of falling badly short of the 'ought'. Small discrepancies that one thinks one can act on can be motivating, so a sense of what is a real possibility and what is unreasonably ambitious can be helpful. Attributions for the causes of things will influence these considerations. Some researchers think it is especially healthy to have a balance of a positive 'expected' self – what one can get to be – and a negative 'feared' self – I'm not like that and I know how to avoid being like that (Harter 2006; Rodriguez, Wigfield and Eccles 2003).

Thus it is thought that possible ideal self-concepts function as standards for real self-concepts, emergent from experience, by middle childhood. Both potential vulnerability and role-taking ability become important here.

Self-concepts in middle childhood show increasing inter-co-ordination, and more appreciation of the view of others, but still tend to be one-dimensional and not hierarchical. These children compared with younger ones show increasing self-control and anticipatory control of their emotions and self-beliefs, and eventually their self-concepts show more counter-balance if their experience allows integration. Negative self-perceptions may become very pervasive and automatic, for example abused children may have dreadful problems in this area (pp. 87, 129–30). Social comparisons are important in middle childhood (Damon and Hart 1988); the age stratification of a school shows up fine differences between individuals, which can't be explained in terms of age and increasingly come to be seen as internal individual differences.

2.4.5 Self-concept in adolescence

Self-concept in adolescence continues to develop in the direction of increasing appeal to abstract, underlying characteristics (Damon and Hart 1988; Harter 2006). Some new dimensions strengthen; a focus on attractiveness (possibly in comparison with the standard for one's own gender, possibly as a consideration of whether one will attract a romantic partner, possibly a conflation of the two); a focus on developing career and lifetime goals; a focus on developing romantic relationships (pp. 180–82; Bouchey 2007; Giordano 2003); an increase in introspection and self-consciousness. Interpersonal characteristics of selves become especially salient, and there is often a strong, even excessive, preoccupation with the nature of one's self, appearance and image (e.g. Harper and Tiggemann 2008; Strahan *et al.* 2008, pp. 223–26).

Adolescents are very much more likely than younger children to express a feeling that they have multiple selves, called out in different social contexts (Bukobza 2007; Ellemers *et al.* 2002). There is theoretical debate stretching back to William James about the multiple self versus unified self. Both he and more modern writers acknowledge the existence of different role-selves, but whereas much Western theory emphasises consistency in the self-concept, in other cultures there may be much less emphasis on a unitary self-concept (Bukobza 2007). Part of the function of self-concept may be as a basis for the recognition of roles, allowing the creation of a positive impression on other people, and preserving relationships (Harter 2006). For Gergen, Lightfoot and Sydow (2004), for example, understanding oneself as a multiple self increases flexibility and resilience; they suggest that in the autobiographical narrative which we all construct, the I-self acts as a continuous and agentic author, organising the Me-self into coherent directional self-narrative.

This is an interesting theoretical distinction and a promising idea for therapy (for example narrative therapy and cognitive–behaviour therapy), but developmentally it may be more than adolescents can easily achieve. The experience of a conflict between 'true-self' and 'false-self' is often a pre-occupation or a concern in adolescence. The protagonists of *The Catcher in the Rye* (Salinger 1951) and *The Bell-Jar* (Plath 1966), and even of *Jane Eyre* (Bronte 1847), are all preoccupied with issues of truth and falsity in other people's selves and in their own. It has been argued that the antecedent of difficulties in this area is a caregiver who doesn't validate the child's true self but forces compliance with external standards of behaviour – a hypothesis which might not generalise to all cultures and historical periods (though it would apply to Jane Eyre). Harter (2006) argues that when significant others only provide support conditionally on the child behaving in the way they approve, irrespective of the child's own needs and wishes, this undermines the child's self-esteem and encourages hopelessness about getting support (Baumeister *et al.* 2003; Ge 1996; McAdams and Olson 2010; Salmivalli *et al.* 1999; Serbin and Karp 2004; Shaw 2003; Thornberry *et al.* 2003). When other people devalue the individual's true self, and the individual devalues it too because of having a looking-glass self constructed from these others' views, a high level of false self-behaviour ensues – a feeling of not knowing one's true self, of presenting an inauthentic self, of lower self-esteem, and of high depression. False self-behaviour involves the suppression of self and of spontaneity. Although Harter (2006) finds no gender difference, Gilligan (1982) suggests this is particularly a problem for young women, and it can be associated with beginning romantic relationships (pp. 180–82; Sippola, Buchanan and Kehoe 2007). Co-rumination (Caselman and Self 2007; Parker *et al.* 2005; Rose 2002; Rose and Rudolph 2006; Rose, Carlson and Waller 2007; pp. 173, 179, 270) may be involved in the problem.

Both sexes are more likely to present more of their true self if they perceive more support by others for their own Voice. Research reviewed by Kling *et al.* (1999) suggests that young women with a more masculine or androgynous orientation feel more confidence in their Voice – traditional femininity is a particular handicap in public contexts, though less so en famille or with close friends. Lack of Voice is felt to be negative, and associated with low self-esteem, depression, and hopelessness (a point which applies in most areas of adult life, not just in adolescence) (Harter 1996; Harter, Low and Whitesell 2003).

Self-consciousness in the sense of continual, awkward, self-awareness and self-evaluation is another self-handicapping behaviour of adolescence. For some, feeling you have multiple selves is a problem rather than merely an enactment of different social roles. Feelings of vacillating between different selves, of not knowing who you really are, of living a 'false self' imposed on one by others, of, eventually, 'anomie' (a complex feeling of alienation, worthlessness and despair) are serious problems for a substantial number of adolescents; probably present but under-diagnosed in younger children too (Goodyer 1990, 2008; Harter *et al.* 1996; Harter, Low and Whitesell 2003;

Harter 2006; Rutter and Smith 1995, pp. 90–93, 125, 142–43). Expressions of negative self-concept tend to increase at times of transitions between schools, at puberty, at leaving home. Students who say they experienced a decline in self-worth when moving between schools also report lower social approval and show a lowered competence; for students who feel an increase in self-worth, their social standing and their competence also seem to improve (Harter 2006). The idea of the self-concept as the 'looking-glass' self comes to mind here; self-reports and reports of others' behaviour directed towards the self are highly likely to be strongly correlated.

Researchers however, see some positive potential in this area. Self-monitoring persons typically present their selves in ways that are appropriate to context, positive to others, and accommodating; this tends to preserve or foster their relationship. These individuals see this self-presentation as different from false-self behaviour, and its connotations are positive not negative (Baumeister 2003; Harter 2006; Nussbaum and Dweck 2008).

2.4.6 Multiple or complex selves: structural and stage models

Even if we stick to the idea that we mainly operate with a 'single' 'true' self, that 'single' 'true' self is not necessarily, or even normally, a single unified and coherent entity. Different theorists carve it up differently. Damon and Hart (1988) present a model of self-understanding in which seven 'schemes' each progress through four levels, not necessarily in synchrony. These 'schemes' are the physical, active, social and psychological selves, which all undergo developmental change, and the continuity, distinctness and agency of the self, which are more continuous. The first level (characteristic of early childhood) involves categorical identifications; the second (middle to late childhood) comparative assessments involving consideration of the self as measured against others; the third (early adolescence) interpersonal implications of the self; the fourth (late adolescence) systematic beliefs, principles and plans. Damon and Hart say that at all ages children have some under-standing of their physical, active, social, and psychological selves. Although one may be more salient than another at a particular time (as in earlier work's account of young children's physical descriptions of the self and older children's psychological ones (Meadows 2006)), this does not mean that one is transformed into the other. Nor do children move neatly from one level to the next on all fronts at once: they are likely to make statements characteristic of several developmental levels at any given time.

Damon and Hart's data derive from 'clinical interviews' of a variety of samples of children and adolescents. They provide some fascinating glimpses of children's ideas about themselves and various other matters. However, there is a possibility in this style of data-gathering that leading questions shape the child's answers, and in this style of data analysis that utterances are fitted to theoretical aspects of the model as much as the other way round. This sort of problem has long been endemic with the complex material elicited in méthode clinique interviews (Meadows 2006).

Interview studies often represent children as immature understanders of persons, dominated by notions which they have to grow out of but which might meanwhile be expected to impair their ability to get along with other people. Some stage or level theorists have seen immature concepts as reflected in inadequate social behaviour (such as Piagetian 'egocentricity'); few of these models look carefully enough at the social milieu that children exist in. More ethnographic studies (e.g. Pollard 1985; Pollard and Filer 1996, 1999; Osborn 2001, 2003) may do more to help us understand the social demands that context makes on self-concept (pp. 211, 212, 218–21). Nor do stage models based on interview explain why children change from one level of understanding to another, a change which would be easier to explain if the later levels of understanding were in some way more useful than the earlier ones. Damon and Hart see comparison between self and others as predominant ('modal') in middle childhood, and see interpersonal relations as modal in early adolescence. Might this reflect the social predicaments of children at these ages, as they are embroiled in first school and getting good grades and then in all the early stages of mating behaviour, the getting dates and going steady which loom large in so many accounts of American adolescence? Erikson (1963, 1968) paints the relation between life stage and self as a series of developmental challenges. The development of self-understanding seems likely to be one of the areas of social cognition where social and cultural factors go a long way toward determining developmental change (pp. 80–84, 97–98, 236–39).

Other theorists prefer to pick up the idea that some aspects of the self are more crucial to the individual than other aspects are (e.g. Harter 2006; Marsh, Ellis and Craven 2002). One distinction (dating back to James) is between core and peripheral aspects of the self. It is much more important to my own self-concept that I am 'intelligent' than that I am 'not keen on team sports', for example. A similar distinction is between aspects that are global and aspects that are domain specific (Harter 2006). There are issues here about the degree to which aspects of self-concept remain in the core or at the periphery; events or moods may lead one to focus intensively for a while on something which was formerly unimportant, and will be again (pp. 173, 179, 270). James (1892/1985) suggested a difference between 'baseline' and 'barometric' self-concept, the latter fluctuating just as barometric pressure fluctuates in association with changes in the weather. (This is actually a metaphor with roots way back in literature; for example in *As You Like It*, in a game of role-playing, flirtation and self-recognition, Rosalind, in disguise as a boy and talking to the young man whom she loves and who has not yet seen through her disguise, says in response to his protestation that he will love the true Rosalind forever: 'No, no, Orlando. Men are April when they woo, but December when they wed; maids are

May while they are maids, but the sky changes when they are wives' (Shakespeare, *As You Like It*; IV, I: 130–154).

Distinction between narrower aspects of self-concept have also been suggested. Marsh and his colleagues (Marsh *et al.* 1983; Marsh and Shavelson 1985; Marsh 1990; Marsh and Yeung 1997), for example, have looked at 'academic self-concept' and suggested that it may be sensible to distinguish even between 'self-concepts' vis-à-vis different curriculum areas. Marsh's Australian and some British samples have provided data that suggests that for some individuals there may be a negative relation between these curriculum-linked self-concepts. These students take the attitude that people in general (and themselves in particular) can only be expected to be good at a limited range of the compulsory school subjects; the arts students blithely say that they are 'no good at maths', the scientists that they have no interest in the arts. Again this is a distinction with roots generations back (Snow 1964; Hudson 1967) that may serve to protect individuals from expectations that are too high and too pervasive, although as it can also result in people believing that there is no point in engaging with extensive areas of the curriculum, or more importantly of human cultural achievement, this is probably a bad thing. It is culturally engendered and culturally specific; Renaissance intellectuals gloried in their simultaneous interest in art, science, architecture, moral philosophy; young children differ in their interests but do not selectively define large parts of the curriculum as beyond them; Greek adolescents feel a social pressure to achieve highly in all school subjects and are certainly not allowed to say their excellence in language makes up for their weakness in maths or would be incompatible with excellence in geography (Koumi 1994). And of course it may be literally gendered in the form of what is and what is not seen as suitable cognition or activities for girls and boys (pp. 191–94, 198–201) – 'girls can't do science', 'boys do football not ballet'.

2.4.7 Stability of self-concept

I have described the changes in self-concept associated with different ages and mentioned links between transitions (through puberty, between schools, from school to work) associated with change in people's lives. Fewer researchers have made longitudinal studies of the stability of self-concepts (McAdams and Olson 2010). This sort of research obviously involves following people over time, and is consequently slow and expensive. Looking at children's self-concepts over time is going to be complicated by both changes in their language and thinking skills and in their familiarity with being interviewed or filling in questionnaires, and by the normative developmental changes or life-stage changes that I have described. Developmentally the longitudinal evidence is congruent with the cross-sectional evidence: individuals tend to have very positive self-concepts when they are little, which get less positive on the move into middle childhood, and less positive still at early adolescence, but improve later in adolescence. Changes are particularly marked at times of transition through school stages and of pubertal change. Throughout, self-concept varies situationally – for most people it is relatively stable, but short-term wobbles by situation are quite normal (I find myself inclined to think that having no wobbles at all would represent a state of pathological insensitivity). On the whole it is during adolescence that fluctuations in self-concept are most flagrant – as we no doubt all remember.

Some individuals do seem to have less stable self-concepts than others (Harter *et al.* 1996; Harter 2006). These fluctuators are sensitive to evaluative events, preoccupied with evaluation, ego-involved, and overreliant on social sources of self-esteem. Inconsistent or overcontrolling approval by significant others is suggested as a source. People with high but unstable self-esteem seek favourable feedback and discount negative feedback; people with low and unstable self-esteem expect continuous negative feedback and avoid it.

2.4.7.1 Entity and incremental theory

Some very interesting work by Carol Dweck (1999; Dweck and Elliot 1983; Hong *et al.* 1999; Grant and Dweck 2003; Blackwell, Trzniewski and Dweck 2007; Ricco and Rodriguez 2006) resonates with this theory of the source of self-esteem, and how to change it. Dweck and her colleagues looked at high-achieving students who were terrified of failing and totally demoralised by any evidence that their performance was less than excellent. The researchers linked this with individuals' theories of intelligence; some students saw it as an attribute that you had a certain fixed and uncontrollable amount of, others as something you could increase through practise. The first group, with their 'entity' theory, would focus on performance as evidence for their amount of intelligence, and were oriented towards approval and avoiding negative feedback; their confidence was eroded if they failed, they would then display learned helplessness, and they avoided challenges because of the risk that they might fail to meet them and so have their confidence reduced. The other group, incremental theorists, who saw intelligence as malleable, were oriented towards learning rather than performance, were optimistic about doing better next time and resilient in the face of failure, and took on challenges with an expectation that they could master them. Dweck has suggested that entity theorists had had too much feedback that praised their particular achievements in too general terms and located the causes of it in the individual rather than the individual's actions – 'Clever girl' rather than 'you did a really good job of remembering that'. Incremental theorists had had more of this 'you did really well on that because you did such and such a thing', and consequently focused more on what they had to do to complete tasks, and less on the implications of success for a fixed and generalised view of their ability. Although there is not an enormous amount of data on the issue, specific task-oriented feedback does seem to be more effective in motivating learners (Denissen *et al.* 2007; Grant and Dweck 2003; Hong *et al.* 1999; Kamins and Dweck 1999).

Obviously part of what is going on here relates to accuracy of self-evaluation. I have already described how young children's early optimism about being able to do almost everything fades as they move through the assessments of school and compare themselves more and more with age mates. To some extent this optimism is justified; if children are aware how much more they can do than a month or year ago, then young children are quite entitled to think that they are learning things and developing new skills very fast. I am inclined to regret that their optimism is squashed out of them, although it could be glossed as an increase in realism. Throughout childhood, adolescence and adulthood, individuals who rate their ability 'accurately', i.e. similarly to the way teachers rate it, tend to select more challenging tasks; under-raters go for low challenge tasks as they think that's what will challenge them, and so do over-raters, who need to avoid contrary evidence. There can be major problems at transition to more challenging educational and social settings (Blackwell, Trzniewski and Dweck 2007; Carver and Connor-Smith 2010; McAdams and Olson 2010). A mild overestimation of one's abilities is probably healthy and protective – depressed people tend to rate their abilities more realistically as well as more negatively (pp. 90–93, 215, 284).

I think it is worth noting that Dweck and colleagues have diversified in recent years into other areas of social cognition, for example ideas about luck and about meaningfulness (Olson *et al.* 2006, 2008; Nussbaum and Dweck 2008; Molden and Dweck 2006), although I will not discuss these here.

2.4.8 Self-conscious emotions – pride, shame, guilt, and embarrassment

Some of the occasions when we think about ourselves lead us to experience social self-conscious emotions, such as confidence, pride, shame, guilt, and embarrassment. These emotions all involve self-evaluation, especially in terms of a comparison with others. They combine appraisal of oneself, of the situation, and of significant others, and the emotional consequences of the comparison – should I be pleased with myself, have I done something that will make other people think the worse of me – and may be powerful both in the particular situation and in general development, especially if we lose control over them (Tangney *et al.* 2007).

These self-conscious emotions are complex and not easily separated. It is also the case that they are linked with other, less explicitly self-referential, emotions, such as feelings of mastery or depression. I do not have space to discuss them all in detail, so I will try to illustrate the central issues by drawing on Mills (2005) and the literature she cites to review the development and the consequences of feelings of shame.

A person who is ashamed feels inadequate, worthless, or disgraced, and may seek to hide or disappear from being evaluated. A socially prescribed standard has not been met, and the shamed person anticipates or sees that other people will think they are inadequate, inferior or wrong in some way, and consequently experiences shame emotions such as embarrassment, mortification, or humiliation. This emotion requires you to have a sense of socially prescribed expectations, a sense of your discrepancy from them, a sense of being responsible for the discrepancy, and a sense that evaluation is coming; and it has been argued therefore that young children would not experience shame. However, some examples of behaviour that resembles that of shamed adults have been found in toddlers. Lewis, Alessandri and Sullivan (1992) observed the reactions of children aged 33 to 37 months to success and failure on easier and harder tasks, and found that failure on the easier tasks was particularly likely to produce behaviour such as collapsed body posture, averted gaze, corners of the mouth drooping downwards, hiding one's face, and expressing a negative evaluation of oneself. Lewis and Ramsay (2002) found cortisol changes similar to those in adults. Long ago, Kagan (1981, 2005) reported distress in toddlers who found themselves to be dirty, or found that they could not complete a task in the conventional way.

The developmental change may be in how long the emotion lasts and what it is understood to imply for the self, rather than whether it is experienced at all. A number of theorists have suggested that shame becomes more internalised and can come to be experienced as a deep sense of defectiveness and inadequacy. The way in which the child is socialised may affect how strongly this sense of shame develops: people with fearful or preoccupied attachment patterns, people who have been abused, people whose parents used shaming as a discipline technique, may be more prone to it (Tangney et al. 2007). There are probably also cultural differences in how far being shamed is a personal experience and how far it expands to include the family or the wider social group – 'letting us all down' is sometimes an important component of the emotional experience of shame (Cole et al. 2002). There may also be temperament-based differences in proneness to complex emotions, with more extraverted, less inhibited individuals being less likely to succumb to shame (Rothbart and Bates 2006).

2.4.9 Self-esteem

It is frequently argued that people who have low 'self-esteem', that is those who see themselves as being not nearly so good as they would like to be, are at high risk of all sorts of poor functioning, such as emotional and social difficulties, both contemporaneously and later (Banaji and Prentice 1994; Baumeister *et al.* 2003; Ge 1996; Harter 2006; Salmivalli *et al.* 1999; Serbin and Karp 2004; Shaw 2003; Thornberry *et al.* 2003). Low self-esteem has been associated with links established between low self-esteem and a range of outcomes, including mental illness, substance abuse, suicidal behaviour and social and adjustment problems (Boden, Fergusson and Horwood 2008; Carver and Connor-Smith 2010; Kim and Cicchetti 2004; McAdams and Olson 2010; McGee and Williams 2000). Possibly self-esteem plays a causal role in life outcomes, with an individual's level of self-esteem being critical in determining success and failure across a range of life tasks; or possibly it is a marker for problems elsewhere which lead to poor life outcomes. If it is itself a major cause, then interventions to improve self-esteem may be highly worthwhile, but if it is weakly associated because it depends on the same background factors as the poor outcomes, it may be better to try to ameliorate the background difficulties rather than to focus on self-esteem.

It is not easy to work out which of these possibilities to prefer. It requires good measures of self-esteem and of a range of potential outcomes, control for the many factors that might affect both self-esteem and outcomes, a large and representative sample, and a reasonably long time period. Boden, Fergusson and Horwood (2008) present analyses drawing on the data from the Christchurch Health and Development Study, which followed a representative cohort in Christchurch, New Zealand, from infancy (Fergusson *et al.* 1989). Although having low levels of self-esteem at age 15 was associated with greater risk of later mental health problems (including depression, anxiety, conduct/antisocial personality disorder, and thinking about suicide), substance dependence problems (including nicotine and alcohol dependence and dependence on illicit drugs), and life and relationship satisfaction issues (including lower levels of life satisfaction, poorer perceived relationship quality, and lower levels of peer attachment), the associations were at best moderate, and they were very much reduced once confounding factors such as previous mental health problems, lower IQ and higher levels of neuroticism, and experience of a number of childhood adversities (including socio-economic disadvantage, family dysfunction, child physical and sexual abuse and impaired parental bonding) were allowed for. Boden, Fergusson and Horwood (2008) (and see also Carvajal *et al.* 2004) suggest that although low self-esteem may have causal influence on poor outcomes, it is only one of a great many other factors that co-occur. Certainly interventions that focus on self-esteem and ignore other factors may not have a major effect.

2.4.10 Cultural differences in self-concept development

So far, I have been treating self-concept as an attribute of the individual at the centre of Bronfenbrenner's contexts. That this is not altogether sensible will have emerged from my discussion of the literature on self-concept as being built up from social interaction and commentary in microsystems (and in the wider social world), and as having social consequences. At the cultural level too there may be pervasive and powerful influences on self-concept, and conceivably individuals' self-concepts may influence their cultures. I will return to this when I discuss cultural systems and children's social being, but this is the place for a brief note on cultural differences in self-concept development.

It may well be that if there are different ideas about social relatedness (individualism and collectivity for example), and different socialisation practices, in different cultures, then there may be cultural differences in what people say about themselves. This is not an exhaustively researched subject and it is conceptually complex (Munro 2005; Toren 1993), but there are some interesting developmental psychology contributions to the debate.

Wang (2006) argues that there are cultural differences in self-concept and in how they develop, and in particular there are differences between traditional Chinese culture and traditional European/American culture in whether individuals focus on their unique personal attributes or on their social roles and relationships when they define or describe themselves. Broadly, traditional Chinese culture emphasised collectivity and relatedness, with people's roles and required behaviour defined by their family and family position, whereas the European/American expectation has been less rigid and more individualistic (pp. 72–74, 97–98, 236–39).

Here are two quotations which illustrate the difference that Wang sees between European–American and Chinese self-descriptions (both from 6 year olds): 'I am a wonderful and very smart person. A funny and hilarious person. A kind and caring person. A good-grade person who is going to go to Cornell. A helpful and cooperative girl'; 'I'm a human being. I'm a child. I like to play cards. I'm my mom and dad's child, my grandma and grandpa's grandson. I'm a hardworking good child' (Wang 2006: 182). The first description includes many cues that hint at the individual's social identity, but her self-description is about her own autonomous traits even when acting on these traits is social and would involve other people. It expresses a very positive evaluation of the self in terms of characteristics that will continue over time and lead to future success and well-being. In contrast, the second one, from a Chinese child, defines the person explicitly in terms of family membership. The self is expressed in terms of specific social relationships, and, implicitly, conformity.

It is impossible to know whether the entire internal emotional states of these two young persons differ in the way these self-descriptions do. However, it is clear that these two children, like most others in all cultures, are guided by the adults who socialise them into functioning acceptably within the cultural norms that the adults themselves learned as children. When discussing parenting, I will argue (pp. 116, 133–34) that discussing personal memories is one of the important 'frames' that parents provide for children. Many families engage in sharing memories, interpretations and evaluations of events (Miller *et al.* 1997; Nelson and Fivush 2004). This event-telling may focus on elaborating personal stories in order to contribute to a unique 'me' identity, or it may prioritise relatedness and collectivity, to instil a sense of belonging and social responsibility. In the examples collected by Wang (2006), European–American mothers elaborated on their young children's remarks and commented on their preferences and their feelings far more than Chinese mothers did; Chinese mothers made far more reference to social norms and expectations for good behaviour. The children's developing narrative skills reflected these parental emphases (Wang and Ross 2005). Heath (1983), painting a similar picture, points out how different styles of narrative about the self are often enacted in public settings, with problematic consequences if the style of the self-narrative and the expectations of others in the setting conflict. Her working-class African–American children, for example, had learned a self-narrative style of bravado and teasing challenge to others which was disastrous for them in school. Her working-class White children had learned to tell stories about themselves that were passive, down-beat and self-belittling, a style that led them to be 'good' conforming pupils in the early years of school, but was not so helpful when they were expected to be autonomous and creative in later education. The literature on gender (pp. 188–92, 198, 200, 238) provides other examples, notably Carolyn Steedman's discussion (Steedman 1982) of a story produced by three eight-year-old girls which reveals their struggles with their identity as working-class females.

2.4.11 Cultural identity and change of cultures

Cultural differences in self-concept and socialisation are particularly interesting in the experience of successive generations of families of immigrant origin as they come to live within the mainstream culture. Family socialisation appears to have a positive effect on adolescents' views of their original ethnicity. Some theorists, and some of those who have lived it themselves, write about the experience as an adaptation to the dominant culture in which individuals lose their original ethnic or national identity, often painfully and with heartfelt regret (Birman 2006; Corby *et al.* 2007; Costigan and Dokis 2006; Farver *et al.* 2007; Garcia-Coll and Szalacha 2004; Mok *et al.* 2007). As with the strengths and problems of maintaining your native language even if it is not much used in your new environment (Meadows 2006), there are sometimes issues about the relative status of immigrant and host cultures which affect the experience of cultural change. Umana-Taylor and Yazedjian (2006: 447) argue that individuals' cultural practices and beliefs can be redefined to allow them to 'maintain the ethnic experience within the framework of the dominant culture' – the redefined culture is a hybrid of the original. Family socialisation plays a major part in this, both through deliberate teaching about the country of origin and through less deliberate practices such as expecting the sort of politeness that was traditional 'back home' and displaying pictures, artefacts and literature about 'the old country'. (It occurs to me that this sort of behaviour is not restricted to immigrants, or perhaps the definition of immigrant needs to be wider; lined up in my hall are a map of Bristol, where I have lived for more than half my life, pictures of the Cornish village we go to for summer holidays – and a map of Cheshire, where I was born.)

Both ethnic identity and adherence to the original culture's language and practices tend to become less salient and less fluent over successive generations, and family socialisation practices like these tend to become weaker. Umana-Taylor and Yazedjian (2006) convened focus groups of US-resident mothers of Puerto Rican and Mexican ethnic origin to discuss what they thought about teaching their children about their 'ethnic background'. This was a matter of great importance for these women, whether or not they had been born in the USA themselves, and they used language, ethnic traditions of dance, music and costume, religion and religious and family festivals and food, as well as reminiscences, books and films, and visits to the old country to help their children to develop a sense of their 'roots'. This did not at all preclude the mothers wishing their children to learn how to get on in mainstream American society; the hope was that the children coming from one society and being enculturated into another would be enriched by each.

Costigan and Dokis (2006), studying families where the parents had emigrated from China to Canada as adults, find differences between public and private values, with the former moving towards the mainstream faster than the latter; and they also find differences between what mothers and fathers value. Immigrant mothers were more traditional than fathers, less in favour of independence for their children, more strongly identified with being Chinese. Children were typically more positive about Canadian culture than their parents, although still expressing as much commitment to Chinese culture. There were higher parent–child resemblances when they described their relationship as warm, particularly in private values where the influence of non-family relationships was not so strong as it was in the public arena. Birman (2006), looking at adolescents who were, with their parents, Jewish refugees emigrated to the USA from the Soviet Union, and found that discord within families was associated with disagreement about public dimensions of acculturation such as American behaviour and using the Russian language.

Cultural change *within* a culture may have major repercussions for individuals within it. Russia after the Revolution and through the development of Stalinism provides examples (pp. 242, 245–49, 252). A positive example comes from Fong (2002) who describes the higher status and self-esteem achieved by urban young women following China's one-child policy. When Chinese families had several children, many parents valued sons over daughters, both because they were more visible contributors to an agricutural economy and because traditionally families were patrilineal and patrilocal, so that when girls married they moved out of their family of rearing and contributed to the welfare of the parents of their husband, not their own. When families were restricted to one child, parents saw that they were going to be reliant on their one child for support in old age, and that therefore this child was valuable to them even if it was a girl. They also saw that their daughter could achieve a well-paid job and social mobility upwards in an urban setting. Urban parents became enthusiastic about their daughters, and the daughters more positive and empowered about themselves and their lives; whether rural daughters have enjoyed such a change is not clear, and it is possible that they have continued to be devalued, maybe to the extent of selective abortion and infanticide of females, and a distortion of the sex ratio of the population, as in parts of India (Srinivasan and Bedi 2008).

2.5 Emotion, social development and the development of well-being

I hope I have made something of a case for regarding the interface of emotional well-being, cognitive models of the world, and social relationships as a key area for an integrated understanding of children's development. This interface has applications both to 'normal' development and to developmental psychopathology. Rather than look at 'emotional', 'social' and 'cognitive' separately, for each one we have to acknowledge that the other two are involved. 'Emotion', for example, involves perception, appraisal and reaction *vis-à-vis* a disturbing event, and in most cases has social implication or social roots. All sorts of complex issues are involved over the conceptual nature of emotion, the identification of the brain areas involved and their interconnections, how affective and cognitive information-processing compare and interact, the specificity or ambiguity of emotional arousal, the accessibility to conscious awareness of affective information-processing, the timing of events in the emotion sequence, how short-term changes in a neural network dealing with an emotional situation are reflected in longer-term ones, and so on. There are processes of establishing, maintaining or disrupting relations between a person and the internal or external environment, when such relations are significant to the individual because they are relevant to goals, or involve emotional communication with other individuals, or have purely hedonic qualities of physical pain, discomfort or pleasure. A cognitive appraisal of the individual's relations with the environment establishes their significance and is a necessary component of emotion. Emotions have interpersonal consequences: they function to maintain, elicit, or end other people's behaviour and to signal to others. For example, the individual's expressions of joy, of success in progressing towards a goal, function to maintain other people's positive interactions, whereas expressions of sadness, of relinquishing a relation with the environment, of individual helplessness when adaptive action is impossible, signal to elicit help and comfort from others. The actual reaction of the others is not of course guaranteed: however, well-meaning interactants are likely to acknowledge each other's emotions even if they cannot themselves share them. Discussion of why emotions are or are not shared or acceptable seems to be an important part of the child's curriculum (pp. 87, 124–25, 129–30). It is also possible to argue that human cognition evolved to a highly complex level because individuals living in large permanent social groups had to lead complex social lives, in which an ability to use emotional signals appropriately, and to attend particularly closely to emotion-arousing situations (as small children do), would be especially important (e.g. Byrne and Whiten 1988; Humphrey 1983).

This view of emotion as being concerned with the relationships of events to an individual's needs and goals links it to motivation, to social interaction, and to cognition. It gives equal status to the person's appreciation of the significance of events, the person's feelings which are monitors of events, and the person's coping strategies, the ways he or she deals with the environment. Such a model necessarily implies developmental change, notably in cognitive appraisal and in coping strategies.

I want to stress again the centrality of emotional regulation, of having to compromise between the perhaps intense and egocentric emotional expression which might come spontaneously (McDowell, O'Neil and Parke 2000), and the perhaps more demure and restricted emotional expression which the culture's rules of etiquette prescribe. (Etiquette may of course prescribe an amplification and exaggeration of a naturally moderate emotional expression; probably the most familiar English middle-class example of this is producing 'thank yous' for gifts which are not especially exciting.) It seems that learning emotional regulation fits very well into the apprentice–master model, as it proceeds by a combination of adults doing it for the infant or young child, adults scaffolding the child's attempts, adult and child discussing and reflecting on what is done, and responsibility passing gradually from the more skilled adult to the becoming-skilled child (pp. 115–16, 130–33, 174; Cole, Martin and Dennis 2004). Similar processes may contribute to the learning of complex social emotions such as guilt or shyness and to recognition of mixed emotions.

What is perhaps of particular developmental interest is what range of individual differences arise from differences in parental handling of the child's emotions. Thompson (1998) includes some interesting reviews of the development of children under abnormal parenting conditions. More recent work on abused children is suggesting changes in neurotransmitters as a result of their exposure to violence and negative emotion that may persist and colour their cognition for many years (Cicchetti 2002, 2004; Cicchetti and Blender 2006; Cicchetti and Curtis 2006; Cicchetti et al. 2007).

I think there is a possibility that people may have 'emotional biases' that influence their cognitive development. I have already presented work that argues that individuals become predisposed to a characteristic chronic mood state; this is a result of biologically based traits, such as temperament, and perhaps genetic vulnerabilities, which are operated on by repetitive social experiences, such as maternal soothing or parental abuse. Certain emotional states are frequent and salient, and become part of feelings about the self, so that they can then influence a wide range of behaviours, such as perception, emotional expression, cognitive processing, and social relations. On the whole, there may be considerable stability in this so that something like a strong and pervasive personality trait is built up over time to operate in a self-perpetuating way (pp. 55–59, 77–78, 88–98, 215–17, 284–87).

There are likely to be developmental changes in the perception, appraisal and regulation of emotional states. Infants react to notable changes with emotion, negatively if their goals are interfered with, positively if goals are reached or confirmed. Emotional expressions are detectable from birth, and there seems to be individual stability in the expression of anger and sadness over the first two years. By nine months of age or thereabouts other people's emotional expression may guide the baby's own expression of affect. In babies there is a fairly clear relationship between their emotion, its expression, and the circumstances which caused it: caregivers perceive, interpret, act on and comment on the child's mood, so sensitising the child to emotional cues and the linkages between expression, behaviour, and causal stimulation. There are stable individual differences here (Dunn et al. 1994) that affect the rate of children's development of emotional discourse and understanding, and of theory of mind. Systematic shaping of children's emotional behaviour may be part of the way in which caregivers influence their development; the range and type of comments which caregivers make about emotional states may determine both the child's emotional expression and the sorts of emotional state that can be communicated to others and to oneself (pp. 65–67, 70, 72–74, 124–25), perhaps to a psychopathological degree. Interpretations of other people's emotions are also likely to be affected by our own emotional experience. Our 'working model' of people has a strong emotional component.

Perhaps because so much of the work that unites social, emotional, and cognitive strands in development stems from a practical interest in developmental psychopathology, which often involved the examination of the mother–child relationship, it focuses on early repeated social interactions with familiar partners as the main source of emotional organisation and cognition. Interaction with caregivers leads to attachment that is secure, or anxious, or ambivalent, or disorganised, and so to 'working models' of relationships. In secure relationships, these models can become more complex and integrated as the child is confident, communicative, and well in tune with the adult partner. The insecurely attached child, whose signals are consistently ignored or misunderstood, whose efforts are not supported or respected, and who does not get useful feedback from the partner, is at risk of more negative emotional states and of building a cognitive model which is less coherent, less accurate and less modifiable (pp. 123–26).

Children who are ill-treated or neglected by their caregivers are one population where the relationship between social, emotional and cognitive development is of particular interest (pp. 129–30). This research supports the idea that different emotional biases arise, largely through social interactions which elicit, emphasise, and allow some emotions more than others. Different 'working models' are built up and cognitive biases contribute to the maintenance of an organisation of cognition and affect and social behaviour through a subjective understanding of the world. This has ramifications for motivation, self-concept, attributional style, metacognition and achievement (pp. 77–78, 88–90, 278).

2.5.1 Mastery

My discussion of what is going on inside the individual child at the centre of Bronfenbrenner's nested developmental systems has moved from self-regulation through temperament and self-efficacy to self-concept as a member of a social group and the development of chronic emotional biases. One of the themes that I have mentioned, and now return to, is mastery. In a very interesting synthesis paper, Bradley and Corwyn (2005) argue that human beings, having evolved a wide and open repertoire of socially embedded behaviour, and being active in their own development, have a strong interest in achieving mastery in their activities. Unlike species who do not have such a strong need to learn and develop new ways of doing things, or to choose between different actions, humans often have to weigh up alternative courses of action that they might do, and often have to evaluate how effective a particular course of action has been. Consequently, there is a lot of scope for concern about whether one did something 'well enough' and for a sense of satisfaction when one sees that the action went well. These contribute to the motivational basis of mastery, and eventually become part of one's social reputation.

Clearly we may each feel more confident in some areas than others, but also individuals may differ in confidence over all their activities. Although these feelings may have very deep roots in biological processes – temperament, maybe self-regulation (pp. 52–59, 64–65) – most current theory focuses on social processes building up a sense of one's own competence over a long period of time. I want to discuss here ways in which this development of a sense of self-efficacy can go well, and then how it can go badly. This needs to be thought about in conjunction with some points about learning in learning communities, such as schools (pp. 210–17).

2.5.1.1 Developing a sense of mastery

From infancy onwards, children often work hard to achieve some goal, and show delight in their own success. Individuals learn to recognise the associations between their actions and the outcomes, and develop the ability to regulate, evaluate, control and correct their actions so as to improve outcomes. Both their own engagement in activity and feedback from others will contribute to this learning. There are signs of mastery motivation and intrinsic motivation even in infancy (e.g. Banerjee and Tamis-LeMonda 2007; Gottfried, Fleming and Gottfried 1998; Messer *et al.* 1986; Shannon, Tamis-LeMonda and Cabrera 2006), and given a rich experience of objects and people which allow exploration, play and mastery the young child can engage with the world and practice all sorts of social, motivational and cognitive skills – attention focusing, planning, controlled action, and succeeding. This can lead to a sense of control, competence, efficacy, and autonomy – and thence into confidence in engaging with further social and cognitive challenges. Although the very young child's achievements may seem small to adults – who are so used to being able to stand, walk, get their sums right, paint a picture, that they may not appreciate what a fantastic thing they are doing – they are massive to the child, and rightly so, especially when you consider how recently they could not achieve anything like so much. Young children are often highly confident about what they will be able to do, sometimes to an unrealistic degree, and optimistic about what they will be able to do in a year's time; children who have been in school for a while show signs of gradually losing this optimism (Stipek 1988; Stipek and Gralinski 1996; Pomerantz and Saxon 2001). I will return to schooling later (pp. 210–17).

The literature on the 'scaffolding' that parents sometimes do with their young children (pp. 94, 130–33) suggests that sensitive responsive child-contingent support for exploration and problem solving is a particularly efficacious way of helping children develop a positive sense of the social role of learner (e.g. Banerjee and Tamis-LeMonda 2007; Dweck 1999; Gauvain 2005; Meadows 2006; Moran, Ghate and van der Merwe 2004; Turner and Berkowitz 2005; Wood 1998). Opportunities for productive activity and achieving success are good for the development of competence (and for the avoidance of behaviour problems (Bradley and Corwyn 2005; CMPO 2008), I discuss this elsewhere (p. 133). I discuss the development of competences in the context of parent–child interaction, (pp. 115–17, 120–21), and in the context of learning in social settings (pp. 206–18). My concern here is how to understand what might be going on inside the child. How should we describe what these experiences do to the child's understanding of mastery, or motivation to mastery, or emotional reaction to mastery?

I think that the components of the learning toolbag here are as follows.

1   An interest in mastery, which is part of our evolutionary inheritance and cultural history: by and large, we are willing to put in some effort to do things well, and not only well enough to survive but at least sometimes to do them better than we have done before (pp. 66, 77–78, 215–17).
2   A personal story of how well we do things, have done things, and will do things in future, which is based on our experience and on what other people tell us. This probably includes a generalised evaluation of ourselves as a person who is effective or is ineffective (pp. 71, 185–86, 278–79).
3   A personal sense of agency and efficacy (pp. 77–78, 214–17).
4   A sense of ability being something you can increase (pp. 77–78, 287).
5   An ability to learn from other people (pp. 214–17).
6   An interest in how other people see us (pp. 175–76, 185–86, 278–79).
7   A learned ability to self-regulate and self-correct (pp. 55, 66, 93, 120–21, 183).

What would differences in these mean for the well-being of the child? Firstly, mastery is satisfying or even fun, as the grin of the baby shows. It figures in theories of personality and motivation, for example ideas about self-actualisation (e.g. Maslow 1987). And a vast amount of theory on cognitive development (Meadows 2006) sees it as a natural part of our developmental machinery (for example Piagetian theory) or as part of our wired-in information-processing systems (for example Case 1985). Engaging in activities that involve mastery often leads to positive emotional states and feelings of satisfaction and relaxation. Secondly, mastery can itself be self-developing – we outdo our previous record, or increase our proficiency a bit, or become slicker and shinier and sexier, or just reach the same result in a different way (though sometimes 'good enough' is good enough). Thirdly, as well as mastery itself being intrinsically motivating and self-developing, we readily engage in the evaluation of our mastery, and the criteria we use often become a bit more demanding. Although we may take a 'been there done that' attitude and settle for not continually pressing to do better, our own mastery is something we often seek to outdo. Fourthly and fifthly, our own mastery and our own evaluation of it are situated in the middle of other people's evaluations of us and other people's degree of mastery. We compare ourselves with others. These comparisons offer us opportunities to learn from others' experience, but also have repercussions for our reputation and our motivation. They may also involve positive emotion – my daughter used to play a computer game ('Where in the

World is Carmen San Diego?') in which the player's role is to be a detective chasing a super criminal round the world. When you successfully catch the criminal, the head of the detective agency comes on screen to praise you – an experience to which Anne reacted with far more overt smiles and blushes than she did when praised by her parents! Others also compare us with the standards they expect or the other people they know – especially, perhaps, in the context of school (pp. 211, 218–24).

2.5.1.2 Developing a sense of what intelligence is

A key part of one's sense of mastery is one's sense of what it derives from, and here research on concepts of intelligence is very relevant (pp. 77–78, 215, 287). Like adults, children in primary school associate intelligence with mastery, with having a lot of knowledge and doing well in school (Meadows 2006), and doing well on academic subjects becomes increasingly often mentioned as a defining characteristic during this phase of schooling (Cain and Dweck 1995; Kinlaw and Kurtz-Costas 2003). Young children include social characteristics in their description of 'intelligence', whereas older children are more likely to differentiate between cognitive strengths and social strengths. Ideas centring on abstract reasoning become more frequent in adolescence (Chen et al. 1988). Good performance on cognitive tasks, and high school grades, are seen as specific and fairly precise signs of 'intelligence', and the reason why you would pick someone to be on your team in an academic competition (Stipek and Gralinski 1996; Stipek and Tannart 1984). Differences in academic performance are taken as signs of difference in 'intelligence' increasingly as school careers wear on; young children (and teachers!) attribute more of the difference in performance to effort, but older pupils are inclined to attribute differential success and failure to differences in ability. Ideas about the self as a learner are obviously relevant here (Burnett 1999; Burnett and Proctor 2002; Dart et al. 2000; Dweck 1999; pp. 213–17).

2.5.2 Depression

Discussion of a sense of mastery leads me to descriptions of functioning when a sense of 'mastery' is chronically lacking: depression, anxiety, shyness. I will be insisting that although we tend to see these as characteristics of the individual, and thus to offer remediation on this basis, this is not really an accurate picture.

Feelings of sadness, helplessness, misery, hopelessness are far from uncommon; for a substantial proportion of individuals these amount to depression (I should say that I am not talking about bipolar disorder here: this may be a different sort of problem so far as causes and remediation are concerned). The factors behind depression range from possible genetic susceptibility to predominantly environmental effects. The psychosocial precursors of depression that are found in many research studies include childhood adversity, vulnerable personality styles, limited social supports, and demanding life events, particularly in combination. Models drawing on ideas about stress and vulnerability (e.g. Brown and Harris 1978; Goodyer 2008; Hankin *et al*. 2007) suggest that exposure to stress at various times over the lifespan is necessary first to predispose people, particularly vulnerable people, to developing depression, and then to precipitate the onset of depressive symptoms.

2.5.2.1 Daily life stresses, brain development and depression

Daily life stresses may have their effect via multiple levels. One such would be effects on the emotion-regulation systems of the central nervous system (pp. 115–16, 130–33). As I have already discussed, if there is excessive, adverse, input in early life, there may be neural changes in the development of the endocrine and behavioural responses to stress. The plasticity of the child's brain development will allow for the establishment of central stress-responsive pathways that normally help the child to cope with the challenges of their environment by creating a central stress response pattern that can be evoked in subsequent times of stress. However, it is possible that this process may become maladaptive, over the lifespan, in those people exposed to excessive childhood stress: for example the child exposed to parental depression may on one level develop attachment problems (pp. 146–47) and on another level build up a hypersensitive neural response to stressful stimuli (Halligan *et al*. 2004; Murray 2006). The dysfunction of central stress-related pathways may produce many of the symptoms of depression because the pathways are involved in the higher order functioning of mood and motivational drive.

2.5.2.2 Personality and depression

Depressive vulnerability may also be seen to lie within a person's internal world; personality style or temperament may predispose to a particular response to social stressors. At-risk personality traits, such as neuroticism, may predispose to a diagnosis of depression, independent of the effect of depression itself in generating a vulnerable personality, because they contribute to a person's perception of their external and social world and thus the manner in which they report on negative aspects of their life. Issues about diagnosis and self-diagnosis of depressive symptoms obviously arise here: not all individuals are equally likely to be seen as being depressed, despite having similar levels of symptoms (Boyce *et al*. 1991; Zahn-Waxler, Klimes-Dougan and Slattery 2000; Goodyer 2008).

2.5.2.3 Social support and depression

People who have, or believe they have, low levels of social support are more likely to feel depressed (Brown and Harris 1978; Cummings, Keller and Davies 2005; Meadows 2006). Having a good relationship with a confidante, a good number of relatives and friends and a good frequency of positive contacts with them, and active participation in social gatherings, religious ceremonies, and organised sports/clubs, all seem to protect against depression. Low levels of social support are strongly associated with risk of depressive symptoms. Raver (2004) argues that differences in such social factors are a component of observed differences in emotional stability. However, discussion in peer groups that dwells excessively on negative issues ('co-rumination', pp. 73, 75, 179, 270) can exacerbate depression rather than reduce it. And being depressed, especially about your social functioning, can impair your social relationships and your social support network (e.g. Ciarrochi and Heaven 2008).

2.5.2.4 Early life events and depression

The classic studies of depression (Brown and Harris 1978; Harris and Brown 1996; see also Cummings and Davies 1994; Meadows 2006) showed that depressed women frequently had histories of unsatisfactory parenting, separation from mothers, and child abuse. A more recent study of Irish and Australian children (O'Sullivan 2004) suggests that experience of bullying and absence of the father are also potent sources of risk for depressive symptoms. Additionally, depressed people reported more adverse childhood experiences of a range of sorts. However, whether depressive symptoms actually existed at the time of the study (a time quite far removed from the childhood events) was primarily down to the existence of adverse life events currently. Low levels of social support preceded the onset of depressive symptoms, and adverse interpersonal events precipitated and maintained the depression.

2.5.2.5 Macrosystem issues and depression

I am focusing here on the centre of Bronfenbrenner's developmental environments. However, microsystem and even macrosystem issues, far wider than the individual, may impinge on their risk of depression. Studies of infants' and children's reponses to stressful situations such as separation or unresponsive parents show that children of all socio-economic statuses can develop excellent responses to such stressors if there is sensitive contingent parenting, but that if there is not, because of socio-economic stresses or pathologies such as depression or chronic drug use, the prognosis for the child may be much less good (e.g. Garner and Spears 2000; Lupien *et al.*

2000; Compas *et al.* 2001; Conger and Donnellan 2007; Evans and English 2002; Grant *et al.* 2003; Hankin *et al.* 2007). Poverty, for example, exposes individuals from conception onwards to a range of risk events that may have long-term impacts on their development of satisfactory emotional regulation (e.g. Newman and Massengill 2006; Raver 2004). There is simply less sign of depression and stress in societies that are economically more equal (e.g. Rutter and Smith 1995; Pickett and Wilkinson 2007; Wilkinson and Pickett 2009).

It appears, therefore, that depression is associated with the combination of several factors: a stress-response system that is not functioning robustly, a developmental history and a current state of adversity and lack of support, the experience of a precipitating life event such as bereavement or job loss, lack of other positive factors in one's current experience, and thought patterns which emphasise the individual's inability to cope.

2.5.3 Anxiety

Everybody will have some area of their lives that they feel anxious about. Almost all children have things they are afraid of (pp. 23–24). We have to learn to cope with these things. Some individuals, however, suffer from feelings of fear and anxiety that are highly intense, out of proportion to the situation as seen by others; painful and disruptive, rather than motivating; persistent, rather than occasional; and felt to be beyond control. Feelings such as these are characteristic of 'internalising' disorders – so-called because the individual who has them looks as though their suffering is turned inwards, mainly hurting themselves rather than others, but also perhaps because the causes of the problem are felt by the sufferer to be their own responsibility.

Internalising problems are very common in children from preschool age onwards (Zahn-Waxler *et al.* 2000; van der Bruggen *et al.* 2008) and often persist through childhood and into adolescence and adulthood. They are sometimes first seen when the child moves from the home setting to daycare or preschool; a number of children have persistent difficulty in coping with the new setting, with separation from their parents, and with adjusting to their peers. Internalising symptoms include crying, depression, worrying, fearfulness, phobias and compulsions, and psychosomatic maladies such as headaches and upset stomachs with no other apparent cause. These sorts of problem are more often seen in girls, but they are by no means uncommon in boys.

Like any other group of disorders, the causes of excessive anxiety are likely to be diverse. Part of what seems to be going on here is a shifting of emotional self-regulation away from a robust balance towards a more wobbly and easily upset position. Some researchers (e.g. Kagan 1997; Kagan and Snidman 1999) link this to early temperament (pp. 52, 64–65).

Difficulty in adjusting to novelty and a low threshold for becoming upset are two characteristics of high inhibition in toddlers and young children – the result is distress and withdrawal as the dominant reaction to unfamiliar situations. Withdrawal may reduce arousal and distress in the short term, but as a coping strategy it has the major disadvantage that the individual won't learn that the novel situation can be a pleasant one, and it will be more difficult to learn more positive coping skills (Rubin, Burgess and Hastings 2002).

Theorists concerned with temperament have always stressed its physiological manifestations (pp. 64–65). One area of interest in the case of anxiety is cardiac vagal tone, which is an index of how the nervous system is regulating heart rate. An arousing event tends to raise heart rate, as the body alerts itself for 'fight or flight': the parasympathetic nervous system modulates this to decrease heart rate, and arousal, as necessary. Individuals differ in how adaptively they can calm themselves – anxious individuals are seen as reaching, and remaining at, a disproportionately high, and disruptive, level of arousal.

The physiological systems that modulate arousal mature over the preschool period, and children become more able to maintain a relatively high and consistent basic vagal tone (Calkins 1997; Calkins and Keane 2004). Lower vagal tone and weaker changes in vagal tone in response to an exciting event may be associated with less adaptive coping with challenges, and with greater anxiety (Calkins 1997; Hastings and De 2008). It is not clear whether this is a direct, mechanical, link, or whether vagal tone is a risk factor only in conjunction with other influences.

Hastings *et al.* (2008) make the case that the association between children's parasympathetic regulation and parental overcontrol could be one such damaging conjunction, leading towards internalising problems. Children of very controlling parents tend to be more anxious and socially withdrawn (Pettit *et al.* 2001; Rubin, Burgess and Hastings 2002; Wood *et al.* 2003). Having had considerable amounts of parental micromanagement they have had fewer opportunities for autonomy and successful self-regulation, skills which need practice. They may also be overdependent on parents emotionally, if the parents have themselves been negatively affected by the child's signs of stress and reacted with protective overcontrol – whether effusive comfort, limiting the child's experience of challenges and thus of opportunities to rise to them successfully, or lack of feedback to the child that they are going to be competent to solve their own problems. Sometimes parental protection is essential for the child's well-being, but too much of it can divert children from increasing satisfaction at their own mastery towards learning that they are incompetent and helpless (e.g. Rubin, Burgess and Hastings 2002; Bayer, Sanson and Hemphill 2006; Hastings and De 2008). Parenting that involves more moderate and scaffolding responses to children's difficulties seems to be associated with better development of autonomy and avoidance of a lapse into anxiety and learned helplessness (Bayer, Sanson and Hemphill 2006; Chen *et al.* 1998; Crockenberg and Leerkes 2003b; Gauvain 2005; Hastings and De 2008; Kärtner 2007; Meadows 2006; Turner and Berkowitz 2005; van der Bruggen *et al.* 2008; Wood 1998).

Obviously here again we have a developmental path of interaction between one's own characteristics and the wider social setting. Individual differences within the child are interacting with layers of the Bronfenbrenner ecosystems further out into the world. Short-term functioning, and longer-term resilience, are developing.

2.5.4 Shyness

Shyness is one of the characteristics of persons that have profound implications for what sort of social persons they are. People who are regarded as 'shy', by themselves or by others, may have different social experiences and different understandings of the social world from those who are regarded as 'sociable'. There is a marked tendency in the literature, and perhaps in common sense discussion, to regard this as a problem (e.g. Chen *et al.* 1995; Coplan *et al.* 2007a and 2007b; Coplan *et al.* 1994; Kerr, Lambert and Bem 1996; Rubin 1999). To see whether it is, we need to unpack the concept of 'shyness' and do some careful looking at the evidence on its causes, consequences, and correlates.

People who are 'shy' generally show a high degree of wariness, possibly even anxiety, when faced with a novel social experience; they may desire to engage socially, but if they do they are inhibited in approaching others or accepting others' social overtures. Being 'shy' may involve feelings of tension and concern about social interactions, worries about others' judgements and reactions, discomfort or inhibition in social situations that seem to be novel or involve evaluation of oneself, and behaviour that reduces social contact or avoids it. Part of the basis of this net of feelings and behaviour is probably a cautious or fearful attitude towards the unfamiliar; as individuals' understanding of themselves and of the social expectations of others develops, feelings of self-consciousness and anxiety about being evaluated negatively become involved. The consequence is that the shy individual behaves with a high degree of reticence and reserve – watching without joining in, avoiding other people's attention, losing confidence and fluency, blushing, stammering and becoming distressed. This is likely to reduce the person's opportunities to practise effective social skills, and if it is seen as an undesirable way to behave, shyness may become associated with a sense of social failure, with consequences such as low self-esteem, depression, social anxiety and withdrawal from social opportunities and demands. This is one reason why shyness is discussed in terms of concern rather than being regarded as part of an arguably sensible preference for independence and solitude. I overstate this as an alternative interpretation

– but before going for an easy judgement that 'shyness' is a bad thing, we need to remember that both the evolutionary pressure to survive despite the attentions of others and the pressures of modern urban life in a crowd would make it important for individuals to deploy skills of caution, reserve and reticence, even of avoidance, when it is appropriate.

2.5.4.1 Causes of shyness

The literature on 'temperament' (Kagan, Reznick and Gibbons 1989; Reznick *et al.* 1986) picks out differences between individuals in their tendency to approach or to hang back from novel situations. The source of these differences is hard to clarify: there is debate about a genetic basis, as whereas pedigree and twin studies typically suggest at least a moderate heritability and animal studies commonly find temperament to be largely heritable, some studies emphasise the role of the environment (e.g. Bouchard 2004; Roisman and Fraley 2006; Hoekstra *et al.* 2008). There may be a physiological basis (Kagan, Reznick and Snidman 1987; Fordham and Stevenson-Hinde 1999); for example there is some emerging evidence that shy children exhibited significantly greater relative right central EEG activation at rest and during the presentation of a fear-eliciting video than non-shy children (Theall-Honey and Schmidt 2006), and that children of parents who suffer from social phobia tend to have higher overall resting frontal EEG activity compared with the children of healthy parents (Campbell *et al.* 2007).

Early attachment experiences have also been suggested as a source of differences in shyness during childhood. If an individual has had insecure attachment relationships as an infant and young child, and is also temperamentally inhibited, it is argued that the result might be a high degree of fearfulness, especially in social situations (Kochanska 1995; Nachmias *et al.* 1996); the combination of temperamental behavioural inhibition and high reactivity to stress as a consequence of insecure attachment is seen as leading to great difficulty in coping with social situations and to a strategy of coping by withdrawing from them. Bohlin, Hagekull and Andersson (2005) in a study of school-age children found that attachment security and shyness in infancy interacted to predict social competence with peers a couple of years later. Although it could be predicted that there would be a similar interaction between attachment and temperament in the area of children's relations with adults in school, Rydell, Bohlin and Thorell (2005) found that attachment status and temperament appeared to have independent effects on five and six-year-olds' relationships with teachers. Children with secure attachment representations had more positive relationships with their teacher (and showed better social competence with peers) than did children with insecure representations. Shy children had less secure teacher relationships and somewhat lower peer competence in terms of social initiative compared with non-shy children, but they also had fewer conflicts with teachers.

A study by Gazelle and Spangler (2007) took a slightly different approach in that it looked at associations between anxious solitude in early childhood and later peer relationships, focusing particularly on the role of maternal sensitivity in mother–child interactions. But their results were consistent with the attachment studies: they found that anxious children whose mothers had behaved towards them with a high degree of sensitivity made many more positive contributions to interaction with their peers and had more friends, and made fewer negative contributions to peer interaction and suffered less peer rejection, compared with anxious children handled with low maternal sensitivity. Nelson et al. (2006) found similar relationships with maternal behaviour in a sample of Chinese children.

It is likely that the nature of the insecurity in attachment is highly relevant. In Rydell, Bohlin and Thorell's (2005) middle-class Swedish sample, children with avoidant representations had more conflictual relationships with teachers and peers and also low levels of prosocial orientation in preschool, compared with children with secure representations. Children whose attachments appeared to be ambivalent or 'bizarre' were not higher in conflict and antisocial behaviour, but they did appear to be somewhat inhibited and withdrawn in their social interactions – possibly being more anxious and less organised in their social behaviour. The authors suggest that one outcome of avoidant attachment may be a weakening propensity for prosocial behaviour, whereas ambivalent-bizarre and ambivalent-resistant attachment may be mainly associated with withdrawal and low initiative (Rydell, Bohlin and Thorell 2005).

This suggests that we should refer back to the issue of whether all sorts of 'shy' behaviour are the same in their implications (Coplan et al. 2007b; Nelson et al. 2006). In particular, the category of 'shy' individuals may include both contented loners and those who would prefer to be social but are unable to relate effectively to others (with subcategories within groups). It may be sensible to try to distinguish between these categories. Interestingly, it appears that even young children do make this distinction. Coplan et al. (2007b) found that six-year-olds discussing hypothetical vignettes of children's behaviour distinguished between shyness (socially fearful children) and unsociability (children who preferred to play alone but could engage socially when required). They felt that unsociability was a choice whereas shyness was less under the individual's control, believed that shy children probably desired to be involved in social interaction, and said they would prefer to play with the hypothetical shy child rather than with the 'unsociable' one. (It was the hypothetical aggressive children who were the least preferred as possible playmates, by a big margin.) They also thought that shyness did not seriously interfere with the social functioning of the group, whereas unsociability might (and aggression definitely upset the group). Thus hypothetical 'shyness' was regarded with some kindness by these young children, even if their preference over all was for socially skilled peers.

It is interesting that there is some evidence that shy and withdrawn children are as likely as normally sociable children to have mutual and stable best friendships, though these best friends were likely also to be relatively withdrawn and to be victimised by other children (Burgess *et al.* 2006). The children in this study were older (fifth grade), however, and being (relatively) unsociable may be more acceptable at some ages than others. It used to be thought that very young children mostly functioned in parallel with other children rather than playing *with* them (Parten 1932), and although more recent observations (Rubin, Maioni and Hornung 1976) of toddlers and preschoolers suggest they are capable of much more social awareness and competence than this model supposed, many theorists regard early solitary play as normal and not predictive of any disorder. Social anxiety in adolescence is relatively common and of more concern – perhaps because this is a period when social contacts and social evaluations are very salient and social identities are very much under review (pp. 174, 177–80, 180–82).

It would be as well to remember also that shyness may be seen as more of a disadvantage for some groups rather than for others. Shyness in girls arouses much less anxiety in parents and much less blame from others than does shyness in boys (Caspi, Elder and Bem 1988; Stevenson-Hinde and Glover 1996). There are cultural similarities (Chen *et al.* 2004) but also cultural differences in the acceptability of shy behaviour. Chen *et al.* (2006) report on the relations between reticent social behaviour and peer initiations and reactions in Canadian and Chinese four-year-olds. Reticent Chinese children received positive responses from their peers, but reticent Canadian children received refusal and disagreement from other children. West and Newman (2007), researching social anxiety among American Indian adolescents in North Carolina, argue that social reticence may be an acceptable behaviour in a culture where internal cohesion and separation from the invading outsider have been, historically, so important.

It should also be noted that there can be discrepancies in different people's views of whether an individual is shy. Spooner and Evans (2005) found that children (theirs were aged ten to twelve years) may self-report as shy but aren't seen as such by their teachers and their peers. Conversely, I remember being surprised and affronted when my form teacher in the first year of secondary school wrote in my report that I was 'at times too reserved'. This sort of discrepancy is not altogether surprising, as different people obviously have different sorts of grounds for their rating of shyness – the 'shy' individual has more evidence of their internal thoughts and feelings and of other occasions which have felt the same, and can introspect, whereas the outsider has to rely more on observable behaviour (which may have causes other than the individual's shyness). All the biases shown up by person perception research may apply; there will be bias in both the actor and the observer. And it could be useful to consider how far 'shyness', like any other personality characteristic, is situation specific.

2.5.4.2 Consequences of shyness

Thus, I think we need to be careful about interpreting data on the relationship between 'shyness' and psychopathologies. There is an extensive body of evidence from a large number of research studies that suggest that shyness is linked to lower social competence, lower popularity and lower self-esteem in childhood, and to various internalising disorders during the period of later childhood into adolescence, and in adulthood (e.g. Caspi *et al.* 1996; Reznick *et al.* 1986; Jaffee *et al.* 2002; Coplan *et al.* 2007b; Moffitt and Caspi 2007). In particular, as much of this evidence suggests that anxiety predisposes to depression (depressed adults are often also anxious), it may be that social anxiety plays a role in linking childhood inhibition and depression. Shyness in childhood may also be associated with experience of more negative relationships with significant adults, and with more exposure to bullying by peers, which would themselves contribute to risk of later depression and anxiety (Gladstone and Parker 2006). If we look at this network of causes from a slightly different angle, it might make sense to suggest that shyness in a child may reduce opportunities to find comfort in social relationships, or to develop supportive affiliations which can be called on for protection when the individual is threatened; thus the shy child, adolescent or adult may not have some of the buffers against 'the slings and arrows of outrageous fortune' which a normally sociable individual enjoys. Or it could be that their reserve may insulate them against casual social harm if they just don't care about the views of their peers, and their self-sufficiency may stand them in good stead if they do not want to engage with novel social situations.

Clearly, being alone more often than is usual can come about for many different reasons, and does not always have just one set of implications for well-being and development. Being socially withdrawn sometimes but not always is associated with later difficulties. Avoiding social interaction, and being both very shy and very sociable, may have particularly strong negative implications, but this is far from certain (Coplan *et al.* 2007b). There are very probably both cultural and historical differences in how negatively shyness is viewed (Chang *et al.* 2005; Chen and French 2007). Altogether, this seems to be a characteristic that probably worries adults more than it needs to, although some extremely shy children might benefit from interventions that reduce their fear and anxiety about social situations and promote more competent social interaction.

Problematic shyness, anxiety and lack of self-esteem seem to be associated, then, with problems with social knowledge. This raises the question of what children know about the social world, and in particular the other people in it. I wrote about some of the enormous amount of research on children's social cognition in an earlier book (Meadows 2006) and there is a recent, accessible and very thoughtful review of the field in Carpendale and Lewis (2006), so I will not repeat the basic material here. Instead I focus on the social roots of moral feelings.

2.6 Children as moral persons

The nature of morality and its relationships with our biology and our society have been debated by philosophers for millennia, and by psychologists for centuries. Their not necessarily compatible musings sometimes include consideration of the evolutionary usefulness of moral reasoning and action, sometimes examine the effect of social pressures and sanctions, and sometimes focus on the internal organisation of the reasoning involved. Judgement and action both need to be considered, and discrepancies between these may be especially important in our complex social world. All these issues are relevant to children's development as moral persons, but in total they amount to far more than I can address at this point, particularly as the issues remain profoundly unresolved. I am going to restrict my discussion to three main points: children's views on the relations between convention and morality; the experiences that lead to different levels of moral judgement; and the importance of emotion in moral action. For a general review of moral development I recommend Turiel (1998) and Nucci (2002).

2.6.1 Models of moral reasoning

The field of moral development has been dominated by a model of morality that emphasised its rationality and to some degree separated it from emotional content. This model began with Piaget (1932) and was developed by Kohlberg (1984). It involved a succession of stages of moral reasoning in which notions of justice and rights were central. Development started from early stages in which children's self-interest and their knowledge of social norms dominated their choice of what was 'right' or 'wrong' and their justifications of their choice, and gradually reached later stages in which principles of moral justice replaced self-interest and convention as the core of moral reasoning. The developmental forces include changes in relationships with parents and peers (especially for Piaget), and an intrinsic drive for coherence and commitment to a key moral principle (Kohlberg). Both researchers used stories about moral dilemmas as a major way to elicit evidence, though Piaget's account also uses charming examples of his own children's response to their moral dilemmas and of children playing games like marbles.

Critics of this approach have debated its methods: does discussion of fictional dilemmas reflect real-life moral reasoning, can children remember all the quite complex information in the stories, is the categorisation of children's answers reliable, can children express their reasoning fluently, are the stages really so clear cut, so coherent, and so sequential. They have disagreed with its depiction of young children as amoral and of many adults as falling far below the final stages of Kohlberg's sequence. They have questioned whether people show consistent levels of reasoning across topics or occasions; identified lapses between reasoning and action. And they have disputed whether valuing justice and respect for human life above all else was the only tenable highest stage of moral reasoning (Emler 1998; Gilligan 1982; Nucci 2002, 2004; Turiel 1998).

2.6.2 Morality, convention and social context

Some of these issues have been developed in more recent work. One of the most important of these new areas has been children's recognition of the moral and the conventional as related, but not identical, domains.

Nucci (2002: 306–307) shows Kohlberg's stages in parallel with the characteristics of children's moral reasoning and understanding of convention. Although understanding moral principles might be, as Kohlberg stressed, a matter of thinking about universal imperatives that apply to everyone whatever their culture or historical period, understanding conventions is a socially based matter. Turiel (1983, 1998) and Smetana *et al.* (1984) demonstrated that children as young as three differentiate between convention and morality, seeing convention as contextually dependent and agreed upon social rules, and morality as less arbitrary, less avoidable, and appealing to universal moral principles. Three-year-old children would agree that although you should participate in 'show and tell' at your nursery school, this was merely because not participating and not abiding by the nursery's conventions would upset social expectations, and it might be quite permissible to keep out of 'show and tell' in 'another country' or 'another planet'; but they would assert that to wreak unprovoked harm on someone would be wrong everywhere, regardless of whether it had been specifically prohibited. Compliance with convention comes to be seen as a good thing (Kalish and Cornelius 2007; Perkins and Turiel 2007), especially if doing so increases social harmony, but it may be seen as problematic if the conventional norms transgress a principle of moral authority or fairness, or of adolescents' autonomy (pp. 139–41, 236–38, 243–45). This may be a matter of social debate, because whereas the link between breaking a moral rule (for example by deliberately shooting someone) and harm to someone is typically immediate and obvious, the link between a social rule (the right to bear arms) and harm to other people (as indexed by the homicide rate) is less immediate, and much more arguable. (There are similar debates about the morality of telling lies (Perkins and Turiel 2007)). In this sort of predicament, individuals have different views, and may have to choose between conventional or post-conventional (principled) moral reasoning; Emler (1998) finds this choice to be linked to political affiliation, with more left-wing people tending to appeal to moral principles and more right-wing people tending to appeal to social convention or outside authority. Readers may wish to interpret this bias pattern in terms of their own political preferences.

2.6.3 Differences in moral reasoning between different social groups

Another area of debate has been over the possibility that different groups have different bases for their moral reasoning. Following critiques of Kohlberg's model after his suggestion that women were less likely to reach higher stages of moral development than men, Gilligan (1982) suggested that the problem was Kohlberg's prioritising of justice as the core principle of moral judgement. She proposed compassion as an alternative, and linked a feminine preference for compassion to socialisation into gender roles. More recent studies (Jaffee and Hyde 2000; Lapsley and Narvaez 2004) show that both males and females reason about both justice and caring, although with a small gender bias in orientation. Again, the justice and compassion might be hoped to go together, rather than one winning out over the other; but here, too, there might be conflicts, with compassion suggesting one course of action and justice another.

Cultural differences are an even more difficult issue. Some theorists emphasise the ways in which individuals' moral reasoning is constrained and constituted by the socially constructed norms that they meet, with cultural emphasis on individuality or on community being one developmentally powerful dimension (e.g. Shweder, Mahapatra and Miller 1990); others see these as superficial differences which conceal universal obligatory moral values. Again, it may be more a matter of what is prioritised rather than what is possible. Children growing up in a highly collectivised society may still feel free to think that they should have a set of values that are personal, private and autonomous (Nucci 2002); and children in a highly individualistic society may nevertheless be desperately anxious to espouse the values of the society and so 'belong' to the desired social group (Power 2004; Wren and Mendoza 2004; Keller 2004a).

Individuals who belong to a minority within a culture may differ in their values from the majority, sometimes in very painful ways. Verkuyten and Slooter (2008), for example, asked twelve to eighteen-year-olds in the Netherlands to indicate their views about issues such as free speech (whether it is permissible to ridicule religion, express racist views, or call for war between Muslims and non-believers), Muslim minority rights (for example to found separate schools or burn flags in a demonstration or protest), and practices based on minority cultural beliefs (such as women wearing a headscarf or female circumcision). They found that all individuals endorsed moral principles of fairness and tolerance of minority rights, but they were not completely consistent across issues. Both Muslim and non-Muslim adolescents were less willing to tolerate action that contravened these values if the perpetrator was from the group they did not themselves belong to, or if the action would negatively affect people like them. This applied also within ethnic groups: the young Muslim women were more hostile to female circumcision than any other group, whereas young Muslim males were the most in favour of male control of women.

Apart from cultural differences in what is acceptable morality, there may be cultural differences in how moral issues are discussed with children. Wang (2008) describe Chinese working class mothers' reaction to their children's transgressions. They very often used social referencing, reminding the child about other children, media characters, authority figures or traditional stories or quotations who were better models. Here are two examples, the second of which seems subtly distinct from what Western parents say:

> . . . the mother took out a box of sweets to treat the visitors. Xiaomei, a 4-year-old girl, grabbed a handful of them.

> *Mother*: Xiaomei, let the guests have the sweets first. You must learn how to be polite. Do you remember Meimei [a cartoon character in a child's TV programme who is very kind, polite and generous to others]?
> *Xiaomei*: (Puts two sweets back in the box)
> *Mother*: Just keep one piece. Give one piece to Aunty Wang and one to Aunty Xu. Put the rest in your hand back in the box. Do you remember that toothless tiger [a cartoon figure] you saw the other day? He lost all his teeth because the little fox tricked him into eating all the sweets. Oh, do you remember Pipi [another cartoon figure]? What happened to him? Did he eat too many sweets? Did he have to go to see the doctor?
> *Xiaomei*: (Runs away)
>
> (Wang 2008: 60)

> Qixing, a 4-year 2-month-old boy is playing with his rice while having lunch.

> *Mother*: Qixing, don't play with the rice! Do you remember what the Tang poem says?
> '*When the sun is hot, the peasants are planting the rice.*
> *While they are planting the rice, their sweat dropped in the field.*
> *Every bit of rice in the plate symbolises the hardship of the peasants.*

Don't waste the rice.
It's not easy to grow it!'
Eat!
Qixing: (Picks up the rice)

(Wang 2008: 62)

There is a fascinating interplay here between the internal feelings of the child, the microsystem of child and mother, and a set of macrosystems at the level of the culture. The first mother appeals to the child on the basis of the feelings of guests present in the room and with reference to three contemporary TV cartoon characters, including reference to the harm that the child might do to herself if she eats too many sweets. The second refers to a didactic poem more than a thousand years old, and perhaps implicitly to more recent solidarity with the workers and peasants. The two cases imply a strong appeal to the timelessness of the need to be respectful of other people's rights, to share and not to waste.

2.6.4 Links between moral reasoning and emotion

A philosophical tradition that can be traced back to the ancient Greeks insists first that morality is not a self-subsistent entity but a part of the functioning of the individual as a whole, integrated with the personality system and so linked to social functioning and motivation; second that it involves questions of intention, identity, power and agency; and third that it is linked to other human ideals such as truth and beauty (Blasi 2004; Nisan 2004). The embedding of moral reasoning within social settings suggests that it will not be free of emotion, and hence that emotion-free accounts of moral development will be missing important issues. Young children recognise the emotional colouring of the situations that involve moral reasoning. In studies by Arsenio and colleagues (Arsenio and Kramer 1992; Arsenio and Lemerise 2001), for example, even kindergarten children thought that people who were doing morally good things, or benefiting from them, or witnessing them (helping another person, sharing out a reward fairly) would have positive emotions: those suffering from or observing an unfair act would feel bad (although the younger children thought the victimiser might feel good about their act if it got them what they wanted): those going against a convention, or witnessing a breach of convention, would feel neither good nor bad about it, although they expected authority figures to be upset. Moral issues are thus associated with emotional outcomes from the beginning, and children's understanding of emotion, for example their difficulties in recognising incompatible emotions, might be an area of relevance to their moral development.

I think there is a case for arguing first that a person's developmental history shapes their emotional stability or vulnerability and second that their emotional states may impact on their moral behaviour. I have discussed elsewhere (pp. 115–16, 130–33) the effects of parents' behaviour and other experiences of the child on their ability to maintain emotional regulation in the face, especially, of difficult situations. One relevant area here is the role of empathy in morality; another is the effects of a history of more or less sensitive parenting, or of neglect or maltreatment (pp. 85–86, 129–30, 141–42).

2.7 Summary

This section has been about the innermost level of the child as a social person. I have looked at a wide range of different issues, and used a number of different approaches to the material. I started with things evolution might have provided to the child that could help with development as a social person. The first set of these involved the fact that the child is immature and capable of change and development. Evolution has provided signals that this is the case, signals that are picked up by the more mature social persons I discuss in the next section in interactions which form the child's development. Evolution has also provided physiological systems, in particular for regulating emotions, which are fine-tuned after birth, in particular in interaction between infant and parent. I think that how these systems of stress management and emotion regulation build up for individual children is one of the most interesting areas of study at present; physiological, behavioural, and cognitive levels of functioning are being brought together in very powerful ways. This is not at all a book about 'how to bring up baby': but if it were an advice book, supporting your child in developing a repertoire of positive ways to cope with stress would be one of the main recommendations.

I moved on from these biological bases to consider theory and research that looks at children's personalities, centring on the self-concept and an assortment of self-conscious emotions that merge into habitual ways of describing oneself. I related these where I could to biological bases and to social processes that may nudge development along more favourable or less favourable paths. Again, many of these points are picked up again when I look at social interactions in the sections on microsystems and macro-systems that follow.

Chapter 3

Qualities of microsystems 1: Child and parents

Despite some attempts to downplay it (e.g. Harris 1995, 1998; Rowe 1994), nobody seriously argues against the proposition that parent–child microsystems provide one of the most important arenas for children's development as social persons. Proverbial wisdom, biographers' practice, individual reminiscence, systematic research all provide countless examples of parental interaction with children having a formative influence on the child (and on the parent, though that is a story I shall largely neglect). For all sorts of reasons stretching from basic biology to the furthest extremes of cultural studies, it would be extraordinary to ignore parents as factors in their children's development. In this chapter, I am going to begin to document some of the multitude of ways in which this all works. I will begin with a brief recapitulation of what evolutionary theory would suggest about parents and children's development; outline some of the ways of looking at what parents do; and review some of the findings about how what parents do affects children.

It will become obvious that I have preferred the gender-neutral term 'parent' to the gender-specific 'mother' and 'father'. In part this is because of my own value system; in part it is because I am talking about parental actions and the accumulated evidence suggests that there is more similarity than difference in the range of parenting activities that mothers and fathers do, and the range of parenting roles that they play, and the ways they affect their children (Lamb 2004), at least in Western cultures. I will say more about cultural and historical differences later.

3.1 Biological foundations of the parent–child microsystem

3.1.1 Strategies for having descendants

Evolutionary theory (Section 1.3) is one of the basic disciplines which we need to apply to the development of children as social persons. It starts from the assumption that 'the ultimate causation that drives all other processes is that of reproductive success' (Beaulieu and Bugental 2007: 72). Individuals are born, live and die. Some of them (all of our ancestors, but not necessarily all of us or all of our descendants) reproduce. It is through our success in reproducing and then the success of our descendants in reproducing that our genes survive. Over the course of evolution, those who succeeded best in producing offspring who then were themselves successful producers of offspring (and so on into successive generations) had their genes become more frequent in the population; those with less success were more at risk of their genes dying out. We would expect, therefore, that there will be all sorts of evolved processes that enable us to do this by having children and rearing them to reproductive maturity.

Obviously, there is more than one way of being an individual who produces offspring who will in their turn produce offspring. Over the course of evolution, different strategies for successful reproduction have emerged. One strategy is to produce a very large number of offspring quickly and cheaply, and accept that only a minority of them will survive – a strategy which most readers will be familiar with in, for example, garden weeds or frogs (British frogs I should say: David Attenborough's television series *Life in Cold Blood* revealed to me that some tropical species of frogs work hard at being parents). Large numbers of offspring (dandelion seeds or frogs' eggs, for example) are generated and thrown into the world to survive or not survive without any further intervention from the parent. Most do not survive, but enough do for the parent frog or dandelion to have a reasonable chance of being a grandparent and great-grandparent. This is wasteful in terms of eggs and seeds, but extremely economical in terms of parental resources. That it is a widely spread strategy suggests that it can work well enough.

The typical evolved human strategy is at the other extreme; a very small number of offspring, produced expensively in terms of time, energy and physical resources, of which most survive to reproductive maturity. The normal human litter size is one, not thousands; individuals rarely have even as many as ten offspring over their lifetime; the gestation period is long, not a few days; the offspring will not have any chance of survival unless looked after until nearly mature; the period of immaturity is very long, indeed humans have been discussed as 'holding on to' immaturity (Gould 1977; Martin 2007; pp. 22–23, 51). Human children are much more expensive to their parents than frog children or dandelion children; and clearly all this has implications for the role of parents and the characteristics of both parents and children. The key implication is that human children need an investment of parenting to have any hope of surviving and reproducing themselves; human parents need to provide parenting to their children (by doing it themselves or finding someone else to do it) if they are to have any hope of being an ancestor. Possibly, beyond this, fine-tuned differences in parenting might increase or decrease the individual's chances of developing successfully.

Cultures have of course also evolved social strategies and ways of investing in the young to enhance their chances of surviving, reproducing, and achieving social success; and they may have different views about what families should be like (Allen *et al.* 2008; Dunbar 2008; Opie and Power 2008; Mace 2008; Patterson and Hastings 2007). I will not discuss these diversities now, but they will crop up in all sorts of areas elsewhere in this book pp. 65, 82–83, 99, 102–03, 117, 127, 139, 152–57, 240–43, 274.

3.1.2 Immaturity and parenting

Human infants are born comparatively immature and grow up very slowly. Some of the reasons for this derive from the evolutionary change from moving around on four feet to moving around on two. This had the consequence that the shape of the pelvis changed and the birth canal became narrow, compared with the unborn baby's head. Thus the head cannot grow too large before birth, lest the baby should be too big to fit through the birth canal and both mother and baby die during the delivery; and the skull may be squashed during birth. These problems result in a tendency for the growth of the head, and the brain inside it, to be restricted before birth and rapid after it. This means that there is a large amount of brain growth and development in the first months and years after birth.

Infants' prolonged period of immaturity and brain development allows an extended period in which they can learn, and requires a prolonged period of protection and nurturance while they are unable to cope alone. Human parents have to parent their offspring, otherwise they will not survive to reproductive age, let alone flourish in a society which has to be learned about. Human parenting is a matter of sustained effort over a long period – that is, it will be worth considering parents' investment as a factor in children's lives. I will first look briefly at who is invested in, and then in more detail at what sorts of investment are necessary.

3.1.3 Infants' ability to evoke parental investment

Immature offspring need to evoke parental care if they are to survive. As I described earlier (pp. 50–51) infants have evolved physical characteristics that enhance their chances of protection and loving care – they look cute and unthreatening, and we react with sympathetic care. But they act in ways that evoke this parental interest too. From very early on indeed, infants selectively attend to human faces and voices, and discriminate the familiar voice of their mother (DeCasper and Fifer 1980; Burnham 1993) and her familiar smell (Macfarlane 1975; Porter 1998) from other non-familiar women. (The very worst moment of my career as a parent came when my daughter became confused over these familiar things. When she was about 15 months old, I left her with her childminder and spent the day mainly at work but also having my hair cut. When I arrived to pick Anne up, she did not recognise me and resisted being put into her buggy to be taken home by someone who clearly looked and smelled like a stranger. Once in the buggy and walking home, she couldn't see me and responded to my voice as familiar; but at home, seeing me again, she acted as if I were a kidnapper, protesting, refusing food, crawling under her cot to get away from me, and eventually crying herself to sleep. Fortunately in the morning somehow I was familiar again, and it was only me who was scarred by the incident. It struck me as very unfair, given that her childminder changed her appearance far more frequently.)

A preference for the parent via such discriminations is likely to convince parents that they are 'special' to their baby. Infants' vocalisations and movements, which do to some extent reveal what they are feeling, are interpreted by adults as quasi-intentional expressions of feeling – they receive social interpretations from caregivers and adults who treat the infant increasingly as an individual who is intending to communicate, as a social being with needs and wishes and intentions that are not unlike their own; and the infant rapidly develops its own social cognition (Johnson, Grossmann and Farroni 2008), attachment relations (Diamond and Fagundes 2008, pp. 121–27), and emotion regulation (pp. 54–59, 128–29).

3.1.4 Parental investment in parenting

The supporters of versions of evolutionary theory that emphasise eliminating any sentimentality from their model suggest that there may be what are effectively cost-benefit analyses of whether parental investment in a particular child is worth it (Mace 2008; Martin 2007). They look for evidence that individuals who are less evolutionarily 'fit' or who are less crucial to their parents' chances of leaving descendants will receive less parental investment. Thus in ancient civilisations children who were handicapped might be exposed at birth, as were illegitimate children in Georgian London as their mothers' chance of a future marriage would be greatly reduced if future partners knew they had already been seduced and become a mother (e.g. de Mause 1976). To this day, children who are handicapped, and step-children, seem to be more at risk of being neglected or abused (e.g. Hershkowitz, Lamb and Horowitz 2007; Jaudes and Mackey-Bilaver 2008; Nordlund and Temrin 2007). The theorists also find evidence that there is often disagreement between parents and children about whether the child still needs parental investment, with parents tending to switch their support from children who could be expected to fend for themselves to younger, less independent, children at a time when the older child would prefer still to draw on parental resources. This is likely to be the fate of everyone except the youngest child, who does not face competition with less mature siblings for parental investment, and may continue to be 'babied' for longer (p. 167).

Differential investment in boys rather than girls sometimes also receives an evolutionary explanation; parents cannot be quite so certain that their son's wife's child is their own grandchild as that their daughter's child is their grandchild (my own mother said that my baby, her sixth grandchild, was 'more exciting' than my brothers' children – although this may have been because it was the first time she had expected an opportunity to be there at the birth). As most psychologists live in societies that are patri-lineal, that is family lineage is reckoned primarily through the male and males may have a higher social staus than females, there has been a focus of discussion on the implications for society of fathers never being quite so certain as mothers can be that they are the biological parent of 'their' child. Basically, much theorising and social practice have been concerned with ways in which males can be more certain of their related-ness to the baby – controlling the female's sexuality by restriction or reward becomes the central issue. But there is another way in which males can be certain about their relationship to a baby; if they and the baby's mother have the same mother, then the male will know for sure that he is related to the baby. This is one of the benefits of matrilineal social organisations (Dunbar 2008; Montgomery 2009; Opie and Power 2008), and it is a pity that uncle–child relationships have not been studied more.

Mace (2008) points out that achieving reproductive success can involve success in all sorts of other developmental areas, for example competition with peers and competition for status as well as competition for mates. Parental investment may be made in co-operative care, education, network-ing, so that children are advantaged in these areas. This means each child costs the parents more than they would if no parenting effort was made, but the effects of the investment may spread beyond the individual child and result in more social investment in systems that can benefit all children – education and health services, for example. Part of what is happening is increased attention to the needs, and eventually the rights, of the child; this will involve the growth of new professions concerned with providing for children, such as teachers and paediatricians, and the institutions that go with them. Although these have to be paid for, the net result seems, his-torically and anthropologically, to be more prosperous societies. (There will be an increase also in the production and consumption of goods for children, who will be equipped with more specialised toys and games, rather than being left to invent their own. The microsystem of parental investment in the child has consequences for the macrosystem of economic activities in production and marketing, which themselves have consequences for the microsystem in what the 'good' parent is expected to provide.)

3.2 How parental investment functions for children

My next question is what forms of parental investment are needed. Again, these can be seen as biological and as cultural. Comparisons between parenting in different species and between different human parents take up a lot of the literature. More extensive or more careful observation has shown richer parenting in non-humans than would have been supposed a few decades ago (as in the tropical frogs I just mentioned, who carefully parent their offspring), and the frames and platforms I am going to discuss are thought to have a biological foundation – but it is an interesting question which of them may be exclusive to humans, and which appear in other species.

3.2.1 Platforms for development

Bugental and Grusec (2006) describe 'biological platforms' for development. The first is the child's *need for protective care* – for safety, nourishment, and comforting. The infant uses evolved behaviours and features such as an expressive face, cries that vary (somewhat) according to the child's needs, patterned activity that the parent can fit in with, etc., to signal its care needs. The parents provide what they can to satisfy their infant. As the child develops language skills and social skills, communications about need become more complex and more acculturated on both sides. The long-term consequences of receiving good protective care are thought to include the fine-tuning of stress/emotion regulation (pp. 54–59, 128–29), positive working models (pp. 124–25), and attachment (pp. 121–27).

Another biological platform is *coalition* – the acquisition and sharing of resources, the development of mutual defence, the development of group identification and in-group behaviours, mutual defence against threat and out-groups. Children learn where they 'belong', who is an ally and who a stranger or potential enemy, and how 'people like us' behave, and move from early favouring of the 'in-group' to later hostility to the 'out-group', generally picking up their parents' prejudices (e.g. Sinclair, Dunn and Lowery 2005). People are categorised by age, gender, and so forth as well as by learned markers of group identification. Socialisation about how to be a member of a group also implies fear of exclusion from the group, a situation which would be seriously damaging to chances of surviving and reproducing. Biological systems such as mirror neurones and imitation (pp. 112–15, 171, 214, 226–31) may form a basis for being able to achieve and maintain coalitions; teaching from parents and others, and everyday observation of them, will also be enormously important.

A third 'biological platform', *hierarchy*, is also social. Individuals have to deal with the hierarchy of their social group, and in many groups each individual has a place that they must keep to if the group is to accept or protect them. Knowing about social status is a condition of safety – thus low status individuals will employ wariness, submission, and 'don't hurt me' signals, and will react differentially to others depending on how much of a threat they may be. Infants show great sensitivity to sounds produced by others, for example, with males' voices more likely than females to be heard as threatening (Bugental and Grusec 2006); vocal signals from adults inhibit children's exuberance and exploration. In social interaction with others, young individuals prepare for dominance, competition, and their place in the group hierarchy – which in many species is dependent on the status of their parents. Dominance and kinship largely explained what animals had the opportunity to eat a fish discovered by a group of macaques (Leca *et al.* 2007), for example. Females' social bonds are strongest to mothers, sisters and other females of similar age and status (e.g. Cheney and Seyfarth 1996; Silk *et al.* 2006). In some primate groups, individuals of higher status can go so far as to take away the infant of a low-status mother to play with it themselves. Individuals of low social status tend to have cortisol levels suggesting they are feeling more stress (e.g. Onyangoa *et al.* 2008; pp. 60, 79, 112).

The last biological platform listed by Bugental and Grusec is also social. It is *mutuality* – sharing, reciprocity, intimacy, friendship, collaboration, group identification. The basis is joint attention, imitation, cheat detection, theory of mind, – all skills which would foster group cohesion and have, it is argued, evolved because of this (e.g. Bjorklund and Pellegrini 2000, 2002; Fenstermacher and Saudino 2006; Tomasello *et al.* 2005; Tomasello and Carpenter 2007; Tomasello, Carpenter and Liskowski 2007). These researchers suggest that earlier mother–infant mutuality facilitates later peer mutuality. Co-regulation with parents and friends leads to increased affiliative behaviour and positive emotion mechanisms. The ability to develop and maintain close interpersonal relationships is an important component of the growth of self-definition and autonomy (pp. 177–80, 180–82, 263).

3.2.1.1 Imitation

If we add another 'biological platform', *imitation* would probably be a good candidate. Human beings, and particularly young ones, are often seen to copy other people's behaviour. Theorists from a whole range of traditions have described imitative behaviour as a key part of children's social lives, contributing enormously to their development (e.g. Piaget 1962; Case 1985; McEwen *et al.* 2007; Fenstermacher and Saudino 2006; Hurley *et al.* 2008). Imitation comes in many forms (and has infinite variety of content), but essentially it involves observing the behaviour of another and then copying it, specifically and possibly deliberately. It goes beyond observing what the other is doing and what the other's goal is, and then yourself doing something which works towards the same goal but not in the same way ('goal emulation'); and it is not a near automatic response to the other's action, such as contagious yawning or sneezing ('movement priming'). It involves copying both goals and means to achieve goals, it can involve a sense of the intentions of the person who is being imitated, and it can even involve a form of identification with the person. It will often involve joint attention, with the original actor and the imitator focusing on the same thing.

Young children, even as babies, tend to do a lot of imitation (Fenstermacher and Saudino 2006; Gergely, Bekkering, and Király 2002; Meltzoff 1988, 1995; Tomasello, Kruger and Ratner 1993; Tomasello et al. 2005). Within the first month of life they have been said to imitate facial gestures. They engage in games with parents that involve taking turns in imitation. They observe actions that achieve desirable outcomes and do the same. They have been seen to imitate actions exactly, even when the actions are obviously inefficient and could easily be modified to work better, in contrast with chimpanzees who observe the action and the goal and change the original action to reach the goal more effectively (Nagell, Olguin and Tomasello 1993). This suggests that the children's imitation is a combination of a biologically programmed set of imitative skills and a social or cultural engagement in doing exactly the same as one's model, as you would in many parent–infant games.

It is worth noting that it can be very difficult not to imitate a social partner, even when imitation is not necessary or particularly appropriate socially; we may have to inhibit ourselves from speaking with a shade of a Welsh accent when we are talking in English to a Welsh speaker, for example, or we take up a similar posture to the person we are talking with. Mirroring posture, in particular, seems to be part of establishing the empathy that fosters good relationships (Iacoboni 2009).

Recent developments in discovering details of brain functioning have discovered that primate brains may be set up in a way that supports imitation. Mirror neurones directly link perception and action; they fire when you do an action yourself and when you perceive someone else doing it (Gallese and Goldman 1998; Gallese, Keysers, and Rizzolatti 2004; Iacoboni 2009). Some of these 'mirror neurones' are activated in the same way when the action seen and the action performed are exactly the same; others – and probably a larger number of them – also fire when the observed and acted actions are not identical but share the same goal or are logically related, which suggests that there is some cognition going on beyond the passive level of 'monkey see, monkey do'. Similarly, mirror neurones may fire if an action that is expected can be inferred to occur, even though it is not actually seen, for example when a hand moves towards a graspable object but a screen hides the actual contact of hand on object. They also seem to react to sounds associated with actions, even when the action itself is not seen (Iacoboni 2009).

Mirror neurones are likely to be highly involved in social action and in imitation in particular (Hamilton, Wolpert and Frith 2004). Possibly their firing when an action is observed links it to the action as it has been, or could be, performed by the observer. Observed movements are compared with the sensory results associated with one's own movements, which could be a foundation for imitating what has been observed. Although this comparison could not of itself provide information about how the observed actions achieve the desired goal, it could be the first step towards carrying out the actions and hence successfully achieving the goal, and an important step also in constructing a flexible coding of one's own and others' actions. It is not hard to see that there could be cognitive benefits (for example in language acquisition and theory of mind) as well as the social ones that I am concerned with now. It is probably worth noting that it seems to be possible that there is a smaller number of functioning mirror neurones in the brains of individuals with autism, and a positive correlation between empathy scores and mirror neurone activity in normal children (Iacoboni 2009).

A tendency to learn from others' behaviour could be a very cost-effective contributor to development, and consequently we might have evolved brain structures which make it easier. Our ancestors had behavioural traits that made it easier for them to survive and reproduce successfully. If these are not genetically heritable, they would have to be reinvented in each generation, except when the offspring have inherited an ability to imitate. Offspring who copy the behaviours that have enhanced their ancestors' reproductive success may increase their fitness, if the environment they have to adapt to is much the same as their ancestors' was. This learning might be a cheap, quick and highly effective way to adapt – especially in a species which has a lot of highly complex stuff to learn.

> Gifted or lucky individuals may discover efficient new means to goals – means that are not readily rediscoverable by independent trial-and-error learning. These would be lost without recombinant imitative learning, which preserves and disseminates valuable instrumental innovations, providing a platform for further innovation. Once imitation evolves genetically, it provides a mechanism of cultural and technological transmission, accumulation, and evolution. The effects of imitative copying and selection intertwine with those of genetic copying and selection; culture and life coevolve.
>
> (Hurley *et al.* 2008: section 2.3.2)

We need to note here that this would be an example of evolutionary selection for something that gives an advantage via social co-operation, rather than through the 'red in tooth and claw' competition between individuals that has been seen as characteristic of evolution via natural selection. Mirror neurones may be an important physical component of a set of abilities that become intimately interwoven with social functioning and social success.

Cultures then would probably develop ways of facilitating imitation of desirable traits and behaviours, for example child–child and parent–child games, social pressure to conform, and formal educational settings (Fenstermacher and Saudino 2006; Mejía-Arauz *et al.* 2007; McEwen *et al.* 2007). But I should note here that it may be sensible to learn from observation *without* imitation. Someone who observes and then imitates selectively could let others take the risk; they may not be the first to get the desired reward but they would avoid setting out on a course of actions with negative consequences. By imitating, individuals may gain access to a high-status social group or goal that they do not themselves deserve to enter. Innovators will have developed ways of stopping good imitators from reaping all the benefits of innovation without incurring any of the costs – using social institutions such as patents, for example, or concealing the details of their actions, or moving on to something new making the behaviour that has been imitated 'so last year' and less desirable, or developing better and better mind reading techniques so that the group can identify those who share the underlying mental causes of the key behaviour not just the ability to produce it imitatively. Here we get into issues of attribution, empathy, and theory of mind that are major components of social development (Carpendale and Lewis 2006, pp. 128–29, 164–66).

3.2.2 Parenting as 'framing' children's activity

Kaye (1984) used a wider conceptualisation of 'functional frames', 'social' as well as 'biological' and explicitly 'cognitive' as well as 'emotional', that parents provide for their children's development, organising for them the world of objects, people and events in ways that reduce potential chaos to intelligible order. Parents *nurture* their children, meeting their needs for nourishment and comfort, both physical and emotional, and in so doing allow and enhance communication and mutual understanding (intersubjectivity or mutuality). They feed them, clean them, keep them warm, cuddle them, reassure them, keep them healthy. They *protect* children from harm, ideally while still allowing them to do things that are not yet quite within their competence – letting the toddler walk along a low wall while walking near by ready to help if her balance falters. They *help* or act as instruments, either doing for children things they cannot yet do themselves or modifying the wished-for activities or objects so that the child can achieve them – cutting up food, providing a safe step up to the washbasin so that the child can clean his teeth. They *provide feedback* on the child's actions so that consequences can be more consistent or more salient or less dangerous than without the parent's action – 'Darling, don't tease the cat, it will scratch you', 'The cat scratched you because she doesn't like being teased'. They *model,* and provide demonstrations of, skills and actions (not always intentionally – I once overheard my small daughter telling off her dolls in a horribly familiar voice – a far too exact imitation of my own). They support and encourage *discourse,* which is a means of sharing and enhancing understanding (and can be seen to be an effective basis for theory of mind and social cognition (pp. 128–29, 164–66, e.g. Carpendale and Lewis 2006; Dunn 1988, 2004; Meadows 2006; Ensor and Hughes 2008). They act as a *memory* for the child (family myths, Bauer 2007; Reese, Hayne and Macdonald 2008) and this helps in the formation of representations and scripts, in the organisation of knowledge and in the fulfilment of plans.

There are, I think, other important frames besides Kaye's. My own additions (Meadows 1986) were that parents *modulate* the child's arousal and that they *invite* participation in culture. Arousal modulation, or regulation, has recently developed into a very interesting topic, with close links to both basic physiology and explanations of lifelong well-being or delinquency, and I have given it a section to itself and some mention in the context of the developmental areas it affects (Bradley and Corwyn 2005, pp. 51–64, 120–21, 127–29). Participation in culture (pp. 82–84, 133–34, 210–12, 233–35, 243–52, 254–56) also crops up elsewhere: cultural participation is still theorised mainly at macrosystem levels, though links to more proximal processes will be involved.

To do all this requires a great deal of adult sensitivity to what the child is feeling and doing, and a great deal of patience, as many, many repetitions of various frames will be required for all the child has to learn. I must also emphasise three things. First, it cannot be a one-way or an unchanging process (Parke and Buriel 2006; Kuczynski and Parkin 2007). Parents do things for children, but children may have elicited the parental behaviour and will respond to it, and both partners build up a history of how to interact and what it means – their roles and functions are interdependent. In their partnership, both sides are causes of each other's behaviour. Their power levels may be asymmetrical, but it is by no means the case that parents have all the power and the child none. Second, every parent–child relationship will change over time (as Bronfenbrenner pointed out). Partly this is because any relationship will change as it develops a history (Hinde 1979), but largely it is because of the child's developmental change. Part of what parents have to do is adjust their parenting to the child's changing skill and the child's changing world, accommodating to these and anticipating them and maybe working towards expected goals. Part of what children have to do is help parents realise what adjustments and accommodations are needed, which parenting habits they have to give up: that if your twenty-year-old undergraduate daughter is setting out for an evening on the town with friends it may not be appropriate for you to say 'You're not going to be warm enough, go and put thicker clothes on'. Third a point I will not elaborate on here; there are likely to be cultural and historical changes in how these 'frames' are emphasised and implemented, as well as individual differences (Bradley and Corwyn 2005; Patterson and Hastings 2007; Shanahan 2000). I would also say that it may be helpful to link the concept of 'frames' to that of 'scaffolding' (Meadows 2006; Turner and Berkowitz 2005).

I find the 'frames' model an especially useful one for considering what is 'good' parenting, and it will be the basis underlying much of this section of this book. In Bronfenbrenner's terms, 'proximal processes' are involved here, recurrent ways of parents behaving towards the child, recurrent occasions where the child elicits or responds to some form of parenting behaviour, and this is the level of analysis I prefer to emphasise. However, the dominant models of individual differences in parenting and of the effects of parenting on child development have been rather different, so I will describe them briefly before reverting to the 'frame' framework. We will look at some concrete examples of proximal processes where there is evidence associating the process with an outcome shortly, after I have briefly dealt with descriptions of differences in parenting in terms of general typologies and styles.

3.2.3 Typologies of parenting

Styles of parenting are sometimes seen as coalescing into types. Although there have been various typologies of parenting, the best known is probably that proposed by Baumrind (1971, 1980). Like earlier theorists, she focused on a combination of warmth and control in parenting. She distinguished three main types: authoritarian, permissive, and authoritative. Authoritarian parenting is rigid, very controlling and coercive, and very demanding about the child's 'good' behaviour; it is also low on warmth and responsiveness. Permissive parenting is the opposite – there are very few restrictions on the child and few demands for mature and responsible behaviour, but there may be great warmth. Authoritative parents combine high demand for maturity and high warmth and responsiveness, and although firm will explain and negotiate far more than either of the other types.

This typology rose from observations of a comparatively small sample of families, but a number of authors reviewing the work done subsequently (e.g. Parke and Buriel 2006; Rothbaum and Trommsdorff 2007) agree that, at least in studies of middle-class European–American samples, the children of authoritative parents are more likely to have positive relationships with their parents, peers and teachers than children whose parenting was authoritarian or permissive, and are more likely to become well-functioning autonomous adolescents. It is not quite so clear that authoritative parenting is advantageous in more traditional or collective social groups, such as Chinese, Arab, Asian, or Hispanic American families (Chao 1994; Cheung and McBride-Chang 2008; Dwairy et al. 2006; Farver et al. 2007; Ho,

Bluestein and Jenkins 2008; Markus and Kitayama 1991; Ng, Pomerantz and Lam 2007; Rothbaum and Trommsdorff 2007; Tamis-LeMonda *et al.* 2008; Zhou *et al.* 2008), or in families living in threatening environments, where it may be that authoritarian parenting protects the child better (Parke and Buriel 2006). However, it is very probable that families where adults and children do not engage positively with each other, where they are hostile, where one or other side has given up attempting to communicate, may not be likely to produce well-functioning individuals.

3.2.4 Descriptions of individual differences in dimensions of parenting

As I've already said, there are several different levels of analysis of parenting that could be used in studies of the 'effects' of parenting on children's development. The most fine-grained specific 'molecular' level looks at detailed behaviours – how much do you talk to your child about other people's feelings, for example, or how much do you talk to them while doing the housework. I will be presenting some examples of studies using these sorts of variables later. However, studies of the molecules of parenting can be ambiguous because families who do a lot of one 'good' sort of parenting often do a lot of another 'good' sort of parenting. Or two 'different' molecules may operate in very similar ways and be indistinguishable on their effects. Only very large samples and sophisticated statistical modelling can make much progress towards attributing the 'effect' of parenting practices appropriately, and these tend to be expensive and therefore rare. They also often feel distant from everyday experience. A substantial number of researchers have focused on 'dimensions' of parenting, where a number of different practices contribute interchangeably to a dimension or 'style'. 'Style' picks up a general quality of parent–child interaction and is argued to moderate the effects of parenting practices on the child and the child's openness to parental influence (Parke and Buriel 2006). 'Warmth' and type of control are key examples of such dimensions.

3.2.4.1 Warmth

'Warmth' is quite easily recognised and far harder to define. Certainly it is not a simple trait or a limited set of behaviours. Typically definitions include parent commitment to the child, responsiveness to the child's signals, actions and needs, willingness to engage with the child in joint activity, particularly activity arising from the child's interests, enthusiasm about the child's achievements and virtues, and sympathy and helpfulness about the child's difficulties and failures, and sensitivity to the child's emotional state. Each of these behaviours would doubtless contribute to a harmonious relationship between parent and child, and such a relationship is likely to involve joint attention, mutual empathy, shared interests, and a low level of conflict. The warmth might be a good thing in itself, or might have an indirect effect through these consequences.

Nobody could provide this sort of parenting all the time, so 'warmth' is relative rather than absolute. It is also likely to be in part a result of the child's characteristics and behaviour – it may be harder to interact in a 'warm' way with a child who is not at all responsive to parental behaviour, as in autism, for example. (Kanner, who first discussed autism as a defined syndrome (Frith 2003, Frith and Hill 2004), talked of 'refrigerator mothers' who had caused the autism by their coldness, a view of its causation that is now seen to mistake cause and effect.) Parents who are relatively high on 'warmth' tend to have children who are relatively high on many prosocial behaviours – securely attached (pp. 122–25), altruistic (pp. 100–02), high in self-esteem (pp. 79–80), compliant with reasonable demands (pp. 236–38, 243–50), conscientious (pp. 100–02) etc. – while if warmth is notably lacking in the parent–child relationship then there is a higher risk that the children will show negative characteristics and a wide range of difficulties (Parke and Buriel 2006; Laible and Thompson 2007; Maccoby and Martin 1983). As a human being, I would not hesitate to believe that children do better in a relationship full of warmth, and that a very cold relationship will not be a comfortable or developmentally productive one; but as a scientist I think there are a lot of questions – about a detailed understanding of 'warmth', for example what sort of warmth, how much is enough, when is it experienced; about the direction of cause and effect between the participants in the relationship; about changes over time; about the place of this warm relationship within other relationships; about the interaction of warmth with other characteristics.

3.2.4.2 Control

Like warmth, 'control' is a prominent dimension of parenting composed of a whole range of behaviours. There is no doubt that children often need to be controlled by their parents; sometimes their own survival may depend on this. The core issues are about how this control is attempted, achieved, and understood, and what balance is achieved between compliance, co-operation, and autonomy. Here too there is a clear take-home message for concerned human beings, but a lot of questions once you start to analyse exactly what is going on. There are major cultural, historical, individual, and situational variations in what is thought to be appropriate here (e.g. Kärtner 2007; Shanahan 2000). However, the literature derived from middle-class European–American samples suggests that, at least in these sorts of families, control practices that include explanation, warmth, responsiveness, and negotiation function better short term and long term than control practices that are intrusive, coercive, negative, or physical (Parke and Buriel 2006;

Laible and Thompson 2007; Patterson *et al.* 1989; Patterson and Sanson 1999; Patterson and Fisher 2002). I will look at some specific control and discipline techniques later, and the sections on antisocial behaviour and delinquency will also address issues of control (pp. 233–34, 264–70, 278–79).

3.2.4.3 Mutually responsive orientation

'Warmth' and 'control' are not, of course, the only dimensions of parenting that could be looked at. An alternative focus developed by Kochanska and her colleagues (Kochanska 2002; Kochanska and Aksan 1995; Kochanska *et al.* 1996, 2005; Kochanska and Murray 2000; Kochanska, Murray and Coy 1997), and related to Tomasello's work on joint attention (Tomasello *et al.* 2005; Tomasello and Carpenter 2007), explicitly recognises the bi-directionality between parental behaviour and child behaviour. They argue that a good relationship between parents and children involves a system of reciprocity and mutual obligation. Children who experience positive responsiveness in their interaction with a parent or caregiver are motivated to respond constructively to their parents' behaviour rather than to be obstructive, to wish to maintain a harmonious relationship with their parent, and to sign up to parents' values (parents may well reciprocate on at least the first two of these). There is a history of responsive positive interaction between the different partners in the relationship that makes the child relatively eager to get on with what the parent wants, and the parent relatively eager to continue a high level of sensitive interaction with the child – both sides have invested heavily in the relationship. Compliance, sensitivity, joint action, communality, empathy, identification as to interests – the possible benefits are enormous.

It appears to be a good thing if parent and child can maintain a 'mutually responsive orientation' (MRO) during interaction. Studies in early child-hood have shown that this is associated with the child enjoying interactions with the mother more, and with the child showing more self-regulated, 'committed' compliance with the mother. In dyads where early MRO was high, mothers used less power-assertive discipline, as if they felt they did not need to resort to forceful discipline to accomplish their disciplinary goals. This seemed to have a positive impact not just on the child's behaviour at the time but also on longer-term moral development (Kochanska *et al.* 1996; Kochanska 2002; Kochanska and Murray 2000; pp. 100–05). 'Power assertion results in the child's shallow processing of the parental message external attributions for compliance, perception of a "threat to autonomy", and resentment and anger toward the parent. Consequently, it leads to a rejection of the parent's values' (Kochanska *et al.* 2008).

In a recent study (Kochanska *et al.* 2008) there was strong evidence from longitudinal data that children who had experienced a high degree of a mutual responsivity relationship (MRO) with their mothers during infancy and toddlerhood had accepted and internalised maternal prohibitions, and showed overall strong self-regulatory capacities, by the time they were four. The mothers who had a positive MRO with their little children tended to rely less on power assertion. The lower rate of power assertion in discipline situations had, in turn, a significant beneficial effect on the children's internalisation and self-regulation. One important thing about this finding was that the families in this study were a relatively low-risk group, and the mothers' levels of power assertion were quite low. The study report suggests that the negative effects of power assertion might be even more marked when there is more of it, as tends to be the case in families which are high risk or stressed or chaotic, and where children do sometimes turn out to have difficulty with internalised self-regulation and with power relationships. An extension of the study's methods into such families would be of interest. So would more examination of other family relationships. Children's self-regulation at age four was also associated with the degree to which they had a mutually responsive relationship with their fathers during the first two years, but the fathers' use of power-assertive discipline did not seem to be involved in the causal sequence in the same way as mothers'. Lamb and Lewis (2004) present a similar argument.

3.3 Attachment

As I mentioned earlier, one of the most important, influential and powerful developmental theories stems from John Bowlby's work on 'attachment'. Bowlby was influenced by a wide range of factors in developing his theory – his own personal history, his observation of deeply troubled children in a school where he taught, his training in and use of psychoanalysis, his interest in animal behaviour, among them (Hinde 2005; Stevenson-Hinde 2005). The key insight is, perhaps, that babies and young children have a strong need for protection, nurturance, care and comforting, with both biological and social bases and consequences. Babies are, normally, born with instinctive behaviours that elicit reward and use nurturing behaviour from their caregivers. The way they look is appealing, they seek to be physically and emotionally close to their caregiver, they increasingly show more positive feelings when the caregiver is near and attending to them. When the caregiver is near, they are visibly calmer and happier; the absence of the caregiver reduces their joy and their playfulness. When they are in distress, they signal a need for the proximity and support of the caregiver, and that proximity and support can help them reduce and control their distress. Being able to do this successfully has both long-term and short-term benefits, and is part of the evolutionary package of social adjustments and possibilities. And the package is all very powerful in maintaining everyday activity, often more powerful than the need for food and warmth and the desire for exploration and mastery that babies also show.

So attachment theory asserts that there is an evolutionary basis to attachment. Because it preserved the safety and well-being of generations of ancestors, babies are born with a capacity to relate to significant others, to seek to be close to them, to rely on them for the fulfilment of their needs for nurture, protection, and relief from distress, to feel happier and more confident when they are within reach. Behaviours such as smiling, watching, seeking to hold the gaze of the other, crying, following, clinging to, snuggling up to, and using as a base and reference point are all biologically programmed to develop and maintain attachment relationships. This is an area of functioning, and of theory, where there is a lively interaction between the biological, the psychological, and the social levels. As Sable (2004) points out, it is considered to be biologically adaptive to form lasting affectional ties, to seek proximity and contact with these figures at times of stress and danger, and to feel increased comfort and security in their presence with benefits also for the psychological well-being of the individuals concerned, and for the functioning of the social group.

3.3.1 Types of attachment relationship

Researchers and clinicians identify a child's attachment on the basis of careful consideration of patterns of behaviour between child and parent or other caregiver (Cummings *et al.* 2000; Goldberg 2000; O'Connor and Byrne 2007). The exact behaviours considered and the setting in which they are looked at depends on the age and abilities of the child – careful observation is supplemented by story-telling and interview as childrens' verbal skills develop. Most babies and young children show an interpretable system of behaviours related to their attachment figure when experiencing a mildly stressful situation, allowing a diagnosis of the security of their attachment. The 'Strange Situation' (Ainsworth *et al.* 1978) is a commonly-used setting for assessing attachment in infants, allowing the observer to see how the child behaves in reaction to the presence, absence and return of the parent and in an unfamiliar environment. Infants who have a 'secure' attachment to their parent or caregiver typically play happily in the unfamiliar room for as long as the parent is present, but this play diminishes when the parent leaves, and the child will probably show signs of distress. When the parent returns, the baby readily makes emotional contact again, seeking contact or proximity or greeting the parent enthusiastically, quickly and smoothly recovers from any distress shown before the parent's return, and returns to play. Typically, securely attached babies have experienced relatively high levels of warmth and responsivity from their attachment figures. Their 'significant others' have expressed emotional warmth towards them, have picked up their signals and responded sensitively, have accepted the baby's initiative even when they were working towards changing what the baby was doing or feeling, and have been co-operative rather than intrusive during play. The baby as a result shows pleasure in the other's presence and is reassured by their return after absence.

Not all babies show this positive, confident pattern. 'Avoidant' babies act as if they feel they cannot rely on the attachment figure. They are not responsive to parental attempts to interact with them, and may even turn away to avoid them. They seem to deliberately divert their attention from anything that would evoke attachment behaviour, and to avoid relying on the attachment figure. If they are distressed by the 'strange situation' they cannot use the parent to recover from their distress; their behaviour is irritable and rejecting. They seem not to be comfortable in turning to the parent when they are under stress, as if they are not confident that the parent will be a reliable source of warmth and comfort. Their interaction with their 'significant others' has been tense, with the adults being rejecting or avoidant or intrusive and overstimulating. The baby's attachment behaviour is 'de-activated' (Bowlby 1977) because it has not been a useful resource.

'Anxious' or 'resistant' babies also act as if the attachment figure is not a source of security, but their behaviour suggests that they are extremely dependent, clingy, demanding, and angry. They are not reassured by parental attention and comforting behaviour, and have great difficulty reducing their distress, so that it is hard for them to regain an emotional equilibrium. They may make excessive demands on the attachment figure and have great difficulty in separating from the attachment figure to play autonomously. Their attachment figures may have been inept or inconsistent rather than rejecting; hard to reach and insensitive rather than too much in opposition to the baby's needs. It is as if the baby's attachment system has become overactivated because at normal levels of activation it has not provided them with a feeling of being reliably supported.

'Disorganised' or 'disoriented' babies have not settled into a consistent attachment strategy. They do not behave coherently, with signs of both avoiding the parent and resisting the parent, as if they had confused expectations or were depressed or afraid. They cling and avoid and resist incoherently, as if they were both confused and fearful, angry and anxious, frightened and unresponsive. Their attachment figure has perhaps maltreated them or suffered from mental illness – really serious depression, for example, can be associated with disorganised attachment in the baby.

3.3.2 Longer-term implications of attachment

Most attachment theorists see the patterning of behaviour between the baby and its caregiver over the first year of life as the key to the baby's attachment both at the time and as it develops through other relationships. A central issue in attachment research concerns how security and patterns of attachment develop and change across time.

Secure attachments are facilitated by responsive, warm, interactions between baby and caregiver, by an emotional environment that is positive in quality. If the caregiver is reliably sensitive to the baby's needs, reliably anticipates what they will be, reliably provides for them, and reliably shows pleasure in the interaction between the baby and the carer, a strong positive attachment is likely to develop between them such that each will feel and show pleasure in each other's company, confidence that the partner is available and supportive and nice to be with, and an ability to cope when stressful circumstances arise. Part of what is crucial here is 'ease of emotional communication', over negative as well as positive feelings (Stevenson-Hinde 2005; Oppenheim *et al.* 2007). In a healthy relationship based on a secure attachment, the partners can express both positive and negative emotions safely, and do not have to censor or distort their emotions lest they put the relationship at risk.

A key part of this is learning how to regulate emotions and stop arousal leading to loss of control (pp. 53, 150, 274–87). Babies have little ability to control their arousal, and caregivers need to look after them in ways that reduce distress and eventually provide the baby with ways to self-comfort. The experiences involved in developing a secure attachment can increase resilience and modulate arousal systems in positive ways, which may be embedded in brain functioning as well as visible in behaviour. The knowledge that one has reliable ways of reducing distress endures throughout subsequent experience. Although of course later experience can modify this certainty, so that enough misfortune may reduce even the person with a history of secure attachment to anger or despair, such a person will typically show more resilience (pp. 209, 283–85) than someone whose early attachment experiences were less than good.

Earlier theorists had of course emphasised the importance of the mother–child relationship for the healthy development of the child. At the time when Bowlby was developing his ideas, this concentration on the mother took some very harsh forms and focused, in any case, on feeding – hence ideas about the infant's 'oral fixation' and 'fixation on the breast' were very current (Stevenson-Hinde 2005). Following Bowlby, the emphasis has shifted very much more to what happens to promote, or to fail to promote, the child's eventual ability to regulate emotion. The optimal caregiver is reliably available and efficacious in helping the child both to avoid extreme distress and to maximise opportunities for positive engagement. With a good responsive caregiver, a frightened child is reassured, soothed and comforted. A child who wants to play is engaged with interesting objects or joint activity, or the caregiver simply acts as a base for the child's independent exploration and activity. Especially, the pattern of interaction gives the child repeated opportunities to cope with negative emotions in ways that restore a positive emotional state. The result is confidence that one's own feelings are both legitimate and manageable, that negative emotions can be dealt with, that significant others can be relied on for support, that emotional closeness to another is positive. Someone who has this sort of sense of self and others is likely to be optimistic when suffering the hassles of everyday life, to persevere under difficult circumstances, to see other people as available and responsive when needed and to believe that they themselves deserve and will receive others' care and support.

For babies and very little children, this attachment is based on feelings, the pattern of interaction, facial expressions, tone of voice, touch, warmth, and so forth. As children develop language and reflect on themselves, cognitive and narrative levels of attachment come into play, but do not displace the non-verbal constituents. Even as adults, we may find it hard to like the colleague who does not smile at us, does not make eye contact, ignores our actions, speaks in a harsh tone; and a working model of such a person as disagreeable and untrustworthy can be hard to change. Similarly although we may cope better with separations from our attachment figure once we understand the reasons for the separation and that their absence is temporary and does not have to be interpreted as a final and irrevocable rejection, such experiences still put us at risk of distress, anxiety, anger, and depression.

A secure attachment developed in infancy and early childhood, then, is seen as a foundation for positive functioning on all fronts thereafter. Obviously, the 'working model' becomes more complex as the child's cognition and language skills become greater, as memory lasts longer, and as wider social worlds open up. Among the signs of greater complexity are: better toleration of separation from the attachment figure; a longer time frame for events; a more varied range of ways of coping with distress and modulating arousal. These continue to contribute to the working model, and as can be seen in Mary Main's work on adult attachment patterns, even people who report problematic early attachments can, in the long term, come to accept them and move beyond them, often with a considerable degree of success (Main et al. 1985, 2005). Relationships with significant others later in life, including therapists, can be a promising route towards redefining and repairing unhelpful working models, and may involve attachments. If such relationships evoke positive emotions, they can give the person new ways of seeing themselves and other people, better ways of managing feelings and relating to others, and a less conflicted sense of one's life story, a new kind of attachment which enhances well-being and the capacity to experience pleasure and positive affect. Even in the shorter term, improvements in parental behaviour can have positive effects on the attachment behaviour that children show (Forbes et al. 2007).

But individuals with a more negative attachment history, who have suffered abuse or neglect or coldness from their caregivers, are likely as a result to have a working model of relationships and of themselves that is not reassuring and which does not reduce their negative emotions. Attachment theorists see insecure attachments as a cause of many psychopathologies, for example anxiety, depression, anger, and inability to relate to other people. Such negative feelings as these can be traced back to earlier reactions to unsatisfying or disrupted attachments, now redirected towards other targets, and perhaps amplified by the history of disappointment at insecure attachment relationships.

3.3.3 Attachment and developmental systems

Bowlby himself pointed out that the attachment between a child and a parent 'turns at each and every stage of the journey on an interaction between the organism as it has developed up to that moment and the environment in which it then finds itself' (Bowlby 1973: 412). More recent researchers, e.g. Carlson and Harwood (2003); Rothbaum et al. (2000); Rothbaum and Trommsdorf (2007); Sroufe (2005); Sroufe et al. (2005a,b), point out that we should not assume that the antecedents, meaning and consequences of attachments are the same across all cultures (and indeed all historical periods, although there obviously is less research on this). The parent–child relationship exists within a nervous system, a family, a community, and a culture, and will be profoundly affected by factors at these levels. I want to mention, briefly, two aspects of this, which are discussed more thoroughly elsewhere in this book: firstly working mothers, childcare and the possibility of multiple attachments, and secondly cultural differences in attachment.

Working mothers have been attacked for leaving their children at risk of broken attachment relationships and long-term emotional damage. Rutter (1981) reviewed the issue of whether infants were capable of multiple attachments, and whether they could comfort themselves with the presence of one attachment figure when another was not available, in the context of the hypothesis that separation of the infant from its mother amounted to maternal deprivation and would damage the child severely. He argued, from a substantial evidence base, that normal infants developed attached relationships with several familiar people (and even objects); and that the attachment relationship with mother was not intrinsically different from attachment relationships with fathers, professional caregivers, or other family members, nor was it necessarily the infant's most important attachment relationship. Infants whose mothers left them in a stable caregiving setting need not be very different in their attachments or their emotional well-being from those whose mothers stayed with them without interruption; nor need there be substantial and pervasive longer-term differences. More recent studies of alternative forms of childcare are discussed later (pp. 208–09), and there is still debate; but *clearly* not all infants and young children need to have access to their mother, and her alone, twenty-four hours a day, seven days a week.

Cultural differences in attachment patterns are an interesting possibility, and there is some evidence that they may exist (Rothbaum and Trommsdorff 2007). For example, longitudinal studies carried out in Germany (Grossman, Grossman and Kindler 2005) used the 'strange situation' assessment and found a higher than expected rate of independence from the mother, which under the conventional interpretation would be considered to show an insecure attachment. The German mothers however valued emotional self-sufficiency in their children, and the children had had frequent experiences of brief separation in which they had learned not to be too distressed by their mother's absence. On the other hand, Japanese mothers (Rothbaum *et al.* 2000) valued *amae*, a continuing emotional dependence of the child on the mother; separations between mother and child were much rarer in their culture (the child sleeping in the same bed as the mother would be common, for example), and they approved of a degree of child dependence on the mother that Anglo–American raters would regard as problematic. Japanese children were expected to be very distressed when their mother left them in the 'strange situation' and very clingy when she returned, even at the age of five: and far more Japanese five-year-olds than American five-year-olds did behave like this.

It is important also to recognise that there might be cultural differences in the parental behaviours that underly attachment. In particular, if mother and child are normally in close proximity, even in physical contact, the mothers may have more cues that the child is about to do something or to need something than if they are physically further apart. Thus mothers may have opportunities to anticipate behaviour sensitively as well as responding to it sensitively. Rothbaum and Trommsdorff (2007) and Cole and Tan (2007) note that most of the research on ways of promoting secure attachments has been done in cultures where sensitive mothers engage in a lot of face-to-face synchronised interchanges, games or conversations or emotional soothing. Mothers who carry their infants on their backs will not so often be able to engage in face-to-face interaction; instead, they frequently touch the infant, for example patting them or jiggling a protruding foot or hand. 'Cultural variations may not influence the importance of achieving a sense of security through responsive caregiving, but the evidence does suggest that the behaviours that constitute responsive or sensitive caregiving and infant security may be culturally variable' (Cole and Tan 2007: 523).

3.4 Focus on parent–child interaction

Although I would not argue that dimensions and typologies are too composite to have any useful function at all, I want to spend some time now on more specific parenting practices and their association with child outcomes. I believe that face-to-face interactions over long periods of time offer opportunities to learn, to rehearse and to refine social skills that can be generalised to other partners in other settings. I am now going to discuss some studies of associations between parenting practices and child outcomes, which illustrate both specificities and spill-over in effects. I will include here some reference to intervention studies that have encouraged parents to change their rate of using particular parenting practices.

3.4.1 Parenting practices that help with learning about emotions

Learning to cope with their emotions is emerging as one of the most interesting and important areas of the child's development as a social person. I discuss emotional self-regulation as a physiological issue in (pp. 52–61, 84–87) and emotions as part of children's experience as social persons in (pp. 61–64); here I look at some of the evidence on parenting practices which help with learning about emotions. Such learning involves not just self-regulation, but also reading other people's emotional expressions, attending to the relevant cues as to causes and consequences, learning display rules for expressing one's own (and evaluating others'), and building up cognitive representations of emotions.

Understanding the expression of emotion is an essential component in knowing what the emotion means, working out what may have caused it, choosing an appropriate response. There is a substantial body of evidence that there is an association between skill at encoding people's emotional expression and social competence (see for example the review by Parke and Buriel 2006). Explicit parental discussion of emotions, and in particular of why emotions are or are not shared or acceptable, is common in many families, and there is a substantial body of evidence that this is associated with children's recognition of others' emotions and their response to them (e.g. Brown and Dunn 1996; Cicchetti 2002; Cole, Martin and Dennis 2004; Cutting and Dunn 1999; Dunn 1987, 1988; Dunn, Maguire, and Brown 1995; Light 1979; Meins and Fernyhough 1999; Zahn-Waxler, Radke-Yarrow and King 1979). It seems that some parents, who demonstrate concern and who act to comfort the distressed, explaining what distress has occurred and why it is appropriate to comfort, tend to have children who as toddlers show more understanding of other people's views and feelings and respond more helpfully to someone else's distress.

What is perhaps of particular developmental interest is what range of individual differences arises from differences in parental handling of the child's emotions. There are stable individual differences here (Dunn 1987) that affect the rate of children's development of emotional discourse and understanding, and of theory of mind (Carpendale and Lewis 2006; Meins 2002; Slaughter et al. 2007). Systematic shaping of children's emotional behaviour may be part of the way in which caregivers influence their development; the range and type of comments which caregivers make about emotional states may determine both the child's emotional expression and the sorts of emotional state that can be communicated to others and to oneself (Bretherton 1990; Lewis and Michalson 1983). Interpretations of other people's emotions are also likely to be affected by our own emotional experience. Our 'working model' of people has a strong emotional component.

3.4.1.1 Emotional functioning and child abuse

Thompson (1998) includes some interesting reviews of the development of children under abnormal parenting conditions. More recent work on abused children is suggesting changes in neurotransmitters as a result of their exposure to violence and negative emotion that may persist and colour their cognition for many years (Cicchetti 2002; Sternberg *et al.* 2006). It seems to be important that the parent's gloss on the child's emotion should be relatively accurate – families where members deny or distort each others' emotions are likely to have damaging effects. Family 'emotional expressiveness' turns up in lots of discussions of developmental psychopathology (e.g. Edwards, Shipman and Brown 2005). It appears that children who are subjected, as Miller (1987) describes, to a regime in which they are only allowed to display socially prescribed emotions, even in situations that evoke different ones, and where the displayed emotions are said to be the true ones and the real ones are denied, are likely to grow up with a distorted understanding of emotion, and indeed distorted emotions. Harris (1990) mentions a study of emotionally disturbed children where egocentric and self-serving displays were better understood than prosocial ones. Preschool children who are abused by their parents are more likely to react to another child's distress with hostility or with distress and fear of their own, and less likely to show active concern (Main and George 1985; Cicchetti 2002). This is not because they do not understand that distressing another child or acting aggressively are serious offences, as they distinguish them quite clearly from minor breaches of convention (Smetana, Kelly and Twentyman 1984). It may perhaps be that abused children have learned less well to inhibit their own aggression, or perhaps they become so disturbed by the other person's distress that they are no longer able to act in a comforting way and even act aggressively in order to get rid of the person whose distress is disturbing them; or perhaps, having seen their parents react to their own distress in non-comforting ways, they have learned to act in the same way themselves, though not yet to assert that causing distress is in the victim's good, or that 'it hurts me more than it hurts you'. Miller (1985, 1987, 1990) argues that denial of the truth of one's own emotions and of other people's is one of the components of abusive parenting and one of the main causes of social psychopathology. Possibly as a result of misperception, possibly for other reasons, children who were habitually aggressive made different appraisals of people's intentions towards them from those of more peaceful children (Dodge *et al.* 1986), and maltreated children and control (non-maltreated) children processed aggressive and non-aggressive stimuli differently (Cicchetti 1990).

3.4.2 Parental expression as to valued styles of social interaction

Most cultures, and within them most social institutions right down to family level, have rules about how emotions can be displayed, and what sort of behaviour is and is not socially acceptable. Children have to learn to operate within these display rules if they are not to be at risk of peer rejection and adult disapproval, or even of poor behavioural outcomes (e.g. Dwairy 2008; Ho, Bluestein and Jenkins 2008; Rothbaum and Trommsdorff 2007; Tamis-LeMonda *et al.* 2008; Zhou *et al.* 2008). Compliance may be especially important in cultures that are relatively collectivist and authoritarian, compared with those that are more tolerant of individuality. Inconsistency about what is acceptable may be a source of difficulty for children and young people (and indeed for parents faced with the child's claim that 'all my friends are allowed to stay up late/get tattoos/not eat their vegetables/ shout at their little sisters'). It has often been argued that if the social system goes to the extreme of denying the reality of people's feelings and perceptions this will result in pathological problems for the person whose views are categorically denied and dismissed (Miller 1985; Bateson 1985). Dwairy (2008) argues that inconsistency in parenting is associated with more experience of anxiety, depression and conduct disorder in the adolescent.

Parents express views of what is suitable behaviour explicitly and implicitly and pervasively. There are obvious examples in gender socialisation (pp. 199–201), domestic rules ('eat up all your veg or you won't get any pudding'), moral teaching ('turn the other cheek'), learning social skills ('if you can't say anything nice don't say anything at all'), and learning about social position ('people like us just don't do that sort of thing . . .'). Contravening these rules will attract social disapproval, and may cause you to be expelled from the in-group whose rule you have broken.

3.4.3 Intersubjectivity, shared activities, and joint involvement

Situations where parent and child play together, talk together, or work side by side are fertile fields for using parental frames and for learning all sorts of social (and cognitive) skills. They involve shared attention, a mutually responsive orientation, mutual adjustment, parental provision of feedback, modelling, discourse, shared memory, and opening up of access to particular cultural areas – in different forms and different proportions depending on the age, interests and abilities of the child, for as long in their lives as they wish to co-operate. When my daughter was tiny I sang her nursery rhymes, nowadays we go to the opera together; when she was little I made cakes and she preferred to eat the cake mixture uncooked, nowadays we discuss limiting the quantity of cake we eat and she makes me stir-fries. Part of the point is the communication, the shared enjoyment, the knowledge of each other that flourish in this sort of activity, and that it would be more difficult to achieve if there was none of it. But as always with parenting, there are going to be issues about whether the shared activity and intersubjectivity in themselves bring about benefits, or whether they are mediating between more biological characteristics and outcomes without having effects of their own (Bradley and Corwyn 2005; Feinberg *et al.* 2007).

There are areas where I think the evidence points rather conclusively to a direct effect of parent–child joint activity on the child's development. One big one is language development (for an introduction, see Meadows 2006: 7–30, 380–382). I argued there that children's preference for listening to mothers' speech, mothers' use of child-directed speech with its special adjustments to the child's competence and attention, the 'name game' that parents and children play, the talk accompanying routines, the joint attention, the nursery rhymes, all combine into a language acquisition support system that cumulatively is an excellent model to learn language from. Joint engagement in child-contingent speech serves short-term ends of making the communication or the activity flow effectively, and has long-term results in improving language and enhancing its role as a useful potent and enjoyable part of social interaction. Children who get very little such experience tend to develop language less fluently than those who engage in it often (Wells 1981, Hart and Risley 1995, Heath 1983, 2004) – often with a precise match between the sort of language that the parent uses more or less of and the level to which the child develops that sort of language – more conditionals, more mind-related language, more knowledge about written language and how to read.

There are similar findings for cognitive development in general and in certain specific areas (Meadows 2006: 382–388). Parents playing number games and modelling counting with their preschoolers seemed to produce children with advanced development of simple mathematical skills. Parents who read a lot to their children generally tend to produce children with few reading problems. The crucial principle is probably not that a larger amount of didactic behaviour is better (though Bradley and Corwyn (2005) make an interesting case that an absence of parental teaching may be a bad thing), but that there should be a match between the amount of stimulation available and the child's ability to use it with enjoyment. Stimulation that is contingent on the child's need, attractive, predictable, and allowing him or her control and independence, that is, stimulation which is like what has been called 'scaffolding' (Vygotsky 1962, 1978, 1981; Kaye 1984; Gauvain 2005; Meadows 2006; Turner and Berkowitz 2005; Wood 1998) is optimal for development; intrusive or non-contingent stimulation (as from the television being on incessantly) may be unhelpful (Jordan 2004). The core is, perhaps, warm participation in socially and intellectually stimulating interactions, with adults showing reciprocity with children, being responsive to them, and providing emotional support but also providing some structured, directed experiences with encouragement and praise (Meins 1997, 1998; Moran, Ghate and van der Merwe 2004; Hubbs-Tait et al. 2002; Petrill and Deater-Deckard 2004). Possibly the child participant in such interaction derives an enhanced sense of being competent and effective as well as receiving good cognitive opportunities and helpful interpretations and support from the adult; it is worth noting that maternal intrusiveness, being very directive and controlling, is associated with the child doing less well. There are quite consistent positive correlations between the amount of adult–child interaction of this sort and the child's cognitive development, which remain even when maternal IQ and educational level are partialled out in an attempt to control for passive genotype–environment interaction effects (Gottfried 1984; Luster and Dubow 1992) and when other demographic variables are controlled (CMPO 2008). It is not entirely clear which components of the parent's behaviour have direct effects, and which are mediated by other factors, and the best balance of behaviour may vary from task to task and age to age (Hubbs-Tait et al. 2002; Bradley and Corwyn 2005), but it does seem to be the case that if the parent–child interaction is characterised by positive emotional support, high cognitive stimulation and low parental intrusiveness the child is likely to do well in terms of both cognition and confidence, whereas the reverse of this pattern is associated with the child doing badly. Thompson (2004) sees parenting and the environment of the home as the basis of individuals' approaches to learning challenges and achievement (pp. 215–17).

It is essential to note that different activities co-exist with different sorts of interaction and talk. For example, the language used by the Bristol children and adults studied by Gordon Wells varied significantly according to the activity being engaged in (Wells 1985). Talk during meals differed from talk outside the home or from talk while looking at story books. A recent British cohort study found amounts of reading to and talking to young children, and outings to 'places of interest' were positively correlated with their cognition, and amount of television watching and outings to department stores and funfairs were negatively correlated, independently of other characteristics of family, child and parents (CMPO 2008). Thus different amounts of engaging in particular activities will give differing opportunities for language and interaction that might facilitate social development.

3.4.3.1 Productive joint activity and positive development

For a number of reasons, children may benefit from their parents' fostering the child's involvement in productive activity. As I said when discussing mastery (pp. 87–90, 215–17), human beings seem to like to have their curiosity satisfied and to achieve a feeling of mastery as a result of having made a bit of an effort. The key idea is that intentional engagement with environmental challenges such that the child develops a sense of agency, a sense of control and a sense of success will have positive consequences. Children with a history of engaging with activities successfully and productively may feel such activities are enjoyable, rewarding, and manageable, and that they themselves are competent and in control. Vygotskian theory (Meadows 2006) argues that adult support through the zone of proximal development is a particularly promising area for succeeding in such engagement and hence for developing the child's skills and the child's ability to learn to learn. As part of the big USA collaborative study of early parenting and early childcare conducted by the NICHD (National Institute of Child Health and Development), Bradley and Corwyn (2005) looked at how parents provided opportunities for engaging in productive activity and whether this affected the rate of behaviour problems in the children. Their results suggest that engaging in productive joint activities and a lower rate of behaviour problems are linked, with a sense of self-regulatory competence being an important mediator. Joint activities will also involve better knowledge of the partner, and potentially shared enjoyment, which should also have positive effects.

3.4.4 Co-constructing the earliest memories

Children hear, and engage in, talk about their own earlier experiences. Differences in this talk have been suggested as contributing to differences in early memories (Bauer 2007; Reese and Newcombe 2007). In a comparison of Chinese mother–preschool child pairs living in China with US-resident first-generation Chinese–American pairs and European–American pairs, Wang (2007) examined what mother and child said when discussing a past shared event. The European–American mothers elaborated children's reminiscences more than either the Chinese–American pairs or the China-resident pairs, and valued their child's development of an autonomous self-concept more highly. The European–American children recalled more facts in their reminiscences about events. Bauer (2007) similarly describes American children's narratives as involving more personal and elaborated talk whereas Chinese children and their parents included more talk about prescriptive moral rules. Reese, Hayne and Macdonald (2008) examined mother–child talk about the child's birth (a highly significant event for both of them) and about more neutral shared autobiographical events in a New

Zealand study, comparing Maori and Pakeha (White European ancestry) mothers and children. The mothers all told detailed, emotive stories about the child's birth compared with the stories they told about recent past events. The quantity of detail in the birth stories, perhaps especially the inclusion of information on time and on internal feelings was strongly linked to the quantity of detail in children's own autobiographical stories. Maori mothers talked about the child's birth in a particularly elaborated and detailed way. The authors suggest that this, plus the cultural emphasis on oral story telling and the cultural experience of many members of the extended family being involved in caregiving and telling the child stories, may surround the Maori child with so many rich stories of their earlier lives that when asked to report an 'earliest memory' they can typically produce one from around age two and a half, a year or so earlier than the norm for most European and American samples. Again, cultural practices were affecting children's development of an autobiographical self (pp. 72–74, 124–25) via the sort of interaction and discourse that mother and child engaged in.

3.4.5 Parental control of children

There are many occasions when 'mother knows best' and parents need to control their children. But children also have a strong drive to function autonomously, or to mastery (pp. 87–90, 120–22), all the way from 'I want to do it my own self' in the preschool years to the adolescent's desire to escape parental control of where they go, who they interact with and what they eat, drink and smoke. Developmentally the crunch points may occur when parents' attempts to direct children's behaviour come into some degree of conflict with the children's desire to develop their autonomy. Parental control tactics come in many forms and are embedded in other qualities of the relationship, and parents use them with different degrees of consistency. Sometimes one discusses, reasons, negotiates, bargains, persuades; sometimes it is a matter of insistence or power assertion or even force or punishment. Sometimes you are pleased that your little darling is thinking for herself, even if the result is a refusal to do what you want; sometimes the merits of blind unquestioning obedience are far more vividly felt. We all know from our own lives that no single technique always works or always fails. But the research literature does suggest that control that stems from a generally warm relationship, clarifies limits, and explains itself, tends to have positive effects, whereas control that is rigid and insensitive, or that implies negative judgements of the child's rights, may be harmful (Kärtner 2007; Parke and Buriel 2006; Grusec and Davidov 2007; Bradley and Corwyn 2005). The warmth and the openness to negotiation of the participants may be what are positive about the former, in contrast to the coldness and inflexibility of the latter. It could also be that discussion and mutual respect are good in themselves and that this applies beyond the control context, provided that they do reach a mutually accepted conclusion, because they allow practice of a host of socially useful skills and demonstrate mutual positive respect. Both inside and outside moments when parent and child are engaged in control issues, individuals prefer some autonomy or at least the alternative of being a valued, if low-power, member of the community.

However, there is one distinction between types of control that resonates with several other areas of theory and research. This is between behavioural control and psychological control (Barber 1996; Grusec and Davidov 2007). Behavioural control focuses directly on behaviour; there are rules for behaviour and behaviour is monitored to ensure that the rules are kept, but if they are not, the matter can generally be regarded as the breaking of a rule by an otherwise worthwhile well-meaning person. The child who persistently fails to wear her hair tied back in school, for example, and gets nagged by her teachers and her mother, may be simultaneously very irritated by their insistence on a rule she sees as petty, and confident that their displeasure (or at least the mother's displeasure) is limited to this particular issue. Psychological control, in contrast, operates by working on the child's emotional state – inducing guilt, highlighting parents' emotional reactions, generalising to the worth of the child elsewhere in their lives. The behaviourally controlling parent would say 'You should tie your hair back, that's the rule and it's not the sort of issue to rebel over', the psychologically controlling parent would say 'You are shaming me', 'I can't love you if you don't do what I want', and so forth. Parents who use high rates of emotional control tend to act manipulatively and intrusively, and may undermine the children's sense of themselves as worthwhile. Children of parents who use a lot of psychological control are at risk of internalising problems such as low self-esteem, guilt and anxiety. But it's not a simple picture on either side; in my example of the girl with the too freely flowing hair, there were some teachers who felt she was flaunting it at them, that this behavioural issue was a much more pervasive one indicative of a general disrespect for their authority. In which feeling they may, looking back, have been absolutely right.

Whatever the sort of control, if it is felt to result from love and concern, it will not carry so much threat to the child's psychological well-being, and may be accepted even if it sets a limit to autonomy. Parental control will be moderated by other factors. Some children are more controllable than others. Having a negative or a highly active or an irritable temperament may mean that parenting that is harsh or intrusive is more than usually likely to lead to behaviour problems, so the child needs patient calming control (Rothbart and Bates 2006). Fearful children respond better to gentle, warm, control. Issues around motivation, self-esteem and sense of autonomy imply that control needs to be adjusted to the age of the child. Parents find it easier to respond to a young child with simple direct control

– saying 'No', moving the child away, using distraction – than it is at later ages, when the child's persistence will have increased and prohibitions are more likely to be taken personally. Conversely, appeals to reason and the child's conscience may work better beyond the preschool years. The danger is that a history of conflict, hostility and mutual negative expectations can build up, so that each little disagreement that occurs is reacted to in terms of the accumulated disagreement of several years of interaction.

Another source of variation in reactions to control is gender (pp. 192, 194, 200–02). The tendency of little girls to seek to stay close to the caregiver and talk to her, whereas little boys show more enthusiasm for vigorous physical activities away from the caregiver, will give the two genders different experiences of control and different practise in coping with other people's demands. Cycles of coercive discipline and coercive response are more likely to occur with boys, and can reach extreme negative levels of antisocial behaviour (e.g. Granic and Patterson 2006; Snyder and Patterson 1995; pp. 176, 182–86, 264–67).

3.4.5.1 Parental monitoring

A substantial body of research suggests that poor parental monitoring may be associated with worse child behaviour (Brody 2003; Kerr and Stattin 2003; Parke and Buriel 2006; Grusec and Davidov 2007; Brook *et al.* 2007). Children are more likely to behave badly when away from parents' supervision, or when parents do not know where they are, who they are with, and what they are doing. It has been argued from this that failures in parental monitoring gave their adolescents the space to behave badly, 'to hang out with deviant peers who will draw them into delinquency and other problem behaviours' (Kerr and Stattin 2003: 122). But obviously there is room for a bi-directional effect here: children who wish to behave badly will undoubtedly seek to evade parental supervision while they do so (Brody 2003). The girl who preferred loose hair at school left home each morning with it tied back, or at least promising to tie it back en route. The child who wishes to steal, set a fire, or torture a cat will probably not do it where an adult can see. There is also room for earlier history to have an effect on monitoring – parents may not monitor a child who has always behaved impeccably, or might try to monitor a troublesome child, or a troublesome area of behaviour, very much more closely; or, faced with a child who persists in behaving undesirably despite their monitoring, they may seek to preserve their relationship with the child rather than risk the child perceiving them as a gaoler – 'you never let me do anything'.

One issue to consider is how the parent might induce the adolescent *not* to want to engage in deviant behaviour. Earlier parental behaviour, or cultural beliefs and practices, might have induced a strong attachment between the child and the parent, so that the child wishes to avoid behaviour that will hurt or embarrass the parent or 'let down' the family honour (hence, it has been suggested, the relatively low rate of delinquency in East Asian adolescents, e.g. Shwalb *et al.* 2004). Consistent parental reasons why certain behaviours are undesirable may help if the family has discussed them and agreed on them. If the child has also internalised the controls that parents or culture offer, they may regulate and supervise themselves. This self-surveillance will be harder for the child to evade than parental surveillance – parents actually spend rather little time where their teenagers are, may have little information about what the teenagers are doing, and may receive only minimal and ungracious answers if they ask for too much information. I think it is very likely that the majority of teenagers prefer it that way.

So if we are considering what will work, it may also be important how the monitoring is done. Clearly it needs to be age-appropriate, in terms of the child's understanding and emotion, in terms of the ecological settings involved, in terms of the cultural expectations of the reference group or groups, and in terms of the degree of autonomy the child can legitimately expect to have (Kärtner 2007). Advice, and a routine of each side keeping the other informed of where they are and what they are doing, may be more positively received than surveillance.

> Effective parenting in the control domain is at least in part a reflection of the ability of parents to know how their children will react to different forms of intervention, that is to accurately identify the meaning of the intervention to their child or the impact of the intervention on the child's sense of autonomy. Good parenting involves problem solving and flexibility in the sense of the parent being able and willing to modify interventions so that they are suited to the current situation (including features of the child, of the behaviour under consideration, and of the context). Parents who are knowledgeable about the child can tailor their interventions accordingly and thus promote positive socialization outcomes. For example, they can accurately assess if their children understand what they are supposed to do, if their children feel they are being treated fairly or noncoercively, whether a particular strategy is seen as a manifestation of caring behaviour or of hostility, or if a power assertive intervention is seen as an indication of the importance of the issue to the parent rather than as an angry outburst. [. . .]
>
> This analysis of effective child-rearing assumes that parents are motivated as well as able to put their knowledge into effect . . . one can ask about the best way to acquire knowledge. Inquiries about thoughts and emotions, done in a noncoercive and accepting way, would be one good approach. Modelling and reciprocation of such sharing by appropriate discussion of the parents' own feelings and thoughts with the child is yet another. Setting the conditions for a positive and warm

relationship or a trusting relationship, which facilitate the child's sharing of information about thoughts, feelings and reactions, is another approach. Parents can also observe their children closely in order to assess their reactions to events. Good relationships also make it easier for both parent and child to spend time with each other, another essential ingredient of knowledge gathering.

(Grusec and Davidov 2007: 296–297)

3.4.6 Adolescents' conflict with parents

One of the most heavily researched topics on adolescence is the nature and quality of adolescents' relationships with parents. In contemporary Western culture, there is what almost amounts to an expectation that adolescents will be moody and difficult, and will rebel against their parents and other adult authority figures. Casual comments about the bad behaviour of adolescents and their conflicts with older people abound in classic authors such as Chaucer and Shakespeare; vivid descriptions of adolescent anger and misery have provided twentieth century classic novels and films (e.g. Salinger 1951, Plath 1966, Lindsay Anderson's film *If*). Theorists have varied in their explanations for this period of difficulty – attributing it to the rapid physical changes of the period, to brain development, to hormonal imbalance, to psychological needs for individuation, to social needs for status – explanations that overlap and rarely exclude each other. Policy makers, educationalists and legislators have varied in their recommendations as to how to treat problematic adolescents – from 'hug a hoodie' to 'hit them with an ASBO'. Parents too may find this a period that feels bewilderingly different from, and more difficult than, what came earlier.

The overwhelming evidence from research over the last fifty years, however, shows that complete alienation from parents, profound rejection of adult values and authority, and serious rebellion are the exception; only a small proportion of adolescents experience emotional turmoil and extremely conflicted relations with parents, and such extreme difficulties typically have their origins prior to adolescence (though of course this troublesome minority may create enormous social difficulties pp. 182–84, 264–67). What normally happens to adult–child relationships during adolescence is a shift in power relations, activity and emotional tone. Adolescents spend less time with their parents than younger children do, and increasing amount of time with their peers. Their relationships with adults become more egalitarian and involve more independent action. This can involve conflict, indeed during early adolescence (ten to thirteen) there is typically a lot of disagreement over everyday issues, amounting according to some theorists to 'a normative and temporary perturbation that is functional in transforming family relationships' (Smetana, Campione-Barr and Metzger 2006: 259). If these conflicts are managed in ways that lead to an amicable settlement and are part of a close and supportive relationship, they might provide useful practise in resolving disagreements. Sustained conflict, or high levels of conflict, or conflicts that are not resolved, or a general context of parent–adult hostility, are more likely to be damaging (Laursen and Collins 1994; Laursen, Coy and Collins 1998; Buehler, Lange and Franck 2007; Deng and Roosa 2007; Zahn-Waxler *et al.* 2008).

Much of the research evidence comes from White Western middle-class samples (Laursen *et al.* 1998). But we would expect there to be cultural variations in conflict, especially in how it is resolved. Members of more individualistic cultures such as the White middle class in the USA may experience more conflicts than members of more collectivist or family-oriented cultures, for example Chinese families in Hong Kong (Fuligni 1998; Yau and Smetana 1996, 2003), but Chinese adolescents still have more conflicts with parents during adolescence than they have earlier or later, just like American ones. There may be differences not so much in the existence of conflict but in how it is resolved. Many conflicts are resolved by the adolescent giving in, or walking away – possibly slamming the door on the way – but it does seem that Western adolescents, or immigrant adolescents who are becoming Westernised, are more likely than adolescents from more collectivist societies to maintain a stubbornly non-compliant attitude until the parent gives in (Phinney *et al.* 2005). Within cultures, conflicts are less likely to be resolved positively in families where there is a high level of conflict between parents, or socio-economic disadvantage or decline (Conger and Donnellan 2007; Grant *et al.* 2003; Smetana 2002; Smetana *et al.* 2006). Warm relationships within the family tend to mean less conflict, but feelings of warmth and closeness tend to decline during adolescence (Allen *et al.* 1998; Buhrmester and Fuhrman 1987; Fuligni 1998). In the framework of parenting dimensions (Baumrind 1971, 1980, pp. 117–20), research findings suggest that parenting that is both demanding and responsive, and 'authoritative' is associated with adolescents who are more socially competent and more psychologically well-adjusted (Steinberg 2001). This may hold across cultural groups, though some researchers argue that if cultural beliefs legitimise a different form of parenting, it may be this that is associated with positive outcomes for the adolescent. Chao (1994), for example, describes the strict parent–child relations that derive from a Confucian commitment to training the young in appropriate behaviour, and judges them to be child-centred rather than punitive. It might be worth 'unpicking' the ways in which the benefits of authoritative parenting may arise to discover more tightly defined behaviours – and acknowledging that the adolescent's behaviour is part of the causal sequence.

One example might be parents' control over the adolescent. As I discussed earlier (pp. 119–21), researchers have found it useful to distinguish between 'psychological control', which involves attempts to control adolescents' thoughts and feelings and tends to be experienced as over-intrusive and demeaning, and 'behavioural control', which regulates, monitors, and manages adolescents' activities without trying to get inside the adolescent's head so much. High levels of psychological control tend to be experienced as unfair (Smetana and Daddis 2002; pp. 119–21, 134–36), and to be associated with high levels of both externalising and internalising problems (Dwairy 2008; Feinberg et al. 2007; Gonzales et al. 2008; Zhou et al. 2008) even in more traditional cultures.

One form of 'behavioural' control, the degree to which parents monitor adolescents' behaviour, has been of interest to researchers, with findings initially suggesting that lack of parental monitoring was associated with worse outcomes for the adolescent. Inadequate parental monitoring is associated with externalising problems such as drug use and alcohol use, truancy and delinquency (Steinberg and Morris 2001; Fletcher et al. 2004; Brook et al. 2007; Deng and Roosa 2007; pp. 233–35, 266–67). A belief that low SES parents are particularly lax about monitoring their children seems to be common among policy makers – a few English parents have been jailed as a response to their children's truancy, more evicted from their housing because of children's antisocial behaviour. However, studies by Luthar and colleagues (Luthar 2003a, 2003b; Luthar and Becker 2002) show that adolescents growing up in conditions of affluence may also lack parental supervision and monitoring, and for them too this appears to increase the risk of negative outcomes such as substance use, anxiety, depression, and lack of emotional closeness with parents.

However, we need to be careful about what we mean by 'monitoring', and we need to recognise that what parents wish to do in the way of monitoring their child, and what they are able to do, cannot be independent of the child's wishes and actions. Kerr and Stattin (2000) found that the association between parents' attempts to know about or control their child's activities and adolescent problem behaviour was much less close than the association between adolescents' willingness to let parents know about their activities and their problematic behaviour. If adolescents were up to no good, they were much less likely to allow their parents to know about it than if their activities and friends were blameless. If parents had some reason to suspect that their adolescents were up to no good, their surveillance efforts tended to increase. There is a two-way pattern of adolescent disclosure and parental surveillance between the adolescent and the parent, and the responsibility for its failure is not always the parent's (Smetana et al. 2005). Similarly, the different participants in the interaction might well say different things about what is going on and what it means; the parent's democratic discussion, for example, might be intrusive nagging in the adolescent's view.

Nevertheless, in adolescence as in earlier parts of life, there are gains to be made from a pattern of interactions that allow participants to express

independent thoughts, desires, needs and feelings but also maintain closeness and connectedness. Where parents and adolescents can make decisions
jointly, and where adolescents can be allowed more autonomy over decisions as they move from middle to late adolescence, there seems to be better
adjustment and less deviance (Fuligni and Eccles 1993; Lamborn *et al.*
1996; Smetana *et al.* 2006) but exactly how this is best done may depend on
the circumstances of the individual family. In a neighbourhood context of
high social risk, for example, more parental control and monitoring may be
especially advantageous because it reduces the amount of time in which the
adolescent can get mixed up with delinquent peers (Hills, Le Grand and
Piachaud 2002; Lamborn *et al.* 1996; McLoyd 1998; McElhany and Allen
2001). Issues about the relative merits of authoritative and authoritarian
parenting may be very relevant here (pp. 62, 154–55, 117–18, 139).

3.4.7 Placing of parent–child in family system

It is important to remember that effects are not just of parents on children;
or even of children on parents. Families are complex groups with interdependent roles and functions. There are both direct and indirect influences,
for example A has an effect on B via A's effect on C, and C's on B. This
means there need to be multiple levels of analysis – individuals, dyads, small
groups, whole families – and a recognition that influence is transactional
not unidirectional, and indirect as well as direct (Chapter 1; Kuczynski
2003; Lamb and Lewis 2004). Additionally, parents manage their children's
environment outside the family – for example they may choose a particular
school, usher the child into particular voluntary groups such as Scouts or
football teams; they chaperone the child and may mediate in peer relationships – roles as gatekeepers and in monitoring. Families are embedded in
other social systems – church, school, and political system (Chapter 5). And
as Bronfenbrenner pointed out, both researchers and parents need to have
developmental perspectives – parents have to accommodate to the child's
developmental changes, anticipating and preparing for changes and goals,
and there may be issues about doing things at times which are socially usual
– having babies when very young or very old, for example. My main focus
here is some examples of the ways in which the parent–child relationships
are affected by problems in parents' other relationships.

3.4.7.1 Child abuse, neglect and maltreatment

Some parents, or parent figures, behave towards children in ways that are
socially agreed to be unacceptable – by inflicting physical harm, by
neglecting them, by using them sexually, by creating emotional damage.
Most children never experience serious and continued abuse, but for the
minority who do, the abuse may have a negative effect on their lives, or

even end them. There are many ways to abuse a child, some common, some less so, some felt by everybody to be abusive, others not universally disapproved of (May-Chahal and Cawson 2005). Using May-Chahal and Cawson's figures, the commonest form of abuse is probably neglect (around ten per cent) – having to look after yourself because your parents had drug problems or were away, no food in the house, no clean clothes, no one to take you for medical care when it was needed. Physical abuse is experienced by around seven per cent – being shaken, hit with a fist or hard object, knocked to the ground, or burned, scalded, or choked. About six per cent are emotionally abused, with a combination of physical domination, psychological domination, humiliation, withdrawal, or terrorising. Sexual abuse is most commonly unwanted fondling or exposure, but comes in other more invasive forms: having some unwanted sexual contact is a very common experience (in their figures about half of girls and twenty per cent of boys), and the prevalence of forced engagement in penetrative sex or masturbation seems to be about sixteen per cent for girls and seven per cent for boys. Different forms of abuse may co-occur.

There are discussions of the damage that these experiences can do to the child, and the possible causal pathways between abuse and effect, throughout this book (pp. 129–30). Summarily, experience of abuse is associated with increased risk of anxiety, depression, suicidal behaviour, school attendance problems, aggression, teenage pregnancy, and being a poor parent yourself. Current and future well-being are undermined, and vulnerability increased.

3.4.7.2 Child exposure to domestic violence

The relationship between parents will have an impact on the child. Although family structure of itself does not seem to have marked effects on children's development – effects being attributable on the whole to functioning within families and the resources that they have (e.g. Golombok 2000; Grusec and Hastings 2007; Lamb 2004; McLanahan and Percheski 2008) – there is substantial evidence (e.g. Amato and Sobolewski 2004; Davies and Cummings 1994; Davies et al. 2002; Katz et al. 2007; Kitzmann et al. 2003; McCloskey and Stuewig 2001; McLanahan and Carlson 2004; Sternberg et al. 2006; Wolfe et al. 1986) that children exposed to domestic violence are at increased risk of mental health problems, poor peer relations, and low emotional security. Their experience may change their views of others' emotional states, their ability to regulate their own emotions, and their understanding of the consequences of their own problematic behaviour (pp. 59, 62). They may also have missed out on the sort of parental discussion of other people's feelings and rights that facilitates children's development of emotional understanding (Dunn 1993; Dunn and Brown 1994; Dunn and Cutting 1999; Katz and Windecker-Nelson 2004; Katz et *al.* 2007; pp. 112–15, 128–29, 164–68). Their ways of coping with their experience of domestic violence and conflict between parents may affect their mental health: O'Brien, Margolin and John (1995) for example suggested that children who coped by tuning out or avoiding parental conflict had better outcomes than those who try to intervene or who blame themselves for their parents' problems, Compas *et al.* (2001) suggested that in a situation of domestic violence it may be best for the child to accept that he or she has little control over events and to focus on reducing and controlling negative emotions. This will not be easy however if the effects of witnessing domestic violence include difficulties in emotion regulation and inability to tolerate negative emotions in oneself or others.

3.4.7.3 Child exposure to parental alcohol abuse

Children of parents with alcohol problems are at greater risk for emotional and behavioural problems, substance use and academic problems (Keller *et al.* 2008). Deficits in child functioning are seen in community samples of problem drinking as well as clinical samples (Keller, Cummings, & Davies 2005), and levels of children's adjustment problems tend to persist even after parental recovery. However, not all children succumb to the increased risk and some cope with adversity very well, indicating the importance of identifying the underlying mechanisms involved. One crucial factor might be changes in the ways in which the children of alcohol abusers are parented compared with children whose parents are not the worse for alcohol.

Parental abuse of alcohol can lead to impaired sensitivity to children, less warmth and more negativity, and poorer monitoring, control, and supervision. It can also be associated with worse relations between adult members of the family, so that the child is more exposed to discord and violence and has less exposure to positive resolutions of disagreements. All these deviations from what is normally seen as 'good' parenting could have an effect on children's risk of poor outcomes (pp. 37, 85–87, 109, 129–30, 240). There might be genetic or prenatal factors such that parents' alcoholism would be associated with poor child outcomes through other routes than parenting, and whether the parents abuse alcohol is also associated with various sorts of social disadvantage. This suggests a complex pathway between parental alcohol use and child outcomes (Keller *et al.* 2005), which may change over time as the child develops. The longitudinal evidence presented by Keller *et al.* (2008) shows a chain of causation involving parenting, such that the father's drinking led to increased marital conflict and family disruption, which led to decreased warmth towards the children, which led to increased problem behaviour on the part of the children. Mothers' drinking had similar effects, but as it was not statistically independent of fathers' drinking, the analyses did not show it having an independent effect. Cummings *et al.* (2004) has similar results.

Hussong *et al.* (2008) investigated why some children of alcoholic parents showed internalising disorders in adolescence and some appeared to be healthy. They argued that internalising symptoms were likely to arise from a combination of genetic risk, greater exposure to stressful environments, and impaired coping strategies. Risk for the child was also higher if the alcohol-abusing parent suffered from depression. They found that if both parents abused alcohol the risk for girls was higher than if only one did, which could indicate both greater genetic risk and greater environmental risk; although the risk was not significantly increased for boys. That the child's internalising problems were assessed in adolescence may be highly relevant here, as depression becomes very much more common in adolescent girls.

3.4.7.4 Children of imprisoned parents

Children are affected by what the state does to their parents (an example of both macrosystem and exosystem influence). A very large number of children experience having a parent imprisoned; Murray (2007) estimates 125,000 children in the UK currently. Case studies and small-scale studies find a substantial amount of disturbance and dysfunction in the children of prisoners – 'children can react to parental imprisonment with internalizing problems such as sleep disturbance, bedwetting, concentration problems, clinging behavior, sadness, low mood, and withdrawal' (Murray and Farrington 2008a: 273). There are important questions about both the short-term and the long-term impact of imprisonment on the prisoner's children, and although most children will never experience this there are two reasons for considering the issues; firstly they illuminate the impact of other disturbances in parent–child relationships and social disadvantage and the causal models that are appropriate, and secondly parental criminality is a powerful predictor of similar difficulties on the child's career, through pathways which careful research is clarifying (Dogan *et al.* 2007; West 1982).

We know that the children of prisoners are at high risk of delinquency and antisocial behaviour (Rutter, Giller and Hagell 1998; Murray, Janson and Farrington 2007). As we have seen throughout this book, there are different models to account for the impact of life events on individuals' development. To recapitulate, some centre on *traumatic events*; here we would look at the separation of the child from the parent under relatively dramatic and emotional circumstances, and with short-term consequences, such as prison visits or being cared for by someone outside the family, that are also unpleasant and might disrupt the child's attachment relationships, habitual experiences, and sense of security. Or we could focus on the long-term consequences of parental imprisonment for the *life course* of the child – social and economic stresses, difficulties for the children's caregivers, having to move house or neighbourhood or school, stigma, bullying – factors which could lead to antisocial behaviour and an increase in children's internalising and externalising problems through the life course (Angold *et al.* 1999). But there is also a possibility that *pre-existing disadvantage or genetic risk* could be associated with both the parent's imprisonment and with the child's problems. Prisoners only rarely come from relatively advantaged families, and the adversities that existed before the child experienced a parent's imprisonment could be the cause of the child's problems irrespective of the incarceration. Or parent and child might share a deleterious genome. Or the authorities may come down harder on child misbehaviour in the family known to have criminal members than they do on people from families who seem otherwise to have avoided all misbehaviour.

There are obviously different ways to begin to sort out this tangle of possibilities. The two that I will illustrate involve looking at child outcomes that are problematic but not disapproved of socially, and looking at complex longitudinal patterns. Murray and Farrington (2008b) report a significant increase in children's internalising problems as well as in anti-social behaviour. Their study recruited more than 400 eight-year-old boys and their families from a working-class inner city area of South London and has followed them up for forty years. They compared five mutually exclusive groups of boys: one group (twenty-three boys) who experienced parental imprisonment in their first ten years of life (for fairly serious offences, for example not for traffic offences or drunkenness, and for a period of at least one month); one group (227 boys) did not experience any separation from a parent (of one month or more) in their first ten years, and their parents were not imprisoned at any time before the boys' eighteenth birthdays; one group (seventy-seven boys) who were separated from a parent by hospitalisation or parental death before the age of ten but the parents were not imprisoned; one group (sixty-one boys) who experienced separation from a parent before age ten because of some sort of family break up or dysfunction but whose parents were not imprisoned; and a final group (seventeen boys) whose parents were imprisoned before the boys' births, but not again between then and the boys' eighteenth birthdays. This allowed comparisons of experience of a whole range of difficulties and disadvantages over a long period of time.

The results showed that parental imprisonment, although associated with antisocial difficulties and with disadvantage, had a significant independent effect on the children's internalising problems. The boys who had been separated from a parent by the parent's imprisonment had significantly more internalising problems, and significantly more persistent and recurrent internalising problems, in both adolescence and adulthood than the boys who were not separated or were separated by hospitalisation or divorce/dysfunction, and higher rates as adults than the boys whose parents were imprisoned before the boys' births. Their internalising problems were more likely to co-exist with antisocial behaviour problems – more than ten times more likely compared with the boys who did not experience separation or only experienced separation because of hospitalisation or death, and four or five times more likely compared with the other two groups (see also Gilliom and Shaw 2004; Marmorstein and Iacono 2004). Other risk factors affected internalising problems – low IQ, low attainment, parental marital relations, poor parental supervision – but parental imprisonment remained an independent risk factor in the development of the child's problems.

What we have here is of great interest for theory and of great importance for policy. Imprisoning criminals puts their children at risk of antisocial behaviour and internalising problems, and therefore creates both short-term trauma for innocent individuals and an increased risk of future criminality. We urgently need better alternatives to imprisonment, especially for criminals who have parental responsibilities, and better support systems to ensure that the harm done to a child by a parent's criminality is reduced to a minimum (Murray 2007; Murray, Janson and Farrington 2007; Smith *et al.* 2007).

3.4.7.5 Parental mental illness and children's development as social persons

Children exposed to the mental illness of a parent are known to be at increased risk of disturbed social and emotional development (Beardslee, Versage and Gladstone 1998; Caspi *et al.* 1995; Goodyer 2008; Maughan and McCarthy 1997; Mowbray *et al.* 2004; Mufson *et al.* 2002). Effects on anxiety, depression, and conduct disorder have been discerned as early as infancy and as late as adulthood. In some cases, the child may have inherited some genetic liability to mental illness from a parent; sometimes the mental illness is associated with the child receiving developmentally dysfunctional experiences, and sometimes with the child missing out on developmentally positive things. Mental illness can damage a family's support network, for example, with direct and indirect effects on the child's development. It is often associated with relative poverty and unstable relationships, with each type of disadvantage tending to reinforce the effects of the others. It may lead to more negative mother–child interaction to insecure attachment, and to family conflict (pp. 37–38, 86–87, 121–27).

Most research has looked at mothers' mental illness, and especially depression, as depressive symptoms are very common indeed among mothers of young children (Cummings, Keller and Davies 2005; Hammen 2003; Meadows 2006). More recently, researchers have looked at fathers. Their mental illness (and their antisocial behaviour) also impacts on the child, possibly not so strongly as the mother's, but more for fathers who are involved with the child than fathers who are not. If the child is living with both a mentally ill mother and a mentally ill father, their rate of disorder is very much increased. The mental health of fathers who do not live with their children does not seem to have much effect on the children's mental health, neither protecting the children from maternal health effects if the father is well but the mother is not, nor damaging the child's mental health if the mother is well and the father is not (Jaffee *et al.* 2003; Meadows *et al.* 2007; Ramchandani *et al.* 2008a, 2008b). Again, this does not rule out genetic explanations for the children's risk, but it does suggest that family systems in general and parenting practices in particular may be at the root of the problem. And they may be more powerful, and more open to intervention, than genetic differences.

3.5 Socio-economic status and theory of family differences

There has been evidence of systematic differences in how children from families of different social status turn out ever since people started to look for it; and for almost all these years there have been disagreements about how to interpret the differences and their causes. Very broadly, the picture is, consistently across time and across cultures, that your chances of many, perhaps most, sorts of psychological, physical and social disadvantage are higher if you are born into a low status, disadvantaged, or poor family than if your family of origin is well off (pp. 150–52). The interpretations of these associations range from strongly hereditarian (e.g. Eysenck 1971; Galton 1978; Harris 1995) through to strongly environmental (e.g. Hills, Le Grand and Piachaud 2002; Ball 2006; Bradley and Corwyn 2002; Brooks-Gunn and Duncan 1997; Palmer *et al.* 2006); and from family experiences being an index of social selection (that might well have had its effects even with different family experiences) to family experiences having a direct causal effect. We need to remember here the methodological difficulty that complicates discussion of the effects of parent–child interaction just as it bedevils the study of heritability. I have talked about the genes–environment debate elsewhere (pp. 25–30); here I focus on the selection–cause debate.

The socio-economic status (SES) of the family is a fairly good predictor of children's academic achievement (Blake 1989; Bornstein and Bradley 2003; Bradley and Corwyn 2002; Conger and Donnellan 2007; Duncan, Brooks-Gunn and Klebanov 1994; Duyme, Dumaret and Tomkiewicz 1999; Hart and Risley 1995; Hoff 2003; Huston and Bentley 2010; Huston, McLoyd and Garcia-Coll 1994; Jencks 1975; McLoyd 1998; Newman and Massengill 2006; Rutter 1985; Schaffer 1992; Smith, Brooks-Gunn and Klebanov 1997; White 1982) and to a lesser extent of their social development. Risk of adverse social outcomes is far higher for people of lower SES, however much we want to think that we are achieving a 'classless' society. Social class differences like these have persisted for generations, and may be getting worse rather than better (Hirsch 2006). Social class may be 'the elephant in the room', the unacknowledged factor behind all sorts of personal decisions (e.g. Ball 2004, 2006) and difficulties in social engineering (Hirsch 2006).

But social class, or SES, is not of itself a causal variable. It is an index based on the occupation of the head of the family, and thus a guide to the family's income, the parents' education, and, less directly, to a wider set of social circumstances. Research on social class or SES sometimes focuses on comparing people from different categories (with different 'social addresses' (Bronfenbrenner 1979, 1986; Bronfenbrenner et al. 1996; Bronfenbrenner and Morris 1998; Bronfenbrenner and Evans 2000)) rather than on the intervening structures or processes that might explain how the address label comes to be associated with different developmental outcomes. Thus its results are often open to several interpretations. Further, the correlations between SES measures and outcomes are not enormously high. Very importantly, social address studies do not adequately rule out genetic factors: studies which try to control for inherited differences in, for example, intelligence by partialling out parents' characteristics, for example the mother's IQ or the parents' educational level, typically find the correlations between family background and children's outcome are reduced (Gottfried 1984; Plomin 1994; Scarr 1996), sometimes to a very insignificant level.

It is not entirely clear, in any case, how a variable like SES affects children's development; what sort of explanatory model is appropriate. The correlation between SES and social development, persistent delinquency for example, might reflect class differences in innate social propensities (Eysenck 1971), although adoption studies (pp. 272–73) suggest it does not. There might be differences in the behaviour that facilitates good social outcomes; there might be different reactions by schools and other social agencies to children differing in SES. There might be different opportunities available to the different social classes (for example better funded schools and leisure in wealthier areas); even in a social system which believes it is meritocratic and open to all those who are talented. There might be differences in health. There might be subjective differences, for example in feelings about whether you can keep up with more prosperous peers, or in what is believed to be attainable (Attree 2006). These possibilities are more likely to be additive than mutually exclusive: the different disadvantages of poverty tend to co-occur (Evans 2004; Huston and Bentley 2010; Micklewright 2002; Newman and Massengill 2006; Palmer et al. 2006). Whichever cause may apply, we surely need to look closely at the moment-by-moment way the effect is brought about. Work that looks at more specific variables than SES may be more useful, and it is these variables which I want to discuss more fully. This strategy will make it easier to address the question of why there is variation *within* classes and other overtly similar backgrounds, and to elucidate causal chains. We cannot however, entirely dismiss class itself as a significant factor in development in so far as it reflects inequalities of health, education, and opportunity (McLanahan and Percheski 2008). Class-based indices may continue to be the most economical predictors of development.

One issue that needs noting at this point is the range of problem outcomes that people suffer. Some problems are common and not very deviant from the norm, others are rarer or more extreme. Extreme outcomes (such as causing virtually a whole country to focus on exterminating groups defined as subhuman) and less extreme ones (such as feelings of in-group favouritism and mild prejudice against out-groups) may need different types of explanation. Our chance of a scientific explanation of Hitler's psychopathology is small, although historians may draw on psychological theory to substantiate their interpretation of what led the baby from rural Austria to become the dictator destroying so many and doing so much damage (Kershaw 2001). Our chance of a good scientific understanding of what influences the development of more normal degrees of prejudice, paranoia, or megalomania is far greater. The difference between the causes of extreme and less extreme disorders is well illustrated in a major study of the sources of cognitive deficit (Broman et al. 1987). This large study suggests different causal patterns for mild retardation (IQ between fifty and sixty-nine) and severe retardation (IQ less than fifty). Severe retardation was likely to be linked to overt central nervous system disorder, mainly Down Syndrome, or the after effects of rubella before birth or meningitis after it. Children who were later diagnosed as severely retarded were more likely to have had problems in the perinatal period; they were more likely to have poor Apgar scores, that is, to be in poor condition immediately after birth, and to be small in size, have low head circumferences and so forth. That is, the severely retarded children commonly showed symptoms of being at risk of abnormal development at or shortly after birth, and their retardation was caused to a significant degree by problems they were born with, or by later overt physical damage.

Different factors seem to be at work for the mildly retarded children. Mild retardation was linked to SES, being very rare in high SES groups, and commoner in Black individuals (4.6 per cent) than White individuals (1.15 per cent). It was associated with lower SES at birth, with lower levels of maternal education, with lower age of the mother at the child's birth, with less maternal care, and with worse housing. There was some association with poor placental functioning, breech deliveries and poorer perinatal condition, factors which predicted severe mental retardation, but these were all less effective than social factors in discriminating between the mildly mentally retarded children and the borderline normal children. White children who were mildly mentally retarded at seven had tended to show poorer early cognitive skills; for example, forty-two per cent of them had abnormal expressive language at the age of three. This earlier indication of problems was less clear in Black children, where seventy-seven per cent of mildly retarded seven-year-olds had had normal language expression at three. Broman *et al.* (1987) conclude that the causes of mild mental retardation are not primarily medical, but that social and environmental factors predominate.

Feinstein and Bynner (2004), using the subjects born in 1970 of the British Cohort Study, examine continuities in cognitive performance over the years of middle childhood, relating change to social class and to economic performance as young adults. The cohort members were assessed on vocabulary and drawing tests at age five and on the British Ability Scale (an IQ measure) and reading at age ten. Just under twelve per cent of children were low scorers (in the bottom quartile) at age five but in the top half at age ten – the 'escapers'; about twelve per cent were in the top quartile at age five but the bottom half at age ten – the 'fallers'. Almost all the 'fallers' came from low SES families. When adult outcomes were examined, individuals who were in the lowest quartile at both five and ten were most likely to suffer outcomes such as low wages, low education, unemployment, criminality, and depression. Escapers were at much less risk of poor outcomes, doing about as well as average children on adult outcomes. Fallers did not do so well as those who were high at both five and ten, suggesting their early high score did not give them protection against later difficulties.

Kim-Cohen *et al.* (2004) looked at how the effects of SES deprivation affected IQ in five-year-old twins. Some children showed resilience in the face of SES adversity, scoring higher on an IQ test and lower on antisocial behaviour than their deprivation would have predicted. There was a genetic component to this resilience, shown by twin similarities, and accounting for a little under half the variance in IQ, but cognitive resilience was also promoted by maternal warmth, stimulating activities, and the child's own sociable temperament. Family cohesiveness, communication and shared meaning may be making important contributions to the children doing better than expected cognitively.

3.5.1 Poverty and the development of the child as a social person: Parenting

As I said in an earlier book (Meadows 2006), an enormous amount of evidence documents an association between poverty and disadvantage, on the one hand, and risk of poorer developmental outcomes in cognition, emotion and behaviour, on the other. Children living in poverty are likely to be subject to a complex, multifaceted and long-term exposure to multiple risks. For example, study after study shows that compared with children from richer families, children living in poverty are more at risk of being in a family where relationships are stressed and violent; where marriages break down and parents are absent; where siblings are delinquent and failing school; where the home has worse physical conditions, for example over-crowding, damp, pollution; where family members' physical and mental health is worse; where the family has less support from neighbours, friends and kin; where daycare and schools have less money, less well-trained staff, fewer resources, and a high proportion of pupils with the same social problems; where there are few positive out-of-school activities; where the neighbourhood has more hazards, more traffic, more crime, more pollution, more physical deterioration; and where even opportunities to access a healthy diet are few and expensive. Even if the economic circumstances of a family in poverty improve, this is most often not a big improvement, the economic respite is often short lived and the associated risks may change even less. The accumulated experience of inadequate or constrained finances, and of all the socio-economic stresses I have just listed, may contribute to feelings of helplessness, of hopelessness, and of being less well off than others; and such feelings no doubt result in 'poverty of aspiration', low expectations of what your life could possibly be, which may further disrupt the use you can make of any positive opportunities that do occur. Exposure to each of these disadvantages may increase the risk of behaviour problems (and poor cognitive development): experience of continued poverty, or of intermittent poverty where the change in income does not take the family far above the official poverty level, can add up to sustained and pervasive disadvantage over a long period, even over successive generations.

We are beginning to be able to go beyond the constituents of poverty to see how each might have an effect on children's development, an essential step in discovering how we can break the cycle of disadvantage. I have therefore included discussion of research on the effects of poverty in a number of sections of this book (pp. 14, 92–93, 148–49). But as it is increasingly being suggested that parenting is one of the key causal mechanisms between the association between poverty and poor outcomes, I am going to address that set of issues here.

Burchinal and her colleagues (2000, 2006) suggest that there is a substantial body of evidence that cognitively stimulating parenting, and parental emotional sensitivity to the child, mediate between social risk factors and children's social and cognitive development (e.g. Ackerman et al. 2007; Belsky et al. 2007b; Bradley and Corwyn 2002, 2005; Brody et al. 2002; Duncan and Brooks-Gunn 1997, 2000; Gutman, Sameroff and Cole 2003; Linver, Brooks-Gunn and Kohen 2002; Lareau 2002; Masten et al. 1995, 1999; Micklewright 2002; Moran, Ghate and van der Merwe 2004; Newman and Massengill 2006; NICHD (National Institute for Child and Health Development) 2003a; Palmer et al. 2006). Families in poverty have fewer chances to provide cognitively stimulating materials and may lack confidence in using them: subsidising poor families increases the amount they spend on child-related items, and so may diminish this, as would providing families with materials direct (Gregg, Harkness and Machin 1999; CMPO 2008). The stresses of poverty increase the risk that there is less warmth and responsiveness and more harshness and withdrawal in interactions between mother and child (and fathers, too, probably) (Brody *et al.* 2002; Burchinal *et al.* 2000, 2006, 2008; Garmezy 1993; Gutman, Sameroff and Eccles 2002; Huston and Bentley 2010; Lamb 2004; Linver, Brookes-Gunn and Kohen 2002; NICHD 2003a). The same association appears in samples of rural and urban children, families of different ethnic groups, children of different ages. Burchinal and her colleagues for example looked at parenting of infants in poor rural communities in the Appalachian mountains (almost all White) and the farmlands of North Carolina (about fifty per cent African–American) (Burchinal *et al.* 2008). They found that there was a pathway from the amount of accumulated risk the family suffered through their measurements of maternal sensitivity and warmth, of how much the parents set up learning and literacy activities for their young child, and of maternal language, through to child outcomes in terms of development and behaviour. They also found that if mothers' behaviour changed between an early assessment (at six months) and a later one (at fifteen months), increases in maternal interaction and language and decreases in maternal harshness predicted improvements in the measurements of the child's outcomes.

The researchers' finding of this association between poverty, risk, parenting and outcomes with such young infants suggests that the differences in outcome for stressed and prosperous families begins very early indeed, and that, if the risk factors continue to be present (as they all too often are), the differences will increase over the child's development – unless there is an early and sustained intervention (e.g. McLanahan and Percheski 2008; Micklewright 2002; Bradley and Corwyn 2005).

3.6 Cultural and historical differences and parenting

I have treated parenting so far in an ahistorical, culture neutral and gender neutral way, as if the characteristics of good or less good parents applied in the same ways in all times and places. This is a view that not everyone would share, indeed I don't feel committed to it myself. Expectations of what good parenting is, and what a good child is, have varied historically, geographically, and culturally, and so have the adaptation issues that individuals have met. I will therefore look briefly at a few of the ways systematic group differences in parenting have been examined. As in other parts of the book, there are many links to other sections.

3.6.1 Mother–father differences in Western samples

Historically, there is evidence of both differential stereotypes and under-lying similarities within and between cultures, historical periods, and individuals (e.g. Dunbar 2008; Montgomery 2009; Pollock 1983; Pleck 2004). The evidence suggests that in late twentieth century and early twenty-first century Europe and North America, both fathers and mothers engage in similar wide ranges of parenting behaviours, but that mothers do more hours of most of them, even when they are in paid employment outside the home (Lamb 2004). The proportions of the parent's parenting time spent in a particular activity may differ consistently – for example it appears that fathers spend a lower proportion of their parenting time on routine cleaning up of children and a higher proportion on rough and tumble play – which may mean that the child associates some activities with one or the other parent; but generally both parents play multiple roles. The ways in which the quality of father–child relationships work seem to resemble the effects of quality of mother–child relationships – being warm and positive, and high on communication and discussion and on enjoyment of shared activities, are developmental good things whichever parent provides them. Parental absence or maltreatment or inadequacy seem to have their impact similarly for mothers and fathers – what matters is if the lack is not made up by anyone else. Absent fathers, for example, are not just missing as potential role models but also, and perhaps more importantly, a hole in the economic and emotional support systems of the family (Amato and Sobolewski 2004; Cummings et al. 2004; Golombok 2000; Holden and Barker 2004; McLanahan and Carlson 2004; pp. 91–92). The family context is often as important as any individual relationship within the family.

Fathers differ in how involved they are in the tasks of parenting. Being the primary family breadwinner can severely limit the time and energy fathers (or, indeed, mothers) have for parenting (Russell and Hwang 2004). Families have to work out a balance of hands on and more distant contributions by their members, and social policy in much of Europe is developing ways to make this easier. Individuals differ in the skills and confidence that they have, and lack of practise may be a genuine reason to hesitate (although it's not altogether credible in all cases – cleaning up the sicked-up feed is not a very expert job, for example). Families and their members differ in how they enact both general social support for each other and participants' access to particular roles. Mothers are often gatekeepers for the father's experience of parenting, often a very fraught issue indeed when the mother–father partnership has broken down (Allen and Hawkins 1999; Amato and Sobolewski 2004; Golombok 2000; McLanahan and Carlson 2004).

So it would be going too far to say that fathers and mothers parent identically in the modern West, but the averages do resemble each other, and the historical trend seems to be towards more hands on and emotionally warm fathering than there used to be. Cultural and subcultural differences still obtain, however, and I want to review some of these briefly, remembering that there is always an enormous variation within cultural groups in behaviour and outcomes. Montgomery (2009) is a good introduction to the anthropological literature.

3.6.2 Cultural differences in fathering

Roopnarine (2004) reviews the US research on African–American and African–Caribbean fathers. These men are often contrasted with their White counterparts in mainly negative terms; there is anxiety, for example, about the higher rate of non-married and non-residential African–American and African–Caribbean fathers compared with White fathers, and the impact of this perhaps reduced rate of contact on the child and the mother. This is often traced back historically to the ways in which slavery and migration disrupted tradition and families, and to the role of endemic racism in individuals' lives. Not all studies take care to compare ethnic groups making sure they are matched for other socio-economic factors (age, educational level and employment, for example) that are likely to affect parenting. Value judgements are expressed in sometimes simplistic terms. All of this complicates the description of cultural differences and their consequences.

It is important to say, then, that African–American and African–Caribbean fatherhood is like White fatherhood in taking a two parent, married partnership as the norm. But social fathering, involving other male relatives or friends as well as or instead of the biological father, is 'an accepted phenomenon' (Roopnarine 2004: 61). (There may be multiple mother figures too, although this is not our focus for the moment.) This sharing of the role of father can include sharing both the parenting and the providing for the family, and tends to vary according to economic circumstances, the man's age or stage in the life cycle, and the other resources that the family can draw on. Beliefs about how to parent have been reported to tend towards higher levels of authoritarianism, power assertion, and harsh, physical, discipline; but this is complicated by the fact that family incomes and educational levels (which are associated with such behaviours in the White population) are on average lower for African–American and African–Caribbean families than for White families; and these families are more likely to live in neighbourhoods where there is a lot of social risk (which again is associated with a parental preference for more controlling parenting). However, particularly for African–Caribbean families there may be specifically cultural factors at work, in beliefs such as 'spare the rod and spoil the child' or 'don't praise the child lest it become too proud', or beliefs that masculinity involves asserting one's power and status, and rejecting an evening out of the family hierarchy.

Cabrera and Garcia-Coll (2004) review the research on Latino fathers. There is less research, and it is clear that Latino fathers come from an even more diverse range of cultures than African–American and African–Caribbean ones. Again, Latino families face greater economic hardship and have lower average educational levels than White individuals, and more of them are comparatively recent migrants to the USA (so they may have adjustment problems, language problems, and dislocations to their family networks). Latino fathers may be focused to a particularly high degree on being the breadwinner for their children rather than engaging in hands on parenting, because that is both an economic priority and a culturally valued choice. The larger family size of Latino groups, and the existence of social roles such as 'compadre' and 'comadre' which are far more substantial than the Anglo equivalent of 'godfather' or 'godmother', may mean that alternative caregivers are available for the children and the father can afford to focus on raising the cash to support them. But here too there seem often to be masculinist value systems ('machismo') and differentiation of gender roles, which might tend to make it unlikely that a Latino father will engage with areas of parenting such as daily childcare, though he may well engage with taking his sons to masculine settings such as outdoor activities. The gradual acculturation of Latino families into the mainstream of American society, and up the socio-economic ladder, may reduce this resistance to gender neutrality in parenting, although it may also weaken the traditional family support networks.

Shwalb et al. (2004) review research on fatherhood in China, Japan, and Korea, all of which are modernising rapidly but are still to some degree Confucian cultures. Again, there are not many substantial research studies, and those that exist are not necessarily representative of the whole of these very large and complex societies. However, it appears that in much of East Asia the father was very much the economically dominant person and the traditional head of the family in a set of largely patriarchal societies. Fathers had to be respected and obeyed, and children were bound to their parents by a sense of filial piety (pp. 156–57). Mothers' roles were defined as different, and subordinate; 'strict father, kind mother' was the general expression. In modern times, this traditional allocation of roles and feelings has had to co-exist with considerable social change, not all of it benevolent. Industrialisation, urbanisation, and economic migration have meant that families have to cope with bringing up children when the breadwinner is absent at work for very long hours (e.g. Japan), or for months at a time (e.g. China). Without an extended family support network to rely on, this can create great difficulties for the parent figures, and may mean a more difficult setting for the child to grow up in. In so far as there is evidence, the historical shift seems to be towards more father involvement in a less hierarchical form, and the effects of greater father involvement in the child's life seem to be as positive as in the West, and to come about in the same ways. The 'One Child' policy in China may have affected expectations of parental involvement and child outcomes in complementary ways (Fong 2002; pp. 84, 200, 238).

3.7 Children's obligations to parents: the example of filial piety

Throughout my discussions of the role of parent–child relationships and interaction in the child's development as a social person, I have concentrated on parents' obligations to children. This is because the culture that I was brought up in and the developmental psychology research that I have read emphasise this rather than its obverse, children's obligations to parents (although my father did joke about how he expected his children to keep him in luxury – 'a gold-plated bath chair' – in his old age). However, I want to note at this point that parent–child relationships, and in particular obligations, are not necessarily one way.

Many cultures say very much more about how children should show respect, obedience, and loyalty to their parents. Perhaps the clearest instance of this is the traditional Chinese emphasis on 'filial piety' (Ikels 2004). This was one of the major cultural values expounded by Confucius in around 500 BCE. The component behaviours were obeying one's parents, caring for them in old age, giving them a properly conducted funeral so that their spirits could join the ancestors, practising ancestor worship, and having descendants (especially or even exclusively male descendants) to continue the family line. Basically people were supposed to feel grateful to their parents and under an obligation to do everything possible for them. There were legal, religious, and political sanctions against anyone who strayed from this set of behaviours, and children were expected to sacrifice themselves in the service of parents' needs. Being 'unfilial' was one of the most serious of crimes, but a 'filial' person would be regarded as reliable, trustworthy and honourable.

It has been argued by psychologists interested in cultural differences that the theory and practise of filial piety within the family, the community and the educational system induced the key psychological characteristics of obedience and conservatism said to be typical of the Chinese character. The Confucian ideal of an individual person as an insignificant self who submits to the larger self of the collectivity is still often expressed (pp. 81, 139, 236–39). It could be argued that this is an internalised self-surveillance device that could account for the low rate of juvenile delinquency in Chinese adolescents (even after emigration to the West).

The novels and memoirs of authors like Jung Chang (1992), Maxine Hong Kingston (1976) and Amy Tan (1991) illustrate what this emphasis on subordinating oneself to 'duty' could be like for daughters, both in China and in families that had emigrated to the USA. Fong (2002) suggests that following the one-child policy in China, girls in urban areas have far more power to challenge patrilineal authority because they are their parents' only investment in the future (where formerly a brother would have been the focus of parental hopes). These only daughters receive more encouragement to pursue education and demanding careers, as they are the only people who can create family success in the next generation. As gender norms emphasise obedience and studiousness for girls, they tend to be highly successful in the education system and to emerge from it well qualified for relatively well-paid jobs (although the 'glass ceiling' clearly exists for them and restricts their access to elite posts). They expect to spend more of their lives in the public sphere of employment than earlier generations of young women, who contributed to their husband's family rather than their own, and were more engaged in the private world of childbearing, childrearing and looking after the aged members of the family – tasks which often precluded them from paid employment. Modern Chinese girls were less tolerant of gender-based inequality. In Fong's survey, girls wanted incomes of their own rather than being reliant on a husband, men were involved in domestic work, and nearly a third of girls said that they hoped to remain childless all their lives. It was increasingly recognised that the work of filial piety could be done as well by women as by men.

Filial piety is a clear example of how the macrosystem influences the microsystem, and how social change has effects at both levels. It is also part of a cultural difference in family obligations and the role of non-family in the care of individuals. Historically the extended family did almost all the caring for the very young and the very old; demographic changes, such as smaller families, increased geographical mobility, and people living longer, and changes in social expectations about how health care and education are provided, have changed the experience of young children and their parents and may also present difficulties for how adult children relate to their ageing parents. The ways in which psychosocial changes and macrosystem changes affect parent–child relationships and obligations are going to be complex.

3.8 Summary

I have discussed the role of parents in the development of the child as social person, structuring the evidence as far as possible around Bronfenbrenner's model of developmental environments and developmental processes. Although we have to recognise that children influence parents and genes influence both, my view is that there is overwhelming evidence that parents, through their parenting practices, have a crucially important influence on the development of the child. The proximal processes of the parent–child microsystem account, I think, for an enormous part of the child's chances of growing up to be a well-functioning social person. Parental behaviour determines to a considerable degree what the child learns about social functioning, what sort of self-concept and understanding of other people emerges, what sort of emotional foundation there is to face later challenges. There are fine differences in what works best at different ages, in different environments, in different cultures, and for particular individuals, but the developmental frames I described earlier apply to all individuals, all individuals will function less well if they are subjected to proximal processes which differ too much from those I have described. And the effects may be extremely hard to put right.

Chapter 4

Qualities of microsystems 2: Child and other children

I move on to discussion of the microsystems that involve the child primarily with other children – siblings, friends and other peers. The child's experience of such microsystems is affected by the child's own characteristics, and the child's characteristics are affected by his or her experience of other children. The interests and activities of such child–child microsystems both resemble and differ from those involving child and parents. Microsystems between children will affect and be affected by other microsystems – for example interaction and relationships with siblings are affected by, and affect, interaction with parents, and peer interaction relationships in school are in tension with relationships with teachers. I have not found much research on the child–sibling relationship involving exosystem or macrosystem levels, although these levels may be visible at the margins of my discussion of children's relationships with peers outside the family. I will talk about siblings first, and then peers.

4.1 Siblings

Most people have brothers and sisters, and for most people their relationships with their brothers and sisters are an important part of their lives during childhood and beyond it. They are very likely to spend more time with their siblings than with their fathers, and perhaps than their mothers; and their relationships with their siblings will affect their relationships with their parents, and vice versa. When they are practising social skills, or comparing themselves with other people, or considering what choices to make about how they live their lives, siblings may be one of the major partners or reference points. Siblings can be seen to do some of the functional framing that I described when I discussed parenting; they can also be seen to compete (pp. 161, 163–67). Siblings' influences feed into one's personal identity (Damon and Hart 1988; Schachter 1982; Steelman *et al.* 2002), one's family system, one's school career, one's friendships, one's romantic relationships, so many aspects of one's life.

I must, early on, make the point that sibling relationships vary just as much as any other type of relationships does. Often sibling relationships have a strong emotional component, with an uninhibited expression of both positive and negative feelings. The illuminating research done in 1950s and 1960s Nottingham by John and Elizabeth Newson (Newson and Newson 1968, 1977) illustrates this; for example they report that there were comparatively uninhibited squabbles and fights between siblings even in families where fighting was disapproved of, even though fighting was strongly discouraged as a way of dealing with disagreements outside the family (Newson and Newson 1976). Often sibling relationships are very intimate – most siblings spend a lot of time together as small children and through to adolescence, may share rooms, toys and friends, know each other very well, compare themselves with each other, are compared by others, and may even be seen sometimes and in some respects as inter-changeable members of the same family. And these are not optional relationships in the way that friendships can be – child siblings who have squabbled cannot say 'I won't be your sister any more', they have to find some other resolution to the disagreement. From very early on children develop ways of coping with these close relationships that make them useful. They know about the relative costs of disagreement with parents, siblings, and friends.

> 'If I take it out on my mum, I've got a chance of getting no money. If I take it out on my friends, you can become like hated at school or big people try and kick you in, if you know what I mean. Whereas if you take it out on your sisters you don't get anything done to you. You get a scratch or a slap but that's not much.' (Daniel 13, oldest)

> 'It's just 'cos you really know them, know their personalities 'cos you've been with them so long and you know what they're like and you don't have to make a good impression on them because you know them well and they're not going to like fall out with you or anything or think you're uncool 'cos I mean they have to live with you, they've got no choice.' (Henrietta 11, oldest)
>
> (Punch 2008: 340, 342)

4.1.1 Genetic and experiential factors in sibling resemblance

Theoretical input from evolutionary psychology reminds us that siblings have shared genes. We may expect family resemblances between siblings in their behaviour, just as we expect them to resemble each other physically. For physical resemblances, the main reasons are genetic – we and our siblings share an inheritance from our parents that causes us to be tall, have long fingers, have our hair grow thin at the temples or the crown of the head, and so forth; although of course there may be non-genetic reasons for some physical resemblances, such as siblings sharing a diet of junk food leading to resemblances in obesity. The reasons for psychological resemblance are more controversial. Developmental behaviour geneticists argue both that family resemblances in personality and adjustment are largely genetic, and that siblings growing up together may develop into very different characters despite apparently sharing the same environment (e.g. Whiteman, McHale and Crouter 2007). At the extreme, this has been argued as all sibling resemblance being due to shared genes, with no shared family effect at all (Harris 1995, 1998). There are serious problems with using the existing evidence to reach such an extreme conclusion, including inadequate statistical methods, poor measures, and inadequate samples. Properly conducted research (e.g. O'Connor *et al.* 1998; Jenkins *et al.* 2005) is developing ways of estimating the relative effects of shared and non-shared family influences and shows that individual differences between sibs in the same family mean that the different sibs have somewhat different experiences within the family, they elicit different responses from other family members, and respond differently to 'shared' stresses or opportunities.

On the whole we would expect siblings to have, in evolutionary terms, shared interests. You can ensure that your own genes have a better chance of passing on to the next generation if you support the reproductive success of your brother or sister, as they have (on average) half of your genes (the same proportion as your child has). Altruistic behaviour is indeed predictable in terms of the genetic relatedness of the actor and the recipient – more helpful behaviour between full sibs than half-sibs or step-sibs, for example – although co-residence and shared interests also predict contact and positive feeling between siblings (e.g. Bowles and Posel 2005; Emlen 1995; Hetherington 1988; Pollet 2007). But evolutionary psychology also sees siblings as being in competition with each other for the resources the parents provide. Sibling rivalry, or at least sibling competition, is found among many species, including European earwigs (Kolliker 2007). Sibling competition for resources may even affect your physical development as well as your social and personal development (Lawson and Mace 2008). Family characteristics may influence the amount of sibling rivalry that occurs: McHale and her colleagues, for example, found that siblings had more positive relationships if parent–child relationships were also positive and parents had strong religious identifications, whereas siblings high in rivalry showed more depression and risky behaviour (McHale *et al.* 2007).

A lot of the research on individual differences in sibling relationships has focused on easily measured variables such as 'family constellation' – gender mixes, birth order, size of age gap, family size. Our stereotype of how sibling relationships work may be exemplified by the family in Louisa May Alcott's *Little Women* (Alcott 1868); four girls, close in age, sharing both games and responsibilities, squabbling and competing but also supporting and consoling each other, and remaining close into adulthood. Here the oldest girl is the conscientious homemaker, the second the rebellious iconoclast, the third self-effacing, the youngest a spoiled darling both resented and petted by her sisters. Alcott drew on her own family to write her novel, so 'Meg', 'Jo', 'Beth' and 'Amy' were real girls as well as prototypes for later girls to imitate.

4.1.2 Birth order and sibling socialisation

There is some evidence that birth order has systematic effects on children's socialisation (Gass, Jenkins and Dunn 2007). The argument is that all the members of a family contribute to how it works and how it affects each member. In the 'confluence' model, which is supported by a brief paper in Science (Kristensen and Bjerkedal 2007) and a commentary on it (Sulloway 2007), the focus is on the family's overall intellectual environment, which gets relatively positive contributions from those who are intellectually well-developed but less positive contributions from those whose intellectual level is low. For the first-born child, the overall effect is positive while he or she is the only one because all the parents' intellectual influence is concentrated on the single child recipient. The birth of a younger child adds in a person with no developed intellectual skills and rearranges parental attention, so the first-born's intellectual environment is degraded. The more skilled first-born, however, adds on to the family environment and has a positive effect on the younger sibling. Once the older child is skilled enough to tutor the younger one, the organisation and reflection of thoughts that tutors need to do benefits their own intellectual level, possibly more than it benefits the learner's.

First-born children have the advantage of a period when their parents' parenting is theirs alone, but then face the unpleasant experience of having to share these benefits with a newcomer. This typically disturbs the older child, who may show aggression towards the new baby, anxiety about being separated from parents, and regression in development, for example reverting to wanting a bottle, or loss of toilet training (Dunn and Kendrick 1982; Dunn 1988, 1993; Dunn et al. 1999; Baydar, Greek and Brooks-Gunn 1997; Baydar, Hyle and Brooks-Gunn 1997). First-born children's feelings of interest, hostility, or affection towards the new baby predict how well the siblings get on (as well as the children's later adjustment in other social settings, which I discuss below (p. 164)). While the children are very young, the feelings of the older child have more effect on the quality of the relationship than the feelings of the younger. As the younger child becomes more of a socialised person, however, able to develop and express views about the older sib, the balance of influence in the relationship will shift. Younger siblings develop their skills of understanding, communicating, and influencing, and become more equal partners in joint play and conflict than they could be when these skills were less mature than their sibs'. For the older sibling, this developmental change may mean anxiety about being overtaken or a 'triumphant sense of always being ahead', as in this example:

C to observer, speaking about her baby brother: He's a walloper. He'll smack me when he's bigger. I'm going to be huge when he's a bit bigger. Up to the ceiling. Like you.
Observer to child: I'm not up to the ceiling.
Child to observer: Well, I'll be up there. I'll grow so much. Up to the ceiling. So high.

(Dunn and Kendrick 1982: 108–109)

Younger siblings, on the other hand, may feel that they are striving to keep up. If the competition becomes too uncomfortable, the sibs may go in for what has been called 'sibling de-identification' (Schachter 1982; Whiteman, McHale and Crouter 2007). Here the siblings avoid comparison and rivalry by defining themselves as 'different' and pursuing different domains of competence and interest, choosing different areas to specialise in so as not to compete too directly. This may be particularly likely to happen where siblings are not naturally differentiated by a big age gap or by prescribed gender roles. Sibling de-identification might affect both short-term relationships with each other and with parents (Feinberg *et al.* 2003), and the long-term career path that individuals take. Younger sibs value the support of older sibs and continue to use them as models, well into adolescence (Buhrmester and Furman 1990, Smetana *et al.* 2006, Whiteman *et al.* 2007). Older sibs may chaperone the younger ones into more adult activities. I remember how thrilled I was aged seven or eight to be allowed to be banker when my older brothers and their friends were playing Monopoly, having what I felt was privileged access to the mysterious and glamorous world of adolescent males.

Younger children seem to carry their relationship with their sib forward into having similar relationships with friends rather more than first-borns do (Tucker *et al.* 1999). Possibly this reflects the fact that less skilled or lower status individuals may learn from more skilled or higher status ones than the reverse, or it may be that the younger sibs have had more opportunities to observe their sibs meeting developmental challenges they haven't yet had to face themselves, such as the challenge of making friends in school or moving into adolescence, something they can learn about vicariously. The older child, having had to be the first of the siblings to learn these things, may have less relevant behaviour to transfer from sibling relationships to the new ones.

There may be advantages to learning from observation in this way, but there can equally be problems (Bard and Rodgers 2003; Shanahan *et al.* 2007; Stormshak *et al.* 1996; Whiteman, McHale and Crouter 2007).

Imitating your older brother may not be a good idea if that older brother is delinquent, for example (Slomkowski *et al.* 2001; pp. 151, 266–67); being expected by teachers to replicate your older sister's success in school may be an unfair demand, if she was overly bookish and your own strengths are different.

4.1.3 Sibling reciprocity and complementarity

Individuals' temperament or personality characteristics may influence the quality of their relationships with their siblings, just as they would any other relationships. The evidence is neither comprehensive nor consistent, but sibling conflict in early childhood may be more common when the children differ in temperament (Gass, Jenkins and Dunn 2007). How time is allocated to different activities is related to the siblings' personal relationship (Shanahan *et al.* 2007). Possibly temperament differences make it more difficult for siblings to maintain reciprocal interactions (Hinde 1979; Meadows 1986), where the different partners do similar things, simultaneously or taking turns, as in children's rough and tumble or chasing games. Siblings often engage in games where they imitate each other, and often share emotions (Dunn and Kendrick 1982); and many a parent has experienced their children ganging up to challenge or deflate their parental authority.

Although reciprocal interaction is commonly found in sibling relationships, there will be complementary action too, where one child's actions are different from but co-ordinated with the other child's. In traditional cultures older siblings are often the official caregiver and substitute parent for the younger ones, responsible for much of the nurturing and socialisation that babies and young children receive (Whiting and Whiting 1975; Zukow-Goldring 1995; Rothbaum and Trommsdorff 2007). This may be the case to some extent in Western cultures too, where older brothers and sisters are given informal responsibility for 'keeping an eye on' their siblings, protecting them in the school playground, letting them tag along when they are with their friends, and so forth. Watching a frightening television programme with an older sibling is less distressing for a preschool child than watching it alone; the older siblings could comfort and calm the younger one, which is just as well as it is more common for siblings to watch television together than for children to watch it with parents (Dubow, Huesmann and Greenwood 2007). Most young children are concerned and helpful about their baby brothers and sisters, indeed if parents can arrange for the toddler to play a helpful role in the care of the new baby this is likely to induce the toddler to be more positive about the baby and the baby to become more attached to its older sib (Dunn and Kendrick 1982). Even young children will adjust their speech to the perceived competence of the baby (Meadows 2006). They exaggerate their intonation, use simpler sentences, and increase their production of repetitions and explanations when talking to the younger child, behaviours which are probably effective in achieving the child's intention of directing the baby's activity, and might help the baby to learn to talk, although this is unlikely to be the sibling's intention. Older siblings do teach the younger ones the skills they have developed themselves, which may help to consolidate their own learning (Light 1983; Gauvain and Perez 2007) or provide them with a partner in their games, as well as increasing the younger sib's repertoire of skills. In a study by Azmitia and Hesser (1993), young children observed their older siblings closely when the older child was working on a problem-solving task in partnership with a friend, and more often sought help from their sibling rather than the sibling's friend, which suggests that these little children saw their older sib as a preferred teacher.

There is a particularly substantial body of evidence about sibs as effective tutors in the area of theory of mind, which involves the development of an understanding that other people have mental states of belief, intention, desire and so forth, that these may not be the same as one's own, and that being able to infer other people's mental states with reasonable accuracy is helpful in interacting with them (McAlister and Peterson 2006; pp. 112–13, 128–29). Experience with sibs seems to contribute to this (Perner, Ruffman and Leekam 1994); indeed it may be that theory of mind starts with familiar family members and especially sibs before it generalises to people elsewhere. Even very young children, well before the usual age of success on theory of mind tasks, have been observed to show a complex understanding of their siblings' mental states, including anticipating their intentions, manipulating their emotions (to improve or worsen them), and sharing an imaginary world. Dunn and Kendrick (1982) provide lovely examples. Here, for example, is Callum, aged 14 months with his older sister, Laura, and below that another insightful extract.

> Callum repeatedly reaches for and manipulates the magnetic letters Laura is playing with. Laura repeatedly says NO gently. Callum continues trying to reach the letters. Finally, Laura picks up the tray containing the letters and carries it to a high table that Callum cannot reach. Callum is furious and starts to cry. He turns and goes straight to the sofa where Laura's comfort objects, a rag doll and a pacifier, are lying. He takes the doll and holds tight, looking at Laura. Laura for the first time is very upset, starts crying, and runs to take the doll.
>
> (Dunn and Kendrick 1982: 116)

Bruce, aged 2–3, says of his baby brother, who is playing with a balloon;

> 'He going to pop it in a minute. And he'll cry. And he'll be frightened of me too. I *like* the pop.'
>
> (Dunn and Kendrick 1982: 106)

These sorts of demonstrations of understanding another person are far more common in sibling relationships than in the formal tests used by theory of mind researchers (Meadows 2006). The familiarity of the other person and the emotional intensity of the relationship make it both easier and more important to know what is going on inside the other's head. Additionally, Dunn's observations show that there is often a lot of talk about people's mental states in the context of sibling conflict and siblings' joint pretend play. It is possible that there is a correlation between the amount of such talk and play and the degree of successful performance on theory of mind tasks (Brown, Donelan-McCall, and Dunn 1996; Carpendale and Lewis 2006; Meins and Fernyhough 1999; Meins 2002, 2003) because children who already have an advanced theory of mind will be better at such conversations and such play, but experiences of shared imaginative play and experiences of discussing other people's mental states in an emotionally relevant context look like important contributors to mental models of other people. Sibling relationships appear to be an important arena for the development of social understanding.

> Siblings have a dynamic relationship characterized by varied types of interaction, ranging from supportive and affectionate exchanges to hostility and conflict. The emotional bonds and high levels of familiarity that siblings have may foster cognitive opportunities by observing and interacting with each other. In addition, siblings, other than twins, have an asymmetry of skill, experience and control. Together, these factors provide fertile ground for children to develop cognitive skills.
>
> (Gauvain and Perez 2007: 594)

4.1.4 Sibling relationships and family conflict

I emphasised when I was presenting Bronfennbrenner's model earlier (Chapter 1) that no single family relationship is completely independent of other relationships (or contexts). Conflict in parent–child relationships is associated with sibling conflict (Brody *et al.* 1992, 1994; Brody 1998; Dunn *et al.* 1999; Erel *et al.* 1998; Smith and Ross 2007), and prosocial relationships between siblings are associated with warm positive parenting. The pathway of causation here is unclear. Parents may be modelling ways to treat people that the children copy with their own siblings; or the parents' positive relationship with their child may improve the child's emotional state and induce the child to treat the siblings well because of their general state of happiness; or the parents may be treating the children with more warmth because the children are so charming as they express their love for their little brothers and sisters (same processes with a negative cast in the case of unhappy or abusive parent–child relationships). Parents' behaviour will be influencing their own relationships with each of their children as well as those children's relationship with each other. Siblings may compete for parents' attention, or they may bond closely with each other when their parents are absent or extremely distant and uninvolved. Children respond to parents' marital conflict differently, with some of them feeling that they are themselves to blame for it (Parke and Buriel 1998; Sternberg *et al.* 2006, p. 161), and within families some children react with more anxiety, anger or depression (Marcus *et al.* 2001; Jenkins *et al.* 2005) while some show less effect. The more children feel that they are to blame, the more likely they are to show symptoms of depressed mood or conduct disorders.

4.1.5 Sibling relationships and fairness issues

Children often feel that their parents treat them and their siblings differently (Dunn 1993; Dunn *et al.* 1999). It is not always clear that this is really the case; many parents say they treat their children alike, and most parents try hard to treat their children fairly. Although this might well mean not treating them identically, outright favouring one of your children over another is generally disapproved of by parents (and by children). Why might child perception and parent perception be different? We could relate it back to the ideas of evolutionary psychology about siblings' competition for resources, as I discussed earlier, but one other factor is that children's comparison of how they are treated and how their siblings are treated often do not allow for the age differences involved. If you see that you are expected to tidy up but your little brother is not, your explanation for this difference in expectations might be parental favouritism or parental adherence to gender stereotypes, and you might regard it as gratuitous and unfair; your parents' explanation might be that this little brother is as yet too young to be able to tidy up, but will have to do it when he grows up a bit. Observers who have seen parents with their successive children so that they can compare how different children were treated at the same age report consistency rather than variation in parents' behaviour (Dunn 1993). Parents' experience of being parents may influence differential treatment of siblings too. Older siblings may see their younger sibs allowed to do something that was forbidden for themselves a few years ago, when they were the same age: the reason might be that the less experienced parents proscribed the forbidden activity because they thought it was dangerous, until the survival of the older child, despite having done it, demonstrates that this was an unnecessary proscription.

Even if the parents' intentions are good, if the children perceive their treatment as different and unfair this is likely to worsen relationships between the siblings short term and long term (Brody 1998; Kowal and Kramer 1997; Parke and Buriel 1998; Stocker 1993; Stocker *et al.* 2002; Volling and Elins 1998). Even young children monitor their parents' interaction with their siblings with an eye to who's getting the better bargain, as in these examples from Dunn and Kendrick (1982).

> John (21 months) and his older sister Annie have pushed stools up to the kitchen counter next to oven, to investigate cooking materials.

> *Mother to John*: Ah ah! Don't touch please. Hot! [removes child].
> *John*: [protest noise]
> *Mother*: Oh I know!
> *John* [angrily]: Annie going there!
> *Mother to Annie*: Annie come right away. Right away.

> (1982: 53)

> Polly (28 months) intervenes in her older sister's conversation with their mother about the sister's pretend game of shopping at Sainsbury's.

> *Polly to sib*: Better get your cheque book.
> *Sib*: Yes . . .
> [Later in pretend game]
> *Sib to mother*: Did I leave my bag there?
> *Mother to sib*: You didn't leave your bag at Sainsbury's, did you?
> *Sib to mother*: What I want?
> *Polly to sib* [Points out mislaid bag]: No at home!
> *Mother to sib*: You left it at home! . . .
> *Sib to mother* [confused about having lost her list and her bag]: Umm – what did I want then?
> *Mother to sib*: What did you want?
> *Polly* [triumphantly]: I got all my shopping list in. I's got my shopping list in my bag.

> (1982: 114–115)

Children may learn a lot from disputes about fairness and the ways that they are resolved (Smith and Ross 2007). The research literature on theory of mind and person understanding (pp. 112–13, 128–29), and on moral development (pp. 120–21), is relevant here.

An extensive research literature shows better or worse relationships with siblings to be correlated with better outcomes for children's adjustment and other social relations (for reviews see Brody 1998; Gass, Jenkins and Dunn 2007) Longitudinal studies (e.g. Dunn *et al.* 1994) showed early sibling conflict predicted children's emotional problems both at the time and at later follow-ups, even when other family influences were allowed for. Here too, the causal pathway is unlikely to be simple. Influences could be from sibling relationships to adjustment, or the reverse, or both ways. Patterson's research on family aggression (Patterson 1986; Snyder and Patterson 1995;

Patterson and Fisher 2002; Patterson, DeGarmo and Forgatch 2004) shows siblings reacting to each other in ways that escalated conflict; such behaviour not only gives children extensive practise, and even encouragement, in being coercive and aggressive; in these families it also offers fewer opportunities than normal to learn to behave in more positive ways. Parents' management of sibling conflict varies between families but also relates to the families' rules about public and private behaviour. Newson and Newson (1976) showed that parents allowed the child to resolve conflicts with siblings more aggressively than was permitted with people outside the family, especially if the child was a girl and especially in middle-class families. Their working-class boys were very likely to be encouraged to settle their differences in active combat, rather than by negotiation or withdrawal.

It could also be that growing up in a conflict-filled atmosphere, with siblings who are aggressive, hostile and disparaging, might cause children's views of themselves to be negative and helpless, with results such as low self-esteem, depression, and anxiety (Bandura 1995, 1997; Zahn-Waxler *et al.* 2008), and perhaps maladaptive changes in neurotransmitters and other stress reduction mechanisms (pp. 54, 56–59). Stocker (1993) and Stocker *et al.* (2002) found that sibling conflict between preschool children predicted adjustment problems after the older child had entered school, which suggests carry-over into a new social context with new challenges. On the other hand, having good relationships with your siblings can help with dealing with stressful life events, such as the death of a grandparent (Dunn *et al.* 1994).

4.1.6 Sibling relationships in adolescence

Sibling relationships are highly salient to adolescents, as they are to younger children (Dunn 1999, Giordano 2003, Smetana *et al.* 2006). Relationships with brothers and sisters can be important sources of companionship, affection, and intimacy; siblings may be valuable sources of information or even sponsors in social interactions with peers, and valuable members of a coalition against adult authority. Although siblings tend to fight each other a lot in early adolescence (Furman and Buhrmester 1985, 1992), as adolescents mature their relationships with siblings become more egalitarian, more reciprocal, and less full of conflict, although also less close as the siblings' social worlds widen and they spend less time together. Sibling involvement in such problem behaviours as early sexual activity and drug use seems to be a risk factor for younger siblings (Slomkowski *et al.* 2001); better relationships and greater support for good behaviour from siblings are associated with lower levels of problem behaviour (Stocker *et al.* 2002, Branje *et al.* 2004).

Siblings' experience of each other will be mixed up with their experience of their parents. Parents' history of experience of parenting their older children is likely to affect the parenting of their younger ones (Whiteman, McHale and Crouter 2003). Older siblings often complain that they were subject to more parental control than younger ones are now; parents reply that they learned from their experience with the first child how much parental control was likely to affect children's behaviour and development. As adolescents are often preoccupied with fairness and autonomy, this can become quite a sore point in the family, between siblings as well as between parent and child.

4.1.7 Summary

It seems to me that sibling microsystems can function in many of the ways that parent–child microsystems do. Evolutionary perspectives on siblings suggest sharing and competing behaviour, which do indeed occur. The characteristics of the individuals involved can be very powerful, and I would not deny that genetic factors are involved. But what seems most salient when we try to examine individual differences in development that could be due to experience of peers, is that there are rather the same sorts of patterns, proximal processes, and outcomes for the participants as we get when we look at parent–child interaction. Sibling relationships allow scope for discussing people's feelings, their rights, their needs; for managing emotions; for joint attention and co-operation; for imaginative play; for learning from others, and teaching others; for negotiation and aggression; for alliances and competition; for chaperoned entry into the wider social world; for enormous amounts of fun. As with parent–child microsystems, prolonged engagement with these proximal processes shapes the developmental pathway.

4.2 Peers and the child as social person

There were times as a parent when I felt with some bitterness that my daughter thought far more about her friends than she did about me. That she showed more preoccupation with them than with me was not unreasonable, however much I disliked it. From the time she went to school, she spent more waking time with friends than with parents, and had far more reason to focus on keeping in with them. She could be confident that her parents would not abandon her or become hostile or behave unpredictably, but friendships were far more volatile and provoked far more anxiety and distress – and, no doubt, more excitement, much useful support, much intimacy. And when I think back to my distant childhood, I still remember my friendships and my not-friendships at least as vividly as I remember my family experiences. My sense is that my family's influence on me was continuous and powerful but gentle; that of my friends more eventful, more exhilarating, and more caustic.

Psychological theory has presented successive accounts of why peer relations are important. Psychoanalytic theorists such as Blos (1967) wrote of a turbulent process of individuation in adolescence when peers became an important influence shaping adolescents' restructuring of their relationships with their parents. Piaget emphasised the contribution of the comparatively equal relationship between peers to moral development and of resolving disagreement between peers to progress on cognitive tasks such as perspective taking and conservation (Piaget 1932). Vygotsky (1978) and Wenger (1998) emphasised the co-operative co-construction of social events as part of the process of development. Peer groups have been discussed as the arenas where much social learning takes place, within the models, rewards, and sanctions that the group provides (e.g. Cairns 1988, 1995). For Harris (1995, 1998), the child devotes every scrap of energy to becoming part of the tribe of other children, reducing other influences (except genetic ones) to near zero, and it is peer normative pressure that shapes development.

Looking at children's lives with their peers involves multiple interwoven levels. We need to consider the characteristics of the individual child, of the interactions and behaviour moment by moment and in retrospect and prospect, of the dyad or larger group, and of the local and wider culture, since group characteristics are not simply the sum of the characteristics of the individual members of the group (cf. Giordano 2003; Hinde 1979; Bronfenbrenner 1979; Mejía-Arauz et al. 2007; Smetana et al. 2006; Fredricks and Eccles 2005; Simpkins et al. 2008). What goes on at one level influences and is constrained by what goes on at other levels. Again we are concerned with mesosystems as well as microsystems (Chapter 1).

4.2.1 Development of peer relations

Even babies notice and are interested in other babies – and there is evidence that increasingly through infancy and the early preschool years they co-ordinate their behaviour with peers, imitate each other and show awareness of being imitated, perform observe–respond and observe–wait–respond interchanges, help and share, and produce responses that are appropriately differentiated to peer characteristics (for reviews see Rubin et al. 1998a, 2006; Hay et al. 1999; Hay, Castle and Davies 2000; NICHD 2003b). When with a familiar peer they behave differently from how they behave with an unfamiliar one. They act reciprocally, including consistent positive interactions involving recollection of previous interactions and perhaps anticipation of future ones – which might well be considered to amount to 'friendships'. Toddlers can develop dominance hierarchies and in-groups, although they are not yet very likely to define and enforce out-groups.

Older preschool children, particularly those who spend time in groups (NICHD 2003a) rapidly develop still more effective social skills. As their social cognition and theory of mind advance (pp. 112–13, 128–29, 160–68), their intersubjectivity improves and they can sustain longer sequences of play and conversation (Werner, Cassidy and Juliano 2006). They still show 'parallel play', playing alongside another child without co-operation or co-ordination, but some of the time they are doing this as part of an effective strategy for being accepted into the play of another child or group. More and more they can co-ordinate thematic and socio-dramatic play (p. 237, Robinson et al. 2003; Göncu, Patt and Kouba 2002); these types of play are thought to provide opportunities for developing and communicating meaning, and opportunities for control, compromise, and negotiation, especially over roles, scripts, rules, and properties. Socio-dramatic play can also provide opportunities for playing out issues with emotional content, for example intimacy, conflict, trust and leadership. There are also increases in prosocial behaviour, in conversation, and in conflict about rights and opinions – whereas conflict over objects decreases as the children develop strategies that make hit and grab unnecessary. Once peers are identified as 'friends', children show a preference for them as playmates, and give and get more positive and supportive behaviour; and where there is more prosocial behaviour, relationships become more stable (Dunn et al. 1999, 2002; Dunn 2004; Berndt 2004). There may well be more incidents of conflict with 'friends' than with 'neutral' children, but this in the preschool years is largely because there is more interaction with friends overall. Comparing conflicts with friends with conflicts with non-friends, conflicts with friends are more likely to be resolved by negotiation, or at worst disengagement, and friends who have temporarily fallen out maintain proximity to each other rather than separating completely.

As middle childhood progresses, peers become still more salient in children's lives. The number of people who are regarded as peers increases, and peers are engaged with in a larger range of settings – home, school, travelling between home and school, sports teams, voluntary groups, on the phone and over the Internet, etc. – and for a larger range of activities – play, conversing, 'hanging out', sports, watching TV, playing computer games, and so forth. Friendships provide experience of give and take and involve joint activities, shared values, shared interests, loyalty, understanding, and disclosure. They are one of the arenas where notions of 'fairness' develop. They become relationships with a history and a future, as well as a present (Hinde 1979). Friends learn about each others' preferred football team, pop star, fashion shop; and the children coerce parents to access what is considered desirable by their peers. Many a mother has had to hang around for hours in fashion shops she would never otherwise have set foot in, while a daughter tries on garment after garment in order to get something that will impress her friends.

The pattern of aggressive behaviour towards peers continues to change through middle childhood; there is less instrumental aggression to settle a moment's disagreement over who has the preferred toy than there was in the toddler and preschool years, and more long-term hostility. Peer relationships include more verbal and relational aggression but less physical aggression, as strategies for asserting oneself and doing down the opponent become more socialised and more verbal, and there is more of a sense of the relationship lasting over time. Children become far more concerned about belonging to the peer group, with acute stress and distress at being excluded from it. Particularly among girls, there is more gossip, and more relational aggression – 'You're not my friend any more', 'I'm not going to let you come to my party' – and derogatory comments on others' appearance and possessions if they are not the most admired look or brand. Girls also, especially as teenagers, engage in more co-rumination with their friends (Caselman and Self 2007; Parker et al. 2005; Rose 2002; Rose and Rudolph 2006; Rose et al. 2007, pp. 73, 179, 270), with long and potentially harmful discussion of negative issues such as weight and relationships. Peer influences on eating disorders and self-harm are a source of concern to specialists.

The breaking off of a friendship is now often a source of great distress (Laursen et al. 1996; Parker and Seal 1998; Wojslawowicz et al. 2006). A chronic lack of friends is associated with greater anxiety and depression, both contemporaneously and later (Ladd and Troop-Gordon 2003). Friends provide amusing companions, confidantes, comforters, protectors against bullying by peers or put-downs from adults (Hodges 1997; Denton and Zarbatany 1996). If friendships go wrong, therefore, the child both loses these benefits and is at risk of hostile revelations if the former friends make new relationships and tell tales about what the child confided in them earlier. Girls seem to be especially prone to such problems as their friendships tend to be both more intimate and more fragile; the bosom friend who turns in a moment to a malevolent gossip spilling out one's most intimate confidences is a blight on many girls' lives in school (and a persistent nuisance to the teachers and parents who have to cope with the swirling animosities) (Zarbatany, McDougall and Hymel 2000; Benenson and Christakos 2003; Crick and Grotpeter 1995). Boys too have mutual antipathies, and some of these involve open warfare (Abecassis et al. 2002; Hartup and Abecassis 2002; Horn 2003), but they may find it possible to develop a state of hostile co-existence.

Boys' friendship groups tend to be larger and less intimate than girls'. Relationships within these groups are often competitive, and issues of power and status are often overt; at this age boys are still using rough and tumble behaviour to sort out dominance hierarchies, and athletic prowess is a great source of status. Group members tend to be similar in levels of school performance and motivation and levels of aggression. There are also strong influences from the surrounding culture, as seen in the study by Knafo et al. (2008) of aggression in Jewish and Arab high school pupils.

Popularity, and lack of popularity, are important in peer groups in middle childhood. Children who are regarded as being 'popular' with peers generally tend to conform to the local social norm, or to differ slightly from it in the favoured direction – just a bit prettier, cleverer, more athletic than the norm. But peer groups also develop sets of roles (Pollard 1985), and one child may fit into a role (such as friendly joker or team coach) which makes them easier to like, whereas another falls into a less attractive one (crybaby, tell-tale, fatty). Popular children tend to be astute in their social cognition; for example they tend to have goals that are seen as positive, they are not too impulsive and unpredictable, they can manage their negative emotions and not engage in negative behaviour, they have effective techniques for making overtures to people and joining in with activities (Bukowski et al. 2007). Children who are rejected or neglected by the peer group have more negative views of their own social self. They are less likely to have a mutual best friend relationship, and what friendships they do have tend to be less supportive, less intimate, and generally of poorer quality.

4.2.2 Attachment and parent influences on peer relations

The early attachment relationships between child and parent seem to predict later peer relationships and friendships (Lyons-Ruth, Easterbrookes and Cibelli 1997; Shaw et al. 1996; Burgess et al. 2003; Schneider, Atkinson and Tardif 2001; Kochanska 1998; Raikes and Thompson 2006; Clark and Ladd 2000). Children who have had secure attachments tend to show more positive behaviour towards peers, whereas those with insecure or disorganised attachments show more negative behaviour – more frustration and inhibition for those with early insecure–ambivalent attachments, and more aggression and anger for those whose attachments were insecure–avoidant or disorganised (Lyons-Ruth, Easterbrookes and Cibelli 1997; Shaw et al. 1996; Burgess et al. 2003; Schneider, Atkinson and Tardif 2001). The suggested linkage between early attachment and later peer relations is complex (pp. 123–26). Rubin, Bukowski and Parker (2006) suggest that the child's early experience of parental warmth, sensitivity and responsivity induces a sense of trust in relationships and of oneself as worthy of a positive response from others. This leads to a secure, confident interaction style and active confident exploration of the world, which facilitate positive play with peers. The next step involves the positive exploration of ideas, perspectives, roles and actions, and thus the development of positive social skills. (One other key part of the sequence might be what Meins and her colleagues (Meins and Fernyhough 1999; Meins 2002, 2003) have called 'mind mindedness'.) Children who have had a poorer attachment experience, on the other hand, might feel and express less trust, more hostility, and more avoidance in their approach to the world.

The parents of unpopular or peer-rejected children tend to use more inept, intrusive and harsh discipline and socialisation techniques. Parents of popular children display more reasoning about feelings, more responsivity, more authoritative control, more child-centred behaviour, more warmth. Children who are aggressive towards peers tend to have parents who model and reinforce aggression, and show high levels of impulsive behaviour, inconsistent discipline, and rejection (Rubin, Bukowski and Parker 2006). An experimental parenting programme, applied to families seen as 'at risk' because an older child was in trouble for aggressive behaviour, successfully reduced young children's physical aggression by increasing parents' responsiveness and play with the child, and decreasing their use of harsh parenting techniques (Brotman *et al.* 2008).

Although this pattern feels credible, the evidence base is limited, the size of the association is small to moderate rather than strong, and the degree to which the attachment pattern and the peer relationships fit into wider social structures and experiences has not been thoroughly explored. What is more, the developmental influences of parents, peers and others interact and modify each other.

Parents' involvement in the development of their children's social skills is linked to the parents' beliefs about the child, about the peers, and about the wider social world. The interview studies of the Newsons bring this out beautifully (Newson and Newson 1968, 1977). The direction of causation is both ways; parents believe something is desirable socially, and try to promote it in the child, in part through seeking to influence their friendships; they also see the child as lacking or needing something, and try to induce or provide it. Either way, considerations of how well the child is meeting the demands of the wider culture, and what effect their peers may be having on this process, can be very powerful. For example, generations of middle-class English boys were sent away to school at very young ages 'to toughen them up'; in the Newsons' studies (Newson and Newson 1977) boys were encouraged to stick up for themselves in disputes outside the family, with physical force, if necessary, whereas girls were supposed never to use physical aggression in public, although it might be accepted in the privacy of the family. Parents also try to coach or manage their child's peer relationships (Pettit *et al.* 1998; Mize and Pettit 1997; Kerns, Cole and Andrews 1998; Eccles 2007), and may become concerned in adolescence with the social networks that their children are introduced to through their peers. Who your peers are may affect what gang you belong to, what possible romantic partners you meet, what access you have in the job market, in short all sorts of social affiliations and life chances. And sometimes peer influence is deeply problematic (e.g. Perret-Clermont *et al.* 2004; pp. 176–77, 178–79, 264–67).

4.2.3 Popularity and teacher views

The peer group microsystem may exist in close relation with the teacher–pupil microsystem. There are associations between peer relations and adjustment to other developmental tasks and in later years (Rubin, Bukowski and Parker 2006). 'Popular' children are more likely to be seen by teachers as being helpful, good students. 'Rejected' or 'aggressive' children are seen as inconsiderate, non-compliant troublemakers, and they are more likely to fail and to absent themselves from school. There is evidence that the peer group you are part of is likely to influence your risk of poor social and academic functioning, in both Western and Chinese samples (e.g. Chen *et al.* 2008; Giordano 2003; Pollard 1985; Pollard and Filer 1996, 1999; Rubin, Bukowski and Parker 2006; Smetana *et al.* 2006). I discuss the mesosystem between individual, peers and teachers later (pp. 218–21).

4.2.4 Peer difficulties and externalising problems

There is a great deal of research that shows an association between aggressive, antisocial behaviour and rejection by peers. Children who are higher than normal on angry, reactive aggression tend to be rejected by their peers, even if the general level of aggression in the peer group is high (Vitaro *et al.* 2002; Patrick 1973; Zhou *et al.* 2008). The causal sequence is not straightforward. It seems likely that underlying behaviour problems contribute to both the peer rejection and the aggression and antisocial behaviour (Caspi, Elder and Bem 1987) but that cumulative peer rejection and absence of friends may make adjustment problems even greater (Bagwell, Newcomb and Bukowski 1998; Deater-Deckard *et al.* 1998; Deater-Deckard 2001; Ladd and Troop-Gordon 2003; Nelson and Dishion 2004). Being rejected by your peers removes opportunities for prosocial and enjoyable behaviour; means you have less protection against bullying; and may mean you dislike school, doubt your own self-worth and attractiveness, and expect negative behaviour from new peers. You may also be left with no companion apart from others who have been rejected. This may mean that your 'friends' are themselves disturbed and unhappy. Membership of a group characterised by antisocial behaviour is likely to further damage one's reputation, achievement, and development (Chen *et al.* 2008; Keenan *et al.* 1995; Kim, Hetherington and Reiss 1999; Simons *et al.* 2001; Vitaro, Brendgen and Waller 2005). This is discussed further in the section on delinquency (pp. 264–71).

Peers' 'deviancy training' includes positive feedback for bad behaviour and contempt for good or normative behaviour (pp. 91–92, 182–86), more experience of conflicts and aggressive conflict resolution, more enticement to mischief, more hostile rumination, and having partners in crime. Being in a social setting, for example a school, with more violent incidents, increases the risk of violent behaviour for the individual (Knafo, Daniel and Khoury-Kassabri (2008) show this for both Jewish and Arab students in Israel).

4.2.5 Peer difficulties and internalising problems

There is consistent evidence (Rubin *et al.* 1998a, 2006) that there is an association between difficulties in peer relations and risk of internalising problems (pp. 61, 90–93, 93–95, 95–100, 124–26). Children who are rejected by their peers are at increased risk of low social status; being victimised; feeling their lack of friends: and suffering anxiety, depression, loneliness, or low self-esteem. The association may be stronger for girls; it is typically worse if the peer rejection is long term. Often peer rejection leaves scars even after the individual begins to have friends or is no longer harassed, and these may even be detectable in adulthood (Hawker and Boulton 2000; Pelkonen *et al.* 2003).

Individuals' personal characteristics are likely to affect not just their risk of peer rejection but also the nature and the duration of the impact of being rejected (Laursen *et al.* 2007). For example, there is some evidence that withdrawn children may get victimised more than aggressive children, and may ruminate more and see peer judgement more accurately (Asher and Paquette 2003; Cillesen *et al.* 1992; Parker *et al.* 2005; Rose 2002; Rose and Rudolph 2006; Rose *et al.* 2007; Zakriski and Coie 1996). Thus they have a lot of negative experiences with peers, know that they are being victimised, and may brood deeply and resentfully about how unfair it all is and how no one appreciates them. Having a good friend is protective against rumination and anxiety/depression (Hodges *et al.* 1999; Hodges 1997), especially if this friend can protect you against bullying. Having no good friend, or a 'friend' who is also rejected and resentful, may be dangerous – this pattern crops up repeatedly in the rare but appalling cases where adolescent boys attack their schools and murder those they associate with their own rejection.

4.2.6 Adolescents and their peers

Typically in the early twenty-first century Western world everyone expects that adolescents will spend a lot of their time 'hanging out' with their peers. Some of this time is spent at school, or at home: more of it than at earlier ages is spent in the more public environment. Shopping malls have emerged as popular places for groups of adolescents to go and do nothing in particular beyond being with other adolescents who are friends or potential friends; the traditional passegiata of Mediterranean Europe is another example, where teenagers would wander about in ways designed to establish who is linked with whom, compete for romantic attention, and generally show themselves off to others. Different environments afford different opportunities for doing these activities in relative safety and comfort, with different implications for individuals' reputation, activities, and development (Clark and Uzzell 2006).

'Getting into bad company' is one of the things that conscientious parents fear for their adolescents. The common view is that adolescents tend to drift (or rush) into larger antisocial groups, who reek havoc in the neighbourhood and disrupt the lives of innocent children and nice old ladies. Currently, there is policy both locally and nationally to prevent groups of teenagers from hanging around in public places, both because they may indeed be 'up to no good' and because older people find them intimidating. One of the public spaces of Bristol (Cathedral on one side and City Council offices on another) is busy with office workers picnicking at lunch time and occasional groups of demonstrators (mainly middle aged and often middle class, depending on the issue), and there is no great public anxiety about them; but the teenagers who practise their skateboarding at one end are continually being discussed in the local media as a worrying social problem. But this picture of adolescent peer groups as mad, bad and dangerous is overwrought. Adolescents are sometimes negatively influenced by their peers, but also sometimes positively: and they are still influenced by their parents and other significant adults, sometimes positively, sometimes negatively. The different reference groups tend to have influence in different areas of adolescents' lives. Peers are especially influential in matters that are part of a specifically adolescent culture or style or identity – choice of music, clothes, amusements (e.g. North *et al.* 2000; Snell and Hodgetts 2007). Adolescents' views of moral issues, political issues, and life path choices are at least as heavily influenced by their parents (Coleman and Hendry 1999) as by their peers – even behaviour like smoking is better predicted by parents' behaviour than by peers'.

It may be important to distinguish between different social structures in adolescence (Giordano 2003; Smetana *et al.* 2006). Adolescents have dyadic relationships with particular friends; they may, with their friends, be part of a wider group of friends who share interests, do things together and form a 'clique'; they may be identified as part of a larger 'crowd' whose members fit the same stereotype and share a similar reputation and perhaps interests, but do not all, in fact, spend much time together or necessarily have personal relationships. Dyads, cliques and crowds differ in the opportunities they offer for joint activities, intimacies and support. You would expect a lot of support from your dyadic friendships, some from your clique, little from your crowd, although even here some in-group/out-group mechanisms may be working. Peer crowds are an important part of demarcating one's individual identity and one's affiliation, even though, ironically, you may be a part of a crowd not because you have chosen to be but because it is the group that others have assigned you to – ethnicity or gender or class can be the basis for crowds whose members might not themselves have actively chosen to belong to it (Brown *et al.* 2008).

Friendships become more intimate and more supportive with age (Furman and Buhrmester 1992). Typically adolescents' friends go to the same school, come from similar backgrounds, and have similar attitudes to school and to peer group choices (Collins and Steinberg 2006), and friends engage in much discussion of shared interests and experiences. Although this may provide much positive support for adolescents, it can be problematic. Girls in particular may focus very much on negative feelings and issues, and brood on them together in 'co-rumination' which can be profoundly unhelpful (Caselman and Self 2007; Parker et al. 2005; Rose 2002; Rose and Rudolph 2006; Rose et al. 2007). Research on anorexia and self-harm, for example, shows that adolescent girls whose friends have difficulties with these issues may be at risk of 'catching' them themselves (e.g. Polivy and Herman 2002; Peterson, Paulson and Williams 2007), or at risk from having to help conceal or otherwise deal with the problem. This may be particularly difficult when the problem is one that responsible adults find difficult; gathering up the courage to tell a teacher that your friend is self-harming, for example, is not going to be made easier by the (justified) perception that the teacher does not have the resources to help the self-harming child, and that this will probably bring in the parents, who are seen by the self-harmer as blaming her and as one of the causes of the self-harm.

Both cliques and crowds may operate with strong exclusionary mechanisms, often based on stereotypes (Horn 2003; Killen et al. 2002; Brown et al. 2008). Members of high-status crowds are more likely to regard it as fair to exclude non-members than members of low-status groups are; and there can be considerable stereotyping of crowds in order to find reasons to treat them as an out-group – what clothing is fashionable is a perennial example. Socially discriminatory mechanisms such as racial prejudice may allocate individuals to a particular crowd that they resemble on one criterion but not on many others. Brown et al. (2008) found that most students in multi-ethnic American schools did not use ethnic differences as the main basis for categorising their peers; however ethnic identity was a salient and positive feature of self-image and peer reputation for many Asian–American and Latino students. Being part of an 'oppositional culture' hostile to school decreases your chances of school success (Downey 2008, pp. 218–21). However, individuals who are excluded from a group may develop ways of coping with this – sometimes constructive, sometimes violent or revolutionary, sometimes on the sour grapes principle that the excluding group wasn't really so wonderful after all.

4.2.6.1 Popularity and unpopularity with peers

Issues about popularity are often salient for adolescents. Reviews (e.g. Rubin et al. 1998a, 2006; Steinberg and Morris 2001; Smetana et al. 2005) present some of the vast quantity of research on the topic. Using sociometric data, the distinctions are usually made between popularity, neglect and rejection. Popular adolescents are generally above average in attractiveness and acceptance by others, and are well known in their social worlds; being outstandingly good at something valued by your peers – sport, music – can be a good route to popularity, provided you pay some attention to the culture's views of how acceptable it is to be better at things than other people (Snell and Hodgetts 2007; Wentzel and Asher 1995; Wentzel et al. 2004). Popular adolescents tend to show better social adaptation and adjustment, but may also slide into the sorts of minor deviant behaviour which is sanctioned by their peer group, including drug and alcohol use and minor delinquency (Allen et al. 2005; Bukowski et al. 2007). Associations between popularity and prosocial or antisocial behaviour vary, with antisocial boys being popular in some cases (LaFontana and Cillesen 2002; Rodkin et al. 2000; Wentzel 2003; Wentzel and Caldwell 1997; Wentzel, McNamara-Barry and Caldwell 2004; Wentzel and Looney 2007). During early adolescence (ten to thirteen years of age) popular girls may engage in a lot of relational aggression – gossiping and spreading rumours, excluding and ignoring others – in ways that set themselves up as a good ally but a dangerous adversary and so control their peers, leading to increased popularity over time (Rose, Swenson and Waller 2004; Bukowski et al. 2007; Wentzel and Looney 2007). Later in adolescence, feeling positive about your popularity predicts good social functioning, even if your sociometric rating is not good, presumably because older adolescents can select a social niche and it is acceptance there rather than general popularity that matters (McElhaney, Antonishak and Allen 2008).

4.2.6.2 Adolescents and romantic relationships

One of the defining features of adolescence is beginning to take part in romantic relationships. Most of us remember this as full of anxieties as well as of delights. There are immense variations in exactly how and when such relationships are undertaken, and they can have major developmental consequences. Some very useful research is emerging in this area (see for example a special issue of the *Journal of Clinical Child & Adolescent Psychology* (2007, Vol 36 Issue 4)) but much remains to be done.

Adolescents' experience in intimate relationships, both close friendships and romantic relationships, is one basis for healthy interpersonal functioning in adulthood. These experiences can have major effects on the long-term development of self-concept, of social skills, and of opportunity to form further relationships, as well as immediate emotional and social impact of an often intense kind. Some relationships are short and others long; duration is not however a good predictor of impact. 'I did but see her passing by/and yet I love her til I die' is poetry (mid-seventeenth century) about a sentiment highly recognisable in adolescent romantic thought.

Stage theorists of personal and social development such as Erikson (1963) see adolescent romantic relationships as deriving from earlier social relationships and leading to better or worse social functioning in later life. Individuals who have already experienced some intimacy in relationships with family and friends, and who have a sense of their identity as family member and friend, are now faced with developing these in romantic relationships, which may when successful involve high degrees of affection, self-disclosure and trust, and provide increased feelings of self-worth, attractiveness, and being emotionally supported (Bouchey 2007; Giordano 2003; Grover et al. 2007). Adolescent romantic relationships may also enhance status with peers – 'My boyfriend is cooler than your boyfriend' – and allow access to new social networks, as well as involving opportunities for sexual activity that are developmentally new (Furman and Wehner 1997).

In societies where adolescents are expected to engage in romantic relationships, there are often issues about timing and about the durability of relationships. The earliest stages of establishing romantic relationships are often full of anxiety about how to make a relationship, and about what sort of relationship to make. Social skills of initiating and maintaining conversation and negotiating conflict may already have been developed in non-romantic relationships, but now have to be applied to a partner with whom there might potentially be an extremely intimate and sexual relationship – thus there are new risks and opportunities, and probably a very visible and perceptive social context (Grover et al. 2007). Individuals who differ in success in initiating potentially romantic relationships tend to differ in micro-level social behaviours such as making eye contact, smiling, and ways of talking. These are the behaviours that signal niceness and attractiveness, and it is not at all surprising that they are at the core of most popular advice on 'how to make friends and influence people'. Romantic relationships may additionally involve handling unrequited longing, physical attraction and sexual intimacy, jealousy and betrayal, and anxiety about displaying a 'false self' (Bouchey 2007; Giordano 2003; Grover and Nangle 2003; Sippola, Buchanan and Kehoe 2007).

There are cultural as well as individual differences in romantic relationships in adolescence. North American and European cultures place more emphasis on them than do more traditional cultures in the Middle East and Latin America, where in some cases they are forbidden and individuals who engage with unrelated members of the opposite sex are subject to extreme social disapproval. Individuals with traditional family backgrounds living in more westernised societies may be torn between different expectations. What solutions they find to these dilemmas will vary, but commonly their behaviour is shifted somewhat towards the majority society's expectations (Upchurch et al. 2001).

Difficulties in adolescent romantic relationships are associated with depression and anxiety, just as relationship difficulties are at other ages (Davila et al. 2004), and may apparently also be a factor in teenage suicide. Being in a good romantic relationship offers protection against such feelings (La Greca and Harrison 2005), although as we all know it is perfectly possible to combine the wonderfulness of being in love with anxieties about whether it is deserved, guilt about being so lucky, and fear that it will not continue – the cultural but universal messages that we are fed, once we have grown out of the initial stories of 'happy ever after', that 'the course of true love never did run smooth'.

4.3 Bullying and aggression

Regrettably, we can all, children included, be thoroughly nasty to each other. Sometimes this behaviour is so pervasive, so serious and so unpleasant that it is defined as 'bullying' – that is behaviour that hurts or harms another person, physically or psychologically; which is intended to do so; which is sustained or repeated; and which involves a power imbalance such that it is difficult for the victim to defend him/herself. Bullying may be physical, for example hitting, kicking, etc.; verbal, for example insults, derogatory judgements, etc.; indirect (relational such as 'I don't like you any more' or 'You're not my friend'); social e.g. malicious gossiping, inciting others to shun or torment an individual, spreading rumours; and other forms such as spoiling other people's schoolwork, purloining pieces of equipment needed in class, setting up the victim for trouble with an adult. Most of us will have experienced such behaviour ourselves, or witnessed it – most of us will even, ourselves, have treated somebody badly at some time.

It is not altogether easy to estimate the prevalence of bullying (Solberg and Olweus 2003; Tomada and Schneider 1997). As we will see the different participants don't always agree over whether an incident is 'bullying' or not, and victims may be ashamed of what has happened to them or be intimidated into not revealing it (Monks and Smith 2006). But it seems to be quite common, and it is seen particularly but not always in school. Some estimates (e.g. Crick 1997; Smith *et al.* 1999) suggest that in British primary school about ten per cent of children admit that they are, at least sometimes, bullies, and twenty-seven per cent say that they have been victims; in secondary school four per cent say they are bullies and twelve per cent victims. Knafo *et al.* (2008) report that thirty-three per cent of Israeli fifteen-year-olds said they had experienced bullying, harassment or molestation in the previous school year. Self-reports of being bullied decline between age eight and age sixteen; self-reports of being a bully oneself do not change so much with age. There is consistent evidence of both differences and similarities between the two genders. Girls and boys report being victims at similar rates, but boys are more likely to give a self-report of being a bully, especially of using physical bullying; boys are not often bullied by girls but girls are bullied by both genders.

There are gender differences in children's preferred modes of bullying. Girls and boys report receiving and dishing out similar amounts of verbal aggression, but boys give and receive more physical aggression; girls give and receive more indirect aggression from later childhood, the period where there is a horribly large amount of 'you can't be friends with us' behaviour (Crick and Grotpeter 1995; Crick 1997; Goodwin 2006; Atwood 1989 for a powerful fictional view). With increasing age both genders shift from physical to indirect aggression, with girls shifting earlier, presumably because their language development tends to run ahead of boys', and they less often play the sort of vigorous physical games in which some excessive physical aggression can slip easily into physical bullying. There is usually a positive correlation between individuals' use of direct and indirect aggression, with bullies having a wide repertoire of ways of getting at their victims.

Bullies often manifest general aggressive non-compliant behaviour to a wide range of people, not just to their victims. Bullying is often a group process. There are bully ringleaders who start the bullying process; there may be assistants who aid and abet but don't start the bullying themselves; and there may be reinforcers who cheer it on (these individuals may sometimes be victims). There are often outsiders who know about the bullying but do nothing, perhaps pretending it's not happening. A smaller number of individuals are defenders who obstruct bullies, or aid or comfort victims, or tell responsible adults. Bullying relationships often involve several bullies ganging up on the victim. Bullies tend to associate with other bullies or assistants or reinforcers; defenders and outsiders associate. Bullies and victims may be in the same social network, indeed some children are both bullies and victims, particularly in the earlier grades of school (Solberg, Olweus and Endresen 2007). Both genders rate defenders as the most popular category of children.

The victims are often targets of repeated aggression. Some researchers (e.g. Olweus 1993) draw a distinction between passive and provocative victims. Passive victims are anxious and insecure, and fail to defend themselves adequately; provocative victims tend to be socially problematic e.g. hyperactive, tension-creating, hot-tempered. Victims tend to be anxious and depressed, and to have low self-esteem and few friends, all characteristics that reduce the amount of support and resource they could call on to defend themselves. Many victims have not told responsible adults such as a teacher or a person at home, either because the bully has frightened them away from doing this, or because the victim has no confidence that adult intervention would be effective in stopping the bullying; a lack of confidence that would be all too realistic. Bullying makes people more vulnerable: bullies pick on vulnerable people (Scholte et al. 2007; Sweeting et al. 2006). Many bullying relationships are comparatively brief, less than one week, but they can last for several years (Smith, Madsen and Moody 1999). Much bullying takes place in school, generally in its public and less supervised places, for example in the playground or in corridors; there is also quite a lot of bullying when children are in transit between home and school, if circumstances permit. Online bullying, or 'cyber-bullying', is a new possibility (Agatson, Kowalski and Limber 2007; Kowalski and Limber 2007).

The stereotype is that bullies are threatening others because they are themselves low in self-esteem. Although this may be true for some bullies, for many it is not. Being seen to be able to bully successfully can have great value in a struggle for dominance or the desired status of being 'hard'. In a study of Israeli fifteen-year-olds (Knafo *et al.* 2008), students whose value system focused on achieving control and dominance over other people and resources, and de-emphasised understanding, appreciating, tolerating, and protecting the welfare of other people, were especially likely to behave violently and to bully others. These bullies are confident and even successful individuals who have reached a high status in their social network by terrorising others, and once they have acquired the status and the admirers that go with it they may no longer have to bully themselves, instead relying on their reputation or their sidekicks to oppress their victims and deter possible defenders. Patrick (1973) describes this vividly in a Glasgow gang that he infiltrated in order to do his PhD. Most pupils say that they don't like bullying but a significant minority say they could join in, and many are unwilling to make themselves conspicuous as defenders.

The role of bullying in establishing roles in a social hierarchy is evident in the 'sampling' behaviour that occurs at transition points such as school transfer, when bullies throw their weight around relatively unselectively at first and then focus on a more limited range of people to victimise (Tomada *et al.* 2005; Schneider 2000; Schneider *et al.* 2008; Smith 1999). Similarly, new members of a group may attempt to bully old ones, or be bullied by old ones, until their role in the group is determined by the status and the alliances they build up.

Bullying occurs in all types and sizes of school. The attitude of teachers in bullying situations, the existence of a school policy about the unacceptability of bullying, and proper supervision of free activities are all important in containing the incidence and the severity of bullying. But schools are not the only social setting that influences bullying. The high rate of violent behaviour found in schools in Israel (Knafo *et al.* 2008) may reflect violence in and around the wider society. Exposure to this violence is correlated with psychiatric consequences (Slone and Shechner 2008).

Read from here.

4.3.1 Developmental experiences associated with risk of becoming a bully or a victim

Certain developmental experiences seem to be associated with risk of becoming a bully or a victim (Olweus 1993; Bukowski *et al.* 2007; Smith 1999). Parenting that is negative, cold, and uninvolved, or permissive without limit setting or monitoring, or very power assertive, and dysfunctional violent families, on the one hand, and early insecure and disorganised attachment on the other, seem to be associated with more physical bullying by boys, and both bullying and victimisation in girls. Maternal overprotectiveness is associated with passive victim boys; maternal hostility with victim girls. Presumably children with these sorts of family backgrounds have learned more about how to conduct negative social relationships and less about how to conduct more positive ones.

Child personality is also worth considering. Early difficult temperament (excessive crying, poor consolability, high reactivity) is associated with more aggression and poor social functioning at later ages. Bullies tend to be high on hostility, victims to be withdrawn; both are likely to be high on neuroticism. Victims tend to be physically weaker, but bullies are not always big and strong. Children with special needs (e.g. stammer, disability, moderate learning difficulty) that are associated with having fewer friends, spending more time alone, and maybe having fewer social skills, are more likely to be victims than individuals whose idiosyncrasies are less stigmatising; although children commonly pick out a characteristic to comment on negatively without taking it as far as sustained bullying, for example having to wear glasses or having red hair may attract occasional unwelcome taunts of 'four-eyes' or 'ginger'. Victims tend to be low on popularity and peer acceptance, and to have fewer friends than normal, or to have friends who are themselves less able to help or protect against bullies. Boy bullies who are aggressive tend to be less popular, especially in later childhood, but may have a group of mates with whom they're popular, to be nuclear members of a small social group which fills their social world; girls who bully tend to be almost as popular as non-bullies.

Bullying may involve both strengths and distortions in social skills and self-esteem. Like all social interaction, it involves encoding social cues in the behaviour of others, and in the social and cultural setting; interpretation of the perceived cues; goal selection, among the range that the situation and the socio-cultural milieu permit; the generation of responses appropriate to the goal and the capabilities of all those involved; the choice of a response; and action. For example, the bully needs to see the victim as·available and safe to attack; to read the victim's behaviour (or mere existence) as in some sense deserving a negative, bullying response; to devise and select a bullying behaviour that will hurt the victim without putting the bully at too much risk of blame or retaliation; to choose the best time, place and method of delivering the bullying behaviour; and to deal out the beating up, or the insult, or the ostracism, or whatever has been selected. A skilled bully will be able to do this very effectively, for example getting through painfully to the victim while still having room to excuse the bullying behaviour as 'it was only a joke' or 'for your own good' (Sluckin 1981).

We know from a considerable amount of research (Crick and Dodge 1996; Crick 1996; Patterson et al. 1989; Patterson and Sanson 1999) that reactively aggressive children see more social behaviours as signals of aggression by the other person, and use fewer cues before making up their minds about what to do. Proactively aggressive children probably don't show so much of a bias in interpretation, but are like reactive aggressors in choosing aggressive solutions more often. Ringleader bullies tend to be quite good on understanding other people's needs, wishes and beliefs (as one would expect, given their ability to get and keep a gang of sidekicks and audience); victims are generally poor at understanding other people's mental states and motivations, which would make it harder for them to avoid or escape other people's bullying. Low self-regard (and behavioural problems) will be associated with being a victim. The self-esteem of bullies may be maintained by the success of their bullying – especially the narciss-istic, self-aggrandising aspects of their self-concepts. Defenders, capable of taking the one altruistic and admirable role in bullying, tend to have high self-esteem.

What seems to be very relevant to both bullying and to ways of reducing it is increasing social skills. In the early years of the development of social skills, many children experience some teasing and mild bullying, but such behaviour is coped with in ways that do not encourage persistence in bullying. Some children however respond less skilfully, lack supportive friends (or have friends who may also be victims), and have personal risk factors; these children may become the focus of bullying, develop low self-esteem and anxiety, be seen as less desirable as a friend, and become more and more vulnerable. It seems likely that bullies' home experience leads them to see relationships as exploitative and to value dominance; they may gather like-minded cronies and exploit victims. In the peer group as a whole there is decreased peer empathy for victims of bullying in adolescence.

4.4 Gender

I have already mentioned gender differences at several points, but for a variety of reasons I am re-integrating these points into a section about gender itself. The main reasons for this repetition lie with the emphasis that both culture and the research literature have long placed on gender roles and gender differences, and with the controversy about what exactly they are and what exactly causes them. From the moment that a child's gender is known, that fact shapes many aspects of his or her subsequent life – even at the very basic level of how long its life continues after it becomes known to the future parents. Very early in their childhoods, children begin to form ideas about gender that guide the activities they undertake, the friends they make, their interests and their goals (Campbell and Muncer 1998; Crouter *et al.* 2007). Parents, families, peers, schools and many social institutions provide information on what gender means, rules about what members of each gender may and may not do, and opportunities to do some things rather than others. All the way from the microsystem to the exosystem, there may be gender roles and gender inequalities. One of the tasks of the child as social person is to move and survive among ideas about gender that are pervasive, intrusive, fought over and extremely hard to escape.

There have been many explanations of gender from an enormous range of theoretical backgrounds. Most call on influences from biology, cognition, social–interpersonal and social–structural factors, acknowledging that there are many causes of gender roles and gender differences, but differing in how these causes are felt to balance and combine. Each type of cause can be at work in the microsystem or as far away as the exosystem or the distant past of the culture or even the species (or divine rules – although I will not discuss these further). To some extent, the most interesting points are not about what basic factors affect gender and the child's role as a gendered person, but about how do children experience and enact the role among such diverse pressures. But before we get to this level of question, we need to examine some of the overarching theories that have been applied in this field.

4.4.1 An evolutionary understanding of human gender differences

Gender differences have been one of the topics that evolutionary psychology (pp. 18–25) focuses on. Partly this is because sexual selection was part of Darwin's core model of evolution. As reproduction is the way to pass on one's own characteristics to future generations and in human history this has involved finding a partner of the opposite gender, successful reproduction involves competition with members of one's own gender to get a good mate from the opposite gender, who will contribute to the success of one's own efforts to reproduce. The potential mate needs to display that he or she is fertile, is healthy, and has those characteristics that one would like one's descendants to have; and that he or she shows no sign of opposite, undesirable, characteristics. This pressure to look like a good potential reproductive partner could have resulted in the selection and elaboration of characteristics that indicate which gender one is, signal fertility, and suggest freedom from characteristics that would reduce one's reproductive potential (Andersson and Simmons 2006). If there is choice of mates and competition for mates, it is advantageous for one's successful reproduction to select a mate with whom one can breed, and who is healthy or advantaged (hence there is often an emphasis first on identifying a person's gender and then on strength, beauty, status and other signs of good reproductive potential). It is very important not to choose badly. It is not hard to find examples of gendered signals of reproductive potential. For example, in species where males fight physically for females, those males who are larger, braver, and tougher may be more successful in finding mates and reproduce more successfully. Female characteristics such as waist to hip ratio and apparent age (as proxy for fertility) are said to be good predictors of the female's attractiveness to males (e.g. Furnham *et al.* 2006).

Some, but not necessarily all, of the 'gender differences' discussed in evolutionary psychology may have come about in this way, although many issues still need to be resolved. Evolutionary psychologists tend to see gender roles and gender differences as marked, stable, and a result of evolution (Beaulieu and Bugental 2007; Bjorklund and Pellegrini 2002; Buss 2005; Dunbar and Barrett 2007; Geary 1998; Halpern *et al.* 2007; Pellegrini 2004). The core argument here is that if gender differences are consistent and ubiquitous, the existence of these differences may have had evolutionary benefits, which in most theories are related to the demands of, and the costs of investment in, reproduction and parenting.

A point often made in evolutionary psychology (Beaulieu and Bugental 2007; Bjorklund and Pellegrini 2002; Buss 2005; Dunbar and Barrett 2007; Geary 1998; Pellegrini 2004) is that reproduction is 'cheaper' for the human male than for the human female. Men produce the sperm; women produce the egg, itself larger and therefore 'higher cost', and then gestate it, a commitment lasting a long time (during which they cannot take up other reproductive opportunities) and costing a lot of energy, nutrition, and risk – death in childbirth has been one of the most common ends of human females' existence for most of our evolutionary history. And then the infant is born unable to look after itself and has to be fed, cared for, and generally parented for more years, although further reproductive opportunities are not entirely ruled out during this time, and the person or persons doing this work need not necessarily be the mother, or even female. A lot of popular evolutionary theory builds these biological facts into arguments for the greater promiscuity of males in the vast majority of human societies, and for a whole variety of laws and customs (Laland and Brown 2002). (Curiously, the costings tend to be based on the cost of producing the single fertilising sperm as compared with the fertilised egg. Counter-costings such as the fact that a male who only produced one sperm per ejaculation would be highly unlikely ever to impregnate his partner, seem not to be considered. Given that men are regarded as 'sub-fertile' at 5 million sperm per millilitre, the 'egg is more expensive than the sperm' claim surely needs to be modified to considerations of whether the single egg is more expensive than 5 million plus sperm. That the parent who gestates and rears the offspring bears a higher personal cost than the parent who does not, I would not dispute.)

4.4.1.1 Sexual selection, competition – and co-operation

However much one might quibble with some of the detail of theories of gender differences, human gender differences in physical size, in musculature, in rate and pattern of physical development, and in other traits are consistent with the view that sexual selection has contributed to some currently observed gender differences. Evolutionary theory undoubtedly applies to human gender differences in rather the same way as it does to those of other species. But, as I said earlier (pp. 24–25, 107, 111), human beings are peculiarly rich in culture, open to learning for virtually all their lives, and immature and in need of a lot of parental care and investment for a protracted period. Thus male competition and female choice are nuanced, in humans, by the existence of female competition and male choice; the two latter components follow from male investment in children. The combination is predicted to result in more subtle and perhaps smaller gender differences in humans than for many other species. The relative importance of evolutionary (including sexual selection) and cultural influences on cognitive, behavioural, and social gender differences is the subject of vigorous debate (Geary 1998; Wood and Eagly 2002).

The process of human reproduction, and of parenting human children to successful reproduction of themselves, requires much adult investment in the young throughout the period where the child's survival is at risk. The human reproductive strategy is, compared with other species, extreme in its reliance on minimal litters, a long period of immaturity, and a prolonged need to teach and nurture the young (Martin 2007, pp. 22, 27, 51, 107–08). A child whose father has left forever after impregnating the mother has less access to resources of all sorts (Lamb 2004; McLanahan and Carlson 2004, pp. 31–32, 153, 253) and is, all other things being equal, quite a lot more likely to grow up socially and economically disadvantaged (which might imply a reproductive disadvantage for the child and hence for the father). Opie and Power (2008) calculate that the cost of feeding a developing fetus and child has been so high ever since the time of pre-human hominids that a female can only produce and rear two or more offspring with support from both a mate and related females (the offsprings' grandmother, aunts, etc.). Recognising this, although simple evolutionary psychology theory says that the female needs to be attractive to get a healthy male, and the male needs to be dominant to get a healthy female, more complex theory says the female needs a healthy *and supportive* mate, (and/or a supportive female group as a substitute or second support system), and the male needs to be dominant of males *and supportive* of his children. Evolutionary psychologists suggest that this could result in females having agentic skills, so that they can persuade their mate and their female friends to help them with the children, whereas males are seen as needing dominance skills and agency with other males (but also, arguably, some sensitivity to the needs of the young and of mothers) (e.g. Buss 2005; Dunbar and Barrett 2007).

There is a somewhat different idea about competition and co-operation, however, in that some evolutionary theorists argue that within-gender competition is more stringent for human males than for human females

(Halpern *et al.* 2007). In many other species, where one gender is more involved in competition than the other, there is high within-gender variation in the characteristics related to competition and choice, and greater risk and mortality for the gender more involved in competition. The pattern appears to be like this in humans too: on many characteristics males are more variable than females, they are more vulnerable to many diseases and other risks, tend to die earlier, and are especially likely to be adversely affected by difficult environments. This is not entirely because males are more likely to be involved in fighting, although this does play a part. In many societies, there is open conflict between social groups over access to resources and to power, with males engaging in most of the conflict. As well as between-group incidents such as low-level manoeuvring to get resources, jockeying for power, trespassing on other people's territory and outright warfare, there will be activities internal to the group, such as forming alliances and dominance hierarchies, building in-group solidarity, maintaining boundaries, developing internal rituals to express group membership, and expressing more negative feelings towards the out-group. Evolutionary psychologists hypothesise that doing these things fell mainly to males from early in evolutionary history, and that generations of patrolling territory, hunting, frightening off incursions, raiding other people's resources, and so forth, selected for males to have brains that were good at navigating across large spaces, fomenting aggression, snatching, grabbing and running away fast, and so forth (Buss 2005; Dunbar *et al.* 2007, Geary 1998).

Not all psychologists agree with this hypothesis (Halpern *et al.* 2007, Wood and Eagly 2002), sometimes because the evidence for there being a gender difference is thin, sometimes because the daily lives of the opposite gender would have included pressures for equivalent skills – hunter–gatherer women foraging for vegetable food would have needed to know their territory quite as well as males hunting animals or enemies, for example. Testing the predictions made by evolutionary psychologists is not straightforward. We cannot do controlled experiments. We do not know when in development an evolved gender difference might appear; if early, then it may be very open to experience, if late, it may be attributed to experience. We know that experience influences variation in characteristics, and could thus exaggerate or mask the extent of evolved gender differences. It will help to make comparisons with other species and to different environments (e.g. Allman *et al.* 1998; Hassett *et al.* 2008; Leigh 1996; Martin 2007; Williams and Pleil 2008), but this cannot ever completely resolve the debates – and because of the political implications, the debates will be (and should be) fervent.

However we consider these matters, it is essential to maintain a developmental perspective. There are some interesting developmental phenomena that are congruent with evolutionary theorists' ideas about male–male competition and female choice. As is the case in other species, human males tend to reach reproductive maturity at a later age, to engage in more risky and aggressive behaviours, and to have a shorter lifespan (Allman *et al.* 1998; Leigh 1996). In many species besides humans, young males engage in rough and tumble play, physical sports, and outright fighting more than young females do; males may show a stronger preference than females for play with toy trucks, and young females may show more interest in playing with babies and cuddly toys (e.g. Hassett *et al.* 2008; Williams and Pleil 2008). Differences such as these are small in the very young, but increase as individuals approach the age at which they could reproduce themselves; all of which is congruent with evolutionary theory (Bjorklund and Pellegrini 2002). But we do have to remember that there is variation between species and within each gender, overlap between the two genders, and evidence of cultural diversity and historical change (Beaulieu and Bugental 2007; Dunbar *et al.* 2007). We know, both from an evolutionary perspective and a psychological one, that nature and nurture are integrally linked and cannot be separated. We go through a lengthy period of development and throughout all of it the traits that we are developing respond to our experience. These characteristics of prolonged development and openness to experience have themselves evolved, presumably because they improved reproductive success (Gould 1977, pp. 22, 27, 51, 189). With our large brains and our highly social ways of living we may be especially able to learn, develop and change from our 'expected' genetic programme to an 'experience-dependent' one (Meadows 2006).

4.4.2 Socio-cultural theories of gender

It is a long time historically since we started living in very complex societies, and there has been plenty of time for gender differences and gender roles to be influenced by factors that are cultural rather than biological. Hyde (2005, 2007) argues that although we focus on gender differences, human males and females are similar on most psychological variables and the majority of measurable psychological gender differences are small or close to zero (or smaller than differences between cultures, e.g. Schwartz and Rubel 2005, Wang 2008). Within-gender variability is greater, typically, than between-gender difference. Cultures can be ranked on how far the whole culture is biased in gender terms (Hofstede 2001, 2005, pp. 47, 72–74, 199–201), and a meta-analysis by Eagly and Wood (1999) suggests that members of cultures that have a big gender gap in status tend to show bigger gender differences than members of cultures with greater equality of status for the two genders. Their view is that whatever minor evolutionary differences there may be at a physical level, it is cultures' division of labour and differentiation of status that amplify such differences and make them a matter of attention. The degree to which the two genders are 'similar' or 'different' will be closely tied to social roles and social stereotypes.

As Bronfenbrenner's model insists, individuals' development is embedded in sets of social structures (pp. 6–18, 249–50) and social interactions. Microsystems, such as the child's interaction with parents or peers, exosystems, such as those that determine parents' working hours or children's access to play opportunities, and macrosystems, such as cultural views of the different roles of each gender, influence the experience of boys and girls daily and profoundly. Analyses of social structure and gender tend to point to gendered inequalities of power displayed in the home, in employment, in politics and in economics. In many cultures, the direction of these differences is more power, status, self-confidence for men, less for women (Wood and Eagly 2002). These differences are expressed in many implicit and explicit ways in all quarters of everyday life – differences in income, in sources of income, in types of employment, in appearance, in where and how each gender is targeted by advertising, in how they are represented in crime statistics, in who speaks where and how and when and about what, in what gender roles are expressed in the mass media, in literature, in the arts. Culturally, they amount to stereotypes (e.g. Bandura 2001; Bandura and Bussey 2004; Martin and Ruble 2004; Scharrer 2005). Children's exposure to such macrosystem expressions will be an important part of their socialisation (Crouter et al. 2007; Wang 2008; Zaff et al. 2008, pp. 198–201), even if they are not discussed as possibly problematic.

> Boys and girls are different by nature. We need to raise them differently . . . sometimes, we need to be more vigilant with boys and a little harsh and rough with them . . . Boys and girls are growing up to be different. Society will look at them and treat them differently . . . I want my daughter to be a woman whom men want to marry . . . I want my daughter to be a good mother who will teach her child to be a good person . . . I cannot let her behave like a boy without telling and showing her what is proper behaviour for women. She will not know her place when she plays with her little male friends unless I tell her. . . .
> (Wang 2008: 64)

This Chinese mother is not questioning the gender stereotyping her daughter will encounter. However, an enormous body of research treats these differences as political, not at all to be taken for granted, not at all to be accepted without a struggle (Richardson and Robinson 2008). We need to be infinitely careful about stereotypes. What we say we value is not always what we act on. And as Goodwin (2006) and Jones and Myhill (2004a and 2004b) argue, the first danger is that we may literally not see behaviour that does not fit our stereotype, and the second is that we may judge it to be both more exceptional and more unacceptable than behaviour that fits the stereotype.

4.4.3 What gender differences are there?

Before we examine the development of gender, we need to do two things: first, acknowledge how very debateable much of the 'evidence' and 'theory' is, and second try to establish what gender differences are found with reasonable reliability. If we are not extremely careful, we may find evidence of a difference between the averages for each of the two genders but overlook within-gender variation and overlap between the male and female distributions – as in height, for example, where the average male height is reliably greater than the average female height, but quite unexceptional women (me, for example) are taller than the average male. Sometimes we simply do not see, let alone talk about, individuals who are just slightly different from the stereotype (e.g. Eagly and Wood 1999, Jones and Myhill 2004a, 2004b). Or researchers may find a gender difference that they interpret as a biological given, when it could alternatively be attributed to social influences on gender differences, for example in access to a social opportunity. (Allowing women to run the marathon was for almost a century thought to be likely to damage them physically, so it was not allowed at all. Once that 'danger' was discredited by women completing marathons successfully, it was thought that women would not be strong enough to run the marathon after they had had a baby – something Paula Radcliffe's win in the 2007 New York Marathon has amply demonstrated was not right either.) Or researchers may find a gender difference at an extreme of the distribution of skills, and infer that there are biological reasons for the difference at the extreme end that also hold throughout the entire range of the distribution. In the early 1980s, I listened to a very distinguished Fellow of the Royal Society argue that the decline in the proportion of women in the ranks of mathematics students from school age to professorial status was biologically based; if the percentage of women maths professors was in the low single figures, he argued, this showed that women were just naturally no good at maths, even though more than half of those successful in maths exams through school (and, nowadays, into university) were female. My point that only a minimally small proportion of *men* were good enough at maths to become maths professors was rejected as 'knee-jerk feminism'! I still think he needed to engage with my point at a rather more intelligent level, and the historical changes there have been in women's performance on tasks they were once thought totally unfit for only strengthen my case (Kurtz-Costes *et al.* 2008; Halpern *et al.* 2007). I do however agree that I might well be called a 'knee-jerk feminist' (and I would be proud to be).

The principal social/psychological dimensions on which there is reasonably credible evidence of gender differences in average score or average behaviour (but considerable within-gender variation and considerable between-gender overlap of distributions) are agency/instrumentality/dominance, which tend to be higher for males, and communion/expressivity/nurturance, which tend to be higher for females. Obviously these dimensions could be measured in an enormous variety of different ways, and have to be seen as very broad collections of characteristics, values and behaviour. However, such differences are found across a range of methods. In self-ratings males tend to rate themselves as more ambitious, dominant, hostile, and females as more sensitive, sympathetic, kind. In personality inventories females tend to score on average higher on anxiety, trust, tender-mindedness, gregariousness, and males to score as more assertive. In observed behaviour males tend to show more aggression, competition, restlessness, and more task contribution, and tend to be more likely to be group leaders, whereas females tend to value benevolence and compassion, to make more socio-emotional contribution to groups, show more non-verbal sensitivity, and appear to have more intense emotional experience (e.g. Lippa 2005; Schwartz and Rubel 2005). (There will be cultural variation in how this is done: for example De Raad *et al.* (2005) asked about the insult terms used by Spanish, Dutch and German young men, and found that although versions of 'stupid' were used in all countries, Spanish men more often used insults about the sexual fidelity of their opponents' mothers, sisters and wives whereas Dutch and German men more often used terms referring to genitals and excretions. I have not found a similar study of young women's insult strategies, although there are occasional graphic examples (pp. 203–04).)

Even if across cultures women typically place more value on the compassionate values of benevolence and universalism, and men on the values of power, stimulation, hedonism and achievement (Schwartz and Rubel 2005) the gender differences are small. And they are not completely consonant with the predictions of either evolutionary psychology or social role theory. Although evolutionary psychology would predict that males would value stimulation, power and competition more highly and females would value benevolence, because evolutionary psychology would relate these values to gender-linked roles as hunters versus gatherers or warriors versus baby minders, it would not predict that females would emphasise universalism and males emphasise self-direction. Expectations about social roles might explain differences in valuing power (males tend to have more access to it), and females' experience of low status, and of the female social role of showing benevolence to those they care for, might generalise into a female view that universalism is important. It is also worth noting that gender differences in values tend to be bigger in societies where men's and women's social roles are more traditional and more separate, that gender role differentiation tends to be smaller in societies which have advanced industrialisation, and that students show smaller gender differences in values than older respondents (Corby, Hodges and Perry 2007; Eagly and Wood 1999; Hofstede 2001, 2005).

Females on average develop fine motor skills earlier, and possibly better, which might possibly be associated with some faster neurological development early on; males on average show greater strength, for example in grip, in rapid movement, and in throwing – again possibly there is a physiological reason for this superiority. However, it is blatantly obvious that whatever physiological basis there is for such differences, firstly there is wide variation within each gender, secondly there is an overlap between the genders, and thirdly the different extent to which these activities are practised is highly likely to make a crucial contribution to the development of these skills. The two most illegible examples of handwriting I am acquainted with have indeed come from males, the two most beautiful scripts from females; but even if neurological development of fine motor movement set the two extremes off on different paths, practise and need (who as adults had secretaries?) for certain exacerbated the divergence.

4.4.4 Development of gender differences in children

The origin of gender is in the individual's genetic material. Although most of this does not differ between males and females, one chromosome out of the 46 chromosomes differs, being a small 'Y' chromosome for the male and a larger 'X' chromosome for the female. Developmentally, from the sixth week of gestation there are differences between male and female fetuses in the balance of the male and female hormones that their bodies produce – male fetuses are normally exposed to more androgen and female fetuses to more progesterone and oestrogen. These differences are thought to lead not just to the formation of different reproductive organs but also to other physical differences – male newborns are on average longer than female ones, the relative lengths of arm bones differ between males and females, there may be subtle structural brain differences (Collaer and Hines 1995). The different hormonal balance continues for a few months after birth, although it subsides to little or no difference through childhood, when both genders have low levels of sex hormones. At adolescence, of course, these low levels rise rapidly and the gender difference in hormone production and levels is high again.

Given that there are hormonal differences in the development of the fetus, there may be some differences in brain development that could underly behavioural differences. Recent advances in neuroscience techniques have led to an expanding body of evidence, but although there is evidence of some anatomical differences, differences in some but not all neurotransmitters, and some differences in the rate of brain development in male and female adolescents, there is much less evidence of differences before adolescence (Giedd et al. 1999; Halpern et al. 2007; Matsuzawa et al. 2001; Shaw et al. 2006). Halpern et al. (2007: 27) summarise the current state of knowledge thus:

In general, females have a higher percentage of gray-matter brain tissue, whereas males have a higher volume of connecting white-matter tissue – with the exception of the splenium of the corpus callosum, which is more bulbous and, thus, larger in females than in males. Furthermore, male brains show greater volumetric asymmetries than female brains do. [. . .] The higher white-matter volume seems associated with better spatial performance in males, while the greater bilateral symmetry seems associated with better language processing in females. Although the advent of noninvasive techniques for functional brain imaging has allowed a rapid increase in the number of studies investigating sex differences in the regional functional specialization for cognition, these studies are in their infancy. Future research of this type should involve larger and more carefully selected sample populations to avoid strong and potentially confounding cohort effects, and should employ longitudinal designs.

There is no question that hormonal differences have substantial effects on behaviour, emotions, and social interactions as well as on our physical development; but most attempts to explain gender differences in terms of hormones alone have been seriously flawed. As with genetic influences, even if hormonal explanations need to be considered they cannot be the whole story in a complex social person.

4.4.4.1 Infancy differences

Adults usually note the child's gender as one of the first things to find out about it. (A recent article in *The Guardian* noted the discomfiture of family and friends when the journalist gave birth to a child whose genitalia were ambiguous in appearance, and a few days elapsed before DNA analysis could disclose the baby's gender – there were almost no congratulatory cards, as such cards are very often explicitly for a girl or a boy, very pink or very blue.) It is really not clear how much gender difference there is in infancy: sometimes parents report differences between boy babies and girl babies (differences that fit the stereotype of softer shyer girls and more active and assertive boys), but strangers cannot usually guess the gender of a baby or toddler except by dress cues or their names. There is some evidence of babies noticing gender-linked characteristics and making a gender-based discrimination, as shown in habituation studies of infants as young as three to four months (Martin, Ruble and Szkrybalo 2002). There is none of infant preference for same-gender-typed objects, and little of differences in activity beyond those 'seen' by people who already know the baby's gender. There is some evidence of differentiation in parents' behaviour – lots of gender-typing in naming, clothes, and toy provision, and encouragement of gender-typed activity, maybe especially for boys; there is rather more conflicting evidence on differentiation of behaviour to stranger babies whose gender is not known. There are few reliable differences in infant measures of behaviour or in the ages at which male and female infants reach developmental milestones such as cutting teeth, sitting up, or walking, although girls may be the more advanced at talking. It usually requires very large samples to detect differences in infancy or the toddler years: for example, Galsworthy and colleagues (2000) found statistically significant gender differences in cognitive tests given to over 3,000 two-year-old twins, but gender accounted for only three per cent of the variance in the toddlers' verbal ability and one per cent of the variance in their non-verbal ability. Differences on this scale are not to be ignored, but typically the literature suggests that early on there are not enormous differences (Spelke 2005).

4.4.4.2 Differences in the preschool and early school years

Once the child is talking, and moving beyond the immediate family, gender can become more salient for all concerned. Children's verbal labelling of people's gender emerges around age two, and gender stereotypes using associations between gender and activities or objects have been elicited from children younger than three. Children at this age may also know which gender label applies to them, and play with this labelling or use gender labelling to upset others. Here is an example, from Judy Dunn's rich data on siblings, of a child playing with the gender categorisation of herself, her baby brother, and her teddy, and also knowing her father's gender.

Child, C. (playing with her teddy) to father, F. Teddy's a man.
F: What are you?
C: You're a boy.
F: Yeah. What are you?
C: A menace.
F: Yeah, a menace. Apart from that are you a boy or a girl?
C: Boy (laughs).
F. Are you? What's Trevor?
C: A girl (laughs).
F. You're silly.

(Dunn and Kendrick 1982: 110–111)

Even at this age, some importance is attached to getting gender labels right – there is a risk of being called 'silly' if you get them wrong. Some preschool children may already feel pressure from others to like or dislike particular activities or things because of their own gender, although recognising whether they are themselves behaving in a gender-typical way, let alone being distressed if what they want to do or be is gender atypical, probably comes after more exposure to a social world with a lot of social comparison and classification. Knowing that your gender is fixed increases over the period age three to age five, with insistence that changes in appearance make no difference to gender coming earlier than knowing that changes in activity make no difference to gender – but children's answers at this age are very dependent on exactly how the questions are asked, and there are often issues about whether they are reporting on 'real' or 'pretend' stereotypes, or on norms. Not conforming to the male stereotype if you are male is seen as more deviant than a girl not conforming to the female stereotype. Most Western children at this age prefer to be the gender they are, although more girls wish to be boys than boys wish to be girls.

Knowing that one's gender is (normally) an attribute that will not change comes to be a factor in deciding one's social identity from the preschool years. Stereotypes of gender typically begin with observable features and activities – 'boys don't wear pink but do play with cars' – and expand into assigning social roles and psychological attributes – 'footballers are boys and girls are gentle'. Clearly at this point social stereotypes kick in with a vengeance, and it is highly likely that the mass media are an enormous influence, more and more as children move into adolescence. Children who watch stereotyped material on television, or read books or papers or magazines which are gender-stereotyped, express stronger gender stereo-types than those who get less exposure to stereotyped media (Friedman, Leaper and Bigler 2007), and early gender stereotyping predicts how gender stereotyped children's views will be later (Golombok *et al.* 2008). And much material is both highly stereotyped and powerful. (For example, my daughter, aged two to three, loved to play Sleeping Beauty or Snow White. Her role in these games was to lie still with her eyes closed, smiling beatifically, while someone else played all the other roles and finally woke her with a kiss. This irritated me into providing an intensive course of stories with more feminist themes, such as Molly Whuppie the giant-killer and various clever girls who outsmart the male baddies (Leeson 1993). Later on, in my continuing war on demeaning gender stereotypes, I made 'sensible' clothes for her Barbie doll. These were not much used: Barbie wore her ballgowns to go rock climbing up the armchair. There was a good long-term outcome in her consciousness of stories and her feminism, although the effect short term was not at all marked.)

The degree to which a child has developed his or her gender identity seems to be associated with more selection of same gender playmates from age two through the primary school (Friedman, Leaper and Bigler 2007). Accurate discrimination of the gender of others, which starts in infancy, means you can select same-gender peers as friends. This allows the estab-lishment of prototypes of male and female behaviour, with peer sensitivity to what's suitable being highly influential. Children show some knowledge of the association between gender stereotypes and activities, objects and attributes in the early preschool years, and this knowledge increases and has stronger social implications as they move through the beginnings of school. Children have little difficulty in making judgements about which roles, possessions, toys, tasks and appearance are gendered. They can express the equivalent of cultural gender stereotypes by age three to five, but their knowledge of gender stereotypes is not very highly correlated with their own personal behaviour.

I started the last paragraph with the phrase 'gender identity'; this is a notion which deserves some unpacking. Egan and Perry (2001), for example, suggested that it has five components: knowledge of one's gender membership; perceived similarity to others of the same gender; satisfaction with one's gender membership; felt pressure (from oneself and from others) to conform to the gender stereotype; and belief that one's own gender is as good as or superior to the other. They further suggested that appraising oneself as not typical of one's gender, not feeling contentment with one's gender membership, and feeling under strong pressure to conform to the stereotype would be associated with worse psychological adjustment, in the shape of low self-esteem, more internalising symptoms, and peer rejection. Responses from White American preadolescent samples supported this prediction (Carver, Yunger and Perry 2003; Egan and Perry 2001; Yunger, Carver and Perry 2004). Corby, Hodges and Perry (2007) replicated these predictions in groups of White, Black and Hispanic preadolescents in Florida, but also found that Hispanic girls who identified closely with the female gender stereotype, or felt high pressure to conform with it, had high levels of the internalising symptoms such as anxiety and passivity that were prominent in the cultural stereotype of femininity. This is a useful reminder, it seems to me, that both conformity to stereotypes and deviance from them may have either costs or benefits, depending on circumstances.

4.4.5 Influences on the development of a gendered social world

4.4.5.1 Parents

Although the early evidence of parent effects on children's gender differences found that parents treated boys and girls with 'a surprising degree of similarity' (Maccoby and Jacklin 1974: 362), Leaper, Anderson and Sanders (1998) argue that this may in part be because the evidence was limited to insensitive research designs. As well as looking at issues such as how parents' talk to girls and boys differs in such broad domains as 'warmth' or 'restrictiveness', we need fine-grained examination of, for example, the sorts of gender roles that parents provide for their children to observe, their explicit instructions about gender roles, the opportunities that they offer for gender-typed activities, and the different ways that brothers and sisters are treated within the same family. And we should expect that there will be variability within individual parents according to the setting and the task that they are engaged in; and differences between parents linked to their social class, economic position, religious affiliation, and educational level – and, in periods of rapid historical change, the social zeitgeist also (Thornton and Young-DeMarco 2001). There are proximal processes at the level of the microsystem and multiple pressures at the level of macro-systems, which combine and collide in the child's experience.

There is some evidence that parents do provide their children with explicit instruction about what is gender-appropriate for them in terms of activities and careers, with children tending to get more of such attention from the parent of the same gender (Harris and Morgan 1991; McHale, Crouter and Tucker 1999; McHale *et al.* 2000; McHale, Crouter and Whiteman 2003; Crouter *et al.* 2007; Martin and Ross 2005). Parents also tend to know more about the everyday activities of their children of the same gender than they do about the children of the opposite gender, partly because they are likely to spend more time with a same-gender child, partly because they may be hoping to involve the child in their own interests, perhaps because they can more easily guess about activities they see as suitable for their own gender. Parents seem to work harder on developing boys' interests than girls' (McHale *et al.* 2000; McHale, Crouter and Whiteman 2003), especially if family resources are restricted. This may be a response to expectations about males' and females' involvement in employment, likely income level, and family maintenance (Crouter *et al.* 2001). Fong (2002) argues that China's one-child policy has led to the empowerment of many young women, because they have not had to compete with brothers for parental investment and they have been able to prove that they are capable of finding well-paid jobs and potentially performing the filial duty of supporting their elderly parents. I suspect that there may be lots of autobiographical evidence of parental pressure or encouragement to develop particular skills, some of them gendered; there could usefully be more systematic research linking specific parental input to long-term outcomes of skill development or career choice, particularly as historical and economic change will be so important to the findings (Eccles and Wigfield 2002; Mello 2008).

Parents do seek influence over their children's developing gender roles, and may try hard to prevent a child from acting too differently from the gender stereotype, particularly if it is the male stereotype that is being challenged by a boy (Lamb 2004; Friedman, Leaper and Bigler 2007). In the West girls who want to do 'boy' things no longer face as much disapproval as they used to, but boys who are perceived as 'girly' are still at risk of severe disapproval, from fathers and male peers especially. It is worth noting that the views of the child about gender-typing do not seem to be highly correlated with those of the parent (Tenenbaum and Leaper 2002). Children's acceptance or rejection or even knowledge of gender stereotypes does not seem to be simply a matter of accepting the indoctrination that their parents supply, although clearly they observe peers, familiar adults, and media images in building up their own discrimination between gendered prototypes. (And of course knowledge about gender stereotypes does not necessarily entail accepting them (Egan and Perry 2001; Liben and Bigler 2002). A study of Muslim and non-Muslim adolescents in Holland (Verkuyten and Slooter 2008) found Muslim girls far more resistant than Muslim boys, and than non-Muslim adolescents of both genders, to parental practices that negatively affected females, such as female circumcision or restrictions on going out. The non-Muslim Dutch teenagers saw these practices as possibly legitimate parts of a culture that they did not themselves belong to, and as non-members they were cautious about disapproving of them. The Muslim boys, on the whole, approved them: the Muslim girls experienced them as discriminatory, and as wrong.)

Parents have gender themselves, and may discuss gender stereotypes and enact gender-stereotyped behaviour, although not necessarily consistently (Leaper and Bigler 2004). Children may have one range of experiences with their mothers, and a somewhat different range with their fathers (Lamb and Lewis 2004). Most of the research evidence finds mothers doing a lot more of the instrumental childcare and teaching whereas fathers spend a higher proportion of their time on play and leisure, although children feel closer to their mothers and more deferential towards their fathers (McHale, Crouter and Whiteman 2003; Lamb 2004; Friedman, Leaper and Bigler 2007). But it is important to acknowledge that children's relation with one parent will be affected by their relationship with the other parent, and indeed with other family members; the whole family system and its place in the wider social world will be the contexts for individual relationships. The research on working mothers, for example, shows that fathers in working mother families tend to increase their involvement with the children, know more about them, spend more time with them, and are more involved in a wider range of childcare than in families where the mother is not employed outside the home – but they still do far less parenting than the employed mother (Crouter and McHale 1993; Crouter et al. 1999a 1999b; Lamb 2004; Russell and Hwang 2004, p. 253).

The quality of the relationships between children's parents may be a powerful influence on their development of gender roles, as it is of other important areas of development (pp. 59, 143). Marital conflict is strongly linked to children's emotional problems and difficulties of adjustment (Holden and Barker 2004; McLanahan and Carlson 2004; Amato and Sobolewski 2004; Cummings et al. 2004; Sternberg et al. 2006).

4.4.5.2 Siblings

We can expect children to learn about gender roles from their siblings, who are likely to be their most common out-of-school companions as well as partners in a long-term relationship (Rust *et al.* 2000; Dunn 1993, 1999; Martin and Ross 2005; p. 159). In an interesting longitudinal study, McHale *et al.* (2001) describe younger siblings modelling their gendered attitudes, personality and activities on their older siblings', with older siblings being a stronger influence than parents. Older sisters, taking on their own stereo-typical role as teachers, were particularly influential – although again the family system as a whole will be important. But as well as modelling that makes siblings more similar in their gendered behaviour, there could be the processes of sibling de-identification described by various theorists (e.g. Schachter 1982; pp. 159, 163), where siblings try to be as different from each other as possible, or influences from being one of several siblings of the same gender in a family where parents wanted both sons and daughters (Golombok 2000).

4.4.5.3 Peers

In the primary school, expressed gender stereotypes may become rigid judgements that contribute to an increasing separation between the two genders in their chosen activities (Maccoby 1998; pp. 170–86). If there is enough choice of people to play with, childhood peer groups in the primary school tend to become single-gender and to have distinctive cultures. Little boys typically play in larger groups, and engage in more rough and tumble play, more play fighting, more 'killing' games, and more competition (and at later ages more violent video games and reckless driving); on average they use their speech more to tease, heckle, boast, and top the other's story, and use more direct commands and make more appeal to rules; they often develop stronger and more explicit dominance hierarchies, place more emphasis on physique and physical strength/skill, and are more focused on agency, power and excitement: and they tend to do less sitting close to mother or to a female teacher. Little girls typically engage in more dyadic or small clique play, more talk, more indirect competition with turn taking; their disputes tend to be more likely to involve appeal to fairness and feelings (rather than rules) and to lead to group break-up – 'I won't be your friend any more'. They more often use domestic themes for play, they engage in more self-disclosure to others, their friends are more matched on characteristics and values, they more often talk to create intimacy, to criticise in a socially acceptable way, to express agreement, to acknowledge others, to exclude others; and they show much more enthusiasm for the company of adult females, hence they spend more time near the (typically female) teacher in nursery/primary school (Friedman, Leaper and Bigler 2007; Maccoby 1998).

Given a choice of playmates, children seem to develop this sort of preference for same gender company quite early – infant school or earlier – and while they are spending more of their time in same-gender groups, there may be greater attention and sensitivity to the opinion of one's same gender peers, which would further increase their influence. This may be one reason why there tends to be increasing self-segregation and exclusion of the opposite gender, through primary school, until the years of adolescence and dating come along. There may be more cross-gender friendships in private or if the choice of playmates is limited than in the age-structured school world, where reputation is so much at risk (pp. 170–86). The mechanisms that lead to separate public worlds for primary school girls and boys – 'almost like two separate cultures' (Ruble, Martin and Berenbaum 2006: 869) – probably include children selecting their friends on the basis of similarity in activities and behaviour, and acting in ways that exclude those who are seen as different, although many cultures have explicit rules about who you can mix with and where you can go (Maccoby 1998; Bussey and Bandura 1999; Rose and Rudolph 2006). Despite these 'separate cultures', individuals may, moment by moment, act in ways which are not gender-stereotyped, sometimes unnoticed by the stereotype police, sometimes with their tolerance, sometimes in ways that lead to conflict.

Girls' social groups tend to be smaller and more intimate than boys' groups are, with less boisterous activity and physical competition and more intimacy, confiding, and backbiting. The social interaction of both little girls and adolescents can be horrifyingly bossy and bitchy, with 'friend-ships' and alliances breaking up and assertions of 'I'm not your friend any more' or 'I won't be your friend if you're friends with her', with negative consequences for the victims' self-esteem and vulnerability to problems such as depression (e.g. Benenson and Christakos 2003; Goodwin 2006; Prinstein *et al.* 2005). In this example from an ethnographic study (Goodwin 2006: 109–110), Dionne and Julia are talking to Angela about what another, younger, group of girls, including Aretha, had earlier told Dionne about Angela, using the reported incident to get at Angela themselves.

Dionne [quoting the other group]: Oh no. We don't like Angela. We think she's so stupid and nothing but a whore and a bitch.
Angela: Sorry. They did not say that.
Aretha: I never even said whore.
Julia: I'm sorry Angela but – like you need to get yourself grounded like Miss Smith – Miss Smith calls it anchoring? Because they just called you fat bitch. And then you're back friends with them? I'm not trying to be mean to you but you're all alone.
Dionne: You're being used.
Aretha: We did not just call her whore.
Dionne: You know you're being used Angela.

In another incident (Goodwin 2006: 219–220), a group of girls plot revenge on Emi who has insulted them by calling Lisa a lesbian and by expecting the group to do what she wanted.

Lisa: She called me a lesbian.
Janis: Emi called you a lesbian?
Lisa: Yes. So fucking lame.
Lisa: I hope they slip off the swing and crack their head open!
Janis: I'll be on your side.
Lisa: Of course you are.
Janis: What's the fight about since you guys have known her for so long.
Lisa: Because um –
Aretha: I want to make Emi jealous.
Janis: Yeah. Let's ignore her.
Ruth (Emi's sister): No you guys.
Janis: And laugh.
Ruth: I don't think that's such a great idea.
Janis: Let's laugh guys.
Lisa: We can do it if we want to. You can't tell us what to do.
Ruth: Okay. Fine. I'm out of this then.
Janis: You guys let's go tell her then.
Aretha: No, but she hasn't got –
Janis: They half laughing.
Janis: Okay. Something really bad.
Janis: What should we do.
Aretha: I know something!
Janis: What.
Aretha: When you guys come over to my house, and she would have to leave by one thirty four kinda time.
Ruth: And so we could say 'Oh I'm so sad that you have to leave.'
Janis: Yeah but will – you guys won't be in a fight by then will you?
Janis: What did she
Ruth: You guys it's gonna become a
Janis: What did she say.
Ruth: A much worse fight.

Margaret Atwood's novel *Cat's Eye* (Atwood 1989) makes a powerful use of the nastiness of girls' friendship groups, and their effects on the confidence of those who dominate or are dominated.

Boys' aggression towards peers is more likely to be confrontational, physical and swiftly resolved: girls use more indirect aggression and negative gossip. Given experience of mixed gender company, girls learn that they may need to use more power-assertive strategies when dealing with boys, and although boys do not so readily use 'female' conflict-mitigation strategies with girls, they may in adolescence turn to girls for emotional support and the possibility of disclosing their inner feelings (Friedman, Leaper and Bigler 2007). Social cognition skills are important in the prevention of aggression (Reitz *et al.* 2007; Werner, Cassidy and Juliano 2006; pp. 172–73, 185–86).

4.4.5.4 Schools

Schools socialise pupils both through being places where a large group of children have to co-exist, and sometimes through their own presentation of gender-stereotyped behaviour and roles. Girls and boys may be social-ised into different beliefs about achievement over the school and post-school years. There is not much difference in the confidence of very young children, or their interest in mastery (pp. 87–90, 215–17), but once in schools low achievement is more visible (and possibly more prevalent) among boys (Dunne and Gazeley 2008; Jones and Myhill 2004a, 2004b). Gender-stereotyped beliefs about areas of achievement seem to develop during primary school, with girls at risk of believing that 'girls can't do maths or science' and boys at risk of believing that doing well at languages is not masculine. Various educational programmes have very much reduced the degree to which such beliefs occur and handicap girls, whose rate of success in school exams is now higher than boys' in all subjects except engineering and computing, and more young women than ever are entering male-dominated subjects and then professions and doing as well as their male fellow students. The under-performance of boys has been more intractable, however; as has anxiety about it, as under-achievement is believed to be associated with problematic social behaviour for boys (e.g. Arnot and Miles 2005; Jones and Myhill 2004a, 2004b).

4.5 Summary

In this section I have looked mainly at children's relationships with other children, developing microsystems between siblings or with peers. The section has also included discussion of bullying and of gender. I have argued that these topics can be considered from both biological and social science perspectives. They are not separate from the relationships with parents that I considered in Chapter 3, nor are they separate from what goes on in larger social settings, such as school.

The proximal processes of child–child microsystems accompany parent–child experiences, I think, to account for an enormous part of the child's chances of growing up to be a well-functioning social person. Parental behaviour starts off what the child learns about social functioning, what sort of self-concept and understanding of other people emerges, what sort of emotional foundation there is to face later challenges, but experience with other children has an enormously significant effect.

Chapter 5

Bigger social systems with child participants

In the earlier parts of this book, I have discussed what may be going on inside the child, and what experiences in microsystems, between the child and one or a few others, may do to the child's development as a social person. The scale of the events I have reviewed is small, mainly a matter of everyday experiences between a very few people, over and over and over again in a limited range of settings. I am confident that these everyday settings and proximal processes are enormously interesting and important. But even the smallest settings are embedded in larger systems: and as children grow older they have increasingly to take part in activities where they are part of large social groups. There are more people to interact with, more impersonal rules, more public roles, more issues about reputation, different amounts of choice, of control, of opportunity, of achievement. I move now to what we know about how children's participation in large-scale social settings influences their development. I begin with the experience of the child in the microsystems that they participate in within large social institutions. The first focus of this section is the child in school, but I go on to discuss the importance of childcare arrangements, children's engagement with the media, and participation in religious belief and practice. I also address some issues about cultural factors in the development of the social person, and some research on the role of mesosystems and exosystems in development.

5.1 School and the child as social person

Children spend a large proportion of their waking hours in school, and interact with many other social persons there to play a range of social roles. The school contains many microsystems within which children engage with others who are often of great emotional and practical significance for them. It is also perhaps the part of their childhood where there are strong macrosystem influences focusing most obviously and explicitly on children:

the culture demands that children should have formal education, requires them to learn specified things in school, and uses their certification from school to determine their opportunities for employment, income, and status. The school, although being a set of microsystems within a macrosystem, also needs to be considered as part of several mesosystems, notably the relationship between the microsystems of home and the microsystems of school, and the relationships between the microsystems of children with fellow pupils and the microsystems of child with teachers. I have already described the complexities of relationships and socialisation within families as highly complex: what goes on in schools is not less complex.

Even if we focus narrowly on schools as places whose purposes are to teach children things and to get children to learn, they are inevitably social settings for the child. All of Bronfenbrenner's levels of developmental contexts come together very visibly around schools. There are multiple microsystems of everyday face-to-face social interactions with school staff and with other pupils. There are everyday face-to-face interactions with parents about school. These all happen within the influence of the community's expectations of schools, pupils and teachers. Most schools, most policy makers, most parents, most commentators also believe that it is part of the school's role to socialise the child. As socialisation is part of the family's role too, there will be a mesosystem of home and school to affect the child's development. Increasingly topics that were once the responsibility of the family are being included in what schools should cover – sex education being one obvious example; newspaper columnists blame schools as well as parents if delinquency rates or teenage pregnancy rates rise. The economic macrosystem develops historically in ways that make schooling and certification ever more crucial for successful functioning in later life. The hours children have to spend in school increase, the curriculum widens, more and more of the population becomes expected to leave school with certification in the form of exam successes, and certification is required for more and more jobs. Lifelong learning becomes a social goal, intended to serve the interests of the individual for a richer, widening and deepening pool of skills and knowledge, but also the demands of the economy for a skilled and effective and flexible labour force.

In order to place some organisation on this complex area, I am going to begin with what children bring to their school from their experience before it. This leads into consideration of the effects of family experience on life in school, and the relative power of school and family in determining children's success in school systems. I then consider how schools define 'competence' before looking at some of the things about schools that make children's achievement of this 'competence' more likely. I end with discussion of pupil identity, as there is a complex relationship between schools as systems and children as social persons.

5.1.1 Preschool experience and school life

A lot of what happens before the child goes to school will have major effects on children's school careers. Indeed, even though education can change people's life chances very much for the better, a great deal about how well a child will do at school is easier to predict if you know about their lives preschool than if you only know about their experience in school. My earlier discussions will have suggested some of the early life factors that affect school experience – inherited characteristics, parental framing, social skills with peers, etc. My next task is to review the literature on these as they can be seen closer to the social contexts of school.

5.1.1.1 Child care, parenting, and school

Throughout evolutionary history, animals that parent have had to provide childcare as well as getting on with their other activities. Nest-building animals leave their young in the nest while they forage for food for themselves and their offspring – in some species the parents take turns, in some it is the work of only one parent. Human parents may carry their infants with them as they work to support themselves, or delegate infant care to particular individuals – sometimes the other parent, sometimes another family member who may be of the parents' generation or the infant's grandparent or older sister, sometimes to professional carers. Historically, most care has kept the child in the normal social community, which could allow the child plentiful opportunities for observing activities in the community, but may often have meant that attention to the child's needs was intermittent because of the demands of the workplace or of domesticity – I am thinking of farm women's babies stashed in the long grass at the edge of the field while the mothers worked to bring in the harvest, or the swaddled infant in a cradle that the mother rocked while she attended to her mending. Rich families have used surrogate, part professional, childcare for centuries – royal children for example would be brought up by whole households of unrelated adults with grandiose titles, and visited by their parents only once or twice a year (e.g. Starkey 2001, 2008). Across history and across cultures, most childcare will have involved fairly small numbers of children who are about the same age, and in most cases (but by no means all) the carers who were employed had a family link to the child or a strong social obligation, and hence a relatively strong commitment to the individual child. Increasingly, twenty-first century infants and young children may spend time in groups with age mates, in settings such as nurseries or play groups, where carers *are in loco parentis* but on a less individualised basis, and are trained professionals rather than family members.

There has been a substantial amount of research on what effect this sort of early out-of-home care has on children. In most preschool groups, attention is paid to some degree to school-like activities, although they may be seen as part of provision for play rather than as preparation for school. The staff in such groups may behave like teachers, be called teachers, even be qualified as teachers, and may have an explicit curriculum of school-like skills for the children to engage with, although education may be the minor partner compared with the need to care for the child. Large-scale studies have been undertaken in the USA and the UK. In both countries there were some grounds for anxiety about the quality of 'educare' provided; but in almost all the research there is consistent evidence of preschool group experience having a favourable effect on children's language and development of the skills needed to work in school classrooms ('school readiness'); the benefits seem to be larger where children have encountered better quality group care (e.g. Blanden and Gregg 2004; NICHD 2003c, 2004a, 2004b, 2006; Osborn and Milbank 1987; Sammons *et al.* 2004). There is a body of rather less consistent evidence that group care may sometimes have an adverse effect on social and emotional development – children with experience of preschool group care are reported to show higher cortisol levels, more aggression or assertion, more anxiety, and poorer relationships with other children (e.g. Belsky 2001; Pluess and Belsky 2009), which may perhaps be grounds for concern about the effects of preschool care, especially on very young children. However, it appears from large-scale studies that this negative effect seems to be most visible with vulnerable children, particularly those with poor family relationships and insecure attachments to their mothers, and with boys (e.g. Belsky *et al.* 2007b; Cote *et al.* 2008; CMPO 2008; Pluess and Belsky 2009).

5.1.1.2 Experience of preschool group interventions

As I described, there is consistent evidence that early experience of pre-school play groups and nursery schools gives children opportunities to learn all sorts of things that make adjustment to school and learning school-based skills a little easier than it seems to be for children with no such experience. The evidence from interventions to reduce the educational disadvantage of children from families with low incomes and low educational achievement (e.g. Meadows 2006) suggests that good experience in preschool groups can help to set children on a more positive trajectory through their school careers, although it cannot inoculate them against the ill-effects of later poorer education. Properly conducted intensive preschool intervention for disadvantaged children can lead to short-term gains in IQ, which are followed by better school performance and better motivation to work in school, especially if parents are involved in it too (Moran, Ghate and van der Merwe 2004; Olds 2005); and there is eventually less risk of failure in school and antisocial behaviour. The much less intense experience of attendance at preschool groups in the UK is also associated with better educational performance in the primary school for the whole social range of children.

Two particularly well-documented projects, the Abecedarian project (Ramey and Ramey 1998) and the Chicago Child–Parent Centers (Reynolds, Ou and Topitzes 2004), show what the causal path between intervention and outcome may be, and that it is probably social as well as cognitive. There are three main possibilities: first, that the intervention improves children's abilities as measured in standardised tests and these improvements initiate a sequence of improved performance on school tasks and tests that culminate in better school achievement; second, that the intervention makes families more likely to support the child's development more effectively; third, that participation in the programme makes the families seek out better schools for their children and use the schools more effectively. The evidence from these two major studies is that all these things happen. Children's cognition was boosted by their preschool experience, and this, plus continuing family support and school support through the later part of their education, led to higher rates of school completion. Programme participation enhanced these little children's cognition and language and their readiness to cope with the demands of formal schooling; this led to higher ratings from teachers, less likelihood of being retained in grade to repeat a year, and more completion of high school. Programme involvement of mothers had a positive effect on both child outcomes and mothers' well-being. School support and family support as they grew older were the major predictors of children avoiding involvement in crime and delinquency. The quality of schooling after the intervention is crucial for the eventual outcome; the early intervention is not so much an 'inoculation' that can prevent failure all by itself, so much as an early advantage that can be built on throughout later schooling, to lead, eventually, to success.

5.1.2 Family experience

The school careers of children generally resemble those of their parents, especially where achievement is concerned. As with other parent–child resemblances, genetic similarities undoubtedly contribute to this, but environmental similarities and parents' goals for their children are at least as important. Almost all parents would like their children to do well in school, almost all say that they are strongly interested in the child (e.g. Hill *et al.* 2004; Jacobs and Harvey 2005; Juang and Silbereisen 2002; Lareau 2000, 2002; Sacker, Schoon and Bartley 2002). Parents may encourage respect for education, or the acquisition of school-related skills, or an expectation that school certification will lead to better opportunities in later life; they may scheme to get their child into a 'better' school or consistently provide experiences designed to complement and deepen what the school offers. Parental commitment to support the child's schooling can be embodied in a lot of additional hours of interaction at home and at school, including direct help with school work, engagement in related activities, provision of materials such as books and educational software, and social networking (e.g. Eccles 2005, 2007; Eccles *et al.* 1998; Eccles and Wigfield 2002; Fredricks and Eccles 2005, 2006, 2008).

The meeting of home language and the school is one of the places where the mesosystem of home and school has been researched. Teachers and children undoubtedly react to each other's language, affecting the teacher's view of the child's skills and probable achievement and the child's view of whether school is a compatible extension of home. Differences in use of language will also result in different shades of expertise in particular uses of language, for example realising that what was meant is not literally the same as what was said, that a comment has the function of a command, that adults do or do not appreciate being challenged, and so forth (e.g. Heath 1983; King 1978). Children whose family experience of language includes it being used in the ways that teachers use language in the classroom tend to settle into school more easily and to do better there than children whose family language is different from the school's. Some of the children whose language or identity is different from school's may reject (or be rejected by) the school because of the difference, and their cognitive skills will thus not incorporate those of the school's curriculum (Downey 2008); others may become users of two dialects, one for home and one for school. Having two dialects or languages may be experienced as potentially or actually alienating (Heath 1983; Rodriguez 1980), particularly if one of them is subject to negative attitudes and discrimination, and if there is no active support for the bilingual child to learn and use both.

Children in school who are using the school's dialect as their own second language, not as native speakers, face a number of disadvantages. Their own language may not have given them so much practice on specialised skills important in the school's language, for example answering display questions, telling or discussing stories, or analysing objects or events; thus they will be less expert in these skills. Their own language may be socially judged as the mark of a stigmatised social group, and stereotypes of that group's behaviour and potential achievement may interfere with recognition of individual children's behaviour and potential. Because teacher and pupil have different languages they may meet communication problems, and at best they may have to translate each other's utterances as well as acting on them. The effort of doing this may divert cognitive resources away from the focus of the interaction, the question the child is to answer or the problem that is to be solved. It may be harder for the teacher to provide help at the appropriate level and for the pupil to internalise the ideas presented in a 'foreign' language. Children from minority groups and from the working class may have to do more work than middle-class children to get the same results. They may be more likely to be labelled as 'stupid' or 'mildly retarded', just as we would all be less likely to shine on a demanding task if we were simultaneously having to translate it from a less familiar language.

5.1.3 School demands for competence

My discussion of schools as places where children are social persons will already have illustrated how many levels of analysis and conceptualisation are potentially involved in discussing children's competence in schools. Bronfenbrenner (1979) makes the crucial point that 'competence' is *context-specific* effectiveness, dependent on the goals, values, self-regulation, and cognitive abilities of the person as they fit with the situation and the system requirements and expectations.

Schools are institutions that expect development in their pupils, and invest in activities which are intended to clarify what is expected of pupils and to shape their behaviour towards what the school wants. In the early years of schooling, for example, teachers engage in a lot of explicit social-isation via stating the rules of classroom behaviour. 'Put your hand up if you know [the answer to the question], otherwise I can't hear you', 'Kind hands don't grab and snatch, they share' are two typical examples of infant school pronouncements (King 1978). The intention of such rules is to make it possible for the class to function productively in a busy crowded situ-ation; teachers see complying with rules like these as good and sensible, since they are supposed to work to the benefit of all involved. Children who have not learned to behave in these socialised ways by the time they are a few years into school will get into trouble. Teachers who cannot achieve a reasonable approximation of a 'busy hum' of engaged learning in their classroom may not be able to feel that they are competent teachers (e.g. Osborn *et al.* 2000; Pollard and Filer 1996, 1999, 2007).

Obviously there may be tension between the individual's goals, values, self-regulation, and cognitive abilities etc. and the school's. Some of the issues around this relate to problems connected with gender (pp. 197–99), peer groups (Chapter 4), delinquency (pp. 264–67), self-esteem (pp. 65–69, 72–75, 79–80), classroom motivation (pp. 87–90), ethnicity (Downey 2008) etc.

If we assume that social psychology is right in suggesting that people work to maintain an advantageous self-image, teachers probably need to see themselves as people who enjoy and control their work, avoiding too much classroom disruption and challenge, coping with demands from head teachers and other assessors, seeing their pupils working and learning productively (Osborn *et al.* 2000). Pupils' self-image can be served by meeting the teacher's (and parent's) expectation that they will be successful learners and diligent pupils, but these, are not their only reference groups. Peers' ideas may not be the same as parents' and teachers'.

Broadly the *really* 'competent' pupil is one who manages to achieve personally valued goals *and* school valued ones *and* peer valued ones; a balancing act that not many will achieve effortlessly. We might want also to specify that the goals and achievement enhance the social functioning of both individuals and the group, leading both to good social acceptance and co-operation and to enhanced self-esteem and psychological well-being.

5.1.3.1 Learning roles and school effectiveness

When I described the ways in which young children interact with their parents and caregivers and learn through social interaction, I used the Vygotskian metaphor of 'scaffolding' (Gauvain 2005; Turner and Berkowitz 2005; Wood 1998; pp. 115–16, 130–33). I argue there (and in Meadows 2006) that this is a peculiarly rich mode of social action and especially conducive to effective learning. Cultural studies (e.g. Lave 1990; Rogoff 2003a, 2003b) identify similar structures in the interaction of apprentices and masters in the learning of cultural crafts and skills. Again, the interaction is typically one expert to one learner (or a very few learners) and involves repeated interaction over a long period of time. I want to consider here what this might have to say for being a learning person in the sort of formal schooling that we are familiar with.

A number of relevant points can be made on the basis of research on what makes for effective learning in school classes (Scheerens and Bosker 1997). Students learn best when they are engaged in academic tasks that are clearly introduced to them and which they can proceed through steadily, making consistent progress with few failures (ideally almost none when they have to work independently, and not many when the teacher is there to provide feedback and guidance); when the teacher has established a class-room orientation towards conscientious academic work, and supervises and instructs actively within the classroom; and when the teacher's behaviour supports students' efforts through behaviour such as question sequences that establish easy facts which have to be combined to answer a harder problem, allowing an appropriate time for a student to produce an answer, providing regular and extensive feedback; praising specifically rather than generally; and acknowledging achievements in a positive but non-intrusive way (Scheerens and Creemers 1989; Scheerens and Bosker 1997; Meadows 2006).

The benefits of this sort of interaction for 'the child as social person in school' presumably centre on the child learning the social role of learner, the child's development of a self-concept as a learner, the social roles experienced by the child vis-à-vis the teacher and the rest of the class. Teachers provide 'scaffolding' which may be analogous to what parents provide, but increasingly pupils have to also provide it for themselves.

.3.2 Learning by social observation

Early scaffolding is not the only social activity that enables learning. We are all able to learn from our observations of other people and our imitations of them: early language learning and early socialisation provide many examples (Meadows 2006, pp. 112–15, 130–33). No one deliberately taught a child less that two years old, who had better remain anonymous, to protest at adults' unwanted intervention in her affairs by shouting 'Shut up' and 'You're really sick, you're really really sick', but observation of older children (in the first case) and television soap opera (in the second) provided sufficient models. Observing and imitating a model's overt behaviour can be a good way to learn; but in practice, if complex behaviour is involved it requires a comparatively clear model, sufficient time to observe it, and perhaps the prior development of many skills that are components of the model's behaviour. The novice often cannot see what the expert is doing, let alone imitate it, let alone appreciate why it is done. An educationally helpful model will do more than merely model: there will be acts which are demonstrations and instructions and comments on the learner's imitations, not simply parts of the normal execution of the skilled behaviour. Such 'educational modelling' behaviour will be especially necessary for learners who only have an immature repertoire of cognitive and metacognitive skills. It is obviously a component of Vygotskian ways of teaching thinking. Media models, peers and siblings might be especially effective models (Anderson *et al.* 2001; Fenstermacher and Saudino 2006; Wang 2008), but parents do it too – my list of parental 'frames' for children included it (pp. 115–16).

5.1.3.3 Social motivation for learning

Here motivational research (Dweck and Elliot 1983; Dweck 1999; Bandura 1995, 1997, 2001; Meadows 2006; Nicholls 1984; Thompson, 2004) is clearly relevant. The long history of research into the academic motivation of children and older students derives from general models of motivation – what energises people to do something, and what direction do they take. Although there are theories that postulate motivation to satisfy drives and instincts, so far as academic motivation is concerned the bases seem to be thought to be competence, autonomy, and relatedness (Pintrich 2000, 2003). It is argued that we wish to have a sense of mastery, a sense of self-determination or autonomy, and a sense of belonging to a social group (pp. 44–48, 88–90, 111, 138–41); without these our motivation and our general well-being will suffer. The effects of these needs on our behaviour or achievement are mediated by social and cognitive constructs such as perceived competence, control beliefs, fear of failure, and regulatory styles.

One fertile stream of research focuses especially on individuals' beliefs in their own efficacy and potential for improvement (Bandura 1995, 1997;

Dweck and Elliot 1983; Dweck 1999; Eccles and Wigfield 2002; Eccles 2007). Students who believe that they can organise themselves effectively and learn the appropriate behaviour tend to do better and remain happier than those who believe they cannot succeed or cannot improve. Students who believe that they will do badly or that the task is uncongenial are relatively unlikely to do well on it, sometimes because they avoid the challenge and make little effort to succeed. Adaptive self-efficacy and competence perceptions motivate students well.

Some learners are very anxious about their role as learner and in particular the implications of failing to succeed – and given education's central role in determining people's career paths and therefore life chances, they may be very right to be concerned. Thompson (2004) argues that one of the major problems leading to under-achievement and thus impeding cognitive development is failure-avoidant behaviour. His picture of how this occurs centres on family environment and brings together several of the themes and the strands of research that I have been describing in this book. Table 5.1 summarises what he thinks is involved.

At the centre is parent–child interaction which is critical and over-controlling, which emphasises high achievement but does not recognise that it has to be worked for, where feedback is not explicit about why something succeeded or failed and what could be done about it: parental teaching, in short, which lacks the child-contingency, the joint activity towards solution, the calibrating of challenges to an amount that the child is likely to cope with, the gradual transfer of responsibility and the warmth that characterise good parental framing and good Vygotskian scaffolding (Meadows 2006, pp. 115–16, 130–33). Parental over-control and parental high demands diminish intrinsic motivation and reduce the scope for internally-led development and finding one's own solution (pp. 119–20, 134–38). These behaviours have consequences for personality characteristics and motivation: the child lacks confidence in his or her own ability, believes that ability is fixed and cannot be augmented (pp. 77–78), that ability is indicated by each success or failure, that effortless success is what should happen, that metacognitive analyses of the specific causes of each success or failure is less relevant than general ability. With this constellation of beliefs, the child may suffer low intrinsic motivation, defensive pessimism, self-handicapping and self-deprecation, passivity and helplessness, fear of challenge, avoidance behaviours, and depression. The authoritarian, demanding, hot-housing sorts of parental behaviour that Thompson describes are thus, perhaps, indicative of ways of teaching that do not improve children's thinking (although evidence from numerous biographies and autobiographies suggests they may sometimes be quite good ways of producing angst and rebellion).

Bradley and Corwyn (2005) suggest that opportunities to work for mastery are also crucially important. In an environment that has been set

Table 5.1 Personal and family factors affecting failure-avoidant behaviour.
Adapted from Thompson 2004: 5, Figure 1.

Person variables – personality	Family environment variables – parenting	Achievement costs – effects on behaviour
• low self-estimates of ability	• family conflict	• diminished intrinsic motivation
• uncertain self-worth	• authoritarian parenting style	• failure to develop effective study skills
• sensitivity to evaluative threat	• parental criticism and over-control	• defensive pessimism
• emphasis on ability as a criterion of self-worth	• socially imposed standards of perfectionism from parents	• propensity to self-handicap in situations of evaluative threat
• view of ability as trait-like and immutable	• emphasis on 'perfection with ease'	• avoidance of challenge
• ability best indicated when success follows	• emphasis on achievement in absence of clear advice as to how it may be achieved	• no persistence if difficulties occur
• low-effort uncertainty about the causes of achievement outcomes	• non-contingent evaluative feedback	• self-presentational costs of self-handicapping
• success viewed as outcome of uncontrollable or external factors	• reinforcement on grounds irrelevant to achievement success	• passivity and helplessness
		• loss of social support networks

up by the caregivers to provide many opportunities for the child to explore safely, children will have more experience of making an effort to do something and gaining a satisfactory outcome as a reward for the effort; and will also have more chance of using feedback from earlier efforts to make adjustments to what they are currently doing. Self-regulation, effective persistence, and competence emerge as children observe those who are more competent than themselves, try to emulate them, and deliberately practise the skill they want to acquire. If the environment is not safe, or if there are few opportunities to combine observation and trying to do it yourself, or if there is no patient supportive feedback or recognition of your achievement, there is less to persuade the child to make an effort, or to plan and direct their activity. Bradley and Corwyn (2005) suggest that these children will become rather passive and unwilling to take risks: they will react to learning challenges and opportunities to become more competent but will not be proactive, and will be at risk of internalised disorders such as apathy, lack of interest, depression and a sense of not being able to be effective (Ryan, Kuhl and Deci 1997). In other cases it may result in the individual having difficulty in engaging with the learning challenges of school at all, let alone adopting them as an exciting opportunity to achieve improving degrees of mastery. Learners have views about the meaning and the meaningfulness of their learning activities, and these can be very problematic if the microsystems of school, home and community do not cohere (Bandura 1995, 1997; Dweck and Elliot 1983; Dweck 1999; Eccles *et al.* 1998; Eccles and Wigfield 2002; Eccles 2007; Ricco and Rodriguez 2006).

5.1.3.4 Learning in the community

An alternative focus to individuals' feelings of efficacy is the sort of achievement goals that they choose to work towards. Theorists in this area assume that people's behaviour is purposeful and intentional and directed towards attaining certain goals, especially goals concerned with competence. By and large, it is believed that individuals, if they can, will select tasks and activities that have value for them and that they think they can succeed on. Task or activity value is comprised of interest or enjoyment value, utility value, attainment value, and cost. Whether you think you can succeed on a task will involve both calculations of how difficult the task is and appraisal of your own abilities and learning power. What may differ between individuals will be the areas in which they seek to be competent, the level of competence they try to reach, and the markers of competence that they see as appropriate to judge what they have attained and what they still need to do. Each of these may or may not fit well with the definitions used by the others concerned with assessing individuals' competence; a student might seek and develop a high level of competence in 'stirring up things with the teacher in ways that amuse my friends', but this is not something that will be well regarded by the adult authorities.

Lave (1990) provides an interesting discussion of the underlying principles of 'understanding-in-practice' and of 'understanding-via-schooling'. She argues that the former is the more powerful source of enculturation:

> Knowledge-in-practice, constituted in the settings of practice, based on rich expectations generated over time about its shape, is the site of the most powerful knowledgeability of people in the lived-in world. The encompassing, synthesizing intentions reflected in a theory of understanding-in-practice make it difficult to argue for the separation of cognition and the social world, the form and content of learning, or of learning and its 'applications'. Internalization is a less important vehicle for transmission of the experience the world has to offer, in this view, than activity in relation with the world.
>
> (Lave 1990: 323)

'Understanding-in-practice' makes the learners constitute the problem for themselves: the child's understanding and goals define the problem, give meaning and value to the subject matter and the process of learning it, and integrate it into the learner's life and activity.

> Given that the development of an understanding about learning and about what is being learned inevitably accompanies learning, in the more conventional sense, it seems probable that learners whose understanding is deeply circumscribed and diminished through processes of explicit and intense 'knowledge transmission' are likely to arrive at an understanding of themselves as 'not understanding' or as 'bad at what they are doing' even when they are not bad at it (such seems the fate of the vast majority of the alumni of school math classes). On the other hand, learners who understand what they are learning in terms that increasingly approach the breadth and depth of understanding of a master practitioner are likely to understand themselves to be active agents in the appropriation of knowledge, and hence may act as active agents on their own behalf.
>
> (Lave 1990: 325)

5.1.4 Identity in school

Being a learner is mixed up with having to perform other social roles along with a large number of other actors with their own vested interests. Peers may be more present and far more vigorous than teachers or other adults in their expectations of what is desirable behaviour for individual pupils, and they may not approve of compliance with the teacher, diligence, or even some sorts of success (Pollard 1985). Some individuals may comply with school's expectations to some extent, but prioritise social goals and denigrate academic ones – as in the views of 'jocks' and 'princesses' about 'nerds' and 'swots' (e.g. Roeser et al. 1996; Roeser and Eccles 1998; Stone et al. 2008; Wentzel and Looney 2007). Sometimes there is a sort of counter-culture of children who are doing less well on the tasks of the school curriculum than their peers, get little intrinsic satisfaction from their 'boring' lessons, and find more enjoyment in 'messing about', 'having a laugh', and a culture of toughness and rejection of mainstream adult values (Pollard 1985). Some pupils may be right in believing that the school system does little for their present happiness and their future prospects: their rejection of it, however, makes it even less likely that schooling could make a positive contribution to their lives.

In a set of case studies of 20 young learners in a British city, Andrew Pollard and Ann Filer (Pollard and Filer 1996, 1999, 2007) explore the interface between identity and learning during the course of schooling. They observed and interviewed their subjects, their families, and some of their teachers through seven years of primary school and five years of secondary school. Focusing on 'pupil careers', they described how children were working to fit in with the demands and expectations of themselves, their families, their peers, and their schools. Over the long period of study, the whole of the children's time in compulsory schooling, each child showed patterns of behaviour that were relatively consistent features of their relationships with parents, siblings, teachers, and peers.

> Children do not act passively in response to changing circumstances and different social contexts, enacting ascribed roles or accommodating to structural imperatives. Rather they respond actively and dynamically in protecting, shaping and maintaining their sense of self and identity as pupils.
>
> (Pollard and Filer 1999: 301)

But alongside this there were significant changes in children's approaches to learning partly associated with individual children's personal histories of adaptation, but also associated with the wider social experience that they encountered. For example, children who had performed well in the primary school sometimes faced difficulties over their identities as learners following transfer into the local comprehensive secondary schools, where there was a wide range of attitudes to school achievement as well as the structural fragmentation and status loss that the shift to secondary school entails – having to relate to many more teachers and peers, becoming the smallest and lowest status people in the school, etc. In these larger schools, with children of more diverse backgrounds and abilities, separate subject departments and teachers, and greater emphasis on relative ability and competition (in contrast with effort and improvement), there were more 'ways to be' open to pupils. They could, for example, go for 'conformity' (compliance, often strategic, with teacher expectations), 'anti-conformity' (deviance and opposition to formal school expectations and rules), 'non-conformity' (independence in relation to formal school expectations, often operating on the margins of mainstream classroom and playground concerns) or 're-defining' (pushing at the boundaries of teachers' expectations, negotiating, challenging and leading their peers) (Osborn, McNess and Pollard 2006). The risk for these children, facing a choice between such different roles and possibilities, was that they could find their identity fragmenting and almost inadvertently fall into maladaptive ways of coping with the demands of school.

> For example, David moved with friends from the working-class environment of Albert Park Primary to his local comprehensive. However, the change resulted in a fragmentation of his pupil identity as his approach to learning was differently valued, and differently valuable

in new context. His established approach to learning was characterised by an enthusiasm for social interaction, group action and group achievement. He thus liked to gain intrinsic satisfaction from tasks while the expectations of teachers and parents were of less concern to him. In out-of-school activities and in areas of responsibility and work in the adult world, his social and learning skills and his facility in developing relationships brought rewards and status. In such contexts he was seen as mature, socially skilled and a leader. However, within secondary school contexts, David's identity was more fragmented. In some curricular subjects and with some teachers, his social and personal skills led to success and affirmation, even in areas such as sport and drama in which he was not necessarily particularly technically skilled. In other school contexts, his practical, active and inclusive approach to learning, and his dislike of solitary study and academic analysis, was interpreted by teachers as 'immature', 'disruptive', 'lazy' and 'underachieving'.

(Pollard and Filer 2007: 451)

Some of the other children in the sample moved into local 'middle-class/ selective/independent school contexts', which typically showed a consensus that pupils in school should be focused on achieving, conforming, and adapting to the school. With less choice between possible identities, and with more agreement between their middle-class home values and their school's achievement orientation, these children's identities as learners and their strategies for functioning as pupils served them better within the school and the peer group. They were considerably less likely to meet other children whose disaffection with schooling was so shared and entrenched as to become a counter-culture. Their rebellion could be like mine many years ago, that is limited to an inconspicuous flouting of marginal rules (those about how long your skirt is or tying your hair back rather than the rules about getting your homework done), writing bad angst-ridden poetry, and refusing to set foot in the school once you had collected your A level results. This sort of rebellion typically has little in the way of negative effects for the 'rebel', whereas not getting your work done to a standard that meets the criteria for exam success is likely to have much longer-term effects.

This sort of picture, of pupils balancing their identities between peer roles, teacher demands, family background pressures, expectations for the future, and own self-interest, appears in many studies, and all over popular representations of school in the media. A common picture differentiates between effort focused on achievement and 'having fun' or 'being cool'. Reay (2006; Reay and Lucey 2000) is typical in finding children tending to believe that being too good at achieving high marks and the teacher's good opinion is socially disastrous as far as the peer group is concerned: 'You can't just say "Oh I don't care about what was on TV last night, let me get on with my writing", because everyone would think you were a saddo' (Reay 2006: 175). But things can get quite complicated when mesosystems involve contradictions, and there are so many ways of getting it wrong: 'One group works really hard ['keeners' or 'boffins'], another group doesn't, they mess around in class. Another group works sometimes and messes around sometimes' (Osborn 2001: 273). An example about what is best for being popular is provided by Reay: 'If you're clever but not too clever and if you're really cool you are popular. But if you are really clever and geeky and always talk about science then you're unpopular. If you're a girlie like Stephanie you're unpopular and if you're an airhead then you're unpopular as well' (Reay 2006: 176).

These issues about identity may well differ between countries and cultures (Ellemers *et al.* 2002; Wang 2006; pp. 46, 174–78). English pupils in the study by Osborn and her colleagues just quoted seemed to perceive their membership of a defined peer group as more salient than their membership of the whole class, in contrast to French and Danish pupils who talked about their class as a whole as their identity group: 'We've got to stand together to make things work . . . you've got to be ready to listen, you've got to help each other' (Osborn 2001: 273). Osborn and her colleagues (e.g. Osborn 2003, Pollard *et al.* 2000) relate this to differences between Denmark, France and England in views about identity, solidarity and difference, depicting Danish society as emphasising solidarity and mutual responsibility and the French as emphasising individualism within equality, whereas the English saw themselves far less cohesively. A similar interaction between the values of the culture and the values of the school, resulting in differences between mainstream and minority ethnic children's behaviour, appears in several studies of American children (e.g. Tharp and Gallimore 1988; Tharp *et al.* 1984; Rogoff 2003b). Schools that valued caring for other people and devalued power assertion protected their pupils somewhat from violent behaviour (Knafo *et al.* 2008).

5.1.5 Interaction between parents, school and child

It seems to be the case that children do better at school if there is a good supportive relationship between the school and the home, and worse if there is not. (As Bronfenbrenner pointed out, 'mesosystems' linking different microsystems need to work effectively for optimal development.) This home–school contact (or even collaboration) seems to be a contributor to the success of early educational interventions such as Head Start and Sure Start (Meadows 2006; Melhuish *et al.* 2008; pp. 34–35, 209) and a major factor in the results of later schooling (e.g. Bandura 2001; Cooper and Crosnoe 2007; Crosnoe 2001; Crosnoe, Mistry and Elder 2002; Crosnoe and Huston 2007; Hill *et al.* 2004; pp. 210–12). Parental involvement in schooling informs the parent about what the child is doing in the classroom (and the teacher about the child's life outside school); facilitates the flow of information between home and school and gives scope for sensible discussions of school between parent and child; gives the parent opportunities to be an advocate for the child; and may influence the teacher's attention to the individual child (Wentzel and Looney 2007). If this helps to support children's academic performance and sense of self-efficacy, and helps them to avoid bad behaviour in school, then this improved performance may contribute to how much the child likes school and engages with the educational process, setting up a positive spiral of engagement and achievement. Parent involvement in the child's schooling is especially tightly coupled with educational progress in lower SES families (Cooper and Crosnoe 2007): presumably because it is a crucial part of the route to doing better educationally than would otherwise be expected.

Teachers commonly feel that it is much harder for them to develop a mutually supportive relationship with parents from lower socio-economic backgrounds, and that this reduces the possibility of school and home combining to support the child's educational progress. A substantial quantity of research reports findings that low SES parents are less likely to attend meetings with teachers, to be involved in parent–teacher associations, to proactively ask about the child's progress, and so forth (Waanders, Mendez and Downer 2007; Wentzel and Looney 2007). This should not be interpreted as reflecting a lack of interest (Hughes et al. 1994; Gillies 2006; Lareau 2000; Raven 1980; Waanders, Mendez and Downer 2007), as there are various other possibilities: financial and time constraints making it difficult to get to meetings; living in a more stressful and dangerous neighbourhood; having to place great emphasis on the child's needs at a survival level; keeping children safe and protected from additional feelings of failure rather than encouraging them to take on the challenges of education more than they inescapably have to do; parents' lack of confidence in their own ability, based on having had a negative experience of school themselves; associating involvement with teachers with the child having got into trouble, rather than with a way of supporting the child; less optimism (on the part of the child as well as the parent) about the contribution that educational success can make to a person's life chances. Raven (1980) describes a particularly telling example of an educational intervention that truly had the interests of the children at heart, but was seen differently by the parents: they saw it as potentially helpful to the child's educational success but also as something which could make them unfit for the tough street life that they were going to have to live.

Learner identities, and problems with identities, may also differ by social class and by gender. Pollard and Filer (2007), for example, describe how greater economic resources allowed wealthier parents to buy private education for their children, and thus avoid some of the exposure to 'anti-conformity' identities which did occur in large state comprehensive schools but were very rare in the private and selective schools: this made meso-system home–school relations easier. Pollard and Filer's working-class parents hoped that their children would do well in school, go into higher education and develop working lives in skilled, well-paid and professional occupations. They were as active as middle class ones in supporting their children's learning, engaged with them in out of school organised activities. This is a contrast with earlier studies such as that of Peter Willmott and Michael Young in the 1950s or Paul Willis a little later (Willmott and Young 1960; Willis 1977) where working-class parents expected their children to be future members of a traditional working class, with employment similar to the parents' own. An unchanging identity as 'working class' did not seem to be strong in the Pollard and Filer case studies. Martin Hughes (e.g. Hughes *et al.* 1994; Hughes and Pollard 2006) similarly emphasises how wrong it is to suppose that working-class parents are not interested in, and supportive of, their children's education: but they may have less confidence in their own activities and, perhaps, too much faith in the schools. Most Westerners would now assume that girls and boys have equal rights to education, even if they expect gender differences in preferred subjects; but some macrosystems limit education for girls, or exclude them from it, despite the evidence that educating women has benefits for them, for their children, and for the wider society.

5.2 Child development and the media

Children are very active as social persons in school; the purposes of schools include being places where children learn *as* social persons and *to be* social persons. But children also come into contact with other parts of the wider social world, and these may have great importance for individual children. I move now to other big social systems where they play a role. The first of these is children's engagement with the mass media.

We are all aware that there have been rapid and enormous changes in the types and the availability of media over the last sixty years. The introduction and spread of new media affects how we spend our lives, and hence how children develop. Always there is both excitement about the potential good and anxiety about possible ill effects; and, consequently, we need good quality research to clarify what effects there really are.

Western children are targets and consumers of media, like television (TV), from a very early age and for a considerable proportion of their time. Reviewers (e.g. Anderson *et al.* 2003; Dubow, Huesmann and Greenwood 2007; Huesmann *et al.* 2003) suggest that it is common for TV to be on 'most of the time' in many US households, and for children to be actually watching it for around three hours per day. The peak of watching TV tends to be at age eleven to thirteen, with substantial individual differences, some associated with social class (e.g. Chowhan 2007). TV is frequently used as an 'electronic babysitter', especially in less well-resourced households. Time spent watching TV reduces time spent reading, studying, and library use, but has less effect on sports and socialising – indeed some researchers have found a positive correlation between amount of sports watched and amount of sports played (e.g. Anderson *et al.* 2001). Heavy users of TV tend to be heavy users of other media. Most American children have access to video games, computers and the internet; teenages are online for an hour a day or more, and use social network and communication sites heavily for instant messaging and social contacts (and for some individuals there is involvement in bullying behaviour (Agatson, Kowalski and Limber 2007; Kowalski and Limber 2007)).

Like the rest of us, teenagers and children choose to watch television to pass time, to be entertained, to seek information, to modulate arousal, and for reasons of social utility, for example keeping up with peer pressure to watch a particular show. This has the important implication for researchers that we need to remember that the young person may seek out a media item to suit these pre-existing needs, hence the apparent influence of the media item on development or behaviour may really be confounded with the pre-existing factors which led to selection of the item.

Parents and commentators frequently criticise the vulgarity, sexualisation, violence, flashiness, and triviality of much television. Research has not yet established whether this criticism is justified in terms of long-term effects on the individuals who watch it. But so far as public anxiety goes, we now have some good reason to worry, I think, about three issues; the contribution of children's use of sedentary electronic amusements to obesity; possible effects on the development of cognitive skills; and, most of all, the role of exposure to media violence in the development of aggressive feelings and behaviour.

5.2.1 Media use, decline in physical activity, diet, and the obesity epidemic

People in many countries across the world are getting fatter, increasingly to a degree that has serious negative implications for their health. The reported rate of health-threatening obesity in the USA is currently over thirty per cent for American adults and expected to rise to over fifty per cent by 2030 (Wang *et al.* 2008) – rates in the UK are said to be similar. Although all sorts of environmental factors have been suggested as causing the 'obesity epidemic' (and I earlier discussed evidence on the possible role of experience in earlier generations influencing the expression of genes in later ones, pp. 28–29), commonly through history people have become too fat because the amount they eat is disproportionately high compared with the amount of physical activity they engage in. There are substantial reasons for worry about modern Western people's diet, which in many cases contains too much fat and sugar. A recent study from the Avon Longitudunal Study of Parents and Children (ALSPAC, Feinstein *et al.* 2008) shows that a diet heavy in junk food prior to age three to four predicts worse educational attainment at ages five to ten, a finding the authors attribute to effects of diet on early brain development (which might imply difficulties in reversing it). In the same study, junk food has been linked to children's behaviour problems in the ALSPAC sample. But the other half of the problem is that many people engage in far less physical activity than previous generations. People drive instead of walking, do less physical labour in their jobs, and in the case of children they are less likely to be let out to exercise themselves roaming the neighbourhood because their parents believe that this would be dangerous – with effects not just on their use of space but on their understanding of it (Rissotto and Giuliani 2006). As a child in the late 1950s I could play as I liked around my suburban home, including in the half-built houses down the road and in fields up to a mile away: and from age seven I daily walked alone a couple of miles to and from my primary school. It is now very unusual for parents to allow their children to do anything like this. Increased rates of traffic, decreased rates of general neighbourhood supervision, and fear of assaults on children mean that many children are near, or in, their family home most of the time. And while there, they may be engaged primarily in sedentary activities, notably watching TV or playing on their computers. Junk foods are much more heavily advertised on TV than healthier foods are, and many families eat in front of the television, with attention fragmented between watching, eating and social engagement. Although children quickly become canny about the purpose and truthfulness of advertising (e.g. Derbaix and Pecheux 2003; Pine and Nash 2003), this combination of effects of TV exposure looks as though it could be contributing considerably to obesity and behaviour problems. There could be a network of choices here contributing to changes in social activities that impacts negatively on health and development.

5.2.2 Media use and the development of cognitive skills

Hours of TV watching appear to be negatively correlated with cognitive development and positively correlated with behaviour problems (Christakis *et al.* 2004; Dubow, Huesmann and Greenwood 2007; CMPO 2008; NICHD 2003d; Schmidt *et al.* 2008; Schmidt and Vandewater 2008). Although there are of course excellent TV programmes aimed at supporting children's learning and socialisation, there is emerging evidence that children's unsupervised engagement with TV in general, and even their exposure to TV as a source of background stimulation that they are not explicitly attending to, may damage their concentration, reduce their engagement in toy play, decrease their social engagement, take up time that could have been filled with parent-provided learning activities, reinforce gender stereotypes, and tend to disrupt what they are doing. Whether this is due to the TV watching in itself, or due to the fact that long exposure to TV is often part of what has been called 'home chaos' (Corapci and Wachs 2002), is not clear. In homes with a lot of unstructured coming and going and high ambient noise, parents tended to be less responsive to their young children, and to have less belief in their own capacity to be effective parents. There may be a relative withdrawal from the parenting role, with consequences for parent–child interaction and for parents' efforts to influence their child's development. Crowded, chaotic homes may make it difficult for parents to be accepting of young children's engagement in vigorous physical activity, and getting them to watch TV may be a way of keeping the children's activity and noise down to bearable levels.

5.2.3 Media and violence

All the way from microsystems to exosystems, people sometimes behave violently and aggressively towards others. Some of the time, this sort of behaviour is admired: more often it disrupts social functioning and is deplored. As well as acting aggressively ourselves, we may witness other people's aggression. Opportunities to observe other people's violence are not new. As well as casual exposure to aggressive behaviours in one's own social circles, many societies have allowed public chastisements in schools, or put people convicted of less serious crimes in the pillory to be hurt and humiliated, or staged events like public executions. These sights were intended both to allow the general populace to express their disapproval of the crime and to deter others from similar criminal behaviour in the future – hence the rituals that accompanied the horrors of executions (e.g. Schama 1989). There were debates about both the effectiveness and the morality of state-sponsored public violence, but not a great deal of evidence of the effects on individual observers' psychological states, beyond some autobiographical accounts of how the observer was disgusted (Thackeray and Dickens), full of pity and terror (Mary Wollstonecraft after seeing Louis XVI driven to the guillotine), filled with thoughts of revenge against the state (Royalist witnesses to the exeution of Charles I), sexually aroused (Thomas Hardy), or deterred from wearing the same sort of clothes as the executed person (it is said that the Victorian murderess Mrs Manning wore a fashionable black satin dress to her public hanging, and so singlehandedly caused the immediate decline of that fabric as a fashion item). However, opinion turned against public violence in the West, and for most of us, most of the time, we mainly see serious violence and aggression in the media. There, it is quite hard to avoid. There is a high level of portrayal of aggression and violence and their consequences in the media – news stories, dramas, cartoons all frequently portray aggressive content. With exposure to the electronic media seeming to expand year on year to cover very many hours of people's lives, great anxiety has grown up about the effects of witnessing violence in the media on viewers' aggression and violence (e.g. Anderson and Bushman 2001; Dill, Brown and Collins 2008).

There has always been a use of portrayals of violence in books and theatre: Greek tragedy, the Bible, Shakespeare, Dostoevsky, through to the late twentieth century 'Theatre of Cruelty'. Film and television have added detail and realism to this, and, arguably, made exposure to portrayals of violence more frequent and perhaps more gripping. Electronic games allow the player to perpetrate the violence, crashing cars, shooting opponents, and so forth. There has been a heated debate over whether exposure to violence in the electronic media caused those exposed to act aggressively, to have aggressive feelings, or to condone aggression to a greater degree than those who were not exposed. Two recent reviews (Anderson *et al.* 2003; Huesmann and Taylor 2006) both clarify the grounds of the argument and argue that there is conclusive evidence that exposure to aggressive acts shown or depicted in the electronic media increases the risk of the observer acting out, feeling or condoning aggression and violence. Undoubtedly, some individuals do aggressive and violent things without any exposure to media violence, and most who are exposed to media violence manage not to act aggressively, but these reviews summarise a vast amount of evidence from different sorts of studies to build a case that the effects of aggression and violence in the media are sufficient for us to worry about them.

For example, surveys that correlate the amount of violence children are exposed to on television and their levels of aggressive behaviour typically find significant positive correlations of the order of about 0.2 between them. This is not an enormously high correlation, explaining about four per cent of the variance in aggression; but Anderson *et al.* (2003) make the point that if a medical intervention made chances of a good outcome four per cent better, we would all be expecting it to be part of health service provision. A more serious problem with this research is that correlational studies cannot establish causation, and it could be that aggressive children and adolescents are attracted to media violence rather than media violence creating aggression, or that some third factor predisposes the same individuals both to watch more violence and to behave more aggressively than average. Controls for third factors typically reduce the correlations between exposure and expression of aggression, but do not eliminate the association. Natural exposure to violence seems to be associated with risk of violence; and natural exposure is common and at a high rate, so these studies might justify us beginning to worry.

In another research approach, a substantial body of well-controlled, randomised experiments has shown that brief exposure to violent dramatic presentations on TV or in films produces short-term increases in aggressive thoughts, emotions, and behaviour in children and adolescents, including in some studies and in some individuals a propensity to commit physically aggressive behaviour serious enough to harm others (Anderson *et al.* 2003; Huesmann and Taylor 2006). The rise in aggressive symptoms after exposure to violence is usually greater for the milder levels of aggression; exposure does increase the risk of more serious aggression but most individuals do not reach serious levels. The effects of exposure may be greater for children or adolescents who have shown high levels of aggression before their participation in the experiment, but even the mildest individuals were not totally immune. The average effect of exposure under experimental conditions appears to be large enough to justify social concern; just as the evidence on non-experimental exposure would suggest.

Almost every Western child has access to electronic media nowadays (Dodge *et al.* 2008), but when television was new some studies of communities where television had just become available suggested that the increase in exposure to depictions of violence this involved could lead to a rise in aggressive and delinquent behaviour (Centerwall 1989, 1992), although Charlton *et al.* (1999) found no real change in the behaviour of very young children on St Helena following the introduction of satellite television. These studies are interesting, but there will always be historical changes beyond the introduction of the new technology which make it difficult for it to be a conclusive research strategy.

If we turn to newer media, although there is less evidence than on television and film violence, there is a body of experimental studies that Anderson *et al.* (2003) and Huesmann and Taylor (2006) believe provides substantial evidence of a link between exposure and aggression. They argue that watching violent music videos creates relatively accepting attitudes and beliefs about violence in young viewers, at least in the short-term setting of the experiments (see also Snell and Hodgetts 2007). Violent lyrics, too, may increase aggressive thinking and emotion (cf. the Marseillaise and the practice of singing the national anthems before international football matches). Similarly, studies of violent video games are quite consistent in suggesting that there is a connection between playing violent video games and increased risk of aggression. In the short term, experimental exposure to violent video games causes increases in aggressive thoughts, emotions, and behaviour; increases in physiological arousal; and decreases in helpful behaviour. The survey evidence links repeated exposure to violent video games with aggressive and violent behavior in the real world. Longitudinal studies suggest long-term effects of repeated exposure to violent video games on late levels of aggression and violence (e.g. Barlett *et al.* 2007), and also on gender stereotyping (e.g. Brenick *et al.* 2007). Subrahmanyam, Smahel and Greenfield (2006) report levels of sexualised language and of associations between violence and sexuality in teenagers' dialogues in chatrooms that they find very alarming.

Is the apparent 'reality' of what is seen important in determining its effect? Much of the violence to be seen on television *is* real – news programmes in particular show 'images which some viewers may find disturbing'. Anecdotal evidence on certain sorts of violence (suicide in particular) suggest that some viewers copy what they have seen on screen or heard about in the news, and although this copycat behaviour has been reported since the reaction to Goethe's novel *The Sorrows of Young Werther* in the eighteenth century, the vividness of television pictures may contribute more powerfully than even the writings of a genius. Alternatively, the blithe violence displayed in non-realistic settings or by cartoons might have powerful effects if the watcher identifies emotionally with the character; something children might be especially likely to do. The violence of superheroes and similar characters may also be presented as justified, or even a good thing, which may make viewers more likely to accept it. There may be an interaction between the nature and setting of the violence shown and the characteristics of the viewer, with young male individuals who already think the world is a violent place being most likely to identify with, condone, and perhaps imitate the violence they see (Anderson *et al.* 2003, Huesmann and Taylor 2006). The degree to which we use television as a way to view the wider world raises a further interesting set of issues.

It is important to stress that nobody is arguing that all or even most aggression is caused by exposure to violence in film, television, music video, lyrics or video games; merely that levels of exposure to such violence seem rather consistently to be associated with a slightly increased risk of aggression and violence. Any effect of exposure to something that increases the risk of aggression could shape the life course of an individual in significant ways (aggression in childhood is a strong predictor of aggression and delinquency in adolescence and young adulthood, pp. 264–67). It also has serious implications for the well-being of society as a whole, both because the societal level of aggression matters for the well-being of us all – it will affect our personal risk of exposure to aggression – and because societal perceptions of aggression matter for individual mental health – we may be more anxious, fearful, unsociable, hostile if we believe that other people are aggressive and unsympathetic (e.g. Anderson *et al.* 2003; Huesmann and Taylor 2006).

5.2.3.1 Psychological processes in response to media violence

What psychological processes lie behind the association of exposure to violence in the media and increases in violent feelings or acts? Probably a set of several different processes, combining in different ways in the short term and the long term. Basic priming, where encountering an event activates links to other similar events, is one likely mechanism behind short-term increases in aggressive feelings and ideas; and if the event (exposure to violence, say) is repeated, the link and the priming may become automatic, so that the individual's feelings of aggression are more and more easily aroused. Extreme acts, like violence, are more exciting to witness than mundane ones (which is one reason they are portrayed in television and other media). There are measurable physical reactions, such as increased heart rate. Being in a state of arousal tends to energise the person so that if they are already feeling aggressive they may become more likely to act aggressively, interpret others as having aggressive intentions, have more difficulty in inhibiting their aggression, or take their aggression a bit further. Thus, people tend to react more violently to provocations immediately after watching exciting films or videos than they do at other times. This kind of effect is usually short lived, perhaps lasting only minutes, but perhaps most marked in those who are already primed for violence (Uhlmann and Swanson 2004). Cumulatively it might bias the ways in which the individual manages their emotional arousal (pp. 62–63, 124) over the much longer term. Chronic or repeated states of high physiological arousal can be very unpleasant, and one of the processes that is involved in coping with them is desensitisation (Carnagey and Anderson 2007; Carnagey, Anderson and Bartholow 2007); this occurs gradually over repeated exposures to the unpleasant event, reducing the initial physiological reaction to a level that is not uncomfortable. This habituation does reduce discomfort, but the discomfort would normally inhibit and reduce disapproval of the violence. People who are desensitised may be more accepting of, and less likely to inhibit, aggressive actions. Carnagey's studies suggest that even relatively brief exposure to media violence can reduce physiological reactions to the sight of real-world violence and can decrease helpful behaviour toward victims of aggression.

Another set of processes which may be behind the effects of media violence in the short term is concerned with imitation. As I argued earlier (pp. 112–15), imitation seems to be one of our basic ways of learning from others, so basic that we may even have our brains wired up to facilitate it, and it is particularly commonly used by children. They may imitate both specific acts (such as martial arts moves) and general scenarios or rules for how to interpet events and how to behave (such as solving disputes through fighting); these may then both guide future behaviour and build into models of what the world is like. Patterson and his colleagues have shown this spiralling into automatic high-level aggression in response to objectively neutral events in their studies of children and adolescents (e.g. Patterson, DeBaryshe and Ramsey 1989; Patterson and Sanson 1999; Patterson and Fisher 2002; Patterson, DeGarmo and Forgatch 2004; Granic and Patterson 2006) with serious control problems.

Finally, effects of exposure to violence on people's wider understanding of the world would be congruent with psychological theories about people's 'scripts' or 'working models' (Meadows 2006). If the sample of experience that we have contains a lot of a particular sort of event, we may build up a model of what the real world is like that includes this sort of event as common or normal or to be expected. We include vicarious experience in this accumulation of 'how things are', and it may be that what we see in the media is dealt with in the same way. If, as is probably the case, the media's attention to the real world is wider than our everyday experience, it may give us a truer picture of the world, but if it were to be biassed in systematic ways, or less considered, then our incorporation of media information might bias our model away from reality. It is not hard to identify examples of this – publicity over sad but rare cases of children being abducted and abused by paedophiles, for example, has led, some argue, to moral panics about 'stranger danger' and curtailing children's freedom to move round their neighbourhood in order to protect them against a risk that most will not encounter; emphasis on feminine grooming and slimness has produced unrealistic expectations of how young women look and made fortunes for the cosmetic and slimming industries; teenage gang members believe that they are under threat from members of other gangs who will shoot or knife them, and react pre-emptively and ferociously. Similarly, the high rate of violence presented in the media may bias us towards expecting normal social relations to include violence as an almost everyday occurrence. Obviously it would be foolish to believe that we exist in a ideal world, and far too many people live among high levels of violence that damage their psychological health (e.g. Barenbaum *et al.* 2004), but there are perhaps real dangers in assuming there is violence imminent when there is not.

5.3 Macrosystems

Macrosystems are the patterns of ideology and behaviour in microsystems, mesosystems and exosystems that tend to make the individual's experience within a culture relatively consistent. Within a macrosystem, Bronfenbrenner says that different individuals will encounter the same range of developmental settings at approximately the same ages, with the various settings being expected to have relatively similar roles, activities, and relations (Bronfenbrenner 1979). The proximal processes in microsystems, which have been my focus for most of this book, may differ very much between individuals, with, I think, relatively clear developmental effects. I do believe, for example, that the ways in which the child learns in the microsystem to maintain something of an emotional equilibrium, or to ask adults questions, impacts on the sorts of mental health or cognitive attitude and skills that they will develop (pp. 62–63, 127). The psychological effects of the ways in which macrosystems hold together microsystems are harder to understand, and evidence on macrosystem effects is by no means plentiful. I will argue that this is partly because macrosystem effects come about through their influence on what happens in microsystems.

Such things as political structures, religious ideologies, and cultural values are examples of macrosystem influences. Historical events such as wars, economic growth or depression, urbanisation and industrialisation, operate at the level of whole societies. Looking at the child and the macrosystem involves searching for the ways that these very widespread factors impinge on individuals. Macrosystems in the sense of ideology and in the sense of consistent practice continually impact on the children (and adults) who live within them. Far too often, the impact is unintended and intensely negative – children are often the most vulnerable victims of poverty, of wars, of colonial exploitation, of pollution or famine or unequal access to education, health, and justice created by regimes that do not sufficiently consider their responsibility to the powerless either in their own country or in the countries that they trade with, ally with, or effectively control. Some macrosystem ideas – for example commitment to human rights, commitment to universal education, protection from work that is dangerous or physically damaging, laws about marriage – have more positive consequences for children, although even here the consequence of a reform may include some loss of whatever advantages the old way of doing things might have provided. Davin (1996) makes this point, discussing changes over the nineteenth and early twentieth century in how understandings of childhood impacted on the London poor.

> From the late eighteenth century the continuing advance of the middle class [. . .] had been characterised by greater separation of gender and age roles, of production and consumption, of public and private: and by a dominant ideology whereby one type of family unit and one set of age and gender relations were increasingly presented as 'natural' and so universally appropriate and desirable. [. . .]
>
> These dominant ideas [. . .] were complemented by the assumption that different customs in the working class implied the inadequacy (or worse) of working-class parents and therefore justified an intervention in family life [. . .] Compulsory school and protective legislation imposed the proper experience of childhood – school, economic dependence and submission to adult (and class) authority – and steadily prolonged its duration. [. . .]
>
> With compulsory education, labour restrictions and protective legislation, the theoretical authority of parent over child ceased to be absolute and the child's potential for any degree of independence was reduced, while new definitions and obligations were established, for parenthood as well as childhood. [. . .] it was increasingly accepted that as children were 'a national asset' the state should take an interest in their health and upbringing.
>
> (Davin 1996: 208)

What I want to focus on is a narrow question: whether there are examples of systematic evidence of macrosystem ideologies and practices, especially political ones, affecting the way that children grow up as social persons. I begin by looking at religion and culture, before moving on to history. I then develop some points about becoming a social person in a democracy, and in totalitarian systems, and look at conflict, social change and inequality.

5.4 Religion and the development of children and youth as social persons

Religious belief and religion-guided action are commonly seen as an influence on people's lives as social persons. Here there is participation in a system of belief and practice which may be probably larger than any other an individual will access, and to those involved it is, presumably, a system whose implications are enormously profound – one's present moral status and future happiness, including one's state after death in some cases, are believed to be determined by one's religious behaviour. Religion can provide reasons for a strong commitment to particular activities or values – prayer, fasting, chastity, the indissolubility of marriage, engagement with what is felt to be sacred or spiritual, for example. Religious affiliation and practice are normally socially determined, with families seeking to make their children adherents to their own religion and belief system, and members of religious groups are generally subject to the moral and practical rules of their religion, which are monitored more or less completely by the other members of the religion, by themselves, and (in many cases) by a God of judgement (omniscient, omnipotent, and inescapable). Religion permeates many cultures, has determined their history, and has created many artefacts and activities – buildings, literature and music, education systems, power relations, for example – that affect the lives of people outside the religion as well as within it.

Research on the role of religion in children's roles as social persons includes examination of children's beliefs about religious issues, their moral development, and the effects of religious commitment on behaviour. In this section I focus on the last of these three. I have discussed cognition about religion in another book (Meadows 2006), and moral development is addressed elsewhere in this one (pp. 120–21).

The main message coming from research on associations between variations in religious behaviour and developmental and psychosocial outcomes is the suggestion that religion, especially religious participation, somewhat enhances the development of positive social behaviour and somewhat reduces the incidence of antisocial behaviour (Baier and Wright 2001; Bartkowski and Xu 2007; Bartkowski, Xu and Levin 2008; Johnson et al. 2000; Pearce and Axinn 1998; Pearce and Haynie 2004; Regnerus 2003a, 2003b; Regnerus and Elder 2003; Smith 2003; Stark 1996). More religious adolescents, and particularly religious adolescents whose parents are also more religious, are rather more likely to be prosocial and rather less likely to be delinquent. This probably applies most to the moderately serious levels of delinquency (e.g. theft rather than either trivial or very serious delinquency). Possibly, the effects are stronger for young people who are at risk, although religious participation also has some protective effect for those who come from more privileged backgrounds (Regnerus and Elder 2003). Religious participants tend to be a bit more compliant than non-religious ones (Cialdini and Goldstein 2004). Most research has been done in the USA and over the last thirty years, which may limit its generalisability: within the present data, the effects of religious commitment and behaviour do not seem to be notably different according to religious denomination.

What is especially interesting, I think, is what proximal processes mediate between the distal factor of religious status and the various outcomes that have been researched. The effect of religion in reducing risk of delinquency might be via the direct impact of religious teaching – 'thou shalt not covet thy neighbour's ox, nor his ass, nor anything that is his', for example: or directly through a sense of a personal relationship with a personal god who is seen as entirely good (or extremely threatening): or through being part of a social institution that monitors and controls your behaviour as a member.

Involvement in religion also involves changes in the social setting – such as spending more time with parents and others engaged in religious activities, and having less opportunity for unsupervised hanging around and getting into trouble. The effect might also be indirect. For example religion might affect the relationships between the child and significant others e.g. attachment or filial piety or obedience to authority or compliance. Or it might change the ways in which significant others behave (since religious systems typically have advice or prescriptions about how parents should treat their children, and marital relations are affected by religious belief; or because it may shift friendship choices towards peers who are also members of the religious community and adherents to its values). Or it might offer and sponsor more activities that could have a positive impact on skills, status or self-esteem (such as choirs, supplementary schools, holiday schemes, and also activities which parents and children share, such as reading sacred books or attending religious ceremonies together). Or it might affect development by giving the child more practise in control over impulsive or highly overactive behaviour. Religions which involve prayer and meditation might induce enhanced emotional self-regulation (or avenues for socially approved or even communal emotional expression, in the case of some charismatic churches and sects).

Being an accepted member of a religious community might give the individual a status and a reputation that have to be maintained and protected against antisocial behaviour, because being seen to behave antisocially would damage both oneself and one's group. Members of religious groups who fail to meet the standards expected by the group are often subjected to rituals of shame and penance before they are readmitted to the group, and extreme transgressions against the rules may result in excommunication. And, in some people's frame of reference, there might be divine guidance of the person towards the good and away from the bad in a virtually hands-on way: famously the footballer Maradona won a crucial football international match by scoring a goal, due he said (metaphorically) to 'the hand of God' – though to the losing side it looked very much like (literally) the hand of Maradona.

It is probably the case that many or most of these direct and indirect effects operate. The existing research findings suggest that commitment to, conformity within, and participation in, religion are all protective against antisocial behaviour. Cumulatively, apart from the special case of a direct relationship with a divine presence, I think the findings suggest that the effect of religious belief and practice on young people's antisocial behaviour is in large part social, and not altogether unlike the effects of other social partnerships. Children and adolescents who are engaged in a religious community may through social learning imitate the behaviour of prosocial models. Their religious participation may clarify their identity and what is expected of them and support them as long as they comply, which could reduce uncertainty and strain. Sharing views and activities with religious others strengthens protection against deviant acts. The religious community may foster commitment to its norms and control aberrant behaviour, offering counselling and support. Although it will also constrain individuals, its rules may reduce the attractiveness of a life that includes bad behaviour. However, on the negative side, individuals who break the rules of their religious community or lose their religion may suffer extreme rejection and exclusion (White 1978; Butler 1903/1973; Winterson 1985 provide fictional or near autobiographical examples; see also Regnerus and Elder 2003). Commitment to one religious in-group may foster hostility towards other religious out-groups (e.g. Cairns *et al.* 2006; Tausch *et al.* 2007; Verkuyten and Slooter 2008). Sometimes religious and secular social institutions do not run easily together (there are many examples in education, for example religious insistence on constraining what children are taught or indeed *which* children are taught; two regrettable examples being the rejection of evolutionary theory and the teaching as 'science' of intelligent design, and the refusal of the Taliban to countenance the education of girls).

5.5 Cultural differences and the development of children and youth as social persons

It is often unclear exactly how the wider culture works on individuals, and attempts to describe what happens are bedevilled by the sorts of issues I raised in my introductory discussion of culture (pp. 44–48). I move now to specific issues about the ways cultures manage social control and what impact this may have on children's development as social persons.

5.5.1 Cultural differences in individualism and collectivism

Although there may be an infinite number of ways to describe cultural differences, one distinction that is much used in developmental psychology is a distinction between individualism and collectivism. Cultures that place a high value on individualism focus on autonomy and personal responsibility for actions and outcomes, whereas cultures that value collectivism place more emphasis on ties to the larger social group, relatedness and interdependence. Cultures deriving from the Protestant capitalist ethic (the USA in particular, and the UK, Northern Europe, Australia, New Zealand) are typically described as more individualistic; and most Asian, Latin, African, and rural, indigenous societies as more collectivist (Fuligni, Tseng and Lam 1999; Harwood, Miller and Irizarry 1995; Hofstede 2001, 2005; Iyengar and Lepper 1999; Kärtner 2007; Rothbaum and Trommsdorff 2007; Ryan and Deci 2000; Smetana 2002; Tamis-LeMonda et al. 2008; Triandis 2001).

Individualism involves valuing personal choice, making the most of one's potential, increasing self-esteem, emphasising self-determination, and being guided by personal goals and intrinisic motivation. So far as possible all individuals should feel autonomous, make their own choices, be intrinsically motivated, feel good about themselves, and realise their full potential. Collectivism, in contrast, is about relatedness and interdependence, about orientation to the larger group, about respect and obedience, and about not standing out as different. The good of the community is more important than the good of any individual member, so individuals must consider the repercussions of their actions for the group when deciding what to do. Members of the group must respect each other, obey authority and maintain the harmony of the group; authority is a matter of status within the group, and will be attached to particular roles or to seniority. Children, therefore, will often be in the position of being 'seen but not heard', and having an important status within the group may come late.

Individualism and collectivism have both been linked to religious value systems, for example Protestantism in the case of individualism and Confucianism in the case of collectivism in east Asia, but no doubt other systems – political, economic, sociological, educational, technological – intertwine to contribute to the overall balance of the culture. It may be a mistake to think of individualism and collectivism as being entirely separate and mutually exclusive values (Tamis-LeMonda et al. 2008). In all cultures, value is placed on both autonomy and relatedness, and an individual who was extremely low on either would be seen as not functioning very well (or at least would be seen as highly unusual). But all cultures are likely to have ways of encouraging or discouraging children's actions according to these values. I discuss this in relation to parenting practices (pp. 115–17, 152–57) and to parents' views of children's friendships (pp. 172–75, 185, 192, 198, 200–201).

5.5.2 Cultural differences in social initiative and social control

The point I have already made about the risks of identifying any particular personality characteristic or social behaviour as 'desirable' or 'undesirable' is reinforced by evidence of cross-cultural differences in how different personalities are evaluated by parents and others concerned with children. One example is cultural differences in the relative value of social initiative and social control (Chen *et al.* 2001; Chen and French 2007; Hofstede 2001, 2005). It is suggested that even concrete behaviours such as amount of peer interaction or amount of socio-dramatic play differ between cultures with different orientations towards initiative or control. For example, there appears to be more, and more active, peer interaction in societies where the desired social behaviour tends towards high levels of individual initiative, such as the USA and Okinawa, rather than cultures that emphasise controlled, collective behaviour, such as China and Indonesia; and there is some evidence that young children in the more individualistic cultures engage in more socio-dramatic play, in comparisons of preschoolers from the USA with Maya, Bedouin, and Korean groups (Chen and French 2007; Farver 1995, 1997). The researchers suggest that socio-dramatic play in particular involves self-expression and self-assertion, which have been differentially encouraged or discouraged in different societies.

Value judgements about behaviours are also structured differently in different societies (Schwartz 1992, 1996; Schwartz and Bardi 2001; Schwartz and Boehnke 2004; Schwartz and Rubel 2005). For example, ratings of sociability are positively correlated with adjustment ratings in US samples, but there are rather different associations in China, where sociability rating predicts social impact, self-regard, not feeling lonely and externalising problems, but not acceptability and adjustment (Rubin *et al.* 1998a, 2006; Chen and French 2007). Western researchers (and parents) typically assume that shy, inhibited, wary, or over-controlled behaviour reflects internal anxiety and immaturity – but there are higher rates of such behaviour in children from East Asian backgrounds (Korean, Chinese etc.) than Anglo–American ones, and where Western parents and theorists tend to be concerned and negative about shyness, Chinese parents are more accepting and approving of 'sensitive', 'modest', 'self-controlled' behaviour (Rubin *et al.* 1998a, 2006; Farver 1995, 1997; Kagan and Fox 2006, Kerr and Stattin 2000; Chen and French 2007; pp. 95–100). Ratings of how 'well-adjusted' the children are tend to be more closely associated with what is culturally acceptable rather than with children's actual behaviour.

Cross-cultural evidence (e.g. Whiting and Edwards 1988; Farver 1995; Tamis-LeMonda *et al.* 2008; Montgomery 2009) also shows that there is more compliance and co-operation by children in societies where family co-operation is the essential economic basis of society, and family responsibilities for children and social commitment to attending to others' needs are valued more. There are differences between children in traditional East Asian cultures, which encourage feelings of obligation as well as, or more than autonomy, and US children, where the balance of priorities is somewhat reversed. Co-operative behaviour is associated with developing self-regulation skills, and with parenting warmth and responsiveness. Girls, who are so often expected to be more helpful domestically, tend to show more compliant and co-operative behaviour in many societies (Larson and Verma 1999; Eisenberg *et al.* 2006; Greenfield 2006).

There is an interaction of culture and gender also in expectations of socially controlled behaviour and responses to children's aggression. Boys are almost always higher in aggressive behaviour than girls, but the gender difference is even greater in patrilineal cultures than non-patrilineal ones (Chen and French 2007), presumably because patrilineal cultures may associate power with gender, and maleness is the source of status in the family. Fong (2002) finds that China's one-child policy has empowered many young women because the absence of brothers has meant that more family resources are focused on them and they are allowed to develop talents that would otherwise have been irrelevant to the family goals in a patrilineal and patrilocal culture. Patriliny itself is in decline in China, she argues, as a result of the emancipation of women. In Nepal, Brahman parents, high-status members of a religion with a strict hierarchy between castes, accept more assertiveness and aggression in their children than Buddhist parents do (Cole 2002, 2006), and children's levels of aggressive behaviour in difficult situations are commensurate with the ways their parents reacted to their earlier aggression. In China, individual aggression is strongly disapproved of by parents and schools and there is an emphasis on contribution to the group (Chen 2000; Chen, Chang and He 2003). There is less peer support for aggression in China than in the USA, and consequently there are adjustment difficulties for aggressive children.

5.5.3 Cultural differences and self-worth

Self-worth or self-esteem was discussed earlier (pp. 79–80): I just note here that the meaning of self-worth, and how it develops, may differ between cultures and subcultures. Briefly, there may be cultural differences in how important it is to think well of oneself, as well as in what aspects of the 'self' one is supposed to be most concerned about. Individualistic cultures seem to place more emphasis on self-worth and individual autonomy than cultures that emphasise collectivity: collectivist cultures can be very hostile towards individuals who have 'got above themselves' and are seen as disagreeably self-important (Rothbaum and Trommsdorff 2007). Collectivist cultures may be more approving of self-abnegation, of sacrificing one's own interests to serve others – and all cultures may see assertive self-worth as more appropriate for some particular individuals, whereas other individuals are expected to serve the interests of others before their own. Cultural differences may also affect views of social conflicts with peers or others; people with more independent world views may feel that conflict is an infringement of their own individual autonomy, and that it is to be resisted assertively, whereas those with a more interdependent world view may be more likely to negotiate, maintain relationships, and minimise disturbance (French 2005; Laursen *et al.* 1996).

5.6 History

The history of childhood is another source of evidence on children as social persons, differing from the mainstream of psychological research in terms of time; just as anthropological work on cultures differs from it in terms of space. Both new perspectives are fascinating in themselves and an invaluable corrective to easy overgeneralisations; we might add a lot to our understanding of how child development works now if we knew how it worked a hundred years ago, or a thousand. But although there have been children growing into social persons in every historical period, and there is literature on ideas about children and their development going back more than a thousand years, there is much debate about what actually happened to children in history and how this affected them, with little of the sort of detailed evidence about proximal processes and effects on personhood that I have drawn on so far. We do have a historical sequence of what could be called 'child development theory' and of books of advice on how to bring up children. We have detailed biographical information about a small number of particular individuals, but many are not entirely typical of children in general, because they are the children of literate parents, or because their parents were concerned about the science or ideology of child development, or because they were royal children being brought up to rule. And ordinary children do turn up in the margins of historical records whose main focus is legal or political or economic, or in social action such as the movement for the abolition of slavery or of child labour in the mines and factories of Victorian England. There is not as much history of childhood as I would like, but there is too much to deal with thoroughly here. I am just going to introduce some points about history that are relevant to the picture of the development of the child as a social person that I have derived from the psychological literature.

5.6.1 History and ideologies of childhood

Some early ideas about childhood saw it as a stage that was part of the whole place of Man in the universe. An early medieval monk writing a natural science textbook about 1080 linked the stages of life to the influence of signs of the Zodiac; the four seasons; the four points of the compass; the four elements of earth, air, fire, and water; and the four humours or temperaments (Burrow 1986; Meadows 1986). This type of model combined Christian and classical Greek influences, and centred on astrology and ideas about the four temperaments. Children differ from adolescents, mature people, or the old because they are dominated by particular parts of the universe, in the case of this particular monk's model by air and fire, wet and hot humours, the astrological signs of Capricorn and Pisces, and west and north; hence children are playful, changeable, and childish. As they grow up, they move into other parts of the universal cycle and come under different cosmic influences, so their personal characteristics change. Their development is not due to their own individual characteristics or their experience within microsystems, but part of the divinely-ordained order of the universe. However ridiculous it may seem to us now, this sort of model continued to be tweaked and written about for hundreds of years (Burrow 1986). We don't really know how much practical influence these theories had on childrearing, although we do know that advice about medical treatment used similar ideas. Early advice books are primarily practical, about feeding and weaning and table manners and disciplining, aiming at fitting the child into the skills he or she would need for adult functioning.

Aries (1962) asserted that there was a major historical change in the whole concept of childhood at around the time of the Enlightenment (late eighteenth century), and hence in how children have been viewed and in what are thought to be appropriate ways to treat them – valuing the innocence and perfectibility of the child took over from a more authoritarian and less romantic view of the child as needing to be coercively trained into adulthood. Other historians have described a slow and limited progress away from extremely harsh treatment of children (infanticide, beating, sexual abuse, high child mortality casually accepted) towards a more caring approach (e.g. de Mause 1976). Some have disputed the views of Aries and de Mause and documented substantial resemblance between the expectations and practices of parents at different times in history (e.g. Pollock 1983, 1987). Part of what is going on here is different sorts of evidence – Aries focusing mainly on formal portraits of children, and Pollock on parents' private diaries and letters, for example.

5.6.2 Prescriptions about childrearing

Ideologies may differ, but prescriptions about childhood are even more contentious, and the gulf between what is advised and what is done is probably impossible to bridge. The evidence is fascinating, but we should probably be very cautious about extrapolating from it to children's actual experience. I can present only a few examples, but here is an American upper-class mother, Nancy Shippen from Philadelphia, writing in 1783 about how she intends to bring up her little daughter.

Some directions concerning a daughter's education.
1st Study well her constitution and genius.
2nd Follow nature and proceed patiently.
3rd Suffer not servants to terrify her with stories of ghosts and goblins.
4th Give her a fine pleasing idea of good, and an ugly frightful one of evil.
5th Keep her to a good and natural regimen of diet.
6th Observe strictly the little seeds of reason in her, and cultivate the first appearance of it diligently.
7th Watch over her childish passions and prejudices, and labour sweetly to cure her of them.
8th Never use any little dissembling arts, either to pacify her or to persuade her to anything.
9th Win her to be in love with openness, in all her acts, and words.
10th Fail not to instil in her an abhorrence of all 'serpentine' words.
11th If she be a brisk witty child, do not applaud her too much.
12th if she be a dull heavy child, do not discourage her at all.
13th Seem not to admire her wit, but rather study to rectify her judgement.
14th Use her to put [get her used to asking] little questions, and give her ready and short answers.
15th Insinuate into her the principles of politeness and true modesty, and Christian humility.
16th Inculcate upon her that most honourable duty and virtue, sincerity.
17th Be sure to possess her with the baseness of telling a lie on any account.
18th Show her the deformity of rage and anger.
[. . .]
28th Discreetly check her desires after things pleasant, and use her [get her used to] frequent disappointments.
29th Let her be instructed to do everything seasonably and in order, and whatever she is set to do let her study to do it well, and peaceably.
30th Teach her to improve everything that nothing may be lost or wasted, nor let her hurry herself about any thing.
31st Let her always be employed about what is profitable or necessary.
32nd Let nothing of what is committed to her care be spoiled by her neglect.

33rd Let her eat deliberately, chew well, and drink in moderate proportions.

34th Let her use exercise in the mornings.

35th Use her [get her used to] rise betimes in the morning, and set before her in the most winning manner an order for the whole day.

(Pollock 1987: 178–179)

By contemporary standards these prescriptions are somewhat controlling and short on spontaneity (and the omitted rules are heavily concerned with religious compliance), but quite a lot of these views from over two hundred years ago about what parents should do when bringing up their children look appropriate to me today. It would not be difficult to fit them into the 'frames' I discussed earlier (pp. 115–16). What is perhaps the most visible change over the samples that Pollock provides is from good parenting as a religious duty owed to society to a more individualistic view, where parenting is a personal investment and its wider social results are considered mainly when the results are bad.

Nancy Shippen is writing about how she hopes to parent her child, and her intentions owe something to contemporary advice books about parenting. Advice books have been available about as long as any other sort of book, and the advice they have provided is a fascinating mixture of idiosyncratic and generally agreed on, kind and harsh, possible and impracticable (e.g. Hardyment 1983). Remarkably similar prescriptions can be made by people whose backgrounds, experience and vested interests contrast very strongly. For example, Bronfenbrenner (1971: 10–11) quotes two Soviet instruction books for parents from the early 1960s, in what was still a collectivist culture: 'First of all a child must be obedient toward his parents and other adults, and treat them with respect . . . The child must fulfil requests that adults make of him – this is the first thing the child must be taught.' And 'Obedience in young children provides the basis for developing that most precious of qualities: self-discipline. [. . .] Where there is no obedience, there is no self-discipline; nor can there be normal development of independence.'

And here is a middle class Englishwoman giving the same advice in 1945:

In a small child instant obedience is absolutely essential. Self-control, directed ultimately by conscience, is our object, and, in order that he may later be able to subordinate his passions and desires to his own will, he must first learn to submit them to another authority.

(Frankenburg 1946: 205)

To do Mrs Frankenburg justice, she follows this authoritarian passage with five or six pages placing severe restrictions on the parent's right to give orders, and recommending in detail ways of making them into positive experiences for the child – 'Give as few orders as possible', 'Be on your guard also never to give an order unless you are sure that the child is not preparing to act on his own initiative', 'An order can often be translated into a suggestion', 'When a child is in a violent temper, orders are rarely advisable', 'A sudden unexpected command is often a cause of distress'. These specifications bring her recommendations much closer to the advice of liberal pundits, such as Dr Spock.

5.7 Children and political systems

Although people are not expected to be voters, legislators or politicians until they are adults, political systems surround children and may be expected to influence their social development. Many of the areas I have talked about already are embedded in political issues relevant to all of us, not just children – gender, for example, or educational experiences, or what is inadequate parenting. But I turn now to look, quickly and selectively, at the literature on children's activity as citizens and within different sorts of political macrosystems. This literature is interesting in itself and also an invaluable complement to the much larger literature on microsystem socialisation. I have argued that it is the proximal processes of micro-systems that do most to shape children's development as social persons, but clearly we need to embed these processes in the wider ecosystems that Bronfenbrenner describes if we are to understand them.

5.7.1 Children growing up in democracies

In the Western democracies that we are familiar with, children may be exposed to a range of different information about politics, from a range of different sources. Even primary school children have displayed considerable thoughtfulness about political issues (Stevens 1982; Emler and Dickinson 1985; Meadows 2006). Many adolescents retain a strong commitment to political 'fairness' or 'freedom', although a worryingly high proportion may pay little attention to politics, or display distrustful or even cynical attitudes (Hahn 1998; Terren 2002): most adolescents rate friends, family, work and leisure as highly important and politics or religion only moderately so (Terren 2002). Where hands-on political participation is optional and much information comes from media that are desperately cynical about politics and politicians, it may be hard for future citizens to develop a sense that it is worthwhile both to be actively involved in politics and to be aware of how everyday life is affected by political processes. The interplay between rights and responsibilities (Sherrod 2008) is important for children as for adults. Family discussion, school 'citizenship' lessons and a range of out-of-school activities can help to build a commitment to being an active member of the state and to practise democratic ways of engaging in politics, and schools and families that do more of these, seem to produce more politically engaged children (Hahn 1998; Hannam 2003; Helwig 1995, 1998; Helwig *et al.* 2003; Print *et al.* 2002; Mannarini and Fedi 2009; Zaff *et al.* 2008). Outstanding events may arouse young people's political enthusiasm and action just as they may arouse older people's. Adolescence is often seen as a time of particularly strong idealism about social issues, but the idealism may be vulnerable to the reality of politics as 'the art of the possible'.

Democracies tend to accept a range of different values and practices. They might therefore be expected to produce a range of different 'social persons', who would perhaps have the common ground of being, on the whole, hostile to the idea of being controlled by a totalitarian state that does not refer to the needs and wants of its citizens, but might differ otherwise in their ways of being prosocial or antisocial, individual or collectivist, and in their political affiliations. I have argued that what goes on in microsystems accounts for much of this sort of variation.

5.7.2 Children's involvement in politics

Young people can be effective political actors; their participation in favour of the civil rights, women's rights, and democracy movements in the twentieth century helped to change the status quo. Many young children show great enthusiasm for campaigns about fairness, green issues, animal welfare and so forth. Historically many political actions have featured students – the anti-capitalism protests in Western Europe in 1968, the pro-democracy protests in China and in Eastern Europe in the 1980s, for example. Students' active participation in radical movements seems to be associated with being less absorbed than adults in the existing economy and attitudes, and with adolescent idealism and energy, and available time; but also with family politicisation. Many of those who marched against the bomb in the 1960s had children who campaigned on green issues in the 1990s. Parents socialise their children politically; children may also socialise their parents. Bloemraad and Trost (2008) describe how whole families took part in immigrant rights rallies in California in 2006. Although most participants discussed attending the rallies with their friends and families before they went, there were some interesting generational differences in the other ways that individuals became involved in the protest marches. Older people typically became involved because of their own experience, or because of their membership in a particular church or workplace. Younger people were recruited to the marches by their peers, at school, in youth groups, or via electronic media such as social networking sites or text messaging. The two generations had different sources of information, but a shared commitment to taking action to promote fairness in social practices. Citizenship education in schools seeks to develop students' engagement with participation in politics, which is an essential part of having a well-functioning democratic state.

5.7.3 Children growing up in totalitarian systems

The clearest examples of macrosystem politics affecting practice and thereby social development come from totalitarian regimes that have a strong and explicit ideology of what people should be like and are hostile to deviations from this ideology. (This is not to say that even totalitarian regimes can succeed in moulding all their citizens into one form; even in fictional dystopias such as *1984* (Orwell 1949) and *Brave New World* (Huxley 1932) there are dissidents.) However, political systems that exert a great deal of control over citizens' everyday affairs have taken an intense interest in ways of producing what they see as 'better' citizens. They do expect to be able to turn most citizens, ideally all, into a very limited range of socially acceptable types of person. For some of these, there are substantial bodies of evidence in the form of biography, memoir, historical studies, the regime's pronouncements, journalism, oral memories and other sources. I am only going to mention a few examples, cautiously because the evidence base is not, on the whole, the sort that psychologists usually handle. We are dealing here mainly with historical sources, and the rules of interpretation may be different.

The Soviet regimes after the Russian Revolution, under Lenin and under Stalin, were concerned to change Russian society from top to bottom. Soviet society was seen as needing to be an organic whole, in which all social institutions worked together to produce ideal citizens and the best society ever. Consequently, things had to be done differently in the family and the school from the ways they had been done before the Revolution, or had been done in the bourgeois West.

> Our family is not a closed-in collective body, like the bourgeois family. It is an organic part of Soviet society, and every attempt it makes to build up its own experience independently of the moral demands of society is bound to result in a disproportion, discordant as an alarm bell.
>
> Our parents are not without authority either, but this authority is only the reflection of social authority. In our country the duty of a father toward his children is a particular form of his duty toward society. It is as if our society said to parents:
>
> 'You have joined together in good will and love, rejoice in your children, and expect to go on rejoicing in them. That is your own personal affair and concerns your own personal happiness. But in this happy process you have given birth to new people. A time will come when these people will cease to be only a joy to you and become independent members of society. It is not at all a matter of indifference to society what kind of people they will be. In handing over to you a certain measure of social authority, the Soviet state demands from you correct upbringing of future citizens.'
>
> (A.S. Makarenko, quoted by Bronfenbrenner 1971: 3)

It is perhaps no accident that visits during the 1960s to the rapidly changing society of Soviet Russia inspired some of Bronfenbrenner's deepest insights about the social contexts of children's development (Bronfenbrenner 1971, 1979). His observations of parenting in Russia suggest some interesting contrasts with the United States. Bronfenbrenner saw that compared with the USA there appeared to be more highly affectionate but highly restrictive contact with young children – holding them much of the time, wrapping them up warmly in many layers of clothes that restrict their movement – and also a high degree of readiness on the part of other people – including complete strangers – to take an active interest in the child, sometimes in the form of social warmth, sometimes in the form of advice, evaluative comment, and outright voluble disapproval. Parents were expected to control their children, and even if reasoning and persuasion were approved of and physical punishment was disapproved of, expressing a sense of having been badly let down by the child, withdrawing attention and affection from the child, or even ceasing to talk to the child for a while, were felt to be appropriate in the USSR. It was also felt to be appropriate to keep referring to the child's misdeeds, even after they had been repented, apologised for, and atoned for. This sort of interest and intervention from outside the family, and these sorts of negativity and shaming behaviour were not recommended, and were not so common, in the West at the time.

There were also differences in the collective settings that cared for, socialised, and educated children. At the beginning of the Soviet period, it was expected that all domestic functions would be managed collectively – communal housing with very little entitlement to private space except temporarily for sexual activity, communal cafeterias rather than personal cooking, communal laundries, and even communal clothes – no guarantee at all of getting even your own underclothes back from the wash, even no concept of having 'your own' underclothes (Figes 2008). Although this 'ideal' was never fully realised in the home, Soviet childrearing was substantially taken over by collective institutions for children from weaning upwards. Caregivers were encouraged to talk to and play with young children in the ways we are familiar with in Western nurseries, but there was a much stronger consistent emphasis on teaching children to share and engage in co-operative activity, and to identify with the peer group. This involved explicit modelling and, if necessary, shaming.

Below are two examples from Bronfenbrenner's fieldnotes, the first a preschool, the second twelve-year-olds:

> Kolya started to pull at the ball Mitya was holding. The action was spotted by a junior staff member who quickly scanned the room and then called out gaily: 'Children, come look! See how Vasya and Marusya are swinging their teddy bear together. They are good comrades.' The

two offenders quickly dropped the ball to join others in observing the praised couple, who now swung harder than ever.

(Bronfenbrenner 1971: 21)

The five elected officers of the *soviet* (council) of class 5-B were having their weekly meeting to evaluate each pupil. [. . .] A month ago, Vova had been warned that he was doing poorly in arithmetic and pulling down his link [class group]. There had been no improvement.

After some discussion, Lyolya proposed: 'I think this problem is serious enough to require action by the entire collective. We can call a special meeting for this afternoon.' [. . .]

At the class meeting, Vova is asked about his homework.

As no mention is made of math, the class officers exchange significant looks. In a stern voice, Chairman Lyolya reminds him: 'A month ago, you were warned to work harder on your math, and now you don't even mention it.'

Vova: 'I didn't have any math homework that night.'

Voice from the class: 'You should have studied it anyway.'

Lyolya asks the class for recommendations. After some discussion:

'I propose that we designate two of our classmates to supervise Vova as he does his math homework every night and give him help as needed.'

Vova objects: 'I don't need them. I can do it by myself. I promise.'

But Lyolya is not impressed. Turning to Vova she says quietly, 'We have seen what you do by yourself. Now two of your classmates will work with you and when they say you are ready to work alone, we'll believe it.'

(Bronfenbrenner 1971: 64–65)

The first example is not unlike Western nursery school practice, but the second is far less familiar. Soviet children who were seen as letting down the collective of children suffered peer pressure to conform and withdrawal of peer approval far in access of what we are used to in British or North American schools – although as I described earlier some European settings also used class solidarity (p. 221).

Bronfenbrenner (1971: 77) considers that the Soviet system did produce a particular type of person. As he saw it, the Soviet children he encountered in the 1950s and 1960s were better behaved, harder working, and more committed to the collective than their American peers at the time. They were less willing to cheat or behave antisocially, particularly if their peers would know – the reverse of the American children who said they would be more inclined to engage in antisocial behaviour if their classmates would know about it. 'Soviet youngsters placed stronger emphasis than any other group on overt propriety, such as being clean, orderly and well-mannered, but gave less weight than the subjects from the other countries to telling the truth and seeking intellectual understanding' (Bronfenbrenner 1971: 81).

The Soviet school system of class collectives and class officers was part of a wide-ranging system of membership, group responsibility and group surveillance that had ramifications across both children's current lives as children and also their futures. Several twentieth-century totalitarian states have deliberately engaged children in institutions designed to produce 'the right sort of' citizens. Hitler, Mao, and Stalin all used youth organisations to socialise children to choose the state, or the peer group over individual or family interests. Typically children came together with age mates to engage in social and physical activities, as well as in sessions of political indoctrination. The organisations had attractive uniforms or membership symbols, engaged their members with communal activities like camping or singing or political rallies, and offered opportunities for social action that were seen as contributors to everyone's good as well as intrinsically fun. They also encouraged the young members in peer group solidarity and in ambitions to join the next level of membership. Much of this was felt by the children involved to be exciting or delightful or as giving high social status (e.g. Grass 2008), and being a member of the in-group was intrinsically desirable. But there were of course two downsides. Members of the in-group were being indoctrinated into an allegiance to the Leader that would stifle their individual conscience and allow them to collude with, or even commit, terrible crimes. And people who were not allowed to become members of the in-group suffered from being non-members. In-group people often felt that non-members had wilfully defined themselves as out-group, as not subscribing to the in-group's values, and therefore that non-members were not full members of society with normal social rights. In Soviet Russia, for example, only 'good' children from socially acceptable families were allowed to become members of the Pioneers (Figes 2008): children whose behaviour was not acceptable, and children whose parents were from backgrounds that were too bourgeois, too rich, insufficiently in political favour, or just ethnically 'unsound' were not allowed in. Members who misbehaved might have to give up their membership, temporarily or permanently, depending on how seriously, or persistently, they had misbehaved. Subsequently, children who had not been members in good standing of the Pioneers had little or no chance of higher education, good jobs, decent housing, or Communist Party membership. Children sometimes had to conceal their family background or even denounce their parents to prosper socially or even to survive. Children who denounced their parents for anti-Soviet activities might be feted and presented as role models for other children. Loyalty to the state was seen as more important than loyalty to family or friends, should they be in conflict. Much the same pattern of indoctrination of the in-group and persecution of the out-group can be seen in memoirs from Maoist China or Hitler's Germany (e.g.

Chang 1992; Grass 2008). Denunciation of family members who offended against the state was socially rewarded, and indeed the state might well persecute the family of people who broke the rules. For example, the teenage children of the army officers who plotted to assassinate Hitler in July 1944 were imprisoned, sent to dangerous battle zones, expelled from university and so forth (e.g. Bruhns 2009; Kershaw 2001).

Memoirs suggest that such experiences developed both strong feelings of commitment to the society, the Leader, the nation or the cause, and also a high degree of reticence and caution about expressing opinions that questioned leader, party or state and might put you into danger – which is why Figes (2008) calls his book *The Whisperers*. This evidence feels compelling, as personal narratives often do. But these studies are not straightforward evidence of psychological effects. The beliefs and feelings of the people at the time may seem incomprehensible to the memoirists writing years after the totalitarian regime had disappeared. Outsiders may feel that a particular sort of personality is characteristic of those who experienced the totalitarian regime, for example the protective secrecy with which Russians conducted their affairs as a result of the surveillance they suffered under Stalinism: but we just do not know how pervasive any such characteristic really was, or whether it was due to that particular political experience or had other roots. What would seem to us to be extreme expressions of loyalty to the state and the leader were apparently common in Germany even before the birth of Hitler, when the Kaiser was the head of state (Bruhns 2009).

I have great respect for Bronfenbrenner's theoretical model (Bronfenbrenner 1979), and confidence in his observations in Russia, but it seems to me that to say that there is conclusive evidence that political ideologies and regimes can produce social persons who are all of the same, ideologically desired, type is to overstate the case. In a chapter called 'The unmaking of the American child' (Bronfenbrenner 1971) Bronfenbrenner shows worrying signs of nostalgia for the days of his own childhood and distaste for the contemporary scene. Here he considers that in 1960s America (and 1960s England) parents spend far less time with their children than they used to, are far less engaged in socialising their children, and show them less attention, less affection, and less companionship than formerly. Age segregation and decline in community contact leave children to be socialised by their peers and television, with disastrous results. William Golding's novel *Lord of the Flies* (Golding 1954) is put forward as an allegory of the sort of society that could be the consequence.

Here there is a contradiction between what Bronfenbrenner sees and what I saw as a child in England at that time. For him, England is 'the home of the Mods and the Rockers, the Beatles, the Rolling Stones, and [America's] principal competitor in tabloid sensationalism, juvenile delinquency, and violence' (Bronfenbrenner 1971: 116). Like most preteens and teenagers, I and my friends were enthusiastic about fashion and music, but did not engage in delinquency or violence: nor were the Beatles and the Stones as revolutionary or as individualistic as they seemed to him. Whereas he as an outsider may have had a wider range of evidence, my experience did not seem to be unlike the experience of my friends and classmates, and it shows for certain that not all parenting, not all child behaviour and not all the social persons who were produced at this time resembled characters from *Lord of the Flies* (which must in any case have been inspired by children Golding observed before 1954 – before television, before rock and roll, before most families having cars, before, as it happens, the demise of Stalinism). It seems unlikely that the institutions he blaims for the bad behaviour of Western teenagers are really to blaim (although tabloid sensationalism clearly still has a lot to answer for).

5.7.4 Children growing up with political conflict

An example from a society that was more recently divided by political conflict reminds us that there are many levels to political indoctrination and to discussion of political action. Leonard (2009) interviewed adolescents about what has been called 'recreational rioting' on the streets of Belfast. This is the street violence that commonly begins with abusive bantering among relatively young children (for example exchange of insults about 'prods' and 'taigs' or about the merits of Rangers and Celtic football teams) and may then escalate into stone throwing, scuffles and more serious rioting. It is more likely to occur in areas where two communities are in some contact, but not really interacting in any positive way, where levels of poverty are relatively high, and where the young people involved spend a lot of time hanging about with nothing particular to do. Several commentators have described this sort of behaviour as having no specific political content – it is not, typically, associated with a clear goal or political agenda – and as arising from boredom or bravado, being undertaken for the excitement of it by young people who are, on the whole, alienated from the normal political process. Some of the comments by the young people that Leonard interviewed supported this view.

> Where I live in North Belfast there is not much to do during the day but at night it's a lot better. To be honest, I think that is when I get into trouble. That's when it's a laugh. Most people that are young enjoy going to riots and fighting with the Catholics and the police (Protestant boy).

> There is a lot of violence and fighting. All my mates and me get a chase of the peelers (police). I like it when there are riots with the peelers (Protestant boy).

I like getting a chase of the police and rioting with Catholics (Protestant girl).

The things I like about living in North Belfast is when the prods (Protestants) and taigs (Catholics) are rioting every day (Catholic girl).

The only good thing about living here is the rioting. It's a terrible thing to say I suppose but rioting is the only thing to do at times. There's nothing else. It's really boring and it breaks the boredom (Catholic boy).

(Leonard 2009)

But Leonard's informants also expressed other views: comments on the danger and disruption that rioting caused, on how confrontations were often about territory or retaliation for earlier offences, on the uneasy relationship between communities and the state apparatus of law and order, and on the continuing sectarianism of the Belfast population. In these accounts of what was going on, the activity of 'recreational rioting' raised serious political issues (although shouting and scuffling and throwing stones are absolutely not the best ways of dealing with them). The label of 'recreational rioting' marginalises the young people's own view of what they are doing and imposes an adult (and middle class) judgement. Political regimes that do not like the activity of protesters have often labelled them as 'hooligans'; but then it was common for the activity of people attending election meetings (for example in the nineteenth century) to include a lot of drunken and disorderly behaviour, and even quite a lot of violence against representatives of the opposite party – this was felt to be part of the fun!

Studies of countries that have experienced late twentieth century wars offer more evidence on how children are affected by political violence. Barber (1999) reports on Palestinian adolescents' involvement in the Intifada, or uprising, of the late 1990s. A very high proportion of male children and adolescents were involved in protests or harassed by Israeli soldiers, and although their accounts do include elements of bravado and seeking out excitement, serious engagement with political issues is also expressed. Involvement in the Intifada expressed feelings of rights and responsibilities on a number of different levels: family, peer group, and religion, for example, as well as nationalism. In Palestine, as in Israel, Croatia and other countries torn by war with neighbours, social cohesion is felt to be required for survival of individuals and their families as well as for the whole society. But experiences of being under attack, of experiencing or witnessing violence, of being displaced from home or separated from parents, have a direct negative effect on children's psychological health (in particular, exposure to violence causes post-traumatic stress disorder and may increase children's violent behaviour) and also affect it indirectly, through changing what parents and other responsible adults are able to do for children and how they deal with emotions (e.g. Barenbaum *et al.* 2004; Even-Chen and Itzhaky 2007; Garbarino and Kostelny 1996; Knafo *et al.* 2008; Kuterovac-Jagodić 2003; Punamäki *et al.* 1997; Qouta *et al.* 2008; Shamai 2001; Slone and Shechner 2008). Being in a social setting, for example a school, with more violent incidents, increases the risk of violent behaviour for the individual; living among widespread violence is associated with increased violence in the home.

5.7.5 Impact of social change on children's relationships and social skills

Bronfenbrenner himself suggested that examination of proximal processes at times of social change could give an especially helpful picture of macrosystem effects (Bronfenbrenner 1979). The first example he discusses is A. R. Luria's studies of social groups at the geographical margin of Soviet Russia, where schooling and literacy were being introduced with consequences for the cognitive and social understanding of those involved.

> The basic forms of cognitive activity begin to go beyond fixation and reproduction of individual practical activity and cease to be purely concrete and situational. Human cognitive activity becomes a part of the more extensive system of general human experience as it has become established in the process of social history, coded in language. [. . .] there are changes in self-awareness of the personality, which advances to the higher level of social awareness and assumes new capabilities for objective, categorical analyses of one's motivation, actions, intrinsic properties and idiosyncracies.
>
> (Luria quoted in Bronfenbrenner 1979: 264)

These psychosocial changes in Uzbekistan and Kirghizia are probably an example of the sorts of changes that are brought about in societies by the introduction of more widespread and formal education. The strength of traditional apprenticeship education is that you learn to do the things that your immediate society values by doing them under supervision in the community: the strength of 'disembedded' formal education may be that it adds the possibility of disembedded understanding processes that can be transferred to new settings rather more readily.

Bronfenbrenner also discusses the sociological studies of Glen Elder, especially his work on the effects on families of the Great Depression. Elder (1974) picked up two samples of adults who had been studied as children at the time when the American stock market crashed, unemployment and homelessness rocketed, and many families were profoundly affected by the economic catastrophe. Data had been gathered at that time from parents, teachers, and the young people themselves, from both interviews and standardised assessments, so that it was possible to assess the ways in which the Depression impacted on individual families, the relationships within the family and between family members and other social settings, and the degree of stability or change that each family experienced. Elder's follow-up studies involved both short-term effects and long-term outcomes, forty years on.

Severe economic loss stressed parents at the time and hence impacted on children. Fathers' loss of employment and income shifted economic responsibility to mothers and other family members, including the children in the first sample (born 1920–1921), who were approaching adolescence at the time of the Depression. It also shifted fathers' views of themselves and children's views of fathers, mothers and the peer group. The fathers who became unemployed lost status to some degree, both in their own eyes and in the eyes of family members. In families where money became very tight children took on far more responsibility for domestic functioning (especially girls) and for paid work (especially boys).

Forty years on, the men from middle-class families who had shouldered these increased responsibilities as teenagers tended to have settled into more mature career choices and more settled career paths than those whose families had not faced so much economic challenge. Men from working-class families that faced great economic stress tended to miss out on opportunities for higher education, and had a relatively high rate of psychological disturbance and drinking problems. The women who had been teenagers in economically stressed families were highly committed to the traditional female roles of mother and homemaker.

Elder and his colleagues also studied a second sample, born in 1928– 1929, and hence very small children at the time of the Depression. The members of this sample experienced economic stress from very early in their lives, and entered adolescence during World War II. Here, coming from a family who had experienced economic hardship reduced chances of higher education, restricted career choice for men, and was associated with worse long-term mental health – even in their thirties and forties they showed less resilience, less commitment to their work, and more problems with impulse control and emotional stability. Women, however, seemed to be more goal-oriented and well-functioning after experiencing prolonged economic hardship. Elder argued that boys suffering deprivation lost more of the positive from their relationships with their fathers than they gained from the increased status of their mothers, whereas girls lost less in their relationship with their fathers and identified with their mothers' increased status in the family.

I would think, incidentally, that increased opportunities for employment for women, and hence their independence, may also have been a factor for Elder's samples. Because so many male workers had been called up for military service, more women were needed for paid work during both the

First and Second World Wars. In order for them to be available for work even if they had children, day nurseries were set up, and it was argued that even young children could benefit from nursery experience. After the end of the wars, there was pressure to get women out of employment so that there would be jobs for the returning men. Riley (1983) argues that this political and economic pressure influenced the new stress on maternal care that pervaded Bowlby's original work on attachment between mothers and children (pp. 121–27). If she is right, then this is an example of the macrosystem visibly influencing theory.

The data from Elder's studies deserve much more than my brief summary: they provide a telling glimpse of how families rise to challenges or are beaten down by them, how this impacts on individuals' views of themselves and of social roles, and how impacts on life choices come about. Microsystems, mesosystems and macrosystems clearly all operate here. And the studies also develop research methods in extremely useful ways (e.g. Giele and Elder 1998; Moen et al. 1995; Elder, Modell and Parke 1993).

5.7.6 Impact of cultural change on children's relationships and social skills

The examples of social change that I have discussed so far have been relatively sudden and substantial – revolutions, wars, major economic upsets. Over the last century or so, many societies whose cultural practices and value systems had been relatively stable (in the sense that even after a period of social upheaval and political change most people's lives continued much as before) have experienced less dramatic but never the less rapid and wide-ranging changes, especially in the direction of increased urbanisation, migration, education, and economic differentiation. Such changes affect the sorts of supports and resources available for children's development, and this can clarify what the demands and the goals of the developmental process are.

In a series of studies in Turkey, for example, Kagitcibasi (Kagitcibasi 2005; Kagitcibasi and Ataca 2005) compared successive generations of parents' values for their children. High-income urban parents placed an increasing emphasis on children developing autonomy compared with parents interviewed in the 1970s, and also expected a warmer, closer and more exuberant relationship with their children. Economic changes over the period have meant that children are seen as people who need to be educated to become future contributors to the needs of the household, rather than the less skilled and effective contributors they could be at present; thus they are not valued so much for their current utilitarian value but their role as a source of enjoyment has increased.

Chen et al. (2005, 2008; Chen and French 2007) describe analogous changes in China. When the basis of the Chinese life was an economy where there were many shortages of basic goods, having utilitarian relationships with others that provided mutual benefits was seen as essential for getting what one needed. With the development of a market economy, or with migration into a market economy, this understanding of relationships or social connections loses significance (Tamis-Lemonda *et al.* 2008). Related-ness becomes valued for itself, for the activities it opens up and the emotional support it can provide, rather than because it provides mutual obligations. If relationships get in the way of individual achievement then a conflict is recognised very much as it would be in Western societies (Helwig *et al.* 2003).

These economic changes may make for changes in what personal characteristics are seen as desirable. Fong (2002) describes the increasing power of urban young women in China following the one-child policy and rapid economic development. Chen *et al.* (2005) found that shy children were rated as highly competent in the early 1990s when accommodating to the group was the core of being a 'good citizen', but by the end of the twentieth century shyness was a problematic characteristic and it was autonomous active children who were rated most highly. British commen-tators on social change have also remarked on the extreme individualism, assertiveness and decline in relatedness fostered by the free market ideology since 1979 – a worldview which may need to change if economic circum-stances have changed for good. The literature about personality structure in different countries (pp. 45–48, 80–84) may need to be considered in the light of historical change – and this is an interesting branch of historical study (Hardyment 1983; Pollock 1983, 1987).

5.7.7 Becoming a social person among social inequality

There is a very substantial amount of evidence that people who live in societies that have a high degree of economic inequality show higher rates of all sorts of social and personal difficulties, even if the societies are adjacent to each other and in many respects very similar, for example Canada and the USA (Willson 2009); or Spain and Portugal (Wilkinson and Pickett 2009). Unequal societies have worse rates of educational failure, low social capital, crime and imprisonment, mental illness, dissatisfaction, obesity, poor health and early death than more equal societies. Individuals who are very much poorer than the average in their society suffer most (pp. 150–52) – they encounter more potentially damaging experiences and they may have fewer resources to deal with challenges to their well-being. But even people who have an income adequate for their needs show worse outcomes in more unequal societies (Pickett and Wilkinson 2007; Wilkinson and Pickett 2007, 2009). Increasing the overall wealth of Western societies has not improved the general well-being of their members, over the last few decades. Wilkinson and Pickett refute the arguments that social status is purely a result of your ability, with those at the bottom of the heap only there because of their own inadequacies, and that raising the average income of the society will help all its members, because wealth will 'trickle down' from the richer to the poorer. They argue instead that social inequality makes societies dysfunctional, reducing the possibility of social mobility, increasing segregation between richer and poorer, increasing chronic social stress, and increasing the risk of social comparisons that make the less privileged resentful and the more privileged anxious about losing their status. There is a negative effect throughout the society; the richest individuals in an unequal society live longer and healthier lives than the poorest in that society, but their lives are shorter and unhealthier than the richest or even the slightly less rich in an equal society.

A recent review (Cemlyn *et al.* 2009) examines the literature on the ways that Gypsy and Traveller communities in Britain are affected by their status on the margins of mainstream society. They have very much worse outcomes in health, literacy, education, involvement in crime, and probably domestic violence and drug and alcohol use, than any other social group in the UK, suffer from racist attitudes and behaviour, and have worse housing, access to education, and access to health care. They may also be torn between traditional cultural values (for example separation, and different status, of males and females in public settings for Roma groups) and the different expectations of mainstream society. Cemlyn and her colleagues point out that there are substantial inadequacies in the way these communities are treated by both individuals and social institutions in the mainstream, with much exclusion and distrust on both sides.

We can begin to infer how social inequality might affect children's development as social persons from what I have said about microsystems (and other social environments) earlier in this book. Children's chances of a stable family life, parenting that enhances their development rather than impairing it, good education and health care, a good repertory of social and cognitive skills, a positive but realistic self-concept, a sense of membership in the wider society, may be better in a more equal society. In unequal societies, the richer part will enjoy these advantages, but because they co-exist with people who have not benefited from them, they are more at risk than if everyone had shared in the social and cultural capital of the society more fairly. We all benefit from being more equal.

5.8 Summary

In this section, I have looked at the child as social person in a number of large-scale social settings. The best-researched setting is the school, which we know is a major factor in children's cognitive development, and is also an arena for playing a range of social roles, not necessarily easily combined. I have also looked at some literature on the effects of other social and cultural institutions that children play an active part in, and on the effects of social and cultural characteristics of systems that affect children without actively including them. This has involved using evidence from anthropology, sociology and history as well as the psychology that has provided most of my sources for this book. On the whole, my feeling about these wider environments is that they make sense in terms of the microsystems they provide: that, for example, Soviet ideology about the importance of the collective led to particular sorts of interaction between children and adults in public and in the family, and it may have been the interaction rather than the ideology that affected children's development as social persons. My money is on proximal processes, certainly when we are within the normal range of experiences, and very possibly even when we are beyond that, as my next section, on risk and resilience, will discuss. To quote Bronfenbrenner on 'molar activities': 'these constitute the principal and most immediate manifestation both of the development of the individual and of the most powerful environmental forces that instigate and influence that development – the actions of other people' (Bronfenbrenner 1979: 45).

Chapter 6

Risk and resilience

In this final section, I want to recapitulate some of the insights about children's development as social persons that arise from the work that I have looked at so far. I have discussed some of the literature on children as social persons in a range of social settings which seem to be associated with better development or more problematic development. I have used Bronfenbrenner's model to illustrate how development is affected by, and affects, microsystems, mesosystems, exosystems, and macrosystems; and especially the importance of proximal processes of interaction experienced day after day over long periods of time.

To help us recapitulate, I now offer discussion of first, children who have suffered from an absence of socialisation in their early lives; second, antisocial behaviour – that is young people behaving badly across social settings; third, some ways of intervening; and fourth, resilience – that is young people turning out well despite their exposure to social settings or experiences that might be expected to bias them towards poor developmental outcomes.

6.1 Children who have suffered from an absence of social support for their development

I have argued that normal human development requires a considerable investment of time and effort by older humans. I have presented some of the microsystem behaviours that seem to be associated with children developing into what I would regard as relatively balanced, happy, prosocial individuals, and some microsystem processes that give rise to problems. But I turn now to another group of children, those who have been subjected to such horrible extremes of neglect, abuse, and social deprivation that they have been thought of as 'feral' children. A total lack of care from birth is unlikely to be something that a child can survive, but extreme lack of care does appear to have happened in a few cases, and for some of these we have detailed information on what sort of functioning such children showed after being rescued.

There are a few famous cases where it has been claimed that the child may have completely lacked any human contact, living with non-human animals and surviving only because they provided substitute parental care, and these 'feral' children are said to resemble 'savages', 'idiots' or 'beasts' (Gesell 1942; Maclean 1979; Newton 2002; Zingg 1940). It is usually claimed that the children behave like the sort of animals that it was believed had enabled them to survive – for example the 'wolf-children' rescued by the Reverend Mr Singh in northern India howled, ran on all fours, and tore at raw meat (Zingg 1940). A few modern children have been reported as having lived much more in animal groups than with their inadequate parents, although most of these seem to have had their earliest years with humans and drifted away from them because the parenting they received was so inadequate. Cases of children living as members of groups of non-human animals are typically badly documented, and both the description of the state of the children when first found, and the treatment they receive in efforts to rehabilitate them, may owe more to the rescuers' preconceptions about what is morally correct than to detailed objective observation, systematic assessment or principled pedagogy. The 'feral' child who is an exception to this, being both well-documented and the recipient of a rehabilitation programme inspired by well thought out educational principles, is the boy known as 'Victor' (Lane 1976).

Victor was captured in the forests of Aveyron in southern France in 1800, not long after the Revolution, when he was aged about thirteen. He had certainly been living wild there for at least three years, and probably his isolation had begun in his early childhood. We do not know how he came to be living in the forests. This was a time of substantial social upheaval, and this may have destroyed the ability of his original family to care for the child. Or he may have been abandoned because his family saw him as in some way problematic – there were scars on his body that might have been a result of an attack by a human rather than caused when he was living wild.

After Victor's capture he was taken to Paris and put into the care of Jean-Marc Itard and his housekeeper, Madame Guerin. Itard was a pioneer in the education of the handicapped and the deaf, and he kept a very detailed record of Victor's development. He devised a system of patient and careful training procedures that remarkably anticipate twentieth-century behaviour modification techniques. Victor, when first rescued, had no language and no social skills, and little emotional display; he functioned at a level of sensorimotor intelligence, sometimes showing extraordinary sensory acuity and sometimes no reaction at all. Under Madame Guerin's care, and with the supervision and training of Itard, he progressed to some conceptual thought and moral feelings, especially of empathy, but his language development was disappointing, his social skills remained rudimentary, and his emerging sexuality and emotions disturbing to both the adults responsible for him and the boy himself. Poor Victor showed so little recovery towards a normal developmental course that it has remained a matter of controversy from his own time to ours whether his defective development might not have had physical roots, not just social ones. Here the question that applies to all children neglected to such a degree has to be faced: is it possible that they were so badly treated because those responsible for them believed that they were in some way abnormal, even before they were abandoned? Consideration of Victor's symptoms and achievements has led some psychologists to suggest that he was probably autistic (Bettelheim 1967; Frith 1990), though Lane (1976) maintains that this diagnosis rests on a selective use of the evidence.

Victor's combination of isolation from human contact and excellent documentation is unique. It has been more common for children to suffer deprivation of social interaction, perceptual stimulation, sensorimotor experience, emotional support or adequate nutrition while still in the care of adults. Not long after Victor was found in post-Revolutionary France, Kaspar Hauser turned up in post-Napoleonic Bavaria (Frith 1990; Masson 1996), another period of history where there had been considerable social upset and also a strong philosophical interest in nature and nurture issues. Kaspar was about sixteen; he had a minute vocabulary, much of it used parrot fashion, but could read and write a little; could barely walk, would eat only bread and water, could not bear strong light but could see in the dark. When (quite rapidly) he was able to talk about his experience, he said that he had always lived in a dark room with a low ceiling, where he sat on straw on the ground. There he never heard a sound or saw a bright light, was supplied with bread and water by a man who stood behind him to do so, and had only a couple of wooden horses for playthings. He made rapid progress with first a foster family and then a tutor; he was an appealing young man with an air of innocence about him, and rumours developed that he was of noble birth. It was thought that perhaps he was an illegitimate son of Napoleon, or the rightful Crown Prince of Baden, kidnapped from his cradle and cruelly imprisoned by his usurper. He became one of the local celebrities, and indeed he was of interest to a wide circle of aristocrats and politicians including an English nobleman who paid for his keep and education. After a while, his cognitive progress slowed down and he was accused of being lazy and inattentive, although whether this was ineradicable deficit or the reaction of a socially petted adolescent to an unsympathetic, even hostile, teacher is unclear. Five years after he first appeared in Nuremberg, he suffered a mysterious knife wound, from which he died. Who he was, where he came from and how he died cannot be known; people's myths about foundlings and the intrigues of courts obscure the case. He may have been a uniquely consummate con artist, but it does seem possible that Kaspar Hauser was made to suffer many years of social and physical deprivation, and that he made a notable recovery when returned to normal life in his late teens.

Some modern cases of social deprivation are documented in a fashion which makes it rather easier to draw inferences about how deprivation affects development. Skuse (1984) reviews four well-known cases of extreme deprivation. The best known is Genie, who was confined to one small bare room by her psychotic father from shortly after her first birthday until she was nearly fourteen, beaten and barked at rather than talked to, tied to a potty-chair or confined in a sleeping bag made like a straitjacket in a crib covered with wire mesh (see also Curtiss 1977; Rymer 1993). Skuse's next case is a pair of monozygotic Czech twins who spent their first year more or less normally in a children's home and the next six months with an aunt, but for the next five and a half years were in the care of a weak-minded father and a stepmother straight out of Grimm's Fairy Tales, who brought up the two little boys in almost total isolation, beating them, locking them up for long periods in the cellar, and never allowing them out of the house (see also Koluchova 1976). Fujinaga *et al.* (1990) report on two Japanese children similarly brought up, kept in a shed near their parents' house and allowed to crawl in the yard, but beaten, never talked to or played with or treated with affection. For all these children, and for four other children, Mary, Alice, Beth, and Louise, who were less cruelly treated and less socially and perceptually deprived (Skuse 1984), fairly detailed information is available on the state they were in when first rescued from their horrible conditions, and on at least some aspects of their later development.

The children are not identical in the deficits they showed initially, nor in how these problems persisted. Some of those who had had very restricted perceptual environments were initially suspected of sensory impairments because their hearing or vision did not fit the usual pattern. For example Genie, who had been kept in a room where she could not see anything further than ten feet away, was short-sighted to exactly this degree. On the whole there was a very rapid development of normal vision and hearing. All the children initially had severely limited spoken language and gesture and their language comprehension was poor. Once they were rescued, and received normal or enhanced language experience, the Czech twins and three of Skuse's less deprived girls rapidly developed virtually normal language skills, and the Japanese siblings made slower but substantial progress. Anna, Genie and the last of Skuse's cases, Mary, remained severely retarded in their language; Anna and Genie also remained far below age-appropriate levels on non-verbal intelligence tests, although in the other cases non-verbal IQs were superior to verbal IQ scores. All of the children developed good or adequate motor skills; the Japanese boy became a successful marathon runner. The Czech twins, the Japanese siblings, and Skuse's cases Alice, Beth, and Louise were able to cope with normal school, and the Czech and Japanese children are known to have held down ordinary jobs.

Skuse suggests that the victims of extreme sensory and social deprivation whom he describes shared a number of characteristic cognitive deficits, emotional and social expression, and social skills. Of these, the language deficit and the social-emotional problems seemed to be most profound, and the rate of improvement in motor and perceptual skills was much faster. Anna, Genie, and Mary, who showed some non-verbal abilities but a complete absence of language, had the worst outcomes; speech therapy and life in a good environment with fostering adults enabled rapid development of language and cognitive abilities in the other children. If anything, cognition recovered rather better than social and emotional skills.

More recent, larger scale, and more systematic data come from a continuing series of systematic longitudinal studies of children who suffered grossly deprived institutional rearing followed by adoption into normal families. In one major stream of this work, the children were all Romanian and placed in orphanages in Romania mainly within the first months of their lives. In these institutions they received inadequate food, no individualised care, and no social or cognitive stimulation, and were kept in bare and dirty cots in bare and dirty rooms. The English and Romanian Adoptees Study Team (ERA) have published a large number of accounts of these children at successive stages from their entry to the UK through to pre-adolescence (e.g. Beckett *et al.* 2006; Castle *et al.* 1999; Chisholm *et al.* 1995; Croft *et al.* 2001; Kaler and Freeman 1994; Kreppner *et al.* 2001, 2007; O'Connor *et al.* 2000, 2003; Roy, Rutter and Pickles 2000; Rutter 1998b; Rutter, Kreppner and O'Connor 2001; Rutter, O'Connor and the ERA study team 2004; Colvert *et al.* 2008). At their rescue, these children showed severe retardation of all cognitive and language measures, retarded physical growth, and socio-emotional problems. Most showed a rapid recovery of cognition and language within the first two years in their adoptive families; by age four those who had been rescued from the orphanages before they were six months old were all scoring near or above the norm for British children. Those who had been in the institutions for longer varied but showed very considerable catch-up. The improvement continued between ages four and six; increases in weight and IQ were often in the normal range, and although head circumference was still somewhat low and there were a lot of residual problems of socio-emotional development, particularly of attachment, most children were functioning well. More recently, Kreppner *et al.* (2001, 2007) identify problems of inattention and overactivity and Colvert *et al.* (2008) of emotional difficulties at age eleven, almost all of them in children who still had high degrees of deficit at age six. Where children had multiple impairments at age eleven, disinhibited attachment behaviour, quasi-autistic behaviour, and cognitive impairment tended to co-occur. This is something of a contrast with multiple problems in children who have not been subject to institutional deprivation, where the problems that co-occur tend to involve conduct disorders, relationship problems, attention problems, and over-activity. Romanian orphan children adopted into the USA, Canada and the Netherlands similarly showed a very high degree of recovery, although possibly with some socio-emotional problems remaining, or emerging, at the onset of adolescence (e.g. Benoit *et al.* 1996; Morison, Ames and Chisholm 1995; Maclean 2003; Wismer Fries and Pollak 2004; Zeanah *et al.* 2003). Kreppner *et al.* (2007) suggest that the pattern of impairment and recovery, and some bits of evidence at the level of neuroscience, suggest that the early extreme deprivation may have had enduring effects on the functioning of the brain and the neuroendocrine system (pp. 14, 54–56, 62–63).

A recent study reports on interventions to improve care of children in orphanages in St Petersburg (McCall *et al.* 2008). Changing the regime of care from one that was acceptable in terms of sanitation, nutrition, safety, and medical care but impersonal and devoid of consistent social relationships, to one which provided more positive and consistent contact with staff who were warm, sensitive and responsive, was associated with a significant positive improvement on the children's cognitive, physical, and socio-emotional development.

> While wards formerly were quiet or had children crying, now they are noisy, filled with talking and excitement. Whereas children once were confined to large playpens or their cribs, now they are actively engaged with toys, their caregivers, and each other on the floor and elsewhere in their rooms. Caregivers pay individualized attention to children, frequently letting the children lead and responding to their overtures. Caregivers sit with children at mealtimes and engage them in conversation, whereas formerly they stood apart and simply watched and maintained order. The caregivers seem relaxed and to enjoy being with the children (they talk, smile, laugh and hug children); before they were dutiful, business-like, and perfunctory. [. . .]
>
> Whereas children once were somber and stoic, now they are alive, constructively engaged, display a variety of emotions including smiling and laughing, and are much more cooperative and interactive with each other and their caregivers. They talk, even describe their experiences and feelings, and stereotypic self-stimulation behaviors, which were once common, have essentially disappeared. They seek out their caregivers for comfort when hurt or upset, whereas this rarely happened before. When strangers enter the room, children no longer stare at them as an object or run up to hug them in indiscriminate friendliness. Instead, toddlers are wary, they back away, and they grab the legs of their caregivers for comfort. Older children, after a few minutes of adjustment, may cautiously introduce themselves to the stranger and ask appropriate questions, whereas before they would greet the stranger with indiscriminate friendliness or point at them yelling, 'Diadia' or 'Teotia' (i.e., 'man' 'woman'). In every way, children [. . .] behave much more similarly to parent-reared children.
>
> (McCall *et al.* 2008: 232)

The distressing cases of individuals who have been grossly neglected, and the studies of orphanage children, suggest that growing up under conditions of extreme social deprivation will prevent the development of normal cognition and language and of social skills. If there is no overt genetic anomaly (as there was in Mary's case) and no gross malnutrition (as in Genie's, and as in the case of some of the Romanian orphans) there may be a rapid improvement in ability, to within the normal range of IQ and cognition, given stimulating loving care in a small group. Thus we can reasonably hope for considerable cognitive improvement, although there may be longer-lasting problems of attention; but it appears that there may be continuing difficulties with overactivity, social skills and attachment for some children.

6.2 Antisocial behaviour

The terms 'delinquency' and 'antisocial behaviour' cover a wide range, in what is done and in terms of severity, persistence, and pervasiveness. There are interesting historical and cultural differences in what is included (Schneider and Schneider 2008). Basically, the terms refer to behaviour that is contrary to the standards of conduct or social expectations of a given group or society (which clearly allows for differences between societies, a point I will return to later). It is antisocial to kick someone into a coma during a fight; it is antisocial to help conceal the goods that your friend has stolen; it is antisocial to pay for a shorter journey on a bus than you actually travel. Some people almost accept some sorts of antisocial behaviour as normal and barely deserving blame – for example littering, riding your bicycle among the pedestrians on the pavement, driving a little faster than the speed limit – whereas other members of the society greatly dislike these behaviours, some other sorts of antisocial behaviour, for example serious physical violence, are universally condemned. Some antisocial acts are one-offs, others are part of a persisting career of delinquent behaviour. And of course, not all delinquencies are detected, let alone officially noted and punished.

Clearly people of all ages may commit an antisocial act. When people are asked to report on their own misbehaviour, the majority of men self-report delinquent acts, mainly minor and fleeting. A substantial minority of men have a criminal record by age thirty-five. But for most people, adolescence is the peak period for misbehaving: in England and Wales in the mid-1990s juveniles (under eighteens) committed twenty-five to thirty-five per cent of recorded offences. The peak age in the UK in 2006 was seventeen for males (when six per cent were offenders) and fifteen for females (two per cent were offenders). The absolute rates of crime and delinquency change somewhat (probably having reduced since the 1980s), but the age and gender patterns remain rather constant.

Female offenders are slightly more likely than males to offend before the age of 21. People aged forty-four and over, particularly women, were much less likely to be found guilty of, or cautioned for, indictable offences. The crime rate climbed steadily from the 1950s to the end of the twentieth century, including particular increases in juvenile crime and in girls' crime: the male : female ratio for offending in England and Wales was 11 : 1 in the 1950s, 4 : 1 in 2006 (Rutter, Giller and Hagell 1998, http://www.statistics.gov.uk/cci/nugget.asp?id=1661). Males almost monopolise burglary, robbery, drug offences, criminal damage, violence against the person, and sexual offences. Females' crime is largely a matter of theft or handling stolen goods, or prostitution. Females are five times more likely than males to be the victims of domestic violence, but males are three times more likely than females to be the victim of violence from a stranger.

Rates of most crimes fell between 1997 and 2006 (both in the official records and in the British Crime Survey, which includes crime that was not officially reported). Most of the crime that young people commit is petty crime, disagreeable but not life-threatening or highly disruptive, and most of it is not repeated. The literature shows that the majority of those who commit antisocial behaviour do so only during adolescence; before, and after, they are pretty much normal citizens. Adolescence-limited antisocial behaviour is strongly associated with peer group norms; teenagers getting together, drinking too much, driving too fast, shoplifting, defying authority, etc. Most people do a little bit of this; most grow out of it. Once the perpetrators are adults, most of them look back on this bad behaviour as something they once did, shouldn't have done, and would not do now. But for a small minority of individuals, their delinquency is serious or persistent.

6.2.1 Personal characteristics of serious persistent delinquents

Whereas pretty much everyone is capable of behaving badly sometimes, a minority of individuals behave antisocially a lot of the time, or to a more extreme degree than others. These individuals commit a disproportionate number of crimes – at least ten per cent, possibly as much as fifty per cent of offences – and cost society a disproportionate amount, in the costs of the havoc they create or in the costs of the police, law, and imprisonment systems that try to stop their crime. A substantial body of research has converged on a consistent description of the personal characteristics of serious/persistent delinquents, the recidivists who persist in antisocial behaviour before, during and after the period of adolescence (Rutter, Giller and Hagell 1998; Silberg et al. 2007).

These individuals are very likely to have a history of being difficult to handle, 'trouble', well before they committed a crime. Both retrospective studies, which obviously could be biased in the direction of reporting early difficulties that were not noticed at the time, and prospective studies, which would not have this problem, suggest that even when they were young children, recidivist delinquents tended to show signs of a difficult temperament – impulsivity, sensation seeking, lacking control, and aggression. They are often seen as hyperactive, with lots of disruptive behaviour; they may be unpopular with other children; and they have been a nuisance to teachers. Some score very low on self-esteem measures. For some there are signs of cognitive impairment – low IQ, poor school performance, maybe specifically poor verbal and planning skills. They may show distorted social information processing – negative attributions for other people's neutral behaviour, high levels of hostility (Krettenauer and Eichler 2006; Granic and Patterson 2006; Rutter, Giller and Hagell 1998). They often come from families with difficulties – ineffective parenting, parental depression, family discord and divorce, coercive discipline, abuse, lack of supervision. In school and in the neighbourhood they tend to associate with similar individuals, in a delinquent peer group. They typically achieve less than they should in school, and have difficulties in finding work, so that they go through life in unstable employment or unemployment. They have less access than normal to positive occupations, for example they are unlikely to enjoy school success, clubs, jobs, and activities with prosocial people; and they may have access to opportunities to behave badly, for example unsupervised neighbourhoods, cheap alcohol or drugs, no one monitoring what they do and expecting them to behave properly. Their general poor functioning may for some subgroups extend into violent, psychopathic behaviour, or serious mental disorders, with social functioning seriously impaired.

6.2.2 Why do badly behaved children tend to have badly behaved parents?

There is substantial evidence of a link between parents' antisocial behaviour and children's antisocial behaviour (Caspi, Elder and Bem 1987; Coie and Dodge 1998; Conger et al. 2003; Eckenrode et al. 2001; Farrington 1987; Brook et al. 2007). Links have been traced over two or more generations both scientifically (e.g. Rutter, Giller and Hagel 1998; Caspi et al. 1987; Thornberry et al. 2003) and in less rigorous popular literature (for example the eugenicists at the turn of the nineteenth into the twentieth century made much use of the case of the contrasted families of the Jukes and the Kallikaks, who were descended from one male ancestor via his legitimate marriage on the one hand and his bastard offspring by a barmaid on the other – no prizes for spotting which 'turned out well' and which 'turned out badly' in this sexist class-bound and determinist analysis).

The reasons for the similar criminal careers of parents and children are not so clear, however. There could be genetic issues, but socio-economic circumstances, parenting styles, peer networks, and drug use are likely to be important.

The commonly found association between persistent antisocial behaviour and the combination of early conduct problems and hyperactivity may have genetic roots or be associated with neurodevelopmental impairment (Jacobson, Prescott and Kendler 2006; Odgers *et al.* 2007, 2008; Silberg *et al.* 2007; Taylor, Iacono and McGue 2000). At present, findings are not altogether clear; different raters may not be consistent in their judgements, and retrospective reports of conduct problems and hyperactivity may be coloured by the present situation. Further research will be required to identify whether there is a case for a biological basis to persistent delinquency and antisocial behaviour, what genes or neural systems are involved, and what if anything can be done to ameliorate the situation.

Parenting is a likely influence on persistent conduct problems (pp. 136, 146–47, 169) – poor monitoring, parental hostility towards the child or young person, coercion, violence, inconsistency, discord, lack of family cohesiveness, and general family stress have all been associated with problems (Dwairy 2008; Sternberg *et al.* 2006). It has to be noted that at least some of the suboptimal parenting might be a consequence of having a difficult child to parent. There could be emerging evidence of an interaction between poor parenting and genetic vulnerability (e.g. Caspi *et al.* 1995, 2002). There certainly is evidence that interventions can break the link between parenting and children's antisocial behaviour (e.g. Eckenrode *et al.* 2001; Brotman *et al.* 2008).

6.2.3 Peer effects and risk of persistent antisocial behaviour

Interactions with delinquent peers (and siblings) can have a negative influence on development (e.g. Reitz *et al.* 2007; pp. 169, 176–77). This applies both to minor delinquency and major persistent delinquency. For most individuals it is a matter of getting into trouble with the group that you hang round with, doing delinquent versions of normal adolescent messing about; drinking too much alcohol and smoking cannabis, for example. More serious delinquency with peers can involve exaggerations of bullying behaviour (pp. 182–86), or of forming gangs: there may be involvement in drug selling and using, threat and warfare between gangs, or, in the case of girls who get into relationships with delinquent young men, in prostitution. There is likely to be a mixture of risk taking, challenging, and protecting against loss of face by becoming more assertive in wrongdoing. Preserving one's reputation as 'hard', and demand for 'respect', may preclude behaving in ways that do not challenge authority. Involvement in delinquent behaviour can both become the easiest option and spiral out of control.

6.3 Adolescent risk taking

The everyday perception of adolescence is that it is a period when people take risks more than at earlier or later ages, even that it is a period when risk taking is expected. Martin (1981) argued that societies can only allow limited amounts of transgressive, disruptive behaviour, so it is restricted to certain social groups or to certain periods of time. Her examples, drawn from mid-twentieth century Britain, include some of the very, very rich (allowed to spend excessively, have flamboyant divorces, look down on the bourgeouisie); some of the very, very poor ('undeserving' or 'feckless', and marginalised, but sentimentalised as 'real characters' or 'the salt of the earth'); and (some of the time) adolescents, who are allowed to 'sow their wild oats', 'gather ye rosebuds while ye may', because 'you're only young once'. Many adolescents live up to this expectation in marginal ways, or sometimes substantial ways: 'The culture of youth is marked by spontaneity, hedonism, immediacy and a kind of self-centred emotional intensity which, from some angles, can resemble individualism, non-conformity, or even rebellion' (Martin 1981: 139).

One implication of all this is that adolescents will be particularly prone to risky behaviour – too much alcohol, drug use, unprotected sex, driving too fast, etc. There are assertions that their brains, or their knowledge, are not sufficiently well-developed for them to cope with risk sensibly (Boyer 2006; Caffray and Schneider 2000; Cooper et al. 2000; Galvan et al. 2006; Reyna and Farley 2006; Vitaro et al. 2001). That they are moving between or out of the control of such microsystems as families and schools, and are not yet subject to the microsystems of employment, means that they may also not be subject to so much individual monitoring as at other and particularly earlier periods of their lives (Carvajal et al. 2004). They may not yet have responsibilities to job, career, spouse, children or mortgage to consider. The intensity of their involvement in peer relations may also increase their susceptibility to risky behaviour (Henry et al. 2007).

There are grounds for anxiety about adolescent risk taking; for example high rates of sexually transmitted infections, of HIV, of unplanned pregnancy, of drug and alcohol abuse, of dangerous driving and injury and death in motoring accidents (Reyna and Farley 2006). Many of the adults with problematic addictions began their harmful behaviour as adolescents, often just experimenting with something that seemed harmless at the time but turned out to be a long-term danger for them. It might indeed therefore be a good idea to reduce risk taking in the teenage years. But are adolescents peculiarly liable to take risks? Reyna and Farley (2006) review the evidence and suggest that we have to be careful both about defining risk and about why adolescents fail to defend themselves against it.

Some risk taking is intentional; for example the individual craves a new and extreme experience. This sort of behaviour might be reduced by better information about risks and benefits, and about whether the intended behaviour is really as common or as 'normal' as the individual believes – for example, if a girl believes that her boyfriend will leave her if she does not have sex with him and be devoted to her if she does; that most girls her age are in sexual relationships; and that being a teenage mother would not be difficult but might, rather, give her someone who would love her unconditionally, she may be more likely to risk unprotected sexual activity than if she believes that having a baby would cripple her chances of educational achievement and employment; that the boyfriend would not make a reliable partner; that her friends would not interrupt their own social lives to support her; and that, generally, parenthood should be postponed.

However, much adolescent risk taking is probably far more unintentional than the calculation I have just used as an example: rather, it may be a spontaneous reaction to an unforeseen situation, or a willingness to take a small risk which then makes it more difficult to protect oneself against the larger one that follows. Adolescents who do not intend to take risks may actually be in more danger than those who have intended to take a risk, because those who knew what they were likely to get into might be more likely to have thought about the possible consequences and taken some precautions. Adolescents who take risks unintentionally might be helped by adult supervision or monitoring, because this would reduce their exposure to temptation to take the risk. Although it could be argued that supervision may reduce their chance of learning about the adverse consequences of the risks they are being prevented from taking, and so prevent learning to avoid risk and self-regulate independently, Reyna and Farley (2006) believe that there is little evidence for this, that thorough monitoring really does diminish risk taking (see also Lahey, Moffitt and Caspi 2003; Vitaro et al. 2001).

Some risk taking can be avoided by thinking ahead and setting things up so that the risk is not present, or is not attractive when it does occur; or by committing oneself in some way to not falling for it (Gibbons et al. 2004; Loewenstein et al. 2001). Many religious and moral teachings use 'self-binding', getting individuals to avoid not only sin but what occasions sin – the individual is committed to avoiding the situation in which they might choose to do what is seen as wrong. Although this can work well, and it can be harder to wriggle out of or reject than monitoring by others, it has three disadvantages: individuals may take no other steps to protect themselves from risk; those who fail to live up to their commitment once may feel that they have broken it for all time and there is no point in further avoidance or other attempts to avoid the risk (it appears that an emphasis on sexual abstinence may be associated with an increased risk of those who lapse from abstinence having unprotected sex); and some individuals or moral systems may coerce one group of people to behave in ways which protect other people from risk (e.g. Jaffee and Hyde 2000; Verkuyten and Slooter 2008). Feeling that one is a valued member of the community tends to reduce risk taking, possibly in part because one has a reputation to protect from social scrutiny or possibly because of feelings of belongingness and communal responsibility; but living in a community where you are in the minority increases it (Bolland *et al.* 2007).

Analyses of adolescent risk taking, using both real life and laboratory settings and a range of methods of assessing attitudes, beliefs and behaviour, include concepts such as perceived risks and benefits, beliefs about social norms, feelings of self-efficacy, and perceived control of the situation – very much the same factors as affect adults' risk taking. Also like adults, adolescents tend to both view themselves as less likely to suffer from taking a risk than a comparable peer ('It won't happen to me'), to think that risks are statistically more likely than they really are, and to overestimate the benefit that taking the risk might bring (Reyna and Farley 2006): a complicated mixture of biases that differs in fine grain from individual to individual. Adolescents who have taken risks and survived apparently unscathed may have more positive feelings about risk taking and fewer negative ones than those who have not engaged in risky behaviour. Individuals who suffer from negative mood (such as depression or low self-esteem) are more likely to engage in risky but mood-changing behaviour, such as thrill seeking or use of drugs or alcohol (Caffray and Schneider 2000; Cooper, Agocha and Sheldon 2000; Bolland *et al.* 2007). 'Sensation seeking', in particular, 'a need for varied, novel, and complex sensations and experiences and the willingness to take physical and social risks for the sake of such experiences' (Zuckerman 1979: 11) is strongly associated with risk-taking behaviour (Crawford *et al.* 2003; Chambers and Potenza 2003; Vitaro *et al.* 2001). Peer involvement in both the 'co-rumination' about negative aspects of one's life (Caselman and Self 2007; Parker *et al.* 2005; Rose 2002; Rose and Rudolph 2006; Rose *et al.* 2007) and in risk taking (Henry *et al.* 2007) may be influential and dangerous.

6.4 Adolescent alcohol abuse

Enoch (2006) reviews alcohol abuse and resilience in adolescents. Adolescent alcohol misuse is a major factor in teen car crashes, homicides, and suicides, and is highly likely to have significant effects even on those who do not come to such extreme and abrupt ends – it is a factor in suffering sexual assaults, in unplanned pregnancy and sexually transmitted diseases, in serious health problems, in long-term physical damage. 'Binge-drinking' by adolescents and young adults makes the areas around pubs and clubs thoroughly unpleasant at the times when their customers emerge. Alcohol abuse is not illegal, but it does have serious social consequences.

The reasons for individual differences in alcohol use and its consequences are known to operate on many different levels. Twin studies suggest that up to half of population variance in use of alcohol (and other addictive substances) is heritable (Enoch 2006). Vulnerability to alcoholism appears to be due in part to the interaction of a large number of gene effects, involving different patterns of neurotransmitters and different neural structures and systems. Genetic effects may well interact with environment, too; recent studies have demonstrated that genetic effects, leading to differences in availability in the central nervous system of the neurotransmitters serotonin, dopamine, and norepinephrine, interact with childhood environmental factors to predict alcoholism and associated psychopathology (Enoch 2006; Gillespie *et al.* 2005; Kaufman *et al.* 2006; Kendler *et al.* 2005; Willis-Owen *et al.* 2005).

Individuals from some ethnic backgrounds have a genetically caused reaction to alcohol that makes it more unpleasant for them, and these individuals are likely to use alcohol much less than those who find its effects pleasant (Enoch 2006). Environmental influences, including parental attitudes, peer pressure and the availability of alcohol, strongly predict if and when a child starts to drink, and adolescents who drink alcohol from a young age or frequently or in large amounts are at more risk of alcoholism and alcohol-related damage to their bodies (Bonomo *et al.* 2004; Grant and Dawson 1998). There are, in particular, effects of alcohol on brain development and functioning that may be especially important during the brain development of adolescence; these include differences in dopamine (which is implicated in the rewarding effects of alcohol) and gamma-aminobutyric acid (GABA), which is implicated in alcohol's sedating effects (De Bellis *et al.* 2000; Schuckit 1994). The relative immaturity of adolescents' brains (pp. 155–62) may make them more vulnerable to addiction to alcohol.

Psychosocial stresses may also contribute to adolescents' alcohol use (pp. 140–267). Many factors such as experience of sexual abuse in childhood, exposure to maternal depression, antisocial behaviour, and teacher-rated conduct problems are associated with increased risk of alcoholism (Enoch 2006; Kim-Cohen *et al.* 2005). Good parent–child relationships, close parental monitoring, higher socio-economic status, and higher educational aspiration all appear to protect against heavy drinking in adolescence, and parents' mental health and family interaction strongly influence the adolescent's own mental health (Cicchetti 2002; Cicchetti and Blender 2006, pp. 267–70). Brook *et al.* (2007) find this sort of pattern in the cities of Colombia, and Zhou *et al.* (2008) in Beijing.

6.5 Helping where social development is going badly

I have been discussing ways in which children's development as social persons can go badly. I hope that this discussion has illustrated how complex both healthy and less healthy development are, how multifaceted and multilayered. The complexity of social development implies that interventions intended to improve individuals' lives and life chances will be complex too. It is unlikely that an intervention will cure all the problems of everybody who experiences it; similarly some interventions may work very well for some individuals and not so well, or even badly, for others. I have already discussed a range of interventions designed to help with parenting, or early education, or difficulties in social functioning. I turn now to the major social intervention of adoption.

6.5.1 Adoption

Some children who are not receiving adequate care from their biological families, are removed from them and adopted into new families who take over parental rights and responsibilities. In most Western societies, adoption for the child's benefit is one of the most complete and radical interventions ever made in children's lives. It transgresses against certain deeply held social beliefs about the importance of bloodlines and of early relationships; there are dubious examples of international adoption which could be viewed as trafficking in children; but it is also an example of 'the kindness of strangers', of a commitment to help a child extending to the deepest emotional levels and to comprehensive sharing of resources. We would expect that it may have a deep impact on children's lives (Harris 2006; Holloway 2006). If it is looked at as a social intervention, what effects does it have?

Broadly, the answer is comparatively well documented. Most large-scale studies (for a meta-analysis see van IJzendoorn and Juffer 2006) show that adoption is generally associated with rather successful outcomes for the adopted child. This is despite the fact that for most adopted children in the West their pre-adoption lives were characterised by difficulties, deprivation and damage, often throughout the developmental periods during which long-lasting effects are laid down, and for some children their difficult early years have led to developmental delays at the time when they are adopted. The general pattern seems to be that for many areas of development, if the child showed delays or difficulties before adoption, after adoption there is a substantial and sometimes rapid catch-up to normal developmental levels. Institutionally reared children for example show a 'massive' catch-up in physical and psychological growth after adoption (Rutter et al. 2007; van IJzendoorn and Juffer 2006) to reach completely normal heights if adopted in infancy and early childhood, and almost normal heights even for those adopted in adolescence after years of deprivation, although some deficits in head size may remain. Language deficits after adoption seem to be concentrated mostly in those children who were very much language delayed at adoption, possibly an index of something having gone badly wrong in the earliest stages of development (Croft et al. 2007). Cognitive deficits, marked in institutionally reared children (Rutter et al. 2007), are also often reduced to little or nothing a couple of years after adoption, particularly where the adopted children are reared in more cognitively stimulating environments than their family of origin provided. Self-esteem, although there are fewer studies and it is harder to measure, seems to be little different from non-adopted children (van IJzendoorn and Juffer 2006). The picture is not quite so good in other social and emotional areas, but there is still enormous improvement. Most adopted children develop more secure attachment relationships with their adoptive parents than they had been able to develop while in institutional care, or with disorganised, abusive, or unresponsive birth parents, but they are still more at risk of insecure attachments than non-adopted children are. The rate of behaviour problems, both inter-nalising and externalising, is a little higher among adopted children than non-adopted ones, and the rate of referral to mental health services is markedly higher; but for all such problems the rate is much lower than for institution-reared children or those living with dysfunctional families of origin. Interestingly, internationally adopted children had lower rates of behavioural difficulties than within-country adopted children, although issues about intake and type of adoptive families as well as earlier experi-ences need to be examined here. For all adopted children, the worse their pre-adoption experiences were, and especially if they lasted for more than a few months, the more they appear to be at risk of worse outcomes after adoption (van IJzendoorn and Juffer 2006; Kreppner et al. 2007; Rutter et al. 2007).

These findings suggest that adoption is an intervention with a very high success rate. Nevertheless, some adopted children do have problems. They may be vulnerable because pre-adoption bad experiences caused damage that cannot be altogether rectified – brain growth or subtly different neuroendocrine fine-tuning, for example. What complicates this interpreta-tion is that those with responsibility for adopted children may behave a little differently from birth parents when they begin to believe the child may have problems. They may refer an adopted child for help at a milder level of problem behaviour because they believe both that the child's early life has created a risk that needs to be addressed before it does substantial damage; and that by early referral of problems they may be protecting the child against ill effects which would have worsened without specialist care.

It must also be remembered that being part of a group that is generally doing rather well, considering earlier difficulties, does not mean that the pre-adoption phase is over or no longer important. The original biological relationship continues to have emotional importance for substantial num-bers of adopted children, and for their birth parents. The child's tempera-ment and attachment may affect how well they settle into their adoptive family (Vorria et al. 2006). And there are major ethical dilemmas for those considering whether adoption is the appropriate intervention, as they try to balance the interests of the child, its birth parents, any sibs who are not adopted, and the eventual adoptive families.

> Adoption is an experience that probably carries some risks (albeit small ones) that stem from it being atypical in all societies. If children who are adopted come from a low-risk background, there are no particular advantages to being adopted. By sharp contrast, however, for children who have been exposed in early life to parental abuse or neglect, adoption can be highly advantageous.
>
> (Rutter 2007b: 7)

Adoption may be a highly successful intervention; but interventions that support the family of origin (or the institution (McCall *et al.* 2008)) so that it can provide the child with good parenting, and ensuring that all children in society enjoy good resources for all aspects of their development, may raise fewer ethical difficulties.

I should note that societies differ in their views of adoption (Montgomery 2009). Some societies prefer 'a clean break' between the child and the family of origin, whereas others forbid adoption that transfers an individual out of all ties with, and obligations to, his or her family of birth, and into a replacement family and new identity. Where children need to be brought up outside their family of origin, arrangements often involve fostering; the child does not change name, does not lose the right to inherit from the birth parents or gain the right to inherit from the foster parents, and has duties and obligations to both families. Often this is done within the extended family so that richer members of the family can give the children of their poorer siblings and cousins a better education or other life chance than the child's own parents can provide. This sort of arrangement may shade into a formal adoption whose purpose is mainly to 'buy in' an heir for the adopting parents (one of Jane Austen's brothers was adopted by a rich and childless aunt and uncle, took their name and inherited their riches – but continued to help his elderly mother and his unmarried sisters financially to the ends of their lives). Or it may be part of a general cultural view that all adults in the group share the responsibility of bringing up the children of the group – 'It takes a village to raise a child'. Experience of living with a foster parent rather than the birth parent may be seen as 'good for' the child because the foster parent is less likely to 'spoil' the child or because it extends the range of social ties and affiliations that the child can call on. Sometimes, however, the foster child is regarded as a worker for the foster family rather than a full member, and the relationship can be harshly exploitative; or the child's role may be to become the caregiver to an elderly family member who has no children to take on that role.

6.6 Resilience

We all encounter all sorts of difficulties and dangers, at different times, in different ways, in different amounts. Difficulties and dangers are followed by different outcomes for different individuals; it is a common observation that there are tremendous individual differences in people's responses to all kinds of hazardous experience or circumstance. Some people's lives are substantially changed or damaged by their experience of a risky or negative event; others seem to survive unscathed by the most painful adversity. These people, who turn out well despite difficulties that would normally be expected to throw their development or their mental health into pathological pathways, are commonly said to show 'resilience'.

It is important to recognise that 'resilience' is not simply a characteristic of an individual. Conceptually, it is concerned with the *combination* of serious risk experiences and a relatively positive psychological outcome despite those experiences. If you encounter serious risk experiences and subsequently show serious damage, you have not shown resilience; if you never encounter serious risk then you have not shown resilience either. There are obviously issues about generalising from how someone coped with a particular life history of risk to how they might have coped with another, and also about whether resilience in the short term and resilience in the long term are the same.

But, broadly, it does seem that people exposed to serious risk come out with different degrees of ill effects. Thus, for example, many children who have suffered serious abuse at the hands of their parents nevertheless grow up to be normal, stable, caring parents themselves (Bifulco and Moran 1998; Corby 2000). Some individuals whose families suffered major financial problems during the Depression of the early 1930s became confident, high-achieving adults whereas others were more anxious, underachieving and unsuccessful (Elder 1974; Elder *et al.* 1993). Some child refugees and asylum seekers have lower levels of post-traumatic stress disorder (PTSD) than others suffer from (e.g. Charuvastra and Cloitre 2008; Fazel *et al.* 2005; Thabet, Abed and Vostanis 2004; Hodes *et al.* 2008). Such variations are of interest on a number of levels. They could help to clarify how development occurs, by identifying both vulnerability factors and protective factors within the individual, or in the microsystems or other contexts that they inhabit, which shift development in better or worse directions. This can lead to identifying the mechanisms or processes that might underlie the associations found between vulnerability or resilience on the one hand and developmental outcomes on the other, and thus to understanding what interventions might modify the negative effects of adverse life circumstances (Carver and Connor-Smith 2010; Cicchetti and Curtis 2007; Cicchetti, Rogosch and Sturge-Apple 2007; Curtis and Cicchetti 2007; Luthar, Sawyer and Brown 2006; Luthar and Brown 2007; Luther, Cicchetti and Becker 2000; McAdams and Olson 2010; Masten and Obradovic 2006; Mills-Koonce *et al.* 2007; Nobile *et al.* 2007; Sameroff and Rosenblum 2006; Schoon 2006; Thapar *et al.* 2007c), an important thing to understand if we are committed to being effective in helping people live and develop well.

The picture is going to be something like this (I will expand on these summary points in the following sections). Resilience is multidimensional, and can involve many different aspects of the individual and many different psychological processes. It is also developmental in nature. What is important about being resilient may differ between particular age periods, as different developmental periods have different developmental tasks: but success in each set of age-related tasks may forecast success in future age-related tasks, even in new domains. Competence and problems are related within and across time for multiple reasons, including: the current problems undermining current competence; failures (or perceived failures) in competence increasing subsequent problems via people's views of their history; failures in competence meaning missed opportunities, which are not available later; and combinations of these reasons. Success or failure in multiple developmental task domains at the same time can have cascading consequences that lead to problems in further domains of adaptation, both internal and external. Interventions to promote success in age-salient developmental tasks have preventive effects on behavioural and emotional problems.

6.6.1 Defining risk, vulnerability, protection, sensitisation, steeling, and resilience

So understanding resilience is obviously an important and exciting enterprise. However, it is not a simple one. Some definitional work needs to be done before we can progress.

When we talk about a 'risk factor', we mean something that makes an experience likely to damage the individual, or something which is statistically predictive of a poor outcome. Obviously in the case of factors that are statistically predictive, we need to clarify how the 'risk factor' leads to the damage; less obviously, we need to try to be specific about this even if the 'risk factor' causes obvious harm. A 'vulnerability factor' is something about an individual that makes damage more likely or more significant, or, again, is statistically predictive of a poor outcome. The term 'protective factor' refers to something that modifies the effects of normally adverse experiences in a positive direction, probably something that is helpful or beneficial, or is statistically predictive of a good outcome. These could be within the individual, for example personality (Carver and Connor-Smith 2010) or outside the individual (for example social support networks, pp. 91–92, 253), or a combination of inside and outside factors (Eby, Maher and Butts 2010). Sometimes 'protective factors' and 'vulnerability factors' lie on the same dimension; for example there is fairly consistent evidence that over many adverse circumstances higher IQ is associated with better outcomes, and lower IQ is associated with vulnerability (Luthar and Brown 2007). However, risk protective or vulnerability factors are not necessarily dimensional, by which I mean that a higher 'dose' has a stronger effect than a moderate dose, and a low dose less than either. In some cases there may be a level of a characteristic that appears to be sufficient for an individual to be able to resist adversity; although the individual below that level is very much at risk, how far he or she is above this threshold does not predict how much or how little damage they suffer. For example, Luthar and her colleagues (Luthar 1999; Luthar and Sexton 2007; Luthar and Brown 2007) found positive links between maternal warmth and child competence in studies of children of mothers with major mental illness or habitual drug abuse. However, the reason for this result was that children who experienced very low levels of maternal warmth were especially likely to end up with particularly low levels of competence; children whose mothers showed average and high levels of warmth were about equally competent. It was not so much that high warmth and closeness were particularly good for the development of competence (although they might well have been good things in themselves): rather, low closeness between mother and child was associated with a significant vulnerability for poorer development (pp. 130–33, 142–43). Similarly, sometimes people who have not encountered a particular risk at all may be, if anything, less well off than people who have encountered and survived a low level of the risk, a 'steeling' effect (Rutter 2006). Infants who have experienced separations from their mothers that were well-managed pleasant experiences in themselves may cope better with less desirable separations than infants whose mothers have always been very near them (pp. 121–26). People who were children during the American Great Depression, but old enough to be constructively involved in coping with sudden family poverty, were better able to cope with later adverse events than people who had been preschool children at the time, and not able to help their families (Elder 1974; Elder et al. 1993, pp. 252–53).

We do not know how often there is a 'steeling effect', nor how it comes about. Some experiences of risk and danger lead, on the contrary, to a sensitisation to the danger – proverbially 'the burned child fears the fire'. Possibly what makes the difference is that for a steeling effect to occur, the person needs to know that they have successfully coped with the challenge, and could therefore have some expectation that they could if necessary cope again (pp. 88–90). The mechanisms could involve how one understands the danger, a sense of self-efficacy, having effective coping strategies, and psychological and physiological habituation. All these are issues discussed in their own right elsewhere in this book.

It is also worth noting that most people who encounter a low rate of risk factors turn out reasonably well. Cases of low risk and poor adaptation are not common; there are only a few individuals whose development goes badly wrong without there being some detectable risk factor (although we need to think carefully about the pitfalls of retrospective evidence in such cases, as it is of course sometimes easier to identify what went wrong after things have turned out badly than when all still seems to be fine). There are also many cases of high risk and good adaptation, people who face challenge but cope well – 'resiliently'. Nevertheless, clearly too many individuals emerge from adverse experiences with damage that may impair their functioning thereafter, and we need to know what processes and circumstances have been involved.

6.6.2 Unpacking factors in resilience

It is obviously going to be useful to unpack the processes involved in risk, vulnerability, and protective factors. For example, there is evidence that maternal warmth contributes to resilience (pp. 142–43, 238); but what exactly is it about maternal warmth that helps development? A stress system that is better modulated, so that the individual can manage emotional arousal? A sense of security, or a positive attachment, or high self-esteem, so that the individual can accept challenges and develop ways to act on them effectively? Better access to mother to learn from her or call on her support? Any or all of these might be good things developmentally, but possibly they would operate in different ways. What complicates analyses is that risk factors tend to coalesce or co-exist. There is an abundance of evidence that much of the variation in psychopathological outcomes can be accounted for by the *accumulating* effects of risk and protective factors, with single factors making small contributions but co-occurring factors ratchetting up big effects (e.g. Burchinal 2008; Burchinal, Vernon-Feagans and Cox 2008; Bradley *et al.* 2001; Bradley and Corwyn 2002). An excellent example is the body of work on delinquency (pp. 233–34, 264–67). A classic study of London boys by West (1982) identified five 'key' risk factors: coming from a low-income family; coming from a large-sized family; having parents whom social workers considered to be inadequate parents; having below average intelligence; and having a parent with a criminal record. Risk of delinquency increased between people with one risk factor and people with two, between people with two risk factors and people with three, between people with three and people with four, such that almost everyone with five risk factors was a persistent delinquent. No single risk factor seemed to be very much stronger than any other, but as they mounted up very few boys subject to multiple risks were able to escape unscathed.

West (1982) made a special study of the few individuals who, despite serious multiple risks, had no criminal convictions in order to discover how it was that they 'had managed to avoid becoming delinquent'. Depressingly, it turned out that there were rather serious limits to the 'resilience' of this group. Some had committed offences without showing up in offical records, that is they were in fact delinquent; most were chronically unemployed or in ill-paid low-status jobs; their housing conditions, social networks and emotional relationships were very poor. West reports on an interview with one young man who had a life history continuing to age twenty-three of all the main risk factors and was currently living with an aged and mentally disturbed mother with virtually no social contacts. 'Asked about offences he replied pathetically: "I can't get into trouble, I never go out"' (West 1982: 95–96).

This case study illustrates the importance of careful attention to outcome measures but also the point that, as I said, risk factors tend to co-occur (Rutter 1987). Educational failure, family discord, continuous unemployment, and very poor housing are not independent of each other. As Bronfenbrenner argued (pp. 6–18) development is often overdetermined. It is likely to be a complex matter to sort out which apparent 'risk factors' or 'protective factors' have an independent effect and which are only powerful in combination with others. For example, maternal drug use often co-occurs with maternal depression, maternal anxiety, maternal lack of social and emotional support, poorer financial and housing conditions, and family stress (Luthar 1999; Luthar and Brown 2007; Luthar and Sexton 2007). Truancy and delinquency often co-occur with a similarly complex list of factors. It is easy to think that the drug abuse is the cause of the children's problems and the fault of the mother, or that delinquency and truancy are caused by children's laziness or by uncaring parents, and to pay less attention to the co-occurring risks and vulnerabilities. Simplistic analyses such as this can stigmatise people unfairly, and can direct interventions in unhelpful, ineffective or even counterproductive ways. They can also lead to us not noticing levels of particular risk behaviours in settings where multiple general risk is thought to be low. Luthar and her colleagues (Luthar and Becker 2002; Luthar and Brown 2007; Luthar and Latendresse 2005; Luthar, Sawyer and Brown 2006) suggest that there are actually higher use of drugs and alcohol, and higher rates of rule breaking, amongst affluent American suburban adolescents than among American adolescents living in poverty. Examination of what risks this behaviour is associated with in the comparatively affluent may help us to understand how it is risky to the poor; and vice versa. That is, we need to look at within-group effects as well as population-wide effects, and to consider interactions and especially synergies between variables. One risk factor may amplify the effect of another, so that both together are more than twice as bad as each singly.

6.6.3 Assessing outcomes

We can also see from studies such as West (1982) that we have to be careful about apparent resilience, as it might be a function not only of variations in risk exposure but also of issues to do with measuring outcomes. Resilience can only be studied effectively when there is evidence of risk, a good measure of the degree of risk, and an adequate range of outcome measures. Apparent resilience might be a consequence of not measuring a wide enough range of outcomes, and so missing some adverse ones. There are all too many examples of research that measures the intended benefits of a drug or an intervention, but not all its 'side-effects' and costs.

We need to consider the types of outcomes that we look at (Moffitt 2005). Outcomes involved in studies of children's resilience most commonly include the degree to which they meet society's expectations in age-related tasks such as educational success, moving into the job market, avoiding delinquency, and so forth, assessed by reports from their teachers, their classmates, and their parents. Outcomes such as accounts of people's feelings are more often used in studies of adults than in studies of children. Luthar, Sawyer and Brown (2006) argue that a wider range of outcomes should be used with both children and adults, and also that the most interesting risk variables to look at are those that can be affected by interventions, that are salient in the risk context, that are enduring in that they affect children for long periods, and that produce a cascading effect, deepening disaster or ratcheting individuals out of risk.

Much research on resilience has focused on psychosocial and economic or environmental factors, such as access to education. These are often salient, amenable to intervention, and produce cascading effects; they will be discussed later. But factors seen at a more biological level may also have these characteristics (Cicchetti and Blender 2006; Hofer 2006a, 2006b), as well as underlying and being affected by the social, economic and personal. Hence we need interdisciplinary research that considers genetic, neuro-chemical, psychological, interpersonal and environmental processes and looks at both the pathways to poor outcomes and the pathways to resilience. We have to recognise that there are multiple levels of processes operating all the time, and limits on our understanding of any one level may seriously impair our understanding of other levels, whereas improvements in understanding one level may help to clarify what is going on at another.

So this is an area where what we want is multifactor studies that can look at both whole populations and more narrowly defined groups and at a range of outcomes of very different sorts. We want to identify lists of risk factors, vulnerability factors, and protective factors but also to go beyond them, both to understanding in detail how they work and to designing and implementing measures that will decrease risk and vulnerability and improve protection and good outcomes. Various levels of theory may inform us about what 'resilience' means. Looking carefully at resilience, recognising the huge individual variation in people's responses to the same experiences, should help us considerably in understanding the whole richness and complexity of development.

6.6.4 Evolution and resilience

Over millennia, species have adapted to the challenges that their environments provide. Individuals have to survive and reproduce, at least, with their own offspring doing the same in the next generation, if their evolutionary lineage is to continue (pp. 18–25). Thus, one of the factors in evolutionary development is the capacity of individuals in each generation to adapt to environmental pressures and change – that is to show 'resilience' to a range of environmental conditions (Cicchetti and Blender 2006; Hofer 2006a, 2006b). Individual development, as a result of organised patterns of genetic programmes and gene regulation orchestrated by events inside and outside the individual organism, will result in better or worse adaptation to the demands of the environment, and this will be central to the individual's success in reproducing and rearing offspring to their own reproductive stage. The development of the species will have involved development of the capacity to generate different developmental courses that are suited to the range of conditions that have been experienced so far. These will, historically, have included some extremely adverse conditions – famine, floods, extreme heat and extreme cold, war, social chaos, etc., as well as the milder adversities which are more commonly experienced. We are certainly not born with easy ways of adapting to extreme adversity, nor with knowledge of how to cope with the challenges that our ancestors faced, nor with an easy resistance to the new stresses that occur, but differences in our resilience are part of the evolutionary process. And diferent ways of being 'resilient' may be more effective against some challenges than others. Evolution should have left us with some of the coping techniques that succeeded for our ancestors, and some scope to develop new ones for new environmental challenges.

6.6.5 Brains and resilience

Brains 'expect' to be fine-tuned by their experience during development and into adult life (Meadows 2006; Greenough, Black and Wallace 1987). Possibly, the nature of the fine-tuning is affected by the child's experience, and there might be a component to 'resilience' at brain level. Some brains might be more able to recover from trauma or adversity than others are; some might be less susceptible to damage in the first place (Cicchetti and Blender 2006). There might possibly be measurable differences in brain structure and function between children who have experienced the same amount of adversity and shown themselves to be 'resilient' or not. Possibly the functioning and processes that lead to resilience use different brain areas or neurotransmitters from the functioning that does not. At a behavioural level, we are identifying psychological processes that help or hinder recovery and developing appropriate therapies (cognitive–behaviour therapy, for example, is an interesting prospect for treating depression

(Butler 2006)), so it would be of great interest to know what is going on at the brain level. It would also be of great interest to know about the reversibility of the effects of adversity on brains (Frewen, Dozois and Lanius 2008), whether there are 'sensitive periods' at which damage is more likely, whether there are 'sensitive periods' at which remediation is more effective. Even when we are thinking about interventions, considerations of brains and neuroscience may be extremely relevant, as in studies by Greenberg (2006) and Dishion and Connell (2006) of interventions to enhance resilience by improving executive control.

Recent research on brain development shows that there are significant changes in the brain during adolescence (Blakemore and Choudhury 2006; Dahl 2004; Romeo and McEwen 2006). We also find that rates of such psychological disorders as anxiety and depression, and of antisocial behaviour, increase rapidly at puberty (Rutter and Smith 1995). As we have seen (pp. 72–74) adolescence is commonly thought of as a period of stress ('sturm und drang') by theorists, parents, the media, and adolescents themselves, and we know that stress during childhood and adolescence can predict susceptibility to anxiety and depression in adulthood (Brown and Harris 1978; Turner and Lloyd 2004; Hankin, Mermelstein and Roesch 2007). Stressors in adulthood, and presumably earlier, can lead to the onset and exacerbation of psychological disorders and to changes in the structure and function of the brain (Romeo and McEwen 2006, pp. 195, 268). A combination of normal developmental change plus stress-induced alterations in the nervous system of the adolescent might contribute to vulnerability to the development of psychopathologies during adolescence.

Exactly what is happening in the brain during adolescence remains to be determined. However, it seems likely that several areas of the brain are affected (Romeo and McEwen 2006). The forebrain and other neurological structures that contribute to judgement and behavioural inhibition are not yet mature, which may put adolescents at risk of making impulsive bad decisions. The hippocampus, which is vitally important for learning and memory, continues to develop well into adolescence and animal studies show that stress affects the volume of connections between its nerve cells, possibly with consequences for memory. Stressful experiences for adolescent and adult rats produce changes in the connectivity and volume of neurones in this brain region, which is crucial for the regulation of emotional behaviours. Stress also affects the amygdala, which plays a central role in emotional memory and fear conditioning, and these changes are associated with high levels of anxious behaviour which do not reverse themselves over time. Some of these changes appear to be long lasting, even permanent, although others are reversible.

Thus adolescence is a time of profound changes in an individual's nervous system, physiology, and behaviour. Although this may make adolescents especially vulnerable to harm, it may also allow for interventions to improve the brain functioning damaged by earlier emotional or physical stress (Andersen 2003). Romeo and McEwen (2006) describe a study where pre-pubertal male animals were operated on to produce a brain lesion that if suffered by adults would irreversibly damage their mating behaviour. Some of the young animals were housed alone and some in groups; the latter showed no effect of the brain damage, suggesting that the quality of the social environment can diminish or even prevent the effects of brain damage. Other research (e.g. Morley-Fletcher 2003; Laviola 2004) suggests that animals suffer deficits in behaviour (high emotional reactivity, anxiety and depression) associated with their mothers being stressed during their gestation, but that being raised in an enriched environment rather than the usual bare laboratory cage substantially reduces these problem behaviours.

6.6.6 Self-regulation and resilience

One core factor in resilience, as in several other topics I have addressed in this book, is self-regulation (pp. 55, 93, 120–21). People whose behaviour is very low on self-regulation are less likely to show resilience in the face of adversity. Self-regulation of emotion, cognition and action may be a key part of developing a set of responses to stress that prevent it from being an overly damaging experience. Appraisal of a stressful situation, judgement of its emotional meaning, and regulation of emotions and arousal so that they do not impede problem-solving behaviour, will all be useful components of positive coping responses, and hence contribute to resilience. Being better at self-regulation, at focusing on the task in hand, and at shifting tactics flexibly if necessary, are all associated with greater resilience (Wachs 2006; Lengua 2002; Lengua and Sandler 1996; Lengua et al. 1999; Ruschena et al. 2005; Wills 2001). Research by Dishion and his colleagues (Dishion et al. 1999; Dishion and Connell 2006) on American adolescents found that those who were showing antisocial behaviour at eleven showed less self-regulation than those whose antisocial behaviour emerged later, and that those who never showed antisocial behaviour had the highest levels of self-regulation. Level of self-regulation predicted delinquent behaviour, as did a history of antisocial behaviour in individuals and in their peer group; these last two factors were more powerful with the individuals who had poor self-regulation than they were with individuals who were quite good or very good at regulating themselves. Zhou et al. (2008) found similar results in Beijing children, and Brook et al. (2007) in Colombia (with drug use in the family being an additional powerful factor). Individuals with poor self-regulation were more likely to be stressed and depressed (Dishion et al. 1999; Dishion and Connell 2006). Finally, experience of parenting and opportunities to meet and rise to challenge are associated with later self-regulation and resilience (Bradley et al. 2001; Bradley and Corwyn 2005; Burchinal 2008; pp. 66, 133, 120–21).

6.6.7 Executive control and resilience

Constructs such as 'executive control', 'planfulness' etc. appear rather frequently in studies of resilience and damage by adversity. For example in a classic study of girls who had been 'in care' (Quinton and Rutter 1988) a substantial proportion of girls with poor outcomes had showed little ability to plan how their lives would go, whereas girls who had planned were much more likely to turn out well. Poor impulse control is one of the risk factors for delinquency (pp. 265–66). Poorly functioning individuals suffering from psychological and social damage may show difficulties with regulating their emotions and their displays of emotion, with inhibiting risky or inappropriate behaviour, with orienting themselves towards the future rather than the immediate present, with thinking about consequences, and with the planning, initiation, and regulation of goal-directed behaviour. These consciously controlled behaviours or 'executive functions' are seen as being dependent on the functioning of the prefrontal cortex (Greenberg 2006) and connected areas, at least in adults; these are areas that are still maturing at adolescence, and which may be associated with the emotional volatility and waywardness that adolescents often show (pp. 195, 268).

The obvious causal pathway from self-regulation and executive control to resilience is differences in coping strategies; children who are persistent and task focused, and able to cope with the emotional arousal caused by struggling, are more likely to work through to a satisfactory solution and to see themselves as efficaceous (Bandura 1997; Dweck 1999; Dweck and Elliot 1983) than children who have difficulty in focusing and persisting, and give up easily. Dweck suggests a role for parents' feedback in convincing people that they can persist and improve, or that effort is futile, and this might perhaps interact with initial temperament differences (Ricco and Rodriguez 2006). This sort of feedback from parents and teachers was identified as a contributor to the underperformance of girls in maths and science and changing it in schools was one of the instigators of significant improvements in whether girls persisted with the traditionally 'masculine' subjects. Children who are highly impulsive and do not reflect on their experience may suffer more adverse events such as physical injuries (Matheny 1986) and be more at risk of substance abuse (Wachs 2006; Enoch 2006; pp. 265–71).

Obviously it is possible to teach people to plan more and act on impulse less. Parents do this all the time with their children; teachers with their pupils. Greenberg (2006) describes an intervention programme that encouraged participants to practise conscious control of problem-solving processes and to regulate their emotions and their social interaction with more explicit language and discussion. Children who engaged with the programme showed decreases in behaviour problems and increases in social and emotional competence. The curriculum was intended to promote inhibitory control and emotion regulation, and Greenberg believes that the changes in behaviour were due to changes measurable, although not actually measured, at the level of brain functioning. Although resilient people have often engaged in planful activity, and people who plan appear to be more resilient, there are issues about causation and about how much 'planfulness' is a good thing. The disadvantages of never being planful or controlled are fairly obvious, as I have just argued; but it may be possible to be too planful, if it edges into rumination and excessive intrapunitiveness. Being able to 'let go' and 'play' is a potent part of creativity and 'flow' (Csikzsentmihalyi and Csikzsentmihalyi 1988; Csikzsentmihalyi and Larson 1984).

6.6.8 Temperament and resilience

I would continue to emphasise that resilience is not a characteristic of individuals that can be used or measured independent of circumstances, rather it is an interactive concept that is concerned with the combination of serious risk experiences and a relatively positive psychological outcome despite those experiences (Rutter 2006). Nevertheless, it is possible firstly that resilient children share particular individual characteristics, and secondly that these shared personality characteristics contribute to their ability to show resilience. Temperament (pp. 64–65) may be one domain of individual characteristics that contribute to individual differences in resilience in children faced with stresses such as living in poverty, major life events, family conflict and divorce, parent substance abuse and mental health problems, peers with problems, and exposure to violence.

Some discussions involve temperament dimensions aggregated into 'easy' and 'difficult' temperament, and the evidence is that 'easy' temperament children consistently tend to have fewer behaviour problems, higher social competence and better adapted behaviour than children with 'difficult' temperaments (Smith and Prior 1995; Tschann et al. 1996; Rothbart and Bates 2006). However, rather than using this simple categorisation of temperament it might be helpful to examine individual temperament dimensions to get a better explanatory grasp of how resilience comes about.

6.6.8.1 Temperament dimensions associated with different outcomes: Positive emotionality, approach and sociability

Children whose assessed temperament shows positive emotions in response to minor life events show more resilience than those whose overall emotional tone is negative, when faced with stresses like substance use (Wills 2001) and family stress and breakdown (Lengua et al. 1999; Lengua 2002). Children whose characteristic temperament shows a positive sociable approach to new situations show lower levels of behaviour problems and higher levels of social competence and emotional adjustment than children whose temperament is low on approach and sociability, following family transitions (Lengua and Sandler 1996; Ruschena *et al.* 2005), in response to financial adversity (Kim-Cohen *et al.* 2004), and in avoiding conduct disorder (Losel and Bliesener 1994; Zhou *et al.* 2008). In all these studies, children with a more open and optimistic outlook were more likely to show resilience than the more pessimistic child. (We probably all know individuals who seem to expect the worst and then get it as expected, with every reaction being one of deep-dyed pessimism – Eeyore in the Winnie the Pooh books is a classic example. In some cultures, however, expecting the worst and then having a good moan about it might be an acceptable coping strategy. There may be some cultural limitations to the evidence that I have just summarised – most of it comes from studies conducted in the USA.)

How does the association between a positive outlook and resilience come about? In a multiplicity of ways, but among these there are several that are of interest. It has been argued that children who are high on negative emotionality or difficult temperament tend to get decreasing involvement with their parents compared with children whose behaviour is more smiley and sociable, which might mean that they get less parental support when a challenge comes along (e.g. Gallagher 2002; Valiente *et al.* 2004). Parents of children who are shy and inhibited may be protective rather than trying to promote their child's independence, which might increase the child's initial tendencies to be cautious and inhibited and decrease the likelihood that the child will become involved with and learn from more boisterous peers, and so be steeled against minor social stresses (Wachs 2006; Rubin 1999; Rubin, Cheah and Fox 2001; Rubin *et al.* 2003; pp. 95–100). Children high in negative emotionality may have stronger reactions to stress and negative events than more emotionally positive children (Belsky, Hseih and Crnic 1998; Lengua *et al.* 1999; Morris *et al.* 2002; Pluess and Belsky 2009; Zhou *et al.* 2008), and different sensitivities to reward and punishment (Colder *et al.* 2002; Derryberry 2003). They may be more likely to employ passive avoidant coping strategies that reduce their opportunities to develop positive solutions to the problems they meet (Wachs 2006; Lengua and Sandler 1996; Lengua *et al.* 1999) and less likely to use flexible, active coping strategies; all of which could make them a little more likely to face the next challenge with an anticipation of difficulty and defeat.

Similarly, children who are more socially oriented elicit more positive responses and support from their parents, peers, and other adults than unsociable individuals, which gives them more positive social experiences and more access to help and encouragement when things turn difficult. Children with better self-regulation and more supportive parenting had better cognitive, behavioural, and social outcomes following parental divorce, for example (Hetherington *et al.* 1999; Feinberg, Kan and Hetherington 2007).

6.6.8.2 Intelligence, mastery and resilience

Resilience may be linked to more positive characteristics than risk proneness, for example intelligence and mastery. What 'intelligence' is has been debated extensively and heatedly (for reviews see e.g. Meadows 2006; Mackintosh 1998), and I am not going to rehearse those arguments here. The characteristics of 'intelligent' people are commonly said to include good comprehension, making good decisions, planning well, being able to apply skills and knowledge to solve problems, good determination of how to achieve goals, and so forth. Not surprisingly, given these characteristics, there is a tendency for more 'intelligent' people to show more resilience when faced with difficulties (Bates and Pettit 2007; Wachs 2006).

At least one theory of 'intelligence' has included something that looks very like the cognitive side of resilience as one of the main components of 'intelligence' (Sternberg 1985). In this model, the 'contextual subtheory' of intelligence outlines different ways in which 'intelligence' is used when real everyday problems and dilemmas arise. The basic processes include modifying oneself to cope better with what the context requires, for example by adopting the dominant ideology and trying to live up to it; attempting to change the context to something more suitable to one's present skills; and opting out and escaping to a different, more congenial, context. This is an interesting model but hard to test.

Mastery experiences (pp. 77–78, 87–90, 215–17) seem to be associated with immediate pleasure, with positive emotional states and feelings of satisfaction and relaxation. They involve a perception of oneself as coping with a challenge, and mastery can itself be self-developing – having survived this once, I can survive it again; having done this thing successfully, I could maybe do it even more successfully. And mastery is often public, even something that is publicly celebrated, and thus involved in other people's evaluations of us. These other people may see us as worth helping, because we do not have a history of difficulty which makes them have little hope that their support can make a difference. All these things are likely to feed into the emotional equilibrium, the planning, the sense of effectiveness, and the range of coping strategies that contribute to 'resilience'. Just as our definitions of 'intelligence' need to acknowledge that 'intelligence is largely the result of a socialisation process, and our understanding and assessment of intelligence must seriously take into account the nature of this process' (Sternberg and Suben 1986: 233), the same is true for our understanding and assessment of resilience.

Chapter 7

Reflections

In this book I have examined our understanding of the child as social person, dealing with material describing children's social functioning, examining dimensions of individual differences, looking at theoretical models and causal influences. The work has been heterogeneous. I have had to piece together evidence from varying approaches in a number of different fields, a process which inevitably means some poorly fitting assemblies and yawning gaps, because the factors affecting development as a social person are numerous, varied, complicated, and hard to fit together. The research methods of many studies, although adequate for the work's immediate purposes, are not adequate for the big developmental questions.

> Behavioural research on children, for the most part, is not geared to investigating transactions, encompassing a multiplicity of influences, measuring environment in non-static and developmental terms, addressing developmental questions developmentally, or accounting for individual differences in development . . . [The] discrepancy between conceptual sophistication, on the one hand, and paradigmatic and methodological insufficiencies, on the other, brings an unsettling dis-equilibrium to developmental research.
>
> (Radke-Yarrow 1991: 391–392)

However, as being in 'an unsettling disequilibrium' could be a major spur to the development of understanding, I want to take this potentially depressing summary as a challenge not as a criticism. So, in this final section, I want to begin to suggest some shifts in research paradigm that may help us tackle the not yet answered questions of the field. The choice of 'questions' reflects my own priorities (on the psychology–education–parenting interface) and my own research experience (a shift from assessment within the Piagetian paradigm to direct and extended observation of behaviour in 'real world' contexts to number-crunching analyses based on a nationally representative cohort study). This is a summary restatement of themes that will have emerged from the earlier chapters of this book, and I hope that people reading this section will refer back to relevant material elsewhere.

Children's development occurs in, and has to be examined in, environments. This is so obvious as to be taken for granted, but although we are making progress towards a good analysis and understanding of environments, especially through Bronfenbrenner's model, only a small proportion of researchers really address the complexity of environments. Many studies ignore most environmental factors, or simplify them, or dismiss them as too variable and arbitrary to be studied scientifically. Or studies deal with single variables, such as structural features of environments, which are assumed to affect all individuals equally and so need no direct measurement. Examples, such as studies of the effect of preschool attendance that do not look at the variation in quality within each preschool setting, and the variation of child characteristcs such as temperament, or of the effects of 'social address' variables such as being part of a one-parent family, come to mind. These studies tell us something about differences between group averages but leave the causal variables underexposed. Even if we do identify distal variables that affect children's development, in many cases their effect comes about through proximal variables. Further research looking at variables within groups, or using variables that are good candidates for bringing about causal change directly, will be necessary.

Environments may be assessed by asking the people who live in them to describe or rate them, a method which can produce very interesting rich subjective 'autobiographical' data or self-categorisation into simple categories provided by the researcher. Using predetermined categories may be the only possible method for large-scale studies (which also often use gross distal variables such as SES or family size), but it is no substitute for fine-grained, systematic and extended observation of interaction in the environment. Such observation may be less subjective than self-description by the participants, but it is unlikely to be free of bias, and the presence of the observer may change the interaction. Each method is, necessarily, an indirect and possibly subjectively biased measure of what the proximal processes in the environment really were. Probably the best we can do is triangulate between different methods and different studies, involving ourselves in replications and meta-analyses.

Careful observation needs to be based on a sensible conceptualisation of the environment, and, because it is likely to be time consuming, expensive, and demanding so far as the environments studied are concerned, it would be wise to embark on it informed by the relevant theoretical literature and by the insights as to variables worth study gained from all the relevant disciplines. Because of the 'economic' problems of systematic observation, samples are likely to be small, and the work may verge on case study. Intensive studies of a small number of cases have made significant contributions in psychology. They will be especially useful for answering questions about children who are unusual, for example children whose early social skills are impaired, or who suffer appalling conditions as they grow up, or who do not respond as usual to training or testing. They may include investigation of several different aspects of behaviour, or several different conditions or life events, which have different effects in combination from their influences singly. Longitudinal case studies can pick up irregularities in the pace of development, which are averaged out of view in large samples, but may provide important clues to the processes of developmental change. But case studies are about individuals, and the questions we can ask and answer about individuals are not the same as the questions that we can ask and answer about populations. All individuals could tell many different stories about themselves: different biographers tell different stories about the same individual subject. Biography, memoir, anthropology, sociology, psychology, are all valuable but they may not be easy to combine. We have to be very careful about how we use the evidence that we have, especially when it comes from different traditions and disciplines. However, the same point about interpretation applies within disciplines too, and sometimes we may achieve a better understanding if we 'triangulate' between several imperfect pictures from different sources. In an ideal world, the subjects of case studies would be in a known position relative to the population as a whole, for example being an intensively studied part of a population study (e.g. Pilling 1990; Dunn et al. 1999) or the researchers would have a very sophisticated understanding of the general population as well as detailed understanding of the key individuals (e.g. Quinton and Rutter 1988; West 1982). This level of study helps to clarify what other research methods suggest, and document the complex histories that lead development down different pathways from childhood to adult life.

Longitudinal studies are going to be an essential part of coming to understand social and personal development. They are more expensive (and much slower) than cross-sectional studies, although they do not always need to extend over very long periods. They require a particularly clear conceptualisation of what are 'continuities' and what are 'changes' in behaviour, various precautions to separate the effects of increases in competence with development from increases in familiarity with and confidence in the research situation, and, inconveniently, a scrupulous and sophisticated understanding of the appropriate statistical techniques for examining the effects of multiple variables. The comparatively intense contact between researcher and subject also brings the ethics of research to the foreground as an issue: a one-off session of testing with a child in school may not require much more than the agreement of all interested parties and careful handling of the child's sensitivities by the tester, but getting data about ecologically real behaviour over a long period of time has to be recognised to be a big demand on subjects for, perhaps, little return. Researchers have to be concerned to minimise the costs and maximise the benefits to their subjects. They also have to recognise that their relationship with their subjects will not be a neutral one, and ethical problems may arise for them as researcher and as morally responsible person. What do you do if the child's answers to your questions suggest experience of sexual abuse from a family member, or if the parents ask for advice on the education of their child? Can you withhold advice that would lead to a change in the child's experience that you would rather exclude from your research design?

I am now almost at the end of this discussion of the child as social person, or rather at the place where my discussion stops for the moment, as further discussion is not just possible but essential. I will end by recapitulating points made in various earlier sections.

1 Children live, as we all do, in a world that presents a particular set of physical, social and conceptual problems in a particular range of settings and experiences. What makes for successful functioning depends on the problem and its context. The ways it is appropriate to relate to your partner are not the same as the ways it is appropriate to relate to your boss or your child or even your best friend. 'Good' and 'poor' functioning are, to a considerable extent, situation specific; and culturally specific also. I am reasonably well functioning as a twentieth century middle-class Englishwoman: I would have great difficulties in Afghanistan or medieval Italy or twenty-first century Hackney if I thought I could behave as I usually do now.

2 The point that there are different sorts of good functioning makes untenable the idea of 'development' as a uni-dimensional progress from less advanced to more advanced functioning, for example more 'complex' social functioning. Evolutionary theory makes a similar point (pp. 21–22, 24–25). In general, evolution has led to more complexity only if more complexity leads to a higher degree of reproductive success. Very simple organisms may persist without any change towards complexity for millions of years if they are successful in reproducing in their environments and there is no relevant environmental change to reduce this success. Development may tend towards better success, but what 'success' is will depend on the environmental challenges that the organism meets.

3 As well as there being different sorts of good functioning reached by different paths, different paths or different means may lead to the same end, more or less effectively or efficiently or happily. Almost all individuals manage to relate happily to others some of the time, but they do so in a number of different ways. Their repertoire of social processes is somewhat related to the path to maturity that they have taken, but paths differ and although some are clearly rockier than others none can really be said to be totally 'good' or 'bad'.

4   Given this co-variation of context, performance and development, what may be important about 'complexity' is the availability of a range of alternative strategies and the ability to select between them as appropriate to the particular situation. People whose repertoire of strategies is very limited or inflexible may do very well if they only encounter familiar problems, but much less well if a problem demands a new or modified strategy. This implies that social and emotional processes have to become somewhat independent from the contexts in which they were first developed, to become at least potentially autonomous tools. Moving from being scaffolded by a more expert person to being able to support one's own emotion regulation is an example of this. The process will never be complete, and being a person is always, I repeat, embedded in a context.

5   We have good reason to believe that the social and interpersonal context is a key part of social and personal functioning. I want to include cognition here too (Meadows 2006). It has been argued that human language and cognition evolved to serve social purposes: primates who live in large permanent groups engage in long-term relationships, multi-party interactions and co-operative alliances, which require cognitive complexity and sophisticated social cognition. We have incontrovertible evidence that much of cognitive development in childhood involves the acquisition of culturally specific cognitive skills through culturally specified social interaction: being observer and apprentice to the work skills of your parent, or being taught to read or do calculus in formal schooling. Even in areas independent of adults there will be social components to the cognition as both the 'non-social' task and the 'individual' thinker are related to a wide range of social tasks and understandings.

We all want to understand ourselves and other people; many of us may want to help ourselves and others to be less unhappy, less aggressive, less unconfident, less socially inept; some of us want to change the social world. We may do these things a little better if we understand the ways in which the biological and social bases of being a person interact and shape development over time. I hope I have conveyed some of the excitement and the achievements as well as some of the problems and complexity, and that this book will help further development of work on 'the child as social person'.

Bibliography

Abe, J. A. and Izard, C. (1999). "A longitudinal study of emotion expression and personality relations in early development." *Journal of Personality and Social Psychology* **77**: 566–577.

Abecassis, M., Hartup, W. W. *et al.* (2002). "Mutual antipathies and their significance in middle childhood and adolescence." *Child Development* **73**: 1543–1556.

Aboud, F. E. (2003). "The formation of in-group favoritism and out-group prejudice in young children: Are they distinct attitudes?" *Developmental Psychology* **39**: 48–60.

Ackerman, B. P., Brown, E. D. and Izard, C. E. (2004). "The relations between persistent poverty and contextual risk and children's behaviour in elementary school." *Developmental Psychology* **40**: 367–377.

Ackerman, B., Izard, C. E. *et al.* (2007). "Relation between reading problems and internalizing behavior in school for preadolescent children from economically disadvantaged families." *Child Development* **78**: 581–596.

Adams, A., Harvey, H. and Prince, R. (2005). "Association of maternal smoking with overweight at age 3 years in American Indian children." *American Journal of Clinical Nutrition* **82**: 393–398.

Adolphs, R. (2009). "The social brain: neural basis of social knowledge." *Annual Review of Psychology* **60**: 693–716.

Agatson, P., Kowalski, R. and Limber, S. (2007). "Students' perspectives on cyberbullying." *Journal of Adolescent Health* **41**: S59–S60.

Ainsworth, M., Blehar, M. *et al.* (1978). *Patterns of Attachment: A Psychological Study of the Strange Situation*. Hillsdale, NJ: Erlbaum.

Al Mamun, A., Lawlor, D. A. *et al.* (2006). "Does maternal smoking during pregnancy have a direct effect on future offspring obesity? Evidence from a prospective birth cohort study." *American Journal of Epidemiology* **164**: 317–325.

Alati, R., Macleod, J. *et al.* (2008). "Intrauterine exposure to alcohol and tobacco use and childhood IQ: findings from a parental-offspring comparison within the Avon Longitudinal Study of Parents and Children." *Pediatric Research* **64**: 659–666.

Alcott, L. (1868). *Little Women*. Boston: Roberts Brothers.

Allen, J. P., Moore, C. *et al.* (1998). "Attachment and adolescent psychosocial functioning." *Child Development* **69**: 1406–1419.

Allen, J. P., Porter, M. R. *et al.* (2005). "Two faces of adolescents' success with peers; adolescent popularity, social adaptation, and deviant behavior." *Child Development* **76**: 747–760.

Allen, N., Callan, H. *et al.* (2008). *Early human kinship: from sex to social reproduction.* Oxford: Blackwell.

Allen, S. and Hawkins, A. (1999). "Maternal gatekeeping: mothers' beliefs and behavior that inhibit greater father involvement in family work." *Journal of Marriage and the Family* **61**: 199–212.

Allman, J., Rosin, A. *et al.* (1998). "Parenting and survival in anthropoid primates: caretakers live longer." *Proceedings of the National Academy of Sciences, USA* **95**: 6866–6869.

Amato, P. and Sobolewski, J. (2004). The effects of divorce on fathers and children: nonresidential fathers and stepfathers. In M. Lamb (ed.), *The Role of the Father in Child Development.* Hoboken, NJ: Wiley.

Andersen, S. L. (2003). "Trajectories of brain development: point of vulnerability or window of opportunity." *Neuroscience and Biobehavioral Reviews* **27**: 3–18.

Anderson, C. and Bushman, B. J. (2001). "Effects of violent video games on aggressive behavior, aggressive cognition, aggressive affect, physiological arousal, and prosocial behavior: A metaanalytic review of the scientific literature." *Psychological Science* **12**: 353–359.

Anderson, C. A. and Bushman, B. J. (2002). "Human Aggression." *Annual Review of Psychology* **53**: 27–51.

Anderson, C., Berkowitz, L. *et al.* (2003). "The influence of media violence on youth." *Psychological Science in the Public Interest* **4**: 81–110.

Anderson, D., Huston, A. C. *et al.* (2001). "Early childhood television viewing and adolescent behavior: the recontact study." *Monographs of the Society for Research in Child Development* **66**: 1–147.

Andersson, M. and Simmons, L. W. (2006). "Sexual selection and mate choice." *Trends in Ecology and Evolution* **21**: 296–302.

Angold, A., Costello, E. *et al.* (1999). "Comorbidity." *Journal of Child Psychology and Psychiatry* **40**: 57–87.

Araya, R., Hu, X. *et al.* (2009). "Effects of stressful life events, maternal depression and 5-HTTLPR genotype on emotional symptoms in pre-adolescent children." *American Journal of Medical Genetics Part B (Neuropsychiatric Genetics)* **150B**: 670–682.

Aries, P. (1962). *Centuries of Childhood.* London: Cape.

Arnot, M. and Miles, P. (2005). "A reconstruction of the gender agenda: the contradictory gender dimensions in New Labour's educational and economic policy." *Oxford Review of Education* **31**: 173–189.

Arsenio, W. and Kramer, R. (1992). "Victimizers and their victims: children's conceptions of the mixed emotional consequences of moral transgressions." *Child Development* **63**: 915–927.

Arsenio, W. and Lemerise, E. (2001). "Varieties of childhood bullying: values, emotion processes and social competence." *Social development* **10**: 59–73.

Asher, S. and Paquette, J. (2003). "Loneliness and peer relations in childhood." *Current Directions in Psyhological Science* **12**: 75–78.

Atkins, R. and Hart, D. (2003). "Neighborhoods, adults, and the development of civic identity in urban youth." *Applied Developmental Science* **3**: 156–164.

Attree, P. (2006). "The social costs of child poverty: a systematic review of the qualitative evidence." *Children and Society* **20**: 54–66.

Atwood, M. (1989). *Cat's Eye*. London: Bloomsbury.

Azmitia, M. and Hesser, J. (1993). Why siblings are important agents of cognitive-development – a comparison of siblings and peers. *Child Development* **64**: 430–444.

Bagwell, C. and Coie, J. (2004). "The best friendships of aggressive boys: relationship quality, conflict managment, and rule-breaking behavior." *Journal of Experimental Child Psychology* **88**: 5–24.

Bagwell, C., Newcomb, A., Bukowski, W. M. (1998). "Preadolescent friendship and peer rejection as predictors of adult adjustment." *Child Development* **69**: 140–153.

Baier, C. and Wright, B. (2001). "'If you love me, keep my commandments': a meta-analysis of the effect of religion on crime." *Journal Of Research In Crime And Delinquency* **38**: 3–21.

Baldwin, J. M. (1895). *Mental Development in the Child and Race*. New York: Macmillan.

Baler, R, Volkow, N. D. *et al.* (2008). "Is fetal brain monoamine oxidase inhibition the missing link between maternal smoking and conduct disorder?" *Journal of Psychiatry and Neuroscience* **33**: 187–195.

Ball, S. (2004). *The Routledge/Falmer Reader in Sociology of Education*. London: Routledge.

Ball, S. (2006). *Education Policy and Social Class: The Selected Works of Stephen J. Ball*. London: Routledge.

Banaji, M. and Prentice, D. (1994). "The self in social contexts." *Annual Review of Psychology* **45**: 297–333.

Bandura, A. (1995). *Self-Efficacy in Changing Societies*. New York: Cambridge University Press.

Bandura, A. (1997). *Self-Efficacy: The Exercise of Control*. New York: Freeman.

Bandura, A. (2001). "Self-efficacy beliefs as shapers of children's aspirations and career trajectories." *Child Development* **72**: 187–206.

Bandura, A. and Bussey, K. (2004). "On broadening the cognitive, motivational, and sociostructural scope of theorizing about gender and functioning: comment on Martin, Ruble, and Szkrybalo." *Psychological Bulletin* **130**: 691–701.

Banerjee, P. and Tamis-LeMonda, C. (2007). "Infants' persistence and mothers' teaching as predictors of toddlers' cognitive development." *Infant behavior and development* **30**: 479–491.

Barber, B. K. (1996). "Parental psychological control: revisiting a neglected construct." *Child Development* **67**: 3296–3319.

Barber, B. K. (1999). "Political violence, family relations, and Palestinian youth functioning" *Journal of Adolescent Research* **14**: 206–230.

Bard, D. and Rodgers, J. (2003). "Sibling influence on smoking behavior: a within-family look at explanations for a birth-order effect." *Journal of Applied Social Psychology* **33**: 1773–1795.

Barenbaum, J., Ruchkin, V. *et al.* (2004). "The psychosocial aspects of children exposed to war." *Journal of Child Psychology and Psychiatry* **45**: 41–62.

Barker, D. (1997). "Fetal nutrition and cardiovascular disease in later life." *British Medical Bulletin* **53**: 96–108.

Barlett, C., Harris, R. *et al.* (2007). "Longer you play, the more hostile you feel:

examination of first person shooter video games and aggression during video game play." *Aggressive Behavior* **33**: 486–497.

Bartkowski, J. and Xu, X. (2007). "Religiosity and teen drug use reconsidered a social capital perspective." *American Journal of Preventive Medicine* **32**: S182–S194.

Bartkowski, J., Xu, X. and Levin, L. L. (2008). "Religion and child development: evidence from the early childhood longitudinal study." *Social Science Research* **37**: 18–36.

Bates, J. and Pettit, G. (2007). Temperament, parenting and socialization. In J. E. Grusec and P. D. Hastings (eds), *Handbook of Socialization*. New York: Guilford.

Bates, J., Pettit, G. *et al.* (1998). "Interaction of temperamental resistance to control and restrictive parenting in the development of externalizing behavior." *Developmental Psychology* **34**: 982–995.

Bateson, G. (1985). *Steps to an Ecology of Mind*. London: Aronson.

Bateson, P., Barker, D. *et al.* (2004). "Developmental plasticity and human health." *Nature* **430**: 419–421.

Bauer, P. (2007). *Remembering the Times of our Lives: Memory in Infancy and Beyond*. Mahwah, NJ: Erlbaum.

Baumeister, D. (1998). The self. In D. Gilbert, S. Fiske and G. Lindzey (eds), *Handbook of Social Psychology*. Boston: McGraw-Hill.

Baumeister, R. (2003). "Does high self-esteem cause better performance, interpersonal success, happiness, or healthier lifestyles?" *Psychological Science in the Public Interest* **4**: 1–44.

Baumrind, D. (1971). "Current patterns of parental authority." *Developmental Monographs* **41**: 1–103.

Baumrind, D. (1980). "New directions in socialization research." *American Psychologist* **35**: 639–652.

Baydar, N., Greek, A. and Brooks-Gunn, J. (1997). A longitudinal study of the effects of the birth of a sibling during the first 6 years of life. *Journal of Marriage and the Family* **59**: 939–956.

Baydar, N., Hyle, P. and Brooks-Gunn, J. (1997). A longitudinal study of the effects of the birth of a sibling during preschool and early grade school years. *Journal of Marriage and the Family* **59**: 957–965.

Bayer, J. K., Sanson, A. V. and Hemphill, S. A. (2006). "Parent influences on early childhood internalizing difficulties." *Journal of Applied Developmental Psychology* **27**: 542–559.

Beardslee, W., Versage, E. and Gladstone T. R. (1998). "Children of affectively ill parents: a review of the past 10 years." *Journal of the American Academy of Child and Adolescent Psychiatry* **37**: 1134–1141.

Beaulieu, D. A. and Bugental, D. B. (2007). An evolutionary approach to socialization. In J. E. Grusec and P. D. Hastings, *Handbook of Socialization Theory and Research*. New York: Guilford Press.

Beckett, C., Maughan, B. *et al.* (2006). "Do the effects of early severe deprivation on cognition persist into early adolescence? Findings from the English and Romanian Adoption Study." *Child Development* **77**: 696–711.

Belsky, J. (2001). "Developmental risks (still) associated with early child care." *Journal of Child Psychology and Psychiatry* **42**: 845–859.

Belsky, J. (2005). Attachment theory and research in ecological perspective: insights from the Pennsylvania Infant and Family Development Project and the NICHD study of early child care. In K. E. Grossman, K. Grossman and E. Waters (eds), *Attachment from Infancy to Adulthood: The Major Longitudinal Studies*. New York: Guilford.

Belsky, J., Hsieh, K. and Crnic, K. (1998). "Mothering, fathering and infant negativity as antecedents of boys' externalising problems and inhibition at 3 years: differential susceptibility to rearing experience?" *Development and Psychopathology* **10**: 301–319.

Belsky, J., Steinberg, L. D. *et al.* (2007a). "Family rearing antecedents of pubertal timing." *Child Development* **78**: 1302–1321.

Belsky, J., Vandell, D. L. *et al.* (2007b). "Are there long-term effects of early child care?" *Child Development* **78**: 681–701.

Benenson, J. and C. Christakos (2003). "The greater fragility of females' versus males' closest Same-sex friendships." *Child Development* **74**: 1123–1129.

Benenson, J., Sinclair, S. *et al.* (2006). "Children's and adolescents' expectations of aggressive responses to provocation: females predict more hostile reactions in compatible dyadic relationships." *Social Development* **15**: 65–81.

Bennett, M. (1999). *Developmental Psychology*. Hove: Psychology Press.

Benoit, T., Jocelyn, L. *et al.* (1996). "Romanian adoption: the Manitoba experience." *Archives of Pediatric and Adolescent Medicine* **150**: 1278–1282.

Berlin, L. J. (2005). Interventions to enhance early attachments. In L. Berlin, Y. Ziv, L. Amaya-Jackson and M. T. Greenberg (eds), *Enhancing Early Attachments*. New York: The Guilford Press.

Berlin, L., Ziv, Y. *et al.* (2005). *Enhancing Early Attachments*. New York: The Guilford Press.

Berndt, T. (2004). "Children's friendships: shifts over a half-century in perspectives in their development and their effects." *Merrill-Palmer Quarterly* **50**: 206–223.

Berndt, T., Hawkins, J. and Jiao, Z. (1999). "Influences of friends and friendships to adjustment to junior high school." *Merrill-Palmer Quarterly* **45**: 13–41.

Bettelheim, B. (1967). *The Empty Fortress: Infantile Autism and the Birth of the Self*. New York: Free Press.

Bierman, K. and Wargo, J. (1995). "Predicting the longitudinal course associated with aggressive-rejected, aggressive (non-rejected) and rejected (non-aggressive) status." *Development and Psychopathology* **7**: 669–682.

Bifulco, A. and Moran, P. (1998). *Wednesday's Child: Research into Women's Experience of Neglect and Abuse in Childhood, and Adult Depression*. London: Routledge.

Bigler, R. S. (2001). "When groups are not created equal: effects of group status on the formation of inter-group attitudes in children." *Child Development* **72**: 1151–1162.

Birch, S. and Ladd, G. (1998). "Children's interpersonal behaviours and the teacher-child relationship." *Developmental Psychology* **34**: 934–946.

Birman, D. (2006). "Acculturation gap and family adjustment findings with Soviet Jewish Refugees in the United States and implications for measurement." *Journal of Cross-Cultural Psychology* **37**: 568–589.

Birnbaum, G. (2007). "Attachment orientations, sexual functioning, and relationship satisfaction in a community sample of women." *Journal of Social and Personal Relationships* **24**: 21–35.

Bishop, E., Cherny, S. S. *et al.* (2003). Development genetic analysis of general cognitive ability from 1 to 12 years in a sample of adoptees, biological siblings, and twins. *Intelligence* **31**: 31–49.

Bjorklund, D. and A. Pellegrini (2000). "Child development and evolutionary psychology." *Child Development* **71**: 1687–1708.

Bjorklund, D. and A. Pellegrini (2002). *The Origins of Human Nature: Evolutionary Developmental Psychology*. Washington, DC: American Psychological Association.

Blackwell, L., Trzesniewski, K. and Dweck, C. S. (2007). "Implicit theories of intelligence predict achievement across an adolescent transition: a longitudinal study and an intervention." *Child Development* **78**: 246–263.

Blake, J. (1989). *Family Size and Achievement*. Berkeley, CA: University of California Press.

Blakemore, S.-J. and Choudhury, S. (2006). "Development of the adolescent brain: implications for executive function and social cognition." *Journal of Child Psychology and Psychiatry* **47**: 296–312.

Blanden, J. and Gregg, P. (2004). "Family income and educational attainment: a review of approaches and evidence for Britain." *Oxford Review of Economic Policy* **20**: 245–263.

Blasi, A. (2004). Moral functioning: moral understanding and personality. In D. Lapsley and D. Narvaez (eds), *Moral Development, Self and Identity*. Mahwah, NJ.: Erlbaum.

Block, J. H., and Block, J. (1980). "The role of ego-control and ego-resiliency in the organization of behavior." *Minnesota Symposium on Child Psychology* **13**: 39–101.

Bloemraad, I. and Trost, C. (2008). "It's a family affair: intergenerational mobilization in the Spring 2006 protests." *American Behavioral Scientist* **52**: 507–532.

Blos, P. (1967). *The Second Individuation Process of Adolescence*. New York: International Universities Press.

Boden, J., Fergusson, D. M. and Horwood, L. J. (2008). "Does adolescent self-esteem predict later life outcomes? A test of the causal role of self-esteem." *Development and Psychopathology* **20**: 319–339.

Bogaert, A. (2005). "Age at puberty and father absence in a national probability sample." *Journal of Adolescence* **28**: 541–546.

Bohlin, G., Hagekull, B. and Andersson, K. (2005). Behavioral inhibition as a precursor of peer social competence in early school age: The interplay with attachment and nonparental care. *Merrill-Palmer Quarterly – Journal of Developmental Psychology* **51**: 1–19.

Bohman, M. I. E. (1996). Genetics of criminal and antisocial behavior. Predispositions to criminality: Swedish adoption studies in retrospect. In G. R. Bock. J. A. Goode (eds), *Genetics of Criminal and Antisocial Behaviour – Ciba Foundation Symposium No. 194*: 99–114. Chichester: Wiley.

Bolland, J. M., Bryant, C. M. *et al.* (2007). "Development and risk behavior among African American, Caucasian and Mixed-race adolescents living in high poverty inner-city neighbourhoods." *American Journal of Community Psychology* **40**: 230–249.

Bonomo, Y. A., Bowes, G. *et al.* (2004). "Teenage drinking and the onset of alcohol dependence: a cohort study over seven years." *Addiction* **99**: 1520–1528.

Borg, M. G. (1999). "The extent and nature of bullying among primary and secondary school children." *Educational Research* **42**: 137–153.

Borge, A. (2004). "Early child care and physical aggression: differentiating social selection and social causation." *Journal of Child Psychology and Psychiatry* **45**: 367–376.

Bornstein, M. and Bradley, R. (2003). *Socioeconomic Status, Parenting and Child Development*. Mahwah, NJ: Erlbaum.

Bouchard, T. J. (2004). "Genetic influence on human psychological traits: a survey." *Current Directions in Psychological Science* **13**: 148–151.

Bouchard, T. J. and Loehlin, J. C. (2001). "Genes, evolution and personality." *Behavior Genetics* **31**: 243–274.

Bouchey, H. (2007). "Perceived romantic competence, importance of romantic domains, and psychosocial adjustment." *Journal of Clinical Child & Adolescent Psychology* **36**: 503–514.

Bouffard, T., Boisvert, T. *et al.* (1995). "The impact of goal orientation on self-regulation and performance among college students." *British Journal of Educational Psychology* **65**: 317–329.

Bowlby, J. (1973). *Attachment and Loss. Vol. 2: Separation: Anxiety and Anger*. New York: Basic Books.

Bowlby, J. (1977). "The making and breaking of affectional bonds." *British Journal of Psychiatry* **130**: 201–210.

Bowlby, J. (1988). *A Secure Base*. New York: Basic Books.

Bowles, S. and Posel, D. (2005). "Genetic relatedness predicts migrants' workers remittances to their families." *Nature* **434**: 380–383.

Boyce, P., Parker, G. *et al.* (1991). "Personality as a vulnerability factor to depression." *British Journal of Psychiatry* **159**: 106–114.

Boyer, T. (2006). "The development of risk-taking: a multi-perspective review." *Developmental Review* **26**: 291–345.

Boyum, L. and Parke, R. (1995). "The role of family emotional expressiveness in the development of children's social competence." *Journal of Marriage and the Family* **57**: 593–608.

Bradley, R. and Corwyn, R. H. (2002). "Socioeconomic status and child development." *Annual Review of Psychology* **53**: 371–399.

Bradley, R. and Corwyn, R. H. (2005). "Productive activity and the prevention of behavior problems." *Developmental Psychology* **41**: 89–98.

Bradley, R. F., Corwyn, R. H. *et al.* (2001). "The home environments of children in the United States Part II: relations with behavioral development through age thirteen." *Child Development* **72**: 1868–1886.

Branje, S., van Lieshout C. *et al.* (2004). "Perceived support in sibling relationships and adolescent adjustment." *Journal of Child Psychology and Psychiatry* **45**: 1385–1396.

Brannen, J. and O'Brien, M. (1995). "Childhood and the sociological gaze: paradigms and paradoxes." *Sociology* **29**: 729–737.

Brendgen, M., Vitaro, F. and Butowski, W. (2000). "Deviant friends and early adolescents' emotional and behavioral adjustment." *Journal of Research on Adolescence* **10**: 173–189.

Brendgen, M., Markiewicz, D. *et al.* (2001). "The relations between friendship quality, ranked friendship preference, and adolescents' behaviour with their friends." *Merrill-Palmer Quarterly* **47**: 395–415.

Brenick, A., Henning, A. *et al.* (2007). "Social evaluations of stereotypic images in video games – Unfair, legitimate, or 'just entertainment'?" *Youth & Society* **38**: 395–419.

Bretherton, I. (1990). Open communication and internal working models: their role in the development of attachment relationships. In R.Thompson (ed.), *Nebraska Symposium on Motivation, Vol 36*. Lincoln: University of Nebraska Press.

Bretherton, I. (2005). In pursuit of the internal working model construct and its relevance to attachment relationships. In K. E. Grossman, K. Grossman and E. Waters (eds), *Attachment from Infancy to Adulthood: The Major Longitudinal Studies*. New York: Guilford.

Brewer, M. B. (1999). "The psychology of prejudice: In-group love or out-group hate?" *Journal of Social Issues* **55**: 429–444.

Brinbaum, G., Reis, H. *et al.* (2006). "When sex is more than just sex: attachment orientations, sexual experience and relationship quality." *Journal of Personality and Social Psychology* **91**: 929–943.

Brody, G. (1998). "Sibling relationship quality: its causes and consequences." *Annual Review of Psychology* **49**: 1–24.

Brody, G. (2003). Parental monitoring: action and reaction. In A. Crouter and A. Booth (ed.), *Children's Influence on Family Dynamics: The Neglected Side of Family Relationships*. Mahwah, NJ: Erlbaum.

Brody, G., Stoneman, Z. *et al.* (1992). "Associations of maternal and paternal direct and differential behaviour with sibling relationships: contemporaneous and longitudinal analyses." *Child Development* **63**: 82–92.

Brody, G., Stoneman, Z. *et al.* (1994). "Forecasting sibling relationships in early adolescence from child temperaments and family processes in middle childhood." *Child Development* **65**: 771–784.

Brody, G. H., Murry, V. M. *et al.* (2002). "Longitudinal pathways to competence and psychological adjustment among African American children living in rural single-parent households." *Child Development* **73**: 1505–1516.

Broman, S., Nichols, P. L. *et al.* (1987). *Retardation in Young Children: A Developmental Study of Cognitive Deficit*. Hillsdale, NJ: Erlbaum.

Bronfenbrenner, U. (1971). *Two Worlds of Childhood: US and USSR*. London: George Allen and Unwin.

Bronfenbrenner, U. (1979). *The Ecology of Human Development*. Cambridge, MA: Harvard University Press.

Bronfenbrenner, U. (1986). Ecology of the family as a context for human development. *Developmental Psychology* **22**: 723–742.

Bronfenbrenner, U. (1994). Who cares for the children? (edited paper from an individual address to UNESCO, Paris, 7 September 1989). In H. Nuba, M. Searson and D. L. Sheiman (eds), *Resources for Early Childhood: A Handbook*: 113–129. New York: Garland.

Bronfenbrenner, U. (1995). Developmental ecology through space and time: A future perspective. In G. E. P. Moen, Jr. and K. Luscher (eds), *Examining Lives in Context: Perspectives on The Ecology of Human Development*. Washington, DC: American Psychological Association.

Bronfenbrenner, U. and Ceci, S. J. (1994). "Nature-nurture reconceptualized in developmental perspective: A bioecological model." *Psychological Review* **101**: 568–586.

Bronfenbrenner, U. and Evans, G. (2000). "Developmental science in the 21st Century." *Social Development* **9**: 115–125.

Bronfenbrenner, U. and Morris, P. (1998). The ecology of developmental process. In W. Damon and R. M. Lerner (ed.), *Handbook of Child Psychology.* New York: Wiley.

Bronfenbrenner, U. and Morris, P. (2006).The bioecological model of Human Development. In L. Damon and R. M Learner (eds), *Handbook of Child Psychology, (6th edn) Vol 1*: 793–828. New York: Wiley.

Bronfenbrenner, U., McClelland, P. D. *et al.* (1996). *The State of Americans: This Generation and the Next.* New York: Free Press.

Bronte, C. (1847). *Jane Eyre.* London: Smith Elder and Co.

Brook, J., Brook, D. *et al.* (2007). "Growing up in a violent society: longitudinal predictors of violence in Colombian adolescents." *American Journal of Community Psychology* **40**: 82–95.

Brooks-Gunn, J. and Duncan, G. T. (1997). "The effects of poverty on children." *Future of Children* **7**: 55–71.

Brotman, L., Gouley, K. K. *et al.* (2003). "Children, stress, and context: integrating basic, clinical, and experimental prevention research." *Child Development* **74**: 1053–1057.

Brotman, L., O'Neal, C. R. *et al.* (2008). "An experimental test of parenting practices as a mediator of early childhood physical aggression." *Journal of Child Psychology and Psychiatry* **50**: 235–245.

Brown, B. (1999). "Optimizing expression of the common human genome for child development." *Current Directions in Psychological Science* **8**: 37–41.

Brown, B. B., Herman, M. *et al.* (2008). "Ethnicity and image: correlates of crowd affiliation among ethnic minority youth." *Child Development* **79**: 529–546.

Brown, G. L., Mangelsdorf, S. C. *et al.* (2008). "Young children's psychological selves: Convergence with maternal reports of child personality." *Social Development* **17**: 161–182.

Brown, G. W. and Harris, T. (1978). *Social Origins of Depression: A Study of Psychiatric Disorders in Women.* London: Tavistock.

Brown, J. R. and Dunn, J. (1996). Continuities in emotion understanding from three to six years. *Child Development* **67**: 789–802.

Brown, J. R., Donelan-McCall, N. and Dunn, J. (1996). Why talk about mental states? The significance of children's conversations with friends, siblings, and mothers. *Child Development* **67**: 836–849.

Brownell, C. (2006). "Becoming a social partner with peers: cooperation and social understanding in one- and two-year olds." *Child Development* **77**: 803–821.

Bruhns, W. (2009). *My Father's Country: The Story of a German Family.* London: Arrow Books.

Buehler, C., Lange, G. and Franck, K. L. (2007). "Adolescents' Cognitive and Emotional Responses to Marital Hostility." *Child Development* **78**: 775–789.

Bugental, D. B. and Beaulieu, D. (2004). "Maltreatment risk among disabled children: A bio-social-cognitive approach." In R. Kail (ed.), *Advances in Child Development and Behavior, Vol 31:* 129–164. New York: Academic Press.

Bugental, D. B. and Grusec, J. E. (2006). Socialization processes. In W. Damon, R.

Lerner, N. Eisenberg (eds), *Handbook of Child Psychology, (6th edn) Vol 3*: 366–428. New York: Wiley.

Bugental, D. B. and Happaney, K. (2004). "Prediciting infant maltreatment in low-income families: The interactive effects of maternal attributions and child status at birth." *Developmental Psychology* **40**: 234–243.

Bugental, D. B. and Johnston, C. (2000). "Parental and child cognitions in the context of the family." *Annual Review of Psychology* **51**: 315–344.

Bugental, D. B., Johnston, C. *et al.* (1998). "Measuring parental attributions: conceptual and methodological issues." *Journal of Family Psychology* **12**: 459–480.

Buhrmester, D. and Furman, W. (1987). "The development of companionship and intimacy." *Child Development* **58**: 1101–1113.

Buhrmester, D. and Furman, W. (1990). "Perceptions of sibling relationships during middle childhood and adolescence." *Child Development* **61**: 1387–1398.

Bukobza, G. (2007). "The epistemological basis of selfhood." *New Ideas in Psychology* **25**: 37–65.

Bukowski, W., Brendgren, M. *et al.* (2007). Peers and socialization: effects on extrenalising and internalising problems. In J. Grusec and P. Hastings (eds), *Handbook of Socialization*. New York: Guilford.

Burchinal, M. (2008). "Social risk and protective factors for African American children's academic achievement and adjustment during the transition to middle school." *Developmental Psychology* **44**: 286–292.

Burchinal, M., Vernon-Feagans, L. and Cox, M. (2008). "Cumulative social risk, parenting, and infant development in rural low-income communities." *Parenting – Science and Practice* **8**: 41–69.

Burchinal, M. R., Roberts, J. E. *et al.* (2000). Social risk and protective child, parenting, and child care factors in early elementary school years. *Parenting-Science and Practice* **6**: 79–113.

Burchinal, M. R., Roberts, J. E. *et al.* (2006). Relating quality of center-based child care to early cognitive and language development longitudinally. *Child Development* **71**: 339–357.

Burgess, K. B., Marshall, P. J. *et al.* (2003). "Infant attachment and temperament as predictors of subsequent behavior problems and psychophysiological functioning." *Journal of Child Psychology and Psychiatry* **44**: 819–831.

Burgess, K. B., Wojslawowicz, J. C. *et al.* (2006). "Social information processing and coping strategies of shy/withdrawn and aggressive children: does friendship matter?" *Child Development* **77**: 371–383.

Burks, V. and Parke, R. (1996). "Parent and child representations of social relationships: Linkages between families and peers." *Merrill-Palmer Quarterly* **42**: 358–378.

Burnett, P. (1999). Children's self-talk and academic self-concepts. *Educational Psychology in Practice* **15**: 195–200.

Burnett, P. and Proctor, R. (2002). "Elementary school students' learner self-concepts, academic self-concepts and approaches to teaching." *Educational Psychology in Practice* **18**: 325–333.

Burnham, D. (1993). "Visual recognition of mother by young infants – facilitation by speech." *Perception* **22**: 1133–1153.

Burrow, J. A. (1986). *The Ages of Man: A Study in Medieval Writing and Thought*. Oxford: Clarendon Press.

Buss, D. (2005). *The Handbook of Evolutionary Psychology*. Hoboken, NJ: John Wiley & Sons.

Bussey, K. and Bandura, A. (1999). "Social cognitive theory of gender development and differentiation." *Psychological Review* **106**: 676–713.

Butler, A. (2006). "The empirical status of cognitive-behavioral therapy: a review of meta-analyses." *Clinical Psychology Review* **26**: 17–31.

Butler N., Goldstein, H. and Ross, E. (1972). "Cigarette smoking in pregnancy: its influence on birth weight and perinatal mortality." *British Medical Journal* **2**: 127–130.

Butler, S. (1903/1973). *The Way of All Flesh*. Harmondsworth: Penguin.

Byrne, R. and Whiten, A. (1988). *Machiavellian Intelligence: Social Expertise and the Evolution of Intellect in Monkeys, Apes and Humans*. Oxford: Clarendon Press.

Byrnes, J. P. (1998). *The Nature and Development of Decision Making: A Self-Regulation Model*. Mahwah, NJ: Erlbaum.

Cabrera, N. and Garcia-Coll, C. (2004). Latino fathers: uncharted territory in need of much exploration. In M Lamb (ed.), *The Role of the Father in Child Development*. Hoboken, NJ: Wiley.

Cadoret, R. J., Cain, C. A. *et al.* (1983). "Evidence for gene-environment interaction in the development of adolescent antisocial behavior." *Behavior Genetics* **13**: 301–310.

Cadoret, R. J., Yates, W. R. *et al.* (1995). "Genetic-environmental interaction in the genesis of aggressivity and conduct disorders." *Archives of General Psychiatry* **52**: 916–924.

Caffray, C. M. and Schneider, S. L. (2000). "Why do they do it? Affective motivators in adolescents' decisions to participate in risk behaviours." *Cognition & Emotion* **14**: 543–576.

Cain, K. and Dweck, C. (1995). "The relation between motivational patterns and achievement cognitions throughout the elementary school years." *Merrill-Palmer Quarterly* **41**: 25–52.

Cairns, E., Kenworthy, J. *et al.* (2006). "The role of in-group identification, religious group membership and intergroup conflict in moderating in-group and out-group affect." *British Journal of Social Psychology* **45**: 701–716.

Cairns, R. (1995). "Friendships and social networks in childhood and adolescence – fluidity, reliability, and interrelations." *Child Development* **66**: 1330–1345.

Cairns, R. (1988). "Social networks and aggressive behavior: peer support or peer rejection?" *Developmental Psychology* **24**: 815–823.

Calkins, S. D. (1997). "Cardiac vagal tone indices of temperamental reactivity and behavioral regulation in young children." *Developmental Psychobiology* **31**: 125–135.

Calkins, S. D. (2002). "Does aversive behavior during toddlerhood matter? The effects of difficult temperament on maternal perception and behavior." *Infant Mental Health Journal* **23**: 381–402.

Calkins, S. D., Keane, S. P. (2004). "Cardiac vagal regulation across the preschool period: Stability, continuity, and implications for childhood adjustment." *Developmental Psychobiology* **45**: 101–112.

Callero, P. (2003). "The sociology of the self." *Annual Review of Sociology* **29**: 115–133.

Cameron, N., Champagne, F. A. *et al.* (2005). "The programming of individual differences in defensive responses and reproductive strategies in the rat through variations in maternal care." *Neuroscience and Biobehavioral Reviews* **29**: 843–856.

Campbell, A. and Muncer, S. (1998). *The Social Child.* Hove: Psychology Press.

Campbell, M. J., Schmidt, L. A. *et al.* (2007). "Behavioral and psychophysiological characteristics of children of parents with social phobia: a pilot study." *International Journal of Neuroscience* **117**: 605–616.

Cardon, L., Fulker, D. W. *et al.* (1992). "Continuity and change in general cognitive ability from 1–7 years of age." *Developmental Psychology* **28**: 64–73.

Carlo, G. (1996). "A cross-national study on the relations between prosocial moral reasoning, gender role orientations, and prosocial behaviors." *Developmental Psychology* **32**: 231–240.

Carlson, E., Sroufe, L. and Egeland, B. (2004). "The construction of experience: a longitudinal study of representation and behavior." *Child Development* **67**: 2217–2226.

Carlson, V. and Harwood, R. (2003). "Attachment, culture, and the caregiving system: the cultural patterning of everyday experiences among Anglo and Puerto Rican mother-infant pairs." *Infant Mental Health Journal* **24**: 53–73.

Carnagey, N. and Anderson, C. (2007). "The effect of video game violence on physiological desensitization to real-life violence." *Journal of Experimental Social Psychology* **43**: 489–496.

Carnagey, N., Anderson, C. and Bartholow, B. D. (2007). "Media violence and social neuroscience: New questions and new opportunities." *Current Directions in Psychological Science* **16**: 178–182.

Carpendale, J. and Lewis, C. (2004). "Constructing an understanding of mind: The development of children's social understanding within social interaction." *Behavioral and Brain Sciences* **27**: 79–96.

Carpendale, J. and Lewis, C. (2006). *How Children Develop Social Understanding.* Oxford: Blackwell.

Carvajal, S. C., Hanson, C. *et al.* (2004). Theory-based determinants of youth smoking: A multiple influence approach. *Journal of Applied Social Psychology* **34**: 59–84.

Carver, C., and Connor-Smith, J. (2010). "Personality and coping." *Annual Review of Psychology* **61**: (in press).

Carver, P., Yunger, J. L and Perry D. G. (2003). "Gender identity and adjustment in middle childhood." *Sex Roles* **49**: 95–109.

Case, R. (1985). *Intellectual Development: Birth to adulthood.* New York: Academic Press.

Caselman, T. and Self, P. (2007). "Adolescent perception of self as a close friend: culture and gendered contexts." *Social Psychology of Education* **10**: 353–373.

Caspi, A. and Silva, P. (1995). "Temperamental qualities at age 3 predict personality traits in young adulthood: Longitudinal evidence from a birth cohort." *Child Development,* **66**: 486–498.

Caspi, A., Elder, G. H. and Bem, D. (1987). "Moving against the world: the life-course patterns of explosive children." *Developmental Psychology* **22**: 308–313.

Caspi, A, Elder, G. H. and Bem, D. J. (1988). "Moving away from the world – life-course patterns of shy children." *Developmental Psychology* **24**: 824–831.

Caspi, A., Henry, B. *et al.* (1995). "Temperamental origins of child and adolescent behavior problems: from age 3 to age 15." *Child Development* **66**: 55–68.

Caspi, A., Moffitt, T. E. *et al.* (1996). "Behavioral observations at age 3 years predict adult psychiatric disorders – Longitudinal evidence from a birth cohort." *Archives of General Psychiatry* **53**: 1033–1039.

Caspi, A., Taylor, A. *et al.* (2000). "Neighbourhood risk affects children's mental health: environmental risks identified in a genetic design." *Psychological Science* **11**: 338–342.

Caspi, A., McClay, A. *et al.* (2002). "Role of genotype in the cycle of violence in maltreated children." *Science* **297**: 851–854.

Caspi, A., Sugden, K. *et al.* (2003). "Influence of life stress on depression: moderation by a polymorphism in the 5-HTT gene." *Science* **301**: 386–389.

Caspi, A., Williams, B. *et al.* (2007). "Moderation of breastfeeding effects on the IQ by genetic variation in fatty acid metabolism." *Proceedings of the National Academy of Sciences of the United States of America* **104**: 18860–18865.

Cassidy, J., Hoffman, K. *et al.* (2005). Examination of the precursors of infant attachment security: implications for early intervention and intervention research. In L. Berlin, Y. Ziv, L. Amaya-Jackson and M. T. Greenberg (eds), *Enhancing Early Attachments*. New York: The Guilford Press.

Castle, J., Groothues, C. *et al.* (1999). "Effects of quality of early institutional care on cognitive attainment." *American Journal of Orthopsychiatry* **69**: 424–437.

Ceci, S. J. and Papierno, P. B. (2005). "The rhetoric and reality of gap closing: when the 'have nots' gain but the 'haves' gain even more." *American Psychologist* **60**: 149–160.

Cemlyn, S., Greenfields, M. *et al.* (2009). *Inequalities Experienced by Gypsy and Traveller Communities: A Review*. Manchester: Equality and Human Rights Commission.

Centerwall, B. S. (1989). "Exposure to television as a risk factor for violence." *American Journal of Epidemiology* **129**: 643–652.

Centerwall, B. S. (1992). "Television and violence: the scale of the problem and where to go from here." *Journal of the American Medical Association* **267**: 3059–3063.

Chambers, R. A. and Potenza, M. N. (2003). "Neurodevelopment, impulsivity, and adolescent gambling." *Journal of Gambling Studies* **19**: 53–84.

Champagne, F., Chretien, P. *et al.* (2004). "Variations in nucleus accumbens dopamine associated with individual differences in maternal behavior in the rat." *Journal of Neuroscience* **24**: 4113–4123.

Chang, J. (1992). *Wild Swans*. London: Harper Collins.

Chang, L., Lei, L. *et al.* (2005). "Peer acceptance and self-perceptions of verbal and behavioural aggression and withdrawal." *International Journal of Behavoral Development* **29**: 49–57.

Chao, R. (1994). "Beyond parental control and authoritarian parenting style: understanding Chinese parenting through the cultural notion of training." *Child Development* **65**: 1111–1119.

Charlton, B. (2006). "The rise of the boy-genius: psychological neoteny, science and modern life." *Medical Hypotheses* **67**: 679–681.

Charlton, T., Coles, D. *et al.* (1999). "Behaviour of nursery class children before and after the availability of broadcast television: A naturalistic study of two cohorts in a remote community." *Journal of Social Behavior and Personality* **14**: 315–324.

Charuvastra, A. and Cloitre, M. (2008). "Social bonds and post-traumatic stress disorder." *Annual Review of Psychology* **59**: 301–328.

Cheah, C. and Rubin, K. (2004). "A cross-cultural examination of maternal beliefs regarding maladaptive behaviors in preschoolers." *International Journal of Behavioral Development* **28**: 83–94.

Chen, W. and Taylor, E. (2006). Resilience and self-control impairment. In S. Goldstein and R. Brooks (eds), *Handbook of Resilience in Children*. New York: Springer.

Chen, X. (2000). "Sociable and prosocial dimensions of social competence in Chinese children: common and unique contributions to social, academic and psychological adjustment." *Developmental Psychology* **36**: 302–314.

Chen, X. (2003). "Compliance in Chinese and Canadian toddlers." *International Journal of Behavioral Development* **27**: 428–436.

Chen, X. (2008). "Effects of the peer group on the development of social functioning and academic achievement: a longitudinal study in Chinese children." *Child Development* **79**: 235–251.

Chen, X. and French, D. C. (2007). "Children's social competence in cultural context." *Annual Review of Psychology* **59**: 591–616.

Chen, X. and Rubin, K. (1994). "Family conditions, parental acceptance, and social competence and aggression in Chinese children." *Social Development* **3**: 269–290.

Chen, X., Chang, L. and He, Y. (2003). "The peer group as a context: mediating and moderating effects on the relations between academic achievement and social functioning in Chinese children." *Child Development* **74**: 710–727.

Chen, X., Rubin, K. and Li, B. (1995). "Social and school adjustment of shy and aggressive children in China." *Development and Psychopathology* **7**: 337–349.

Chen, X., Hastings, P. D. *et al.* (1998). "Child-rearing practices and behavioral inhibition in Chinese and Canadian toddlers: a cross-cultural study." *Developmental Psychology* **34**: 677–686.

Chen, X., Chen, H. *et al.* (2001). "Group social functioning and individual socio-emotional and school adjustment in Chinese children." *Merrill-Palmer Quarterly* **47**: 264–299.

Chen, X. Y., He, Y. F. *et al.* (2004). "Loneliness and social adaptation in Brazilian, Canadian, Chinese and Italian children: a multi-national comparative study." *Journal of Child Psychology and Psychiatry* **45**: 1373–1384.

Chen, X., Cen, G. Z. *et al.* (2005). "Social functioning and adjustment in Chinese children: The imprint of historical time." *Child Development* **76**: 182–195.

Chen, X., Desouza, A. T. *et al.* (2006). "Reticent behaviour and experiences in peer interactions in Canadian and Chinese children." *Developmental Psychology* **42**: 656–665.

Chen, X., Chang, L. *et al.* (2008). "Effects of the peer group on the development of social functioning and academic achievement: a longitudinal study in Chinese children." *Child Development* **79**: 235–251.

Cheney, D. and Seyfarth, R. (1996). "The recognition of social alliances by vervet monkeys." *Animal Behavior* **34**: 1722–1731.

Cheung, C. S. and McBride-Chang, C. (2008). "Relations of perceived maternal parenting style, practices and learning motivation to academic competence in Chinese children." *Merrill-Palmer Quarterly* **54**: 1–22.

Chisholm, K., Carter C. *et al.* (1995). "Attachment security and indiscriminate friendly behaviour in children adopted from Romanian orphanages." *Development and Psychopathology* **7**: 283–294.

Cho, G., Sandel, T. L. *et al.* (2005). "What do grandmothers think about self-esteem? American and Taiwanese folk theories revisited." *Social Development* **14**: 701–721.

Chodorow, N. (1978). *The Reproduction of Mothering: Psychoanalysis and the Sociology of Gender.* Berkeley, CA: University of California Press.

Chowhan, J. and Stewart, J. (2007). "Television and the behavior of adolescents: does socio-economic status moderate the link?" *Social Science and Medicine* **65**: 1324–1336.

Christakis, D., Zimmerman, F. J. *et al.* (2004). "Early television exposure and subsequent attentional problems in children." *Pediatrics* **113**: 708–713.

Christensen, P. and James, A. (2008). *Research with Children: Perspectives and Practices.* New York: Routledge.

Church M., Elliot A. *et al.* (2001). "Perceptions of classroom environment, achievement goals, and achievement outcomes." *Journal of Educational Psychology* **93**: 43–54.

Cialdini, R. B. and N. J. Goldstein (2004). "Social influence: compliance and conformity." *Annual Review of Psychology* **55**: 591–621.

Ciarrochi, J. and Heaven, P. C. L. (2008). "Learned social hopelessness: the role of explanatory style in predicting social support during adolescnce." *Journal of Child Psychology and Psychiatry* **49**: 1279–1286.

Cicchetti, D. (1990). The organisation and coherence of socioemotional, cognitive and representational development: illustrations through a developmental psychopathology perspective on Down's syndrome and child maltreatment. In R. Thompson (ed.), *Nebraska Symposium on Motivation, Vol 36.* Lincoln: University of Nebraska Press.

Cicchetti, D. (2002). How a child builds a brain: insights from normality and psychopathology. In W. Hartup and R. A. Weinberg (eds), *Minnesota Symposia on Child Psychology: Child Psychology in Retrospect and Prospect, Vol 32.* Mahwah, NJ: Lawrence Erlbaum Associates.

Cicchetti, D. (2004). "An odyssey of discovery: lessons learned through 3 decades of research on child maltreatment." *American Psychologist* **59**: 728–741.

Cicchetti, D. and Blender, J. (2006). "A multiple-levels-of-analysis perspective on resilience. Implications for the developing brain, neural plasticity, and preventive interventions." *Annals of the New York Academy of Sciences* **1094**: 248–258.

Cicchetti, D. and Curtis, W. J. (2006). The developing brain and neural plasticity: Implications for normality, psychopathology, and resilience. In D. J. Cohen and D. Cicchetti (eds), *Developmental Psychopathology: Developmental neuroscience (2nd edn), Vol 2*: 1–64. New York: Wiley.

Cicchetti, D. and Curtis, W. J. (2007). "A multilevel approach to resilience." *Development and Psychopathology* (special issue) **19**: 627–955.

Cicchetti, D., Rogosch, F. A., Sturge-Apple, M. L. (2007). "Interactions of child maltreatment and serotonin transporter and monoamine oxidase A polymorphisms: depressive symptomatology among adolescents from low socioeconomic status backgrounds." *Development and Psychopathology* (special issue) **19**: 1161–1180.

Cillesen, A., van Ijkendoorn, H. W. *et al.* (1992). "Heterogeneity among peer-rejected boys: subtypes and stabilities." *Child Development* **63**: 893–905.

Clark, C. and Uzzell, D. (2006). The socio-environmental affordances of adolescents' environments. In C. Spencer and M. Blades (eds), *Children and their Environments*. Cambridge: Cambridge University Press.

Clark, K. and Ladd, G. W. (2000). "Connectedness and autonomy support in parent–child relationships: Links to children's socioeconomic orientation and peer relationships." *Developmental Psychology* **36**: 485–498.

CMPO (Centre for Market and Public Organisation) Research Team. (2008). *Up to Age 7: Family Background and Child Development up to age 7 in the Avon Longitudinal Study of Parents and Children (ALSPAC). Research report No808a.* Bristol: University of Bristol.

Coie, J. and Dodge, K. (1998). Antisocial behaviour. In W.Damon and N.Eisenberg (eds), *Handbook of Child Psychology, Vol 3.* New York: Wiley.

Coie, J., Terry R. *et al.* (1995). "Childhood peer rejection and aggression as predictors of stable patterns of adolescent disorder." *Development and Psychopathology* **7**: 697–714.

Colder, C., Mott, J. *et al.* (2002). "The interactive effects of infant activity level and fear on growth trajectories of early childhood behavior problems." *Development and Psychopathology* **14**: 1–23.

Cole, M. (1996). *Cultural Psychology.* Cambridge, MA: Harvard.

Cole, P. C. (2002). "Cultural differences in children's reaction to difficult situations." *Child Development* **73**: 983–996.

Cole, P. (2006). "Cultural variations in the socialisation of young children's anger and shame." *Child Development* **77**: 1237–1251.

Cole, P. and Tan, P. (2007). Emotion socialization from a cultural perspective. In J. Grusec and P. Hastings (eds), *Handbook of Socialization.* New York: Guilford.

Cole, P. M., Martin, S. E. and Dennis, T. A. (2004). "Emotion regulation as a scientific construct: methodological challenges and directions for child development research." *Child Development* **75**: 317–333.

Cole, P., Bruschi, C. *et al.* (2002). "Cultural differences in children's emotional reactions to difficult situations." *Child Development* **73**: 983–996.

Coleman, J. and Hendry, L. (1999). *The Nature of Adolescence.* London: Routledge.

Collaer, M. and Hines, M. (1995). "Human behavioural sex differences: a role for gonadal hormones during early development?" *Psychological Bulletin* **118**: 55–107.

Collins, N. and Read, S. (1990). "Adult attachment, working models and relationship quality in dating couples." *Journal of Personality and Social Psychology* **58**: 644–663.

Collins, W. (2003). "More than a myth: the developmental significance of romantic relationships during adolescence." *Journal of Research in Adolescence* **13**: 1–24.

Collins, W. and Steinberg, L. (2006). Adolescent development in interpersonal context. In W. Damon, R. Lerner, N. Eisenberg (eds), *Handbook of Child Psychology, Vol 3.* New York: Wiley.

Collins, W. A., Maccoby, E. E. *et al.* (2000). "Contemporary research on parenting: the case of nature and nurture." *American Psychologist,* **55**: 218–232.

Colvert, E., Rutter, M. *et al.* (2008). "Emotional difficulties in early adolescence following severe early deprivation: Findings from the English and Romanian adoptees study." *Development and Psychopathology* **20**: 547–567.

Compas, B., Conner-Smith, J. *et al.* (2001). "Coping with stress during childhood and adolescence: problems, progress, and potential in theory and research." *Psychological Bulletin* **127**: 87–127.

Conger, K., Conger, R. *et al.* (1997). "Parents, siblings, psychological control, and adolescent adjustment." *Journal of Adolescence Research* **12**: 113–138.

Conger, R. D. and Conger, K. (2002). "Resilience in MidWestern families: selected findings from the first decade of a prospective, longitudinal study." *Journal of Marriage and the Family* **64**: 361–373.

Conger, R. and Donnellan, M. (2007). "An interactionist perspective on the socioeconomic context of human development." *Annual Review of Psychology* **58**: 175–199.

Conger, R. D., Conger, K. *et al.* (1993). "Family economic stress and adjustment of early adolescent girls." *Developmental Psychology* **29**: 206–219.

Conger, R. D., Ge, X. *et al.* (1994). "Economic stress, coercive family process, and developmental problems of adolescents." *Child Development* **65**: 541–561.

Conger, R. D., Neppl, T. *et al.* (2003). "Angry and aggressive behavior across three generations: A prospective, longitudinal study of parents and children." *Journal of Abnormal Child Psychology* **31**: 143–160.

Conn, W. (1997). "Understanding the self in self-transcendence." *Pastoral Psychology* **46**: 3–17.

Connolly, J., Furman, W. *et al.* (2000). "The role of peers in the emergence of heterosexual romantic relationships in adolescence." *Child Development* **71**: 1395–1408.

Cook, W. (2001). "Interpersonal influences in family systems: a social relaions model analysis." *Child Development* **72**: 1179–1197.

Cooper, C. E. and Crosnoe, R. (2007). "The engagement in schooling of economically disadvantaged parents and children." *Youth & Society* **38**: 372–391.

Cooper, M. L., Agocha, B. and Sheldon, M. S. (2000). "A motivational perspective on risky behaviors: The role of personality and affect regulatory process." *Journal of Personality* **68**: 1059–1088.

Coplan, R., Rubin, K. H. *et al.* (1994). "Being alone, playing alone, and acting alone – distinguishing among reticence and passive and active solitude in young children." *Child Development* **65**: 129–137.

Coplan, R., Wilson, J. *et al.* (2006). "A person-oriented analysis of behavioral inhibition and behavioral activation in children." *Personality and Individual Differences* **41**: 917–927.

Coplan, R., Closson, L. *et al.* (2007a). "Gender differences in the behavioral associates of loneliness and social dissatisfaction in kindergarten." *Journal of Child Psychology and Psychiatry* **48**: 988–995.

Coplan, R., Girardi, A. *et al.* (2007b). "Understanding solitude: young children's attitudes and responses toward hypothetical socially withdrawn peers." *Social Development* **16**: 390–409.

Coplan, R., Arbeau, K. *et al.* (2008). "Don't fret, be supportive! maternal characteristics linking child shyness to psychosocial and school adjustment in kindergarten." *Journal of Abnormal Child Psychology* **36**: 359–371.

Corapci, F. and Wachs, T. (2002). "Does parental mood or efficacy mediate the influence of environmental chaos upon parenting behavior?" *Merrill-Palmer Quarterly* **48**: 182–201.

Corby, B. (2000). *Child Abuse: Towards a Knowledge Base*. Buckingham: Open University Press.

Corby, B., Hodges, E. and Perry, D. G. (2007). "Gender identity and adjustment in Black, Hispanic and White preadolescents." *Developmental Psychology* **43**: 261–266.

Corsaro, W. (2005). *The Sociology of Childhood*. Thousand Oaks, CA: Pine Forge Press.

Costello, E. (2003). "Relationships between poverty and psychopathology: a natural experiment." *JAMA* **290**: 2023–2029.

Costigan, C. and Dokis, D. (2006). "Similarities and differences in acculturation among mothers, fathers, and children in immigrant chinese families." *Journal of Cross-Cultural Psychology* **37**: 723–741.

Côté, S. (2008). "Nonmaternal Care in Infancy and Emotional/Behavioral Difficulties at 4 Years Old: moderation by Family Risk Characteristics." *Developmental Psychology* **44**: 155–168.

Cote, S. M., Borge, A. I. *et al.* (2008). "Nonmaternal care in infancy and emotional/behavioral difficulties at 4 years old: Moderation by family risk characteristics." *Developmental Psychology* **44**: 155–168.

Cotterell, J. (1996). *Social Networks and Social Influences in Adolescence*. London: Routledge.

Cox, M. J., Owen, M. T. *et al.* (1992). "Prediction of infant-mother and infant-father attachment." *Developmental Psychology* **28**: 474–483.

Crawford, A. M., Pentz, M. A. *et al.* (2003). "Parallel developmental trajectories of sensation seeking and regular substance use in adolescents." *Psychology of Addictive Behaviors* **17**: 179–192.

Crick, N. (1996). "The role of overt aggression, relational aggression, and prosocial behavior in the prediction of children's future social adjustment." *Child Development* **67**: 2317–2327.

Crick, N. (1997). "Engagement in gender normative versus nonnormative forms of aggression: Links to social-psychological adjustment." *Developmental Psychology* **33**: 610–617.

Crick, N. and Dodge, K. (1996). "Social information-processing mechanisms in reactive and proactive aggression." *Child Development* **67**: 993–1002.

Crick, N. and Grotpeter, J. (1995). "Relational aggression, gender, and social-psychological adjustment." *Child Development* **66**: 710–722.

Crockenberg, S. B. (1981). "Infant irritability, mother responsiveness, and social support influences on the security of infant-mother attachment." *Child Development* **52**: 857–865.

Crockenberg, S. (2003). "Rescuing the baby from the bathwater: how gender and temperament (may) influence how child care affects child development." *Child Development* **74**: 1034–1038.

Crockenberg, S. and Leerkes, E. (2003a). "Parental acceptance, postpartum depression, and maternal sensitivity: Mediating and moderating processes." *Journal of Family Psychology* **17**: 80–93.

Crockenberg, S. and Leerkes, E. (2003b). Infant negative emotionality,caregiving, and family relationships. In A. Crouter and A. Booth (eds), *Children's Influence on Family Dynamics: The Neglected Side of Family Relationships*. Mahwah, NJ: Erlbaum.

Croft, C., O'Connor T. G. *et al.* (2001). "Longitudinal change in parenting associated with developmental delay and catch-up." *Journal of Child Psychology and Psychiatry* **42**: 649–659.

Croft, C., Beckett, C. *et al.* (2007). "Early adolescent outcomes of institutionally deprived and non-deprived adoptees: Language as a protective factor and vulnerable outcome." *Journal of Child Psychology and Psychiatry* **48**: 31–44.

Crone, E. A. and van der Molen, M. W. (2004). "Developmental changes in real life decision-making: Performance on a gambling task previously shown to depend on the ventromedial prefrontal cortex." *Developmental Neuropsychology* **25**: 251–279.

Crosnoe, R. (2001). "Academic orientation and parental involement in education during high school." *Sociology of Education* **74**: 210–230.

Crosnoe, R. and Huston, A. (2007). "Socioeconomic status, schooling, and the developmental trajectories of adolescents." *Developmental Psychology* **43**: 1097–1110.

Crosnoe, R., Mistry, R. S. and Elder, G. H. (2002). "Economic disadvantage, family dynamics, and adolescent enrollment in higher education." *Journal of Marriage and Family* **64**: 690–702.

Crouter, A. and Booth, A. (2006). *Romance and Sex in Adolescence and Emerging Adulthood*. Mahwah, NJ: Erlbaum.

Crouter, A. C. and McHale, S. M. (1993). "Temporal rhythms of family-life: Seasonal variation in the relation between parental work and family processes." *Developmental Psychology*. **29**: 198–205.

Crouter, A. C., Bumpus, M. F. *et al.* (1999a). "Linking parents' work pressure and adolescents' well-being: Insights into dynamics in dual-earner families." *Developmental Psychology* **35**: 1453–1461.

Crouter, A. C., Helms-Erikson, H. H. *et al.* (1999b). "Conditions underlying parents' knowledge about children's daily lives in middle childhood: between- and within-family comparisons." *Child Development* **70**: 246–259.

Crouter, A. C., Head, M. R. *et al.* (2001). "Under what conditions do mothers lean on daughters?" *New Directions in Child Development* **94**: 23–42.

Crouter, A., Whiteman, S. *et al.* (2007). "Development of Gender Attitude Traditionality Across Middle Childhood and Adolescence." *Child Development* **78**: 911–926.

Crowell, J. and Waters, E. (2005). Attachment representations, secure-base behavior, and the evolution of adult relationships: the Stony Brook Adult Relationship Project. In K. E. Grossman, K. Grossman and E. Waters (eds), *Attachment from Infancy to Adulthood: The Major Longitudinal Studies*. New York: Guilford.

Csikszentmihalyi, M. and Csikszentmihalyi, I. S. (1988). *Optimal Experience: Psychological Studies of Flow in Consciousness*. Cambridge: Cambridge University Press.

Csikszentmihalyi, M. and Larson, R. (1984). *Being Adolescent: Conflict and Growth in the Teenage Years*. New York: Basic Books.

Cummings, E. and Davies, P (1994). "Maternal depression and child development." *Journal of Child Psychology and Psychiatry* **35**: 73–112.

Cummings, E., Keller, P. S. and Davies P. T. (2005). "Towards a family process model of maternal and paternal depressive symptoms: exploring multiple relations with child and family functioning." *Journal of Child Psychology and Psychiatry* **46**: 479–489.

Cummings, E. M., Davies, P. T. *et al.* (2000). *Developmental Psychopathology and Family Process*. New York: The Guilford Press.

Cummings, E. M., Goeke-Morey, M. *et al.* (2004). Fathering in family context: effects of marital quality and marital conflict. In M. Lamb (ed.), *The Role of the Father in Child Development*. Hoboken, NJ: Wiley.

Curtis, W. J. and Cicchetti, D. (2003). "Moving research on resilience into the 21st century: Theoretical and methodological considerations in examining the biological contributors to resilience." *Development and Psychopathology* (special issue) **15**: 773–810.

Curtis, W. J. and Cicchetti, D. (2007). "Emotion and resilience: A multilevel investigation of hemispheric electroencephalogram asymmetry and emotion regulation in maltreated and nonmaltreated children." *Development and Psychopathology* **19**: 811–840.

Curtiss, S. (1977). *Genie: A Psycholinguisitic Study of a Modern-Day 'Wild Child'*. New York: Aacademic Press.

Cutting, A. L and Dunn, J. (1999). Theory of mind, emotion understanding, language, and family background: Individual differences and interrelations. *Child Development* **70**: 853–865.

Dahl, R. E. (2004). "Adolescent brain development: a period of vulnerabilities and opportunities." *Annals of the New York Academy of Sciences* **1021**: 1–22.

Damon, W. and Hart, D. (1988). *Self-understanding in childhood and adolescence*. Cambridge: Cambridge University Press.

Darling, N. and Steinberg, L. (1993). "Parenting style as context: an integrative model." *Psychological Bulletin* **113**: 487–496.

Dart, B., Burnett, P. C. *et al.* (2000). Students' conceptions of learning, the classroom environment, and approaches to learning. *Journal of Educational Research* **93**: 262–270.

Davies, P. and Cummings, E. M. (1994). "Marital conflict and child adjustment: an emotional security hypothesis." *Psychological Bulletin* **116**: 387–411.

Davies, P. T. and Windle, M. (1997). "Gender-specific pathways between maternal depressive symptoms, family discord, and adolescent adjustment." *Developmental Psychology* **33**: 657–668.

Davies, P. T., Dumenci, L. and Windle, M. (1999). "The interplay between maternal depressive symptoms and marital distress in the prediction of adolescent adjustment." *Journal of Marriage and the Family* **61**: 238–254.

Davies, P., Harold, G. T. *et al.* (2002). "Child emotional security and interparental conflict." *Monographs of the Society for Research in Child Development* **67**: 1–115.

Davila, J., Steinberg, S. J. *et al.* (2004). "Romantic involvement and depressive symptoms in early and late adolescence: The role of a preoccupied relational style." *Personal Relationships* **11**: 161–178.

Davin, A. (1996). *Growing Up Poor*. London: Rivers Oram Press.

Davis, E. P. and Glynn, L. M. (2007). "Prenatal exposure to maternal depression and cortisol influences infant temperament." *Journal of American Academy of Child and Adolescent Psychiatry* **46**: 737–746.

Davis, H. (2001). "The quality and impact of relationships between elementary school students and teachers." *Contemporary Educational Psychology* **26**: 431–453.

Davis-Kean, P. and Sandler, H. (2001). "A meta-analysis of measures of self-esteem for young children: A framework for future measures." *Child Development* **72**: 887–906.

Dawkins, R. (2005). *The Ancestor's Tale: A Pilgrimage to the Dawn of Life*. London: Phoenix.

Dawson, G. and Ashman, S. (1999). On the origins of a vulnerability to depression: the influence of the early social environment on the development of psycho-biological systems related to risk for affective disorder. In C. A. Nelson (ed.), *Effects of Early Adversity on Neurobehavioral Development. Minnesota Symposium on Child Psychology, Vol 31*: 245–279. Mahwah, NJ: Lawrence Erlbaum Associates.

Dawson, G. and Frey, K. *et al.* (1999). "Infants of depressed mothers exhibit atypical frontal electrical brain activity during interactions with mother and with a familiar, nondepressed adult." *Child Development* **70**: 1058–1066.

Dawson, G., Ashman, S. *et al.* (2001). "Autonomic and brain electrical activity in securely- and insecurely-attached infants of depressed mothers." *Infant Behavior and Development* **24**: 135–149.

De Bellis, M., Clark, D. *et al.* (2000). "Hippocampal volume in adolescent-onset alcohol use disorders." *American Journal of Psychiatry* **157**: 737–744.

De Botton, A. (2000). *The Consolations of Philosophy*. London: Hamish Hamilton.

de Mause, L. (1976). *The History of Childhood*. London: Souvenir Press.

De Raad, B., van Oudenhoven, J. P. *et al.* (2005). "Personality terms of abuse in three cultures: type nouns between description and insult." *European Journal of Personality* **19**: 153–165.

Deater-Deckard, K. (2001). "Annotation: Recent research examining the role of peer relations in the development of psychopathology." *Journal of Child Psychology and Psychiatry* **42**: 565–579.

Deater-Deckard, K., and O'Connor, T. (2000). "Parent–child mutuality in early childhood: Two behavior-genetic studies." *Developmental Psychology* **16**: 1561–1570.

Deater-Deckard, K., Ivy, L., Smith, J. (2006). Resilience in gene-environment transactions. In S. Goldstein and R. Brooks (eds), *Handbook of Resilience in Children*. New York: Springer.

Deater-Deckard, K., Dodge, K. A. *et al.* (1998). Multiple risk factors in the development of externalizing behavior problems: Group and individual differences. *Development And Psychopathology* **10**: 469–493.

DeCasper, A. and Fifer, W. (1980). "Of human bonding – newborns prefer their mothers voices." *Science* **208**: 1174–1176.

Dempster, F. N. (1992). "The rise and fall of the inhibitory mechanism: toward a unified theory of cognitive development and aging." *Developmental Review* **12**: 45–75.

Deng, S. and Roosa, M. (2007). "Family influences on adolescent delinquent behaviors: applying the social development model to a Chinese sample." *American Journal of Community Psychology* **40**: 333–344.

Denissen, J., Zarrett, N. *et al.* (2007). "I like to do it, I'm able, and I know I am: longitudinal couplings between domain-specific achievement, self-concept, and interest." *Child Development* **78**: 430–447.

Denton, K. and Zarbatany, L. (1996). "Age differences in support processes in conversations between friends." *Child Development* **67**: 1360–1373.

Depue, R. A. and Collins, P. F. (1999). "Neurobiology of the structure of personality: Dopamine, facilitation of incentive motivation, and extraversion." *Behavioral and Brain Sciences* **22**: 491–569.

Derbaix, C. and Pecheux, C. (2003). "A new scale to assess children's attitude towards TV advertising." *Journal of Advertising Research* **43**: 390–399.

DeRosier, M., Kupersmidt, J. and Patterson, C. (1994). "Children's academic and behavioral adjustment as a function of the chronicity and proximity of peer rejection." *Child Development* **32**: 159–173.

Derryberry, D. (2003). "Temperament and coping: advantages of an individual differences perspective." *Development and Psychopathology* **15**: 1049–1066.

DeVore, E. R. and Ginsburg, K. R. (2005). "The protective effects of good parenting on adolescents." *Current Opinion in Pediatrics* **17**: 460–465.

deVries, M. (1984). "Temperament and infant mortality among the Masai of East Africa." *American Journal of Psychiatry* **141**: 1189–1194.

Diamond, L. M. and Fagundes, C. P. (2008). "Developmental perspectives on links between attachment and affect regulation over the lifespan." *Advances in Child Development and Behavior* **36**: 83–134.

Dill, K., Brown, B. and Collins, M. A. (2008). "Effects of exposure to sex-stereotyped video game characters on tolerance of sexual harassment." *Journal of Experimental Social Psychology* **44**: 1402–1408.

Dishion, T. J. and Connell, A. (2006). "Adolescents' resilience as a self-regulatory process – Promising themes for linking intervention with developmental science." *Annals of the New York Academy of Sciences* **1094**: 125–138.

Dishion, T., McCord, J. and Poulin, F. (1999). "When interventions fail: peer groups and problem behavior." *American Psychologist* **54**: 755–764.

Dodge, K., Pettit, G. S. *et al.* (1986). "Social competence in children." *Monographs of the Society for Research in Child Development* **51**: 1–80.

Dodge, K., Lansford J. E. *et al.* (2003). "Peer rejection and social information-processing factors in the development of aggressive behavior problems in children." *Child Development* **74**: 374–393.

Dodge, T., Barab, S. *et al.* (2008). "Children's sense of self: learning and meaning in the digital age." *Journal of Interactive Learning Research* **19**: 225–249.

Dogan, S. J., Conger, R. D. *et al.* (2007). "Cognitive and parenting pathways in the transmission of antisocial behavior from parents to adolescents." *Child Development* **78**: 335–349.

Dornbusch, S. M., Ritter, P. L. *et al.* (1987). "The relation of parenting style to adolescent school performance." *Child Development* **58**: 1244–1257.

Downey, D. (2008). "Black/White differences in school performance: the oppositional culture explanation." *Annual Review of Sociology* **34**: 107–126.

Dubow, E. F., Huesmann, L. R. and Greenwood, D. (2007). Media and youth socialization: underlying processes and mediators of effects. In J. Grusec and P. Hastings (eds), *Handbook of Socialization*. New York: Guilford.

Dunbar, R. (2008). Kinship in biological perspective. In N. Allen, H. Callan, R. Dunbar and W. James (eds), *Early Human Kinship: From Sex to Social Reproduction*. Oxford, Blackwell.

Dunbar, R. and Barrett, L. (2007). *Oxford Handbook of Evolutionary Psychology*. Oxford: Oxford University Press.

Duncan, G. and Brooks-Gunn, J. (1997). *Consequences of Growing Up Poor*. New York: Russell Sage Foundation.

Duncan, G. and Brooks-Gunn, J. (2000). "Family poverty, welfare reform, and child development." *Child Development* **71**: 188–196.

Duncan, G., Brooks-Gunn, J. and Klebanov P. K. (1994). "Economic deprivation and early-childhood development." *Child Development* **65**: 296–318.

Dunn, J. (1987). Understanding feelings: the early stages. In J. Bruner and H. Haste (eds), *Making Sense: The Child's Construction of the World*. London: Methuen.

Dunn, J. (1988). *The Beginnings of Social Understanding*. Oxford: Blackwell.

Dunn, J. (1993). *Young Children's Close Relationships: Beyond Attachment*. Newbury Park, CA: Sage.

Dunn, J. (1999). Siblings, friends, and the development of social understanding. *Relationships As Developmental Contexts* **30**: 263–279.

Dunn, J. (2004). *Children's Friendships*. Oxford, Blackwell.

Dunn, J. and Brown, J (1994). "Affect expression in the family, children's understanding of emotions and their interactions with others." *Merrill-Palmer Quarterly* **40**: 120–137.

Dunn, J. and Cutting, A. (1999). "Understanding others and individual differences in friendship interaction in young children." *Social Development* **8**: 201–219.

Dunn, J. and Kendrick, C. (1982). *Siblings: Love, Envy and Understanding*. London: Grant McIntyre.

Dunn, J., Cutting, A. and Fisher, N. (2002). "Old friends, new friends: predictors of children's perspective on their friends at school." *Child Development* **73**: 621–635.

Dunn, J., Maguire, M. and Brown, J. (1995). The development of children's moral sensibility – individual-differences and emotion understanding. *Developmental Psychology* **31**: 649–659.

Dunn, J., Slomkowski, C. et al. (1994). "Adjustment in middle childhood and early adolescence: Links with earlier and contemporary sibling relationships." *Journal of Child Psychology and Psychiatry* **35**: 491–504.

Dunn, J., Deater-Decker, K et al. (1999). "Siblings, parents and partners: Family relationships within a longitudinal community sample." *Journal of Child Psychology and Psychiatry* **40**: 1025–1037.

Dunne, M. and Gazeley, L. (2008). "Teachers, social class and underachievement." *British Journal of Sociology of Education* **29**: 451–463.

DuRocher-Studlich, T. and Cummings, E. (2003). "Parental dysphoria and children's internalizing symptoms: Marital conflict styles as mediators of risk." *Child Development* **74**: 1667–1681.

Duyme, M., Dumaret, A. and Tomkiewicz, S. (1999). How much can we boost IQs of dull children? A late adoption study. *Proceedings of the National Academy of Sciences* **96**: 8790–8794.

Dwairy, M. (2008). "Parental inconsistency versus parental authoritarianism:

Associations with symptoms of psychological disorders." *Journal of Youth and Adolescence* **37**: 616–626.

Dwairy, M., Achoui, M. *et al.* (2006). "Parenting styles, individuation, and mental health of Arab adolescents." *Journal of Cross-cultural Psychology* **37**: 262–272.

Dweck, C. (1999). *Self Theories*. Hove: Psychology Press.

Dweck, C. S. and Elliot, E. S. (1983). Achievement motivation. In E. Hetherington (ed.), *Handbook of Child Psychology, Vol 3: Socialization, Personality, and Social Development*. New York: Wiley.

Eagly, A. H. and Wood, W. (1999). "The origins of sex differences in human behavior: evolved dispositions versus social roles." *American Psychologist* **54**: 408–423.

Eaves, L., Silberg, J. *et al.* (2003). "Resolving multiple epigenetic pathways to adolescent depression." *Journal of Child Psychology and Psychiatry* **44**: 1006–1014.

Eby, L., Maher, C. and Butts, M. (2010). "The intersection of work and family life: the role of affect." *Annual Review of Psychology* **61**: (in press).

Eccles, J (2005). "Studying the development of learning and task motivation." *Learning and Instruction* **15**: 161–171.

Eccles, J. (2007). Families, schools and developing achievement-related motivations and engagement. In J. Grusec and P. Hastings (eds), *Handbook of Socialization*. New York: Guilford.

Eccles, J. and Wigfield, A. (2002). "Motivational beliefs, values, and goals." *Annual Review of Psychology* **53**: 109–132.

Eccles, J., Wigfield, A. *et al.* (1998). Motivation to achieve. In W. Damon and N Eisberg (eds), *Handbook of Child Psychology, Vol 3*. New York: Wiley.

Eckenrode, J., Zielinkski, D. *et al.* (2001). "Child maltreatment and the early onset of problem behaviors." *Development and Psychopathology* **13**: 873–890.

Edwards, A., Shipman, K. and Brown, A. (2005). "The socialization of emotional understanding: A comparison of neglected and nonneglectful mothers and their children." *Child maltreatment* **10**: 293–304.

Egan, S. and Perry, D. (2001). "Gender identity: a multidimensional analysis with implications for psychosocial adjustment." *Developmental Psychology* **37**: 451–463.

Eisenberg, N. (2000). "Emotion, regulation and moral development." *Annual Review of Psychology* **51**: 665–697.

Eisenberg, N. (2001). "The longitudinal relations of regulation and emotionality to quality of Indonesian children's social functioning." *Child Development* **72**: 1747–1763.

Eisenberg, N., Cumberland, A. and Spinrad, T. (1998). "Parental socialization of emotion." *Psychological Inquiry* **9**: 241–273.

Eisenberg, N., Pidada, S. and Liew, J. (2001). "The relations of regulation and emotionality to children's externalizing and intenalizing problem behavior." *Child Development* **72**: 1112–1134.

Eisenberg, N., Spinrad, T. L. *et al.* (2004). "The relations of effortful control and impulsivity to children's resiliency and adjustment." *Child Development* **75**: 25–46.

Eisenberg, N., Fabes, R. *et al.* (2006). Prosocial development. In W. Damon, R.

Lerner, N. Eisenberg (eds), *Handbook of Child Psychology, (6th edn) Vol 3: Social, Emotional and Personality Development*. New York: Wiley.

Elander, J., Rutter, M. *et al.* (2000). "Explanations for apparent late onset criminality in a high-risk sample of children followed-up in adult life." *British Journal of Criminology* **40**: 497–509.

Elder, G. H. (1974). *Children of the Great Depression*. Chicago, CA: University of Chicago Press.

Elder, G., Modell, J. and Parke, R. D. (1993). *Children in Time and Place: Developmental and Historical Insights*. Cambridge: Cambridge University Press.

Ellemers, N., Spears, R. *et al.* (2002). "Self and social identity." *Annual Review of Psychology* **53**: 161–186.

Elliot, A. and Harackiewicz, J. (1996). "Approach and avoidance achievement goals and intrinsic motivation: a mediational analysis." *Journal of Personality and Social Psychology* **70**: 461–475.

Elliot, A. J. and Church, M. A. (1997). "A hierarchical model of approach and avoidance achievement motivation." *Journal of Personality and Social Psychology* **72**: 218–232.

Elliot, E. and Dweck, C. (1988). "Goals: an approach to motivation and achievement." *Journal of Personality and Social Psychology* **54**: 5–12.

Ellis, B. and Garber, J. (2000). "Psychosocial antecedents of variation in girls' pubertal timing: Maternal depression, stepfather presence, and marital and family stress" *Child Development* **71**: 485–501.

Emlen, S. (1995). "An evolutionary theory of the family." *Proceedings of the National Academy of Science of the United States of America* **92**: 8092–8099.

Emler, N. (1998). Sociomoral understanding. In A. Campbell and S. Muncer (eds), *The Social Child*. Hove: Psychology Press.

Emler, N. and Dickinson, J. (1985). "Children's representation of social inequalities: the effects of social class." *British Journal of Developmental Psychology* **3**: 191–198.

Ennett, S. and Bauman, K. (1996). "Adolescent social networks: school, demographic, and longitudinal considerations." *Journal of Adolescent Research* **11**: 194–215.

Enoch, M. A. (2006). "Genetic and environmental influences on the development of alcoholism – Resilience vs. risk." *Annals of the New York Academy of Sciences* **1094**: 193–201.

Ensor, R. and Hughes, C. (2008). "Content or connectedness? Mother–child talk and early social understanding." *Child Development* **79**: 201–216.

Erel, O. and Burman, B. (1995). "Interrelatedness of marital relations and parent–child relations: A meta-analytic review." *Psychological Bulletin* **118**: 108–132.

Erel, O., Margolin, G. *et al.* (1998). "Observed sibling interaction: links with the marital and the mother–child relationship." *Developmental Psychology* **34**: 288–298.

Erikson, E. (1963). *Childhood and Society*. Harmondsworth: Penguin.

Erikson, E. (1968). *Identity, Youth and Crisis*. London: Faber.

Escobar-Chaves, S. (2008). "Media and risky behaviors." *The Future of Children* **18**: 147–180.

Espinosa, M., Beckwith, L. *et al.* (2001). "Maternal psychopathology and attachment in toddlers of heavy cocaine-using mothers." *Infant Mental Health Journal* **22**: 316–333.

Evans, G. (2004). "The environment of childhood poverty." *American Psychologist* **59**: 77–92.

Evans, G. (2006). "Child development and the physical environment." *Annual Review of Psychology* **57**: 423–451.

Evans, G. and English, K. (2002). "The environment of poverty: multiple stressor exposure, psychophysiological stress, and socioemotional adjustment." *Child Development* **73**: 1238–1248.

Even-Chen, M. and Itzhaky, H. (2007). "Exposure to terrorism and violent behavior among adolescents in Israel." *Journal of Community Psychology* **35**: 43–55.

Eysenck, H. (1967). *The Biological Basis of Personality*. Springfield, IL: Charles C. Thomas.

Eysenck, H. (1971). *Race, Intelligence and Education*. London: Temple Smith.

Fabes, R., Hanish, L. *et al.* (2003). "Children at play: the role of peers in understanding the effects of child care." *Child Development* **74**: 976–1005.

Farrington, D. P. (1987). "Predicting Individual Crime Rates." *Crime And Justice – A Review of Research* **9**: 53–101.

Farrington, D. and Coid, J. E. (2003). *Early Prevention of Adult Antisocial Behaviour*. Cambridge: Cambridge University Press.

Farver, J. (1995). "Cultural differences in Korean- and Anglo-American preschoolers: social interaction and play behaviours." *Child Development* **66**: 1088–1099.

Farver, J. (1997). "Social pretend play in Korean- and Anglo-American preschoolers." *Child Development* **68**: 544–556.

Farver, J., Xu, Y. *et al.* (2007). "Ethnic identity, acculturation, parenting beliefs and adolescent adjustment." *Merrill-Palmer Quarterly* **53**: 184–215.

Fazel, M., Wheeler, J. *et al.* (2005). "Prevalence of serious mental disorder in 7000 refugees resettled in western countries: a systematic review." *The Lancet* **365**: 1309–1314.

Feeney, J., Noller, P. *et al.* (1993). "Adolescents' interaction with the opposite sex: influence of attachment style and gender." *Journal of Adolescence* **16**: 169–186.

Feeney, J., Peterson, C. *et al.* (2000). "Attachment style as a predictor of sexual attitudes and behavior in late adolescence." *Psychology and Health* **14**: 1105–1122.

Feinberg, M. E., Kan, M. L. and Hetherington, E. M. (2007). "The longitudinal influence of coparenting conflict on parental negativity and adolescent maladjustment." *Journal of Marriage and the Family* **69**: 687–702.

Feinberg, M., McHale, S. *et al.* (2003). "Sibling differentiation: sibling and parent relationship trajectories in adolescence." *Child Development* **74**: 1261–1274.

Feinberg, M. E., Button, T. M. *et al.* (2007). "Parenting and adolescent antisocial behavior and depression: evidence of genotype – parenting environment interaction." *Archives of General Psychiatry* **64**: 457–465.

Feiner, R. (2006). Poverty in childhood and adolescence. In S. Goldstein and R. Brooks (eds), *Handbook of Resilience in Children*. New York: Springer.

Feinstein, L. and Bynner, J. (2004). The importance of cognitive development in middle childhood for adult socio-economic status, mental health, and problem behaviour. *Child Development* **75**: 1329–1339.

Feinstein, L., Sabates, R. *et al.* (2008). "Dietary patterns related to attainment in school: the importance of early eating patterns." *Journal of Epidemiology and Community Health* **62**: 734–739.

Feldman, R. (2007). "Parent-infant synchrony and the construction of shared timing; physiological precursors, developmental outcomes, and risk conditions." *Journal of Child Psychology and Psychiatry* **48**: 329–354.

Feldman, R., Weller, A. *et al.* (2002). "Skin-to-skin contact (kangaroo care) promotes self-regulation in premature infants: sleep-wake cyclicity, arousal modulation, and sustained exploration." *Developmental Psychology* **38**: 194–207.

Fenstermacher, S. and Saudino, K. (2006). "Understanding individual differences in young children's imitative behavior." *Developmental Review* **26**: 346–364.

Fergusson, D. M., Horwood, L. J. *et al.* (1989). "The Christchurch Child Development Study: a review of epidemiological findings." *Paediatric and Perinatal Epidemiology* **3**: 278–301.

Fiese, B. and Marjinsky, K. (1999). "Dinnertime stories: Connecting family practices with relationship beliefs and child adjustment." *Monographs of the Society for Research in Child Development* **64**: 52–68.

Fiese, B., Tomcho, T. *et al.* (2002). "A review of 50 years of research on naturally occurring family routines and rituals: Cause for celebration?" *Journal of Family Psychology* **16**: 381–390.

Figes, O. (2008). *The Whisperers*. London: Penguin.

Figueredo, A. (2006). "Consilience and life history theory: from genes to brain to reproductive strategy." *Developmental Review* **26**: 243–275.

Figueredo, A. (2007). "The K-factor, covitality, and personality: a psychometric test of life history theory." *Human Nature* **18**: 47–73.

Fivush, R. and K. Nelson (2004). "Culture and language in the emergence of autobiographical memory." *Psychological Science* **15**: 573–577.

Fivush, R. Haden, C. A. and Reese, E. (2006). "Elaborating on elaborations: Role of maternal reminiscing style in cognitive and socioemotional development." *Child Development* **77**: 1568–1588.

Flanagan, C. A., Gallay, L. S. *et al.* (2005). "What does democracy mean? Correlates of adolescents' views." *Journal of Adolescence Resarch* **20**: 193–218.

Fletcher, A., Darling, N. *et al.* (1995). "The company they keep: relation of adolescents' adjustment and behavior to their friends' perceptions of authoritative parenting in the social network." *Developmental Psychology*, **31**: 300–310.

Fletcher, A., Steinberg, L. *et al.* (2004). "Parental influences on adolescent problem behavior: revisiting Stattin and Kerr." *Child Development* **75**: 781–796.

Flook, L. and Fuligni, A. (2008). "Family and school spillover in adolescents' daily lives." *Child Development* **79**: 776–787.

Foley, D. L., Eaves, L. J. *et al.* (2004). "Childhood adversity, monoamine oxidase a genotype, and risk for conduct disorder." *Archives of General Psychiatry* **61**: 738–744.

Fong, V. (2002). "China's One-Child policy and the empowerment of urban daughters." *American Anthropologist* **104**: 1098–1109.

Forbes, L., Evans, E. *et al.* (2007). "Change in atypical maternal behavior predicts change in attachment disorganization from 12 to 24 months in a high-risk sample." *Child Development* **78**: 955–971.

Fordham, K. and Stevenson-Hinde, J. (1999). Shyness, friendship quality, and adjustment during middle childhood. *Journal of Child Psychology and Psychiatry* **40**: 757–768.

Forgatch, M. S. and DeGarmo, D. S. (1999). "Parenting through change: an effective prevention program for single mothers." *Journal of Consulting and Clinical Psychology* **67**: 711–724.

Forsyth, J. S., Willatts, P. *et al.* (2003a). "Long chain polyunsaturated fatty acid supplementation in infant formula and blood pressure in later childhood: follow up of a randomised controlled trial." *British Medical Journal* **326**: 953–955.

Forsyth, J. S., Willatts, P. *et al.* (2003b). "Relationship of prenatal LCPUFA status to infant visual and cognitive function." *Journal of Reproductive and Infant Psychology* **21**: 253.

Forsyth, J. S., Willatts, P. *et al.* (2003c). "Long-chain polyunsaturated fatty acid supplementation in infancy and cognitive function in later childhood." *Journal of Reproductive and Infant Psychology* **21**: 257–258.

Fowler, P., Cassie, S. *et al.* (2008). "Maternal smoking during pregnancy specifically reduces human fetal desert hedgehog gene expression during testis development." *The Journal of Clinical Endocrinology and Metabolism* **93**: 619–626.

Fox, H. (2005). "Behavioral inhibition: linking biology and behavior within a developmental framework." *Annual Review of Psychology* **56**: 235–262.

Francis, M. and Lorenzo, R. (2006). Children and city design: proactive process and the 'renewal' of childhood. In C. Spencer and M. Blades (eds), *Children and their Environments*. Cambridge: Cambridge University Press.

Frankenburg, M. S. (1946). *Common Sense in the Nursery*. Harmondsworth: Penguin.

Fredricks, J. and J. Eccles (2005). "Developmental benefits of extracurricular involvement: Do peer characteristics mediate the link between activities and youth outcomes?" *Journal of Youth and Adolescence* **34**: 507–520.

Fredricks, J. and Eccles, J. (2006). "Is extracurricular participation associated with beneficial outcomes? Concurrent and longitudinal relations." *Developmental Psychology* **42**: 698–713.

Fredricks, J. and Eccles, J. (2008). "Participation in extracurricular activities in the middle school years: Are there developmental benefits for African American and European American youth?" *Journal of Youth and Adolescence* **37**: 1029–1043.

Freese, J., Li, J.-C. A. *et al.* (2003). "The potential relevances of biology to social inquiry." *Annual Review of Sociology* **29**: 233–256.

French, D. (2005). "Reported peer conflicts of children in the United States and Indonesia." *Social Development* **14**: 458–472.

Frewen, P., Dozois, D. J. A. and Lanius, R. A. (2008). "Neuroimaging studies of psychological interventions for mood and anxiety disorders: Empirical and methodological review." *Clinical Psychology Review* **28**: 228–246.

Friedlmeyer, W., Chakkarath, P. and Schwartz, B. (2005). *Culture and Human Development*. Hove: Psychology Press.

Friedman, C. K., Leaper, C. and Bigler, R. S. (2007). "Do mothers' gender-related attitudes or comments predict young children's gender beliefs?" *Parenting-Science and Practice* **7**: 357–366.

Frith, U. (1990). *Autism*. Oxford: Blackwell.

Frith, U. (2003). *Autism: Explaining the Enigma, (2nd edn)*. Oxford: Blackwell.

Frith, U. and Frith, C. (2001). "The biological basis of social interaction." *Current Directions in Psychological Science* **10**: 151–155.

Frith, U. and Hill, E. (2004). *Autism: Mind and Brain*. Oxford: Oxford University Press.

Frydenberg, E. (1997). *Adolescent Coping: Theoretical and Research Perspectives*. London: Routledge.

Fujinaga, T., Kasugat, T. et al. (1990). "Long-term follow-up study of children developmentally retarded by early environmental deprivation." *Genetic, social and general psychology monographs* **116**: 37–104.

Fuligni, A. (1998). "Authority, autonomy, and parent-adolescent conflict and cohesion: a study of adolescents from Mexican, Chinese, Filipino, and European backgrounds." *Developmental Psychology* **34**: 782–792.

Fuligni, A. and Eccles, J. (1993). "Perceived parent–child relationships and early adolescents' orientations toward peers." *Developmental Psychology* **29**: 622–632.

Fuligni, A. J., Tseng, V. and Lam, M. (1999). "Attitudes toward family obligations among American adolescents with Asian, Latin American, and European backgrounds." *Child Development* **70**: 1030–1044.

Furman, W. and Buhrmester, D. (1985). "Children's perceptions of the personal relationships in their social networks." *Developmental Psychology* **21**: 1016–1024.

Furman, W. and Buhrmester, D. (1992). "Age and sex in perceptions of networks of personal relationships." *Child Development* **63**: 103–115.

Furman, W. and Wehner, E. (1997). Adolescent romantic relationships: a developmental perspective. In S. Shulman and W. Collins (eds), *New Directions for Child Development: Adolescent Romantic Relationships*. San Francisco: Jossey-Bass.

Furman, W., Simon, V. A. et al. (2002). "Adolescents' working models and styles for relationships with parents, friends, and romantic partners." *Child Development* **73**: 241–255.

Furnham, A., Swami, V. et al. (2006). "Body weight, waist-to-hip ratio and breast size correlates of ratings of attractiveness and health." *Personality and Individual Differences* **41**: 443–454.

Gale C. R., O'Callaghan F. J. et al. (2006). "The influence of head growth in fetal life, infancy, and childhood on intelligence at the ages of 4 and 8 years." *Pediatrics* **118**: 1486–1492.

Gallagher, K. (2002). "Does child temperament moderate the influence of parenting on adjustment?" *Developmental Review* **22**: 623–643.

Gallese, V. and Goldman, A. (1998). "Mirror neurons and the simulation theory of mind-reading." *Trends in Cognitive Sciences* **2**: 493–501.

Gallese, V., Keysers, C. and Rizzolatti, G. (2004). "A unifying view of the basis of social cognition." *Trends in Cognitive Sciences* **8**: 396–403.

Galsworthy, M. J., Dionne, G. et al. (2000). "Sex differences in early verbal and non-verbal cognitive development." *Developmental Science* **3**: 206–215.

Galton, F. (1978). *Hereditary Genius*. London: Friedmann.

Galvan, A., Hare, T. A. et al. (2006). "Earlier development of the accumbens relative to orbitofrontal cortex might underlie risk-taking behavior in adolescents." *Journal of Neuroscience* **26**: 6885–6892.

Garbarino, J. and Kostelny, K. (1996). "The effects of political violence on Palestinian children's behavior problems: A risk accumulation model." *Child Development* **67**: 33–45.

Garcia-Coll, C. and Szalacha, L. (2004). "The multiple contexts of middle childhood." *The Future of Children* **14**: 80–97.

Gardenfors, P. (2003). *How Homo Became Sapiens.* Oxford: Oxford University Press.

Gardner, J. M. M., Grantham-McGregor, S. M. *et al.* (1999). "Behaviour and development of stunted and nonstunted Jamaican children." *Journal of Child Psychology and Psychiatry and Allied Disciplines* **40**: 819–827.

Garmezy, N. (1993). "Children in poverty – resilience despite risk." *Psychiatry – Interpersonal and Biological Processes* **56**: 127–136.

Garmezy, N., Masten, A. *et al.* (1984). "The study of stress and competence in children: a building block of developmental psychopathology." *Child Development* **55**: 97–111.

Garner, P. and Spears, F. (2000). "Emotion regulation in low-income preschool children." *Social Development* **9**: 246–264.

Gass, K., Jenkins, J. and Dunn, J. (2007). Are sibling relationships protective? A longitudinal study. *Journal of Child Psychology and Psychiatry* **48**: 167–175.

Gauvain, M. (2005). "Scaffolding in socialization." *New Ideas in Psychology* **23**: 129–139.

Gauvain, M. and S. Perez (2007). The socialization of cognition. In J. Grusec and P. Hastings (eds), *Handbook of Socialization Theory and Research.* New York: Guilford.

Gazelle, H. and Spangler, T. (2007). "Early childhood anxious solitude and subsequent peer relationships: Maternal and cognitive moderators." *Journal of Applied Developmental Psychology* **28**: 515–535.

Ge, X. (1996). "The developmental interface between nature and nurture: a mutual influence model of child antisocial behavior and parent behaviors." *Developmental Psychology* **32**: 574–589.

Ge, X., Donnellan, M. *et al.* (2003). Are we finally ready to move beyond "Nature vs, Nurture"? In A. Crouter and A. Booth (eds), *Children's Influence on Family Dynamics: The Neglected Side of Family Relationships.* Mahwah, NJ: Erlbaum.

Geary, D. C. (1998). *Male, Female: The Evolution of Human Sex Differences.* Washington, DC: American Psychological Association.

Gergely, G., Bekkering, H. and Király, I. (2002). "Rational imitation in preverbal infants." *Nature* **415**: 755–765.

Gergen, K., Lightfoot, C. and Sydow, L. (2004). "Social construction: vistas in clinical child and adolescent psychology." *Journal of Clinical Child and Adolescent Psychology* **33**: 389–399.

Gesell, A. (1942). *Wolf Child and Human Child.* London: The Scientific Book Club.

Gibbons, F. X., Gerrard, M. *et al.* (2004). "Context and cognitions: Environmental risk, social influence, and adolescent substance use." *Personality and Social Psychology Bulletin* **30**: 1048–1061.

Giedd, J. N., Blumenthal, J. *et al.* (1999). "Brain development during childhood and adolescence: a longitudinal MRI study." *Nature Neuroscience* **2**: 861–863.

Giele, J. and Elder, G. (1998). *Methods of Life Course Research: Qualitative and Quantitative Approaches.* Thousand Oaks, CA: Sage.

Gillespie, N. A., Whitfield, J. B. *et al.* (2005). "The relationship between stressful life events, the serotonin transporter (5-HTTLPR) genotype, and major depression." *Psychological Medicine* **35**: 101–111.

Gillies, V. (2006). "Working class mothers and school life: exploring the role of emotional capital." *Gender and Education* **18**: 281–293.

Gilligan, C. (1982). *In a Different Voice: Psychological Theory and Women's Development.* Cambridge, MA: Harvard University Press.

Gilliom, M. and Shaw, D. (2004). "Codevelopment of externalizing and internalizing problems in early childhood." *Development and Psychopathology* **16**: 313–333.

Giordano, P. (2003). "Relationships in adolescence." *Annual Review of Sociology* **29**: 257–281.

Gladstone, G. L. and Parker, G. B. (2006). "Is behavioral inhibition a risk factor for depression?" *Journal of Affective Disorders* **95**: 85–94.

Goldberg, S. (2000). *Attachment and Development.* London: Arnold.

Golding, W. (1954). *Lord of the Flies.* London: Faber.

Goldsmith, H. H., Buss, K. A. and Lemery, K. S. (1997). "Toddler and childhood temperament: Expanded content, stronger genetic evidence, new evidence for the importance of environment." *Developmental Psychology* **33**: 891–905.

Goldstein, S. and Brooks, R. (2006). *Handbook of Resilience in Children.* New York: Springer.

Golombok, S. (2000). *Parenting: What Really Counts?* London: Routledge.

Golombok, S., Rust, J. *et al.* (2008). "Developmental trajectories of sex-typed behavior in boys and girls: a longitudinal general population study of children aged 2.5–8 years." *Child Development* **79**: 1583–1593.

Göncu, A., Patt, M. B. and Kouba, E. (2002). Understanding young children's pretend play in context. In P. K. Smith, C. Hart (eds), *Blackwell Handbook of Childhood Social Development.* Oxford: Blackwell.

Gonzales, N. A., Germán, M. *et al.* (2008). "Mexican American adolescents' cultural orientation, externalizing behavior and academic engagement: the role of traditional cultural values." *American Journal of Community Psychology* **41**: 151–164.

Goodwin, M. H. (2006). *The Hidden Life of Girls: Games of Stance, Status and Exclusion.* Oxford: Blackwell.

Goodyer, I. (1990). *Life Experiences, Development and Childhood Psychopathology.* New York: Wiley.

Goodyer, I. (2008). "Early onset depressions – meanings, mechanisms and processes." *Journal of Child Psychology and Psychiatry* **49**: 1239–1256.

Goswami, U. (2006). "The foundations of psychological understanding." *Developmental Science* **9**: 545–550.

Gottesman, I. I. and Hanson, D. R. (2005). "Human development: biological and genetic processes." *Annual Review of Psychology* **56**: 263–286.

Gottfried, A. W. (1984). *Home Environment and Early Cognitive Development: Longitudinal Research.* New York: Academic Press.

Gottfried, A., Fleming, J. and Gottfried, A. W. (1998). "Role of cognitively stimulating home environment in children's academic intrinsic motivation: A longitudinal study." *Child Development* **69**: 1448–1460.

Gottlieb, G, Wahlsten, D. and Lickliter, R. (1998). The significance of biology for human development: a developmental psychobiological systems view. In R. M. Lerner (ed.), *Handbook of Child Psychology, Vol 1*: 233–273. New York: Wiley.

Gould, S. J. (1977). *Ontogeny and Phylogeny*. Cambridge, MA: Belknap Press of Harvard University Press.

Granger, D. A. and Kivlighan, K. (2003). "Integrating biological, behavioral, and social levels of analysis in early child development: Progress, problems, and prospects." *Child Development* **74**: 1058–1063.

Granic, I. and Patterson, G. (2006). "Towards a comprehensive model of antisocial development." *Psychological Review* **113**: 101–131.

Grant, B. F. and Dawson, D. (1998). "Age of onset of drug use and its association with DSM-IV drug abuse and dependence: results from the National Longitudinal Alcohol Epidemiologic Survey." *Journal of Substance Abuse* **10**: 163–173.

Grant, H. and Dweck, C. (2003). "Clarifying achievement goals and their impact." *Journal of Personality and Social Psychology* **85**: 541–553.

Grant, K., Compas, B. *et al.* (2003). "Stressors and child and adolescent psychopathology: moving from markers to mechanisms of risk." *Psychological Bulletin* **129**: 447–466.

Grass, G. (2008). *Peeling the Onion*. London: Vintage.

Green, J. and Goldwyn, R. (2002). "Annotation: Attachment disorganisation and psychopathology – New findings in attachment research and their potential implications for developmental psychopathology in childhood." *Journal of Child Psychology and Psychiatry and Allied Disciplines* **43**: 835–846.

Greenberg, M. T. (2005). Enhancing early attachments: synthesis and recommendations for research, practice and policy. In L. Berlin, Y. Ziv, L. Amaya-Jackson and M. T. Greenberg (eds), *Enhancing Early Attachments*. New York: The Guilford Press.

Greenberg, M. (2006). "Promoting resilience in children and youth. Preventive interventions and their interface with neuroscience." *Annals of the New York Academy of Sciences* **1094**: 139–150.

Greene, B., Miller, R. B *et al.* (2004). "Predicting high school students' cognitive engagement and achievement: contributions of classroom perceptions and motivation." *Contemporary Educational Psychology* **29**: 499–517.

Greenfield, P. (2006). Cultural pathways through human development. In L. Damon, R. E. Lerner, K. A. Renninger, I. E. Sigel (eds), *Handbook of Child Psychology, Vol 4*. New York: Wiley.

Greenough, W., Black, J. and Wallace, C. (1987). "Experience and brain development." *Child Development* **58**: 539–559.

Gregg, P., Harkness, S. and Machin, S. (1999). *Child Poverty and its Consequences*. York: Joseph Rowntree Foundation.

Gregg, P., Propper, C. and Washbrook, E. (2008). *Understanding the relationship between parental income and multiple child outcomes: a decomposition analysis. CMPO working paper series(08/193)*. London: Centre for Analysis of Social Exclusion (CASE).

Grossman, K. E., Grossman, K. and Kindler, H. (2005). Early care and the roots of attachment and partnership representations: the Bielefeld and Regensburg longitudinal studies. In K. E. Grossman, K. Grossman and E. Waters (eds),

Attachment from Infancy to Adulthood: The Major Longitudinal Studies. New York: Guilford.

Grossman, K. E., Grossmann, K. and Waters, E. (2005). *Attachment from Infancy to Adulthood: The Major Longitudinal Studies.* New York: The Guilford Press.

Grotevant, H. (1998). Adolescent development in family contexts. In W. Damon and N Eisberg (eds), *Handbook of Child Psychology Vol 3.* New York: Wiley.

Grover, R. and Nangle, D. (2003). "Adolescent perceptions of problematic heterosocial situations: A focus group study." *Journal of Youth and Adolescence* **32**: 129–139.

Grover, R, Nangle, D. W. *et al.* (2007). "Girl friend, boy friend, girlfriend, boyfriend: broadening our understanding of heterosocial competence." *Journal of Clinical Child & Adolescent Psychology* **36**: 491–502.

Grusec, J. and Davidov, M. (2007). Socialization in the family: the role of parents. In J.Grusec and P.Hastings (eds), *Handbook of Socialization.* New York: Guilford.

Grusec, J. and Goodnow, J. (1994). "Impact of parental discipline methods on the child's internalization of values: A reconceptualization of currrent points of view." *Developmental Psychology* **30**: 4–19.

Grusec, J. and Hastings, P. (2007). *Handbook of Socialization Theory and Research.* New York: Guilford.

Grych, J. and Fincham, F. (2001). *Child Development and Interparental Conflict: Theory, Research and Applications.* New York: Cambridge University Press.

Gunnar, M. R. and Cheatham, C. L. (2003). "Brain and behavior interface: stress and the developing brain." *Infant Mental Health Journal* **24**: 195–211.

Gunnar, M. and Donzella, B. (2002). "Social regulation of the cortisol levels in early human development." *Psychoneuroendocrinology* **27**: 199–220.

Gunnar, M. and Quevedo, K. (2007). "The neurobiology of stress and development." *Annual Review of Psychology* **58**: 145–173.

Gunnar, M. and Vazquez, D. (2006). Stress neurobiology and developmental psychology. In D. Cicchetti and D. Cohen (eds), *Developmental Psychopathology, Developmental Neuroscience.* New York: Wiley.

Gunnar, M. R., Sebanc, A. M. *et al.* (2003). "Peer rejection, temperament and cortisol activity in preschoolers." *Developmental Psychobiology* **43**: 346–358.

Gutman, L. M. and Eccles, J. (1999). "Financial strain, parenting behaviors, and adolescent achievement: testing model equivalence between African American and European American single- and two-parent families." *Child Development* **70**: 1464–1476.

Gutman, L. and Feinstein, L. (2008). *Children's Well-Being in Primary School: Pupil and School Effects. Centre for Research on the Wider Benefits of LearningResearch Reports Bristol, CMPO: 25.* Nottingham: DCSF.

Gutman, L. M., Sameroff, A. J. and Cole, R. (2003). "Academic growth curve trajectories from first to twelfth grades: effects of multiple social risk and preschool child factors." *Developmental Psychology* **39**: 777–790.

Gutman, L. M., Sameroff, A. J. and Eccles, J. S. (2002). "The academic achievement of African American students during early adolescence: An examination of multiple risk, promotive, and protective factors." *American Journal of Community Psychology* **30**: 367–399.

Hahn, C. (1998). *Becoming Political: Comparative Perspectives on Citizenship Education.* Albany, NY: State University of New York Press.

Hair, E. C. and Graziano, W. G. (2003). "Self-esteem and personality in high school students: A prospective longitudinal study in Texas." *Journal of Personality* **71**: 971–994.

Halligan, S., Herbert, J. *et al.* (2004). "Exposure to postnatal depression predicts elevated cortisol in adolescent offspring." *Biological Psychiatry* **55**: 376–381.

Halpern, D., Benbow, C. P *et al.* (2007). "The Science of Sex Differences in Science and Mathematics." *Psychological Science in the Public Interest* **8**: 1–51.

Hamilton, A., Wolpert, D. and Frith, U. (2004). "Your own action influences how you perceive another person's action." *Current Biology* **14**: 493–498.

Hammen, C. (2003). Risk and protective factors for children of depressed parents. In S. Luthar (ed.), *Resilience and Vulnerability*. Cambridge: Cambridge University Press.

Hankin, B., Mermelstein, R. and Roesch, L. (2007). "Sex differences in adolescent depression: stress exposure and reactivity models." *Child Development* **78**: 279–295.

Hannam, D. (2003). "Participation and responsible action for all students – the crucial ingredient for success." *Teaching Citizenship* **5**: 24–33.

Hanson, D. and Gottesman, I. (2007). Choreographing genetic, epigenetic and stochastic steps in the dances of developmental psychopathology. In A.Masten (ed.), *Minnesota Symposium on Child Development*. Mahwah, NJ: Erlbaum.

Harackiewicz, J., Barron, K. E *et al.* (2000). "Short-term and long-term consequences of achievement goals: predicting interest and performance over time." *Journal of Educational Psychology* **92**: 316–330.

Harding, D. (2003). "Counterfactual models of neighborhood effects: the effect of neighborhood poverty on dropping out and teenage pregnancy." *American Journal of Sociology* **109**: 676–719.

Hardyment, C. (1983). *Dream Babies: From Locke to Spock*. London: Cape.

Harkness, S. and Super, C. M. (2002). Culture and Parenting. In M. R. Bornstein (ed.), *Handbook of Parenting, Vol 2: Biology and Ecology of Parenting*. Mahwah, NJ: Erlbaum.

Harper, B. and Tiggemann, M. (2008). "The effect of thin ideal media images on women's self-objectification, mood, and body image." *Sex Roles* **58**: 649–657.

Harris, J. (1995). "Where is the child's environment? A group socialisation theory of development." *Psychological Review* **102**: 458–489.

Harris, J. R. (1998). *The Nurture Assumption*. New York: Free Press.

Harris, K. M. and Morgan, S. P. (1991). "Fathers, sons, and daughters: Differential parental involvement in parenting." *Journal of Marriage and the Family* **53**: 531–544.

Harris, P. (1990). Children's understanding of mixed emotions. In A. de Ribaupierre (ed.), *Transition Mechanisms in Child Development: The Longitudinal Perspective*. Cambridge: Cambridge University Press.

Harris, P. (2006). *In Search of Belonging: Reflections of Transracially Adopted People*. London: British Association of Adoption and Fostering.

Harris, T. O. and Brown, G. W. (1996). "Social causes of depression." *Current Opinion In Psychiatry* **9**: 3–10.

Hart, B. and Risley, T. (1995). *Meaningful Differences in the Everyday Experience of Young American Children*. Baltimore: Brookes.

Hart, D., Atkins, R. and Fegley, S. (2003). "Personality and development during childhood: a person-centred approach." *Monographs of the Society for Research in Child Development* **68**: 74–85.

Harter, S. (2006). "The Self." In W. Damon, R. Lerner, N. Eisenberg (eds), *Handbook of Child Psychology, (6th edn) Vol 3*: 505–571. New York: Wiley.

Harter, S., Low, S. M. and Whitesell, N. R. (2003). "What have we learned from Columbine? The impact of the self-system on suicidal and violent ideation amongst adolescents." *Journal of Youth Violence* **2**: 3–26.

Harter, S., Marold, D. H. *et al.* (1996). "A model of the effects of parental and peer support on adolescent false-self behavior." *Child Development* **55**: 1969–1982.

Hartup, W. and Abecassis, M. (2002). Friends and enemies. In P. K. Smith and C. Hart (eds), *Blackwell Handbook of Childhood Social Development*. Oxford: Blackwell.

Hartup, W. and Stevens, N. (1997). "Friendships and adaptation in the life course." *Psychological Bulletin* **121**: 355–370.

Harwood, R., Miller, J. G. and Irizarry, N. L. (1995). *Culture and Attachment: Perceptions of the Child in Context*. New York: Guilford.

Hasselmann, M. and Reichenheim, M. (2006). "Parental violence and the occurrence of severe and acute malnutrition in childhood." *Paediatric and Perinatal Epidemiology* **20**: 299–311.

Hassett, J. M., Siebert, E. R. and Wallen, K. (2008). "Sex differences in rhesus monkey toy preferences parallel those of children." *Hormones and Behavior* **54**: 359–364.

Hastings, P. and De, I. (2008). "Parasympathetic regulation and parental socialization of emotion: Biopsychosocial processes of adjustment in preschoolers." *Social Development* **17**: 211–238.

Hastings, P. and Rubin, K. (1999). "Predicting mothers' beliefs about preschool-aged children's social behavior: Evidence for maternal attitudes moderating child effects." *Child Development* **70**: 722–741.

Hastings, P., Utendale, W. *et al.* (2007). The socialization of prosocial development. In J. Grusec and P. Hastings (eds), *Handbook of Socialization*. New York: Guilford.

Hawker, D. and Boulton, M. (2000). "Twenty years' research on peer victimisation and psychosocial maladjustment: A meta-analytic review of cross-sectional studies." *Journal of Child Psychology and Psychiatry* **41**: 441–455.

Hay, D., Castle, J. and Davies, L. (2000). "Toddlers' use of force against familiar peers: A precursor of serious aggression?" *Child Development* **71**: 457–467.

Hay, D., Payne, A. and Chadwick, A. (2004). "Peer relations in childhood." *Journal of Child Psychology and Psychiatry* **45**: 84–108.

Hay, D., Castle, J. *et al.* (1999). "Prosocial action in very early childhood." *Journal of Child Psychology and Psychiatry* **40**: 905–916.

Hayne, H. (2004). "Infant memory development: Implications for childhood amnesia." *Developmental Review* **24**: 33–73.

Heath, S. (1983). *Ways with Words*. Cambridge: Cambridge University Press.

Heath, S. B. (2004). The children of Trackton's children: spoken and written language in social change. In R. Ruddell and N. Unrau (eds), *Theoretical Models and Processes of Reading*. Newark, NJ: International Reading Association.

Helwig, C. C. (1995). "Adolescents' and young adults' conceptions of civil liberties: freedom of speech and religion." *Child Development* **66**: 152–166.

Helwig, C. (1998). "Children's conceptions of fair government and freedom of speech." *Child Development* **69**: 518–531.

Helwig, C. C., Arnold, M. L. *et al.* (2003). "Chinese adolescents' reasoning about democratic and authority-based decision making in peer, family, and school contexts." *Child Development* **74**: 783–800.

Henry, D., Schoeny, M. *et al.* (2007). "Peer selection and socialization effects on adolescent intercourse without a condom and attitudes about the costs of sex." *Child Development* **78**: 825–838.

Herrick, R. (1989). D. Jesson-Dibley (ed.), *Selected Poems*. Manchester: Carcanet Press.

Hershkowitz, I., Lamb, M. E. and Horowitz, D. (2007). "Victimization of children with disabilities." *American Journal of Orthopsychiatry* **77**: 629–635.

Hetherington, E. M. (1988). Parents, children and siblings six years after divorce. In R. Hinde and J. S. Hinde (eds), *Relationships within the Family: Mutual Influences*: 311–331. Oxford: Clarendon Press.

Hetherington, E, Henderson, S. and Reiss, D. (1999). "Adolescent siblings in stepfamilies: Family functioning and adolescent adjustment." *Monographs of the Society for Research in Child Development* **64**: 1–209.

Hewlett, B. (2004). Fathering in forager, farmer and pastoral cultures. In M Lamb (ed.), *The Role of the Father in Child Development*. Hoboken, NJ: Wiley.

Hewstone, M., Rubin, M. *et al.* (2002). "Intergroup Bias." *Annual Review of Psychology* **53**: 575–604.

Heywood, C. (2001). *A History of Childhood: Children and Childhood in the West from Medieval to Modern Times*. Malden, MA: Polity Press.

Higgins, E. T. and Pittman, T. (2008). "Motives of the human animal: Comprehending, managing and sharing inner states." *Annual Review of Psychology* **59**: 361–383.

Hill, N. and Herman-Stahl, M. (2002). "Neighbourhood safety and social involvement: Associations with parenting behaviors and depressive symptoms among African-American and Euro-American mothers." *Journal of Family Psychology* **16**: 209–219.

Hill, N. E., Castellino, D. R. *et al.* (2004). "Parent academic involvement as related to school behavior, achievement, and aspirations: Demographic variations across adolescence." *Child Development* **75**: 1491–1509.

Hills, J., Le Grand, J. and Piachaud, D. (2002). *Understanding Social Exclusion*. Oxford: Oxford University Press.

Hinde, R. (1979). *Towards Understanding Relationships*. London: Academic Press.

Hinde, R. (1982). *Ethology*. London: Fontana.

Hinde, R. A. (1987). *Individuals, Relationships and Culture*. Cambridge: Cambridge University Press.

Hinde, R. (2005). Ethology and attachment theory. In K. E. Grossman, K. Grossman and E. Waters (eds), *Attachment from Infancy to Adulthood: The Major Longitudinal Studies*. New York: Guilford.

Hirsch, D. (2006). *Where Poverty Intersects with Social Exclusion: Evidence and Features of Solutions*. York: Joseph Rowntree Foundation.

Ho, C., Bluestein, D. and Jenkins, J. M. (2008). "Cultural differences in the relationship between parenting style and children's behavior." *Developmental Psychology* **44**: 507–522.

Hodes, M., Jagdev, D. *et al.* (2008). "Risk and resilience for psychological distress amongst unaccompanied asylum seeking adolescents." *Journal of Child Psychology and Psychiatry* **49**: 723–732.

Hodges, E. (1997). "Individual risk and social risk as interacting determinants of victimization in the peer group." *Developmental Psychology* **33**: 1032–1039.

Hodges, E., Boivin, M. *et al.* (1999). "The power of friendship: protection against an escalating cycle of peer victimisation." *Developmental Psychology* **35**: 94–101.

Hoekstra, R., Bartels, M. *et al.* (2008). "Genetic and environmental influences on the stability of withdrawn behavior in children: a longitudinal, multi-informant twin study." *Behavior Genetics* **38**: 447–461.

Hofer, M. (2006a). "Evolutionary basis of adaptation in resilience and vulnerability. Response to Cicchetti and Blender." *Annals of the New York Academy of Sciences* **1094**: 259–262.

Hofer, M. (2006b). "Psychobioloigcal roots of early attachment." *Current Directions in Psychological Science* **15**: 84–88.

Hoff, E. (2003). The specificity of environmental influence: socio-economic status affects early vocabulary development via maternal speech. *Child Development* **74**: 1368–1378.

Hofstede, G. (2001). *Culture's Consequences: Comparing Values, Behaviors, Institutions, and Organizations across Nations.* London: Sage.

Hofstede, G. (2005). *Cultures and Organizations: Software of the Mind.* New York: McGraw-Hill.

Holden, G. and Barker, T. (2004). Fathers in violent homes. In M Lamb (ed.), *The Role of the Father in Child Development.* Hoboken, NJ: Wiley.

Holland, S. (2003). *Bioethics: A Philosophical Introduction.* Cambridge: Polity Press.

Holloway, S. (2006). *Family Wanted: True Stories of Adoption.* London: Granta.

Homer, B. and Tamis-LeMonda, C. (2005). *The Development of Social Cognition and Communication.* Mahwah, NJ: Erlbaum.

Hong, Y., Chiu, C. *et al.* (1999). "Implicit theories, attributions, and coping: a meaning system approach." *Journal of Personality and Social Psychology.* **77**: 588–599.

Hooper, C. J., Luciana, M. *et al.* (2004). "Adolescents' performance on the Iowa Gambling Task: Implications for the development of decision-making and ventromedial prefrontal cortex." *Developmental Psychology* **40**: 1148–1158.

Horgan, G. (2007). *The Impact of Poverty on Young Children's Experience of School.* York: Joseph Rowntree Foundation.

Horn, S. (2003). "Adolescents' reasoning about exclusion from social groups." *Developmental Psychology* **39**: 71–84.

Houshyar, S. and Kaufman, J. (2006). Resiliency in maltreated children. In S. Goldstein and R. Brooks (eds), *Handbook of Resilience in Children.* New York: Springer.

Howe, M. L. (2003). "Memories from the cradle." *Psychological Science* **12**: 62–65.

Hrdy, S. B. (1999). *Mother Nature: Maternal Instincts and How They Shape the Human Species.* New York: Ballantine.

Hubbs-Tait L., Culp, A. M. *et al.* (2002). "Relation of maternal cognitive stimulation, emotional support, and intrusive behaviour during Head Start to children's kindergarten coping strategies." *Child Development* **73**: 110–131.

Hubbs-Tait, L., Nation, J. *et al.* (2005). "Neurotoxicants, micronutrients, and social

environments. Individual and combined effects on children's development."
Psychological Science in the Public Interest **6**: 57–121.

Hudson, L. (1967). *Contrary Imaginations: A Psychological Study of the English Schoolboy.* Harmondsworth: Penguin.

Huesmann, L. and Taylor, L. (2006). "The role of media violence in violent behavior." *Annual Review of Public Health* **27**: 393–415.

Huesmann, L. R., Moise-Titus, J. *et al.* (2003). "Longitudinal relations between children's exposure to TV violence and their aggressive and violent behavior in young adulthood: 1977–1992." *Developmental Psychology* **39**: 201–221.

Hughes, M. and Pollard, A. (2006). "Home-school knowledge exchange in context." *Educational Review* **58**: 385–395.

Hughes, M., Wikeley, F. *et al.* (1994). *Parents and their Children's Schools.* Oxford: Blackwell.

Humphrey, N. (1983). *Consciousness Regained: Chapters in the Development of the Mind.* Oxford: Oxford University Press.

Hur, Y., McGue, M. and Iacono, W. G. (1998). "The structure of self-concept in female pre-adolescent twins: A behavior-genetic study." *Journal of Personality and Social Psychology* **74**: 1069–1077.

Hurley, S., Clark, A. and Kiverstein, J. (2008). "The shared circuits model (SCM): How control, mirroring, and simulation can enable imitation, deliberation, and mindreading." *Behavioral and Brain Sciences* **31**: 1–22.

Hussong, A., Flora, D. *et al.* (2008). "Defining risk heterogeneity for internalizing symptoms among children of alcoholic parents." *Development and Psychopathology* **20**: 165–193.

Huston, A. (2005). "Impacts on children of a policy to promote employment and reduce poverty for low-income parents." *Developmental Psychology* **41**: 902–918.

Huston, A. and Aronson, S. (2005). "Mothers' time with infant and time in employment as predictors of mother–child relationships and children's early development." *Child Development* **76**: 467–482.

Huston, A., and Bentley, A. (2010). "Human Development in societal context." *Annual Review of Psychology* **61**: (in press).

Huston, A., McLoyd, V. and Garcia-Coll, C. (1994). Children in poverty. *Child Development* (special issue) **65**: 275–282.

Huxley, A. (1932). *Brave New World.* London: Chatto and Windus.

Hyde, J. (2004). "Children's temperament and behaviour problems predict their employed mothers' work functioning." *Child Development* **75**: 580–594.

Hyde, J. S. (2005). "The gender similarities hypothesis." *American Psychologist* **60**: 581–592.

Hyde, J. (2007). "New directions in the study of gender similarities and differences." *Current Directions in Psychological Science* **16**: 259–263.

Iacoboni, M. (2009). "Imitation, empathy, and mirror neurons." *Annual Review of Psychology* **60**: 653–670.

Ikels, C. (2004). *Filial Piety: Practice and Discourse in Contemporary East Asia.* Stanford, CA: Stanford University.

Isaksen, K. and Roper, S. (2008). "The Impact of Branding on Low-Income Adolescents: A Vicious Cycle?" *Psychology and Marketing* **25**: 1063–1087.

Iyengar, S. and Lepper, M. (1999). "Rethinking the value of choice: a cultural perspective on intrinsic motivation." *Journal of Personality and Social Psychology* **76**: 349–366.

Jacobs, N. and Harvey, D. (2005). "Do parents make a difference to children's academic achievement? Differences between parents of higher and lower achieving students." *Educational Studies* **31**: 431–448.

Jacobson, K. C., Prescott, C. A. and Kendler, K. S. (2006). "Sex differences in the genetic and environmental influences on the development of antisocial behavior." *Development and Psychopathology* **14**: 395–416.

Jaffe, S. (2006). Family violence and parental psychopathology. In S. Goldstein and R. Brooks (eds), *Handbook of Resilience in Children*. New York: Springer.

Jaffee, S. and Hyde, J. S. (2000). "Gender differences in moral orientation: a meta-analysis." *Psychological Bulletin* **126**: 703–726.

Jaffee, S. R., Moffitt, T. E. *et al.* (2002). "Differences in early childhood risk factors for juvenile-onset and adult-onset depression." *Archives of General Psychiatry* **59**: 215–222.

Jaffee, S. R., Moffitt, T. E. *et al.* (2003). "Life with (or without) father: the benefits of living with two biological parents depend on the father's antisocial behavior." *Child Development* **74**: 109–126.

Jaffee, S. R., Caspi, A. *et al.* (2005). "Nature x nurture: genetic vulnerabilities interact with physical maltreatment to promote conduct problems." *Development and Psychopathology* **17**: 67–84.

James, A. and James, A. L. (2004). *Constructing Childhood*. London: Palgrave Macmillan.

James, A. and Jenks, C. (1996). "Public perceptions of childhood criminality." *British Journal of Sociology* **47**: 315–333.

James, A., Jenks, C. and Prout, A. (1998). *Theorizing Childhood*. Cambridge: Polity Press.

James, W. (1890). *The Principles of Psychology*. New York: Dover.

James, W. (1892/1985). *Psychology: The Briefer Course*. Notre Dame, IN: University of Notre Dame Press.

Jaudes, P. and Mackey-Bilaver, L. (2008). "Do chronic conditions increase young children's risk of being maltreated?" *Child Abuse and Neglect* **32**: 671–681.

Jencks, C. (1975). *Inequality: A Reassessment of the Effects of Family and Schooling in America*. Harmondsworth: Penguin.

Jenkins, J., Simpson, A. *et al.* (2005). "The mutual influence of marital conflict and children's behaviour problems: shared and non-shared family risks." *Child Development* **76**: 24–39.

Jenks, C. (2005). *Childhood*. London: Routledge.

Jennings, K., Sandberg, I. *et al.* (2008). "Understanding of self and maternal warmth predict later self-regulation in toddlers." *International Journal of Behavioral Development* **32**: 108–118.

Johnson, B., Li, S. *et al.* (2000). "A systematic review of the religiosity and delinquency literature." *Journal of Contemporary Criminal Justice* **16**: 32–52.

Johnson, M., Grossmann, T. and Farroni, T. (2008). "The social cognitive neuroscience of infancy: Illuminating the early development of social brain functions." *Advances in Child Development and Behavior* **36**: 331–372.

Johnson M. K., Beebe, T. *et al.* (1998). "Volunteerism in adolescence: a process perspective." *Journal of Research in Adolescence* **8**: 309–332.

Jokela, M., Keltikangas-Jarvinen, L. *et al.* (2007). "Serotonin receptor 2A gene and the influence of childhood maternal nurturance on adulthood depressive symptoms." *Archives of General Psychiatry.* **64**: 356–360.

Jones, N. A., Field, T. *et al.* (1998). "Newborns of mothers with depressive symptoms are physiologically less developed." *Infant Behavior and Development* **21**: 537–541.

Jones, S. and Myhill, D. (2004a). "Seeing things differently: teachers' constructions of underachievement." *Gender and Education* **16**: 531–546.

Jones, S. and Myhill, D. (2004b). "'Troublesome boys' and 'compliant girls': gender identity and perceptions of achievement and underachievement." *British Journal of Sociology of Education* **25**: 547–561.

Jordan, A. (2004). "The role of media in children's development: an ecological perspective." *Journal of Developmental and Behavioral Pediatrics* **25**: 196–206.

Jordan, J. (2006). Relational resilience in girls. In S. Goldstein and R. Brooks (eds), *Handbook of Resilience in Children.* New York: Springer.

Juang, L. P. and Silbereisen, R. K. (2002). "The relationship between adolescent academic capability beliefs, parenting and school grades." *Journal of Adolescence* **25**: 3–18.

Juvonen, J., Nishina, A. *et al.* (2000). "Peer harassment, psychological adjustment, and school functioning in early adolescence." *Journal of Educational Psychology* **92**: 349–359.

Kaati, G., Bygren, L. *et al.* (2007). "Transgenerational response to nutrition, early life circumstances and longevity." *European Journal of Human Genetics* **15**: 784–790.

Kaffman, A. and Meaney, M. J. (2007). "Neurodevelopmental sequelae of postnatal maternal care in rodents: clinical and research implications." *Journal of Child Psychology and Psychiatry* **48**: 224–244.

Kagan, J. (1981). *The Second Year.* Cambridge: Cambridge University Press.

Kagan, J. (1997). "Conceptualizing psychopathology: The importance of developmental profiles." *Development and Psychopathology* **9**: 321–334.

Kagan, J. (2005). "Human morality and temperament." *Nebraska Symposium on Motivation* **51**: 1–32.

Kagan, J. and Fox, N. A. (2006). Biology, culture and temperamental biases. In W. Damon, R. Lerner, N. Eisenberg (eds), *Handbook of Child Psychology, (6th edn) Vol 3*: 167–225. New York: Wiley.

Kagan, J. and Snidman, N. (1999). "Early childhood predictors of adult anxiety disorders." *Biological Psychiatry* **46**: 1536–1541.

Kagan, J., Reznick, J. S. and Snidman, N. (1987). "The physiology and psychology of behavioral-inhibition in children." *Child Development* **58**: 1459–1473.

Kagan, J., Reznick, J. S. and Gibbons, J. (1989). "Inhibited and uninhibited types of children." *Child Development* **60**: 838–845.

Kagitcibasi, C. (2005). "Autonomy and relatedness in cultural context – Implications for self and family." *Journal of Cross-Cultural Psychology* **36**: 403–422.

Kagitcibasi, C. and Ataca, B. (2005). "Value of children and family change: a three-decade portrait from Turkey." *Applied Psychology – An International Review* **54**: 317–337.

Kaler, S. and Freeman, B. (1994). Analysis of environmental deprivation: cognitive and social development in Romanian orphans. *Journal of Child Psychology and Psychiatry* **35**: 769–781.

Kalish, C. and Cornelius, R. (2007). "What is to be done? Children's ascriptions of conventional obligations." *Child Development* **78**: 859–878.

Kamins, M. and Dweck, C. (1999). "Person versus process praise and criticism: implications for contingent self-worth and coping." *Developmental Psychology* **35**: 835–847.

Kaplan, A., Gheen, M. *et al.* (2002). "Classroom goal structure and student disruptive behaviour." *British Journal of Educational Psychology* **72**: 191–212.

Karmiloff-Smith, A. and Thomas, M. (2003). "What can developmental disorders tell us about the neurocomputational constraints that shape development? The case of Williams syndrome." *Development and Psychopathology* **15**: 969–990.

Kärtner, J. (2007). "Manifestations of autonomy and relatedness in mothers' accounts of their ethnotheories regarding child care across five cultural communities." *Journal of Cross-Cultural Psychology* **38**: 613–628.

Kashani, J. H., Daniel, A. E. *et al.* (1992). "Family violence: impact on children." *Journal of the American Academy of Child and Adolescent Psychiatry* **31**: 181–189.

Katz, L. and Windecker-Nelson, B. (2004). "Parental meta-emotion philosophy in families with conduct-problem children: Links with peer relations." *Journal of Abnormal Child Psychology* **32**: 385–398.

Katz, L. F. and Woodin, E. M. (2002). "Hostility, hostile detachment, and conflict engagement in marriages: Effects on child and family functioning." *Child Development* **73**: 636–651.

Katz, L., Hessler, D. *et al.* (2007). "Domestic violence, emotional competence, and child adjustment." *Social Development* **16**: 513–538.

Kaufman, J., Yang, B.-Z. *et al.* (2006). "Brain-derived neurotrophic factor-5-HHTLPR gene interactions and environmental modifiers of depression in children." *Biological Psychiatry* **59**: 673–680.

Kaufman, S. R. and Morgan, L. M. (2005). "The anthropology of the beginnings and ends of life." *Annual Review of Anthropology* **34**: 317–341.

Kaye, K. (1984). *The Mental and Social Life of Babies*. London: Methuen.

Keenan, K., Loeber, R. *et al.* (1995). "The influence of deviant peers on boys' disruptive and delinquent behaviour: A temporal analysis." *Development and Psychopathology* **7**: 715–726.

Keller, H. (2004b). "Developmental consequences of early parenting experiences: self-recognition and self-regulation in three cultural communities." *Child Development* **75**: 1745–1760.

Keller, M. (2004a). Self in relationship. In D. Lapsley and D. Narvaez (eds), *Moral Development, Self and Identity*. Mahwah, NJ: Erlbaum.

Keller, P. S., Cummings, E. M. and Davies P. T. (2005). "The role of marital discord and parenting in relations between parental problem drinking and child adjustment." *Journal of Child Psychology and Psychiatry* **46**: 943–951.

Keller, P., Cummings, E. M. *et al.* (2008). "Longitudinal relations between parental drinking problems, family functioning, and child adjustment." *Development and Psychopathology* **20**: 195–212.

Keller, T., Catalano, R. *et al.* (2002). "Parent figure transitions and delinquency and drug use among early adolescent children of substance abusers." *American Journal of Drug and Alcohol Abuse* **28**: 399–427.

Kendler, K. (2005). "'A gene for . . .' The nature of gene action in psychiatric disorders." *American Journal of Psychiatry* **162**: 1243–1252.

Kendler, K. S., Kessler, R. C. *et al.* (1993). "The prediction of major depression in women: Toward an integrated etiologic model." *American Journal of Psychiatry* **150**: 1139–1148.

Kendler, K., Kessler, R. C. *et al.* (1995). "Stressful life events, genetic liability and onset of an episode of major depression in women." *American Journal of Psychiatry* **152**: 833–842.

Kendler, K., Gardner, C. *et al.* (2002). "Toward a comprehensive developmental model for major depression in women." *American Journal of Psychiatry* **159**: 1133–1145.

Kendler, K. S., Kuhn, J. W. *et al.* (2005). "The interaction of stressful life events and serotonin polymorphism in the prediction of episodes of major depression." *Archives of General Psychiatry* **62**: 529–535.

Kerns, K., Cole, A. K. and Andrews, P. B. (1998). "Attachment security, parent peer management practices, and peer relationships in preschoolers." *Merrill-Palmer Quarterly* **44**: 504–522.

Kerr, M., and Stattin, H. (2000). "What parents know, how they know it, and several forms of adolescent adjustment: Further support for a reinterpretation of monitoring." *Developmental Psychology* **36**: 366–380.

Kerr, M. and Stattin, H. (2003). Parenting of adolescents: action or reaction? In A. Crouter and A. Booth (eds), *Children's influence on family dynamics: the neglected side of family relationships*. Mahwah, NJ: Erlbaum.

Kerr, M., Lambert, W. W. and Bem, D. J. (1996). "Lifecourse sequelae of childhood shyness in Sweden: comparison with the United States." *Developmental Psychology* **32**: 1100–1105.

Kershaw, I. (2001). *Hitler*. Harlow: Longman.

Killen, M. and Stangor, C. (2001). "Children's reasoning about social inclusion and exclusion in peer group contexts." *Child Development* **72**: 174–186.

Killen, M., Lee-Kim, J. *et al.* (2002). "How children and adolescents evaluate gender and racial exclusion." *Monographs of the Society for Research on Child Development.* **67**: 1–180.

Kim, J. and Cicchetti, D. (2004). "A longitudinal study of child maltreatment, mother–child relationship quality and maladjustment: The role of self-esteem and social competence." *Journal of Abnormal Child Psychology* **32**: 341–354.

Kim, J., Hetherington, E. M. and Reiss, D. (1999). "Associations among family relationships, antisocial peers, and adolescents' externalisising behaviors: Gender and family type differences." *Child Development* **70**: 1209–1230.

Kim-Cohen, J., Moffitt, T. *et al.* (2004). "Genetic and environmental processes in young children's resilience and vulnerability to socioeconomic deprivation." *Child Development* **75**: 651–668.

Kim-Cohen, J., Moffitt, T. E. *et al.* (2005). "Maternal depression and children's antisocial behavior: nature and nurture effects." *Archives of General Psychiatry* **62**: 173–181.

Kim-Cohen, J., Caspi, A. *et al.* (2006). "MAOA, maltreatment, and gene-environment interaction predicting children's mental health: new evidence and a meta-analysis." *Molecular Psychiatry* **11**: 903–913.

King, M. (2007). "The sociology of childhood as scientific communication: observations from a social systems perspective." *Childhood* **14**: 193–213.

King, R. (1978). *All Things Bright and Beautiful?* London: Wiley.

Kingston, M. H. (1976). *The Woman Warrior*. London: Picador.

Kinlaw, C. and Kurtz-Costas, B. (2003). The development of children's beliefs about intelligence. *Developmental Review* **23**: 125–161.

Kirkorian, H., Wartella, E. *et al*. (2008). "Media and young children's learning." *The Future of Children* **18**: 39–61.

Kitzmann, K., Gaylord, N. *et al*. (2003). "Child witnesses to domestic violence: a meta-analytic review." *Journal of Consulting and Clinical Psychology* **71**: 339–352.

Klebanov, P. and Brooks-Gunn, J. (2006). "Cumulative, human capital, and psychological risk in the context of early intervention. Links with IQ at ages 3, 5, and 8." *Annals of the New York Academy of Sciences* **1094**: 63–82.

Klebanov, P. K., Brooks-Gunn, J. *et al*. (1994). "Does neighborhood and family poverty affect mothers' parenting, mental health and social support?" *Journal of Marriage and the Family*, **56**: 441–455.

Kling, K. C., Hyde, J. S. *et al*. (1999). "Gender differences in self-esteem: A meta-analysis." *Psychological Bulletin* **125**: 470–500.

Knafo, A., Daniel, E. and Khoury-Kassabri, M. (2008). "Values as protective factors against violent behavior in Jewish and Arab high schools in Israel." *Child Development* **79**: 652–667.

Knyazev, G., Zupancic, M. *et al*. (2008). "Child personality in Slovenia and Russia: Structure and mean level of traits in parent and self-ratings." *Journal of Cross-cultural Psychology* **39**: 317–334.

Kochanska, G. (1995). "Children's temperament, mothers' discipline, and security of attachment – multiple pathways to emerging internalization." *Child Development* **66**: 597–615.

Kochanska, G. (1997a). "Children's temperament, mothers' discipline, and security of attachment: Multiple pathways to emerging internalisation." *Developmental Psychology* **64**: 325–347.

Kochanska, G. (1997b). "Multiple pathways to conscience for children with different temperaments: From toddlerhood to age 5." *Developmental Psychology* **33**: 228–240.

Kochanska, G. (1998). "Mother–child relationship, child fearfulness, and emerging attachment: A short-term longitudinal study." *Developmental Psychology* **34**: 480–490.

Kochanska, G. (2001). "Emotional development in children with different attachment histories: The first three years." *Child Development* **72**: 474–490.

Kochanska, G. (2002). "Mutually responsive orientation between mothers and their young children: A context for the early development of conscience." *Current Directions in Psychological Science* **11**: 191–195.

Kochanska G. and Aksan, N. (1995). "Mother–child mutually positive affect, the quality of child compliance to requests and prohibitions, and maternal control as correlates of early internalization." *Child Development* **66**: 236–54.

Kochanska, G. and Murray, K. T. (2000). "Mother–child mutually responsive orientation and conscience development: From toddler to early school age." *Child Development* **71**: 417–431.

Kochanska, G., Murray, K. and Coy, K. C. (1997). "Inhibitory control as a contributor to conscience in childhood: From toddler to early school age." *Child Development* **68**: 263–277.

Kochanska, G., Murray, K. *et al.* (1996). "Inhibitory control in young children and its role in emerging internalization." *Child Development* **67**: 490–507.

Kochanska, G., Coy, K. *et al.* (2001). "The development of self-regulation in the first four years of life." *Child Development* **72**: 1091–1111.

Kochanska, G., Forman, D. R. *et al.* (2005). "Pathways to conscience: early mother–child mutually responsive orientation and children's moral emotion, conduct, and cognition." *Journal of Child Psychology and Psychiatry* **46**: 19–34.

Kochanska, G., Aksan, N. *et al.* (2007). "Children's fearfulness as a moderator of parenting in early socialization: two longitudinal studies." *Developmental Psychology* **43**: 222–237.

Kochanska, G., Barry, R. A. *et al.* (2008). "A developmental model of maternal and child contributions to disruptive conduct: the first six years." *Journal of Child Psychology and Psychiatry* **49**: 1220–1227.

Kohlberg, L. (1984). *Essays on Moral Development: vol. 2. The Psychology of Moral Development*. San Francisco: Harper and Row.

Kolliker, M. (2007). "Benefits and costs of earwig (Forficula auricularia) family life." *Behavioral ecology and sociobiology* **28**: 176–185.

Koluchova, J. (1976). Severe deprivation in twins: a case study. In A. Clarke and A. Clarke (eds), *Early Experience: Myth and Reality*. London: Open Books.

Koumi, I. (1994). *Self-Values and Academic Self-Concept of Greek Secondary School Pupils*. Unpublished PhD from University of Bristol.

Kowal, A. and Kramer, L. (1997). "Children's understanding of parental differential treatment." *Child Development* **68**: 113–126.

Kowalski, R. and Limber, S. (2007). "Electronic bullying among middle school students." *Journal of Adolescent Health* **41**: S22–S30.

Kramer, M., Aboud, F. *et al.* (2008). "Breastfeeding and child cognitive development – New evidence from a large randomized trial." *Archives of General Psychiatry* **65**: 578–584.

Kreppner, J., O'Connor, T. *et al.* (2001). "Can inattention/overactivity be an institutional deprivation syndrome?" *Journal of Abnormal Child Psychology* **29**: 513–528.

Kreppner, J., Rutter, M. *et al.* (2007). "Normality and impairment following profound early institutional deprivation: a longitudinal follow-up into early adolescence." *Developmental Psychology* **43**: 931–946.

Krettenauer, T. and Eichler, D. (2006). "Adolescents' self-attributed moral emotions following a moral transgression: Relations with delinquency, confidence in moral judgment and age." *British Journal of Developmental Psychology* **24**: 489–506.

Kristensen, P. and Bjerkedal, T. (2007). "Explaining the Relation Between Birth Order and Intelligence." *Science* **316**: 1717.

Kubzansky, L. D., Martin, L. T. and Buka, S. L. (2004). "Early manifestations of personality and adult functioning." *Emotion* **4**: 364–377.

Kuczynski, L. (2003). *Handbook of Dynamics in Parent-Child Relations*. Thousand Oaks, CA: Sage.

Kuczynski, T. and Parkin, M. (2007). Agency and bidirectionality in socialization:

Interactions, transactions, and relational dialectics. In J. Grusec and P. Hastings (eds), *Handbook of Socialization*. New York: Guilford Press.

Kurtz-Costes, B., Rowley, S. J *et al.* (2008). "Gender stereotypes about mathematics and science and self-perceptions of ability in late childhood and early adolescence." *Merrill-Palmer Quarterly* **54**: 386–409.

Kuterovac-Jagodić, G. (2003). "Posttraumatic stress symptoms in Croatian children exposed to war: A prospective study." *Journal of Clinical Psychology* **59**: 9–25.

Kuttler, A., Parker, J. and LaGreca, M. (2002). "Developmental and gender differences in preadolescents' judgments of the veracity of gossip." *Merrill-Palmer Quarterly* **48**: 105–132.

La Greca, A. and Harrison, H. (2005). "Adolescent peer relations, friendships, and romantic relationships: do they predict social anxiety and depression?" *Journal of Clinical Child and Adolescent Psychology* **34**: 49–61.

Ladd, G. and Troop-Gordon, W. (2003). "The role of chronic peer difficulties in the development of children's psychological adjustment problems." *Child Development* **74**: 1344–1367.

LaFontana, K. and Cillessen, A. (2002). "Children's perceptions of popular and unpopular peers: a multimethod assessment." *Developmental Psychology* **38**: 635–647.

Lahey, B. B., Gordon, R. A. *et al.* (1999). "Boys who join gangs: A prospective study of predictors of first gang entry." *Journal of Abnormal Child Psychology* **27**: 261–276.

Lahey, B., Moffitt, T. E. and Caspi, A. (2003). *Causes of Conduct Disorder and Juvenile Delinquency*. New York: Guilford.

Laible, D. and Thompson, R. A. (2007). Early socialization: A relationship perspective. In J. Grusec and P. Hastings (eds), *Handbook of Socialization*. New York: Guilford.

Laland, K. and Brown, G. (2002). *Sense and Nonsense: Evolutionary Perspectives on Human Behaviour*. Oxford: Oxford University Press.

Lamb, M. (1998). Nonparental care: context, quality, correlates. In W. Damon, Siegel, I. and Renninger, K (eds), *Handbook of Child Psychology, Vol 4*. New York: Wiley.

Lamb, M., Ed. (2004). *The Role of the Father in Child Development*. Hoboken, NJ: Wiley.

Lamb, M. and Lewis, C. (2004). The development and significance of father–child relationships in two-parent families. In M. Lamb (ed.), *The Role of the Father in Child Development*. Hoboken, NJ: Wiley.

Lamborn, S., Dornbusch, S. *et al.* (1996). "Ethnicity and community context as moderators of the relation between family decision-making and adolescent adjustment." *Child Development* **66**: 283–301.

Lane, H. (1976). *The Wild Boy of Aveyron*. London: George Allen and Unwin.

Lapsley, D. and Narvaez, D. (2004). *Moral Development, Self and Identity*. Mahwah, NJ: Erlbaum.

Lareau, A. (2000). *Home advantage: Social Class and Parental Intervention in Elementary Education*. Lanham, MD: Rowman & Littlefield.

Lareau, A. (2002). "Invisible inequality: social class and childbearing in black families and white families." *American Sociological Review* **67**: 747–776.

Larson, R. W. (2000). "Toward a psychology of positive youth development." *American Psychologist* **55**: 170–183.

Larson, R. and Verma, S. (1999). "How children and adolescents spend time across the world: work, play and developmental opportunities." *Psychological Bulletin* **125**: 701–736.

Lau, J., Gregory, A. M. *et al.* (2007). "Assessing gene-environment interactions on anxiety symptom subtypes across childhood and adolescence." *Development and Psychopathology* **19**: 1129–1146.

Lau, S., Lew, W. J. F. *et al.* (1990). "Relations among perceived parental control, warmth, indulgence, and family harmony of Chinese in Mainland China." *Developmental Psychology* **26**: 674–677.

Laursen, B. and Collins, W. (1994). "Interpersonal conflict during adolescence." *Psychological Bulletin* **115**: 197–209.

Laursen, B., Coy, K. C. and Collins, W. A. (1998). "Reconsidering changes in parent–child conflict across adolescence: a meta-analysis." *Child Development* **69**: 817–832.

Laursen, B., Hartup, W. and Koplas, A. (1996). "Towards understanding peer conflict." *Merrill-Palmer Quarterly* **42**: 76–102.

Laursen, B., Bukowski, W. M. *et al.* (2007). "Friendship moderates prospective associations between social isolation and adjustment problems in young children." *Child Development* **78**: 1395–1404.

Lave, J. (1990). The culture of acquisition and the practice of understanding. In J. W. Stigler, R. A. Shwerder and G. S. Herdt (eds), *Cultural Psychology: Essays on Comparative Human Development*. Cambridge: Cambridge University Press.

Laviola, G. (2004). "Beneficial effects of enriched environment on adolescent rats from stressed pregnancies." *European Journal of Neuroscience* **20**: 1655–1664.

Lawson, D. and Mace, R. (2008). "Sibling configuration and childhood growth in contemporary British families." *International Journal of Epidemiology* **37**: 1408–1421.

Leaper, C. and Bigler, R. (2004). Gendered language and sexist thought. *Monographs of the Society for Research in Child Development* **69**: 128–142.

Leaper, C., Anderson, K. and Sanders, P. (1998). "Moderators of gender effects on parents' talk to their children: a meta-analysis." *Developmental Psychology* **34**: 3–27.

Leary, M. (2007). "Motivational and emotional aspects of the self." *Annual Review of Psychology* **58**: 317–344.

Leary, S., Smith, G. D. *et al.* (2006a). "Smoking during pregnancy and offspring fat and lean mass in childhood." *Obesity (Silver Spring)* **14**: 2284–2293.

Leary, S., Smith, G. D. *et al.* (2006b). "Smoking during pregnancy and components of stature in offspring." *American Journal of Human Biology* **18**: 502–512.

Leca, J.-B., Gunst, N. *et al.* (2007). "A new case of fish-eating in Japanese macaques: implications for social constraints on the diffusion of feeding innovation." *American Journal of Primatology* **69**: 821–828.

Lee, V. and Burkham, D. (2003). "Dropping out of high school: the role of school organisation and structure." *American Educational Research Journal* **40**: 353–393.

Lee, V. and Loeb, S. (2000). "School size in Chicago elementary schools: effects on teachers' attitudes and students' achievement." *American Educational Research Journal* **37**: 3–31.

Leeson, R. (1993). *Smart Girls*. London: Walker Books.

Leigh, S. R. (1996). "Evolution of human growth spurts." *American Journal of Physical Anthropology* **101**: 455–474.

Lengua, L. (2002). "The contribution of emotionality and self-regulation to the understanding of children's response to multiple risk." *Child Development* **73**: 144–161.

Lengua, L. and Sandler, I. (1996). "Self-regulation as a moderator of the relation between coping and symptomatology in children of divorce." *Journal of Abnormal Child Psychology* **24**: 681–701.

Lengua, L. J., Sandler, I. N. *et al.* (1999). "Emotionality and self-regulation, threat appraisal, and coping in children of divorce." *Development and Psychopathology* **11**: 15–37.

Leonard, M. (2009). "What's recreational about 'recreational rioting'? Children on the streets in Belfast." *Children & Society* (epublication ahead of print).

Lerner, R. M., Fisher, C. B. *et al.* (2000). "Toward a science for and of the people: promoting civil society through the application of developmental science." *Child Development* **71**: 11–20.

Leventhal, T. and Brookes-Gunn, J. (2000). "The neighbourhoods they live in: The effects of neighbourhood residence on child and adolescent outcomes." *Psychological Bulletin* **126**: 309–337.

Leventhal, T. and Brookes-Gunn, J. (2005). "Neighbourhood poverty and public policy: a five-year follow-up of children's educational outcomes in the New York City Moving to Opportunity demonstration." *Developmental Psychology* **41**: 933–952.

LeVine, R. (2003). *Childhood Socialization: Comparative Studies of Parenting, Learning and Educational Change*. Hong Kong, Comparative Education Research Centre, The University of Hong Kong.

LeVine, R. and New, R. (2008). *Anthropology and Child Development: A Cross-Cultural Reader*. Oxford: Blackwell.

Lewis, M. and Michalson, L. (1983). *Children's Emotions and Moods: Developmental Theory and Measurement*. New York: Plenum Press.

Lewis, M. and Ramsay, D. (2002). "Cortisol response to embarrassment and shame." *Child Development* **73**: 1034–1045.

Lewis, M., Alessandri, S. M. and Sullivan, M. W. (1992). "Differences in shame and pride as a function of children's gender and task difficulty." *Child Development* **63**: 630–638.

Lewis, M. D., Lamm, C. *et al.* (2006). "Neurophysiological correlates of emotion regulation in children and adolescents." *Journal of Cognitive Neuroscience* **18**: 430–443.

Liben, L. and Bigler, R. (2002). "The developmental core of gender differentiation: conceptualizing, measuring and evaluating constructs and pathways." *Monographs of the Society for Research in Child Development* **67**: 1–147.

Lieberman, A. F. and Amaya-Jackson, L. (2005). Reciprocal influences of attachment and trauma. In L. Berlin, Y. Ziv, L. Amaya-Jackson and M. T. Greenberg (eds), *Enhancing Early Attachments*. New York: The Guilford Press.

Light, P. (1979). *The Development of Social Sensitivity*. Cambridge: Cambridge University Press.

Light, P. (1983). Social interaction and cognitive development: a review of post-Piagetian research. In S. Meadows (ed.), *Developing Thinking*. London: Methuen.

Linnet, K., Dalsgaard, S. *et al.* (2003). "Maternal life style factors in pregnancy risk of Attention Deficit Hyperactivity Disorder and associated behaviours: review of the current evidence." *American Journal of Psychiatry* **160**: 1028–1040.

Linver, M., Brooks-Gunn, J. and Kohen, D. E. (2002). "Family processes as pathway from income to children's development." *Developmental Psychology* **38**: 719–734.

Lippa, R. (2005). *Gender, Nature, and Nurture*. Mahwah, NJ: Erlbaum.

Loeb, S., Fuller, B. *et al.* (2004). "Child care in poor communities: early learning effects of type, quality, and stability." *Child Development*, **75**: 47–65.

Loewenstein, G. F., Weber, E. U. *et al.* (2001). "Risk as feelings." *Psychological Bulletin* **127**: 267–286.

Lok, S. and McMahon, C. (2006). "Mothers' thoughts about their children: Links between mind-mindedness and emotional availability." *British Journal of Developmental Psychology* **24**: 477–488.

Losel, F. and Bliesener, T. (1994). "Some high-risk adolescents do not develop conduct problems: a study of protective factors." *International Journal of Behavioral Development* **17**: 753–777.

Love, J., Harrison, L. *et al.* (2003). "Child care quality matters: how conclusions may vary with context." *Child Development* **74**: 1021–1033.

Lupien, S., King, S. *et al.* (2000). "Child's stress hormone levels correlate with mother's socioeconomic status and depressive state." *Biological Psychiatry* **48**: 976–980.

Luster, T. and Dubow, E. (1992). Home environment and maternal intelligence as predictors of verbal intelligence: a comparison of preschool and school-age children. *Merrill-Palmer Quarterly* **38**: 151–175.

Luthar, S. (1997). *Developmental Psychopathology: Perspectives on Adjusment, Risk, and Disorder*. Cambridge: Cambridge University Press.

Luthar, S. (1999). *Poverty and Children's Adjustment*. London: Sage.

Luthar, S. (2003a). "The culture of affluence: psychological costs of material wealth." *Child Development* **74**: 1581–1593.

Luthar, S. (2003b). *Resilience and Vulnerability: Adaptation in the Context of Childhood Adversities*. New York: Cambridge University Press.

Luthar, S. and Becker, B. (2002)." Privileged but pressured? A study of affluent youth." *Child Development* **73**: 1593–1610.

Luthar, S. S. and Brown, P. J. (2007). "Maximizing resilience through diverse levels of inquiry: prevailing paradigms, possibilities, and priorities for the future." *Development and Psychopathology* (special issue) **19**: 931–955.

Luthar, S. S. and Cicchetti, D. (2000). "The construct of resilience: implications for intervention and social policy." *Development and Psychopathology* (special issue) **12**: 857–885.

Luthar, S. S. and D'Avanzo, K. (1999). "Contextual factors in substance use: a study of suburban and inner-city adolescents." *Development and Psychopathology* **11**: 845–867.

Luthar, S. and Latendresse, S. (2005). "Children of the affluent: Challenges to well-being." *Current Directions in Psychological Science* **14**: 49–53.

Luthar, S. and Sexton, C. (2007). "Maternal drug abuse versus maternal depression:

Vulnerability and resilience among school-age and adolescent offspring." *Development and Psychopathology* **19**: 205–225.

Luthar, S. S., Cicchetti, D. and Becker, B. (2000). "The construct of resilience: a critical evaluation and guidelines for future work." *Child Development* **71**: 543–562.

Luthar, S. S., Sawyer, J. and Brown, P. J. (2006). "Conceptual issues in studies of resilience. Past, present, and future research." *Annals of the New York Academy of Sciences* **1094**: 105–115.

Luthar, S. S., D'Avanzo, D. *et al.* (2003). Parental substance abuse: risks and resilience. In S. S. Luthar (ed.), *Resilience and Vulnerability. Adaptation in the Context of Childhood Adversities*. New York: Cambridge University Press.

Lyons-Ruth, K., Easterbrookes, M. A. and Cibelli, C. D. (1997). "Infant attachment strategies, infant mental lag, and maternal depressive symptoms: Predictors of internalizing and externalizing problems at age seven." *Developmental Psychology* **33**: 681–692.

McAdams, D., and Olson, B. (2010). "Personality development: continuity and change over the life course." *Annual Review of Psychology* **61**: (in press).

McAlister, A. and Peterson, C. (2006). "Mental playmates: siblings, executive functioning and theory of mind." *British Journal of Developmental Psychology* **24**: 733–751.

McCall, R., Groark, C. J. *et al.* (St. Petersburg-USA Orphanage Research Team). (2008). "The effects of early social-emotional and relationship experience on the development of young orphanage children." *Monographs of the Society for Research in Child Development*, **73**: 1–262.

McCartney, K. (2003). On the meaning of models: a signal amongst the noise. In A. Crouter and A. Booth (eds), *Children's Influence on Family Dynamics: The Neglected Side of Family Relationships*. Mahwah, NJ: Erlbaum.

McCloskey, L. and Stuewig, J. (2001). "The quality of peer relationships among children exposed to family violence." *Development and Psychopathology* **13**: 83–96.

Maccoby, E. (1998). *The Two Sexes: Growing Up Apart, Coming Together*. Cambridge, MA: Belknap Press of Harvard University Press.

Maccoby, E. (2000). "Parenting and its effects on children: on reading and misreading behaviour genetics." *Annual Review of Psychology* **51**: 1–27.

Maccoby, E. (2003). The gender of child and parent as factors in family dynamics. In A. Crouter and A. Booth (eds), *Children's Influence on Family Dynamics: The Neglected Side of Family Relationships*. Mahwah, NJ: Erlbaum.

Maccoby, E. and Jacklin, C. (1974). *The Psychology of Sex Differences*. Stanford, CA: Stanford University Press.

Maccoby, E. and Martin, J. (1983). Socialisation in the context of the family: parent–child interaction. In E. M.Hetherington (ed.), *Handbook of Child Psychology, Vol 4*. New York: Wiley.

McDowell, D. and Parke, R. (2000). "Differential knowledge of display rules for positive and negative emotions: Influences from parents, influences on peers." *Social Development* **9**: 415–432.

McDowell, D. and Parke, R. (2005). "Parental control and affect as predictors of children's display rule use and social competence with peers." *Social Development* **14**: 440–457.

McDowell, D., O'Neil, R. and Parke, R. (2000). "Display rule application in a disappointing situation and children's emotional reactivity: relations with social competence." *Merrill-Palmer Quarterly* **46**: 306–324.

McDowell, D., Parke, R. and Spitzer, S. (2002). "Parent and child cognitive representations of social situations and children's social competence." *Social Development* **4**: 486–496.

McDowell, D., Parke, R. and Wang, S. (2003). "Differences between mothers' and fathers' advice-giving style and content: relations with social competence and psychological functioning in middle childhood." *Merrill-Palmer Quarterly* **49**: 55–76.

Mace, R. (2008). "Reproducing in cities." *Science* **319**: 764–766.

McElhaney, K. and Allen, J. P. (2001). "Autonomy and adolescent social functioning: the moderating effect of risk." *Child Development* **72**: 220–235.

McElhaney, K., Antonishak, J. and Allen, J. P. (2008). "'They like me, they like me not': popularity and adolescents' perceptions of acceptance predicting social functioning overtime." *Child Development* **79**: 720–731.

McEwen, F., Happé, F. *et al.* (2007). "Origins of individual differences in imitation: links with language, pretend play, and socially insightful behavior in two-year-old twins." *Child Development* **78**: 474–492.

Macfarlane, A. (1975). "Olfaction in the development of social preferences in the human neonate." *Ciba Foundation Symposium* **33**: 103–117.

McGee, R. and Williams, S. (2000). "Does low self-esteem predict health compromising behaviours among adolescents?" *Journal of Adolescence* **23**: 569–582.

McGuire, S., Manke, B. *et al.* (1999). "Perceived competence and self-worth during adolescence: a longitudinal behavior-genetic study." *Child Development* **70**: 1283–1296.

McHale, J. and Rasmussen, J. (1998). "Coparental and family group-level dynamics during infancy. Early family predictors of child and family functioning during preschool." *Development and Psychopathology* **10**: 39–58.

McHale, S. and Crouter, A. (2003). How do children exert an impact on family life? In A. Crouter and A. Booth (eds), *Children's Influence on Family Dynamics: The Neglected Side of Family Relationships*. Mahwah, NJ: Erlbaum.

McHale, S. M., Crouter, A. C. and Tucker, C. J. (1999). "Family context and gender role socialization in middle childhood: comparing girls to boys and sisters to brothers." *Child Development* **70**: 990–1104.

McHale, S., Crouter, A. and Whiteman, S. (2003). "The family contexts of gender development in childhood and adolescence." *Social Development* **12**: 125–148.

McHale, S. M., Updegraff, K. A. *et al.* (2000). "When does parents' differential treatment have negative implications for siblings?" *Social Development* **9**: 149–172.

McHale, S. M., Updegraff, K. A. *et al.* (2001). "Sibling influences on gender development in middle childhood and adolescence." *Developmental Psychology* **37**: 115–125.

McHale, S., Whiteman, S. *et al.* (2007). "Characteristics and correlates of sibling relationships in two-parent African American families." *Journal of Family Psychology* **21**: 227–235.

Mackintosh, N. (1998). *IQ and Human Intelligence*. Cambridge: Cambridge University Press.

McLanahan, S. and Carlson, M. (2004). Fathers in fragile families. In M. Lamb (ed.), *The Role of the Father in Child Development*. Hoboken, NJ: Wiley.

McLanahan, S. and Percheski, C. (2008). "Family structure and the reproduction of inequalities." *Annual Review of Sociology* **14**: 257–276.

McLaughlin, A., Campbell, F. *et al.* (2007). "Depressive symptoms in young adults: the influences of the early home environment and early educational child care." *Child Development* **78**: 746–756.

Maclean, C. (1979). *The Wolf Children*. Harmondsworth: Penguin.

Maclean, K. (2003). "The impact of institutionalisation on child development." *Development and Psychopathology* **15**: 853–884.

McLoyd, V. (1998). "Socioeconomic disadvantage and child development." *American Psychologist* **53**: 185–204.

Maestripieri, D. (2005). "Early experience affects the intergenerational transmission of infant abuse in rhesus monkeys." *Proceedings of the National Academy of Sciences USA* **102**: 9726–9729.

Mahler, M., Pine, F. and Bergman, A. (1975). *The Psychological Birth of the Human Infant: Symbiosis and Individuation*. London: Hutchinson.

Main, M. and George, C. (1985). Responses of abused and disadvantaged toddlers to distress in agemates: a study in the day care setting. *Developmental Psychology* **21**: 407–412.

Main, M., Kaplan, N. *et al.* (1985). "Security in infancy, childhood and adulthood: a move to the level of representation. Growing points in attachment theory and research." *Monographs of the Society for Research in Child Development*. **50**: 66–106.

Main, M., Hesse, E. *et al.* (2005). Predictability of attachment behavior and representational processes at 1, 6 and 19 years of age: the Berkeley Longitudinal Project. In K. E. Grossman, K. Grossman and E. Waters (eds), *Attachment from Infancy to Adulthood: The Major Longitudinal Studies*. New York: Guilford.

Malle, B. and Hodges, S. (2005). *Other Minds: How Humans Bridge the Divide between Self and Others*. New York: The Guilford Press.

Mallett, J. (2004). "The peppered moth: a black and white story after all." *Genetics Society News* **50**: 34–38.

Malouff, J., Rooke, S. *et al.* (2008). "The heritability of human behavior: results of aggregating meta-analyses." *Current Psychology: A Journal for Diverse Perspectives on Diverse Psychological Issues* **27**: 153–161.

Mannarini, T. and Fedi, A. (2009). "Multiple senses of community: the experience and meaning of community." *Journal of Community Psychology* **37**: 211–227.

Marcus, N., Lindahl, K. *et al.* (2001). "Interparental conflict, children's social cognitions, and child aggression: a test of a mediational model." *Journal of Family Psychology* **15**: 315–333.

Markus, H. and Kitayama, S. (1991). "Culture and the self: implications for cognition, emotion and motivation." *Psychological Review* **98**: 224–253.

Marmorstein, N. R. and Iacono, W. G. (2004). "Major depression and conduct disorder in youth: Associations with parental psychopathology and parent–child conflict." *Journal of Child Psychology and Psychiatry* **45**: 377–386.

Marsh, H. (1990). "The structure of academic self-concept: the Marsh-Shavelson model." *Journal of Educational Psychology* **82**: 623–636.

Marsh, H. and Shavelson, R. (1985). "Self-concept: its multifaceted, hierarchical structure." *Educational Psychology* **20**: 107–123.

Marsh, H. and Yeung, A. S. (1997). "Causal effects of academic self-concept on academic achievement: Structural equation models of longitudinal data." *Journal of Educational Psychology* **89**: 41–54.

Marsh, H., Ellis, L. and Craven, R. G. (2002). "How do preschool children feel about themselves? Unraveling measurement and multidimensional self-concept structure." *Developmental Psychology* **38**: 376–393.

Marsh, H., Smith, I. D. *et al.* (1983). "Self-concept: reliability, stability, dimensionality, validity and the measurement of change." *Journal of Educational Psychology* **75**: 772–790.

Martin, B. (1981). *A Sociology of Contemporary Cultural Change*. Oxford: Blackwell.

Martin, C. L. and Ruble, D. (2004). "Children's search for gender cues: cognitive perspectives on gender development." *Current Directions in Psychological Science* **13**: 67–70.

Martin, C. L., Ruble, D. N. and Szkrybalo, J. (2002). "Cognitive theories of early gender development." *Psychological Bulletin* **128**: 903–933.

Martin, C., Fabes, R. A. *et al.* (2005). "Social dynamics in the preschool." *Developmental Review* **25**: 299–327.

Martin, J. and Ross, H. (2005). "Sibling aggression: sex differences and parents' reactions." *International Journal of Behavioral Development* **29**: 129–138.

Martin, R. (2007). "The evolution of human reproduction: a primatological perspective." *American Journal of Physical Anthropology* **134** (S45): 59–84.

Mashburn, A., Pianta, R. C. *et al.* (2008). "Measures of classroom quality in prekindergarten and children's development of academic, language and social skills." *Child Development* **79**: 732–749.

Maslow, A. (1987). *Motivation and Personality*. New York: Longman.

Masson, J. (1996). *The Lost Prince: The Unsolved Mystery of Kaspar Hauser*. New York: Simon and Schuster.

Masten, A. S. (2001). "Ordinary magic: resilience processes in development." *American Psychologist* **56**: 227–238.

Masten, A. S. (2004). "Regulatory processes, risk and resilience in adolescent development." *Annals of the New York Academy of Sciences* **1021**: 310–319.

Masten, A. S. (2005). "Developmental cascades: linking academic achievement, externalizing and internalizing symptoms over 20 years." *Developmental Psychology* **41**: 733–746.

Masten, A. S. and Coatsworth, J. D. (1998). "The development of competence in favorable and unfavorable environments." *American Psychologist* **53**: 205–220.

Masten, A. and Obradovic, J. (2006). "Competence and resilience in development." *Annals of the New York Academy of Sciences* **1094**: 13–27.

Masten, A., Coatsworth, J. D. *et al.* (1995). "The structure and coherence of competence from childhood through adolescence." *Child Development* **66**: 1635–1659.

Masten, A. S., Hubbard, J. *et al.* (1999). "Competence in the context of adversity: Pathways to resilience and maladaptation from childhood to late aolescence." *Development and Psychopathology* **11**: 143–169.

Matheny, A. (1986). "Injuries among toddlers." *Journal of Pediatric Psychology* **11**: 161–176.

Matsuzawa, M., Matsui, M. *et al.* (2001). "Age-related volumetric changes of brain gray and white matter in healthy infants and children." *Cerebral Cortex* **11**: 335–342.

Maughan, A. and Cicchetti, D. (2002). "The impact of child maltreatment and interadult violence on children's emotion regulation abilities and socioemotional adjustment." *Child Development* **73**: 1525–1542.

Maughan, B. and McCarthy, G. (1997). "Childhood adversities and psychosocial disorders." *British Medical Bulletin* **53**: 153–169.

Maughan, B., Rowe, R. *et al.* (2006). "Conduct disorder and oppositional defiant disorder in a national sample: developmental epidemiology." *Journal of Child Psychology and Psychiatry* **45**: 609–620.

Mayall, B. (2002). *Towards a Sociology for Childhood.* Maidenhead: Open University Press.

May-Chahal, C. and Cawson, P. (2005). "Measuring child maltreatment in the United Kingdom (UK): A study of the prevalence of child abuse and neglect." *Child Abuse & Neglect* **29**: 969–984.

Mayer, J., Roberts, R. *et al.* (2008). "Human abilities: Emotional Intelligence." *Annual Review of Psychology* **59**: 507–536.

Mayer, S. (1997). *What Money Can't Buy: Family Income and Children's Life Chances.* Cambridge, MA: Harvard University Press.

Mead, G. H. (1934). *Mind, Self and Society.* Chicago, IL: University of Chicago Press.

Meadows, S. (1986). *Understanding Child Development.* London: Unwin.

Meadows, S. (2006). *The Child as Thinker.* London: Routledge.

Meadows, S. O., McLanahan, S. *et al.* (2007). "Parental depression and anxiety and early childhood behavior problems across family types." *Journal of Marriage and Family* **69**: 1162–1177.

Meece, J. and Miller, S. (2001). "A longitudinal analysis of elementary school students' achievement goals in literacy activities." *Contemporary Educational Psychology* **26**: 454–480.

Meece, J., Anderman, E. *et al.* (2006). "Classroom goal structure, student motivation and academic achievement." *Annual Review of Psychology* **57**: 487–503.

Meehan, B., Hughes, J. *et al.* (2003). "Teacher-student relationships as compensatory resources for aggressive children." *Child Development* **74**: 1145–1157.

Meins, E. (1997). Security of attachment and maternal tutoring strategies: interaction within the zone of proximal development. *British Journal of Developmental Psychology* **15**: 129–144.

Meins, E. (1998). The effects of security of attachment and maternal attributes of meaning on children's linguistic acquisitional style. *Infant Behavior and Development* **21**: 237–252.

Meins, E. (2002). "Maternal mind-mindedness and attachment security as predictors of theory of mind understanding." *Child Development* **73**: 1715–1726.

Meins, E. (2003). "Pathways to understanding mind: Construct validity and predictive validity of maternal mind-mindedness." *Child Development* **74**: 1194–1211.

Meins, E. and Fernyhough, C. (1999). "Linguistic acquisitional style and mentalising development: the role of maternal mind-mindedness." *Cognitive Development* **14**: 363–380.

Mejía-Arauz, R., Rogoff, B. *et al.* (2007). "Cultural variation in children's social organization." *Child Development* **78**: 1001–1014.

Melhuish, E., Belsky, J. *et al.* (2008). "Effects of fully-established Sure Start local programmes on 3-year-old children and their families living in England: a quasi-experimental observational study." *The Lancet* **372**: 1641–1647.

Mello, Z. (2008). "Gender variation in developmental trajectories of educational and occupational expectations and attainment from adolescence to adulthood." *Developmental Psychology* **44**: 1069–1080.

Meltzoff, A. N. (1988). "Infant imitation after a 1-week delay – long-term-memory for novel acts and multiple stimuli." *Developmental Psychology* **24**: 470–476.

Meltzoff, A. N. (1995). "Understanding the intentions of others – reenactment of intended acts by 18-month-old children." *Developmental Psychology* **31**: 838–850.

Menaghan, E. (2003). On the brink: stability and change in parent–child relationships in adolescence. In A. Crouter and A. Booth (eds), *Children's Influence on Family Dynamics: The Neglected Side of Family Relationships*. Mahwah, NJ: Erlbaum.

Mendez, M., Torrent, M. *et al.* (2008). "Maternal smoking very early in pregnancy is related to child overweight at age 5–7 years." *American Journal of Clinical Nutrition* **87**: 1906–1913.

Messer, D., McCarthy, M. *et al.* (1986). "Relation between mastery behavior in infancy and competence in early-childhood." *Developmental Psychology* **22**: 366–372.

Micklewright, J. (2002). *Social exclusion and children: a European view of a US debate. CASE paper: 51*. London: Centre for Analysis of Social Exclusion.

Midgley, C., Kaplan, A. *et al.* (2001). "Performance-approach goals: good for what, for whom, under what circumstances, and at what cost?" *Journal of Educational Psychology* **93**: 77–86.

Miller, A. (1985). *Thou Shalt Not be Aware: Society's Betrayal of the Child*. London: Pluto Press.

Miller, A. (1987). *For Your Own Good: Hidden Cruelty in Child-Rearing and the Roots of Violence*. London: Virago.

Miller, A. (1990). *The Untouched Key: Tracing Childhood Trauma in Creativity and Destructiveness*. London: Virago.

Miller, J. G. (2002). "Bringing culture to basic psychological theory: Beyond individualism and collectivisim – Comment on Oyserman *et al.* (2002)." *Psychological Bulletin* **128**: 97–109.

Miller, P. J., Wiley, A. R. *et al.* (1997). "Personal storytelling as a medium of socialization in Chinese and American families." *Child Development* **68**: 557–568.

Mills, R. (2005). "Taking stock of the developmental literature on shame." *Developmental Review* **25**: 26–63.

Mills, R. and Duck, S. (2000). *The Developmental Psychology of Personal Relationships*. New York: Wiley.

Mills, R. and Piotrowski, C. (2000). Emotional communication and children's learning about conflict. In R. Mills and S. Duck (eds), *The Developmental Psychology of Personal Relationships*. New York: Wiley.

Mills-Koonce, W., Propper, C. B. *et al.* (2007). "Bidirectional genetic and environmental influences on mother and child behavior: The family system as the unit of analyses." *Development and Psychopathology* (special issue) **19**: 1073–1087.

Mithen, S. (1996). *The Prehistory of the Mind*. London: Thames and Hudson.

Mize, J. and Pettit, G. (1997). "Mothers' social coaching, mother–child relationship style, and children's peer competence: Is the medium the message?" *Child Development* **68**: 312–322.

Moen, P., Elder, G. *et al.* (1995). *Examining Lives in Context: Perspectives on the Ecology of Human Development*. Washington, DC: American Psychological Association.

Moffitt, T. and Caspi, A. (2007). Evidence from behavioural genetics for environmental contributions to antisocial conduct. In J.Grusec and P. Hastings (eds), *Handbook of Socialization*: 96–123. New York: Guilford Press.

Moffitt, T. E. (2001). *Sex Differences in Antisocial Behaviour: Conduct Disorder, Delinquency, and Violence in the Dunedin Longitudinal Study*. Cambridge: Cambridge University Press.

Moffitt, T. E. (2005). "The new look of behavioral genetics in developmental psychopathology: gene-environment interplay in antisocial behaviors." *Psychological Bulletin* **131**: 533–554.

Moffitt, T. E., Caspi, A. and Rutter, M. (2005). "Strategy of investigating interactions between measured genes and measured environments." *Archives of General Psychiatry* **67**: 473–481.

Moffitt, T. E., Caspi, A. *et al.* (2006). "Measured gene-environment interactions in psychopathology." *Perspectives on Psychological Science* **1**: 5–27.

Mok, A., Morris, M. W. *et al.* (2007). "Embracing American culture: structures of social identity and social networks among first-generation biculturals." *Journal of Cross-Cultural Psychology* **38**: 613–628.

Molden, D. and Dweck. C. (2006). "Finding 'meaning' in psychology – A lay theories approach to self-regulation, social perception, and social development." *American Psychologist* **61**: 192–203.

Molden, D., Plaks, J. *et al.* (2006). "'Meaningful' social inferences: effects of implicit theories on inferential processes." *Journal of experimental social psychology* **42**: 738–752.

Molitor, A., Mays, L. *et al.* (2003). "Emotion regulation behavior during a separation procedure in 18-month-old children of mothers using cocaine and other drugs." *Development and Psychopathology* **15**: 39–54.

Monks, C. and Smith, P. K. (2000). The social relationships of children involved in bully/victim problems at school. In R. Mills and S. Duck (eds), *The Developmental Psychology of Personal Relationships*. New York: Wiley.

Monks, C. and Smith, P. K. (2006). "Definitions of bullying: age differences in understanding of the term, and the role of experience." *British Journal of Developmental Psychology* **24**: 801–821.

Montgomery, H. (2009). *An Introdution to Childhood: Anthropological Perspectives on Children's Lives*. Chichester: Wiley-Blackwell.

Moran, P., Ghate, D. and van der Merwe, A. (2004). *What Works in Parenting Support? A Review of the International Evidence*. London: DfES.

Morison, S. J., Ames, E. W. and Chisholm, K. (1995). "The development of children adopted from Romanian orphanages." *Merrill-Palmer Quarterly* **41**: 411–430.

Morley-Fletcher, S. (2003). "Environmental enrichment during adolescence reverses the effects of prenatal stress on play behaviour and HPA axis reactivity in rats." *European Journal of Neuroscience* **18**: 3367–3374.

Morris, A. S., Silk, J. *et al.* (2002). "Temperamental vulnerability and negative parenting as interacting predictors of child adjustment." *Journal of Marriage and the Family* **64**: 461–471.

Mounts, N. (2001). "Young adolescents' perceptions of parental managment of peer relationships." *Journal of Early Adolescence* **21**: 92–122.

Mounts, N. (2002). "Parental management of adolescent peer relationships in context: the role of parenting style." *Journal of Family Psychology* **16**: 58–69.

Mowbray, C., Bybee, D. *et al.* (2004). "Diversity of outcomes among adolescent children of mothers with mental illness." *Journal of Emotional and Behavior Disorders* **12**: 206–221.

M'Rabet, L., Vos, A. P. *et al.* (2008). "Breast-feeding and its role in early development of the immune system in infants: consequences for health later in life." *Journal of Nutrition* **138**: 1782S-90S.

Mufson, L., Nomura, Y. *et al.* (2002). "The relationship between parental diagnosis, offspring temperament and offspring psychopathology: a longitudinal analysis." *Journal of Affective Disorders*, **71**: 61–69.

Muijs, R. (1997). "Predictors of academic achievement and academic self-concept; a longitudinal perspective." *British Journal of Educational Psychology* **67**: 263–277.

Munafo, M., Durrant, C. *et al.* (2009). "Gene x environment interactions at the serotonin transporter locus." *Biological Psychiatry* **65**: 211–219.

Munro, R. (2005). "Partial organization: Marilyn Strathern and the elicitation of relations." *Sociological Review* **53**: 245–266.

Murray, J. (2007). "The cycle of punishment: social exclusion of prisoners and their children." *Criminology and Criminal Justice* **7**: 55–81.

Murray, J. and Farrington, D. (2006). "Parental imprisonment: effects on boys' antisocial behaviour and delinquency through the life-course." *Journal of Child Psychology and Psychiatry* **46**: 1269–1278.

Murray, J. and Farrington, D. (2008a). "Parental imprisonment: long-lasting effects on boys' internalizing problems through the life course." *Development and Psychopathology* 2008 **20**: 273–290.

Murray, J. and Farrington, D. P. (2008b). "The effects of parental imprisonment on children." *Crime and Justice: A Review of Research* **37**: 133–206.

Murray, J., Janson, C.-G. and Farrington, D. P. (2007). "Crime in adult offspring of prisoners – A cross-national comparison of two longitudinal samples." *Criminal Justice and Behavior* **34**: 133–149.

Murray, J., Janson, C.-G. *et al.* (2007). "Crime in adult offspring of prisoners: a cross-national comparison of two longitudinal samples." *Criminal Justice and Behavior* **34**: 133–149.

Murray, L. (2006). "Socioemotional development in adolescents at risk of depression: the role of maternal depression and attachment style." *Development and Psychopathology* **18**: 489–516.

Nachmias, M., Gunnar, M. *et al.* (1996). "Behavioral inhibition and stress reactivity: the moderating role of attachment security." *Child Development* **67**: 508–522.

Nagell, K., Olguin, R. and Tomasello, M. (1993). "Processes of social-learning in the tool use of chimpanzees (Pan-Troglodytes) and human children (Homo-Sapiens)." *Journal of Comparative Psychology* **107**: 174–186.

Neiss, M. B., Sedikides, C. and Stevenson, J. (2002). "Self-esteem: a behavior-genetic prespective." *European Journal of Personality* **16**: 351–367.

Nelson, K. (2003). "Self and social functions: individual autobiographical memory and collective narrative." *Memory* **11**: 125–136.

Nelson, K. and Fivush, R. (2004). "The emergence of autobiographical memory: a social cultural developmental theory." *Psychological Review* **111**: 486–511.

Nelson, S. E. and Dishion, T. J. (2004). "From boys to men: Predicting adult adaptation from middle childhood sociometric status." *Development and Psychopathology* **16**: 441–459.

Nelson, L., Hart, C. H. *et al.* (2006). "Relations between Chinese mothers' parenting practices and social withdrawal in early childhood." *International Journal of Behavioral Development* **30**: 261–271.

Newman, K. and Massengill, R. (2006). "The texture of hardship: qualitative sociology of poverty 1995–2005." *Annual Review of Sociology* **32**: 423–446.

Newson, J. and Newson, E. (1968). *Four Years Old in an Urban Community.* London: George Allen and Unwin.

Newson, J. and Newson, E. (1976). *Seven Years Old in the Home Environment.* London: George Allen and Unwin.

Newson, J. and Newson, E. (1977). *Perspectives on School at Seven Years Old.* London: Allen and Unwin.

Newton, M. (2002). *Savage Girls and Wild Boys: A History of Feral Children.* London: Faber.

Ng, F.-Y., Pomerantz, E. and Lam, S. (2007). "European American and Chinese parents' responses to children's success and failure: implications for children's responses." *Developmental Psychology* **43**: 1239–1255.

NICHD (National Institute for Child and Health Development) Early Child Care Research Network. (2001). "Child care and children's peer interaction at 24 and 36 months: the National Institute of Child Health and Human Development Early Child Care Study of Early Child Care." *Child Development* **72**: 1478–1500.

NICHD (National Institute for Child and Health Development) Early Child Care Research Network. (2003a). "Social functioning in first grade: associations with earlier home and child care predictors and with current classroom experiences." *Child Development* **74**: 1639–1662.

NICHD (National Institute for Child and Health Development) Early Child Care Research Network. (2003b). "Does amount of time spent in child-care predict socioemotional adjustment during the transition to kindergarten?" *Child Development* **74**: 976–1005.

NICHD (National Institute for Child and Health Development) Early Child Care Research Network. (2003c). "Does quality of childcare affect child outcomes at age 41/2?" *Developmental Psychology* **39**: 451–469.

NICHD (National Institute for Child and Health Development) Early Child Care Research Network. (2003d). "Do children's attention processes mediate the link between family predictors and school readiness?" *Developmental Psychology* **39**: 381–593.

NICHD (National Institute for Child and Health Development) Early Child Care

Research Network. (2004a). "Multiple pathways to early academic achievement." *Harvard Educational Review* **74**: 1–29.

NICHD (National Institute for Child and Health Development) Early Child Care Research Network. (2004b). "Trajectories of physical aggression from toddlerhood to middle childhood." *Monographs of the Society for Research on Child Development* **69**: 1–269.

NICHD (National Institute for Child and Health Development) Early Child Care Research Network. (2005). "Predicting individual differences in attention, memory, and planning in first graders from experiences at home, child care, and school." *Developmental Psychology* **41**: 99–114.

NICHD (National Institute for Child and Health Development) Early Child Care Research Network. (2006). "Child-care effect sizes for the NICHD Study of Early Child Care and Youth Development." *American Psychologist* **61**: 99–116.

Nicholls, J. G. (1984). "Achievement motivation: conception of ability, subjective experience, task choice, and performance." *Psychological Review* **91**: 328–346.

Nicolopoulou, A. and Richner, E. S. (2007). "From actors to agents to persons: the development of character representation in young children's narratives." *Child Development* **78**: 412–429.

Nisan, M. (2004). Judgment and choice in moral functioning. In D. Lapsley and D. Narvaez (eds), *Moral Development, Self and Identity*. Mahwah, NJ: Erlbaum.

Nishina, A. and Juvonen, J. (2005). "Daily reports of witnessing and experiencing peer harassment in middle school." *Child Development* **76**: 435–450.

Nobile, M., Giorda, R. *et al.* (2007). "Socioeconomic status mediates the genetic contribution of the dopamine receptor D4 and serotonin transporter linked promoter region repeat polymorphisms to externalization in preadolescence." *Development and Psychopathology* (special issue) **19**: 1147–1160.

Nordlund, J. and Temrin, H. (2007). "Do characteristics of parental child homicide in sweden fit evolutionary predictions?" *Ethology* **113**: 1029–1037.

North, A., Hargreaves, D. *et al.* (2000). "The importance of music to adolescents." *British Journal of Educational Psychology* **70**: 255–272.

Nucci, L. (2002). The development of moral reasoning. In U. Goswami (ed.), *Blackwell Handbook of Cognitive Development*. Oxford: Blackwell.

Nucci, L. (2004). Reflections on the moral self construct. In D. Lapsley and D. Narvaez (eds), *Moral Development, Self, and Identity*. Mahwah, NJ: Erlbaum.

Nussbaum, A. and Dweck, C. (2008). "Defensiveness versus remediation: Self-theories and modes of self-esteem maintenance." *Personality and Social Psychology Bulletin* **34**: 599–612.

O'Brien, M. (2004). Social science and public policy perspectives on fatherhood in the European Union. In M. Lamb (ed.), *The Role of the Father in Child Development*. Hoboken, NJ: Wiley.

O'Brien, M., Margolin, G. and John, S. (1995). "Relation among marital conflict, child coping, and child adjustment." *Journal of Clinical Child Psychology* **24**: 346–361.

O'Connor, T. and Byrne, J. G. (2007). "Attachment measures for research and practice." *Child and Adolescent Mental Health* **12**: 187–192.

O'Connor, T. and Nilsen, W. J. (2005). Models versus metaphors in translating attachment theory to the clinic and community. In L. Berlin, Y. Ziv, L. Amaya-

Jackson and M. T. Greenberg (eds), *Enhancing Early Attachments*. New York: The Guilford Press.

O'Connor, T. and Scott, S. (2007). *Parenting and Outcomes for Children*. York: Joseph Rowntree Foundation.

O'Connor, T., Thomas, G. *et al.* (1998). "Genotype-environment correlations in late childhood and early adolescence: Antisocial behavior problems and coercive parenting." *Developmental Psychology* **34**: 970–981.

O'Connor, T., Rutter, M. *et al.* (2000). "The effects of global severe privation on cognitive competence: extension and longitudinal follow-up." *Child Development* **71**: 376–390.

O'Connor, T., Caspi, A. *et al.* (2003). "Genotype-environment interaction in children's adjustment to parental separation." *Journal of Child Psychology and Psychiatry, and Allied Disciplines* **44**: 849–856.

Odgers, C., Milner, B. J. *et al.* (2007). "Predicting prognosis for the conduct-problem boy: Can family history help?" *Journal of the American Academy of Child and Adolescent Psychiatry* **46**: 1240–1249.

Odgers, C., Moffitt, T. E. *et al.* (2008). "Female and male antisocial trajectories: From childhood origins to adult outcomes." *Development and Psychopathology* **20**: 673–716.

Olds, D. (2005). The nurse-family partnership: foundations in attachment theory and epidemiology. In L. Berlin, Y. Ziv, L. Amaya-Jackson and M. T. Greenberg (eds), *Enhancing Early Attachments*. New York: The Guilford Press.

Olson, K., Banaji, M. R. *et al.* (2006). "Children's biased evaluations of lucky versus unlucky people and their social groups." *Psychological Science* **17**: 845–846.

Olson, K., Dweck, C. *et al.* (2008). "Judgments of the lucky across development and culture." *Journal of Personality and Social Psychology* **94**: 757–776.

Olweus, D. (1993). *Bullying at School*. Oxford: Blackwell.

O'Neil, R., Parke, R. and McDowell, D. (2001). "Objective and subjective features of children's neighbourhoods: relations to parental regulatory strategies and children's social competence." *Journal of Applied Developmental Psychology* **22**: 135–155.

Ong, K., Preece, M. A. *et al.* (2002). "Size at birth and early childhood growth in relation to maternal smoking, parity and infant breast-feeding: longitudinal birth cohort study and analysis." *Pediatric Research* **52**: 863–867.

Ontai, L. and Thompson, R. A. (2008). "Attachment, parent–child discourse and theory-of-mind development." *Social Development* **17**: 47–60.

Onyangoa, P., Gesquiere, L. R. *et al.* (2008). "Persistence of maternal effects in baboons: Mother's dominance rank at son's conception predicts stress hormone levels in subadult males." *Hormones and Behavior* **54**: 319–324.

Opie, K. and Power, C. (2008). Grandmothering and female coalitions: a basis for matrilineal priority? In N. Allen, H. Callan, R. Dunbar and W. James (eds), *Early Human Kinship: From Sex to Social Reproduction*. Oxford, Blackwell.

Oppenheim, D., Koren-Karie, N. *et al.* (2007). "Emotion dialogues between mothers and children at 4.5 and 7.5 years: relations with children's attachment at 1 year." *Child Development* **78**: 38–52.

Orwell, G. (1949). *1984*. London: Secker and Warburg.

Osborn, A. and Milbank, J. (1987). *The Effects of Early Education*. Oxford: Clarendon.

Osborn, M. (2001). "Constants and contexts in pupil experience of learning and schooling: comparing learners in England, France and Denmark." *Comparative Education* **37**: 267–278.

Osborn, M. (2003). *A World of Difference: Comparing Learners across Europe.* Buckingham: Open University Press.

Osborn, M., McNess, E. and Pollard, A. (2006). "Identity and transfer: a new focus for home-school knowledge exchange." *Educational Review* **58**: 415–433.

Osborn, M., McNess, E. *et al.* (2000). *What Teachers Do: Changing Policy and Practice in Primary Education.* London: Continuum.

O'Sullivan, C. (2004). "The psychosocial determinants of depression: a lifespan perspective." *Journal of Nervous and Mental Disease* **192**: 585–594.

Owens, E. B. and Shaw, D. S. (2003). "Predicting growth curves of externalizing behavior across the preschool years." *Journal of Abnormal Child Psychology* **31**: 575–590.

Oyserman, D., Coon, H. M. *et al.* (2002). "Rethinking individualism and collectivism: evaluation of theoretical assumptions and meta-analyses." *Psychological Bulletin* **128**: 3–72.

Painter, R., Osmond, C. *et al.* (2008). "Transgenerational effects of prenatal exposure to the Dutch famine on neonatal adiposity and health in later life." *BJOG: An International Journal of Obstetrics & Gynaecology* **115**: 1243–1249.

Palmer, G., MacInnes, T. *et al.* (2006). *Monitoring Poverty and Social Exclusion 2006.* York: Joseph Rowntree Foundation.

Papero, A. (2005). "Is early, high-quality daycare an asset for the children of low-income, depressed mothers?" *Developmental Review* **25**: 181–211.

Parke, R. (2004). Fathering and children's peer relationships. In M Lamb (ed.), *The Role of the Father in Child Development.* Hoboken, NJ: Wiley.

Parke, R. and Buriel, R. (1998). Socialization in the family. In E. Hetherington (ed.), *Handbook of Child Psychology, Vol 3.* New York: Wiley.

Parke, R. and Buriel, R. (2004). "Development in the family." *Annual Review of Psychology* **55**: 365–399.

Parke, R. and Buriel, R. (2006). Socialization in the family: ethnic and ecological perspectives. In W. Damon, R. Lerner, N. Eisenberg (eds), *Handbook of Child Psychology, (6th edn) Vol 3:* 429–504. New York: Wiley.

Parke, R., O'Neil *et al.* (2000). The influence of significant others on learning about relationships: from family to friends. In R. Mills and S. Duck (eds), *The Developmental Psychology of Personal Relationships.* New York: Wiley.

Parker, J. and Seal, J. (1998). "Forming, losing, renewing and replacing friendships: Applying temporal parameters to the assessment of children's friendship experience." *Child Development* **67**: 2248–2268.

Parker, J. G., Low, C. M. *et al.* (2005). "Friendship jealousy in young adolescents: individual differences and links to sex, self-esteem, aggression and social adjustment." *Developmental Psychology* **41**: 235–250.

Parten, M. (1932). "Social participation among preschool children." *Journal of Abnormal Psychology* **27**: 243–269.

Patrick, J. (1973). *A Glasgow Gang Observed.* London: Eyre Methuen.

Patterson, C. (2004). Gay fathers. In M Lamb (ed.), *The Role of the Father in Child Development.* Hoboken, NJ: Wiley.

Patterson, C. and Hastings, P. (2007). Socialization in the context of family diversity. In J.Grusec and P. Hastings (eds), *Handbook of Socialization*. New York: Guilford Press.

Patterson, G. (1986). The contribution of siblings to training for fighting: a microsocial analysis. In D.Olweus, J. Block and M.Radke-Yarrow (eds), *Development of Antisocial and Prosocial Behaviour*. New York: Academic Press.

Patterson, G. and Sanson, A. (1999). "The association of behavioral adjustment to temperament, parenting and family characteristics among 5-year-old children." *Social Development* **8**: 293–309.

Patterson, G. R. and Fisher, P. A. (2002). Recent developments in our understanding of parenting: bidirectional effects, causal models, and the search for parsimony. In M. R. Bornstein (ed.), *Handbook of Parenting, Vol 3*: 59–88. Mahwah, NJ: Erlbaum.

Patterson, G. R., DeBaryshe, B. D. and Ramsey, E. (1989). "A developmental perspective on antisocial behavior." *American Psychologist* **44**: 329–335.

Patterson, G. R., DeGarmo, D. and Forgatch, M. S. (2004). "Systematic changes in families following prevention trials." *Journal of Abnormal Child Psychology* **32**: 621–633.

Pearce, L. and Axinn, W. (1998). "The impact of family religious life on the quality of mother–child relations." *American Sociological Review* **63**: 810–828.

Pearce, L. and Haynie, D. (2004). "Intergenerational religious dynamics and adolescent delinquency." *Social Forces* **82**: 1553–1572.

Peisner-Feinberg, E., Burchinal, M. R. *et al.* (2001). "The relation of preschool child care quality to children's cognitive and social development trajectories through second grade." *Child Development* **72**: 1534–1553.

Pelkonen, M., Marttunen, M. *et al.* (2003). "Risk for depression: a 6-year follow-up of Finnish adolescents." *Journal of Affective Disorders* **77**: 41–51.

Pellegrini, A. D. (2004). "Sexual segregation in childhood: a review of evidence for two hypotheses." *Animal Behaviour* **68**: 435–443.

Pellegrini, A. and Bartini, M. (2000). "A longitudinal study of bullying, victimisation and peer affiliation during the transition from primary school to middle school." *American Educational Research Journal* **37**: 699–725.

Pellegrini, A. and Blatchford, P. (2000). *The Child at School*. London: Arnold.

Pembrey, M. (2004). "The Avon Longitudinal Study of Parents and Children (ALSPAC): a resource for genetic epidemiology." *European Journal of Endocrinology* **151**: U125–U129.

Pembrey, M., Bygren L *et al.* (2006). "Sex-specific, male-line transgenerational responses in humans." *European Journal of Human Genetics* **14**: 159–166.

Penner, L. A., Dovidio, J. F. *et al.* (2005). "Prosocial behavior: multilevel perspectives." *Annual Review of Psychology* **56**: 365–392.

Perkins, S. and Turiel, E. (2007). "To lie or not to lie: to whom and under what circumstances." *Child Development* **78**: 609–621.

Perlman, M. (2000). An analysis of sources of power in children's conflict interactions. In R. Mills and S. Duck (eds), *The Developmental Psychology of Personal Relationships*. New York: Wiley.

Perner, J., Ruffman, T. and Leekam, S. (1994). Theory Of Mind is contagious – you catch it from your sibs. *Child Development* **65**: 1228–1238.

Perren, S. and Alsaker, F. (2006). "Social behaviour and peer relationships of victims, bully-victims and bullies in kindergarten." *Journal of Child Psychology and Psychiatry* **47**: 45–57.

Perret-Clermont, A.-N., Pontecorro, C. *et al.* (2004). *Joining Society: Social Interaction and Learning in Adolescence and Youth.* Cambridge: Cambridge University Press.

Peterson, K., Paulson, S. and Williams, K. K. (2007). "Relations of Eating Disorder Symptomology with Perceptions of Pressures from Mother, Peers, and Media in Adolescent Girls and Boys." *Sex Roles* **57**: 629–639.

Petrill, S. and Deater-Deckard, K. (2004). Task orientation, parental warmth and SES account for a significant proportion of the shared environmental variance in general cognitive ability in early childhood: evidence from a twin study. *Developmental Science* **7**: 25–32.

Pettit, G., Brown, E. G. *et al.* (1998). "Mothers' and fathers' socializing behavior in three contexts: Links with children's peer competence." *Merrill-Palmer Quarterly* **44**: 173–193.

Pettit, G. S., Laird, R. D. *et al.* (2001). "Antecedents and behavior-problem outcomes of parental monitoring and psychological control in early adolescence." *Child Development* **72**: 583–598.

Phinney, J., Kim-Jo, T. *et al.* (2005). "Autonomy-relatedness in adolescent-parent disagreements: ethnic and developmental factors." *Journal of Adolescent Research* **20**: 8–39.

Piaget, J. (1932). *The Moral Judgment of the Child.* Harmondsworth: Penguin Books.

Piaget, J. (1962). *Play, Dreams and Imitation in Childhood.* New York: Norton.

Piaget, J. (1971). *Biology and Knowledge.* Edinburgh: Edinburgh University Press.

Pianta, R. C. and Walsh, D. J. (1996). *High-Risk Children in Schools.* London: Routledge.

Pickett, K. and Wilkinson, R. (2007). "Child wellbeing and income inequality in rich societies: ecological cross sectional study." *British Medical Journal* **335**: 1080.

Pilling, D. (1990). *Escape from Disadvantage.* London: Falmer Press.

Pine, K. and Nash, A. (2003). "Barbie or Betty? Children's preference for branded products and evidence for gender-linked differences." *Developmental and Behavioral Pediatrics* **24**: 219–224.

Pintrich, P. (2000). "Multiple goals, multiple pathways: the role of goal orientation in learning and achievement." *Journal of Educational Psychology* **92**: 544–555.

Pintrich, P. (2003). "A motivational science perspective on the role of student motivation in learning and teaching contexts." *Journal of Educational Psychology* **95**: 667–686.

Pittman, L. and Chase-Lindsay, P. (2001). "African American adolescent girls in impoverished communities: parenting style and adolescent outcomes." *Journal of Research on Adolescence* **11**: 199–224.

Plath, S. (1966). *The Bell Jar.* London: Faber.

Pleck, E. (2004). Two dimensions of fatherhood: a history of the good dad-bad dad complex. In M. Lamb (ed.), *The Role of the Father in Child Development.* New York: Wiley.

Plomin, R. (1994). *Genetics and Experience: The Interplay between Nature and Nurture.* London: Sage.

Plomin, R. and Rutter, M. (1998). "Child development, molecular genetics, and what to do with genes when they are found." *Child Development* **69**: 1221–1240.

Pluess, M. and Belsky, J. (2009). "Differential susceptibility to rearing experience: the case of childcare." *Journal of Child Psychology and Psychiatry* **50**: 396–404.

Polivy, J. and Herman, C. P. (2002). "Causes of eating disorders." *Annual Review of Psychology* **53**: 187–213.

Pollack, W. (2006). Sustaining and reframing vulnerability and connection: creating genuine resilience in boys and young males. In S. Goldstein and R. Brooks *Handbook of Resilience in Children*. New York: Springer.

Pollard, A. (1985). *The Social World of the Primary School*. London: Holt, Rinehart & Winston.

Pollard, A. (2000). *What Pupils Say: Changing Policy and Practice in Primary Education*. London: Continuum.

Pollard, A. and Filer, A. (1996). *The Social World of Children's Learning*. London: Continuum.

Pollard, A. and Filer, A. (1999). *The Social World of Pupil Career*. London: Continuum.

Pollard, A. and Filer, A. (2007). "Learning, differentiation and strategic action in secondary education: analyses from the Identity and Learning Programme." *British Journal of Sociology of Education* **28**: 441–458.

Pollet, T. V. (2007). "Genetic relatedness and sibling relationship characteristics in a modem society." *Evolution And Human Behavior* **28**: 176–185.

Pollock, L. (1983). *Forgotten Children*. Cambridge: Cambridge University Press.

Pollock, L. (1987). *A Lasting Relationship: Parents and Children over Three Centuries*. Hanover: University Press of New England.

Pomerantz, E. and Saxon, J. (2001). Conceptions of ability as stable and self-evaluative processes: a longitudinal examination. *Child Development* **72**: 152–173.

Porter, R. (1998). "Olfaction and human kin recognition." *Genetica* **104**: 259–263.

Posner, M. I. and Rothbart, M. (2000). "Developing mechanisms of self-regulations." *Development and Psychopathology* **12**: 427–441.

Power, C. and Jefferis, B. (2002). "Fetal environment and subsequent obesity: a study of maternal smoking." *International Journal of Epidemiology* **31**: 413–419.

Power, F. (2004). The moral self in community. In D. Lapsley and D. Narvaez (eds), *Moral development, self and identity*. Mahwah, NJ: Erlbaum.

Pratt, M. and Fiese, B. (2004). *Family Stories and the Life Course: Across Time and Generations*. Mahwah, NJ: Erlbaum.

Prinstein, M., Borelli, J. *et al.* (2005). "Adolescent girls' interpersonal vulnerability to depressive symptoms: a longitudinal examination of reassurance-seeking and peer relationships." *Journal of Abnormal Psychology* **114**: 676–688.

Print, M., Ornstrom, S. *et al.* (2002). "Education for Democratic Processes in Schools and Classrooms." *European Journal of Education* **37**: 193–210.

Propper, C. and Moore, G. (2006). "The influence of parenting on infant emotionality: A multi-level psychobiological perspective." *Developmental Review* **26**: 427–460.

Punamäki, R., Qouta, S. *et al.* (1997). "Models of traumatic experiences and children's psychological adjustment: the roles of perceived parenting and children's own resources and activity." *Child Development* **68**: 718–728.

Punch, S. (2008). "'You can do nasty things to your brothers and sisters without a reason': siblings' backstage behaviour." *Children and Society* **22**: 333–344.

Putnam, F. W. (2005). The developmental neurobiology of disrupted attachment: lessons from animal models and child abuse research. In: L. Berlin, Y. Ziv, L. Amaya-Jackson and M. T. Greenberg (eds), *Enhancing Early Attachments*. New York: The Guilford Press.

Qouta, S., Punamäki, R. *et al.* (2008). "Does war beget child aggression? Military violence, gender, age and aggressive behavior in two Palestinian samples." *Aggressive Behavior* **34**: 231–244.

Quinton, D. and Rutter, M. (1988). *Parenting Breakdown: The Making and Breaking of Inter-generational Links*. Aldershot: Avebury.

Radke-Yarrow, M. (1991). The individual and the environment in human behavioural development. In P.Bateson (ed.), *The Development and Integration of Behaviour*. Cambridge: Cambridge University Press.

Raikes, H. A. and Thompson, R. A. (2006). "Family emotional climate, attachment security and young children's emotion knowledge in a high risk sample." *British Journal of Developmental Psychology* **24**: 89–104.

Ramchandani, P., Stein, A. *et al.* (2008a). "Depression in men in the postnatal period and later child psychopathology: A population cohort study." *Journal of the American Academy of Child and Adolescent Psychiatry* **47**: 390–398.

Ramchandani, P., O'Connor, T. G. *et al.* (2008b). "The effects of pre- and postnatal depression in fathers: a natural experiment comparing the effects of exposure to depression on offspring." *Journal of Child Psychology and Psychiatry* **49**: 1069–1078.

Ramey, C. and Ramey, S. (1998). "Early intervention and early experience." *American Psychologist* **53**: 109–120.

Raven, J. (1980). *Parents, Teachers and Children: A Study of an Educational Home-Visiting Scheme*. London: Hodder and Stoughton.

Raver, C. (2004). "Placing emotional self-regulation in socioeconomic and socio-cultural contexts." *Child Development* **75**: 346–353.

Reader, S. (2003). "Innovation and social learning: individual variation and brain evolution." *Animal Biology* **53**: 147–158.

Reay, D. (2001). "'Spice girls', 'nice girls', 'girlies', and 'tomboys': gender discourses, girls' cultures and femininities in the primary classroom." *Gender and Education* **13**: 153–166.

Reay, D. (2002). "Shaun's Story: troubling discourses of white working-class masculinities." *Gender and Education* **14**: 221–234.

Reay, D. (2006). "I'm not seen as one of the clever children: consulting primary school pupils about the social conditions of learning." *Educational Review* **58** 171–181.

Reay, D. and Lucey, H. (2000). "Children, school choice and social differences." *Educational Studies* **26**: 83–100.

Reese, E. and Newcombe, R. (2007). "Training mothers in elaborative reminiscing enhances children's autobiographical memory and narrative." *Child Development*, **78**: 1153–1170.

Reese, E., Hayne, H. and Macdonald, S. (2008). "Looking back to the future: Maori and Pakeha mother–child birth stories." *Child Development* **79**: 114–125.

Regnerus, M. (2003a). "Moral communities and adolescent delinquency: Religious contexts and community social control." *Sociological Quarterly* **44**: 523–554.

Regnerus, M. (2003b). "Religion and positive adolescent outcomes: a review of research and theory." *Review of Religious Research* **44**: 394–413.

Regnerus, M. and Elder, G. (2003). "Religion and vulnerability among low-risk adolescents." *Social Science Research* **32**: 633–658.

Reiss, D. (2003). Child effects on family systems: behavioral genetic strategies. In A. Crouter and A. Booth (eds), *Children's Influence on Family Dynamics: The Neglected Side of Family Relationships*. Mahwah, NJ: Erlbaum.

Reiss, D. and Leve, L. (2007). "Genetic expression outside the skin: clues to mechanisms of Genotype x Environment interaction." *Development and Psychopathology* **19**: 1005–1027.

Reiss, D., Cederblad, M. *et al.* (2001). "Genetic probes of three theories of maternal adjustment: II. Genetic and environmental influences." *Family Process* **40**: 261–272.

Reitz, E., Prinzie, P. *et al.* (2007). "The role of peer contacts in the relationship between parental knowledge and adolescents' externalizing behaviors: a latent growth curve modeling approach." *Journal of Youth and Adolescence* **36**: 623–634.

Repetti, R., Taylor, S. E. and Saxbe, D. (2007). The influence of early socialization experiences on the development of biological systems. In J. E. Grusec and P. D. Hastings (eds), *Handbook of Socialization*. New York: Guilford Press.

Reyna, V. and Farley, F. (2006). "Risk and rationality in adolescent decision making: implications for theory, practice, and public policy." *Psychological Science in the Public Interest* **7**: 1–44.

Reynolds, A., Ou, S.-R. and Topitzes, J. W. (2004). "Paths of effects of early childhood intervention on educational attainment and delinquency." *Child Development* **75**: 1299–1328.

Reznick, J. S, Kagan, J *et al.* (1986). "Inhibited and uninhibited children – a follow-up-study." *Child Development* **57**: 660–680.

Ricco, R. and Rodriguez, P. (2006). "The relation of personal epistemology to parenting style and goal orientation in college mothers." *Social Psychology of Education* **9**: 159–178.

Rice, F., Harold, G. T. *et al.* (2006). "Family conflict interacts with genetic liability in predicting childhood and adolescent depression." *Journal of the American Academy of Child & Adolescent Psychiatry* **45**: 841–848.

Richards, M. H., Crowe P. A. *et al.* (1998). "Developmental patterns and gender differences in the experience of peer companionship during adolescence." *Child Development* **69**: 154–163.

Richardson, D. and Robinson, V. (2008). *Introducing Gender and Women's Studies*. Basingstoke: Palgrave Macmillan.

Rickard, I. and Lummaa, V. (2007). "The predictive adaptive response and metabolic syndrome: challenges for the hypothesis." *Trends in Endocrinology and Metabolism* **18**: 94–99.

Riggins-Caspers, K. M., Cadoret, R. J. *et al.* (2003). "Biology-environment inter-action and evocative biology-environment correlation: Contributions of harsh discipline and parental psychopathology to problem adolescent behaviors." *Behavior Genetics* **33**: 205–220.

Riggs, N. R., Blair, C. and Greenberg, M. T. (2003). "Concurrent and 2-year longitudinal relations between executive function and the behavior of 1st and 2nd grade children." *Child Neuropsychology* **9**: 267–276.

Riley, D. (1983). *War in the Nursery: Theories of the Child and Mother*. London: Virago.

Rissotto, A. and Giuliani, M. (2006). Learning neighbourhood environments: the loss of experience in a modern world. In C. Spencer and M. Blades (eds), *Children and Their Environments*. Cambridge: Cambridge University Press.

Roberts, B. W. and DelVecchio, W. (2000). "The rank-order consistency of personality traits from childhood to old age: A quantitative review of longitudinal studies." *Psychological Bulletin* **126**: 3–25.

Roberts, B. W., Caspi, A., and Moffitt, T. E. (2001). "The kids are alright: growth and stability in personality development from adolescence to adulthood." *Journal of Personality and Social Psychology* **81**: 582–583.

Roberts, D. and Foehr, U. (2008). "Trends in media use." *The Future of Children* **18**: 11–37.

Robinson, C. C., Anderson, G. T. *et al.* (2003). Sequential transition patterns of preschoolers' social interactions during child-initiated play: Is parallel-aware play a bidirectional bridge to other play states? *Early Childhood Research Quarterly* **18**: 3–21.

Rodkin, P., Farmer, T. *et al.* (2000). "Heterogeneity of popular boys: antisocial and prosocial configurations." *Developmental Psychology* **36**: 14–24.

Rodriguez, D., Wigfield, A. and Eccles, J. S. (2003). "Changing competence perceptions, changing values: implications for youth sport." *Journal of Applied Sports Psychology* **15**: 67–81.

Rodriguez, R. (1980). An education in language. In L. Michaels and C. Ricks (eds), *The State of the Language*. Berkeley, CA: University of California Press.

Roeser, R. W. and Eccles, J. S. (1998). "Adolescents' perceptions of middle school: relation to longitudinal changes in academic and psychological adjustment." *Journal of Research in Adolescence* **8**: 123–158.

Roeser, R., Midgley, C. *et al.* (1996). "Perceptions of the school psychological environment and early adolescents' psychological and behavioral functioning in school: the mediating role of goals and belonging." *Journal of Educational Psychology* **88**: 408–422.

Rogoff, B. (2003a). "Firsthand learning through intent participation." *Annual Review of Psychology* **54**: 175–203.

Rogoff, B. (2003b). *The Cultural Nature of Human Development*. New York: Oxford.

Roisman, G. and Fraley, C. (2006). "The limits of genetic influence: a behavior-genetic analysis of infant-caregiver relationship quality and temperament." *Child Development* **77**: 1656–1667.

Romeo, R. and McEwen, B. (2006). "Stress and the adolescent brain." *Annals of the New York Academy of Sciences* **1094**: 202–214.

Roopnarine, J. (2004). African American and African Caribbean fathers: level, quality and meaning of involvement. In M. Lamb (ed.), *The Role of the Father in Child Development*. Hoboken, NJ: Wiley.

Rose, A. (2002). "Co-rumination in the friendships of girls and boys." *Child Development* **73**: 1830–1843.

Rose, A. and Rudolph, K. (2006). "A review of sex differences in peer relationship processes: potential trade-offs for the emotional and behavioral development of girls and boys." *Psychological Bulletin* **132**: 98–131.

Rose, A., Carlson, W. and Waller, E. M. (2007). "Prospective associations of co-rumination with friendship and emotional adjustment." *Developmental Psychology* **43**: 1019–1031.

Rose, A. J., Swenson, L. P. and Waller, E. M. (2004). "Overt and relational aggression and perceived popularity: developmental differences in concurrent and prospective relations." *Developmental Psychology* **40**: 378–387.

Rose, S. (1998). *Lifelines: Biology, Freedom, Determinism*. Harmondsworth: Penguin.

Rothbart, M. K. and Bates, J. (2006). Temperament. In W. Damon, R. Lerner, N. Eisenberg (eds), *Handbook of Child Psychology, (6th edn) Vol 3*. New York: Wiley.

Rothbart, M. K., Ahadi, S. A. *et al.* (2001). "Investigation of temperament at 3 to 7 years: the children's behavior questionnaire." *Child Development* **72**: 1394–1408.

Rothbaum, F. and Trommsdorff, G. (2007). Do roots and wings complement or oppose one another? The socialization of relatedness and autonomy in cultural context. In J. Grusec and P. Hastings (eds), *Handbook of Socialization*. New York: Guilford.

Rothbaum, F., Pott, M. *et al.* (2000). "The development of close relationships in Japan and the United States: Paths of symbiotic harmony and generative tension." *Child Development* **71**: 1121–1142.

Rousseau, J.-J. (1995). *Emilius: or, an Essay on Education*. Bristol: Thoemmes Press.

Rowe, D. (1994). *The Limits of Family Influence*. New York: Guilford.

Roy, P., Rutter, M. and Pickles, A. (2000). "Institutional care: risk from family background or pattern of rearing?" *Journal of Child Psychology and Psychiatry* **49**: 139–141.

Rubin, K. (1999). "The transaction between parents' perceptions of their children's shyness and their parenting styles." *International Journal of Behavioral Development* **23**: 937–958.

Rubin, K., Bukowski, W. and Parker, J. (2006). Peer interactions, relationships and groups. In W. Damon, R. Lerner, N. Eisenberg (eds), *Handbook of Child Psychology, (6th edn) Vol 3*: 571–645. New York: Wiley.

Rubin, K., Burgess, K. and Hastings, P. (2002). "Stability and social-behavioral consequences of toddlers' inhibited temperament and parenting." *Child Development* **73**: 483–495.

Rubin, K., Cheah, C. and Fox, N. (2001). "Emotion regulation, parenting, and the display of social reticence in preschoolers." *Early Education and Development* **12**: 97–115.

Rubin, K., Maioni, T. L. and Hornung, M. (1976). "Free play behaviors in middle-class and lower-class preschoolers – Parten and Piaget revisited." *Child Development* **47**: 414–419.

Rubin, K., Bukowski, W. *et al.* (1998a). Peer interactions, relationships and groups. In W. Damon and N Eisberg (eds), *Handbook of Child Psychology Volume 3*. New York: Wiley.

Rubin, K., Hastings, P. *et al.* (1998b). "Intrapersonal and maternal correlates of aggression, conflict and externalizing problems in toddlers." *Child Development* **69**: 1614–1629.

Rubin, K., Burgess *et al.* (2003). "Predicting preschoolers' externalizing behaviours from toddler temperament, conflict and maternal negativity." *Developmental Psychology* **39**: 164–176.

Ruble, D., Martin, C. and Berenbaum, S. (2006). Gender Development. In W. Damon, R. Lerner, N. Eisenberg (eds), *Handbook of Child Psychology, Vol 3*. New York: Wiley

Rusbult, C. E. and Van Lange, P. A. M. (2003). "Interdependence, interaction, and relationships." *Annual Review of Psychology* **54**: 351–375.

Ruschena, E., Prior, M. *et al.* (2005). "A longitudinal study of adolescent adjustment following family transitions." *Journal of Child Psychology and Psychiatry* **46**: 353–363.

Russell, G. and Finnie, V. (1990). "Preschool children's social status and maternal instruction to assist group entry." *Developmental Psychology* **26**: 603–611.

Russell, G. and Hwang, C. (2004). The impact of workplace practices on father involvement. In M. Lamb (ed.), *The Role of the Father in Child Development*. Hoboken, NJ: Wiley.

Rust, J., Golombok, S. *et al.* (2000). "The role of brothers and sisters in the gender development of preschool children." *Journal of Experimental Child Psychology* **77**: 292–303.

Rutter, M. (1981). *Maternal Deprivation Reassessed*. Harmondsworth: Penguin.

Rutter, M. (1985). Family and school influences on cognitive development. *Journal of Child Psychology and Psychiatry* **26**: 349–368.

Rutter, M. (1987). "Psychosocial resilience and protective mechanisms." *American Journal of Orthopsychiatry* **57**: 316–331.

Rutter, M. (1988a). *Studies of Psychosocial Risk: The Power of Longitudinal Data*. Cambridge: Cambridge University Press.

Rutter, M. (1998b). "Developmental catch-up, and deficit, following adoption after severe global early privation." *Journal of Child Psychology and Psychiatry and Allied Disciplines* **39**: 465–476.

Rutter, M. (2006). *Genes and behaviour: Nature-nurture interplay explained*. Oxford: Blackwell.

Rutter, M. (2007a). Gene-environment interplay and developmental psychopathology. In A. Masten (ed.), *Minnesota Symposium on Child Psychology, Vol 34*: 1–26. Mahwah, NJ: Erlbaum.

Rutter, M. (2007b). "Implications of resilience concepts for scientific understanding." *Annals of the New York Academy of Sciences* **1094**: 1–12.

Rutter, M. and Silberg, J. (2002). "Gene-Environment Interplay in Relation to Emotional and Behavioral Disturbance." *Annual Review of Psychology* **53**: 463–490.

Rutter, M. and Smith, D. J. (1995). *Psychosocial Disorders in Young People*. New York: Wiley.

Rutter, M., Giller, H. and Hagel, A. (1998). *Antisocial Behaviour by Young People*. Cambridge: Cambridge University Press.

Rutter, M., Kreppner, J. M. and O'Connor, T. G. (2001). "Specificity and heterogeneity in children's response to severe privation." *British Journal of Psychiatry* **179**: 97–103.

Rutter, M., O'Connor T. G. and the English and Romanian Adoptees (ERA) Study Team (2004). "Are there biological programming effects for psychological development? Findings from a study of Romanian adoptees." *Developmental Psychology* **40**: 81–94.

Rutter, M., Silberg, J. *et al.* (1999a). "Genetics and child psychiatry: 1 advances in quantitative and molecular genetics." *Journal of Child Psychology and Psychiatry* **40**: 3–18.

Rutter, M., Silberg, J. *et al.* (1999b). "Genetics and child psychiatry: 2 empirical research findings." *Journal of Child Psychology and Psychiatry* **40**: 19–56.

Rutter, M., Moffitt, T. E. *et al.* (2006). "Gene-environment interplay and psychopathology: Multiple varieties but real effects." *Journal of Child Psychology and Psychiatry* **47**: 226–261.

Rutter, M., Kreppner, J. *et al.* (2007). "Early adolescent outcomes for institutionally-deprived and non-deprived adoptees." *Journal of Child Psychology and Psychiatry* **48**: 17–30.

Ryan, R. and Deci, E. (2000). "Self-determination theory and the facilitation of intrinsic motivation, social development, and well-being." *American Psychologist* **55**: 1093–1104.

Ryan, R. M., Kuhl, J. and Deci, E. L. (1997). "Nature and autonomy: an organizational view of social and neurobiological aspects of self-regulation in behavior and development." *Development and Psychopathology* **9**: 701–728.

Rydell, A. M., Bohlin, G. and Thorell, L. B. (2005). "Representations of attachment to parents and shyness as predictors of children's relationships with teachers and peer competence in preschool." *Attachment & Human Development* **7**: 187–202.

Rymer, R. (1993). *Genie: Escape from a Silent Childhood.* London: Michael Joseph.

Sable, P. (2004). "Attachment, ethology and adult psychotherapy." *Attachment & Human Development* **6**: 3–19.

Sacker, A., Schoon, I. and Bartley, M. (2002). "Social inequality in educational achievement and psychosocial adjustment throughout childhood: magnitude and mechanisms." *Social Science & Medicine* **55**: 863–880.

Salinger, J. D. (1951). *The Catcher in the Rye.* London: Hamish Hamilton.

Salmivalli, C., Kaukiainen, A. *et al.* (1999). "Self-evaluated self-esteem, peer-evaluated self-esteem, and defensive egotism as predictors of adolescents' participation in bullying situations." *Personality and Social Psychology Bulletin* **25**: 1268–1278.

Sameroff, A. and Rosenblum, K. (2006). "Psychosocial Constraints on the Development of Resilience." *Annals of the New York Academy of Sciences* **1094**: 116–124.

Sameroff, A., Seifer, R. *et al.* (1993). "Stability of intelligence from preschool to adolescence: the influence of social and family risk factors." *Child Development* **64**: 80–97.

Sammons, P., Karen, E. *et al.* (2004). "The impact of pre-school on young children's cognitive attainments at entry to reception." *British Educational Research Journal* **30**: 691–712.

Sandstrom, M. and Coie, J. (1999). "A developmental perspective on peer rejection: Mechanisms of stability and change." *Child Development* **70**: 955–966.

Sanson, A., Hemphill, S. A. and Smart, D. (2004). "Connections between temperament and social development: A review." *Social Development* **13**: 142–170.

Saudino, K. and Plomin, R. (2007). "Why are hyperactivity and academic achievement related?" *Child Development* **78**: 972–986.

Scarr, S. (1992). "Developmental theories for the 1990s: development and individual differences." *Child Development* **63**: 1–19.

Scarr, S. (1996). "How people make their own environments: implications for parents and policy makers." *Psychology, Public Policy and Law* **2**: 204–228.

Scerif, G. and Karmiloff-Smith, A. (2005). The dawn of cognitive genetics? Crucial developmental caveats. *Trends In Cognitive Sciences* **9**: 126–135.

Schachter, F. (1982). Sibling deidentification and split-parent identification: a family trend. In M. Lamb and B. Sutton-Smith (eds), *Sibling Relationships*. Hillsdale, NJ: Erlbaum.

Schaffer, H. R. (1992). Early experience and the parent–child relation ship: genetic and environmental interactions as developmental determinants. In B. Tizard and V. Varma (eds), *Vulnerability and Resilience in Human Development*. London: Jessica Kingsley.

Schaffer, H. R. (1998). *Making Decisions about Children*. Oxford: Blackwell.

Schama, S. (1989). *Citizens: A Chronicle of the French Revolution*. London: Viking.

Scharrer, E. (2005). "Hypermasculinity, aggression and television violence: an experiment." *Media Psychology* **7**: 353–376.

Scheerens, J. and Bosker, R. (1997). *The Foundations of Educational Effectiveness*. Oxford: Elsevier.

Scheerens, J. and Creemers, B. (1989). "Conceptualising school effectiveness." *International Journal of Educational Research* **13**: 691–706.

Schmidt, L., Fox, N. and Hamer, D. H. (2007). "Evidence for a gene-gene interaction in predicting children's behavior problems: Association of serotonin transporter short and dopamine receptor D4 long genotypes with internalizing and externalizing behaviors in typically developing 7-year-olds." *Development and Psychopathology* **19**: 1105–1116.

Schmidt, M., Pempek, T. A. *et al.* (2008). "The effects of background television on the toy play behavior of very young children." *Child Development* **79**: 1137–1151.

Schmidt, M. and E. Vandewater (2008). "Media and attention, cognition and school achievement." *The Future of Children* **18**: 63–85.

Schneider, B. H. (2000). *Friends and Enemies: Peer Relations in Childhood*. London: Hodder and Stoughton.

Schneider, B., Atkinson, L. and Tardif, C. (2001). "Child-parent attachment and children's peer relations: A quantitative review." *Developmental Psychology* **37**: 86–100.

Schneider, B., Attili, G. *et al.* (1997). "A comparison of middle-class English-Canadian and Italian mothers' beliefs about children's peer-directed aggression and social withdrawal." *International Journal of Behavioral Development* **21**: 133–154.

Schneider, B., Tomada, G. *et al.* (2008). "Social support as a predictor of school bonding and academic motivation following the transition to Italian middle school." *Journal of Social and Personal Relationships* **25**: 287–310.

Schneider, J. and Schneider, P. (2008). "The anthropology of crime and criminalization." *Annual Review of Anthropology* **37**: 351–373.

Scholte, R., Engels, R. *et al.* (2007). "Stability in bullying and victimization and its association with social adjustment in childhood and adolescence." *Journal of Abnormal Child Psychology* **35**: 217–228.

Schoon, I. (2006). *Risk and Resilience: Adaptations in Changing Times*. Cambridge: Cambridge University Press.

Schuckit, M. A. (1994). "Low level of response to alcohol as a predictor of future alcoholism." *American Journal of Psychiatry* **151**: 184–189.

Schwartz, S. (1992). "Universals in the content and structure of values: theoretical advances and empirical tests in 20 countries." *Advances in Experimental Social Psychology* **25**: 1–65.

Schwartz, S. (1996). *Value Priorities and Behavior*. In C. Seligman, J. M. Olson and M. P. Zanna (eds), *The Psychology of Values: The Ontario Symposium, Vol 8*: 1–24. Hillsdale, NJ: Erlbaum.

Schwartz, S. and Bardi, A. (2001). "Value hierarchies across cultures: taking a similarities perspective." *Journal of Cross-Cultural Psychology* **32**: 268–290.

Schwartz, S. and Boehnke, K. (2004). "Evaluating the structure of human values with confirmatory factor analysis." *Journal of Research in Personality* **38**: 230–255.

Schwartz, S. and Rubel, T. (2005). "Sex differences in value priorities: cross-cultural and multimethod studies." *Journal of Personality and Social Psychology*. **89**: 1010–1028.

Scott, J. (2006). *Jean Jacques Rousseau*. New York: Routledge.

Seidman, E. (1994). "The impact of school transitions in early adolescence on the self-esteem and perceived social context of poor urban youth." *Child Development* **65**: 507–522.

Serbin, L. A. and Karp, J. (2004). "The intergenerational transfer of psychosocial risk: mediators of vulnerability and resilience." *Annual Review of Psychology* **55**: 333–363.

Shamai, M. (2001). "Parents' perceptions of their children in a context of shared political uncertainty." *Child & Family Social Work* **6**: 249–260.

Shamir-Essakow, G., Ungerer, J. A. *et al.* (2004). "Caregiving representations of mothers of behaviorally inhibited and uninhibited preschool children." *Developmental Psychology* **40**: 899–910.

Shanahan, L., Kim, J.-Y. *et al.* (2007). "Sibling similarities and differences in time use: a pattern-analytic, within-family approach." *Social Development* **16**: 662–681.

Shanahan, M. (2000). "Pathways to adulthood in changing societies: Variability and mechanisms in life course perspective." *Annual Review of Sociology* **26**: 667–692.

Shanahan, S. (2007). "Lost and found: the sociological ambivalence towards childhood." *Annual Review of Sociology* **33**: 407–428.

Shannon, J., Tamis-LeMonda, C. and Cabrera, N. J. (2006). "Fathering in infancy: mutuality and stability between 8 and 16 months." *Parenting – Science and Practice* **6**: 167–188.

Shaw, D. S. (2003). "Advancing our understanding of intergenerational continuity in anti-social behavior." *Journal of Abnormal Child Psychology* **31**: 193–199.

Shaw, D., Owens, E. B. *et al.* (1996). "Early risk factors and pathways in the development of early disruptive behavior problems." *Development and Psychopathology* **8**: 679–699.

Shaw, P., Greenstein, D. *et al.* (2006). "Intellectual ability and cortical development in children and adolescents." *Nature* **440**: 676–679.

Sheridan, S., Eagle, J. W. and Dowd, S. E. (2006). Families as contexts for children's adaptation. In S. Goldstein and R. Brooks (ed.), *Handbook of Resilience in Children.* New York: Springer.

Sherrod, L. (2008). "Adolescents' perceptions of rights as reflected in their views of Citizenship." *Journal of Social Issues* **64**: 771–790.

Sherrod, L., Flanagan, C. *et al.* (2002). "Dimensions of citizenship and opportunities for youth development: the what, why, when, where, and who of citizenship development." *Applied Developmental Science* **6**: 264–272.

Shiner, R. L. (1998). "How shall we speak of children's personalities in middle childhood? A preliminary taxonomy." *Psychological Bulletin* **124**: 308–322.

Shiner, R. L. and Caspi, A. (2003). "Personality differences in childhood and adulthood: Measurement, development and consequences." *Journal of Child Psychology and Psychiatry and Allied Disciplines* **44**: 2–32.

Shwalb, D., Nakawaza, J. *et al.* (2004). Fathering in Japanese, Chinese and Korean cultures. In M. Lamb (ed.), *The Role of the Father in Child Development.* Hoboken, NJ: Wiley.

Shweder, R. A., Mahapatra, M. and Miller, J. G. (1990). Culture and moral development. In W. Stigler, R. A. Shweder and G. H. Herdt (eds), *Cultural Psychology: Essays on Comparative Human Development.* Cambridge, Cambridge University Press.

Silberg, J., Rutter, M. *et al.* (2007). "Etiological heterogeneity in the development of antisocial behavior: the Virginia twin study of adolescent behavioral development and the young adult follow-up." *Psychological Medicine* **37**: 1193–1202.

Silk, J., Alberts, S. *et al.* (2006). "Social relationships among adult female baboons (Papio cynocephalus) II. Variation in the quality and stability of social bonds." *Behavioral Ecology and Sociobiology* **61**: 197–204.

Simons, R., Chao, W. *et al.* (2001). "Quality of parenting as a mediator of the effect of childhood defiance on adolescent friendship choices and delinquency: a growth curve analysis." *Journal of Marriage and the Family* **63**: 63–79.

Simpkins, S., Eccles, J. *et al.* (2008). "The mediational role of adolescents' friends in relations between activity breadth and adjustment." *Developmental Psychology* **44**: 1081–1094.

Sinclair, S., Dunn, E. and Lowery, B. S. (2005). "The relationship between parental racial attitudes and children's implicit prejudice." *Journal of Experimental Social Psychology* **41**: 283–289.

Sippola, L., Buchanan, C. M. and Kehoe, S. (2007). "Correlates of false self in adolescent romantic relationships." *Journal of Clinical Child & Adolescent Psychology* **36**: 515–521.

Skinner, E. and Zimmer-Gembeck, M. (2007). "The development of coping." *Annual Review of Psychology* **58**: 119–144.

Skinner, E., Edge, A. *et al.* (2003). "Searching for the structure of coping: a review and critique of category systems for classifying ways of coping." *Psychological Bulletin* **129**: 216–269.

Skuse, D. (1984). "Extreme deprivation in early childhood, I: diverse outcomes for three children in an extraordinary family: II: theoretical issues and a comparative review." *Journal of Child Psychology and Psychiatry* **25**: 523–542, 543–572.

Slaughter, V., Peterson, C. *et al.* (2007). "Mind what mother says: narrative input and theory of mind in typical children and those on the autism spectrum." *Child Development* **78**: 839–858.

Slomkowski, C., Rende, R. *et al.* (2001). "Sisters, brothers and delinquency: evaluating social influence during middle childhood and adolescence." *Child Development* **72**: 271–283.

Slone, M. and Shechner, T. (2008). "Psychiatric consequences for Israeli adolescents of protracted political violence: 1998–2004." *Journal of Child Psychology and Psychiatry*: 280–289.

Sluckin, A. (1981). *Growing Up in the Playground*. London: Routledge & Kegan Paul.

Smetana, J. (2002). Culture, autonomy, and personal jurisdiction. In R.Kail and H.Reese (eds), *Advances in Child Development and Behaviour*. New York: Academic Press.

Smetana, J. and Daddis, C. (2002). "Domain-specific antecedents of psychological control and parental monitoring: the role of parenting beliefs and practices." *Child Development* **73**: 563–580.

Smetana, J., Campione-Barr, N. and Metzger, A. (2006). "Adolescent development in interpersonal and societal context." *Annual Review of Psychology* **57**: 255–284.

Smetana, J., Kelly, M. and Twentyman, C. T. (1984). "Abused, neglected and nonmaltreated children's conceptions of moral and socio-conventional transgressions." *Child Development* **55**: 277–287.

Smetana, J., Metzger, A. *et al.* (2005). "Disclosure and secrecy in adolescent-parent relationships." *Child Development* **77**: 201–217.

Smith, A., Jussim, L. *et al.* (1999). "Do self-fulfilling prophecies accumulate, dissipate or remain stable over time?" *Journal of Personality and Social Psychology* **77**: 548–565.

Smith, C. (2003). "Theorizing religious effects among American adolescents." *Journal for the Scientific Study of Religion* **42**: 17–30.

Smith, I., Beasley, M. *et al.* (1990). "Intelligence and quality of dietary treatment in phenylketonuria." *Archives of Disease in Childhood* **65**: 472–478.

Smith, I., Beasley, M. *et al.* (1991). "Effect on intelligence of relaxing the low phenylalanine diet in phenylketonuria." *Archives of Disease in Childhood* **66**: 311–316.

Smith, J. and Prior, M. (1995). "Temperament and stress resilience in school-age children: a within-families study." *Journal of American Academy of Child and Adolescent Psychiatry* **34**: 168–179.

Smith, J. and Ross, H. (2007). "Training parents to mediate sibling disputes affects children's negotiation and conflict understanding." *Child Development* **78**: 790–805.

Smith, J., Brooks-Gunn, J. and Klebanov, P. (1997). Consequences of living in poverty for young children's verbal and cognitive ability and early school achievement. In G. Duncan and J. Brooks-Gunn (eds), *Consequences of Growing Up Poor*. New York: Russell Sage Foundation.

Smith, P. K. (1999). *The Nature of School Bullying; A Cross-national Perspective*. London: Routledge.

Smith, P. K., Madsen, K. C. and Moody, J. C. (1999). "What causes the age decline in reports of being bullied at school? Towards a developmental analysis of risks of being bullied." *Educational Research* **41**: 267–285.

Smith, R., Grimshaw, R. *et al.* (2007). *Poverty and Disadvantage amongst Prisoners' Families.* York: Joseph Rowntree Foundation.

Snell, D. and Hodgetts, D. (2007). "Heavy Metal, identity and the social negotiation of a community of practice." *Journal of Community and Applied Social Psychology* **17**: 430–445.

Snow, C. P. (1964). *The Two Cultures and the Scientific Revolution.* Cambridge: Cambridge University Press.

Snyder, J. and Patterson, G. (1995). Individual differences in social aggression. *Behavior Therapy* **26**: 371–391.

Soenens, B., Vansteenkiste, M. *et al.* (2006). "Parenting and adolescent problem behavior: An integrated model with adolescent self-disclosure and perceived parental knowledge as intervening variables." *Developmental Psychology* **42**: 305–318.

Solberg, M. and Olweus, D. (2003). "Prevalence estimation of school bullying with the Olweus Bully Victim Questionnaire." *Aggressive Behavior* **29**: 239–268.

Solberg, M., Olweus, D., Endresen, I. (2007). "Bullies and victims at school: Are they the same pupils?" *British Journal of Educational Psychology* **77**: 441–464.

Spelke, E. S. (2005). "Sex differences in intrinsic aptitude for mathematics and science? A critical review." *American Psychologist* **60**: 950–958.

Spencer, C. and Blades, M. (2006). *Children and their Environments.* Cambridge: Cambridge University Press.

Spooner, A. L. and Evans, M. A. (2005). "Hidden shyness in children: Discrepancies between self-perceptions and the perceptions of parents and teachers." *Merrill-Palmer Quarterly-Journal of Developmental Psychology* **51**: 437–466.

Srinivasan, S. and Bedi, A. S. (2008). "Daughter elimination in Tamil Nadu, India: a tale of two ratios." *Journal of Development Studies* **44**: 961–990.

Sroufe, L. A. (2005). "Attachment and development: a prospective, longitudinal study from birth to adulthood." *Attachment & Human Development* **7**: 349–367.

Sroufe, L. A., Egeland, B. *et al.* (2005a). *The Development of the Person: The Minnesota Study of Risk and Adaptation From Birth to Adulthood.* New York: Guilford.

Sroufe, L. A., Egeland, B. *et al.* (2005b). Placing early attachment experiences in developmental context: the Minnesota Longitudinal Study. In K. E. Grossman, K. Grossman and E. Waters (eds), *Attachment from Infancy to Adulthood: The Major Longitudinal Studies.* New York: Guilford.

Stams, G. J. M., Juffer, F. and van Ijzendoorn, M. H. (2002). "Maternal sensitivity, infant attachment and temperament in early childhood predict adjustment in middle childhood: The case of adopted children and their biologically unrelated parents." *Developmental Pyschology* **38**: 806–821.

Stanton, B., M. Cole *et al.* (2004). "Randomized trial of a parent intervention: parents can make a difference in long-term adolescent risk behaviors, perceptions, and knowledge." *Archives of Pediatrics and Adolescent Medicine* **10**: 947–955.

Stark, R. (1996). "Religion as context: Hellfire and delinquency one more time." *Sociology of religion* **57**: 163–173.

Starkey, D. (2001). *Elizabeth: The Struggle for the Throne.* New York: HarperCollins.

Starkey, D. (2008). *Henry: Virtuous Prince*. London: Harper Press.

Stattin, H. and Kerr, M. (2000). "Parental monitoring: a reinterpretation." *Child Development* **71**: 1072–1085.

Steedman, C. (1982). *The Tidy House*. London: Virago.

Steele, H. and Steele. M. (2005). Understanding and resolving emotional conflict: the London Parent-Child Project. In E. Grossman, K. Grossman and E. Waters (eds), *Attachment from Infancy to Adulthood: The Major Longitudinal Studies*. New York: Guilford.

Steelman, L., Powell, B. *et al.* (2002). "Reconsidering the effects of sibling configuration: recent advances and challenges." *Annual Review of Sociology* **28**: 243–269.

Steinberg, L. (2001). "We know some things: adolescent-parent relationships in retrospect and prospect." *Journal of Research in Adolescence* **11**: 1–19.

Steinberg, L. (2005). "Cognitive and affective development in adolescence." *Trends in Cognitive Science* **9**: 69–74.

Steinberg, L. and Morris, A. (2001). "Adolescent development." *Annual Review of Psychology* **52**: 83–110.

Steinberg, L., Lamborn, S. D. *et al.* (1992). "Impact of parenting practices on adolescent achievement: authoritative parenting, school involvement, and encouragement to succeed." *Child Development*. **63**: 1266–1281.

Sternberg, K., Baradaran, L. P. *et al.* (2006). "Type of violence, age, and gender differences in the effects of family violence on children's behavior problems: A mega-analysis." *Developmental Review* **26**: 89–112.

Sternberg, R. (1985). *Beyond IQ: A Triarchic Theory of Human Intelligence*. Cambridge: Cambridge University Press.

Sternberg, R. J. and Suben, J. G. (1986). "The socialization of intelligence." *Minnesota Symposia on Child Psychology* **19**: 201–235.

Stevens, O. (1982). *Children Talking Politics: Political Learning in Childhood*. Oxford: Martin Robertson.

Stevenson-Hinde, J. (2005). The interplay between attachment, temperament and maternal style: a Madingley perspective. In K. E. Grossman, K. Grossman and E. Waters (eds), *Attachment from Infancy to Adulthood: The Major Longitudinal Studies*. New York: Guilford.

Stevenson-Hinde, J. and Glover, A. (1996). "Shy girls and boys: A new look." *Journal of Child Psychology and Psychiatry and Allied Disciplines* **37**: 181–187.

Stice, E. and Gonzales, N. (1998). "Adolescent temperament moderates the relation of parenting to antisocial behavior and substance use." *Journal of Adolescent Research* **13**: 5–31.

Stipek, D. (1988). "Declining perceptions of competence: a consequence of changes in the child or in the educational environment." *Journal of Educational Psychology* **80**: 352–356.

Stipek, D. and Gralinski, J. (1996). "Children's beliefs about intelligence and school performance." *Journal of Educational Psychology* **88**: 397–407.

Stipek, D. and Tannart, L. (1984). "Children's judgments of their own and their peers' academic competence." *Journal of Educational Psychology* **76**: 75–84.

Stocker, C. (1993). "Siblings' adjustment in middle childhood: Links with mother–child relationships." *Journal of Applied Developmental Psychology* **14**: 485–499.

Stocker, C., Burwell, R. *et al.* (2002). "Sibling conflict in middle childhood predicts children's adjustment in early adolescence." *Journal of Family Psychology* **16**: 50–57.

Stone, M., Barber, B. *et al.* (2008). "We knew them when: Sixth grade characteristics that predict adolescent high school social identities." *Journal of Early Adolescence* **28**: 304–328.

Stoolmiller, M. (2001). "Synergistic interaction of child manageability problems and parent discipline tactics in predicting future growth in externalising behavior for boys." *Developmental Psychology* **37**: 814–825.

Stormshak, E., Bellanti, C. and Bierman, K. L. (1996). "The quality of sibling relationships and the development of social competence and behavioral control in aggressive children." *Developmental Psychology* **32**: 79–89.

Strahan, E., Lafrance, A. *et al.* (2008). "Victoria's dirty secret: how sociocultural norms influence adolescent girls and women." *Personality and Social Psychology Bulletin* **34**: 288–301.

Sturge-Apple, M. L., Davies, P. T. and Cummings, M. E. (2006). "Impact of hostility and withdrawal in interparental conflict on parental emotional unavailability and children's adjustment difficulties." *Child Development* **77**: 1623–1641.

Subrahmanyam, K. and Greenfield, P. (2008). "Online communication and adolescent relationships." *The Future of Children* **18**: 119–146.

Subrahmanyam, K., Smahel, D. and Greenfield, P. (2006). "Connecting developmental constructions to the Internet: identity presentation and sexual exploration in online teen chat rooms." *Developmental Psychology* **42**: 395–408.

Sulloway, F. (2007). "Birth order and intelligence." *Science* **316**: 1711–1712.

Suomi, S. J. (2006). "Risk, resilience, and gene: environment interactions in Rhesus Monkeys." *Annals of the New York Academy of Sciences* **1094**: 52–62.

Sutton, J., Smith, P. K. *et al.* (1999). "Bullying and 'Theory of Mind': A critique of the 'social skills deficit' view of anti-social behaviour." *Social Development* **8**: 117–127.

Swain, J. E. and Lorberbaum, J. P. (2007). "Brain basis of early parent-infant interactions: psychology, physiology, and in vivo functional neuroimaging studies." *Journal of Child Psychology and Psychiatry* **48**: 262–287.

Sweeting, H., Young, R *et al.* (2006). "Peer victimization and depression in early-mid adolescence: a longitudinal study." *British Journal of Educational Psychology* **76**: 577–594.

Talge, N. M., Neal, C. *et al.* (2007). "Antenatal maternal stress and long-term effects on child neurodevelopment: how and why?" *Journal of Child Psychology and Psychiatry* **48**: 245–261.

Tamis-LeMonda, C. S., Way, N. *et al.* (2008). "Parents' goals for children: the dynamic coexistence of individualism and collectivism in cultures and individuals." *Social Development* **17**: 183–209.

Tan, M. (1991). *The Kitchen God's Wife.* London: Harper Collins.

Tangney, J., Stuewig, J. *et al.* (2007). "Moral emotions and moral behavior." *Annual Review of Psychology* **58**: 345–372.

Tausch, N., Tam, T. *et al.* (2007). "Individual-level and group-level mediators of contact effects in Northern Ireland: the moderating role of social identification." *British Journal of Social Psychology* **46**: 541–556.

Taylor, A. and Kim-Cohen, J. (2007). "Meta-analysis of gene-environment interactions in developmental psychopathology." *Development and Psychopathology* **19**: 1029–1037.

Taylor, J., Iacono, W. G. and McGue, M. (2000). "Evidence for a genetic etiology for early-onset delinquency." *Journal of Abnormal Psychology* **109**: 634–643.

Tenenbaum, H. and Leaper, C. (2002). "Are parents' gender schemas related to their children's gender-related cognitions? A meta-analysis." *Developmental Psychology* **38**: 615–630.

Terren, E. (2002). "Post-modern attitudes: a challenge to democratic education." *European Journal of Education* **37**: 161–177.

Teti, D. and Gelfand, D. (1991). "Behavioral competence among mothers of infants in the first year: the mediational role of maternal self-efficacy." *Child Development* **62**: 918–929.

Thabet, A., Abed, Y. and Vostanis, P. (2004). "Co-morbidity of PTSD and depression among refugee children during war conflict." *Journal of Child Psychology and Psychiatry* **45**: 533–542.

Thapar, A., Fowler, T. *et al.* (2003). "Maternal smoking during pregnancy and attention deficit hyperactivity disorder symptoms in offspring." *American Journal of Psychiatry* **160**: 1985–1989.

Thapar, A., Langley, K. *et al.* (2007a). "Gene-environment interplay in attention-deficit hyperactivity disorder and the importance of a developmental perspective." *British Journal of Psychiatry* **190**: 1–3.

Thapar, A., Langley, K. *et al.* (2007b). "Advances in genetic findings on attention deficit hyperactivity disorder." *Psychological Medicine* **37**: 1681–1692.

Thapar, A., Harold, G *et al.* (2007c). "The contribution of gene-environment interaction to psychopathology." *Development and Psychopathology* **19**: 989–1004.

Tharp, R. and Gallimore, R. (1988). *Rousing Minds to Life*. Cambridge: Cambridge University Press.

Tharp, R. G., Jordan, C. *et al.* (1984). Product and process in applied developmental research: education and the children of a minority. In A. Brown, M. Lamb and B. Rogoff (eds), *Advances in Developmental Psychology, Vol 3*. Hillsdale, NJ: Erlbaum.

Theall-Honey, L. A. and Schmidt, L. A. (2006). "Do temperamentally shy children process emotion differently than nonshy children? Behavioral, psychophysiological, and gender differences in reticent preschoolers." *Developmental Psychobiology* **48**: 187–196.

Thompson, R. A. (1998). Early sociopersonality development. In W. Damon, R. Lerner, N. Eisenberg (eds), *Handbook of Child Psychology, (6th edn) Vol 3*. New York: Wiley.

Thompson, T. (2004). "Failure avoidance: parenting, the achievement environment of the home, and strategies for reduction." *Learning and Instruction* **14**: 3–26.

Thornberry, T. P., Freeman-Gallant, A. *et al.* (2003). "Linked lives: the intergenerational transmission of antisocial behavior." *Journal of Abnormal Child Psychology* **31**: 171–184.

Thornton, A. and Young-DeMarco, L. (2001). "Four decades of trends in attitudes toward family issues in the United States: the 1960s through the 1990s." *Journal of Marriage and the Family* **63**: 1009–1037.

Tienari, P., Wynne, L. C. *et al.* (1994). "The Finnish adoptive family study of schizophrenia: Implications for family research." *British Journal of Psychiatry* **23**: 20–26.

Tolan, P., Gorman-Smith, D. *et al.* (2006). "Family violence." *Annual Review of Psychology* **57**: 557–583.

Tomada, G. and Schneider, B. (1997). "Relational aggression, gender, and peer acceptance: Invariance across culture, stability over time, and concordance among informants." *Developmental Psychology* **33**: 601–609.

Tomada, G., Schneider, B. H. *et al.* (2005). "Friendship as a predictor of adjustment following a transition to formal academic instruction and evaluation." *International Journal of Behavioral Development* **29**: 314–322.

Tomasello, M. and Carpenter, M. (2007). "Shared intentionality." *Developmental Science* **10**: 121–125.

Tomasello, M., Carpenter, M. and Liszkowski, U. (2007). "A new look at infant pointing." *Child Development* **78**: 705–722.

Tomasello, M., Kruger, A. C. and Ratner, H. H. (1993). "Cultural learning." *Behavioral and Brain Sciences* **16**: 495–511.

Tomasello, M., Carpenter, M. *et al.* (2005). "Understanding and sharing intentions: the origins of cultural cognition." *Behavioral and Brain Sciences* **28**: 675–735.

Toren, C. (1993). "Making history: the significance of childhood cognition for a comparative anthropology of mind." *Man* **28**: 461–478.

Trevarthen, C. and Aitken, K. (2003). "Infant Intersubjectivity: Research, Theory, and Clinical Applications." *Journal of Child Psychology and Psychiatry and Allied Disciplines* **42**: 3–48.

Triandis, H. (2001). "Individualism-collectivism and personality." *Journal of Personality* **69**: 907–924.

Trzesniewski, K. H., Donnellan, M. and Robins, R. W. (2003). "Stability of self-esteem across the life-span." *Journal of Personality and Social Psychology* **84**: 205–220.

Tschann, J. M., Kaiser, P. *et al.* (1996). "Resilience and vulnerability among preschool children: family functioning, temperament, and behavior problems." *Journal of American Academy of Child and Adolescent Psychiatry* **35**: 184–192.

Tucker, C. J., Updegraff, K. A. *et al.* (1999). "Older siblings as socializers of younger siblings empathy." *Journal of Early Adolescence* **19**: 176–198.

Turiel, E. (1983). *The Development of Social Knowledge.* New York: Cambridge University Press.

Turiel, E. (1998). The development of morality. In W. Damon and N. Eisberg (eds), *Handbook of Child Psychology Vol 2: Social, Emotional and Personality Development.* New York: Wiley.

Turkheimer, E., Haley, A. *et al.* (2003). "Socioeconomic status modifies heritability of IQ in young children." *Psychological Science* **14**: 623–628.

Turner, R. J. and Lloyd, D. (2004). "Stress burden and the lifetime incidence of psychiatric disorder in young adults." *Archives of General Psychiatry* **61**: 481–488.

Turner, V. and Berkowitz, M. (2005). "Scaffolding morality: positioning a socio-cultural construct." *New Ideas in Psychology* **23**: 174–184.

Udry, J. (2003). How to spin straw into gold. In A. Crouter and A. Booth (eds),

Children's Influence on Family Dynamics: The Neglected Side of Family Relationships. Mahwah, NJ: Erlbaum.

Uhlmann, E. and Swanson, J. (2004). "Exposure to violent video games increases automatic aggressiveness." *Journal of Adolescence* **27**: 41–52.

Umana-Taylor, A. J. and Yazedjian, A. (2006). "Generational differences and similarities among Puerto Rican and Mexican mothers' experiences with familial ethnic socialization." *Journal of Social And Personal Relationships* **23**: 445–464.

Upchurch, D., Aneshensel, C. S. *et al.* (2001). "Sociocultural contexts of time to first sex among Hispanic adolescents." *Journal of Marriage and the Family* **63**: 1158–1169.

Updegraff, K. A. and Obeidallah, D. A. (1999). "Young adolescents' patterns of involvement with siblings and friends." *Social Development* **8**: 53–69.

Updegraff, K. A., McHale, S. M. and Crouter, A. C. (2002). "Adolescents' siblings relationships and friendship experiences: Developmental patterns and relationship linkages." *Social Development* **11**: 182–204.

Urdan, T. (2004). "Predictors of academic self-handicapping and achievement: examining achievement goals, classroom goal structures, and culture." *Journal of Educational Psychology* **96**: 251–264.

Valentino, K., Cicchetti, D. *et al.* (2008). "Memory, maternal representations, and internalizing symptomatology among abused, neglected and nonmaltreated children." *Child Development* **79**: 705–719.

Valeski, T. and Stipek, D. J. (2001). "Young children's feelings about school." *Child Development* **72**: 1198–1213.

Valiente, C., Eisenberg, N. *et al.* (2002). "Prediction of children's empathy-related responding from their effortful control and parents' expressivity." *Developmental Psychology* **40**: 911–926.

Valiente, C., Fabes, R. A. *et al.* (2004). "The relations of parental expressivity and support to children's coping with daily stress." *Journal of Family Psychology* **18**: 97–106.

Van de Vliert, E. (2007). "Climatoeconomic roots of survival versus self-expression cultures." *Journal of Cross-Cultural Psychology* **38**: 156–172.

van den Boom, D. C. (1994). "The influence of temperament and mothering on attachment and exploration: an experimental manipulation of sensitive responsiveness among lower-class mothers with irritable infants." *Child Development* **65**: 1457–1477.

van den Boom, D. C. (1997). "Sensitivity and attachment: next steps for developmentalists." *Child Development* **68**: 592–594.

van der Bruggen, C. (2008). "The relation between child and parent anxiety and parental control: a meta-analytic review." *Journal of Child Psychology and Psychiatry* **49**: 1257–1269.

van IJzendoorn, M. and F. Juffer (2006). "Adoption as intervention." *Journal of Child Psychology and Psychiatry* **47**: 1228–1245.

van IJzendoorn, M., Bakermans-Kranenburg, M. J. and Juffer, F. (2005). Why less is more: from the Dodo bird verdict to evidence-based interventions on sensitivity and early attachments. In L. J. Berlin, Y. Ziv, L. Amaya-Jackson and M. T. Greenberg (eds), *Enhancing Early Attachments*. New York: The Guilford Press.

van Lieshout, C. (2000). "Lifespan personality development: self-organising goal-oriented agents and developmental outcome." *International Journal of Behavioral Development* **24**: 276–288.

Vaughn, B. E., Colvin, T. N. *et al.* (2001). "Dyadic analyses of friendship in a sample of preschool-age children attending Head Start: correspondence between measures and implications for social competence." *Child Development* **72**: 862–878.

Verkuyten, M. and Slooter, L. (2008). "Muslim and non-Muslim adolescents' reasoning about freedom of speech and minority rights." *Child Development* **79**: 514–528.

Vitaro, F., Brendgen, M. and Tremblay, R. (2002). "Reactively and proactively aggressive children: antecedent and subsequent characteristics." *Journal of Child Psychology and Psychiatry* **43**: 495–506.

Vitaro, F., Brendgen, M. and Waller, B. (2005). "Patterns of affiliation with delinquent friends during late childhood and early adolescence: correlates and consequences." *Social Development* **14**: 82–108.

Vitaro, F., Brendgen, M. *et al.* (2001). "Gambling, delinquency, and drug use during adolescence: mutual influences and common risk factors." *Journal of Gambling Studies* **17**: 171–190.

Volling, B. and Elins, J. (1998). "Family relationships and children's emotional adjustments as correlates of maternal and paternal differential treatment: a replication with toddler and preschool siblings." *Child Development* **69**: 1640–1656.

Volling, B. L., McElwain, N. L. and Miller, A. L. (2002). "Emotion regulation in context: the jealousy complex between young siblings and its relations with child and family characteristics." *Child Development* **73**: 581–600.

von Kries, R., Bolte, G. *et al.* (2008). "Parental smoking and childhood obesity – is maternal smoking in pregnancy the critical exposure?" *International Journal of Epidemiology* **37**: 210–216.

Von Salisch, M. (2000). The emotional side of sharing, social support and conflict negotiation between siblings and between friends. In R. Mills and S. Duck (eds), *The Developmental Psychology of Personal Relationships*. New York: Wiley.

Vorria, P., Papaligoura, Z. *et al.* (2006). "The development of adopted children after institutional care: a follow-up study." *Journal of Child Psychology and Psychiatry* **47**: 1246–1253.

Vygotsky, L. (1962). *Thought and Language*. Cambridge, MA: MIT Press.

Vygotsky, L. (1978). *Mind in Society*. Cambridge, MA: Harvard University Press.

Vygotsky, L. (1981). The genesis of higher mental functions. In J. Wertsch (ed.), *The Concept of Activity in Soviet Psychology*. Armont, NY: M. E. Sharpe.

Waanders, C., Mendez, J. and Downer, J. T. (2007). "Parent characteristics, economic stress and neighbourhood context as predictors of parent involvement in preschool children's education." *Journal of School Psychology* **45**: 619–636.

Wachs, T. (2006). "Contributions of temperament to buffering and sensitization processes in children's development." *Annals of the New York Academy of Sciences* **1094**: 28–39.

Wachs, T. and Bates, J. (2001). Temperament. In G. Bremner and A. Fogel (ed.), *Handbook of Infant Development*. Oxford: Blackwell.

Wang, Q. (2006). "Culture and the development of self-knowledge." *Current Directions in Psychological Science* **15**: 182–187.

Wang, Q. (2007). "'Remember when you got the big, big bulldozer?' Mother–child reminiscing over time and across cultures." *Social Cognition* **25**: 455–471.

Wang, Q. and Ross, M. (2005). "What we remember and what we tell: The effects of culture and self-priming on memory representations and narratives." *Memory* **13**: 594–606.

Wang, X. (2008). "Responding to children's everyday transgressions in Chinese working-class families." *Journal of Moral Education* **37**: 55–79.

Wang, Y., Beydoun, M. A. *et al.* (2008). "Will all Americans become overweight or obese? Estimating the progression and cost of the US obesity epidemic." *Obesity* **16**: 2323–2330.

Want, S. C. and Harris, P. L (2002). "How do children ape? Applying concepts from the study of non-human primates to the development of 'imitation' in children." *Psychological Science* **5**: 1–13.

Watson, A. (1999). "Social interaction skills and theory of mind in young children." *Developmental Psychology* **35**: 386–391.

Weaver, I., Cervoni, N *et al.* (2004). "Epigenetic programming by maternal behavior." *Nature Neuroscience* **7**: 847–854.

Wells, C. G. (1981). "Some antecedents of early educational attainment." *British Journal of Sociology of Education* **2**: 181–200.

Wells, C. G. (1985). Preschool literacy-related activities and success in school. In D. Olson, N. Torrance and A. Hildyard (eds), *Literacy, Language and Learning: The Nature and Consequences of Reading And Writing*. Cambridge: Cambridge University Press.

Wenger, E. (1998). *Communities of Practice*. New York: Cambridge University Press.

Wenner, J., Burch, M. M. *et al.* (2008). "Becoming a teller of tales: Associations between children's fictional narratives and parent–child reminiscence narratives." *Journal of Experimental Child Psychology* **101**: 1–19.

Wentzel, J. (2003). "Sociometric status and adjustment in middle school: a longitudinal study." *Journal of Early Adolescence* **23**: 5–28.

Wentzel, J., McNamara-Barry, C. and Caldwell, K. (2004). "Friendships in middle school: Influences on motivation and school adjustment." *Journal of Educational Psychology* **96**: 195–203.

Wentzel, K. (2002). "Are effective teachers like good parents? Interpersonal predictors of school adjustment in early adolescence." *Child Development* **73**: 287–301.

Wentzel, K. and Asher, S. (1995). "The academic lives of neglected, rejected, popular and controversial children." *Child Development* **66**: 754–763.

Wentzel, K. R. and Caldwell, K. (1997). "Friendships, peer acceptance, and group membership: Relations to academic achievement in middle school." *Child Development* **68**: 1198–1209.

Wentzel, K. and Looney, L. (2007). Socialization in school settings. In J. Grusec and P. Hastings (eds), *Handbook of Socialization*. New York: Guilford.

Werner, E. (2006). What can we learn about resilience from large-scale longitudinal studies? In S. Goldstein and R. Brooks (eds), *Handbook of Resilience in Children*. New York: Springer.

Werner, R., Cassidy, K and Juliano, M. (2006). "The role of social-cognitive abilities in preschoolers' aggressive behaviour." *British Journal of Developmental Psychology* **24**: 775–799.

West, A. E. and Newman, D. L. (2007). "Childhood behavioral inhibition and the experience of social anxiety in American Indian adolescents." *Cultural Diversity and Ethnic Minority Psychology* **13**: 197–206.

West, D. (1982). *Delinquency: Its Roots, Careers and Prospects*. London: Heinemann.

White, A. (1978). *Frost in May*. London: Virago.

White, K. (1982). "The relation between socioeconomic status and academic achievement." *Psychological Bulletin* **91**: 461–488.

Whiteman, S., McHale, S. and Crouter, A. (2003). "What parents learn from experience: the first child as a first draft?" *Journal of Marriage and the Family* **65**: 608–621.

Whiteman, S., McHale, S. and Crouter, A. (2007). "Competing processes of sibling influence: observational learning and sibling deidentification." *Social Development* **16** 642–661.

Whiting, B. and Edwards, C. (1988). *Children of Different Worlds*. Cambridge, MA: Harvard.

Whiting, B. and Whiting, J. (1975). *Children of Six Cultures*. Cambridge, MA: Harvard University Press.

Wiles, N., Peters, T. J. *et al.* (2006). "Fetal growth and childhood behavioral problems: results from the ALSPAC cohort." *American Journal of Epidemiology* **163**: 829–837.

Wilhelm, K., Franz, P. B. *et al.* (2006). "Life events, first depression onset, and the serotonin transporter gene." *British Journal of Psychiatry* **188**: 210–215.

Wilkinson, R. and Pickett, K. (2007). "The problems of relative deprivation: Why some societies do better than others." *Social Science & Medicine* **65**: 1965–1978.

Wilkinson, R. and Pickett, K. (2009). *The Spirit Level: Why More Equal Societies Almost Always Do Better*. London: Allen Lane.

Willatts, P. (2003). "Feeding children's minds: long-chain polyunsaturated fatty acids and cognitive development." *Journal of Reproductive and Infant Psychology* **21**: 259–260.

Willatts, P., Forsyth, J. S. *et al.* (1998). "Effect of long-chain polyunsaturated fatty acids in infant formula on problem solving at 10 months of age." *Lancet* **352**: 688–691.

Williams, C. and Pleil, K. (2008). "Toy story: Why do monkey and human males prefer trucks?" *Hormones and Behavior* **54**: 355–358.

Williams, S., Conger, K. *et al.* (2007). "The development of interpersonal aggression during adolescence: The importance of parents, siblings, and family economics." *Child Development* **78**: 1526–1542.

Willis, P. (1977). *Learning to Labour: How Working Class Kids get Working Class Jobs*. Farnborough: Saxon House.

Willis-Owen, S., Turri, M. G. *et al.* (2005). "The serotonin transporter length polymorphism, neuroticism and depression: a comprehensive assessment of association." *Biological Psychiatry* **58**: 451–456.

Willmott, P. and Young, M. (1960). *Family and Class in a London Suburb*. London: Routledge and Kegan Paul.

Wills, T. (2001). "Family risk factors and adolescent substance use: moderation effects for temperament dimensions." *Developmental Psychology* 37: 283–297.

Wilson, A. (2009). "'Fundamental causes' of health disparities: A comparative analysis of Canada and the United States." *International Sociology* 24: 93–113.

Wilson, B. J. (2003). "The role of attentional processes in children's prosocial behavior with peers: Attention shifting and emotion." *Development and Psychopathology* 15: 313–329.

Wilson, B. (2008). "Media and children's aggression, fear and altruism." *The Future of Children* 18: 87–118.

Winterson, J. (1985). *Oranges are Not the Only Fruit*. London: Pandora.

Wismer Fries, A. and Pollak, S. (2004). "Emotion understanding in postinstitutionalized Eastern European children." *Development and Psychopathology* 16: 355–369.

Wohlwill, J. (1973). *The Study of Behavioral Development*. New York: Academic Press.

Wojslawowicz, J., Rubin, K H. *et al.* (2006). "Behavioral characteristics associated with stable and fluid best friends patterns in middle childhood." *Merrill-Palmer Quarterly* 52: 671–693.

Wolfe, D., Zak, L. *et al.* (1986). "Child witnesses to violence between parents: critical issues in behavioral and social adjustment." *Journal of Abnormal Child Psychology* 14: 95–104.

Wolters, C. (2004). "Advancing achievement goal theory: using goal structures and goal orientations to predict students' motivation, cognition, and achievement." *Journal of Educational Psychology* 96: 236–250.

Woo, S. (1991). Molecular genetic analysis of phenylketonuria and mental retardation. In P. McHugh and V. McKusick (eds), *Genes, Brain and Behavior*. New York: Raven Press.

Wood, D. (1998). *How Children Think and Learn*. Oxford: Blackwell.

Wood, J. J., McLeod, B. D. *et al.* (2003). "Parenting and childhood anxiety: theory, empirical findings, and future directions." *Journal of Child Psychology and Psychiatry and Allied Disciplines* 44: 134–151.

Wood, W. and Eagly, A. (2002). "A cross-cultural analysis of the behavior of men and women: Implications for the origins of sex differences." *Psychological Bulletin* 128: 699–727.

Wren, T. and Mendoza, C. (2004). Cultural identity and personal identity; philosophical reflections on the identity discourse of social psychology. In D. Lapsley and D. Narvaez (eds), *Moral Development, Self and Identity*. Mahwah, NJ: Erlbaum.

Yates, M. and Youniss, J. (1996). "Community service and political-moral identity in adolescents." *Journal of Research in Adolescence* 54: 248–261.

Yau, J. and Smetana, J. (1996). "Adolescent-parent conflict among Chinese adolescents in Hong Kong." *Child Development* 67: 1262–1275.

Yau, J. and Smetana, J. (2003). "Adolescent-parent conflict in Hong Kong and Mainland China: a comparison of youth in two cultural contexts." *International Journal of Behavioral Development* 27: 201–211.

Yeung, J., Linver, M. and Brook-Gunn, J. (2002). "How money matters for young children's development: parental investment and family processes." *Child Development* 73: 1861–1879.

Youniss, J. and Yates, M. (1999). "Youth service and moral-civic identity: a case for everyday morality." *Educational Psychology Review* **14**: 361–376.

Youniss, J., McLellan, J. A. and Yates, M. (1999). "Religion, community service, and identity in American youth." *Journal of Adolescence* **22**: 243–253.

Yunger, J. L., Carver, P. R. and Perry, D. G. (2004). "Does gender identity influence children's psychological well-being?" *Developmental Psychology* **40**: 572–582.

Zaff, J., Malanchuk, O. *et al.* (2008). "Predicting positive citizenship from adolescence to young adulthood: The effects of a civic context." *Applied Developmental Science* **12**: 38–53.

Zahn-Waxler, C., Klimes-Dougan, B. and Slattery, M. J. (2000). "Internalizing problems of childhood and adolescence: Prospects, pitfalls, and progress in understanding the development of anxiety and depression." *Development and Psychopathology* **12**: 443–466.

Zahn-Waxler, C., Radke-Yarrow, M. and King, R. (1979). "Child-rearing and children's prosocial dispositions towards victims of distress." *Child Development* **50**: 319–313.

Zahn-Waxler, C., Park, J.-H. *et al.* (2008). "Young children's representations of conflict and distress: A longitudinal study of boys and girls with disruptive behavior problems." *Development and Psychopathology* **20**: 99–119.

Zakriski, A. and Coie, J. (1996). "A comparison of aggressive-rejected and non-aggressive rejected children's interpretations of self-directed and other-directed rejection." *Child Development* **67**: 1048–1070.

Zarbatany, L. (2000). "Gender-differentiated experience in the peer culture: Links to intimacy in preadolescence." *Social Development* **9**: 62–79.

Zarbatany, L., McDougall, P. and Hymel, S. (2000). "Gender-differentiated experience in the peer culture: links to intimacy in preadolescence." *Social Development* **9**: 62–79.

Zeanah, C., Nelson, C. A. *et al.* (2003). "Designing research to study the effects of institutionalization on brain and behavioural development: the Bucharest Early Intervention Project." *Development and Psychopathology* **15**: 885–907.

Zhou, Q., Wang, Y. *et al.* (2008). "Relations of parenting and temperament to Chinese children's experience of negative life events, coping efficacy, and externalising problems." *Child Development* **79**: 403–513.

Zingg, R. (1940). "Feral children and cases of extreme isolation." *American Journal of Psychology* **53**: 487–517.

Zuckerman, M. (1979). *Sensation Seeking: Beyond the Optimal Level of Arousal.* Hillsdale, NJ: Erlbaum.

Zukow-Goldring, P. (1995). Sibling caregiving. In M.Bornstein (ed.), *Handbook of Parenting, Vol 3.* Hillsdale, NJ: Erlbaum.

Author index

Subject index

Abecedarian project 209
absent fathers 92, 153
abuse: and attachment 85–87; child 37, 79, 109, 240, 39, 85–87, 129–130, 141–144; and emotional functioning 129–130; family system and neglect 141–144; and interaction with gene effect 37, 334; historical examples of 109; by macaque mothers 58–59; *see also* child abuse
academic achievement 147
academic self concept 76, 213–217
adaptation: and evolution 20–22, 36
adaptation: to the dominant culture 82–84, 87
ADHD 37–38, 39
adolescence 72–74, 244: and alcohol abuse 268, 269, 270; and brain development 195, 268; and conflict with parents 138; and control 136; and cultural differences 178–179; and emotional difficulties 138; and non-conformity 268; and peers 177–180; and risk-taking 267–270; and romantic relationships 180–182
adoption 38, 148, 272–274
adrenocorticotrophic hormones 53, 59
adult protection of young 22, 41, 94, 108, 121, 122
affluence 140, 279
African American and African Caribbean fathers 154
African families 38, 46, 236
age differences between siblings 167
age differences in delinquency rates 264
agency 42–43, 66, 89, 104, 133, 189, 191–194, 202

aggression 61, 97, 142, 169, 172–173, 175, 176–177, 226–231, 238
alcohol use: and adolescence 268–279; and delinquency 266–267; and parental monitoring 140; by parents 143–144; and popularity 180; and self esteem 80; and stress 56; by Travellers 256
alleles 26, 31, 36
altruistic behaviour 119, 161, 186; *see also* kin selection; prosocial behaviour
amae 127
ambivalent or 'bizarre' attachments 97, 174
anger 61, 86, 120, 124–125, 138, 167, 241
animal studies 58, 63
anorexia and self-harm 178–179
anthropology 44
antisocial behaviour 145, 264–267, 283
anxiety 36, 53, 93–95, 124–125, 140, 142, 146, 173, 281
approach 64, 95, 96, 285–286
approaches to learning 219–220
arousal 93, 124, 226–231
assertiveness 255
attachment 38–39, 54, 56, 59, 70, 79, 86–87, 91, 96, 111, 120–121, 122–127, 209, 273, 278–279; adult patterns 125; anxious 123, 125; biological bases 122–123; evolutionary functions 122–123; longer term implications 123–126; and parent influences on peer relations 174–175; types of relationship 122–127; *see also* secure